7 STEPS *to a* COMPREHENSIVE LITERATURE REVIEW

SAGE was founded in 1965 by Sara Miller McCune to support the dissemination of usable knowledge by publishing innovative and high-quality research and teaching content. Today, we publish over 900 journals, including those of more than 400 learned societies, more than 800 new books per year, and a growing range of library products including archives, data, case studies, reports, and video. SAGE remains majority-owned by our founder, and after Sara's lifetime will become owned by a charitable trust that secures our continued independence.

Los Angeles | London | New Delhi | Singapore | Washington DC

Anthony J Onwuegbuzie
& Rebecca Frels

7

STEPS *to a*
COMPREHENSIVE
LITERATURE
REVIEW

A Multimodal & Cultural Approach

Los Angeles | London | New Delhi
Singapore | Washington DC

Los Angeles | London | New Delhi
Singapore | Washington DC

SAGE Publications Ltd
1 Oliver's Yard
55 City Road
London EC1Y 1SP

SAGE Publications Inc.
2455 Teller Road
Thousand Oaks, California 91320

SAGE Publications India Pvt Ltd
B 1/I 1 Mohan Cooperative Industrial Area
Mathura Road
New Delhi 110 044

SAGE Publications Asia-Pacific Pte Ltd
3 Church Street
#10-04 Samsung Hub
Singapore 049483

Editor: Mila Steele
Assistant editor: James Piper
Production editor: Rachel Burrons
Marketing manager: Ben Sherwood
Cover design: Francis Kenney
Typeset by: C&M Digitals (P) Ltd, Chennai, India
Printed and bound by CPI Group (UK) Ltd,
Croydon, CR0 4YY

MIX
Paper from
responsible sources
FSC® C013604

© Anthony J. Onwuegbuzie and Rebecca Frels 2016

First published 2016

Library of Congress Control Number: 2015942962

British Library Cataloguing in Publication data

A catalogue record for this book is available from the British Library

ISBN 978-1-4462-4891-1
ISBN 978-1-4462-4892-8 (pbk)

At SAGE we take sustainability seriously. Most of our products are printed in the UK using FSC papers and boards. When we print overseas we ensure sustainable papers are used as measured by the PREPS grading system. We undertake an annual audit to monitor our sustainability.

For Agatha N. Onwuegbuzie, a unique mother.

TABLE OF CONTENTS

ABOUT THE AUTHORS

Anthony J. Onwuegbuzie is Professor in the Department of Educational Leadership at Sam Houston State University, Texas, USA. He teaches doctoral-level courses in qualitative, quantitative, and mixed research. His research areas include disadvantaged and under-served populations. Additionally, he writes extensively on an array of qualitative, quantitative, and mixed methodological topics. With a current *h-index* of 66, Dr. Onwuegbuzie has secured the publication of more than 400 works, including more than 300 journal articles, 50 book chapters, and three books. Additionally, he has delivered more than 750 presentations and 100 workshops worldwide that include more than 30 keynote addresses across six continents. He has received numerous outstanding paper awards, as well as national and international teaching recognitions. Dr. Onwuegbuzie is former Editor of *Educational Researcher* (*ER*), being part of the editor team (2006–2010) that secured a first impact factor of 3.774. He is currently a Co-Editor of *Research in the Schools*, and has been Guest Editor of six mixed research special issues. Many of his articles have been the most read and cited among articles in their respective journals. For example, his mixed research article published in *ER* is the most cited *ER* article ever. His overall goal is to be a role model for beginning researchers and students worldwide.

Rebecca Frels is a Licensed Professional Counselor-Supervisor and Counselor Educator at Lamar University, Texas, USA. A former music educator and school counselor, her research and scholarship is in the areas of research methodology, mentoring, and student success. She has written or co-authored more than 30 articles and three book chapters. She has served as Production Editor for *Research in the Schools* and Guest Co-Editor for the *International Journal of Multiple Research Approaches*. International experience includes facilitating research courses for the Organization for Social Science Research in Eastern and Southern Africa (OSSREA) in Kenya, Uganda, and Tanzania and courses with the Universidad de Iberoamérica (UNIBE), San Jose, Costa Rica and Universidad IberoAmericana in Puebla, Mexico. Recently, she combined her passion for both mixed methods and mentoring, creating for *Oxford Handbook for Mixed and Multiple Method Research* a book chapter titled "Mentoring the next generation of mixed and multiple method researchers." She and her co-author Anthony Onwuegbuzie have developed the critical dialectical pluralistic approach for mixed research for promoting the voice of participants as decision makers and co-researchers in the research process. Currently, she is conducting research in the area of peer mentoring in higher education—incorporating outreach through technology and social media.

INTRODUCTION

An overall theme in this book is integration—integrating the *products* and the *processes*. When conducting the literature review of our own in designing this textbook, we recognized that although many excellent textbooks have addressed how to conduct a literature review, few have emphasized how the literature review should incorporate research practices for a transparent process. Moreover, we discovered that few textbook authors have tackled how to address the rapidly growing Web 2.0 digital technologies and instant communications that are situated in a cultural and historical context. Considering that throughout the world, people are becoming experts at information-seeking, we are confident in saying that the literature review can be accomplished with rigor and include myriad sources—taking what might be considered as the traditional review to a new level.

WHY ANOTHER BOOK ON CONDUCTING THE LITERATURE REVIEW?

The literature review in social, behavioral, and health sciences can take on various roles and can serve multiple purposes. For example, at the undergraduate level, the literature review is a type of desk research, often termed a book report or desk research project. At the master's and doctoral levels, a major literature review is conducted primarily at the end of a program when the student undertakes either a thesis or dissertation. However, as contended by Boote and Beile (2005), programs in higher education do not give credence to the importance of understanding how to conduct the literature review. Yet, in the social sciences, the sharing of knowledge, specifically evidence-based knowledge, is the driving force for advances in the field. Furthermore, in the academic realm, the phrase *publish or perish* (circa 1950; Sojka & Maryland, 1993) is all too familiar to even prolific researchers. Boote and Beile (2005) posited:

> acquiring the skills and knowledge required to be education scholars should be the focal, integrative activity of predissertation doctoral education. Preparing students as researchers to analyze and synthesize research in a field of specialization is crucial to understanding educational ideas. (p. 3)

In using the term *comprehensive* in our textbook title, we do not claim or suggest that a literature review can be exhaustive toward a totality of literature on any given topic. Similar to that of a primary research study, the literature reviewer-as-researcher must bind the study and document the guiding criteria when doing so. As such, a literature review should be comprehensive inasmuch as it contains all the most important elements of literature reviews (e.g., including quantitative and qualitative information). The word *comprehensive* also should connote that rigorous techniques such as mixed research techniques are used to collect and to analyze information, and using sampling theory to determine when the information used is representative of the complete set of information that is available on the topic (cf. Chapter 6).

In addition, to interpret historically and culturally the relevancy of authors' works, we have integrated reflective practices for seeking many perspectives—hence, the subtitle of our book: "A culturally progressive, ethical, and multimodal approach." This approach balances the intent of the original sources with the intent of the literature reviewer. Finally, our use of the phrase "Seven Steps" in the textbook title should indicate that our book represents an organized and sequential approach to literature reviews. Also, the word *steps* should connote that the elements are distinct, although representing an inter-related and a sequential approach by no means implies that the steps are linear, but rather that the process can be approached in a sequence. The steps, after being visited for the first time, become dynamic, integrated parts that require reflection and revisiting upon each new step.

WHO MIGHT USE THIS BOOK?

This book was designed to be a tool and guide for master's-level students, doctoral-level students, and new and experienced researchers. In fact, we believe that any person who is a scholar will find the book helpful for conducting, documenting, and presenting the literature review. We have designed this book to work as either a supplemental textbook in a research methodology course or as a stand-alone textbook for a research methodology course. In particular, if you are an emergent scholar at the doctoral level, this book will help guide you through the literature review process for your thesis or dissertation and also provide valuable support for your research. Finally, this book will be helpful to methodologists and scholars alike as a bridging meta-framework, inclusive of best practices in research.

HOW IS THIS BOOK UNIQUE?

IT IS ABOUT CULTURE

When considering how long the practice of literature reviewing has been part of scholarship, to our surprise, there has been virtually no mention of culture and how it influences not only *what* is found, but also *why* one literature reviewer selects particular works and not others. A culturally progressive literature reviewer considers the idea that knowledge sources stem from people (i.e., participants) and are generated by people (i.e., researchers, authors) who represent all cultures, races, ethnic backgrounds, languages, classes, religions, and other diversity attributes.

As a result, our approach to the literature review involves the literature reviewer engaging in reflective practices to become intimately aware of his/her own cultural attributes better to recognize, to acknowledge, to affirm, and to value the worth of all participants and researchers/authors to capture their voices. As such, the crux of the Comprehensive Literature Review (CLR) is what is often referred to as *cultural competence*. This awareness of biases and personal values and how these elements might influence decisions made at every step of the literature review process is what we term a *culturally progressive approach*.

IT SPEAKS TO ETHICAL RESEARCH STANDARDS

Broadly speaking, ethics incorporate moral principles and best practices pertaining to both research and subject discipline topics. Ethics provide the essence that overflows into every component of the literature review process. When conducting a Comprehensive Literature Review, the literature reviewer practices professional competence and undertakes tasks within recognized skill sets relating to the topic explored and the results reported. Ethical research in the literature review includes integrity, scholarly responsibility, social responsibility, and respecting rights, dignity, and diversity.

IT IS A MIXED METHODS LITERATURE REVIEW (TO BE APPROACHED WITHOUT FEAR!)

As a mixed methods approach, the Comprehensive Literature Review is conducted using mixed research techniques—that is, by collecting and analyzing *both* quantitative and qualitative information within the same literature review. Due to this integrative nature, we explain that the literature reviewer does not merely *summarize* the extant literature and the information extracted from this literature (dispelling one of the many myths over time), but he/she *synthesizes* the qualitative information (e.g., data stemming from qualitative studies) and quantitative information (e.g., data stemming from quantitative studies) thematically, resulting in a final report or presentation that recognizes how one type of data illuminates the understanding or contradictions of another. There you have it—the use of mixed research techniques!

IT EXTENDS THE LITERATURE REVIEW TO INCLUDE OTHER SOURCES

The Comprehensive Literature Review process reflects the multimodal nature of text in the Web 2.0 era by initially using published articles as a starting point, and then extending the search to include multimodal texts and settings, referred to as MODES: Media, Observation(s), Documents, Expert(s) in the field, and Secondary data. After beginning the search through traditional literature, or published journal articles via the search in library databases, we explain how to use guiding criteria for evaluating the most up-to-date knowledge using new literacies, or what is referred to as multimodal literacy, associated with a topic (especially considering that there is always a time lag between when the information is first conceptualized/written and when it becomes accessible [e.g., by being published]) to present a holistic picture and, thus, an integrated literature review.

THE SEVEN STEPS MAKE THE PROCESS DO-ABLE

Upon first glance, the word *comprehensive* might give the illusion that the literature review is some daunting task, or is quite insurmountable. Therefore, we simplify the literature review process by breaking the review into the following seven overlapping but distinct steps: (a) Step 1: Exploring Beliefs and Topics; (b) Step 2: Initiating the Search; (c) Step 3: Storing and Organizing Information; (d) Step 4: Selecting/Deselecting Information; (e) Step 5: Expanding the Search (MODES); (f) Step 6: Analyzing and Synthesizing Information; and (g) Step 7: Presenting the CLR Report. These seven steps are multidimensional, interactive, emergent, iterative, dynamic, holistic, and synergistic—because each step informs all other steps. Each step concludes with what we describe as the CORE of the process, which is Critical examination, Organization, Reflections, and Evaluation via the evaluation checklist. Yes, a comprehensive literature review is do-able!

IT IS A META-FRAMEWORK

The literature review involves activities such as identifying, recording, understanding, meaning-making, and transmitting information. In its optimal form, the literature review not only represents a study; it represents a mixed research study facilitated by using mixed research techniques—that is, by collecting and analyzing *both* quantitative and qualitative information from collected sources, as a literature synthesis. Whether the literature review is conducted to inform primary research or is a stand-alone work, it involves the literature reviewer making meta-inferences within multiple steps.

IT PROVIDES NUMEROUS EXAMPLES AND TOOLS

By using one example of a literature review topic as a common thread for the steps, this textbook becomes a practical resource for conducting a literature review. In addition, we have created numerous typologies, resource guides, and frameworks using visual displays for facilitating understanding and application of the Seven-Step Model.

HOW IS THIS BOOK ORGANIZED?

FOUNDATIONS

We begin this book in Chapter 1 by reviewing some basic elements and terminology relating to research through the quantitative, qualitative, and mixed methods research traditions. We then move into the myths that have surrounded the literature review process so that the literature reviewer might not fall into these traps when beginning the journey. Furthermore, we outline the reasons and objective of the literature review.

OVERVIEWS

In the next two chapters, we provide the overall summary of the Comprehensive Literature Review and the Seven-Step Model. We explain how, within the meta-framework, the Comprehensive Literature Review is a methodology, method, tool, and multimodal (or new literacies) approach. We also highlight the identity of the literature reviewer as an original thinker, critical thinker, reflexive researcher, ethical researcher, and most of all—a culturally progressive researcher.

CHAPTER STEPS

The next eight chapters present the steps, one-by-one (with two chapters representing the seventh step). After presenting these 11 chapters, we end our textbook with a postscript in which we provide five examples as to how to conduct theory-driven and model-driven CLRs—a pathway that when integrated with the Seven-Step Model provides one of the more exciting areas for the further development of CLRs. At the end of each chapter, we present evaluation questions that pertain to the knowledge discovered, and critique the products that have evolved as a result of the step. It involves what is happening emotionally and cognitively. In short, it examines *the what* and *why this*?

We have based the guiding questions after each chapter on what is commonly known as Socratic questioning, as a form of inquiry and debate. For reflexivity purposes, we present questions for self-dialogue to challenge biases and viewpoints. Additionally, this type of challenge is dialectical, and by exposing any contradictions, might lead to a strengthening of the literature reviewer's identity and illuminate ideas for the next step. The critical thinking questions are categorized into six types (Paul & Elder, 2006) and presented in a table such as the one below (Table I.1), and are designed to judge assumptions and actions.

Table I.1 Examples of six types of Socratic questions to be used after each step of the Seven-Step Model

Type of Question	Question(s)
Clarification	Why did you select or state what you stated in this step?
Assumptions	What might you be assuming to be true?
Reason and evidence	What do you think caused you to select or say that?
Viewpoint and perspective	What might be an alternative viewpoint?
Implications and consequences	What are the strengths and weaknesses of what I select or say? What are some generalizations?
About the questions themselves	What was the point of this question? What did I seek to know and why?

We also created a CORE process so that the reflexivity for the literature reviewer might take a meaningful direction (Figure I.1). In the CORE, the C presents Critical examination, the O presents Organizing ideas, the R presents Reflection questions, and the E presents some Evaluation points.

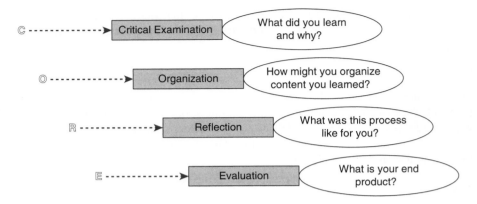

Figure I.1   The CORE process

We hope that you find this textbook useful as both a resource for research methodology and also the literature review!

PART ONE

OVERVIEW

1

FOUNDATIONS OF THE LITERATURE REVIEW

CHAPTER 1 ROADMAP

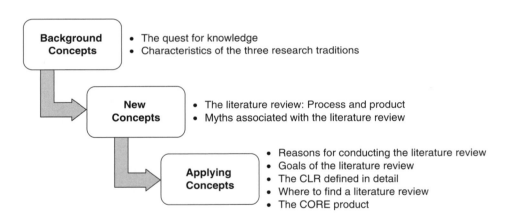

Background Concepts
- The quest for knowledge
- Characteristics of the three research traditions

New Concepts
- The literature review: Process and product
- Myths associated with the literature review

Applying Concepts
- Reasons for conducting the literature review
- Goals of the literature review
- The CLR defined in detail
- Where to find a literature review
- The CORE product

BACKGROUND CONCEPTS

Knowledge broadly represents a degree of familiarity—somewhere between awareness and expertise—with someone or something that is acquired through education (i.e., study) or experience. Although no single agreed-upon definition of knowledge exists, its importance has never been in doubt. In fact, many famous people have extolled the virtues of knowledge. Major fields of study are labeled using the word *science* or *sciences*, such as social sciences (e.g., psychology, sociology, cultural and ethnic studies), health sciences (e.g., nursing, dentistry, occupational therapy), natural sciences (e.g., chemistry, physics), applied sciences (e.g., law, social work, education), and formal sciences (e.g., mathematics, statistics, computer sciences). It should not be surprising why the word *science* is so prevalent here when we examine the origin of this word. Interestingly, the word *science* comes from the Latin word *scientia*, which means "knowledge." Thus, as eloquently stated by Johnson and Christensen (2010, p. 16), it is reasonable to define science as "an approach for the generation of knowledge that places high regard for empirical data and follows certain norms and practices that develop over time because of their usefulness." As Johnson and Christensen (2010, p. 15), surmised, "Science includes any systematic or carefully done actions that are carried out to answer research questions or meet other needs of a developing research domain (e.g., describing things, exploring, experiencing, explaining, predicting)" and "includes many methods and activities that are carried out by researchers as they attempt to generate scientific knowledge." Also, many ways exist for generating knowledge, including experience (i.e., formally known as empiricism), which stems from observation and perception, expert judgment, and reasoning (i.e., formally known as rationalism), which primarily includes deductive reasoning (i.e., arriving at specific conclusions based on a set of premises or hypotheses), inductive reasoning (i.e., making generalizations based on a specific number of observations), and abductive reasoning (i.e., starting from a set of accepted facts and determining their best explanations).

THE QUEST FOR KNOWLEDGE

Because science results in an accumulation of knowledge over time, science can be seen as cumulative. Thus, it behooves us always to find out what we know about a topic of interest and then to use what we know as a starting point. Indeed, failure to do so could lead us unnecessarily to "re-invent the wheel"—an idiomatic metaphor used wherein the wheel is symbolic for human ingenuity and creativity. Moreover, a lack of awareness of existing knowledge might lead us to utilize practices that have been found previously to be ineffective. This is especially the case for the field of research. For example, if a primary school teacher decides to use a teaching strategy that researchers previously have demonstrated as being not only ineffective but also detrimental to academic achievement, this likely would have dire consequences. In such a case, before using the strategy, the teacher should find out as much as possible about it before adopting it. The best way to do so is via what has been traditionally called a *literature review* or *review of the literature*. In fact, regardless of the academic discipline, the most common way of acquiring knowledge is by searching out what has already been done—through the literature review.

Many authors of research methodology textbooks inadvertently perpetuate myths about the literature review process by understating what the literature review entails. Unfortunately, it is likely that these myths explain why many researchers—as many as 40% (Onwuegbuzie & Daniel, 2005)—who submit articles for possible publication in journals write inadequate literature reviews. The literature review involves activities such as identifying, recording, understanding, meaning-making, and transmitting information. To some degree, the literature review represents a study that seeks to represent what is known (or not known) on a particular topic, and optimally it includes *both* quantitative and qualitative information from collected sources, as a literature synthesis. Whether the literature review is conducted to inform primary research or is a stand-alone work, it involves the literature reviewer making meta-inferences within multiple steps.

DEFINITION OF THE CLR

Throughout this book, we present some of the same rigorous techniques that are utilized within the mixed methods research tradition—which are referred to as mixed methods research. We outline this literature review via a series of "steps." However, although the steps are presented in sequence, they are not linear. Rather, the steps are dynamic integrated parts of a comprehensive process for searching and reflecting on the new knowledge acquired in creating a literature review. Specifically, these steps are a meta-framework for a new, *comprehensive literature review*, to which is referred as the CLR. Later in this chapter, we provide you with some of the essential components involved in this definition using a more detailed verbiage for understanding the CLR.

BOX 1.1

THE COMPREHENSIVE LITERATURE REVIEW (CLR)

The Comprehensive Literature Review (CLR) is a methodology, conducted either to stand alone or to inform primary research at multiple stages of the research process, which optimally involves the use of mixed research techniques inclusive of culture, ethics, and multimodal texts and settings in a systematic, holistic, synergistic, and cyclical process of exploring, interpreting, synthesizing, and communicating published and/or unpublished information.

CHARACTERISTICS OF THE THREE RESEARCH TRADITIONS

Virtually all researchers belonging to the three major research traditions or approaches use the literature review to inform their research, or what we often refer to as primary research. A **research tradition** often might be referred to as a research paradigm, and is **quantitative research**, **qualitative research**, or a combination of both—what is called **mixed methods research**. As you will see throughout this book, what is most interesting about the literature review process is that many of the methods associated with each of these research traditions, such as data collection techniques and data analysis techniques, also help researchers to conduct a CLR. All three research traditions yield empirical research studies. Broadly speaking, empirical research studies represent research wherein data are generated via direct observation or experiment in order to address one or more research questions (i.e., interrogative statements that the researcher attempts to answer using research techniques) and/or to test one or more hypotheses (i.e., proposed explanations of observable phenomena that can be tested via research). As such, findings from empirical research studies are based on actual evidence, as opposed to theory, assumptions, or speculations.

Quantitative research studies primarily involve the collection, analysis, and interpretation of numeric data, with goals that include describing, explaining, and predicting phenomena. In contrast, **qualitative research** studies primarily involve the collection, analysis, and interpretation of non-numeric data that naturally occur from one or more of the following sources: documents, talk, observations, and drawings/photographs/videos. Finally, **mixed methods research**, or what is more aptly called **mixed research** (to denote the fact that more than just methods are mixed), as noted by Johnson and Onwuegbuzie (2004), involves mixing or combining quantitative and qualitative research approaches (e.g., collection, analysis, interpretation) within the same study. Table A.1, Table A.2, and Table A.3 located in Appendix A toward the end of this book provide an overview of the major quantitative research designs, qualitative research designs, and mixed research designs, respectively. We encourage you to take some time and review the differences among the research traditions to prepare yourself as a literature reviewer.

With the three traditions in mind, primary research represents a quantitative, qualitative, or mixed research study conducted by a researcher(s) that is informed by, and informs, the literature review. One feature that these three types of studies have in common is that they all involve the following four phases: research conceptualization, research planning, research implementation, and research dissemination. In the research conceptualization phase, researchers representing all three traditions decide on the **goal of the study**, or the desired end-point of the study such as to examine the past, to measure change, or to test a theory; the **objective of the study**, or the action that will result from the study such as explanation; the **rationale of the study**, which is why the study is needed and the gap in our knowledge that the research findings will be helping to fill; and the **purpose of the study**, or what the researcher intends to study. Further, research questions play an important role for all three research traditions. Most notably, for all three research traditions, research questions provide researchers with a framework for conducting the study; help researchers to organize their research studies; help researchers to bound their research studies; help researchers to determine the type of data that should be collected, analyzed, and interpreted; and give research studies relevance, direction, and coherence, thereby helping to keep the researcher focused during the course of the study.

In the research conceptualization phase, all three sets of researchers—that is, quantitative researchers, qualitative researchers, and mixed researchers—plan the study that will address the research question(s), particularly the **sampling design**, or the number of participants selected and the sampling scheme used to select them (e.g., random vs. non-random), and

research **design**, or the framework (e.g., outline or plan) that is used to address the research question(s). In fact, a common mistake of beginning researchers is not recognizing the central role that research questions play in determining the appropriate research tradition. As a literature reviewer, similar to those conducting research, you might have questions in mind as you conduct a literature review.

In the research implementation phase, researchers belonging to all three traditions collect their data, analyze their data, validate or legitimate their data, and interpret their data. This is the phase where all the research planning and designing undertaken by the research is actualized. For all three research traditions, the length of time needed to complete each of these steps varies from one study to the next, and is dependent on the decisions made in the research conceptualization phase (e.g., research questions) and the research planning phase (i.e., sample design, research design), as well as on the scope of the study and available resources (e.g., time, money).

Finally, in the research dissemination phase, all three sets of researchers share their research findings orally (e.g., presenting their findings in class; presenting their findings at a research conference), visually (e.g., performance ethnography wherein the research findings are performed via dramatic representations such as plays), or, most commonly, in writing. Typically, the goal here is to make the findings available to one or more others. In the classroom context, the research findings are shared with the classroom instructor. Beyond the classroom—including master's theses and doctoral dissertations—the printed and/or digital form of the research report will be stored somewhere, such as the library or a bibliographic database. Future researchers representing all three traditions then can use this latest research report, alongside other available works, to inform their own literature reviews and studies. And, thus, the cycle of knowledge generation continues…

NEW CONCEPTS

At this point, you might be asking yourself why this information is important. We maintain that ethics in research, or the guiding moral principles of research, help the literature reviewer incorporate best practices pertaining to understanding the sources that they selected, the information that they extract from these sources, and how it relates to any one or more subject discipline topics.

TOOL: A SUMMARY TABLE OF RESEARCH TRADITIONS

Table 1.1 provides a summary of the major differences among quantitative, qualitative, and mixed research so that you might be able to compare the three traditions with respect to goals, reasoning, and, data collection; and, more so, when you begin to review sources, you might recognize unique and common characteristics of each tradition.

The three major research traditions can be viewed as lying on a continuum—with quantitative research, in its purest form, located on the left side of the continuum; qualitative research, in its purest form, located on the right side of the continuum; and mixed research lying somewhere between the extreme ends.

Table 1.1   Comparison of quantitative, mixed, and qualitative research

Component	Quantitative Research	Mixed Research	Qualitative Research
Dominant research goal	Confirmatory (i.e., a priori or *top down*): The researcher tests hypotheses and theory by collecting, analyzing, and interpreting data	Exploratory and Confirmatory (i.e., iterative): The researcher collects, analyzes, and interprets data to generate hypotheses that are subsequently tested	Exploratory (i.e., a posteriori or *bottom up*): The researcher collects, analyzes, and interprets data (e.g., via interviews, observations) and generates (grounded) theory and/or hypotheses
Reasoning	Deductive: The researcher arrives at specific conclusions based on a set of premises or hypotheses	Abductive: The researcher converts observations into theories and then assesses those theories through subsequent collection, analysis, and interpretation of data	Inductive: The researcher makes generalizations based on a specific number of observations
Relationship to the research process	Objective: The researcher is independent of the knowledge sought (i.e., researcher and knowledge sought cannot be separated)	Intersubjective: The researcher conducts a study under the assumption or belief that knowledge is both constructed and based on the reality of the world we experience and in which we live	Subjective: Researchers strive to eliminate their biases and remain emotionally detached and uninvolved with the knowledge sought; knowledge is socially constructed
Dominant research objectives	Describe, explain, predict, influence	Explore, describe, explain, predict, influence	Explore, describe

Component	Quantitative Research	Mixed Research	Qualitative Research
Research questions	The researcher poses questions that tend to be very specific in nature and can be descriptive (i.e., seek to quantify responses on one or more variables; e.g., begin with the words *What is...* or *What are...*), comparative (i.e., seek to compare two or more groups on some outcome variable; e.g., use words such as *differ* and *compare*), or relationship (i.e., concerned with trends between/among two [or more] variables; e.g., use words such as *relate*, *relationship*, *association*, and "trend")	The researcher poses questions that combine or mix both quantitative and qualitative research questions and that necessitate that both quantitative data and qualitative data be collected and analyzed concurrently, sequentially, or iteratively	The researcher poses questions that tend to be open-ended, non-directional, and emergent. They tend to address "what" and "how" questions, and comprise either grand tour questions (i.e., representing broad or central questions) or specific subquestions (i.e., issue subquestions, which address the major concerns and complexities to be resolved [e.g., "What does it mean for a researcher to conduct a literature review?"] and topical subquestions, which arise from a need for information for the description of the case [e.g., "What do researchers do when they conduct a literature review?"])
Focus	Numeric: The researcher collects numeric data using structured and validated data-collection instruments such as standardized tests and rating scales	Multiple forms: The researcher uses instruments that generate numeric and/or non-numeric data (e.g., words, observations, images)	Breadth and depth: The researcher investigates the breadth and depth of a phenomenon
Nature of observation	Controlled setting: The researcher attempts to examine a phenomenon under as controlled a condition as possible, attempting to examine causal effect of outcomes of interest	Multiple settings: The researcher examines a phenomenon in multiple contexts, conditions, or perspectives	Natural setting: The researcher examines a phenomenon in its natural environment, examining the context in which this phenomenon occurs
Type of data	Numeric: The researcher collects numeric data using structured and validated data-collection instruments such as standardized tests and rating scales	Multiple forms: The researcher uses instruments that generate numeric and/or non-numeric data (e.g., words, observations, images)	Words, observations, and images: The researcher collects qualitative-based data from sources such as interviews, focus groups, observations, field notes, and documents; the researcher is the primary data-collection instrument

TOOL: A DEPICTION OF THE RESEARCH CONTINUUM

Figure 1.1 illustrates the research traditions and various combinations of research traditions that are used in mixed research.

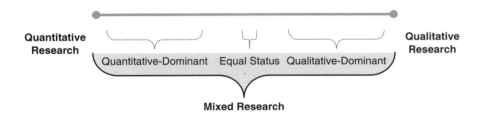

Figure 1.1   The research continuum

As seen in Figure 1.1, mixed research, in its most interactive and integrative form, lies in the center. This form of mixed research is called equal-status mixed research, which represents approximately equal use of quantitative and qualitative approaches (Johnson, Onwuegbuzie, & Turner, 2007). The more quantitative-dominant mixed research lies somewhere on the left half of the continuum (but not at the far left). The farthest left of the continuum is quantitative research in its purest form. In contrast, the more qualitative-dominant mixed research lies somewhere on the right half of the continuum.

As you look over the figure, keep in mind that qualitative-dominant mixed research involves mixed research studies in which the researcher(s) places more weight on the qualitative research phase or component than on the quantitative research phase or component. How much weight the researcher(s) places in a mixed research study depends on the researcher's philosophical belief about the degree that quantitative and qualitative approaches can and should be mixed, research question(s), sample design used (i.e., sample size and how the participants are selected for each component/phase [e.g., random vs. non-random sampling]), and practical (e.g., available resources) and situational (e.g., research setting) considerations. The converse is true for quantitative-dominant mixed research. Thus, (empirical) research studies representing all three traditions fall somewhere on this continuum. As a result, the literature (studies in published form) is an anthology of varying degrees of quantitative, qualitative, or mixed inquiry. Undoubtedly, the biggest commonality among all three traditions is the researchers' attempt to build on prior knowledge. The best way to obtain this prior knowledge is by conducting the literature review. As such, the literature review represents the most important step of the research process, regardless of which tradition is used.

THE LITERATURE REVIEW: PROCESS AND PRODUCT

The literature review is the most effective way of becoming familiar not only with previous findings but also with the research methodology used in previous research. Most commonly, the literature review appears either within an introduction section of a research report, or is a section presented just after the introduction section if the review was conducted to inform primary research. We discuss, through our own literature review of common myths presented in this chapter, that the words *literature review* include much more than just reporting on other published research studies on a topic. When considering the process of the literature review, we recognize that not only is the final product to be considered (including sources beyond printed literature), but much like the research process, also the overall process is to be considered, including all the decisions that a literature reviewer makes along the way.

MYTHS ASSOCIATED WITH THE LITERATURE REVIEW

A myth is a false collected belief that is passed through time. In this case, due to the many myths associated with the literature review, researchers are misled into believing that the literature review is a type of report that simply describes prior studies. In fact, many research methodology textbooks unfortunately give the false impression that "the review of the literature is a preliminary, cursory exercise that must be endured prior to the start of the 'real' study" (Dellinger, 2005, p. 52) and that "writing a literature review is no more complicated than writing a high school term paper" (Boote & Beile, 2005, p. 5). In fact, building on the work of Onwuegbuzie, Collins, Leech, Dellinger, and Jiao (2010), we have identified 10 myths about literature reviews that are promulgated in the literature, particularly in research methodology textbooks. The 10 myths relate to each other with respect to three elements: scope, sequence, and identity. The first five myths are misconceptions pertaining to the scope of the literature review; the next three myths are misconceptions pertaining to sequence of the literature review. The final two myths, which include the number-one myth of the literature review, pertain to the mis-identity of the literature review. We present these myths in descending order—in countdown fashion.

MYTHS OF SCOPE

THE TENTH MYTH: THE LITERATURE REVIEW HAS ONE GOAL. Some researchers and textbook authors mistakenly believe that literature reviews are conducted only to inform primary research—that is, to inform a qualitative, quantitative, or mixed research study conducted by a researcher. Yet, the review of the literature can be an end in itself—that is, as a stand-alone work. In fact, the literature review can be conducted to inform practice or to provide a comprehensive understanding of what is known about a topic or issue.

EXAMPLE: THE LITERATURE REVIEW AS A STAND-ALONE PROJECT

When one of the author's (Tony's) father experienced a brain aneurysm, while he lay in a coma, I had to conduct a thorough review of the literature to decide which of the several brain surgery options provided to my family by the brain surgeon my father should undergo. This review led to us selecting a technique known as keyhole brain surgery, which, fortunately, turned out to be successful. As such, there are two major goals for literature reviews: (a) as a stand-alone review, or an end in itself (i.e., independent work) and (b) as an informative review for primary research at one or more phases of the research process (i.e., research conceptualization phase, research planning phase, research implementation phase, and research dissemination phase).

THE NINTH MYTH: THE LITERATURE REVIEW ALWAYS VARIES WITH THE TYPE OF PRIMARY STUDY. Quite often, authors of textbooks misrepresent the literature review by stating that the literature review is different depending on the type of primary study that is intended to be conducted, with the literature review particularly being different for quantitative and qualitative research studies. For example, it is a mistake to believe that *all* qualitative researchers do not conduct their literature review until their study is well under way—in particular, after some or even all the data have been collected. However, literature reviews are needed for virtually all qualitative research designs, at the very least, for the researcher to understand better the context of the study. One notable exception is grounded theory research, which represents a study involving a rigorous set of systematic procedures to produce substantive theory of social phenomena from data (Glaser & Strauss, 1967), wherein some proponents argue against an initial literature review being conducted before data collection. Interestingly, however, some grounded theorists hold the opposite view (for an excellent discussion of the advantages and disadvantages of conducting a literature review prior to collecting data in grounded theory research, see McGhee, Marland, & Atkinson, 2007).

Another misrepresentation that falls under this second myth stems from authors who state or imply that qualitative research studies only necessitate including qualitative studies in the literature review section. Yet, citing quantitative research studies in the literature review section—or anywhere else in the article for that matter—does not prevent a primary study from being classified as qualitative research. Moreover, conducting research—whether quantitative, qualitative, or mixed research—without adequate knowledge of previous, relevant methodology and empirical findings represents poor practice.

These ideas that the literature reviews for qualitative research studies are different than are those for quantitative research studies are misleading because there are many published qualitative research studies that have detailed literature reviews that inform the study. For example, Astor, Meyer, and Behre (1999) conducted a qualitative research study in which they asked students and teachers in five high schools to identify the "locations and times of the most violent events and most dangerous areas in and around the school" and "to identify the ages and genders of the perpetrators/victims of the violent events" (p. 3). These researchers then interviewed the students and teachers about why they believed violence occurred in the locations and times that they had identified. Despite the fact that this study represented qualitative research, the authors conducted an in-depth literature review—that occupied more than 7.5 pages of the 40-page article (i.e., 18.8%). Thus, in most instances, the onset of a rigorous review of the literature occurs before the primary quantitative, qualitative, or mixed research study begins. However, as explained in the third myth, the literature review does more than only inform the primary study.

THE EIGHTH MYTH: THE AMOUNT OF LITERATURE DETERMINES THE IMPORTANCE OF THE TOPIC. It is a common misbelief of some research methodology textbook authors that the importance of a research topic is determined by the amount of available literature. This is not at all the case. In fact, a sparse number of available works in an area might well mean that there is comparatively scant available literature and that the researcher has identified a new important area to research. Believing this myth, over the years, some of our graduate students unwisely decided to abandon their research topics after

their literature reviews revealed scant literature on their topic. When they have notified us of their intentions beforehand, we have been able to persuade them not to do so, informing them that their lack of literature was a *desirable* outcome because it made it obvious that there was a gap in our knowledge base in this area.

Further, we inform our students that even if little or no literature exists on a research topic, by searching for related topics, the researcher can still conduct a rigorous literature review. For example, when one of the authors of this textbook (i.e., Tony) was conducting a literature review for his dissertation research on statistics anxiety nearly two decades ago, he identified only a handful of works published in this area. However, on reviewing the numerous works published on the related areas of mathematics anxiety, test anxiety, and general anxiety, and using these works to inform the construct of statistics anxiety, he was able to conduct an extensive review of the literature (cf. Onwuegbuzie, 1993).

THE SEVENTH MYTH: LITERATURE REVIEWS ARE VALUE NEUTRAL. An additional myth perpetuated by textbook authors that involves the scope of the literature review is that it represents the body of information in a neutral way. However, the scope is much broader because, when writing literature reviews, authors make a series of decisions such as what literature is included and excluded, what literature is emphasized or criticized, and so on. Therefore, oftentimes inadvertently, a literature review is inclusive of a perspective—in some way or another. Rather than attempting to be neutral, reviewers should strive to be **systematic.**

We define *systematic* as a set of rigorous routines, documentation of such routines, and the way the literature reviewer negotiates particular biases throughout these routines. This means that you should bring the same level of rigor to your review as you would if you were producing primary research evidence, and include transparent procedures to find, to evaluate, and to synthesize the results of relevant research. However, differing from some of the health science field definitions of "systematic literature reviews," we believe that a literature reviewer cannot maintain a fully neutral position in literature research, but is guided by philosophical assumptions and belief systems that impact decisions in the literature review process.

However, most importantly, as we will discuss in the next chapter, literature reviews are shaped by, and shape, your cultural lens. For example, a reviewer representing one culture (e.g., an indigenous background) might interpret the literature on a culture-based topic differently than might a reviewer representing another culture.

THE SIXTH MYTH: THE LITERATURE REVIEW IS A SUMMARY OF THE EXTANT LITERATURE.
Another myth associated with the literature review is that the literature review represents only a *summary* of the extant literature. Yet, the review of the literature involves much more than summarizing information. Indeed, if the reviewer only summarizes each piece of information (e.g., each research article), then he/she likely will end up summarizing information that is incomplete and perhaps even misleading. In addition to summarizing each piece of information, as previously noted, a reviewer should evaluate and analyze information before deciding whether to include the works in the final set of information pieces that are combined into a coherent whole that informs the literature review—a process known as **synthesizing**. After investigating various sources, or evidence of previous research findings, the literature reviewer interprets the collection of previous research findings through summarizing, analyzing, evaluating, and synthesizing. These four objectives will be discussed in more depth in Step 5.

MYTHS OF SEQUENCE

THE FIFTH MYTH: THE LITERATURE REVIEW IN QUANTITATIVE RESEARCH ENDS AT THE ONSET OF THE PRIMARY STUDY.
Another misinterpretation of the literature review is that in quantitative research, the search for related literature should be completed before the primary study begins. This statement falsely gives the impression that the literature review has an ending point before the primary research study begins and is not revisited. The literature review typically should take place throughout the research process—that is, before, during, and after the research study. For instance, whenever an unexpected finding emerges in quantitative, qualitative, or mixed research studies, the researcher should re-examine the literature in an attempt to contextualize it.

EXAMPLE: CONTINUING A LITERATURE REVIEW THROUGHOUT PRIMARY RESEARCH

Onwuegbuzie, Collins, and Elbedour (2003) conducted a quantitative research study wherein they investigated the role of group composition on the quality of a research article critique and research proposal written by 70 cooperative learning groups of graduate students (ranging in size from 2 to 7) enrolled in 15 sections of an introductory-level education research methodology course. These researchers observed a positive relationship between research aptitude (i.e., mean midterm and final examination scores) and group outcomes (i.e., scores on the research article critique and research proposal assignments), wherein "groups that contained high-achieving students on an individual level tended to produce better group outcomes than did their low-achieving counterparts" (p. 226). As a result of this relationship, these researchers conducted a review of the literature to ascertain whether this phenomenon had been identified by other researchers in other contexts.

This literature review led these researchers to label the relationship that emerged in their study as a *Matthew effect*, which is a phrase given to connote the idea of the "rich getting richer"—in their study, it represented the finding that groups with the highest average individual achievement level (i.e., the richest) tended to produce the greatest group-based research article critiques and research proposals (i.e., became richer), and vice versa. These researchers then went on to discuss the origin and evolution of the use of the Matthew effect, as well as hypothesize why the Matthew effect might have occurred.

In fact, the assertion that the literature review ends at the onset of the primary study stems from erroneous beliefs that (a) research is a linear process, instead of being interactive, fluid, and iterative; (b) literature reviews are static rather than representing evolving and continuous processes; and (c) literature reviews are one-dimensional in terms of their function (i.e., only to provide information about the topic) rather than being multidimensional (i.e., they can be used to provide information about all aspects of the research process). In fact, it is such erroneous beliefs that led Nobel Laureate Sir Peter Medawar (1964, p. 42) to call the conventional scientific paper "a fraud" because it portrays "a totally mistaken conception, even a travesty, of the nature of scientific thought."

Interestingly, when Onwuegbuzie et al. (2003) originally submitted their manuscript to the *Journal of Educational Research* for review for possible publication, several of the journal reviewers questioned the fact that the Matthew effect was not discussed in the literature review section of the manuscript and was presented only in the discussion section. Because of this criticism, the editor recommended that these authors insert a discussion of the Matthew effect in the literature review section of the revised version of their manuscript. However, in revising their manuscript, the researchers had to argue in their cover letter that to insert such a discussion would be misleading because it would give the impression that the decision to discuss the Matthew effect came to the fore prior to the collection and analysis of data. Wisely, the editor agreed with the researchers' argument and agreed that the presentation of the Matthew effect should occur only in the discussion section to reflect when it originated.

THE FOURTH MYTH: THE LITERATURE REVIEW IS A LINEAR PROCESS.

A myth advanced by authors of research methodology textbooks is that the literature review represents a linear process, with the literature review always preceding the reviewer's own primary research study. Although the literature review tends to precede the primary research study in most instances, there is no reason why research cannot oscillate between the primary research study and the extant information. As a methodology, the literature review is iterative and is influenced by, and influences, the researcher's belief systems, values, and philosophical assumptions (i.e., claims about knowledge and how it can be obtained that guide research). The idea that the literature review is a non-linear process is consistent with Bates's (1989) concept of berrypicking, wherein literature reviewers

> begin with just one feature of a broader topic, or just one relevant reference, and move through a variety of sources. Each new piece of information they encounter gives them new ideas and directions to follow and, consequently, a new conception of the query…Furthermore, at each stage, with each different conception of the query, the user may identify useful information and references. In other words, the query is satisfied not by a single final retrieved set, but by a series of selections of individual references and bits of information at each stage of the ever-modifying search. A bit-at-a-time retrieval of this sort is here called berrypicking. This term is used by analogy to picking huckleberries or blueberries in the forest. The berries are scattered on the

bushes; they do not come in bunches. One must pick them one at a time. One could do berrypicking of information without the search need itself changing (evolving). (¶ 23)

This concept of non-linearity will be discussed in our forthcoming definition of the literature review.

THE THIRD MYTH: THE LITERATURE REVIEW IS ONLY ONE PHASE IN THE RESEARCH PROCESS.

Another myth advanced by virtually all authors of research methodology textbooks is that the literature review represents only one phase of the research process. Yet, as we outline in the next chapter, the literature review represents a study in its own right. Indeed, in what they termed the research synthesis, Onwuegbuzie, Collins, et al. (2010) mapped the 13 steps of the mixed research process—as conceptualized by Collins, Onwuegbuzie, and Sutton (2006)—onto the literature review process. Thus, Onwuegbuzie, Collins, et al. (2010) outlined the literature review process as representing a study that contains 13 steps.

At this point, the number of steps involved in a literature review is not as important as is the recognition that the literature review process is tantamount to a study. In fact, as we will discuss later in this book, the literature review process can represent a quantitative research study (e.g., a meta-analysis, which involves summarizing or aggregating the results of individual quantitative research studies obtained from a literature review that address one or more related research hypotheses; Glass, 1976); a qualitative research study (e.g., meta-synthesis, which "is a form of systematic review or integration of qualitative research findings in a target domain that are themselves interpretive syntheses of data"; Sandelowski & Barroso, 2003, p. 227); or a mixed research study (e.g., combining meta-analyses and meta-syntheses)—although we recommend that the most rigorous of literature reviews utilize mixed research techniques and, thus, represent mixed research studies. With this in mind, we contend that whenever researchers conduct an empirical study, the literature review process essentially turns that study into two studies—a literature review study and the primary study. This might be somewhat scary to a beginning researcher; however, as you will see throughout this textbook, the literature review study actually helps researchers to optimize their primary research studies by facilitating the decisions that they make at *every* stage of the primary research process.

MYTHS OF IDENTITY

THE SECOND MYTH: THE LITERATURE REVIEW INVOLVES THE REVIEW OF ONLY PUBLISHED WORKS. An extremely common myth that permeates research methodology textbooks is that the literature review involves the review of *only* published works. Unfortunately, this myth is perpetuated beyond research methodology textbooks. For example, a University of Toronto website defines the literature review as follows: "A literature review is an account of what has been *published* on a topic by accredited scholars and researchers" [emphasis added]. In fact, most research methodology textbooks provide excellent information about how to search for relevant published works (e.g., via library subscription databases), but no information as to how to search for *unpublished* works.

Yet, unpublished works, otherwise known as *grey* (or *gray*) *literature*, represent a very important source of information. Interestingly, representatives of the Sixth International Conference on Grey Literature which was held in New York, in 2004, defined grey literature as follows: "That which is produced on all levels of government, academics, business and industry in print and electronic formats, but which is not controlled by commercial publishers, i.e. where publishing is not the primary activity of the producing body" (Grey Literature Conference Program, 2004). Grey literature represents works that are not usually attainable through conventional channels. However, grey literature "is frequently original and usually recent" (Debachere, 1995, p. 94). The *grey* in grey literature refers to the brain's *grey matter* because so much of this literature is extremely intellectual in nature and, thus, is significant for making knowledge claims in many subject areas. Grey literature as a genre has a long history, dating back to at least the 1920s, particularly among scientific circles in Europe (Augur, 1989).

In general, grey literature items represent non-conventional and sometimes ephemeral works that include the following: reports (e.g., pre-prints, preliminary progress and advanced reports, technical reports from government agencies or scientific research groups, statistical reports, memoranda, state-of-the-art reports, market research reports, working papers from research groups or committees, white papers), conference proceedings, technical reports, technical specifications and standards, non-commercial translations, bibliographies, technical and commercial documentation, and official documents that have not been published commercially (e.g., government reports and documents) (Alberani, Pietrangeli, & Mazza, 1990), with translations and reports constituting a major portion of grey literature (Augur, 1989). According to Augur (1989), the following types of organizations issue grey literature: associations, churches, county councils, educational establishments, federations, institutes, institutions, laboratories, libraries, museums, private publishers, research establishments, societies, trade unions, trusts, and universities.

The fact that, to date, there have been 15 international conferences on grey literature (cf. http://www.textrelease.com/gl15conference/organizations.html) and seven volumes of a journal devoted to grey literature, called *The Grey Journal: An International Journal on Grey Literature*, which appears in both print and electronic formats (cf. http://www.textrelease.com/publications/journal.html)—with the first volume appearing in 2005—and a recent book on grey literature (Farace & Schöpfel, 2010) provides compelling evidence of the importance of unpublished works.

THE FIRST MYTH: THE LITERATURE REVIEW INVOLVES *ONLY* THE COLLECTION OF LITERATURE. Undoubtedly, the most prevalent myth perpetuated by authors of research methodology textbooks is that the literature review involves *only* the collection of literature that already exists either in printed or digital forms. However, with the Web 2.0 technology available for literature reviewers, information does not have to represent only literature. Multimodality, as noted by Kress (2010), refers to **semiotics** (i.e., the study of communication through signs and symbols) and the dissemination of messages through modes, or various levels of media. Within multimodal texts and settings, Kress (2010) explains that "a society, its cultures and the representations of their meanings form a tightly and integrated whole, at a certain level of generality" (p. 8). As such, because we believe that culture is important in understanding literature and other sources, the inclusion of modes as culturally embedded representations are important resources for literature reviews.

Further, Web 2.0 tools have allowed literature reviewers access to databases, images, guidebooks, maps, and other tools, simply by the click of a mouse. Thus, in Chapter 8, we expand the concept of multimodal texts and settings to include any of the following five major MODES—**M**edia, **O**bservation(s), **D**ocuments, **E**xpert(s) in the field, and **S**econdary data—as an extension of the literature search. In this chapter, we present some guiding criteria for evaluating electronic sources in Step 5 of our model. Indeed, because literature (i.e., documents) represents only one of these five MODES, we prefer the term *research synthesis* of literature as opposed to the traditional term—*review* of literature. The traditional term *review* promulgates this first myth. However, to keep the peace (for now), we are using the term literature review. But keep in mind that particular philosophical assumptions and belief systems, situated in cultural traditions, drive the decisions throughout the review process.

TOOL: A SUMMARY OF TEN MYTHS TO AVOID

Table 1.2 presents a short review of the 10 myths.

Table 1.2   Summary table of myths associated with conducting the literature review

Type		Label
Scope	Myth 10	The Literature Review has One Goal
	Myth 9	The Literature Review Always Varies with the Type of Primary Study
	Myth 8	The Amount of Literature Determines the Importance of the Topic
	Myth 7	Literature Reviews are Value Neutral
	Myth 6	The Literature Review is a Summary of the Extant Literature
Sequence	Myth 5	The Literature Review in Quantitative Research Ends at the Onset of the Primary Study
	Myth 4	The Literature Review is a Linear Process
	Myth 3	The Literature Review is Only One Phase in the Research Process
Identity	Myth 2	The Literature Review Involves the Review of Only Published Works
	Myth 1	The Literature Review Involves *Only* the Collection of Literature

APPLYING CONCEPTS

Now that we have explored the broader picture—the pursuit of furthering knowledge in any specific subject area and the pitfalls perpetuated by the 10 myths, we turn to the practical and specific reasons that you might have for conducting a literature review.

REASONS FOR CONDUCTING THE LITERATURE REVIEW

Perhaps your review is intentional—that is, you have been assigned a topic, say, by your course instructor, to explain a particular phenomenon. Or, perhaps your review is exploratory, whereby you are seeking to inform your primary research or thesis/dissertation study, but you are not quite sure exactly where to begin. In many graduate-level programs, the literature review is incorporated into research methodology courses, and often becomes the foundation for your

TOOL: A REVIEW OF REASONS TO CONDUCT A LITERATURE REVIEW

Figure 1.2 presents a typology of the most common reasons that researchers use to conduct the literature review. We have categorized these reasons into three major areas: topic-driven focused, method-driven focused, and connection-driven focused.

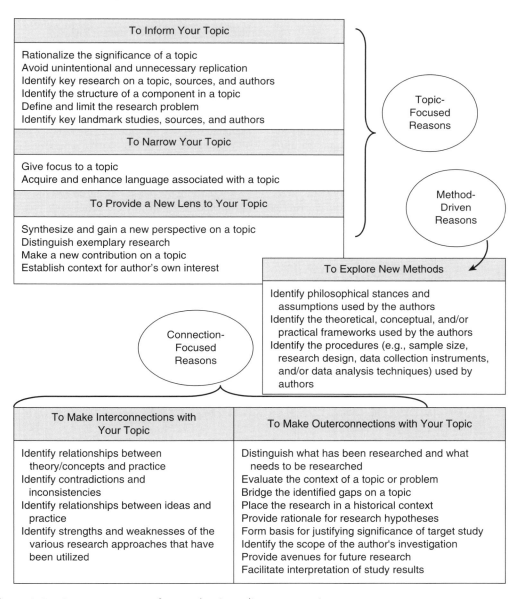

Figure 1.2   Common reasons for conducting a literature review

primary research as a rite of passage in a thesis/dissertation toward graduation. Regardless, the literature review will help you to become extremely knowledgeable about a topic by knowing what has been addressed already, what key issues influence it, and the main criticisms associated with it.

GOALS OF THE LITERATURE REVIEW

Before the literature review even begins, the reviewer must determine its goal. As noted previously, the goal of the literature review can be twofold: (a) a stand-alone study, or an end in itself, or (b) a study to inform primary research. Regardless of the goal, the literature review does not only represent a high level of scholarship, but also represents an original and unique product impacted by the sum of our experiences, education, training, values, morals, and spiritual influences, which, at times, are negotiated through the practice of **reflexivity**. Reflexivity is a circular process of observing the effects of the research process on the researcher (or literature reviewer) and how this effect influences the researched. Whatever the goal of the literature review (i.e., as an end in itself, to inform primary research), and whatever the topic area, literature reviewers should be **rigorous.** By rigorous, we mean conducting a literature review that is (a) **defensible** (i.e., integrates a rationale for decisions of inquiry, strategies, and designs), (b)

systematic (i.e., follows a set of guidelines such as the model that we outline in subsequent chapters), (c) **evaluative** (i.e., whereby every step of the process is evaluated for relevancy and credibility), and (d) **transparent** (i.e., documenting beliefs, values, and philosophical assumptions and stances pertaining to decisions).

THE IMPORTANCE OF TRANSPARENCY

Literature reviews should be reproducible to some extent with respect to the decisions made during the process by leaving what qualitative researchers call an **audit trail**—a strategy advanced by Halpern (1983) and Schwandt and Halpern (1988). In the context of literature reviews, an audit trail is a detailed description of the steps taken from the start of a literature review to its end, which includes the presentation of the review. Simply put, an audit trail represents records that are kept regarding the procedures used and the steps taken during the literature review process. It is like a trail of bread crumbs on a path, which might lead another researcher to understand her/his journey in collecting sources for her/his review. In particular, when developing an audit trail, Halpern (1983) noted particular categories for documenting information related to **credibility**, or what might also be known as **internal validity**, which, pertaining to the literature review, is the reviewer's reconstruction or representation of the views of an author and include:

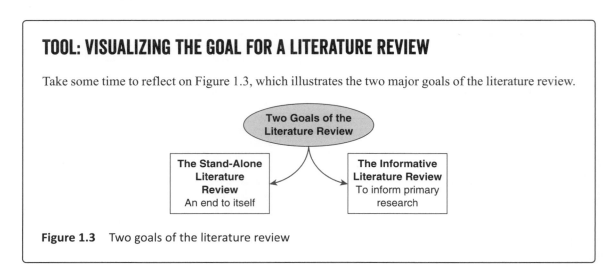

TOOL: VISUALIZING THE GOAL FOR A LITERATURE REVIEW

Take some time to reflect on Figure 1.3, which illustrates the two major goals of the literature review.

Two Goals of the Literature Review

The Stand-Alone Literature Review
An end to itself

The Informative Literature Review
To inform primary research

Figure 1.3   Two goals of the literature review

- raw data (e.g., all selected literature, written field notes)
- data reduction and analysis products (e.g., summaries such as condensed notes, quantitative summaries, qualitative summaries, and theoretical notes)
- process notes that include methodological notes (e.g., procedures, strategies, rationales, designs) and trustworthiness notes (i.e., relating to credibility, validity, and appropriateness of the information collected)
- materials relating to intentions and dispositions that include personal notes (e.g., reflexive notes whereby the literature reviewers document their ideas, thoughts, experiences, concerns, challenges, and motivations) and expectations (e.g., predictions and intentions)

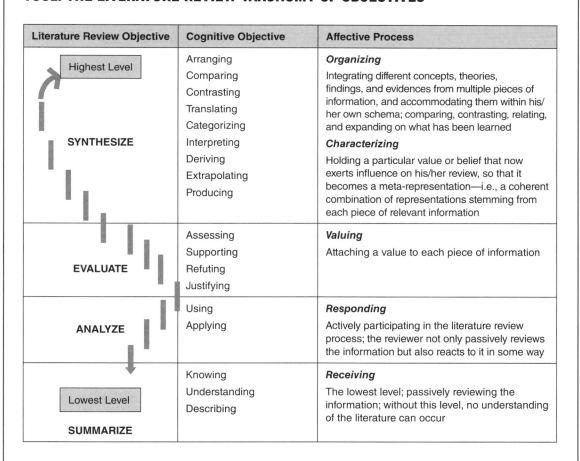

TOOL: THE LITERATURE REVIEW TAXONOMY OF OBJECTIVES

Literature Review Objective	Cognitive Objective	Affective Process
Highest Level / SYNTHESIZE	Arranging, Comparing, Contrasting, Translating, Categorizing, Interpreting, Deriving, Extrapolating, Producing	**Organizing** — Integrating different concepts, theories, findings, and evidences from multiple pieces of information, and accommodating them within his/her own schema; comparing, contrasting, relating, and expanding on what has been learned **Characterizing** — Holding a particular value or belief that now exerts influence on his/her review, so that it becomes a meta-representation—i.e., a coherent combination of representations stemming from each piece of relevant information
EVALUATE	Assessing, Supporting, Refuting, Justifying	**Valuing** — Attaching a value to each piece of information
ANALYZE	Using, Applying	**Responding** — Actively participating in the literature review process; the reviewer not only passively reviews the information but also reacts to it in some way
Lowest Level / SUMMARIZE	Knowing, Understanding, Describing	**Receiving** — The lowest level; passively reviewing the information; without this level, no understanding of the literature can occur

Figure 1.4 Literature review taxonomy of objectives mapped onto Bloom's taxonomy of cognitive objectives and affective processes. Adapted from "Literature review taxonomy of objectives," by A. J. Onwuegbuzie, 2010, unpublished manuscript, Sam Houston State University, Huntsville, TX. Copyright 2010 by A. J. Onwuegbuzie.

OBJECTIVES OF THE LITERATURE REVIEW

Now that we have introduced the idea that a literature review is much more than just a review or report of the literature, and that a literature can stand alone as an end in itself or can serve to inform primary research, it is noteworthy to establish some internal objectives within these two goals. Based on Bloom, Engelhart, Furst, Hill, and Krathwohl's (1956) and Krathwohl, Bloom, and Masia's (1964) taxonomy of learning, we have built on the idea from Onwuegbuzie, Collins, et al. (2010) that a literature review process involves the four factors of summarizing, analyzing, evaluating, and synthesizing (Krathwohl, 2002). As such, we present what Onwuegbuzie (2010) calls the *Literature Review Taxonomy of Objectives*, which is displayed in Figure 1.4. This figure is appropriate for understanding objectives as relating to Bloom et al.'s (1956) taxonomy of cognitive objectives and affective processes.

As you will experience conducting a literature review, you will have action-based inputs, such as searching the literature and storing the literature. However, the four objectives—summarize, analyze, evaluate, and synthesize—are cognitive and affective responses that, in turn, influence your final report. These four objectives form a hierarchy, with summarizing being the lowest level of a literature review and synthesizing being the highest level. Thus, the literature reviewer should strive for this high level of integration.

THE COMPREHENSIVE LITERATURE REVIEW (CLR) DEFINED IN DETAIL

As we previously discussed in the definition of the CLR, the integrated process of the seven steps represents a methodology, which yields a synthesis of information that can stand alone as a type of "desk" research, or can inform primary research. Early in this chapter, we presented a (macro) definition of the CLR:

> The Comprehensive Literature Review (CLR) is a methodology, conducted either to stand alone or to inform primary research at multiple stages of the research process, which optimally involves the use of mixed research techniques inclusive of culture, ethics, and multimodal texts and settings in a systematic, holistic, synergistic, and cyclical process of exploring, interpreting, synthesizing, and communicating published and/or unpublished information.

EXTENDED DEFINITION OF THE CLR

Expanding on our macro definition, and addressing each of the 10 aforementioned myths, the following more specific (micro) definition completes our vision for incorporating a rigorous and ethical process, awareness of culture, and multimodal sources.

BOX 1.2

CLR MICRO DEFINITION

The Comprehensive Literature Review (CLR) is a methodological, culturally progressive approach involving the practice of documenting the process of inquiry into the current state of knowledge about a selected topic as related to philosophical assumptions/beliefs, inquiry (method), and guidelines of practice (organization, summarization, analysis, synthesis, reflection, and evaluation), resulting in a product that is a logical argument of an interpretation of relevant published and/or unpublished information on the selected topic from multimodal texts and settings that primarily comprise five MODES (i.e., **M**edia, **O**bservation(s), **D**ocuments, **E**xpert(s) in the field, and **S**econdary sources). In addition to representing a continuous, iterative, interactive, and dynamic process, the CLR also is holistic and synergistic. The final product, which either stands alone or is used to inform primary quantitative, qualitative, and mixed research, is situated in society for influencing future ways of knowing.

It can be seen that both the general (i.e., macro) and specific (i.e., micro) definitions refute all 10 myths. Specifically, both the tenth myth (i.e., "The Literature Review has One Goal") and the ninth myth (i.e., "The Literature Review Always Varies with the Type of Primary Study") are dismantled by the following phrase "which either represents an end in itself or is used to inform primary quantitative, qualitative, and mixed research." The fifth myth (i.e., "The Literature Review in Quantitative Research Ends at the Onset of the Primary Study") and fourth myth (i.e., "The Literature Review is a Linear Process") are refuted via the following sentence: "In addition to representing a continuous, iterative, interactive, and dynamic process, the CLR also is holistic and synergistic." The eighth myth (i.e., "The Amount of Literature Determines the Importance of the Topic") is addressed by the phrase "is situated in society for influencing future ways of knowing."

The seventh myth (i.e., "Literature Reviews are Value Neutral") is countered by the phrase "The Comprehensive Literature Review (CLR) is a... culturally progressive approach." The sixth myth (i.e., "The Literature Review is a Summary of the Extant Literature") is rebutted by the following phrase: "organization, summarization, analysis, synthesis, reflection, and evaluation." The third myth (i.e., "The Literature Review is Only One Phase in the Research Process") is refuted via the opening statement, "The Comprehensive Literature Review (CLR) is a methodological...approach." The second myth (i.e., "The Literature Review Involves the Review of Only Published Works") is countered by the following phrase: "an interpretation of relevant published and/or unpublished information." Finally, the first myth (i.e., "The Literature Review Involves *Only* the Collection of Literature") is invalidated by the following phrase: "resulting in a product that is a logical argument of an interpretation of relevant published and/or unpublished information on the selected topic from multimodal texts and settings that primarily comprise five MODES (i.e., Media, Observation(s), Documents, Expert(s) in the field, and Secondary sources)."

WHERE TO FIND A LITERATURE REVIEW

Although empirical primary research article designs might vary from journal to journal, typically, research articles include some variation of the following major sections: title, author(s) and affiliation(s), introduction, method, results, discussion, references, and appendices. As we explained when dispelling some of the myths of the literature review, the literature review informs many parts of primary research. If the literature review is an end in itself, it is in fact the parts of the research. Therefore, although we work toward a rigorous design for the literature as a whole, it is not uncommon that a literature review uses parts of the review in more than one section of a research report.

Figure 1.5 presents the eight major parts of a primary research report. For the most part, the research synthesis is situated within the first narrative section, the introduction section (cf. American Psychological Association, 2010), throughout four major parts: (a) introduction and explanation of the problem; (b) exploration of the importance of the problem; (c) description of the synthesis of relevant scholarship (i.e., the literature review report); and (d) statement of hypotheses and the correspondence to the forthcoming research design. As can be seen in Figure 1.5, although the introduction section is the focal presentation of the research synthesis report, other parts of the introduction and other parts of the primary research report (if the literature review is intended to inform primary research) depend on the argument that you will build through your literature review report—within the primary research report.

CONCLUSIONS

It is important to recognize that you will become extremely knowledgeable in the literature review process as a researcher. In short, you will learn how to conduct rigorous and transparent research during your literature review process by providing an audit trail and by reflecting on your beliefs and philosophical assumptions. Everything you do in your reviewing of literature is a result of cultural competence, ethics, philosophical assumptions, and your beliefs on a topic.

Review these foundational ideas:

- The quest for knowledge is the basis for research and is presented through literature.
- The three research traditions (quantitative, qualitative, and mixed) differ in approach to understanding knowledge and lie on a continuum.

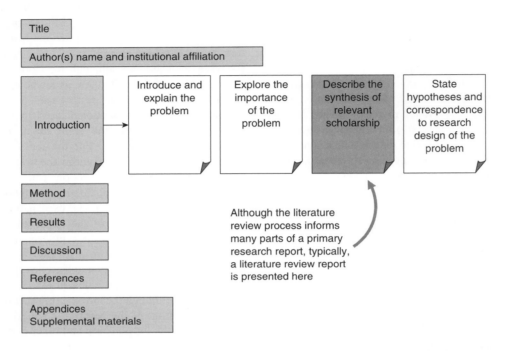

TOOL: A MAP OF THE SECTIONS OF A TYPICAL PRIMARY RESEARCH REPORT

Title

Author(s) name and institutional affiliation

Introduction → Introduce and explain the problem | Explore the importance of the problem | Describe the synthesis of relevant scholarship | State hypotheses and correspondence to research design of the problem

Method

Results

Discussion

References

Appendices
Supplemental materials

Although the literature review process informs many parts of a primary research report, typically, a literature review report is presented here

Figure 1.5 The major parts of a primary research report and where to find the literature review

- The literature review is the most important component of the research process because it builds on prior knowledge. Therefore, it is important to maintain that the literature review, as a process and product, in essence, is a methodology.
- It is important to recognize the 10 common myths surrounding traditional literature reviews so that you might avoid adopting these misbeliefs.
- The common reasons that researchers use for conducting literature reviews are numerous, and can add knowledge on both a topic and methodology pertaining to the investigation.
- The literature review should be defensible, evaluative, systematic, and transparent. There are two major goals of a literature review: as an end in itself, or as the means to inform primary research. In the latter case, the literature review flows throughout the study.

- Objectives of the literature review extend to many phases in research: background, method, analysis, and discussion sections.
- The CLR underscores the interacting concepts of documentation of your process and inquiry, and extends your search to include other modes as needed.

THE CORE PRODUCT

At the end of each chapter, we provide a guide for reflexivity so that the literature reviewer might recognize potential biases and also potential opportunities to revisit the search. This process is what we term the CORE of the literature reviewer—reflexivity, specifically: Critical examination, Organization, Reflections, and Evaluation. We encourage the use of CORE

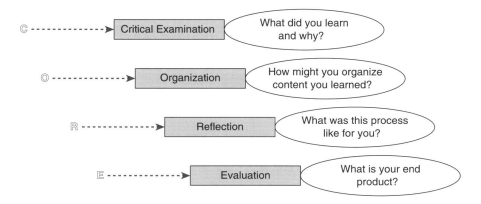

Figure 1.6 The CORE reflection

critically to examine both the process and the product of the literature review. Figure 1.6 describes this CORE process.

In short, CORE helps you to examine the *what?* and *why this?* We have based the guiding questions in each chapter on what is commonly known as Socratic questioning. Socrates, the classical Greek philosopher, would engage in questioning dialogue with a colleague as a form of inquiry and debate. For reflexivity purposes, we present questions for self-dialogue to challenge biases, viewpoints, assumptions, and subsequent actions (Paul & Elder, 2006). In the next chapter, we build on these foundations and discuss the critical ingredients in your identity as a literature reviewer and introduce the Seven-Step Model that will guide you in your quest for knowledge.

CHAPTER 1 EVALUATION CHECKLIST

CORE	Guiding Questions and Tasks
Critical Examination	What are two or more myths you see perpetuated in literature that you read? As a myth-buster, how might a comprehensive literature review be valuable in your field/discipline?
Organization	Consider some of the research that you have read in the past. To what extent did the author(s) contribute to the background of the research using prior knowledge? Create a table of reasons, which might help you conceptualize your experiences.
Reflections	Think about the research tradition of which you are most familiar. How do you know and what ideas associated with it resonate with you?
Evaluation	When considering Bloom et al.'s (1956) taxonomy, why might the literature reviewer want to avoid simply describing the literature?

2

THE LITERATURE REVIEW

CHAPTER 2 ROADMAP

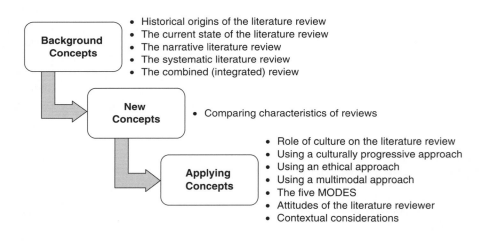

Background Concepts
- Historical origins of the literature review
- The current state of the literature review
- The narrative literature review
- The systematic literature review
- The combined (integrated) review

New Concepts
- Comparing characteristics of reviews

Applying Concepts
- Role of culture on the literature review
- Using a culturally progressive approach
- Using an ethical approach
- Using a multimodal approach
- The five MODES
- Attitudes of the literature reviewer
- Contextual considerations

HISTORICAL ORIGINS OF THE LITERATURE REVIEW

The formal review of the literature can be traced back 350 years, starting with the publication of the first academic journal in the English language on March 6, 1665 by Henry Oldenburg, who was the Corresponding Secretary of the Royal Society. This journal, which Henry Oldenburg edited and published at his own expense, was called the *Philosophical Transactions of the Royal Society*. Interestingly, this journal appeared approximately 200 years after print technology first had been used by Gutenberg and exactly 30 years after King Charles I officially opened the royal postal service to the public in 1635 (Willinsky, 2005). The use of the word *philosophical* in the title stems from the phrase "natural philosophy," which, at the time of the journal's onset, was synonymous with the word *science*. This journal immediately became an important source for scientific information and has been ever since. In 1887, the journal expanded and was subdivided into two separate journals: one journal pertaining to the field of physical sciences (i.e., *Philosophical Transactions of the Royal Society A: Physical, Mathematical and Engineering Sciences*) and the other journal pertaining to the field of life sciences (*Philosophical Transactions of the Royal Society B: Biological Sciences*).

Over their long and illustrious histories, many landmark scientific discoveries have been published in these journals, which were authored by famous scientists such as Charles Darwin, Isaac Newton, and Michael Faraday. Interestingly, when we conducted a citation analysis using Harzing's (2009) *Publish or Perish* software, we discovered that articles published in these journals have been cited in more than 200,000 published works!

THE CURRENT STATE OF THE LITERATURE REVIEW

Since the publication of the first academic journal, the number of journals has increased exponentially. Indeed, according to Ware (2006),

> There are approximately 23,000 scholarly journals in the world, collectively publishing 1.4 million articles a year. The number of articles published each year and the number of journals have both grown steadily for over two centuries, by about 3% and 3.5% per year respectively. The reason is the equally persistent growth in the number of researchers, which has also grown at about 3% per year and now stands at around 5.5 million. (p. 3)

In fact, Jinha (2010) estimated that between 1,477,382 and 1,504,600 scholarly articles were published worldwide in 2009. Moreover, currently, there are an estimated 50 million published scholarly journal articles in existence (Jinha, 2010). For many decades, two major branches of traditional literature reviews have appeared in journals and other works (e.g., books): narrative literature reviews and systematic literature reviews. Each of these branches is discussed in the following two sections.

THE NARRATIVE LITERATURE REVIEW

A narrative literature review is a written report that summarizes—and optimally critiques—the literature on a particular topic, without providing any integration of either quantitative findings or qualitative findings. (We will describe ways of integrating quantitative findings and integrating qualitative findings a little later when we define an integrative literature review.)

TOOL: CATEGORIZING NARRATIVE, SYSTEMATIC, AND INTEGRATIVE REVIEWS

Figure 2.1 represents these two branches of traditional literature reviews, which are described in detail in the following sections.

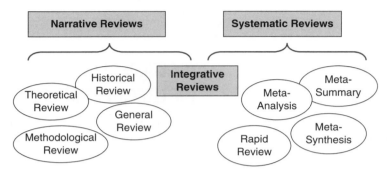

Figure 2.1 Four major types of narrative reviews, four major types of systematic reviews, and one major type of combined narrative review and systematic review

Narrative reviews, which represent the most common class of literature review, typically provide a broad overview of a topic, rather than addressing a specific question such as how effective an intervention is in producing a desired outcome.

At their most comprehensive, narrative reviews cover a wide range of issues within a given topic. Also, at their most trustworthy, each selected work that is included in the literature review has been subjected to some form of critical analysis by the literature reviewer regarding its appropriateness; however, readers typically are not made privy to the literature reviewer's decision-making. Further, narrative reviews do not provide any information about how the search for literature was conducted, how many studies were selected, what criteria were used to decide which studies to include, or how valid or trustworthy the findings are that are yielded from each selected study.

EXAMPLE: FOUR COMMON TYPES OF NARRATIVE REVIEWS

Four common types of narrative reviews are *general reviews, theoretical reviews, methodological reviews,*

and *historical reviews.* Figure 2.2 presents these four types of review.

A *general literature review* is a traditional literature review comprising a body of text or account that provides a review of the salient and critical aspects of the most current knowledge regarding a topic of interest. The information that drives a general review typically is extracted from the body of extant literature, which includes substantive findings, as well as conceptual, theoretical, and/or methodological contributions to a particular topic. Although a general literature review can represent a stand-alone work, most often, it is part of the introduction to a research report, thesis, dissertation, or essay. As a scholarly work, the literature review must be defined by a guiding concept (e.g., the research objective, the underlying problem or issue, or the reviewer's argumentative thesis).

In a *theoretical literature review*, the literature reviewer examines how theory shapes research. As specified by the editor of the *Review of Educational Research* (2011), "To the extent that research is cited and interpreted, it [theoretical literature review] is in the service of the specification, explication, and illumination of a theory" (¶ 3). Theoretical reviews primarily represent how a theory is used to frame research and meaning-making. A *methodological literature review* is a description of research design and methods (e.g., sampling size, sampling scheme, instrumentation, procedures, analysis) that have been used in research studies—typically research studies addressing a particular research question

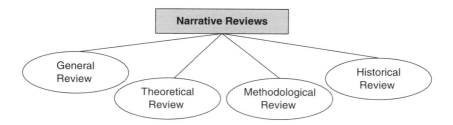

Figure 2.2 Typology of narrative reviews

or examining a phenomenon. These methodological reviews should outline the strengths and weaknesses of the methods used and provide future directions. In a ***historical literature review***, the literature reviewer situates the extant literature in historical contexts. Further, explanations for phenomena are framed within historical events.

THE SYSTEMATIC LITERATURE REVIEW

In contrast to a narrative literature review, a ***systematic literature review*** is a critical assessment and evaluation of all research studies that address a particular research question on a research topic. The literature reviewer transparently uses an organized method of identifying, collecting, and evaluating a body of literature on this topic using a predetermined set of specific criteria. A systematic review typically includes a description of the selected body of research studies and integrates the findings of each work in some way. Unlike the case for narrative research, the procedures underlying the systematic review are explicitly defined in advance, in order to ensure that the systematic review is transparent and can be replicated. Studies included in a systematic review are screened for appropriateness—in particular, studies are selected if they are deemed valid or trustworthy by the literature reviewer. Specifically, a systematic review must have four attributes:

- explicit inclusion/exclusion criteria
- a transparent search strategy
- systematic coding and analysis of included studies
- some form of synthesis of the findings

Systematic literature reviews are most common in the field of health science. In 1993, The Cochrane Collaboration was established, and named after the British epidemiologist, Archie Cochrane (The Cochrane Collaboration, 2012). This international, multidisciplinary organization represented a group of more than 28,000 volunteer specialists in healthcare from more than 100 countries who review the effects of healthcare interventions that are tested via randomized control trials. The results of these systematic reviews are published in what are known as *Cochrane Reviews*, which are published in *The Cochrane Database of Systematic Reviews* section of the Cochrane Library (Cochrane Library, 2012).

META-ANALYSIS

In a ***meta-analysis***—an analysis that was first coined by Glass (1976)—the literature reviewer combines quantitative findings from as many available individual quantitative research studies as possible that address a set of related research hypotheses for the purpose of integrating the results. There are two major goals in meta-analyses. The first goal is to estimate the mean ***effect size*** across the selected studies. For example, Di Castelnuovo, Rotondo, Iacoviello, Donati, and Gaetano (2002), who conducted a meta-analysis of 13 studies examining the relationship between wine consumption and cardiovascular disease, reported that "From 13 studies involving 209,418 persons, the relative risk of vascular disease associated with wine intake was 0.68 (95% confidence interval, 0.59 to 0.77) relative to nondrinkers" (p. 2836). This 0.68 figure is called the ***odds ratio*** (i.e., an effect-size measure describing the strength of association or non-independence between dichotomous variables—in this case, wine consumption [i.e., yes vs. no] and vascular disease [i.e., yes vs. no]). Di Castelnuovo et al.'s finding indicates that, across these 13 studies, participants who drank wine

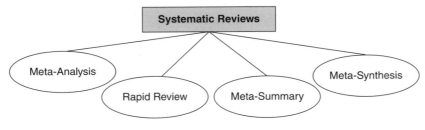
were, on average, two-thirds (i.e., 0.68) less likely to experience vascular disease than were the non-wine drinkers. This finding certainly makes a person want to drink wine right now! However, it might be difficult to finish writing this chapter if we as authors did.

The second goal of meta-analysis is to examine the variability of effect sizes across studies as a function of study design effects (e.g., whether the effect size varied as a function of gender; whether the effect size was different for experimental studies where randomization took place vs. studies where randomization did not take place)—a technique known as homogeneity analyses (Onwuegbuzie & Leech, 2003). For instance, in the wine example, the researchers could have investigated whether the odds ratio of 0.68 was different for males than for females, or whether the effect size varied as a function of the quality of the study.

RAPID REVIEW

A *rapid review* is a literature review that represents an accelerated or streamlined systematic review (Grant & Booth, 2009). The goal of a rapid review is to synthesize evidence within a shortened timeframe. Rapid reviews typically are targeted to audiences such as government policymakers, healthcare administrators, and health professionals (e.g., Hailey, 2007). Rapid review methodologies might be determined by clinical urgency or they might be motivated by insufficient

time and resources to conduct full systematic reviews (Ganann, Ciliska, & Thomas, 2010; Watt et al., 2008). Whereas systematic reviews usually take a minimum of 6 months to 1 year to complete (Ganann et al., 2010), rapid reviews can take as little as a few weeks or even a few days. Some methodological strategies for rapid reviews include limited searching by years, databases, language, and sources beyond electronic searches; using one reviewer for title and abstract reviewing; reviewing full text sources only; and assessing methodological quality (Ganann et al., 2010).

EXAMPLE: RAPID REVIEW

An example of a rapid review can be found in Heyvaert, Maes, and Onghena's (2011) article, which was published in the journal for which we serve as editors, namely, *Research in the Schools*. These researchers conducted a rapid review to determine the current works on mixing qualitative and quantitative methods at the synthesis level (i.e., the phase at which information from the collected works is synthesized). Specifically, these researchers developed a search strategy that comprised (a) a search of three relevant electronic databases (i.e., Web of Science, PsycINFO, and ERIC); (b) a hand search of two journals that routinely published mixed research articles (i.e., *Journal of Mixed Methods Research* and *Quality & Quantity: International Journal of Methodology*); and (c) a search of the reference lists of all the identified relevant articles. They used two groups of search terms: (a) *mixed method* and *multi-method*; and (b) *synthesis*, *review*, *meta*, and *aggregated*. This rapid review led to the identification of six elaborated synthesis frameworks that applied the principles of mixed research.

META-SUMMARY

As stated by Sandelowski and Barroso (2003), a **qualitative meta-summary** is "a form of systematic review or integration of qualitative findings in a target domain that are themselves topical or thematic summaries or surveys of data" (p. 227).

EXAMPLE: META-SUMMARY

Sandelowski and Barroso's (2003) qualitative meta-summary of 45 published and unpublished reports of qualitative studies of HIV-positive women resulted in 800 findings being extracted that were reduced to 93 findings, from which effect sizes were determined. Effect sizes in qualitative research—a phrase coined by Onwuegbuzie (2003a)—represent a "quantitative transformation of qualitative data in the service of extracting more meaning from those data and verifying the presence of a pattern or theme" (Sandelowski & Barroso, 2003, p. 231). An example of effect sizes stemming from qualitative data is represented by counts of observations or themes. Sandelowski and Barroso documented that five results had effect sizes ranging from 25% to 60%, with both published and unpublished qualitative research studies contributing approximately equally to the strength of these findings. Further, a total of 73 findings had effect sizes that were less than 9%, with 47 of them having effect sizes of only 2%.

META-SYNTHESIS

As noted by Sandelowski and Barroso (2003), a **meta-synthesis** (also known as metasynthesis, qualitative meta-analysis, meta-study, meta-ethnography, grounded formal theory, and aggregated analysis; Zimmer, 2006) is

> a form of systematic review or integration of qualitative research findings in a target domain that are themselves interpretive syntheses of data, including phenomenologies,

ethnographies, grounded theories, and other integrated and coherent descriptions or explanations of phenomena, events, or cases. (p. 227)

The first meta-synthesis likely was conducted by sociologists Glaser and Strauss, who developed grounded theory (Glaser & Strauss, 1967), during the late 1960s and early 1970s, which led to their study entitled *Status Passage* (Glaser & Strauss, 1971). This study represented a synthesis of four studies in which they examined the process of dying and various other major life transitions. However, Glaser and Strauss did not refer to their study as representing any kind of synthesis but rather simply representing an extension of grounded theory with the codes and themes extracted from one study being compared to codes and categories emerging from the three other studies.

The phrase *meta-synthesis* was first coined approximately one quarter of a century ago, specifically in 1985 by Stern and Harris—a little less than a decade after the phrase *meta-analysis* was coined by Glass (1976). The term meta-synthesis is very appropriate because the prefix *meta* is derived from the Greek meaning *beyond* or *transcending*, and the word *synthesis*, which also is derived from Greek, means *a merging* or a *bringing together*. Thus, by definition, the overarching goal of a meta-synthesis is to transcend the findings of a collection of qualitative research studies. As such, meta-syntheses are more aligned to the concept of holism (i.e., referring to the system or phenomenon as a whole essentially determining how its component parts function), than to the concept of reductionism (i.e., all the elements of a system or a phenomenon can be reduced or explained by its component parts alone).

Stern and Harris (1985) used a meta-synthesis to develop an explanatory theory or model that explained the results stemming from a group of distinct but related qualitative studies. A meta-synthesis is similar to meta-analysis inasmuch as it represents the integration of findings from two or more studies in an attempt to make findings more accessible for application in practice. However, a meta-synthesis is different from a meta-analysis in four important ways. First, a meta-analysis involves the integration of *qualitative* findings, as opposed to a meta-analysis, which involves the integration of *quantitative* findings. Second, a meta-synthesis represents an interpretive analysis, in contrast to a meta-analysis, which involves aggregating quantitative findings (e.g., effect sizes). Third, whereas an important goal of meta-synthesis is *theory development*, a major goal of a meta-analysis is *theory testing*. Fourth, whereas the overall goal of meta-analysis is to increase the analyst's confidence in making cause-and-effect conclusions regarding a phenomenon of interest, in meta-syntheses, the overall goal is more hermeneutic, aiming to understand and to explain phenomena. In other words, meta-syntheses provide pathways and spaces for new knowledge via new insights and understandings that incorporate and distill the meanings extracted from constituent studies, which implies that a meta-synthesis represents an ever-expanding, space-opening analysis (Sandelowski, Docherty, & Emden, 1997; Sherwood, 1997a, 1997b).

Perhaps the most important type of meta-synthesis is what Noblit and Hare (1988) coined as a **meta-ethnography**. According to these authors, a meta-ethnography represents a synthesis of linked ethnographies. As we define in Appendix Table A.2, in ethnography, the researcher describes and interprets cultural phenomena that reflect the knowledge, beliefs, behaviors, and/or system of meanings that represent the life of a cultural group. Noblit and Hare (1988) describe a meta-ethnography as follows:

> Our meta-ethnographic approach enables a rigorous procedure for deriving substantive interpretations about any set of ethnographic or interpretive studies.... A meta-ethnography can be considered a complete study in itself. [Meta-ethnography] compares and analyzes texts, creating new interpretations in the process. It is much more than what we usually mean by a literature review. (p. 9)

Interestingly, Noblit and Hare (1988) refer to a meta-ethnography as representing "a complete study in itself" which refutes Myth 10 (i.e., "The Literature Review has One Goal"), Myth 6 (i.e., "The Literature Review is a Summary of the Extant Literature"), and Myth 3 (i.e., "The Literature Review is Only One Phase in the Research Process"). Indeed, their statement here is consistent with our contention that the literature review represents a study. We will discuss this concept of literature review-as-a-study in Chapter 3.

EXAMPLE: META-SYNTHESIS

An excellent example of a meta-synthesis is provided by Pielstick (1998), who conducted a meta-ethnographic study of transformational leadership, presenting an overview of what had been learned about transforming leaders over a 20-year period (i.e., 1978–1998). Pielstick's (1998) meta-ethnography yielded the following results:

> The research findings clustered into seven major themes: (1) creating a shared vision, (2) communicating the vision, (3) building relationships, (4) developing a supporting organizational culture, (5) guiding implementation, (6) exhibiting character, and (7) achieving results. These have been reframed into the following model. A shared vision of the future is supported by the four pillars of leading: communicating regularly with followers, building a web of relationships with and among followers, creating a sense of community based on shared values and beliefs, and guiding achievement of the vision through empowerment and other actions. The pillars rest on a solid foundation of exceptional character. (pp. 20–31)

A meta-synthesis involves translating the findings of one study into another. These translations lie on a translation continuum, with one end of the continuum representing studies that can be translated using metaphors, concepts, and themes that are common to both—or what can be referred to as **reciprocal translations**. At the other end of the translation continuum are studies that contain findings that are in opposition to each other, or that represent contradictions or paradoxes—or what can be referred to as **refutational translations** (cf. Noblit & Hare, 1988). In between these two poles are studies that overlap without being substitutional—or what can be referred to as **overlapping translations**. Importantly, both refutation and overlap might yield other emergent categories or understandings that have not been identified in the original accounts.

THE COMBINED (INTEGRATED) REVIEW

So far, we have discussed four major types of narrative review (i.e., general reviews, theoretical

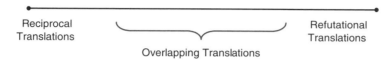
reviews, methodological reviews, and historical reviews), and four major types of systematic reviews (i.e., meta-analysis, rapid review, meta-summary, and meta-synthesis). Interestingly, there is one type of literature review—an ***integrative review***—that can be classified as both a narrative review and a systematic review.

As outlined by the editor of the *Review of Educational Research* (2011),

> Integrative reviews pull together the existing work on an educational topic and work to understand trends in that body of scholarship. In such a review, the author describes how the issue is conceptualized within the literature, how research methods and theories have shaped the outcomes of scholarship, and what the strengths and weaknesses of the literature are. (¶ 2)

This form of review is integrative because it combines the review of both the extant empirical and theoretical literature to obtain a more comprehensive understanding of a particular phenomenon. Moreover, integrative reviews allow for the review of studies using diverse methodologies including both quantitative-based (e.g., experimental) and qualitative-based (e.g., grounded theory) methodologies. For example, meta-analyses can be "accompanied by an interpretive framework that takes the article beyond the reporting of effect sizes and the bibliographic outcome of a computer search" (*Review of Educational Research*, 2011, ¶ 2). Further, integrative reviews "incorporate a wide range of purposes: to define concepts, to review issues of a particular topic" (Whittemore & Knafl, 2005, pp. 547–548). As such, integrative reviews, to date, represent the broadest type of literature review.

COMPARING CHARACTERISTICS OF REVIEWS

When conducted optimally (e.g., being as transparent as possible in the search strategies used), both narrative reviews and systematic reviews have many strengths. For example, narrative reviews, being interpretive in nature, optimally help literature reviewers to extract meaning of the phenomenon, under the assumption that the literature reviewer's own understandings, and the narrative-based literature review techniques used, occur within and are the products of the same contextual network or frame. These contextually based meanings might primarily lead to analytic generalizations (i.e., applied to wider theory; Curtis, Gesler, Smith, & Washburn, 2000), which represent knowledge claims that can be interpreted only in the context of the individual (i.e., particularistic) information sources.

TOOL: VISUALIZING THE INTEGRATIVE REVIEW

Figure 2.5 presents the nature of combining the narrative and systematic literature review, which can be on varying degrees.

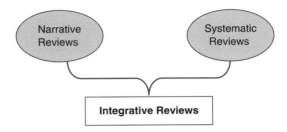

Figure 2.5   The integrative review as a combination of narrative and systematic reviews

NEW CONCEPTS

As can be seen, currently, there are nine types of literature reviews, comprising four major types of narrative review (i.e., general reviews, theoretical reviews, methodological reviews, and historical reviews), four major types of systematic reviews (i.e., meta-analysis, rapid review, meta-summary, and meta-synthesis), and one type of literature review that potentially combines narrative review techniques and systematic review techniques (i.e., integrative reviews).

To apply the concepts introduced in this chapter for added meaning, we present some tools in the way of visual displays whereby we distinguished, compared, integrated, and classified literature reviews so that we also create something new and innovative. These tools might help you to reflect on the importance of your own CLR in that no matter what type of review it most closely resembles, it is the result of a rigorous, transparent, culturally progressive process as endless as your imagination.

TOOL: COMPARING 11 CHARACTERISTICS OF NARRATIVE AND SYSTEMATIC REVIEWS

Figure 2.6 is a visual representation of the two extremes representing narrative reviews and systematic reviews based on the characteristics of narrative reviews and systematic reviews.

At the extreme end of the narrative review spectrum are literature reviews that are non-exhaustive, that represent a sample of literature, that are selected in a non-linear manner, that involve the literature reviewer adopting a reflexive stance while selecting literature, in which the criteria for including/excluding literature are not explicit, wherein no formal appraisal criteria are used for assessing

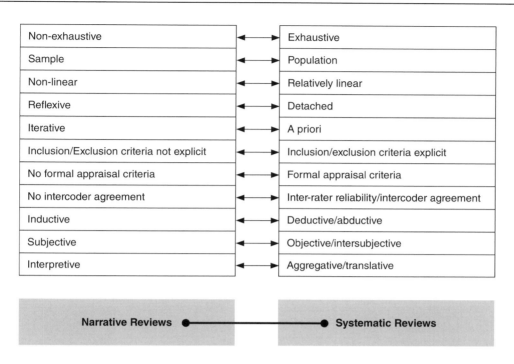

Non-exhaustive	Exhaustive
Sample	Population
Non-linear	Relatively linear
Reflexive	Detached
Iterative	A priori
Inclusion/Exclusion criteria not explicit	Inclusion/exclusion criteria explicit
No formal appraisal criteria	Formal appraisal criteria
No intercoder agreement	Inter-rater reliability/intercoder agreement
Inductive	Deductive/abductive
Subjective	Objective/intersubjective
Interpretive	Aggregative/translative

Narrative Reviews ●————————————● **Systematic Reviews**

Figure 2.6 Characteristics of narrative reviews and systematic reviews

each selected work, in which intercoder agreement regarding the selection of literature cannot be ascertained (either because one reviewer is used or because the selection strategy is not systematic), in which inductive reasoning techniques are used to extract meaning from each literature source, in which subjectivity underlies the literature review process, and in which an interpretive approach is used to conduct the literature review.

In stark contrast, at the extreme end of the systematic review spectrum are literature reviews that are exhaustive, that represent the whole population of literature, that are selected in a (relatively) linear manner, that involve the literature reviewer adopting a detached or neutral stance while selecting literature, in which the criteria for including/excluding literature are explicit and transparent, wherein formal appraisal criteria are used for assessing each selected work, in which inter-rater reliability pertaining to the selection of quantitative studies and intercoder agreement pertaining to the selection of qualitative studies are obtainable, wherein deductive reasoning techniques (for quantitative-based systematic reviews such as meta-analyses) and abductive reasoning techniques (for qualitative-based systematic reviews such as meta-syntheses) are used to extract meaning from each literature source, in which objectivity (for quantitative-based systematic reviews such as meta-analyses) and/or inter-subjectivity (for qualitative-based systematic reviews such as meta-syntheses) underlie the literature review process, and wherein an aggregative approach (for quantitative-based systematic reviews such as meta-analyses) and/or a translative approach (for qualitative-based systematic reviews such as meta-syntheses) are used to conduct the literature review.

In contrast, systematic reviews, by their use of formal critical appraisal techniques to facilitate a comprehensive search for relevant primary studies, in the case of meta-synthesis and meta-summary, can promote *theory building* (i.e., increasing the level of theory beyond the level possible using information from only one study), *theory explication* (i.e., whereby an abstract concept stemming from one study is enhanced via the findings stemming from other studies), and/or *theory development* (i.e., whereby findings are synthesized into a [more] complete and coherent theory); and, in the case of meta-analysis, can advance *theory testing* and external (statistical) generalizations (i.e., making inferences or predictions to a population of interest based on information obtained from a representative selection of works; Onwuegbuzie, Slate, Leech, & Collins, 2009). Notwithstanding, an important flaw associated with all nine types of literature reviews is that they do not reflect adequately three elements that are essential for 21st-century literature reviews: the cultural context of literature review, the ethical nature of literature reviews, and the multimodal nature of information.

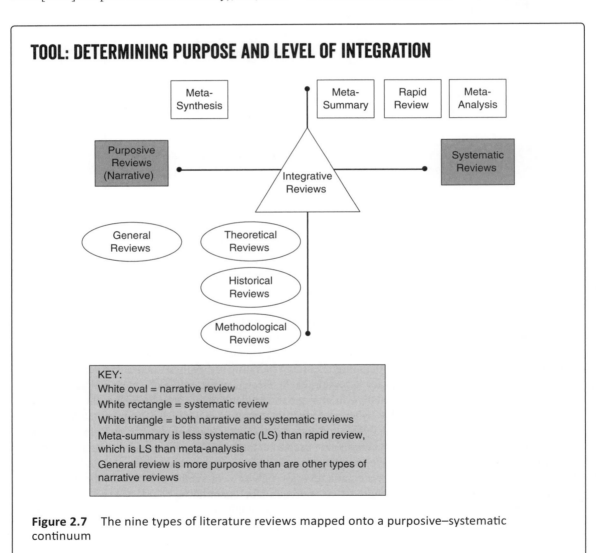

Figure 2.7 The nine types of literature reviews mapped onto a purposive–systematic continuum

Figure 2.7 maps the nine types of literature reviews according to where they lie on the purposive–systematic continuum. By purposive, we mean non-systematic, with the selection of literature or the rationale used not being adequately transparent—much like the narrative literature review. For example, general reviews are the most purposive (i.e., the least systematic), with meta-analyses being the most systematic. Interestingly, integrative reviews are placed at the origin because they often involve a combination of findings from a body of studies that are systematically reviewed and combined with conceptual, theoretical, and/or methodological works that are reviewed purposively.

TOOL: CLASSIFYING REVIEWS USING A LITERATURE REVIEW GRID

Following the figure of the purposive–systematic continuum, Figure 2.8 represents what we call a *literature review grid*. This figure illustrates how specific forms of literature reviews can be classified. The figure represents a two-dimensional diagram portraying two sets of poles, namely: (a) a horizontal line representing how exhaustive the literature review search is, with selective reviews and exhaustive reviews at the opposite ends of the continuum; and (b) a vertical pole representing the type of literature review study, with stand-alone literature review studies (i.e., literature review as an end in itself) and embedded literature review studies (i.e., literature review that informs a primary research study) at the opposite ends of the continuum.

In Figure 2.8, the upper left quadrant, labeled as "(1)," represents a literature review that informs a larger work such as a theoretical, conceptual, or methodological article/chapter that is informed by selective (i.e., non-exhaustive) extant works. The upper right quadrant, labeled as "(2)," represents an exhaustive (or, at least, an extensive) literature review that informs an empirical work such as a thesis,

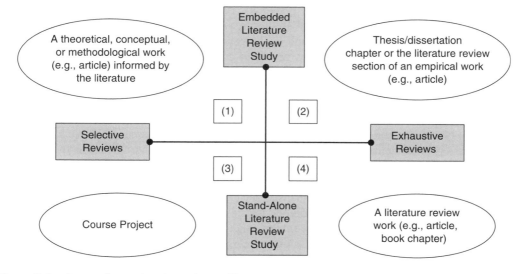

Figure 2.8   A two-dimensional typology of literature reviews

(Continued)

(Continued)

a dissertation, or an empirical (quantitative, qualitative, or mixed research) article that appears in a journal which contains generous page/word-count limits. The lower left quadrant, labeled as "(3)," represents a review of selective (i.e., non-exhaustive) extant works that serves as an end in itself such as a course project or assignment. Finally, the lower right quadrant, labeled as "(4)," represents a review of an exhaustive (or, at least, an extensive) body of extant works that serves as an end in itself such as an article or a book chapter containing a historical review, theoretical review, or a methodological review.

TOOL: A THREE-DIMENSIONAL MODEL FOR CATEGORIZING/ORGANIZING

Figure 2.9 presents our three-dimensional model for categorizing and organizing literature reviews. Specifically, as can be seen, the model contains three dimensions, each focused upon a given set of perspectives for conducting literature reviews, and each positioned at 90-degree angles to the other two.

Dimension 1 (level of systematic review) can be conceptualized as classifying how systematic the selection of information sources is, with purposive (i.e., non-systematic) being located at one end of the continuum and systematic being located at the other end of the continuum. The midpoint of the continuum represents the place where an equal combination of purposive and systematic techniques is used. This might include an integrative study in which the quantitative studies that address a particular problem statement or research questions are selected for a systematic review, and key qualitative articles addressing the same or related problem statement or research questions are selected and subjected to a narrative review or a meta-synthesis. All other points of the continuum represent some level of systematic review. In Dimension 2 (type of literature review study), stand-alone literature review studies lie at one end of the continuum and embedded literature review studies lie at the other end of the continuum. By stand-alone literature review studies, we mean that the literature review serves as an end in itself. In contrast, by embedded literature review studies, we mean that for empirical studies, the literature serves as a study that is embedded within the primary research study. All other points of the continuum represent some level of a literature review study.

In Dimension 3 (comprehensiveness of literature review), selective literature reviews lie at one extreme of the continuum and exhaustive literature reviews lie at the other end, with the mid-point of the continuum representing the place where the balance between a selective and exhaustive literature review is equal—as might be the case for a rapid review. All other points of the continuum represent some level of selective (i.e., non-exhaustive) review. Using this model, a given literature review—including the nine types of literature reviews discussed earlier—can be positioned somewhere within the three-dimensional space, which indicates the multidimensional complexity or sophistication of literature reviews. For example, a literature review might represent a systematic (i.e., Dimension 1) and exhaustive (i.e., Dimension 3) study that informs a primary research study (i.e., embedded study; Dimension 2), as might be the case for a meta-analysis. Alternatively, a literature review might represent a selective (i.e., Dimension 3), purposive (i.e., Dimension 1), and stand-alone study (i.e., Dimension 2).

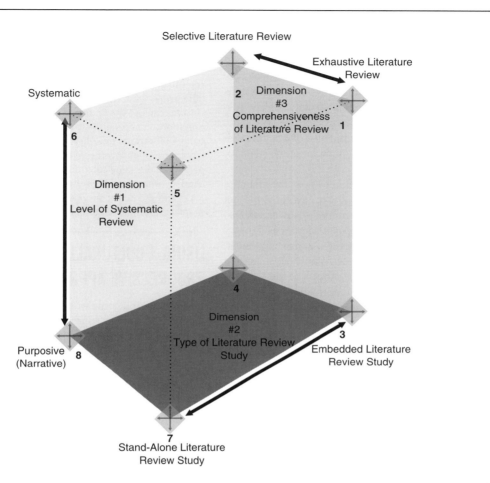

Figure 2.9 A three-dimensional model for categorizing and organizing literature reviews

[a]Directionality of the continua across each dimension is arbitrary. There is no intentionality of suggesting superiority of one continuum point or extreme over another. Rather, the appropriateness of the continuum point depends on the literature review goal, literature review objective, and literature review question(s). Encircled numbers represent eight possible combinations of the extreme points on the three dimensions of level of systematic review, type of literature review study, and exhaustiveness of literature review.

APPLYING CONCEPTS

ROLE OF CULTURE ON THE LITERATURE REVIEW

Regardless of the type of literature review, because they are written in a specific time and context, the authors are subject to particular codes of behavior, values, norms, beliefs, and customs that impact their communications—which is cultural. A **culture** is a set of experiences, learned traditions, principles, and guides of behavior that are shared among members of a particular group that are dynamic and influential in communication. Therefore, knowledge is learned through a social and cultural context with many dimensions.

Culture also is very broad and can include many "cultures within cultures." Ethnic groups have culture within culture, as do businesses, neighborhoods, and so forth. As a result, there is much diversity within cultures, and culture changes over time and is central to political, economic, social, and individual identities. It then stands to reason that even researchers have cultures! The role of culture is important to consider before you begin the literature review. Keep in mind that the authors of the sources that you examine might be of the same, or different, culture from you.

As a methodology situated in culture, the literature review is unique because it involves synthesizing not only the cultural lens of the literature reviewer, but also the many voices of the information sources as a meaning-making endeavor that provides a final argument, or pervasive report. As a result, the most important aspect of the literature review process is the recognition that literature and other information sources are deeply embedded in culture. In fact, many learning theorists have described the important role that culture plays in the acquisition of knowledge. As social contexts change, it is likely that interpretations of content change. For example, Lev Vygotsky's (1978) social development theory focuses on the learner's utilization of the signs and symbols that are associated with the culture as a basis for knowledge acquisition.

According to Vygotsky, human beings create cultures through the use of signs and symbols. In turn, culture determines both what knowledge is valuable and how this knowledge is acquired. Thus, culture drives knowledge acquisition. Every research study is (a) conducted on one or more cultural groups (e.g., ethnic groups, age groups, neighborhoods, businesses, educational institutions); (b) conducted *by* one or more researchers representing one or more cultural groups; and (c) a product that is consumed (e.g., read, replicated, applied) by people representing one or more cultural groups.

EXAMPLE: INFORMATION SITUATED IN CULTURE

To understand better how culture is inherent in knowledge, consider the western historical story of Columbus discovering the new world. If written from the perspective of indigenous people of this region, the story looks much different from the account told in many history books. Therefore, participants representing different cultures can yield substantively different findings; two researchers representing different cultures can interpret the same findings differently; and two consumers representing different cultures can use the findings and/or the researcher's interpretations in substantively different ways. For example, a study that reports on subgroups of children performing at lower academic levels might be interpreted and used by parents of the same subgroups to study harder. It might be used by other parents of the same subgroups to advocate for better academic services from the school. The same findings—but different interpretations.

USING A CULTURALLY PROGRESSIVE APPROACH

By recognizing some of the human bias that accompanies information sources, a culturally progressive approach for the CLR includes what many research organizations refer to as *cultural competence*, which is not a mastery of culture but instead focuses on the stance taken toward respecting diversity of cultures. Building on Gallegos, Tindall, and Gallegos's (2008) conceptualization of cultural competence in research, we offer the following definition of a *culturally progressive literature reviewer*—toward which we believe that all literature reviewers should strive:

A culturally progressive literature reviewer responds respectfully and effectively to research and other knowledge sources stemming from people (i.e., participants) and generated by people (i.e., researchers, authors) who represent all cultures, races, ethnic backgrounds, languages, classes, religions, and other diversity attributes in a way that recognizes, acknowledges, affirms, and values the worth of all participants and researchers/authors and protects and preserves their dignity. Further, a culturally progressive literature reviewer maintains a high degree of self-awareness for understanding how her/his own backgrounds and other experiences might serve as assets or limitations when searching and interpreting literature and other sources of information.

By also adapting the American Psychological Association's (2003) Multicultural Guidelines, a culturally progressive literature reviewer continually should strive toward (a) *cultural awareness of beliefs* by being sensitive about her or his biases and personal values and how these elements might influence her or his decisions made at every step of the literature review process in general and the interpretation of the literature and other information sources in particular; (b) *cultural knowledge*, acquiring knowledge of the cultural context of each knowledge source (e.g., culture of each participant and each author/researcher) and the role that the cultural context plays in generating the knowledge claims made by the authors/researchers; and (c) *cultural skills*, being able to communicate the literature review report in a manner that is both culturally sensitive and culturally relevant. As such, assuming a culturally progressive approach goes even beyond a culturally competent approach by including the adoption of a proactive stance to the role that culture plays in the literature review process.

EXAMPLE: AVOIDING BIAS AND DEFICIT RESEARCH INTERPRETATIONS

As an example, a literature reviewer who does not adopt a culturally progressive approach might synthesize findings about a certain cultural or ethnic group from the literature and elsewhere that unconsciously or unintentionally promotes the cultural deficit model. Research from a deficit model is interpreting solely negative outcomes associated with the culture or ethnicity under study, as stemming, exclusively or in large part, from characteristics rooted in their cultures, instead of contextualizing these findings within a broader sociocultural context that recognizes power dynamics, institutional barriers, and other relevant issues that are not in the control of the culture, as well as affirming the cultural richness present in this community. One example of the deficit model occurred in the United States with the publishing of a book titled *The Bell Curve* (Herrnstein & Murray, 1994), whereby intelligence scores were presented in a negative perspective relating to genetics, giving the false impression that a cognitively elite group exists based on genetics.

On a lighter level, one potential way that a literature reviewer might unconsciously or unintentionally promote the cultural deficit model is by exclusively or predominantly synthesizing quantitative research studies—which are useful for "answering questions of who, where, how many, how much, and what is the relationship between specific variables" (Adler, 1996, p. 5)—and largely ignoring qualitative studies—which are more optimal than are quantitative studies for answering why and how questions. Recently, in the United States, the American Evaluation Association (2011) expressed in a public, published statement that evaluations cannot be culture free and that those who engage in evaluation must attend to becoming culturally competent, recognizing one's own cultural position, others' positions, and ways to interact genuinely (cf. http://www.eval.org/ccstatement.asp). Similarly, literature reviews cannot be culture free and literature reviewers must strive to adopt a culturally progressive approach. Therefore, by attending to your literature review process and reflecting on your mores (e.g., traditions, ethnicity, way of life), you will be a part of the new generation of culturally progressive literature reviewers who recognize that the literature review is a holistic and cultural process wherein a person experiences a range of emotions, increased awareness, and innovative conceptualizations.

USING AN ETHICAL APPROACH

Broadly speaking, *ethics* incorporate moral principles and best practices pertaining to both research and subject discipline topics. Ethics provide the essence that overflows into every component of the literature review process. First and foremost, the literature reviewer must be an ethical literature reviewer. In general, ethics incorporate moral principles and best practices (i.e., standards) pertaining to both research and subject discipline topics. Among many subject disciplines and organizations within the disciplines, there are multiple codes of ethics that are constantly being updated to reflect changes in the field and new issues.

TOOL: INCORPORATING RESEARCH ETHICS

Most notably, ethics include moral principles including but not limited to:

- **Non-maleficence**: the concept of not causing harm to others
- **Beneficence**: action that is undertaken for the benefit of others; beneficent actions can be undertaken to help remove or to prevent harm or to improve the situation of others
- **Justice**: decisions that are made, based on universal principles and rules, in an impartial and warranted manner in order to ensure fair and equitable treatment of all people
- **Fidelity**: the act of loyalty, faithfulness, and fulfilling commitment

In addition, the ethical researcher considers best practices in not only research but also the subject discipline of the topic explored. We have adapted some of the important researcher guidelines into the literature reviewer identity:

- **Professional competence**: recognizing limitations and undertaking tasks within your set of skills and knowledge of the topic explored and the results reported
- **Integrity**: being fair, honest, and respectful of others' works and representing their works appropriately
- **Scholarly responsibility**: adhering to best practices through documentation (i.e., the audit trail) and reflecting on choices made when selecting and deselecting documents
- **Respecting rights, dignity, and diversity**: striving to eliminate bias for misrepresenting others' scholarship and not discriminating based on age, gender, race, ethnicity, national origin, religion, sexual orientation, disability, and so forth
- **Social responsibility**: applying awareness of the social dimensions of a subject

Of the many approaches to ethics, the two approaches that are most pertinent for literature reviewers are *virtue ethics* and *pragmatic ethics*. In the context of literature reviews, **virtue ethics** refer to the *character* of the literature reviewer as the impetus for ethical behavior, as opposed to focusing on rules. You, as a virtue ethicist literature reviewer, would focus less on the report that ensues from the literature review process and instead would consider what the decisions made at each step of the literature review process indicate about the character and integrity (e.g., benevolent vs. malevolent) of the literature reviewer. Thus, a virtual ethicist literature reviewer would assess each literature review that they conduct on a case-by-case basis. In contrast, you as a literature reviewer who adheres to **pragmatic ethics** would assess the literature review using the standards set by society under the premise that society is progressing morally in line with the progression of scientific knowledge.

Ethical research is of great importance for the literature reviewer because the reviewer must honor the works of others and be careful not to misrepresent the voices of those sources reviewed. Therefore, when integrating *all* of the inherent components of one source as a research synthesis, the literature reviewer attends to a two-level responsibility: the ethics of representation of the sources identified and the ethics of transparency in the literature review process.

USING A MULTIMODAL APPROACH

In Chapter 1, we pointed out that the most prevalent myth perpetuated by authors of research methodology textbooks is that the literature review involves *only* the collection of literature that already exists either in printed or digital forms (i.e., Myth 1). This form of information—especially traditional print-based texts, for the most part—represents what can be called *monomodal texts*, which primarily involve the linguistic (i.e., verbal) semiotic system, comprising aspects such as vocabulary and grammar of the written language. Yet, all societies worldwide are composed of *multimodal texts*.

As noted in Chapter 1, a text is multimodal when it combines or mixes two or more modes of communication (e.g., text, image, sound) into a single information source, forming a composite, unified, and coherent whole. Each mode of communication might transmit a message that is independent of the other mode(s). As a set, the underlying modes produce interpretation and meaning-making that, on the part of the reader, are different than does any single mode considered on its own. Alternatively stated, a text is multimodal when it combines or mixes two or more semiotic systems. In turn, a *semiotic system* is an arrangement of signs and sign processes. Anstey and Bull (2010) identified the following five semiotic systems:

1. *Linguistic*: comprising elements such as vocabulary and the grammar of written and oral language
2. *Visual*: comprising elements such as color, vectors, and location in still and moving images
3. *Audio*: comprising elements such as pitch, volume, and rhythm of music and other sound effects
4. *Spatial*: comprising elements such as proximity, direction, location, and organization of objects in space
5. *Gestural*: comprising elements such as movement, speed, and stillness in facial expression and body language

Virtually all Web 2.0 sources contain two or more of these semiotic systems. For example, a webpage might contain semiotic systems such as linguistics (e.g., written language), visual (e.g., pictures), audio (e.g., music, sound effects), spatial (e.g., maps), and gestural (e.g., moving images)—representing all five semiotic systems.

READING PATH

In the context of multimodal texts, Kress (2010) refers to the term *reading path*, which he describes as "the route of interest, attention, engagement, prompt, [and] framing" (p. 176). With traditional,

print-based text (e.g., printed journal articles, books), the reading path for the literature reviewer-as-reader depends on culturally constructed rules and conventions (Kress, 2003), such as texts being read from left to right in certain cultures (e.g., Western cultures) and right to left in certain other cultures (e.g., Chinese; Japanese; cultures that speak Arabic, Hebrew, Yiddish, Urdu). In contrast, in digital (i.e., Web 2.0) environments, the reading path largely is determined by the literature reviewer-as-reader's purpose for reading, interest, and modal cues (Karchmer-Klein & Shinas, 2010).

Thus, in digital environments, the literature reviewer-as-reader might interpret the information differently than the writer/creator of the text intended. The decisions that the literature reviewer-as-reader must make to determine a reading path when reading a multimodal text places additional demands on the literature reviewer, such as a propensity for modal scanning and identifying the most relevant mode(s) for meaning-making (Karchmer-Klein & Shinas, 2010). Not only must literature reviewers adopt a culturally progressive approach to enhance appropriate levels of understanding and meaning-making via the cultural perspectives that they bring to the information source, but also they must adopt an ethical approach in determining reading paths. Thus, in digital environments, the literature reviewer's culturally progressive approach, ethical research approach, and multimodal approach are inextricably intertwined.

THE FIVE MODES

The CLR process reflects the multimodal nature of text in the Web 2.0 era. As we noted in Chapter 1, we extend the concept of multimodal texts and settings to include the following five major MODES: **M**edia, **O**bservation(s), **D**ocuments, **E**xpert(s) in the field, and **S**econdary data. That is, in order to conduct a CLR, the literature reviewer should not only adopt both a culturally progressive approach and ethical research approach, but also they should strive to obtain information from as many of these five MODES as possible. We provide much more information about each MODE in Chapter 8: Expanding the Search.

MEDIA

Media are visual representations such as photographs, videos, and drawings/paintings. You might have heard of the adage "a picture is worth a thousand words." This saying also is true when searching for meaning during the CLR process. For example, photographs and videos can help to provide contextual information. In particular, photographs and videos provide a visual representation of a moment in time, often referred to as a snapshot, or static state of this representation to help create meaning in your literature review. Computer-mediated communication (CMC) and Web 2.0 tools can play an important role in facilitating meaning-making. These include: YouTube (i.e., a video sharing tool that allows literature reviewers to upload, to view, and to share video clips), Flickr (i.e., a tool that provides access to both videos and photographs), Panoramio (i.e., a photo sharing tool), iMovie (i.e., a video editing software application), and iTunes (i.e., a tool used for playing and organizing digital music and video files).

OBSERVATIONS

Literature reviewers can obtain useful information by collecting observations as an extension after examining documents in an initial search. This MODE also helps you, as the literature reviewer, to create meaning in your writing. For instance, if a literature reviewer was interested in understanding what is known about characteristics of effective schools (e.g., elementary schools, secondary schools), he/she could obtain more contextual information by actually visiting the location of one or more schools that have been rated as being effective by a reputable organization (e.g., accreditation agency). Once there, the reviewer could examine the sociocultural context of these schools by observing aspects of these schools (e.g., size, location, levels of crime, available security measures) that can be integrated with the extant literature. Also, while at these locations—and assuming that no laws or ethics are violated—the reviewer could collect media data by taking photographs or videotaping relevant settings. A reviewer can go even further by mapping locations of a school district, state, county, province, region, or even country where effective schools reside. Additionally, a reviewer can examine empirical research articles that have been published on the topic of effective schools and map the regions where any identified effective school is located, so that the findings from the extant literature can be contextualized geographically.

DOCUMENTS

As noted earlier, literature reviewers typically have at their disposal both printed and digital texts. With technology advances in Web 2.0, literature reviewers have resources such as Facebook (circa 2004), Myspace.com (circa 2003), Ning (circa 2005), Second Life (circa 2003), Bebo (circa 2005), Friendster (circa 2002), and Orkut (circa 2008). These social networking forums allow literature reviewers to socialize and to exchange information in many forms (e.g., documents, photographs). These media can provide contextual information that can be incorporated into literature reviews. Examining the social network sites of prolific authors potentially is a useful avenue for expanding the literature review. In recent years, a form of digital document that has grown in popularity is what is commonly referred to as a blog (a term that represents a blending of the term *web log*).

A ***blog*** is a type of website or part of a website that is updated with new content (e.g., commentary, description of events, pictures, videos) by one or more individuals as needed, with entries typically displayed in reverse-chronological order. At their optimum, blogs are interactive, allowing other people to respond to previous blog postings. In addition, bloggers can send messages to each other via graphical user interfaces (GUIs)—making blogging an alternative type of social networking. Blogs might contain semiotic systems such as linguistics (e.g., text), visual (e.g., images, webpages), audio (e.g., music, sound effects), and spatial (e.g., maps). In addition to textual blogs, blogs can focus on art (i.e., art blog), photographs (i.e., photoblog), videos (i.e., video blogging or vlogging), music (i.e., MP3 blog), and audio (i.e., podcasting). Microblogging is another type of blogging, which involves very short blog posts. Because many blogs provide commentary on a particular subject—and with more than 150 million public blogs in existence—they are potentially a fruitful avenue for literature reviewers. One advantage that blogs have over printed text (e.g., journal articles, books) is that, whereas printed text always has a time lag between the emergence of information (e.g., findings from a study) and when this information is made available to the public (e.g., when the article is published), blogs often can provide information almost instantaneously, with minimal time lag. In addition, *RSS technologies* (circa 1999) allow literature reviewers to be updated when new (research) works have been released. Most library subscription databases (e.g., Education Full Text, PsycINFO) allow literature reviewers to set up an RSS feed based on their search criteria. As such, literature reviewers will be notified of any new research articles that are of interest to them. Literature reviewers also can aggregate feeds from many sites into one place. RSS feeds can be read using software that is commonly referred to as an *RSS reader* (also called *feed reader* or *aggregator*), which can be web-based, desktop-based, or mobile-device-based.

EXPERTS

An extremely effective way of expanding the CLR is by interviewing or talking directly—either formally or informally—with some of the leading and/or prolific authors that the literature reviewer identified during the course of her/his literature review. In these interviews/talks, the literature reviewer should attempt to obtain the authors' latest thinking on the topic of interest. Optimally, the literature reviewer would conduct either individual face-to-face interviews with the selected prolific authors, or face-to-face (focus) group interviews with two or more of these authors. Alternatively, if the literature reviewer does not live or work in close proximity to an author, he/she can ask this author to conduct what some researchers refer to as *virtual interviewing*, which involves using some form of CMC and Web 2.0 tools, either asynchronously (e.g., email, blogs) or synchronously (e.g., chatrooms, instant messaging, Second Life, and Short Message Service [SMS] via mobile telephones).

SECONDARY DATA

A fifth effective way of ensuring that the CLR is undertaken is by using available secondary data and incorporating relevant information into the literature review report. *Secondary data* represent information that is collected by someone other than the literature reviewer. Popular secondary data for the social science field include surveys, censuses, and records collected by organizations (e.g., educational institutions, accreditation agencies). An important utility of secondary data is that it saves time that would have been spent otherwise if the literature reviewer had collected data himself/herself. Another important aspect of secondary data is, typically, that they have a pre-established degree of validity/legitimation and reliability/dependability that does not need to be re-examined by the literature reviewer who is re-using such data. Also, secondary data can provide baseline data that literature reviewers can compare to the primary data that they collect subsequently.

Public domain-based secondary data abound across disciplines, across fields, across regions, across countries, and across continents. The challenge is not only to locate them but also to locate the most recent versions of these data. One way of accomplishing this is by using keyword strings such as *National Data and "name of country"* or *National Statistics and "name of country."* For example, using the search string *National Data and England* on the Google search engine identified the United Kingdom (UK) National Statistics Publication Homepage, with secondary data centered around the following themes:

- Agriculture and environment
- Business and energy
- Children, education and skills
- Crime and justice
- Economy
- Government
- Health and social care
- Labor market
- People and places
- Population
- Travel and transport
- Equality and diversity
- Migration

As a literature reviewer, it is practical to say that, ultimately, you are a researcher. As both a literature reviewer and researcher, it is important to recognize

TOOL: POTENTIAL WEB 2.0 PATHWAYS TO LOCATE EXPERTS

Figure 2.10 provides a summary chart of potential tools that can be used with respect to experts.

Web 2.0 Tool	Definition	Use	Advantages
Twitter (circa 2006)	A free online social networking and microblogging service, with more than 380 million users worldwide	Enables literature reviewers to send and to read text-based posts of up to 140 characters (i.e., *tweets*) to prolific authors, selected researchers, or relevant stakeholders who utilize this tool	Literature reviewers can tweet via the Twitter website, compatible external applications (e.g., smartphones), or by SMS available in certain countries. Moreover, literature reviewers can subscribe to prolific authors' tweets, a practice called *following*
Internet-based social bookmarking services (circa 1996)	An Internet method to organize and to manage hot-linked bookmarks of online resources	Enables literature reviewers, by joining the network of a prolific author/researcher, to have access to the author's/researcher's links to webpages	Unlike file sharing repositories such as Google Docs, the online resources themselves are not shared; rather, bookmarks are provided that reference these resources, with metadata providing tags (similar to keywords), descriptions of these resources, and short critiques or summaries of important information
Delicious (circa 2003)	A social bookmarking service	Allows literature reviewers to build a community of authors/researchers and colleagues who can share, observe, and critique tag patterns across bookmarked material	Literature reviewers can develop their own online literature review identities, whereby they earn a reputation for their literature review-based bookmark collections and critiques of information sources on a particular subject(s)
CiteULike (circa 2004)	A free academic-oriented social bibliography site	Allows literature reviewers to manage and to discover scholarly references, as well as to save books and articles online	Literature reviewers can use this service to store references that they find online, to discover new articles and resources, to receive automated article recommendations, to share references with other users, to find out who is reading the same articles and resources, and to store and search pdf files. CiteULike contains more than 5 million references
LinkedIn (circa 2003)	Professionally focused social networking site available in many languages and which hosts more than 135 million registered users from more than 200 countries and territories	Enables literature reviewers to monitor who within the community has added new resources. Most importantly, literature reviewers can use this tool to build relationships with other literature reviewers who cite similar resources	Literature reviewers can maintain a list of contact details of people with whom they have some level of relationship, called *connections*

Figure 2.10   Tools for contacting experts on a topic

the many identities and responsibilities inherent in the research process. As such, you wear many hats, three of which we have already discussed as important to consider: (a) cultural context, (b) research ethics, and (c) up-to-date multimodal resources. In addition, being a literature reviewer involves critical thinking—inspecting all aspects of the process and product—and attending to any biases that might be part of interpreting research. We highlight some additional attributes that are important to keep in mind for the literature review.

ATTITUDES OF THE LITERATURE REVIEWER

ORIGINALITY

Being an *original thinker* is critical in academic research because in order to advance knowledge within a field or subject discipline, it is important not merely to replicate what has already been undertaken or what is already known, but also to add in a significant way to further understanding, even if it is only in a small increment. Remember, as a literature reviewer, you are not simply restating or reporting on research in a specific topic area; you are combining it with original thoughts for an original, purposeful, and "logical argument of an interpretation of relevant published and/or unpublished information on the selected topic from multimodal texts and settings that primarily comprise five modes"—as per our micro definition of the CLR that we introduced in Chapter 1. Also, as an original thinker, when you explore databases, you will create a unique combination of key terms using your imagination and creativity in a type of mixing of ideas—revealing new knowledge. In the Seven-Step Model, we present to you ways to extend your search beyond the library subscription database and Internet sources for locating and integrating some of the obvious places for ideas, concepts, or articles. In this process, driven by culturally progressive, ethical research, and multimodal approaches, you cannot discard the fact that your individual experiences, education, training, values, morals, and spirituality influence your identity as an original thinker.

REFLEXIVITY

In addition, the literature reviewer is a *critical thinker*, who engages in evaluation of each identified source AND engages in evaluation of the discovery of the sources. That is, the critical thinker critiques each source identified in the literature review and each step of the process in the act of finding—before, during, and as a result of the literature review. This is accomplished through critiquing and *reflexivity*. Reflexivity is attending to the cognitive and emotional changes and sometimes even social changes—all of which represent some form of transformation—that you might experience in your literature review research.

TOOL: USING REFLEXIVITY IN THE CLR PROCESS

As noted in the introduction to the Seven-Step Model, we have embedded a guide for reflexivity to examine potential biases as well as to revisit aspects of each step. Figure 2.11 illustrates what we termed the CORE of the literature reviewer—reflexivity, specifically: Critical examination, Organization, Reflections, and Evaluation.

In essence, your audit trail, or decisions that you made throughout your literature review, needs to be communicated in your final report so that your findings and interpretations make sense to a person who did not "walk in your shoes." In fact, the extent to which you communicate *how* you critically collected, examined, and interpreted the literature is the extent to which you influence the knowledge base of not only your topic but also the identity of the reflexive researcher. As such, the literature reviewer serves as the main *instrument* when conducting the literature review.

(Continued)

(Continued)

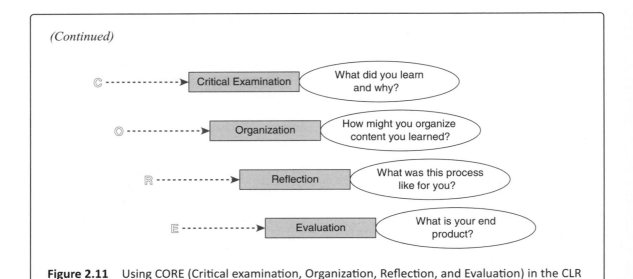

Figure 2.11 Using CORE (Critical examination, Organization, Reflection, and Evaluation) in the CLR

TOOL: VISUALIZING YOUR ROLE AS A RESEARCHER AND LITERATURE REVIEWER

Figure 2.12 illustrates your role as a literature reviewer as it influences the process and the final literature review report.

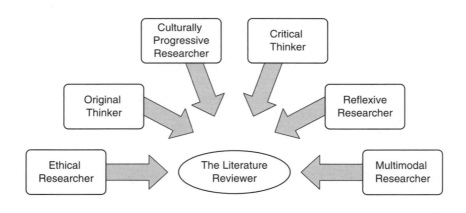

Figure 2.12 The identity of the literature reviewer

TOOL: VISUALIZING YOUR ROLE IN REVIEWING OTHER SOURCES

Figure 2.13 portrays the identity of the literature reviewer with respect to multiple sources (e.g., articles, information) and the historical and cultural nuances involved. As a researcher seeking to create new knowledge from the sources in your literature review, you will attend to this process for every work or source of information compiled. As seen in this figure, the literature reviewer as a researcher considers many inputs, and must negotiate the multiple contexts of these inputs through his/her lens, or culturally situation. Then, after conducting the literature review using the Seven-Step Model, the literature reviewer presents a final product that is cognizant of ethics, culture, and multiple modes.

Both cultural progressiveness and ethical responsibility is addressed through the ongoing reflective practices of the literature reviewer. Figure 2.13 illustrates how the CLR involves the adoption of a culturally progressive and ethical research approach, as well as a multimodal literature review approach. All of the elements in Figure 2.13 are negotiated by your reflexivity, which includes the formal examination of the literature review process and your identity as a researcher. Oftentimes, it is

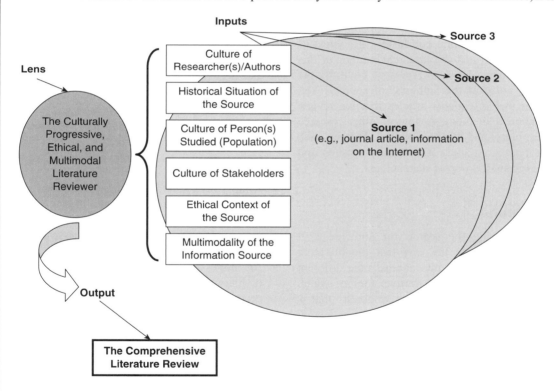

Figure 2.13 The many layers, or ways that the literature reviewer considers the voice(s) of many sources as situated in culture, history, culture of the persons studied, culture of stakeholders, the ethical context of the source, and the multimodal information sources as negotiated by the same components as the lens for interpretation

(Continued)

(Continued)

by just being aware of some potential biases you might have that launches your own unique way to be reflexive with the sources upon which you happen. It is important to recognize that you will not only become extremely knowledgeable in your area of literature, but, in your process of acquiring knowledge, you will also grow as a researcher. In this role, integrity is key. Therefore, it is a culturally progressive, ethical, and multimodal research approach that drives each step presented in the following chapters.

CONTEXTUAL CONSIDERATIONS

If the literature reviewer neglects any one or more of the aforementioned identities, the passing-on of knowledge might become a narrow process that is stagnant and simply restates content that is not sensitive to the sociocultural and historical context of both the research and the researcher/author of this information. The idea is to represent faithfully the intent and voice of the author(s) of sources. Yet, remember that oftentimes articles that we review also contain a literature review of other research that was interpreted by the author(s). Further, each empirical research study is culturally situated and targeted toward a group of stakeholders.

CONCLUSIONS

When considering the search for knowledge, it is interesting to note the way that the literature review has transformed into at least nine different types: four of which are narrative, four of which are systematic, and one integrative identity that is a combination of both. Therefore, the three research traditions (i.e., quantitative, qualitative, and mixed) might depend on any one of these types of literature reviews to inform its direction. In addition, as an end in itself, the stand-alone literature review also might be accomplished through one of these typologies. We designed the Seven-Step Model, which we begin in Chapter 4, based on the definition of the CLR as an integrative literature review. In fact, because the literature review might have varying degrees of many typologies, the three-dimensional model, Figure 2.9, allows a way to plot the individuality of the many forms, or identities, that a literature review might take. As an integrative review, and when you begin the Seven-Step Model, your final product will fall somewhere on this dimensional plot.

Review these ideas relating to the identity of the literature review:

- For many decades, there have been two major branches of traditional literature reviews: narrative literature reviews and systematic literature reviews.
- General reviews, theoretical reviews, methodological reviews, and historical reviews, and meta-synthesis, meta-summary, rapid reviews, meta-analysis, and integrative reviews, are nine types of literature review.
- A rapid review is a literature review that represents an accelerated or streamlined systematic review. Types of systematic reviews also include: meta-summary, meta-synthesis, meta-analysis, meta-ethnography, and integrative.
- An important flaw associated with all types of literature reviews is that they do not reflect adequately three elements that are essential for 21st-century literature reviews: the cultural context of literature reviews, the ethical nature of literature reviews, and the multimodal nature of information.
- When conducted optimally (e.g., being as transparent as possible in the search strategies used), both narrative reviews and systematic reviews have many strengths.
- Culture is a set of experiences, learned traditions, principles, and guides of behavior that are shared among members of a particular group that are dynamic and influential in communication.

Cultural competence, which is not a mastery of culture, focuses on the stance taken toward respecting diversity of cultures.

- Broadly speaking, *ethics* incorporate moral principles and best practices pertaining to both research and subject discipline topics.
- A text is multimodal when it combines or mixes two or more semiotic systems, and to conduct the review, the literature reviewer should not only adopt both a culturally progressive approach and ethical research approach, but also strive to obtain information from as many of these five MODES as possible.
- The literature reviewer serves as the main instrument when conducting the review and must negotiate the multiple contexts of sources, or inputs through his/her lens, or cultural situation.

CHAPTER 2 EVALUATION CHECKLIST

CORE	Guiding Questions and Tasks
Critical Examination	What are the strengths of the narrative literature review and the systematic literature review and in what contexts would you conduct each?
	How might you explain why ethics are important to consider as a literature reviewer when interpreting sources?
Organization	For the chapters to date, create a list of items on which you need greater clarity. For any resources you use, create an electronic file for storage.
	Of the multimodal texts discussed, with which are you most familiar, and which might you want to explore further?
	For any resources you collect, be sure to keep them in an electronic file and organize the information.
Reflections	As a literature reviewer, why might you consider transparency to be important in presenting your report, whether it be a stand-alone literature review or one to inform your primary research?
	Why might a literature review be original when it considers other authors' works?
Evaluation	Discern the characteristics and comparisons of the literature review. Of these reviews, identify any trends for the literature review in your discipline and profession.
	What new ideas do you have for interpreting evidence-based research with respect to particular populations? How has your mindset improved?

3

METHODOLOGY OF THE LITERATURE REVIEW

CHAPTER 3 ROADMAP

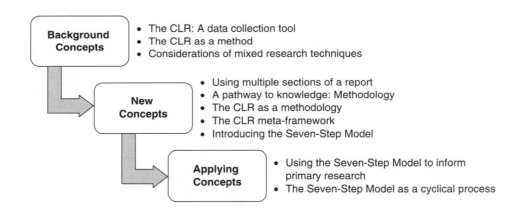

Background Concepts
- The CLR: A data collection tool
- The CLR as a method
- Considerations of mixed research techniques

New Concepts
- Using multiple sections of a report
- A pathway to knowledge: Methodology
- The CLR as a methodology
- The CLR meta-framework
- Introducing the Seven-Step Model

Applying Concepts
- Using the Seven-Step Model to inform primary research
- The Seven-Step Model as a cyclical process

BACKGROUND CONCEPTS

THE CLR: A DATA COLLECTION TOOL

The word *data* refers to a body of information. This body of information can be extracted from many sources such as words, numbers, images, hyperlinks, audio, and video. Therefore, the information that the literature reviewer collects to inform a literature review represents data. Thus, it stands to reason that the literature review process can be viewed as a data collection tool—that is, as a means of collecting a body of information pertinent to a topic of interest. As a data collection tool, the literature review involves activities such as identifying, recording, understanding, meaning-making, and transmitting information. Indeed, the literature review process is actualized through data collection. In its optimal form, the literature review represents a formal data collection process wherein information is gathered in a comprehensive way.

THE CLR AS A METHOD

In the field of research, the term *method* represents the specific approaches and procedures that the researcher systematically utilizes that are manifested in the research design, sampling design, data collection, data analysis, data interpretation, and so forth. The literature review represents a method because the literature reviewer chooses from an array of strategies and procedures for identifying, recording, understanding, meaning-making, and transmitting information pertinent to a topic of interest. Moreover, as asserted by Onwuegbuzie, Leech, and Collins (2011), conducting a literature review is equivalent to conducting a research study, with the information that the literature reviewer collects representing the data. In fact, as is the case for *all* studies, the literature review involves the following four phases that we discussed in Chapter 1, namely, conceptualization, planning, implementation, and dissemination. As such, when the literature review stands alone (i.e., independent work), then the literature review represents a single research study that ends when the literature review process ends. In contrast, when the goal of the literature review is to inform primary research, then the literature review represents an embedded study. Therefore, essentially, all studies that contain a review of the literature, however large or small, actually involve the conduct of two studies: a study of the previous knowledge (i.e., review of the literature) and the primary research study conducted by the researcher(s)—with the literature review study being embedded within the primary research study. With this in mind, as we stated in Chapter 1, researchers should no longer view the literature review as one step of the many steps that underlie a research study; rather, the researcher should view the literature review as representing an embedded study.

CONSIDERATIONS OF MIXED RESEARCH TECHNIQUES

As you will see in the subsequent chapters, in its optimal form, the literature review not only represents a study; it also represents a mixed research study. In other words, the CLR is facilitated by using *mixed research techniques*—that is, by collecting and analyzing *both* quantitative and qualitative information within the same literature review. Traditionally, as noted in Chapter 1, many textbook authors give the impression that the literature review always varies with the type of primary study (Myth 9) and that it involves not only just *summarizing* the extant literature (Myth 6) but also merely summarizing the *findings* of previous (related) studies. Such myths falsely give the impression that only quantitative data should be summarized in quantitative research-based works and only qualitative data should be summarized in qualitative research-based works. As such, a literature reviewer who summarizes only quantitative research findings only will use quantitative data to inform the literature review. As discussed in Chapter 2, a literature reviewer prescribing to this myth likely might conduct what Gene Glass (1976) coined a meta-analysis, wherein the literature reviewer combines quantitative findings from as many available individual quantitative research studies as possible that address a set of related research hypotheses for the purpose of integrating the results. Conversely, a literature reviewer who summarizes only qualitative research findings only will use qualitative data to inform the literature review. For instance, a literature reviewer belonging to this camp might conduct what Sandelowski and Barroso (2006) refer to as a meta-synthesis, whereby the literature reviewer integrates qualitative research findings from selected qualitative research studies that represent interpretive syntheses of data addressing a set of related research questions for the purpose of integrating the results.

NEW CONCEPTS

A literature review in its most *comprehensive form* includes a synthesis of quantitative findings stemming from quantitative research studies and qualitative findings stemming from qualitative research studies. Synthesizing both quantitative and qualitative findings within the same literature review automatically renders the literature review process as a mixed research study (Onwuegbuzie, Collins, et al., 2010).

USING MULTIPLE SECTIONS OF A REPORT

The CLR as a mixed research study is enhanced by recognizing that meaning-making can occur from any aspect of a work (e.g., research article, book chapter, book), including the title, abstract, literature review section, theoretical or conceptual framework, purpose statement(s), research question(s), hypotheses, statement of the educational significance, method section (e.g., participants, instruments, procedure, research design, analysis), results section, and discussion section. These sections contain quantitative and/or qualitative information. For example, at the very least, the following elements contain quantitative information:

- findings pertaining to each quantitative study presented in the literature review section of the source
- sample size(s) pertaining to one or more of the studies
- quantitative and/or qualitative studies presented in the literature review section of the source
- findings in the results section of each quantitative study selected for the literature review section

Also, the following elements of the research study contain qualitative information:

- findings pertaining to each qualitative study presented in the literature review section of the source
- the literature review section of each quantitative, qualitative, or mixed research study presented in the literature review section of the source

- information about the sample characteristics pertaining to each quantitative, qualitative, or mixed research study presented in the literature review section of the source
- conclusion section of each quantitative, qualitative, or mixed research study presented in the literature review section of the source; and findings in the results section of each qualitative study presented in the literature review section

Because of the array of quantitative and qualitative data that are potentially inherent in each work, *every* literature review lends itself simultaneously to the analysis of quantitative and qualitative information. As such, every literature review optimally involves using mixed research techniques. Simply put, then, the literature review represents a mixed research study. A literature reviewer might use quantitative research approaches to synthesize quantitative-based works and qualitative research approaches to synthesize qualitative-based works. With regard to quantitative research techniques, for instance, a literature reviewer might utilize **correlational research techniques** to examine, across studies, the relationship between the size of the effect of a reading intervention on reading achievement and the mean age of the students exposed to the intervention. With respect to qualitative research approaches, for example, a literature reviewer might utilize case study techniques for the collection of qualitative information, wherein each source represents a case. And, adopting Stake's (2005) typology, the literature review can be framed as an **intrinsic case study** (i.e., the literature review is designed to select sources of information that highlight particular cases of interest [e.g., illustrative case, deviant case]), an *instrumental case study* (i.e., the literature review is designed to examine a particular case for the main purpose of providing insight into a phenomenon or issue, or to obtain a generalization), or a *collective/multiple case study* (i.e., the literature review is designed to examine multiple cases in an attempt to examine a phenomenon)—with the instrumental case study being the most common qualitative method that can be mapped onto the literature review process.

In fact, literature reviewers have at their disposal many quantitative and qualitative research designs, which have been identified in Chapter 1. In any case, whatever combination of quantitative and qualitative research approaches is used to conduct the literature review, it is clear that the CLR represents a mixed research study. Thus, bearing in mind the 350-year history of formal literature reviews, we are surprised that the literature review has not been framed as a mixed research study until recently. In fact, building on the seminal work of Heyvaert et al. (2011), similar to the typologies presented in Chapter 2 of narrative and systematic reviews, we have identified only seven frameworks that apply the principles of mixed research, namely, what (a) Whittemore and Knafl (2005) called *integrative review*; (b) Gaber (2000) called *meta-needs assessment*; (c) Harden and Thomas (2010) called *mixed methods synthesis*; (d) Sandelowski, Voils, and Barroso (2006) called *mixed research synthesis*; (e) Pluye, Gagnon, Griffiths, and Johnson-Lafleur (2009) called *mixed studies review*; (f) Pawson, Greenhalgh, Harvey, and Walshe (2005) called *realist review*; and, most recently, (g) Onwuegbuzie, Collins, et al. (2010) also called a mixed research synthesis.

A PATHWAY TO KNOWLEDGE: METHODOLOGY

One aspect that all cultures have shared throughout time is a quest for knowledge. An important pathway to knowledge is via a framework called *methodology*. There are many ways of defining methodology. For example, methodology can be defined as "the branch of logic that deals with the principles of the formation of knowledge" (*American Heritage Dictionary*, 1993, p. 858) or as "a body of practices, procedures, and rules in

a discipline or an inquiry"; also, as "a set of working methods" or "the study or theoretical analysis of such working methods" (p. 858). Alternatively stated, a methodology is a broad approach to scientific inquiry that contains a system or set of practices, methods, rules, and principles within a given field (e.g., social and behavioral science) or discipline (e.g., sociology). Some authors use *methodology* and *methods* interchangeably; yet, these two concepts are very different. In fact, methods represent merely one component of methodology.

METHODOLOGY CONCEPTUALIZED

In her seminal article, Greene (2006) conceptualized that the development of a methodology for the study of human beings necessitates consideration of the following four inter-related but conceptually distinct domains: (a) philosophical assumptions and stances, (b) inquiry logics, (c) guidelines for research practice, and (d) sociopolitical commitments (see also Greene, 2008). The first domain, *philosophical assumptions and stances*, refers to the core philosophical or epistemological beliefs associated with the methodology. This domain also includes beliefs regarding axiomatic elements, including the following: *epistemology* (i.e., study of the nature and scope of knowledge), pertaining to issues such as the relationship between the knower and the known; *ontology* (i.e., nature of reality), relating to issues such as single versus multiple-constructed realities, and subjectivity versus objectivity; and *axiology* (i.e., study of values), pertaining to issues such as the role of values in research. Consequently, the domain of philosophical assumptions and stances "guides the inquirer's gaze to look at particular things in particular ways and offers appropriate philosophical and theoretical justification for this way of seeing, observing, and interpreting" (Greene, 2006, p. 93).

According to Greene (2006), *inquiry logics*, the second domain, involve the identification of appropriate research goals, research objectives, research purposes, and research questions; appropriate sampling designs; broad research designs and procedures; criteria of quality for inferences; and standards for reporting findings. In addition, this domain involves identifying logics of justification for each of these research strategies, with an overall logic connecting all the research elements in a coherent way.

The third domain, *guidelines for research practice*, provides specific research strategies. Here, the philosophical assumptions and stances (Domain 1) and logics of inquiry (Domain 2) are translated into specific research procedures. Thus, guidelines for research practice represent the *how to* of research, which includes procedures relating to sampling schemes, research designs, data collection, data analysis, and data interpretation that emanate from Domain 2. Domain 3 also includes specific procedures for collecting (e.g., surveys, interviews), analyzing (e.g., correlation, method of constant comparison), interpreting, and reporting data. Therefore, guidelines for research practice provide the nuts and bolts of the research study.

The fourth domain, *sociopolitical commitments*, addresses whose interests should be served by the particular research approach, where the investigation is situated in society, whether the study contributes to collective theoretical knowledge, whether the investigation generates knowledge, whether the study informs governmental decision makers and stakeholders, whether the study is located in a protected space that is free from political dispute, and whether the study lies somewhere among competing elements that represent social critique or advocacy for particular interests, viewpoints, and subgroups. The domain of sociopolitical commitments plays an important role in situating the research in society. According to Greene

TOOL: OVERVIEW OF FOUR DOMAINS OF A METHODOLOGY

The four domains are summarized in Table 3.1. As a set, these four domains provide a unified and interactive framework and a set of practical guidelines for a methodology. Also, these domains have been fully developed with respect to both the quantitative and qualitative research traditions. In recent years, these domains have begun to be fully developed with respect to mixed research, which still represents an emerging methodology.

Table 3.1   Four domains that drive the development of a methodology

Domain	Description
Philosophical assumptions and stances	This domain refers to the core philosophical or epistemological assumptions of the methodology. This domain "guides the inquirer's gaze to look at particular things in particular ways and offers appropriate philosophical and theoretical justification for this way of seeing, observing, and interpreting" (Greene, 2006, p. 93).
Inquiry logics	This domain pertains to what traditionally is called *methodology*. It guides the researcher's "gaze" such that "what is important to see…is observed, recorded, and understood or explained in defensible ways" (Greene, 2006, p. 93).
Guidelines for research practice	This domain provides specific strategies for inquiry practice. Here, the first two domains are converted into specific research procedures. Thus, guidelines for research practice represent the *how to* of research, including procedures pertaining to sampling schemes, research designs, data collection, and data analysis that emanate from Domain 2.
Sociopolitical commitments	This domain involves delineation and justification of how the research is located in society. It "importantly directs the inquirer's journey toward a particular destination, as it identifies priority roles for social science in society and provides values-based rationales and meanings for the practice of social inquiry. While values are present in all four domains, they are proclaimed in Domain 4" (Greene, 2006, p. 94).

Source: "Toward a methodology of mixed methods social inquiry," by J. C. Greene, 2006, *Research in the Schools, 13*(1), pp. 93–98.

(2006), "While values are present in all four domains, they are proclaimed in Domain 4" (p. 94).

THE CLR AS A METHODOLOGY

When conceptualizing the definition of the literature review, we consider further the following ideas of Greene (2006):

> A methodology for social inquiry gains credibility and persuasiveness when all of these domains act in concert with one another, when their interlocking connections are smooth and well oiled, when the overall presentation is strong, coherent, well articulated and thus persuasive. (p. 94)

We contend that the CLR is a methodology because of its potential to have a "coherent foundation for inquiry with tightly interconnected logics of justification, positioning, procedures, and rationales" (Greene, 2006, p. 94). Specifically, the literature review has at its root several research philosophies (Domain 1), some of which will be discussed in more detail in the next chapter.

EXAMPLE: POSTPOSITIVIST PHILOSOPHICAL FRAME

A literature review might be rooted in a *postpositivist philosophy*, which advocates an objective, although fallible, stance on social knowledge. Reviewers who adopt a postpositivist approach to literature reviews likely would place more emphasis on quantitative findings than on qualitative findings. Moreover, postpositivist literature reviewers would place high value on developing, testing, modifying, and expanding theory (Domain 4). So, central questions and hypotheses that drive literature reviews are represented by causal questions about the effects or outcomes of a certain human action, behavior, experience, or intervention. Further, systematic reviews are viewed by postpositivists as representing the best literature review analysis techniques for testing causal hypotheses (Domain 2), because they lead to generalizations. Underlying these systematic reviews are techniques with a long tradition such as meta-analysis (Domain 3).

EXAMPLE: CONSTRUCTIVIST PHILOSOPHICAL FRAME

A literature review might be rooted in a *constructivist philosophy* (e.g., social constructivists/constructionists), which often is associated with a claim that multiple, contradictory, but equally valid accounts of the same phenomenon—known as *multiple realities*—can coexist. Literature reviewers who adopt some form of constructivist approach to literature reviews likely would place more emphasis on qualitative findings than on quantitative findings. Moreover, constructivist literature reviewers would place high value on obtaining local, contextual understanding and meaning-making regarding the human experience (Domain 4). Central questions revolve around contextuality and meaning and guide the literature reviewer to construct and to reinterpret from the literature review an emic (i.e., insider's) view of meaningfulness within the underlying context (Domain 2). Constructivist-based literature reviews are guided by well-established tenets such as inductive reasoning, detailed rich and thick description, and reflexivity (Domain 3).

THE INTER-DIALOGUE OF METHODOLOGY

To understand better the concept of methodology and the literature review, we might regard how music is expressed through multiple genres, such as pop music, jazz music, classical music, and so on. Oftentimes, musicians will compose and perform fusion music, which is a combination of many genres and philosophies, as well as methods. Thus, the methodology in the literature review process is similar to fusion music, and after conducting the literature review, you will have left your mark in time—like a carbon footprint. Even though you, as the literature reviewer, will explore and determine your own philosophical stance in Step 1 of the Seven-Step Model, we regard our own philosophical stances in creating this book as what Johnson (2011) recently termed *dialectical pluralism*, which is a thoughtful, eclectic integration of methods and perspectives. Dialectical pluralism is a research stance that is inspired by the way mixed methods, or multiple data, inform one and other. At times, when we study a topic that focuses directly on the lives and experiences of underserved and marginalized persons or groups, such as children/adolescents or adults needing mentoring, we use a philosophical lens that we conceptualized ourselves, which we call **critical dialectical pluralism** (Onwuegbuzie & Frels, 2013a). Critical dialectical pluralism represents a social justice paradigm, the goal of which is to give voice and to empower the people who are being studied (Onwuegbuzie & Frels, 2013a). Thus, rather than viewing the literature review as only a phase in the research study, we should view the literature review as a methodology. We built our concept of methodology on the words stated by Onwuegbuzie, Leech, et al. (2011):

> the literature review represents a methodology because it represents a broad approach to scientific research that encompasses a set of research objectives, research purposes, and research questions, as well as methods and procedures, criteria of quality, and standards for reporting. Each individual component of the literature review (e.g., selecting a topic, searching the literature, developing the argument, surveying the literature, critiquing the literature, and writing the review; see, for e.g., Machi & McEvoy, 2009) must be compatible for the process to be optimal. (p. 187)

THE CLR META-FRAMEWORK

As you have seen in previous chapters, there are many ways that the literature review reveals itself throughout history and involves the use of one of the three research traditions (i.e., quantitative, qualitative, mixed). In this chapter, we have discussed ways that the literature review represents a data collection tool, a method, a mixed research study, and, most of all, a methodology. Further, because oftentimes a methodology can be an abstract process, a methodology needs some type of mechanism, or process, to bring it to fruition. This would be a framework. By now, you might be asking, then why a meta-framework? The prefix *meta* is used to mean *about (its own category)* and one example would be to say metadata are data about data. Definitely, there are many frameworks within the Seven-Step Model, such as steps within steps. Therefore, the CLR is a **meta-framework**. For example, in Step 1: Exploring Beliefs and Topics, we provide many parts of the belief system, such as worldview, field/discipline-specific

beliefs, and topic-specific beliefs. We imagine that if a person holds many beliefs on one issue, he/she might have a meta-belief system.

Returning to the metaphor of music genre as methodology, there are various frameworks for a symphony orchestra. The composer of the music itself uses a framework: perhaps a traditional three movement symphony, or four movement symphony, or a symphonic poem to convey the compositional ideas. Each section of the orchestra and each musician within the section uses a framework to interpret the composition, and the conductor has particular steps to begin and to end the concert of this music. As a result, the concert itself is a meta-framework of many steps, procedures, approaches, and ideas.

INTRODUCING THE SEVEN-STEP MODEL

As we have discussed throughout this chapter, the literature review involves culture, ethics, multimodalities, and your identity as a researcher—inclusive of your values, beliefs, and experiences. As the phrase suggests, the Seven-Step Model of the CLR comprises seven steps: (a) Step 1: Exploring Beliefs and Topics; (b) Step 2: Initiating the Search; (c) Step 3: Storing and Organizing Information; (d) Step 4: Selecting/Deselecting Information; (e) Step 5: Expanding the Search to Include One or More MODES (**M**edia, **O**bservation(s), **D**ocuments, **E**xpert(s), **S**econdary Data); (f) Step 6: Analyze and Synthesize Information; and (g) Step 7: Present the CLR Report. These seven steps are multidimensional, interactive, emergent, iterative, dynamic, holistic, and synergistic.

By *multidimensional*, we mean that each of the steps has multiple components or dimensions. By *interactive*, we mean that each step is dependent on all the other steps. That is, each step is related to each of the other steps by going back and forth at different stages of the review. By *emergent*, we mean that leads should be followed as they emerge, such as good detectives following all leads. For example, as we discussed earlier and will discuss in more detail in Chapter 8, whenever possible, as part of the literature review, prolific authors should be interviewed by the reviewer to find out about these authors' latest unpublished works, ongoing works, and/or future works (Step 5). The information that these authors provide

TOOL: THE META-FRAMEWORK OF THE SEVEN STEPS

Figure 3.1 depicts what we have been discussing as a meta-framework of the concepts described in the first three chapters. As a literature reviewer, it is important that you understand the bigger picture because, as a culturally progressive researcher, it is an ethical responsibility to be able to justify each decision that you make and, moreover, to be able to convey your literature review to others, through your own lens, without changing the original intentions of the authors whose sources you synthesize.

As seen in Figure 3.1, the core of the meta-framework is the core of our Seven-Step Model, the cultural progressive approach that drives the literature review process. Layered within the model are the ethical approach, multimodal texts and settings, and the identity of the literature reviewer, as an original thinker, critical thinker, and reflexive literature reviewer.

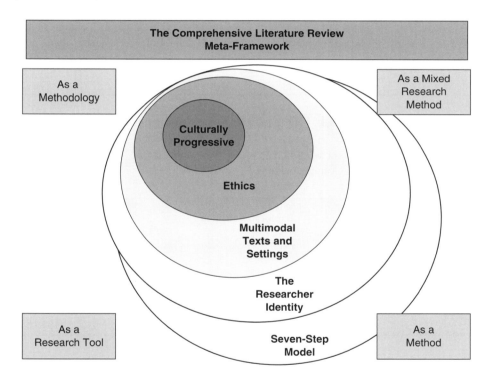

Figure 3.1   A conceptualization of a meta-framework and systems within systems

would be maximally emergent. By *iterative*, we mean that the steps are recursive. That is, any or even all of the steps can be repeated, as many times as is needed. Further, the reviewer often oscillates (i.e., moves back and forth) between some or all of these steps. For instance, the literature reviewer might receive information from one or more prolific authors (i.e., Step 5) that might lead the reviewer to focus the search further (i.e., return to Step 2) or to select/deselect literature (i.e., return to Step 4). By *dynamic*, we mean that the CLR is vibrant, energetic, lively, and eventful—and, hence, exciting. By *holistic*, we mean that the literature reviewer should incorporate as many semiotic systems as possible. Finally, by *synergistic*, we mean that the CLR follows Hall and Howard's (2008) four core principles for synergistic approaches:

- synthesizing information obtained from as many of the five MODES as possible culminates in a literature review that is more comprehensive than would have been obtained if a traditional literature review has been conducted
- using a dialectic approach to conducting the literature review, wherein multiple philosophical assumptions and stances are intertwined, when applicable
- considering of equal importance quantitative and qualitative research techniques for conducting the literature review in general and synthesizing the information in particular

- balancing the multiple roles of the literature reviewer (i.e., culturally progressive, ethical, multimodal, original thinker, critical thinker, reflexive researcher)

EXPLORATION, INTERPRETATION, AND COMMUNICATION PHASES

The first phase, Exploration, involves a series of investigative steps. In particular, optimally, literature reviewers should explore an array of their belief systems, including their worldviews, research philosophical beliefs, discipline-specific beliefs, and topic-specific beliefs, as well as the inter-relationships among these belief systems (Step 1). In addition, literature reviewers should explore their topics of interest, using various means (e.g., personal beliefs, knowledge, and experiences;

TOOL: THE THREE PHASES OF THE SEVEN-STEP MODEL

Figure 3.2 presents the seven steps of the CLR process subdivided into the following three phases: Exploration, Interpretation, and Communication.

Exploration Phase

Step 1: Exploring Beliefs and Topics

Step 2: Initiating the Search

Step 3: Storing and Organizing Information

Step 4: Selecting/Deselecting Information

Step 5: Expanding the Search to Include One or More MODES (Media, Observation(s), Documents, Expert(s), Secondary Data)

Interpretation Phase

Step 6: Analyzing and Synthesizing Information

Communication Phase

Step 7: Presenting the CLR Report

Figure 3.2   The three phases of the Comprehensive Literature Review

professional beliefs, knowledge, and experiences) to explore initial key terms associated with this topic to inform their information searches (Step 1). Further, literature reviewers should explore potential information databases, and then, once appropriate databases have been identified, they should search these databases to explore information about the topic and to identify the most appropriate key terms to help focus the search (Step 2). Literature reviewers also should explore what information to select and what information to deselect (Step 4) and expand the search by incorporating one or more of the five MODES (Step 5). While making their journeys to and through Step 5—the final step of the Exploration Phase—literature reviewers should explore how to store and to organize information.

The second phase, Interpretation, involves literature reviewers interpreting the selected information that they extracted via the previous five steps. This interpretation occurs through analysis and synthesis pathways. As the word suggests, this interpretation phase is interpretive because it is the culmination of the analysis, evaluation, and interpretation of selected information sources, which are then synthesized, leading to what Tashakkori and Teddlie (1998) refer to as *meta-inferences*, which represent inferences from each information source that are combined into a coherent narrative.

The third and final phase, Communication, involves literature reviewers disseminating their literature reviewer reports to the appropriate audience. This dissemination might take the form of a presentation that is delivered via **A**cting (e.g., performance ethnography wherein the literature review report is performed via dramatic representations such as plays), **V**isually (e.g., via drawings, paintings, photographs, videos, multimedia), **O**rally (e.g., presenting the literature review report in class; presenting the literature review report as part of a thesis/dissertation defense; presenting the literature review report at a research conference by itself, or as part of the presentation of a primary research report), or, most importantly, in **W**riting (e.g., via a class assignment, thesis/dissertation chapter, research article, book chapter, blog, website, or Internet-based social bookmarking service)—with the printed and/or digital form of the literature review report being stored somewhere (e.g., library, bibliographic database, website). Typically,

the goal here is to make the research report available to one or more others, thereby contributing to the cycle of knowledge generation.

USING THE SEVEN-STEP MODEL TO INFORM PRIMARY RESEARCH

As seen in Figure 3.4, the Seven-Step Model can be applied to any or all of the 12 components of a primary research report: problem statement, background, theoretical/conceptual framework, research question(s), hypotheses, participants, instruments, procedure, analyses, interpretation of the findings, directions for future research, and implications for the field. The following sections provide an overview of these applications.

PROBLEM STATEMENT

An effective (i.e., research-worthy) **problem statement** (also called the *statement of the problem*) is the description of a current and important challenge (i.e., problem) that is confronted by researchers and/or practitioners for which there are no adequate solutions available from the extant literature. Further, a research-worthy problem statement should make clear the nature and scope of the problem that has been identified. More specifically, the problem statement is a section in a research report that contains the topic for the study, the research problem within this topic, a justification for the problem based on past research and practice, deficiencies or shortcomings of past research or practical knowledge, and the importance of addressing the problem for diverse audiences (Creswell, 2002, p. 650). Clearly, to obtain "a justification for the problem based on past research" and to identify "deficiencies or shortcomings of past research," a Comprehensive Literature Review is needed.

BACKGROUND

It should be obvious that a literature reviewer needs to provide adequate background information to be able to write the literature review section of a primary research report. Thus, we do not need to provide a further explanation here as we hope it is implied!

TOOL: OVERVIEW OF THE SEVEN-STEP MODEL

Figure 3.3 illustrates the flow of the Seven-Step Model. This figure also reflects the exploration, interpretation, and communication phases.

As you can see from this figure, Step 3 (Storing and Organizing Information) plays a pivotal role in the literature review process because every selected information source needs to be stored and organized, at least initially. Thus, as can be seen, arrows go from Step 2, Step 4, and Step 5 to Step 3, which indicates that information obtained during Step 2, Step 4, and Step 5 must be stored and organized. Also, arrows go from Step 3 to Step 4, Step 5 (i.e., via Step 4), and Step 6, which indicates that information obtained in previous stages should be stored and organized before moving to Step 4, Step 5, and Step 6. In the following chapters, you will learn about each of the seven steps to conduct the CLR.

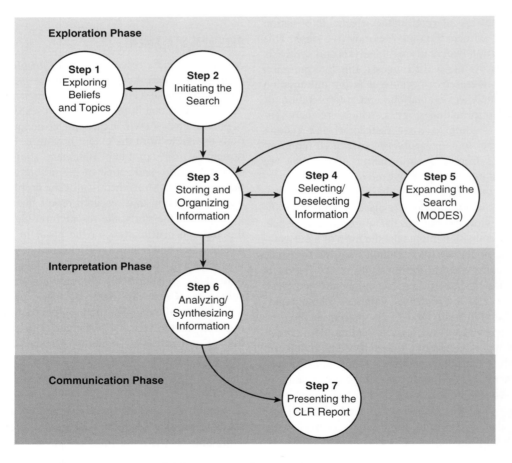

Figure 3.3   The Seven-Step Model for a Comprehensive Literature Review

TOOL: SEVEN-STEP MODEL TO INFORM PRIMARY RESEARCH AREAS

Figure 3.4 presents how the Seven-Step Model might be used to inform the various components of the primary research study.

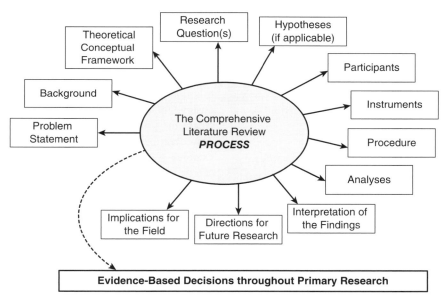

Figure 3.4   The Comprehensive Literature Review process as it informs the various components of a primary research report

THEORETICAL/CONCEPTUAL FRAMEWORK

As noted by Lester (2005), a ***theoretical framework*** guides the research process via the use of formal theory "developed by using an established, coherent explanation of certain sorts of phenomena and relationships" (p. 458). In contrast, a ***conceptual framework*** is "an argument that the concepts chosen for investigation, and any anticipated relationships among them, will be appropriate and useful given the research problem under investigation" (p. 460). Virtually all quantitative, qualitative, and mixed research studies are driven, at least to some degree, by a theoretical framework and/or a conceptual framework. In order to identify an "established, coherent explanation of certain sorts of phenomena and relationships" (i.e., theoretical framework) or to determine whether the "concepts chosen for investigation, and any anticipated relationships among them, will be appropriate and useful" (i.e., conceptual framework), the literature reviewer must be familiar with the extant body of information.

RESEARCH QUESTION(S)

A *research question* is an interrogative statement that the researcher attempts to answer using research techniques. In most instances, research questions stem from the literature because they represent a narrowing of the purpose statement, which, in turn, reflects a gap in our knowledge base. Even if the research question stems from practical experience, it is always a good idea to examine the literature not only to contextualize the research question, but also to check to determine whether this research question has not already been addressed by one or more other teams of researchers. Thus, a literature review helps a researcher finalize his/her research question(s).

HYPOTHESES

The research *hypothesis* is a proposed explanation of an observable phenomenon that can be tested via research. Alternatively stated, a hypothesis is a declarative statement wherein the researcher—typically in quantitative research studies or the quantitative phase(s) of mixed research studies—makes a prediction or judgment about the relationship that exists among the variables of interest. As stated by Johnson and Christensen (2010), "the stated hypothesis typically emerges from the literature review or from theory" (p. 77). Thus, a literature reviewer needs to conduct a literature review to be able to finalize his/her hypotheses.

PARTICIPANTS

In the *participants section* of a research report, at a minimum, authors describe the sample/population size, sampling scheme (how the sample was selected), and characteristics of the sample/population members. It is always a good idea to examine the literature to contextualize all the sampling decisions made. For example,

in quantitative research, wherein hypotheses are tested, the appropriateness of the sample size needed for determining whether these relationships exist (i.e., what is called *statistical power*) depends, in part, on the size of the relationship expected among the variables that underlie the hypothesis (i.e., known as the *effect size*). Information regarding the expected size of the relationship among the variables of interest can be gleaned from the size of the relationships among the same or similar variables that has been documented in previous empirical reports. Consequently, the literature review can play an important role in helping the literature reviewer make sound decisions regarding his/her choice of participants.

INSTRUMENTS

In a research study, *instruments* are tools used for facilitating the fulfillment of one or more of the following research objectives: explore, describe, explain, predict, influence (see Figure 1.4 in Chapter 1). For example, in quantitative research, where the primary research objectives are to describe, to explain, to predict, or to influence data, instruments are used to measure, to observe, or to document data. In qualitative research, where the primary research objectives are to explore or to describe, instruments are used to document or to examine phenomena. In mixed research, instruments can be used for any of the reasons for which they are used in both quantitative and qualitative research. The literature review plays a vital role in helping the literature reviewer select the most appropriate instrument(s) for a primary research study. Unfortunately, in our experience, we have noticed that many researchers—especially beginning researchers—do not thoroughly investigate the instruments that they have selected.

EXAMPLE: USING THE CLR TO SELECT AN INSTRUMENT

Gibson and Dembo (1984) contended that their Teacher Efficacy Scale (TES) was developed based on Bandura's (1977) theory of self-efficacy. However, Dellinger (2005) demonstrated that this assertion had been contradicted repeatedly in the literature. Further, Dellinger (2005) documented that numerous researchers had empirically demonstrated that the TES has poor psychometric properties (e.g., Coladarci & Fink, 1995; Guskey & Passaro, 1994; Henson, 2002, 2003; Tschannen-Moran, Woolfolk Hoy, & Hoy, 1998; Witcher et al., 2006) and, thus, subsequently questioned the dimensionality of the TES. In particular, they concluded that the TES had more than the two subscales that were claimed by its developers. Yet, despite the poor measurement validity associated with the TES, as well as its inadequate foundational validity (i.e., reflecting "researchers' prior understanding of a construct and/or phenomenon under study"; Dellinger & Leech, 2007, p. 323) and historical validity (i.e., reflecting the "type of validity evidence that accrues through utilization and cited relevance in the extant literature"; Dellinger, 2005, p. 44), many researchers still use the TES. In fact, at the time of writing, Proquest Dissertations and Theses (PQDT) databases revealed 666 dissertations wherein this scale was used either to collect efficacy data (the overwhelming majority of articles) or to assess/discuss the psychometric properties of the TES, which is consistent with Henson, Kogan, and Vache-Haase's (2001) declaration that the TES is "the most frequently used instrument in the area" (p. 404)—despite its questionable psychometric properties, which might invalidate any findings stemming from the use of this instrument. The documented problems with the TES instrument provide just one example of how not conducting the literature review can lead to an inappropriate choice of instrument by the researcher.

PROCEDURE

The **procedure section** is "the section of the research report that describes how the study will be executed" (Johnson & Christensen, 2010, p. 592). This section also includes a delineation of the research design, which, as we defined in the previous chapter, is the framework (e.g., outline or plan) that is used to address the research question(s). As is the case for the participants and instrument sections, a literature review can play an important role in helping the literature reviewer make sound procedural decisions.

ANALYSES

In the context of research, an **analysis** involves breaking the underlying data into smaller parts to gain a better understanding of the phenomenon represented by these data. In addition to examining methodological sources to determine appropriate ways to analyze the data, given the research question(s) and/or hypotheses, the literature reviewer should examine reports that are similar to the primary study to ascertain the analyses that were

conducted, as well as any problems experienced by the analysts. For example, for quantitative research studies, it would be useful to find out how different researchers dealt with missing data during their analyses (i.e., information that was not obtained from one or more participants). In qualitative research, it might be useful to find out what analytical techniques led to data saturation (e.g., the analysis led to the emergence of themes or categories such that the analyst concludes that new data will not provide any new information or insights for developing these themes or categories; Morse, 1995). Thus, the literature review can play an important role in helping the literature reviewer make sound analytical decisions.

INTERPRETATIONS OF THE FINDINGS

As we discussed in the previous chapter, when debunking Myth 3, researchers are unable to contextualize their findings without incorporating relevant information from the extant body of works. Therefore, researchers include a section to discuss the **implications of the findings**. Even more importantly, when serendipitous (i.e., unexpected) findings emerge, it is even more important to use the extant body of works to help explain these findings. For instance, in the previous chapter, we described how Onwuegbuzie et al. (2003) conducted a literature review during the interpretation phase of their study, which led to them identifying a phenomenon that they labeled a *Matthew effect* to describe the performance of cooperative learning groups in introductory-level education research methodology courses. Therefore, the literature review during the interpretation phase helps to rule in or rule out rival explanations.

DIRECTIONS FOR FUTURE RESEARCH

It should be obvious that a literature reviewer needs to conduct a literature review to provide useful **directions for future research** that does not lead to unnecessary, redundant research being conducted in the future. As such, we do not need to provide a further explanation here but will keep this feature as our final thoughts on the subject.

IMPLICATIONS FOR THE FIELD

In interpreting their findings, it is essential that the literature reviewer does not provide recommendations that have been demonstrated previously as being inappropriate. Thus, the literature reviewer needs to conduct a review to help make thoughtful and ethical recommendations that are culturally progressive. The *implications for the field* section of a research report allows the literature reviewer to include ideas for the future research on this topic.

THE SEVEN-STEP MODEL AS A CYCLICAL PROCESS

As we have discussed, the Seven-Step Model can be used to inform at least 12 components of a primary research report. For primary studies, the Seven-Step Model should serve as a cyclical process, wherein the literature reviewer undergoes the seven steps as many times as is needed to inform adequately all components of a research report. This does not mean that the Seven-Step Model needs to be applied on at least 12 occasions. In fact, it is possible that several, if not most, of these components can be informed within the same seven-step cycle by carefully coding each information source. We will show you how to accomplish this in Step 3 of the Seven-Step Model (i.e., Chapter 6).

Remembering that although here we discuss the literature review as informing many parts of a primary research study, the literature review also can stand alone and, in this case, it is also a cyclical process. In fact, in writing this book on the literature review, we conducted our own information research to inform our report as a stand-alone literature review. We considered the research problem, which was the misrepresentation of the literature review in the social sciences. Next, we knew that simply describing the literature review through time would not add to the knowledge base; yet, we determined that we needed to synthesize this information toward a new definition. Thus, the CLR was born!

CONCLUSIONS

In closing, it is important to remember that as a literature reviewer, you should be aware of your identity as a culturally competent and ethical researcher, and that your comprehensive literature review might become someone else's basis for future research or for establishing a best practice in your field. Indeed, a literature review is a methodology. Therefore, as a methodology, method, and more, the literature review holds an important place in "the literature," and can impact stakeholders in your field or discipline. Now that we have discussed many ways to consider research tradition and tied these ideas to the literature review in Chapters 1 and 2, it is time to embark on your all-important literature review journey. In the next chapter, you will begin Step 1 and explore your worldview and research philosophical beliefs, topic-based beliefs, and discipline-based beliefs. In addition, in Step 1, we begin to guide you in documenting your step through the reflective practice, or what we call the CORE product. We suggest that you review these important chapter concepts before moving on:

- The literature review represents a data collection tool, a method, a mixed research method, and, above all, a methodology.
- When the literature review serves as an end in itself (i.e., stand-alone), then the literature review represents a single research study that ends when the literature review process ends.
- When the goal of the literature review is to inform primary research, then the literature review represents an embedded study.
- The CLR is facilitated by using mixed research techniques—that is, by collecting and analyzing *both* quantitative and qualitative information within the same literature review.
- The literature review can be framed as an intrinsic case study (i.e., the literature review is designed to select sources of information that highlight particular cases of interest [e.g., illustrative case, deviant case]).
- The literature review also can be an instrumental case study (i.e., the literature review is designed to examine a particular case for the main purpose of providing insight into a phenomenon or issue, or to obtain a generalization).
- The literature review can be a collective/multiple case study too (i.e., the literature review is designed to examine multiple cases in an attempt to examine a phenomenon).
- A methodology is a broad approach to scientific inquiry that contains a system or set of practices, methods, rules, and principles within a given field. These assumptions apply to the CLR.

TOOL: EXAMPLE OF USING THE SEVEN STEPS

Figure 3.5 represents a synopsis of our own literature review for designing the Seven-Step Model. As seen in this figure and in Step 7, we revisited the steps as needed when writing the final report, which is our textbook.

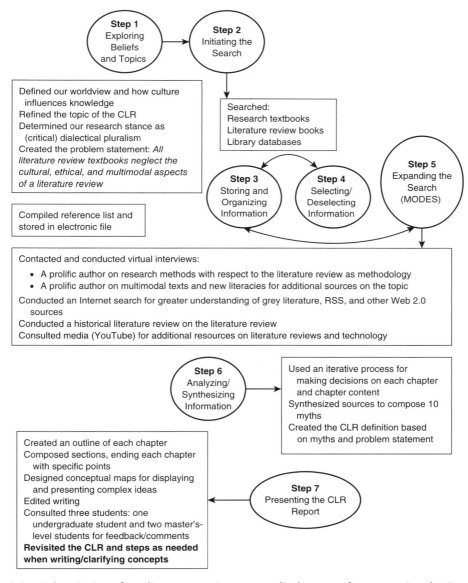

Figure 3.5 A description of our literature review as a cyclical process for presenting the Seven-Step Model and chapters of this textbook

CHAPTER 3 EVALUATION CHECKLIST

CORE	Guiding Questions and Tasks
Critical Examination	Think of one specific piece of knowledge, perhaps a historical fact or concept. Why do you think culture influences the way this knowledge was communicated?
Organization	Consider your experience reading research studies. Are particular sections of the report more interesting to you than others? Could it be that new jargon is an obstacle for you?
	Collect some resources to help you in the reading of the more difficult sections.
Reflections	In what ways is it important to consider the CLR as a methodology? In what ways might methodological variations of research influence the way it is conducted?
Evaluation	Discuss a time that you gathered both qualitative and quantitative data to understand a new topic, such as a medical procedure or at what restaurant to eat. How did one tradition add meaning to your understanding of the other?

PART TWO

EXPLORATION

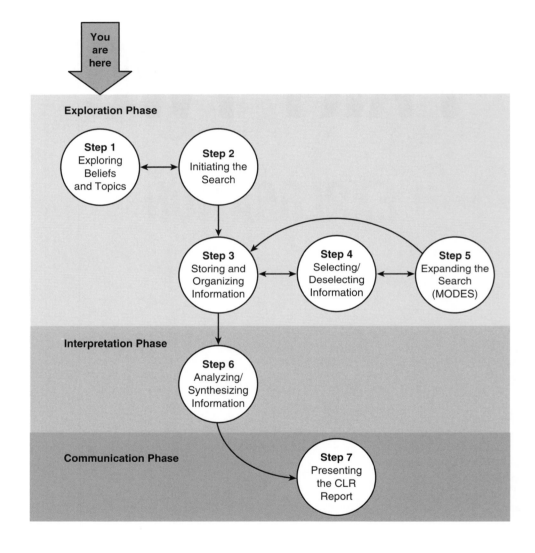

4

STEP 1: EXPLORING BELIEFS AND TOPICS

CHAPTER 4 ROADMAP

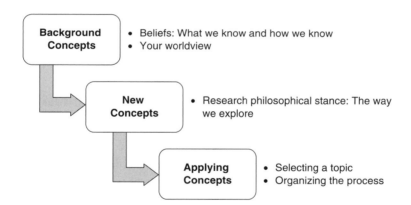

Background Concepts
- Beliefs: What we know and how we know
- Your worldview

New Concepts
- Research philosophical stance: The way we explore

Applying Concepts
- Selecting a topic
- Organizing the process

BACKGROUND CONCEPTS

BELIEFS: WHAT WE KNOW AND HOW WE KNOW

When we begin to consider beliefs, we turn again to culture and ask the question—How do we know what we know? In our experiences, it is possible that we have absorbed the beliefs of our parents, beliefs of our society or culture, beliefs of our traditions, moral teachings, and spirituality. As we move through life, we have experiences that might either affirm or challenge our beliefs. Further, in the field of philosophy, the term *philosophical thinking* moves us to look into the thinking that forms our beliefs and their logical connections with other beliefs.

For the purpose of Step 1: Exploring Beliefs and Topics, we do not propose that you change your core beliefs nor do we presume to challenge your belief systems. However, we do want you to begin the step of critical reflection so that you are aware of why you lean toward particular ideas and why you negotiate some of these ideas with reason. Therefore, we posit that all research is culturally situated in culture and our belief systems—we decide what problems to study, what and where to search for answers to these problems, what to highlight and how to highlight our findings, and how we shape the discussion of our findings. In fact, no one flips a coin or spins a wheel to select a topic randomly. You will choose an idea that resonates with what you care about, what you are interested in, or what captures your attention. You might not even know why you have selected or refined a topic, to a certain extent. Getting started with Step 1 involves exploring your beliefs and how these beliefs influence your literature review. Although there are many belief systems, for Step 1, we highlight the epistemology and axiology of knowing, as they influence and are influenced by your personal worldview. Next, we discuss how your worldview is the lens for the way that you embrace a particular research philosophical belief or beliefs, discipline-specific beliefs, and topic-specific beliefs.

TOOL: DISCOVERING YOUR INTERACTING BELIEF SYSTEMS

Figure 4.1 illustrates the interacting belief systems for selecting and approaching your literature review topic.

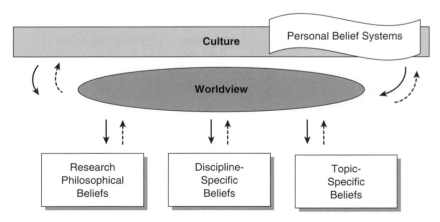

Figure 4.1   The interactive process of culture, belief systems, worldview, and approach in the Comprehensive Literature Review

YOUR WORLDVIEW

As discussed in Chapter 2, culture is the overarching influence for the literature review. In Figure 4.1, we have illustrated how culture, which is changing and evolving with life, is the influencing factor in our belief systems for composing what we term your *worldview*. The term worldview is a calque of the German word *Weltanschauung,* comprising the word *Welt* ("world") and *Anschauung* ("view" or "outlook"). Your worldview is the philosophical stance that provides a basic set of beliefs for guiding a researcher's actions (Denzin & Lincoln, 1994). A worldview is influenced by the following components:

- *Epistemology*, or the nature of knowledge and justification. For example, proponents of empiricist epistemology posit that knowledge comes from sense experience. Proponents of rationalist epistemology argue that through reasoning comes knowledge (Schwandt, 2007).
- *Ontology*, or the study of reality or being, to understand the kinds of things that are part of the world. For example, *idealism* is the idea that nothing exists but minds and the experience within minds. *Phenomenology* is concerned with the essential structures of a conscious experience.
- *Axiology*, or the idea that values influence the way that knowledge is acquired, includes social and cultural norms either for the researcher or for the ideas or persons (i.e., respondents) researched.
- *Verstehen*, the German term for understanding, is used to reference the aim of human science including the method used to understand in a social, historical, and cultural context (Schwandt, 2007).

A worldview also might be regarded as a person's philosophy, mindset, overarching philosophy of life, values, outlook on life, formula for life, ideology, or even faith. Broadly speaking, a worldview might be considered the overall lens through which a person sees and interprets, and becomes certain that what he/she knows is real—simply put, a worldview represents the entirety of the individual. Alternatively stated, a worldview is the framework of beliefs, perceptions, attitudes, and ideas through which the individual interprets the world and interacts with it. However, a worldview is not static. It is influenced by a person's beliefs and influences other types of beliefs. Concurrently, worldview influences a selected research philosophy, discipline-specific beliefs, and topic-specific beliefs—which, in turn, and to varying degrees, reshape a worldview, which also influences a person's culture to some degree (the solid arrows in Figure 4.1 indicate a *definite* influence, whereas the broken arrows in Figure 4.1 indicate only a *possible* influence). It is a living and breathing process!

EPISTEMOLOGICAL BELIEFS: KNOWING

One traditional explanation of knowing is that a person knows information to be true when: (a) a person is certain of the information; (b) the information, in fact, is true; and (c) that the person is justified in believing the information is true. Ayer (1956), one of the most influential philosophers in the 20th century, explained that these three conditions are the necessary and sufficient conditions for knowledge. Concerning your beliefs and knowing, you might hold that the only true basis for knowledge is empirical evidence derived from your own sensory experiences, or that reason is the supreme influence in your knowing.

Perhaps you consider that authority, in the form of literature or influential people, is the best way to account for what is true. On the other hand, you might depend on intuition to be certain of information, or knowing. Concerning beliefs, it is typical that because they are part of your thinking and perception process, if you believe that Germany never won a World Cup soccer trophy, you think that Germany really never won this honor. It is important to distinguish (especially if you live in Germany) that there is a difference between a belief and what philosophers would call a truth statement. Going back to understanding the third necessary and sufficient condition for knowledge, you can *justify* a statement that you make because it actually is true.

Your epistemology, or your negotiation of *being sure* of what you know, affects what you accept as valid evidence—what you are willing to believe about the sources that you investigate in a literature review. Your **epistemological beliefs** affect the significance that you ascribe to empirical evidence, reason, intuition, and information sources and the risks that you will take when you synthesize that knowledge. By listing a few ways that you are sure that information is true *and how* you recognized information as being true, you have just identified your epistemological belief system. This is one of the pieces of your worldview.

AXIOLOGICAL BELIEFS: VALUES

The concept of values is as diverse as is the unique composition of each person. Although people, in general, have traits much like each other, each person's expression is bound by a specific DNA genetic code. Likewise, we might have beliefs that might be common to the beliefs of a sister, brother, spouse, or best friend; yet, values take our beliefs into different areas such as moral and non-moral values, traditional values, objective and subjective values, and absolute and relative values. As a result of investigating our *axiological beliefs*, or the worth of beliefs, either personal or societal, we begin to recognize another piece of our worldview.

We have been discussing the nature of knowing, and ways that people, in a social context, develop beliefs. As a result, people all approach life and life tasks through different perceptions, thinking, knowing, and doing—or overall worldview.

Worldview is an interactive cyclical process that changes as you incorporate new knowledge and cultural understanding. As discussed in previous sections, your general beliefs are influenced by your upbringing, culture, social milieu, and life experiences. These beliefs have an influential role throughout the research process and especially when you consider a research topic. It is highly doubtful that even if you are assigned a research topic, no other researcher or literature reviewer will explore it in exactly the same way that you will, due to your unique worldview. This is why we state that the literature reviewer is the major instrument in the literature review process—a reality that, heretofore, has not been acknowledged by authors of literature review books and book chapters. In fact, we have coined the statement, "You cannot take the literature reviewer out of the literature review!"

Moreover, general beliefs play an important role throughout the literature review process, influencing virtually every decision made. For example, general beliefs affect, at least in part, whether a source (e.g., article) is selected and perceived as important to you. Specifically, you might choose not to include an article that contains statements made, a theory proposed, or findings reported by the author that are outside your belief systems, or your values, or ways of knowing through experience. While reflecting on your beliefs, it is critical that you also examine and negotiate what we discussed at the core of the CLR: a culturally progressive stance, ethics, and multimodal sources—specifically how cultural components are revealed in the sources that you select, as well as how your culture influences the sources that you select.

At this point, we want to introduce you to the topic that we selected for most of the examples of the seven steps throughout this book. This topic is based on some of our own values and is the topic of mentorship. Box 4.1 presents an overview of Rebecca's research in the area of mentoring (Frels, 2010), which we use throughout this book for examples of a CLR. We refer to this study as the Dyadic Mentoring Study.

BOX 4.1

THE DYADIC MENTORING STUDY

Throughout this book, we use the Dyadic Mentoring Study (Frels, 2010) and other examples related to mentoring to help explain the Seven-Step Model and to provide practical illustrations for the CLR. The term *mentor* in this particular context refers to a caring adult who provides academic and emotional support to a younger person. The term *school-based mentor* refers to a caring adult who meets with the younger person in a public or private school setting so that the academic environment is part of their interactions.

DISCIPLINE-SPECIFIC AND TOPIC-SPECIFIC BELIEFS

Reviewers also should explore their discipline-specific philosophies (e.g., education, psychology, sociology). *Discipline-specific beliefs* are the ideas that drive how we think about the field or discipline, what we consider most important in the field, and how we arrived at this knowledge. For example, in conducting a literature review on "effective teaching," the literature reviewer should examine her/his beliefs about her/his own preferences, such as relationship experiences with teachers who encompassed particular teaching styles, structured assignments versus creative assignments, or general attitudes about cooperative learning and individual or group assignments. Being cognizant of such beliefs would, in turn, allow the literature reviewer to consider the cultural and societal tenets in his/her experiences, and, in turn, awareness of these biases will help in documenting decisions about the sources that were retained and the sources discarded when beginning the literature review search.

Topic-specific beliefs, similar to discipline-specific beliefs, are more focused in one aspect within the field and are based on how we think, what we think, and how we acquired this understanding. Topic-specific beliefs typically allow people to "voice an opinion" of which they can often be very passionate.

EXAMPLE: PRESENTING THE BELIEF SYSTEMS IN WRITING

Box 4.2 presents an excerpt that Rebecca wrote to identify her worldview, discipline-specific views, and topic-specific views. As a psychotherapist in the United States, she explained that her view is a result of her belief that effective teachers work best through relationships.

RESEARCH PHILOSOPHICAL STANCE: THE WAY WE EXPLORE

Perhaps even more subtly, a research *philosophical stance* influences the decision made by a reviewer regarding whether to include a certain type of study (e.g., qualitative) in the set of selected sources that inform the literature review, and how much emphasis to place on studies that represent this genre, if selected. Also, research philosophy influences the way that the literature reviewer contextualizes information gleaned

---

BOX 4.2

AN EXAMPLE OF NOTATING A WORLDVIEW, BUILT ON THE VIEWS OF THE DISCIPLINE, OR FIELD OF EDUCATION, AND THE TOPIC OF TEACHING

I identified my worldview philosophy to be humanistic and existential in approach, whereby a person living authentically acknowledges responsibility for his or her life and is mindful of the responsibility for oneself and the world (Yalom, 1980). I believe that this concept is relevant in education (my discipline-specific view), that if a teacher establishes a strong relationship with a student, he/she will be able to be mindful of responsibility and feel better connected to the class, the coursework, and his or her best self. Humanistic, existential theory as outlined by May (1983) illuminates relationships on different levels: (a) the level of real persons (a teacher is pleased to see a mentee and vice-versa to relieve a loneliness to which all humans experience); (b) the level of friends (two individuals trust each other and have a genuine concern for listening and understanding); and (c) the level of esteem (a teacher and student possess a capacity for self-transcending concern for one another).

With respect to the topic of teaching, my philosophy is built on my professional experiences as a school counselor and psychotherapist to believe that both teachers and students have the potential to benefit from the teaching and learning experience. Further, I believe that this perspective is important to effective teaching. These ideas provide the overall lens within which I might conduct my literature review.

from the sources selected. As we have discussed the ideas of what we know, how we know, and the values that contribute to our overall worldview, it is important to recognize that philosophical debates have been a part of our history dating back to ancient times that witnessed the emergence of proto-rationalists (absolutists who looked for certainty in entities; e.g., Plato [429–347 BCE]; Socrates [470–399 BCE]), sophists (ontological relativists; e.g., Protagora [490–420 BCE]), and proto-empiricists (realists whose goal was to obtain understanding of what humans see and experience in their everyday lives; e.g., Aristotle [384–322 BCE]) (Johnson & Gray, 2010). These three sets of philosophers differed with respect to their philosophies and theories of (universal) truth, with proto-rationalists viewing truth as unchanging, sophists viewing truth as being changing and relative, and proto-empiricists deeming intersubjectivity to be a facet of truth (Johnson & Gray, 2010).

Johnson and Gray (2010) posited that the proto-rationalists could be viewed as proto-*quanti*tative, whereas the sophists could be viewed as proto-*quali*tative, which implies that debates about how to approach the nature of truth have existed for a very long time. In the 20th century, the pursuit of knowledge, generally speaking, fell into three camps—associated with the three research traditions (i.e., quantitative, qualitative, mixed research)—modeled on natural science (quantitative research), human science and subjectivity (qualitative research), and a checks-and-balance system of the two (mixed research). (For an excellent review of the history of philosophical and theoretical issues, see Johnson & Gray, 2010.)

One general stance relates to *postpositivism*, which theorizes that facts are theory-laden, value-laden, and include some social constructs. Another general way to explore is based on *constructivism*, either radical constructivism or social constructivism (Schwandt, 2007). *Radical constructivism* holds that human knowledge cannot accurately represent or faithfully copy an external reality and is an unending series of cognitive constructions. This stance is based on concepts posited by Piaget (1896–1980) and Kant (1724–1804). Contrastingly, *social constructivism* focuses more on the social processes and interactions and seeks to understand how social influences result in an intersubjective understanding of life and life's circumstances.

Finally, *pragmatism-of-the-middle*, based on the works of James (1842–1910), Dewey (1859–1952), and Peirce (1839–1914) and, in its general form (there are many branches of pragmatism; cf. Biesta, 2010; Johnson & Onwuegbuzie, 2004; Johnson et al., 2007), views knowledge as an instrument for organizing experiences while considering the impact of traditions, perspective, and philosophical orientations (Schwandt, 2007). It is also important to note that we, as authors of this chapter, composed this information with our own philosophical stance, which is a variation on pragmatism. This research stance, similar to pragmatism, is (*critical*) *dialectical pluralism*—an integrative mixed research (social justice) approach to synthesizing the sources collected.

EXAMPLE: PRESENTING THE RESEARCH STANCE

Box 4.3 on page 75 presents an excerpt of how we would report our own research stance when building this very textbook on literature reviews and creating the CLR meta-framework.

After the literature reviewer has invested some time recognizing how beliefs and values are particular to culture and experiences, it is probable that there is a general topic area in mind to research. It is also important to consider your field of interest and the collective need-to-know. By approaching the selection of a topic via considering your field of interest (emanating, at least in part, from your discipline-specific beliefs) and the academic community, you will build the body of knowledge for future research. Therefore, spending some time discussing your potential topic area with other academic scholars in your field provides you not only with the needs of the community, but also with some of the hot topic areas, as well as with some of the language specific to the topic. This discussion also will be helpful to you when beginning Step 2 of the process when documenting key terms for your initial search.

SELECTING A TOPIC

A topic area also might stem from practical problems that you encounter in your everyday work environment,

---

TOOL: COMMON RESEARCH PHILOSOPHY CHART

Table 4.1 is a brief overview of some of the most common research philosophical stances (also referred to as paradigms) and although there are variations and branches of each, these stances might help you understand the various ways that literature reviewers might tend to explore and to report new knowledge. (For a more extensive overview of some of the most common research philosophical stances, we refer you to Onwuegbuzie, Johnson, & Collins, 2009.)

It might be helpful to remember that although philosophical stances have differences, they have some common characteristics such that you might agree and align with more than one stance. We like to use the metaphor of cuisine on a buffet serving line in a restaurant. Upon first visit, it is not uncommon to try and even to like many dishes; yet, some items do not complement others and would not belong on the same plate. Also, after visiting the buffet frequently, you might gravitate toward one or two items, and if the buffet were not offered you would select the one item that you enjoy the most. Likewise, after some time, you will gravitate toward a research stance and begin to search the literature and conduct research through this interpretative lens of knowing. Bon appétit!

As seen via the different research perspectives, a quantitative researcher who holds the philosophy of postpositivism to its highest degree would be skeptical about the value of qualitative research and likely would be reluctant to include qualitative research articles as a part of the arsenal of sources to inform the literature review, and, at best, would include a disproportionally low number of qualitative research articles and/or provide minimal discussion of them, relative to the selected quantitative research articles. In addition, literature reviewers with a strong postpositivist (quantitative) orientation might be more inclined to report numerical data contained in a source (e.g., empirical article) than narrative data.

Conversely, a qualitative researcher with a strong constructivist orientation would less likely explore particular databases, such as those representing the medical field, possibly believing that the database contains mostly quantitative research works. Similar to artwork whereby an artist does not sign a print with his/her style of art (e.g., impressionist, contemporary), it is not likely that you will read a journal article or a textbook whereby the author explicitly states that he/she is a postpositivist or a constructivist (although we wish that they would specify their research philosophies). It is for this reason that as a culturally progressive literature reviewer, you will be able to read the method, findings, and results of empirical research and the views of conceptual writers with a critical eye, similar to an art critic.

(Continued)

(Continued)

Table 4.1   Contemporary research stances (paradigms) and characteristics

	Postpositivism	Pragmatism-of-the-Middle	Constructivism	Critical Theory	Participatory
Most Closely Aligned Research Tradition	Quantitative	Mixed research	Qualitative	Qualitative	Qualitative
Epistemology	Researchers are neutral, emotionally detached, and should eliminate biases and seek empirically to justify stated hypotheses	Knowledge is based on reality of the world and constructed through experience; justification comes through warranted assertions	Meaning is co-created. Knowledge is subjective and is not separable between researcher and research participant(s)	Values are mediated in the findings	Findings are co-created, experiential, and practical for practice
Ontology	Ascertains that social science inquiry should be objective	Traditional dualism is rejected. It regards the influence of the inner world of human experiences in action	Multiple contradictory but equally valid accounts of the same phenomenon represent multiple realities	Reality is impacted through social, political, cultural, ethnic, racial, economic, and gender values that evolve over time	The mind and given world order are co-created through subjective-objective reality
Methodology	Generalizations are time- and context-free; real causes of social scientific outcomes can be determined reliably and validly via dominantly quantitative (and sometimes qualitative) methods	Uses a thoughtful/dialectical eclecticism and pluralism of methods and perspectives; values what works in practice and seeks to solve individual and social problems	Uses a dialectical (i.e., dual sides in conversation) approach and inductive reasoning and regards that time- and context-free generalizations are neither desirable nor possible	Uses a dialogue or dialectical approach	Regards political participation for collaborative action research and emphasizes the practical

APPLYING CONCEPTS

In the Seven-Step Model, we encourage the literature reviewer to negotiate his/her cultural biases with the historical and practical implications of sources explored. This is why a literature reviewer optimally seeks to adopt a (critical) dialectical pluralist stance when searching sources, wherein research studies are selected for inclusion in the set of sources that inform the literature review based on the *quality* of information that they provide (e.g., reliability, validity, trustworthiness, dependability, confirmability, transferability, authenticity, appropriateness, utility) and not based on their genre. In this sense, a folk tale originating in India comes to mind. In this Buddhist tale, men who are blind examine an elephant and stand only near one part. One man feels the leg and states that an elephant is similar to a pillar; another man examines only the tail and states that an elephant is like a rope; another examines the trunk and states that an elephant is like a tree branch, and so on. Finally, after listening carefully, the king explains how all of the men are correct and that the reason for the discrepancies is that each man is only touching one part of the elephant.

The moral of the story is that people with different belief systems can work harmoniously, or as later explained by Rumi, a 13th-century Sufi poet, an individual perspective is inherently limited. Therefore, it is important to remember these points:

- Your cultural progressive stance includes recognizing that researchers have biases
- You can negotiate an author's bias and your own bias through keeping an open mind and critical reflection
- Recognizing your philosophical research stance is the first step to *being aware* before navigating through the literature review process

BOX 4.3

AN EXAMPLE OF NOTATING A RESEARCH STANCE BASED ON THE TOPIC OF LITERATURE REVIEWS

The research philosophical stance for our literature review when exploring literature for this textbook was what Johnson (2011) recently labeled as *dialectical pluralism*, referring to an epistemology that requires the researcher to incorporate multiple perspectives within the same inquiry. We believed that our dialectical research philosophical stance is compatible with a literature review and, specifically, a comprehensive literature review, whereby transparency in research is highly regarded. In addition, it resonates with our topic area of teaching based on Fink's (2003) model of integrated course design. As noted by Fink (2003), integration in teaching "builds on and incorporates many ideas that already exist in the published literature on instructional design and good teaching" (p. xiii).

with the search for solutions culminating in viable topics coming to the fore. Or an attempt to address a practical problem in your home or familial environment might lead to potential topics emerging. For example, you might recall that in Chapter 1 Tony's father experiencing a brain aneurysm led to Tony conducting a thorough review of the literature to decide which of the several brain surgery options provided to his family by the brain surgeon his father should undergo.

Personal interest represents another source for a research topic. For example, both Rebecca and Tony are big fans of the most popular sport played in the

United States, namely, the National Football League (NFL), avidly supporting the Houston Texans and the San Francisco 49ers, respectively. In fact, both Tony and Rebecca were fortunate to attend the Super Bowl XLVII game between the San Francisco 49ers and the Baltimore Ravens in New Orleans, USA, in which, unfortunately, the San Francisco 49ers lost in a very close finish (i.e., 34–31). (Tony is still receiving therapy for his team losing!) Interestingly, many of Tony's friends have accused him of causing the power outage that lasted for more than 30 minutes during this match when the San Francisco 49ers were losing by 22 points. To this accusation, Tony has refused to comment. Anyway, several years ago, Tony was interested in finding out whether the offensive players of a team make a greater contribution to the success of their team than do the defensive players. This curiosity led Tony to conduct a comprehensive literature review, which, after not being able to obtain a definitive answer to this question from the extant literature, subsequently led to him conducting two studies that were published in academic journals (i.e., Onwuegbuzie, 1999, 2000b) that yielded the finding that "the attainments of the defense are more important than are the offensive attainments in predicting the success of NFL teams" (Onwuegbuzie, 1999, p. 151). Tony conducted a similar sports-related literature review to inform a study that examined factors that predicted success among professional basketball teams in the United States, which also was published in an academic journal (Onwuegbuzie, 2000a), and he is in the process of conducting a comprehensive literature review on the most popular sport in the world—football (or what some people call "soccer"). In any case, this shows how the topic for literature reviews can stem directly from interests or hobbies, and can even be conducted for fun!

Considering how the literature reviewer utilizes prior conducted research from traditions—quantitative, qualitative, or mixed research—as well as opinion papers, conceptual articles, and other sources (which we explain as MODES in Step 5), the literature reviewer should be cognizant to incorporate, at least to some extent, each of these sources. Typically, in quantitative research, the research problem is associated with explaining, predicting, or describing a phenomenon. In qualitative research, most often, the problem is associated with events or phenomena

and tends to explore what or why a phenomenon is occurring. As such, mixed research leads to an investigation of research problems as a combination in varying degrees of both traditions.

If the literature review is to inform primary research, selecting a topic is directly related to what is known as the *statement of the problem* or *problem statement*. A statement of the problem is based on an issue or dilemma, or a lack of knowing something within a general topic area linked to primary research. In fact, even if the literature review is an end in itself, the literature reviewer will want to create a problem statement so that he/she can address how the review might inform the field/discipline and her/his own knowledge base. By associating one or more problems in a general topic area, the literature reviewer maintains a *critical stance*, which is an open mind in investigating opposing views on the topic: the cultural, historical, and practical knowledge acquired on the topic. In fact, the research questions (if conducting the review to inform primary research) might guide the literature review and, in turn, if the research question is known prior to conducting the literature review, it might be modified as a result of the literature review. Alternatively, if the research question is not known prior to conducting the literature review, then the literature reviewer can use the knowledge gleaned from the CLR to identify the gap in our knowledge base and, hence, arrive at one or more research questions that, if addressed adequately, will begin to fill this void.

At this point in the Seven-Step Model, the topic area is very broad because it has not yet been refined or narrowed through an initial search of databases. Yet, a general idea is established that is linked to the worldview, discipline-specific beliefs, and topic-specific beliefs—based on culture, experiences, and problems identified to explore. The topic will become focused through the subsequent steps of the literature review. Consequently, the problem statement also might evolve as the literature reviewer moves through the subsequent steps. Further, the problem statement can be modified to develop the guiding criteria for the initial search and the tentative (research) question(s) to guide the initial search. For example, Rebecca's experiences as a school counselor in the United States led her to examine the role of adult mentors with students who needed additional academic or emotional support in the school setting. Her research, the Dyadic Mentoring Study, was a result of her worldview that relationships are important for educational success. In addition, her discipline-specific beliefs stemmed from her work in the school setting (that program services reach a broader population of students and are efficient and effective). Therefore, the idea of researching mentoring as part of a school-based program became more focused as she searched the literature and discovered the topic of dyadic mentoring. For the purposes of selecting a topic—and this topic also is subject to change—it is important to hold an inquisitive position. Johnson and Christensen (2010) propose that literature reviewers begin by exploring everyday life, practical issues, or past research.

EXAMPLE: COMPOSING A PROBLEM STATEMENT

A problem statement was created for the Dyadic Mentoring Study; the problem statements were:

Some mentoring programs are effective and some are not

Some mentoring programs retain mentors and some do not

These problem statements could be transformed into CLR (tentative) focus questions:

What are some components of successful dyadic mentoring programs in a school setting? What are some characteristics of programs that yield sustainable dyadic mentoring relationships?

Revisiting Box 4.2 helps to identify how the Dyadic Mentoring Study topic was formed based on worldview and experiences and explained in a final CLR report. In Chapter 3, we distinguished the literature reviewer as an original thinker—combining some type of knowledge with original thoughts for an original, purposeful, and "logical argument of an interpretation of relevant published and/or unpublished information on the selected topic from multimodal texts and settings that primarily comprise five modes." This type of thinking involves imagination and curiosity.

TOOL: FLOWCHART TO AID IN SELECTING A TOPIC

The following matrix, Figure 4.2, presents a guide for your brainstorming in selecting a general topic, which provides a conceptual framework to the CLR. After reviewing this figure, it is helpful to create one or more problem statements and potential questions that will guide your initial search of databases in Step 2.

As seen in this figure, the literature reviewer begins in a field or discipline of interest based on past experiences and role in life. After selecting a general area, the literature reviewer depends upon creativity, open-mindedness, imagination of new possibilities, and a questioning stance to adopt an original idea. Next, the literature reviewer frames this new idea, which might be in the form of a question or a predetermined problem statement. Remember that this process is subject to change and, in fact, as a culturally progressive reviewer who is critically thinking, the process is iterative—moving in cycles.

Also, as seen in this figure, after using questions to guide the selection of a topic, it is important to recognize the philosophical assumptions that are associated with both the researcher and the field/discipline in which he/she is researching as well as the political standpoints and moral standpoints. Next, before determining the general topic, the literature reviewer should review the reasons for conducting the literature review (see Figure 1.2 in Chapter 1). These reasons, which are topic-focused, method-focused, or connection-focused, actually drive the literature review research. Being disciplined and organized as you begin this process is key. The following section provides some tools as you begin this process.

(Continued)

(Continued)

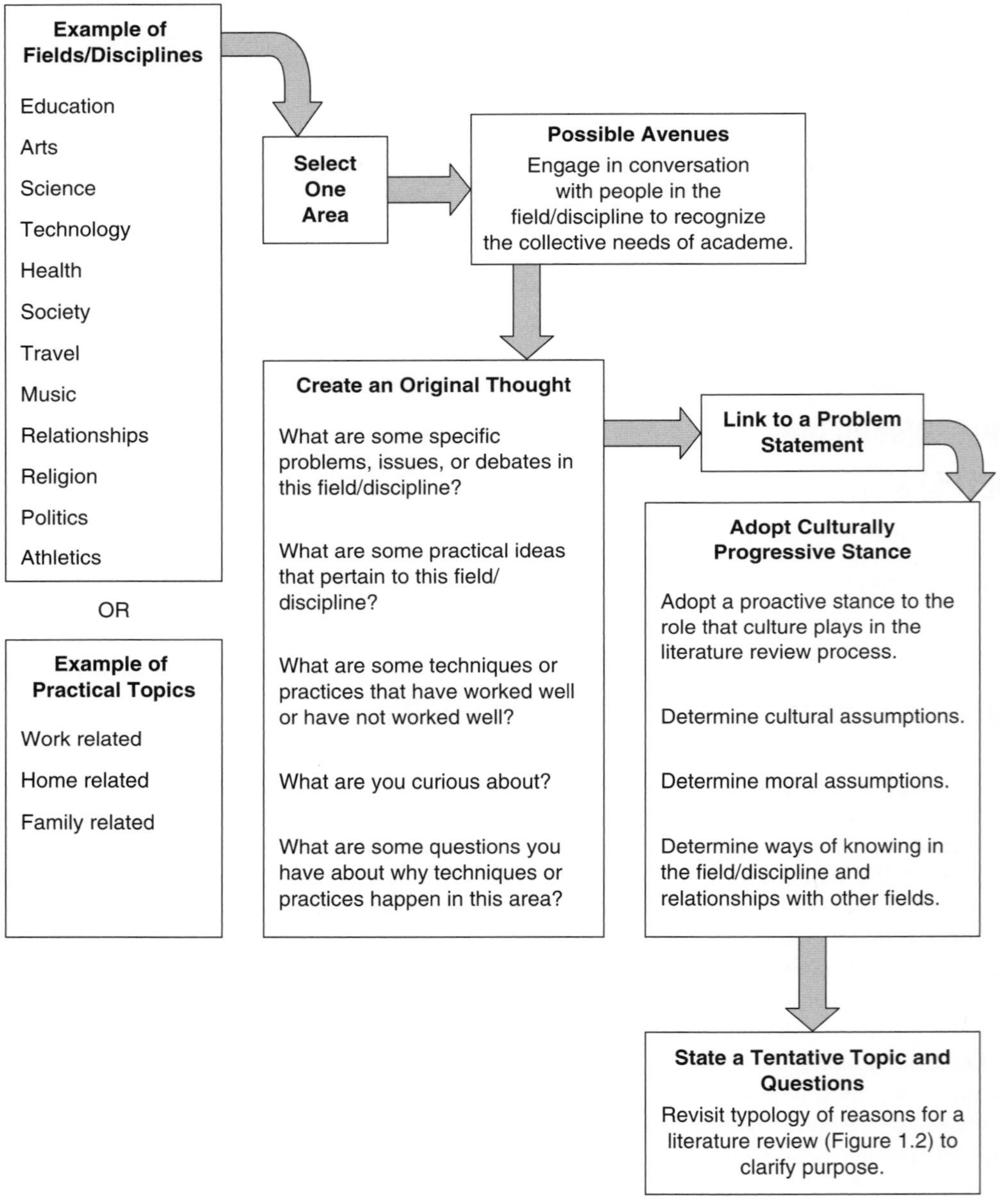

Example of Fields/Disciplines

Education

Arts

Science

Technology

Health

Society

Travel

Music

Relationships

Religion

Politics

Athletics

OR

Example of Practical Topics

Work related

Home related

Family related

Select One Area

Possible Avenues
Engage in conversation with people in the field/discipline to recognize the collective needs of academe.

Create an Original Thought

What are some specific problems, issues, or debates in this field/discipline?

What are some practical ideas that pertain to this field/ discipline?

What are some techniques or practices that have worked well or have not worked well?

What are you curious about?

What are some questions you have about why techniques or practices happen in this area?

Link to a Problem Statement

Adopt Culturally Progressive Stance

Adopt a proactive stance to the role that culture plays in the literature review process.

Determine cultural assumptions.

Determine moral assumptions.

Determine ways of knowing in the field/discipline and relationships with other fields.

State a Tentative Topic and Questions
Revisit typology of reasons for a literature review (Figure 1.2) to clarify purpose.

Figure 4.2 A guide to selecting a topic, based on worldview, research philosophical beliefs, discipline-specific beliefs, and topic-specific beliefs

ORGANIZING THE PROCESS

TOOL: FLOWCHART TO ORGANIZE STEP 1

Figure 4.3 provides a flowchart to explore your understanding and strengths with respect to Step 1 and the information in this chapter to help organize your thoughts about selecting a topic.

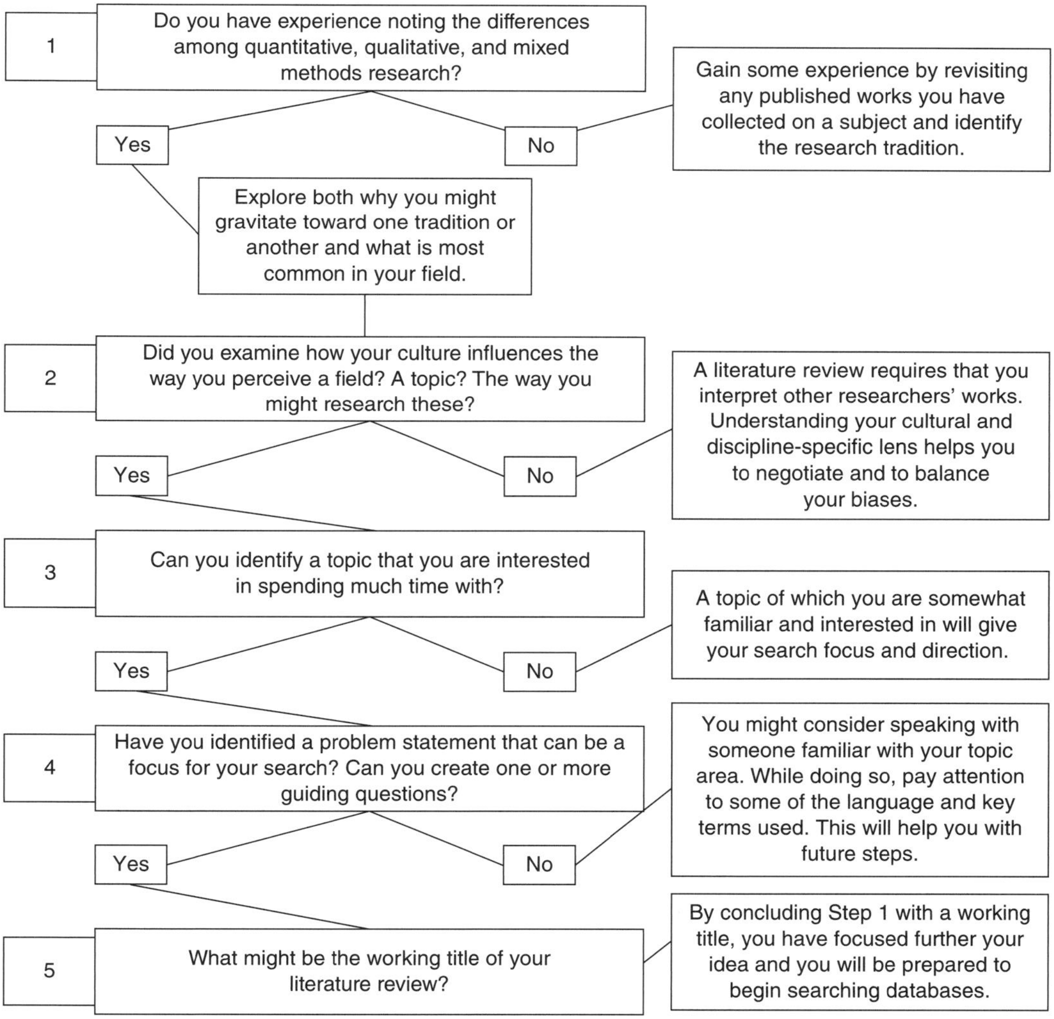

1 — Do you have experience noting the differences among quantitative, qualitative, and mixed methods research?

- Yes
- No → Gain some experience by revisiting any published works you have collected on a subject and identify the research tradition.

Explore both why you might gravitate toward one tradition or another and what is most common in your field.

2 — Did you examine how your culture influences the way you perceive a field? A topic? The way you might research these?

- Yes
- No → A literature review requires that you interpret other researchers' works. Understanding your cultural and discipline-specific lens helps you to negotiate and to balance your biases.

3 — Can you identify a topic that you are interested in spending much time with?

- Yes
- No → A topic of which you are somewhat familiar and interested in will give your search focus and direction.

4 — Have you identified a problem statement that can be a focus for your search? Can you create one or more guiding questions?

- Yes
- No → You might consider speaking with someone familiar with your topic area. While doing so, pay attention to some of the language and key terms used. This will help you with future steps.

5 — What might be the working title of your literature review? → By concluding Step 1 with a working title, you have focused further your idea and you will be prepared to begin searching databases.

Figure 4.3 Flowchart of the Step 1 process

TOOL: QUESTIONS TO AID IN FORMULATING BELIEFS

Table 4.2 is provided as a reflective process so that you might begin to articulate some of the decisions associated with selecting a particular topic area. You might decide to keep a journal about some of your ponderings for a deeper reflection on your topic area.

Table 4.2 Overview of some of the most common research philosophical stances

Challenging Areas	Question(s) to Ask Yourself	
Clarification	Why did you select or state what you stated?	*Your topic*. What led you to select this topic?
Assumptions	What might you be assuming to be true?	*Your beliefs*. What are some *truths* in your topic area?
Reason and evidence	What do you think caused you to select or say that?	*Your culture*. In what ways have your experiences helped you to believe particular tenets within your topic area?
Viewpoint and perspective	What might be an alternative viewpoint? What might someone of a different culture see?	*Your values*. What might be some opposing views to your topic beliefs?
Implications and consequences	What are the strengths and weaknesses of what I select or say? What are some generalizations? How might what I say affect others?	*Your worldview*. What are some generalizations that are culturally related to your topic and the way it has been researched?
About the questions themselves	What was the point of this question? What did I seek to know and why?	*Your philosophical stance*. Why explore this topic? Why do you see particular issues or problems associated with it?

In Step 1, you should organize your electronic filing system and create your electronic artifacts. For your electronic workspace, we suggest that you familiarize yourself with the concept of using folders to store sources and working drafts of your manuscript. The following screenshots display how we created folders. In the first screenshot (Figure 4.4), we created a folder titled: The CLR.

Next, to begin your reflections as a literature reviewer, begin a folder inside this folder. We titled this folder: Reflections (Figure 4.5). The artifact that you are creating for Step 1 is one or two brief paragraphs stating your (a) overall worldview, (b) topic-specific belief, (c) field/discipline-specific belief, and (d) research philosophy/stance (see Box 4.2 for an example of this paragraph). You might store this artifact in a folder titled Beliefs Step 1.

In this chapter, we outline the first step to embark on for a comprehensive literature review that is similar to the saying to "know thyself," and which includes philosophical exploration of how a person sees and understands the world and human condition. We emphasize that you select a topic based on many assumptions, including values, experiences, interests, and beliefs about how knowledge is acquired. Through reflexivity, which includes your awareness of these attributes, you can begin to negotiate your own biases inherent in your comprehensive literature review.

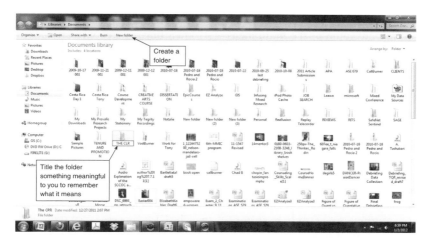

Figure 4.4 Creating folders helps you to organize your electronic artifacts

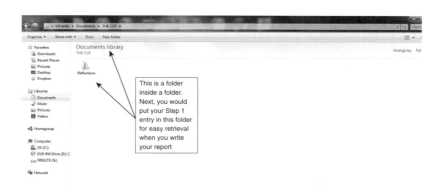

Figure 4.5 A file is dedicated to reflections of the content learned in each chapter

CONCLUSIONS

After reading the content of this chapter, or Step 1: Exploring Beliefs and Topics, remember the saying: "Rome wasn't built in a day." In Chapter 1, we discussed the three research traditions, how the quest for knowledge can be expressed in many ways, and the common reasons for the literature review. In Chapter 2, we provided the cornerstone of the literature review process—the literature reviewer—as a culturally progressive, ethical, and multimodal explorer. Next, Chapter 3 extended the

definition and understanding of the new and comprehensive literature review as a tool for research, a method, a mixed method, and a methodology—yielding a meta-framework. All of these chapters were foundational for beginning the seven steps of the CLR. In this chapter, we presented the first of the seven steps, which determines the direction that you will take for all of the subsequent steps because beliefs influence the way that we interpret literature. To close this chapter and at the end of each chapter relating to the seven steps, we offer reflection questions to help compose some of your thoughts for journaling or discussion points. Before moving on, review some of the main ideas presented in this chapter.

- Worldview is a philosophical stance that provides a basic set of beliefs for guiding a literature reviewer's actions and includes research beliefs, discipline-specific beliefs, and topic-specific beliefs.
- A culturally progressive stance includes maintaining a high degree of self-awareness for understanding how your own background and other experiences might serve as assets or limitations when searching and interpreting literature and other sources of information, as well as striving to develop cultural awareness and beliefs, cultural knowledge, and cultural skills.

- You can negotiate an author's bias and your own bias by keeping an open mind and critical reflection.
- By approaching the selection of a topic by considering your field of interest and the academic community, you will build the body of knowledge for future inquiry by other literature reviewers.
- The literature review is typically linked to a problem statement.
- Spending some time discussing your potential topic area with other academic scholars in your field is helpful.
- The CLR process is not static and, in fact, for a culturally progressive reviewer who is critically thinking, the process is iterative—moving in cycles.

CHAPTER 4 EVALUATION CHECKLIST

CORE	Guiding Questions and Tasks
Critical Examination	To what extent did you identify the cultural underpinnings relating to your view of the topic area?
	How do you see yourself in the cultural context with others who are knowledgeable in your topic area? What might be some limitations of your literature review that are culturally related?
Organization	To what extent did you write and store your paragraph describing your worldview, topic-specific beliefs, and research stance (see Box 4.2)?
	To what extent did you create an electronic filing system for your artifacts to establish an audit trail?
	What are three beliefs you have about "credible" research? To what extent do you lean more toward one tradition than another? Why?
Reflections	To what extent did you list one challenge you recognize that is culturally related?
Evaluation	To what extent did you come to any new understandings of how your culture and worldview might influence many of your decisions and perceptions of others' decisions?

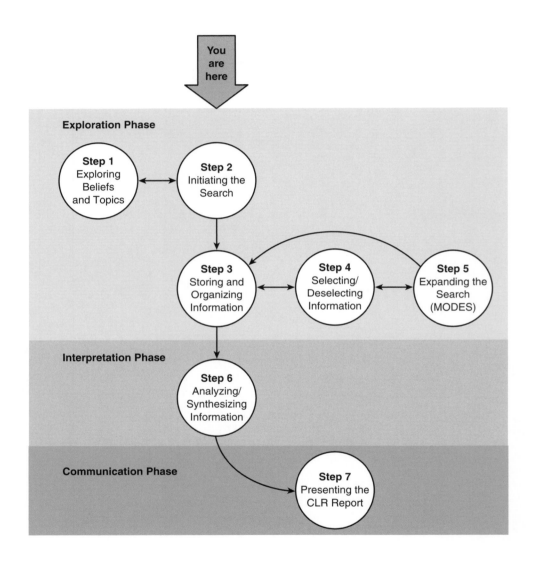

5

STEP 2: INITIATING THE SEARCH

CHAPTER 5 ROADMAP

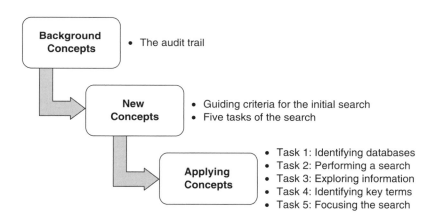

Background Concepts
- The audit trail

New Concepts
- Guiding criteria for the initial search
- Five tasks of the search

Applying Concepts
- Task 1: Identifying databases
- Task 2: Performing a search
- Task 3: Exploring information
- Task 4: Identifying key terms
- Task 5: Focusing the search

BACKGROUND CONCEPTS

All licensed taxicab drivers in London are expected immediately to be able to determine the most appropriate route from memory and with ease in response to a passenger's request, incorporating relevant factors such as weather and traffic conditions, rather than looking at a map, relying on satellite navigation, asking the taxicab controller via radio, or asking the passenger himself or herself. As such, in order to be licensed to drive a black taxicab anywhere in London (i.e., a *Green Badge driver*), all drivers must pass a special test called the *Knowledge*. The Knowledge, which originated in 1865, requires each taxicab driver to have a detailed knowledge of London. More specifically, the Knowledge requires taxicab drivers to study in depth 320 pre-set London street routes comprising 25,000 streets and 20,000 landmarks and places of interest within the six-mile radius of Charing Cross, which is located in the center of London. Consequently, the Knowledge is the world's most demanding and rigorous training course for taxicab drivers, and it typically takes between 2 and 4 years to pass the examination.

Recall that in Chapter 1 we defined the CLR, in that although we use the term *comprehensive*, we do not imply that a reviewer should collect and use everything written on a particular topic. Not only is this impossible, it would not be appropriate. As a methodology, collecting only the salient information, which includes using mixed research (quantitative research and qualitative research) techniques, speaks to the comprehensive nature of the process—not that all information sources are used. Further, as a culturally progressive approach, the CLR reflects the importance of understanding how information is situated in culture, context, and time and, therefore, might not be appropriate to use, even if it is on the topic being researched. Consider the taxicab driver and the Knowledge of London. Some streets might be dated, involve obstacles, or could be inappropriate to travel. Some routes are affected by particular traffic at certain times of the day, some older roads might be impacted by heavy rain, and some roads have been established as traditional routes to and from a historical marker. Using the very same map would be a stagnant approach for the driver. In fact, the Knowledge is a fluid, time-sensitive information source, situated in both tradition and progressive trends. Appropriately, we have provided a map for an overview of background concepts to keep in mind for Step 2, new concepts relating to Step 2, and concepts related to applying Step 2. Next, we list the examples of Step 2 that are provided throughout the chapter.

Acquiring knowledge of London street routes and being multimodal is very similar to acquiring knowledge about a topic of interest via conducting a literature review. In particular, both sets of knowledge necessitate a rigorous examination of numerous pathways to obtain a comprehensive state of knowing. Just as the knowledge required for London taxicab drivers increases as the number of streets and landmarks examined increase, so too does knowledge of a topic representing a field (e.g., social science, applied science) or a discipline (e.g., education, mathematics, psychology) increase as the number of sources examined increases. The ability to initiate and to conduct database searches (Step 2) is a vital next step after identifying a potential topic, which was guided by belief systems and worldview. The greater the extent to which a literature reviewer searches databases, the more likely it will be for the reviewer to reach a point of saturation, or the likelihood that enough *salient* information was collected, which results in a collection of likely sources to address aspects important to the selected topic.

THE AUDIT TRAIL

Initiating the search involves several tasks that include: identifying potential literature databases, performing an initial search, exploring information about the selected topic, identifying the key terms associated with this topic, and focusing the search. Moreover, this step involves detailed documentation of each of the aforementioned areas. These details speak to the role of ethics for the CLR, presented in Chapter 2, especially in the area of *scholarly responsibility*, which is adhering to best practices through documenting and reflecting on decisions made throughout the CLR process. Further, the documentation process, or audit trail, addresses the role of the literature reviewer as an original and critical thinker who inspects and reflects on all aspects of the process and product.

TOOL: LIST OF TASKS FOR STEP 2

Figure 5.1 illustrates the flow of Step 2, the associated tasks, and how these tasks interact and flow into the next step of the Seven-Step Model.

By revisiting the example of a problem statement and focus questions from Step 1 and the Dyadic Mentoring Study introduced in Chapter 4, you should recognize how to create guiding criteria as a search is initiated and evolves. One problem that sparked Rebecca's interest in a literature review about mentoring was that some school-based mentoring programs seemed to be effective and some programs did not. This problem statement helped her to initiate a literature search based on the (tentative) focus question for exploring some components of successful dyadic mentoring programs. As seen in Figure 5.1, initiating the search begins with the focus question in mind by identifying potential literature databases. During this task, *creating a map* as an audit trail of the search is important, which would mean tracking each search strand, term used to search, and database. Next, the initial search using initial keywords will yield some information sources (Task 2). For each keyword, documenting the number of works (i.e., hits) that are identified with each keyword might be in the form of recording simple notes, or a log. After a collection of potential information sources resulting from the initial search, it is likely that these works lend additional ideas for exploring other information about the selected topic (Task 3). Again, an audit trail of the information develops when documenting each additional idea. The information that emerges also helps to create the most appropriate keywords (Task 4). Tracking of the keywords is the means to compare and to contrast them with your initial set of keywords. This new set of keywords then should be used to focus the search (Task 5).

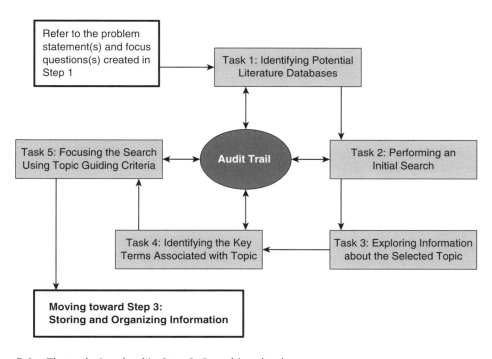

Figure 5.1   The tasks involved in Step 2: Searching databases

NEW CONCEPTS

GUIDING CRITERIA FOR THE INITIAL SEARCH

As the initial search progresses, some characteristics emerge that distinguish some sources to be potential information sources rather than others. The characteristics that are distinguished to focus the search become the topic guiding criteria. *Topic guiding criteria* are guidelines that facilitate a focused search for potentially the most suitable information sources for a selected topic. These topic guiding criteria provide a rationale as to the direction that an initial search takes. That is, some criteria emerge from your beliefs about the topic, field, and/or discipline and initiating the search. Other delineating criteria might emerge as you go. These criteria develop as you move through a search, and evolve from the initial problem statement(s) and question(s) from Step 1. They provide tentative boundaries in the search and help the literature reviewer in narrowing the search, or keeping the search focused. Much like a taxicab driver who decides why some routes might be better than others, the literature reviewer documents ideas that guide the initial search, which becomes the audit trail of Step 2.

As described in Chapter 2, where we outlined the identity of the literature reviewer, cultural progressiveness and ethical responsibility are addressed through ongoing reflective practices. By reflecting and documenting criteria at this step of the CLR process, and documenting attributes, populations, contexts, and concepts that are situated in sources, the literature reviewer as the main instrument for the search establishes integrity for what will be the results. Also, when performing the initial search, it is important to document everything because everything matters. Irrelevant information can be set aside at a later time (i.e., Step 4) but it cannot ever be reproduced if it is not documented. The information sources located and collected from the focused search and the topic guiding criteria will be stored and organized, which leads to Step 3, described in Chapter 6.

FIVE TASKS OF THE SEARCH

In order to address research ethics and, in particular, rigor, we have outlined the minimal tasks in creating the audit trail for Step 2. Figure 5.1 highlights the audit trail, which is positioned in the center of the five tasks because it plays a central role. As a general rule, the audit trail record should be sufficiently detailed that the steps of the initial and subsequent searches can be retraced not only weeks and months later but also even years later! Also seen in Figure 5.1, the arrows go to and from audit trail to each of the five tasks. The arrows going from each task to audit trail indicate that each task is subjected to an audit trail. In contrast, the arrows going from audit trail to each task indicate that the audit trail (which includes documenting your evaluation of each task, such as the process notes and/or personal notes) helps to determine whether that task has been undertaken adequately enough to move on to the next task, or to continue working on this task or even to return to a prior task, if needed. For example, if the initial search (Task 2) does not yield a sufficient number of works to provide adequate information about a selected topic (Task 3), then it likely would be beneficial to return to the previous task (Task 1) by identifying more potential literature databases. Thus, at the very least, the initial search, involving five tasks, will involve five evaluations—a minimum of one evaluation phase per task, with each evaluation including an audit trail. Each of these five tasks is described in more detail in the following sections.

TASK 1: IDENTIFYING DATABASES

Fields and disciplines are recognized by the academic journals in which research is published. Thus, identifying potential literature databases involves selecting databases that represent multiple fields/disciplines, yielding what we refer to as a *multidisciplinary* (i.e., involving databases that represent multiple disciplines; e.g., Academic Search Premier [EBSCOhost]), *interdisciplinary* (i.e., involving databases that combine two or more disciplines; e.g., MEDLINE), and *transdisciplinary* (i.e., involving databases that cross two or more disciplines; e.g., ProQuest Statistical Insight) initial searches. For all of the disciplinary databases, two major types of literature databases are used: library subscription databases and public Internet sources.

LIBRARY SUBSCRIPTION DATABASES

A library subscription database is an organized, and typically exhaustive, collection of electronic information that allows a user to search for a specific topic, title of work, article(s), thesis, dissertation, and/or book(s) in a variety of ways (e.g., subject, title, author, keyword). Each library subscription database usually contains from thousands to millions of works. Whereas many databases contain only citations, or citations and abstracts, some databases contain the full text of works published in journals, magazines, newspapers, or electronic repositories, as well as books. Full-text means that the entire text contained in a work (e.g., journal article, book, magazine, newspaper article) is available from the library subscription database for viewing, copying, downloading, and printing.

A library subscription database can be multidisciplinary, interdisciplinary, and/or transdisciplinary. As the word *subscription* suggests, much of the information contained in library subscription databases contains information that is copyrighted, licensed, and proprietary, and, consequently, is not free. However, libraries of many colleges and universities pay yearly subscription fees for an array of databases, with the larger institutions tending to pay subscription fees for more databases than do smaller institutions. Thus, if a university pays a subscription fee for a database of interest, then students and faculty members would not have to pay for full-text works contained in this database.

Libraries also pay subscription fees for non-electronic sources of information such as print journals, magazines, and newspapers. Although library subscription databases use the Internet as a delivery system, they are not considered Internet sources. Indeed, many, if not most, of the published resources found in the library subscription databases are not (freely) available on open web (i.e., information that can be accessed on the web free of charge, often without having to log in), unless they represent articles that have been published in open-access journals (i.e., journals that contain articles that are digital, online, free of charge, and free of most copyright and licensing restrictions; for a directory of more than 8,000 open-access journals, see http://www.doaj.org/). You will need to check with the library of your institution to find out to which databases it subscribes.

PUBLIC INTERNET SOURCES

In contrast, a public Internet source represents electronic information that stems directly from the Internet, which is a global system of interconnected computer networks that billions of users worldwide can access, either wirelessly or via a cable, using an array of electronic, wireless, and optical devices such as desktop computers, laptop/notebook computers, tablet computers, and smartphones. Public Internet sources typically are represented via one of three tools: subject directories, search engines, and meta-search engines.

SUBJECT DIRECTORIES. A subject directory is a catalogue of websites that have been collected and organized by humans. More specifically, subject directories often are called *subject trees* because they begin with a few major categories and then branch out into subcategories, topics, and subtopics. For example, to find resources on Egyptology (i.e., the study of ancient Egyptian history, art, language, literature, and religion) from the Internet Public Library directory (www.ipl.org)—a useful subject directory for scholarly research—you would select "Resources by Subject" at the top level (see Figure 5.2), "Social Sciences" at the next level, and then "Egyptology Resources" at the third level. As such, subject directories are very useful as a starting point for your topic. Subject directories also are useful for browsing a topic when you do not have a clear idea of the information that you need. Many subject directories include a keyword search option that often eradicates the need for you to work through multiple levels of topics and subtopics.

EXAMPLE: INTERNET DIRECTORIES

If you insert the term "Egyptology" at the first level of the Internet Public Library directory, you will see a link for "Egyptology Resources" that will take you to the "Egyptology Resources" website (see Figures 5.2–5.3). Interestingly, Yahoo! is the largest subject directory currently on the

Internet and is a very useful website for finding topics that are popular among the general public. In general, because subject directories represent only a small portion of websites that are available on the Internet, they are most useful for finding general information on subjects of interest.

SEARCH ENGINES. If, on the other hand, obtaining specific information on a topic is important rather than using a subject directory, it would be more useful to use a search engine or a meta-search engine. Search engines (circa 1990) are large databases of webpages connected by software called *spiders* or *web crawlers*. When typing in a subject keyword or keywords (i.e., search string) on a search engine such as Google (www.google.com), the search engine rummages through the thousands and even millions of pages contained in its directory to find information—including real-time information—that contains this keyword. Then, using a combined ranking algorithm that takes into account the relevance, the number of times it has been cited in other scholarly literature (the most important factor), and publication date, the search engine provides a listing of the best-matching webpages that contain this keyword (with the "best" typically being presented first according to the search engine's criteria), usually with the title of the document and the website address of each webpage, as well as a brief summary or excerpt (typically one or two lines) that includes the keyword.

Figure 5.2 Screenshot showing how to use the Internet Public Library directory to find information on the topic of Egyptology

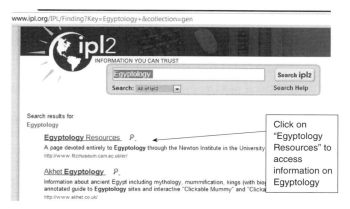

Figure 5.3 Screenshot showing the website page on the Internet Public Library directory after entering the search term "Egyptology"

Depending on how extensive the topic that the keyword underlies is, this listing of webpages can be presented on as little as one page or as many as hundreds of pages. This listing of webpages often is referred to as search engine results pages (SERPs). For example, using the keyword "research" on the Google search engine will yield more than one half a billion results. Of the numerous search engines, we recommend the use of scholarly Internet sources—with Google Scholar (https://www.scholar.google.com) being the most comprehensive database. A particular appeal of Google Scholar is that it is available freely to anyone around the world with Internet access. However, it should be noted that although Google Scholar freely provides the citation of scholarly works (e.g., journal article, book), as well as the abstract of most scholarly journal articles, the user would have to pay to obtain the full text of most of these works, unless the library of the user's institution subscribes to the source (e.g., journal) that contains the selected work(s).

META-SEARCH ENGINES. In contrast, meta-search engines are search tools that submit a search to several search engines and/or databases simultaneously and then aggregate the results into a single list or display the results according to their source (e.g., search engine). Because these meta-search engines search multiple search engines and combine the results from these search engines, they can reduce substantially the user's time spent searching a topic by decreasing the need for the user to search multiple search engines separately. Each meta-search engine is substantively different from all other meta-search engines because each one searches a different set of search engines (e.g., the most popular search engines vs. the lesser-known engines vs. other databases), searches a unique number of search engines, and presents the results in a unique way.

For example, the Dogpile meta-search engine (www.dogpile.com) searches the following search engines: Google, Yahoo, Bing, and Ask.com. Although meta-search engines allow a reviewer to conduct extensive searches, a drawback of using them is that they provide a lot of information that is irrelevant, untrustworthy, and even misleading—much of which has not been subjected to any kind of peer review or validity check—through which the reviewer would have to wade before finding a sufficient amount of relevant and trustworthy information. Thus, meta-search engines should be used with caution.

TASK 2: PERFORMING A SEARCH

Once the topic, although tentative, is selected (Step 1), and potential databases and library subscription databases have been identified for initiating the search, the second task of Step 2 begins. This task involves performing an initial search of your selected topic.

TOOL: PUBLIC INTERNET SEARCH TOOLS LISTED IN CHRONOLOGICAL ORDER

Table 5.1 provides several search tools for each of the three types of public Internet sources: subject directories, search engines, and meta-search engines. Also provided in this table are the web addresses for each tool, as well as the year of conception. This list is by no means exhaustive, but these search tools represent many of the most popular tools. However, keep in mind that new search tools will continue to be developed, so new electronic search tools are likely to be available as they are developed.

Table 5.1 Public Internet search tools listed in chronological order

Type of Internet Search Tool	Internet Address	Year of Conception
Subject Directory		
Virtual Reference Shelf	http://www.loc.gov/rr/askalib/virtualref.html	Mid-1980s
The WWW Virtual Library	http://vlib.org/	1991
Yahoo!	http://www.yahoo.com	1994
InfoMine	http://infomine.ucr.edu/	1994
Internet Public Library	http://www.ipl.org	1995
Best Information on the Net	http://library.sau.edu/bestinfo/	1995
LookSmart	http://www.looksmart.com/	1995
About.com	http://www.about.com	1996
Digital Librarian	http://www.digital-librarian.com/	1996
CompletePlanet: The Deep Web Academic Info	http://www.academicinfo.net/subject-guides	1998
Open Directory Project	http://www.dmoz.org/	1998
Intute	http://www.intute.ac.uk/search.html	2006
A1WebDirectory.org	http://www.a1webdirectory.org/	2007
Search Engines		
Yahoo!	http://www.yahoo.com	1994
Lycos (Advanced Search)	http://www.lycos.com/	1994
AltaVista (Advanced Search)	http://www.altavista.com/	1995
Google (Advanced Search)	http://www.google.com/	1996
HotBot	http://www.hotbot.com/	1996
Ask (Advanced Search)	http://www.ask.com/	1996
Soso.com (Chinese)	http://www.soso.com/	1998
Gigablast (Advanced Search)	http://www.gigablast.com/	2000
Exalead	http://www.exalead.com/search/	2000
Baidu (Chinese, Japanese)	http://www.baidu.com/	2000

Type of Internet Search Tool	Internet Address	Year of Conception
Hakia	http://hakia.com/	2004
Sogou.com (Chinese)	http://www.sogou.com/	2004
DuckDuckGo	http://duckduckgo.com/	2006
Google Scholar	http://scholar.google.com/	2007
Youdao (Chinese)	http://www.youdao.com/	2007
Bing	http://www.bing.com/	2009
Yandex (Russian)	http://www.yandex.com	2010
Blekko	http://www.blekko.com	2010
Volunia.com (Multilingual)	http://www.volunia.com/	2012
Meta-Search Engines		
WebCrawler	http://www.webcrawler.com/	1994
MetaCrawler	http://www.metacrawler.com/info.metac.a/search/home	1994
Excite	http://www.excite.com/	1995
Dogpile	http://www.dogpile.com/info.dogpl/search/home	1996
Beaucoup	http://www.beaucoup.com/	1996
Mamma	http://www.mamma.com/	1996
Ixquick Metasearch	https://www.ixquick.com/	1998
Monster Crawler	http://monstercrawler.com/	1999
MetaEUREKA	http://www.metaeureka.com/	2000
Info.com	http://www.info.com/	2003
Findelio	http://www.findelio.com/	2005
Quintura	http://www.quintura.com/	2005
DeeperWeb	http://deeperweb.com/	2009
Yippy (formerly Clusty)	http://www.yippy.com/	2010

EXAMPLE: CREATING GUIDING CRITERIA

To illustrate this task, as an example for Step 2: Initiating the Search, the topic of *mentoring* was selected because the topic is relevant in some capacity to virtually all students and teachers around the world, regardless of field or discipline. Further, to focus the search, other characteristics, or guiding criteria, help in delineating a focused topic. If we wanted a topic to be most relevant for readers of this book, the guiding criteria might include the characteristic that a source should be relevant to the audience of students, researchers, and faculty members (including supervisors/advisors and mentors) as the audience for this book. Thus, the focus of a search would be to delineate information sources pertinent to *mentoring of college students*, as opposed to mentoring of primary school or secondary school students. Therefore, two guiding criteria that should be documented in the audit trail would be: (a) information was selected that focused on mentoring relationships and (b) mentoring context was the post-secondary, or university level.

TOOL: A COMPARISON OF LIBRARY DATABASES

Figure 5.4 presents a comparison of library subscription databases and Internet search engines.

   Because of the overall advantages of using library subscription databases compared to Internet sources, we recommend that whenever possible you use library subscription databases as a starting point for your literature search. If access to library subscription databases is not available, the use of Google Scholar is a plausible second choice for the initial search.

Library Subscription Databases	Internet Search Engines/Meta-Search Engines
Availability/Cost	
Library database subscriptions for many journals/periodicals are paid for by numerous colleges and universities. Check with librarians to determine which databases are freely accessible. Library databases cannot be accessed via search engines or the open web.	Most search engines are free of charge, as is much of the information extracted by the search engines, including full-text articles published in open-access journals (for a directory of more than 8,000 open-access journals, see http://www.doaj.org/). Full-text articles from non-open-access journals and books typically are not freely available. At best, the information that could be obtained from articles published in non-open-access journals is the title, abstract, and citation. Some websites identified through Internet search engines contain licensed, proprietary information that compels users to log on via a user account. Logging on may or may not necessitate payment of a subscription.
When Most Appropriate to Use	
Library databases are most appropriate to use for scholarly/academic research. They are also appropriate to use when you need to obtain trustworthy information. They are particularly useful too when you do not want to have to wade through irrelevant information. They are particularly useful when you want to conduct a search without any advertisements being seen.	Internet search engines are particularly useful when you are interested in the most current information because most articles published in journals have a lag time. They are also most appropriate when you are interested in non-scholarly/academic information such as entertainment news. They are also appropriate to use when you want information that you can pass on to others without violating any license or copyright laws. They are also appropriate to use when you have sufficient time to wade through all the information provided and to evaluate each piece of information for validity.
Type of Information Retrieved	
Scholarly journal articles Theses and dissertations Books Reference works (e.g., encyclopedias) Newspaper articles Special collections University archives Government documents Digital collections Free access to works via your university's interlibrary loan (ILL) system	Limited number of free scholarly journal articles (i.e., from open-access journals) Educational websites (e.g., Educational App Store) Interactive/social websites (e.g., Wikipedia, blogs, Facebook) Government websites (e.g., Library of Congress; UK Government Web Archive) Commercial websites (e.g., Amazon) Statistics websites (e.g., National Center for Educational Statistics; United Nations Statistics Division) Websites of learned societies (e.g., International Association for Mixed Methods Research) Current news and information (e.g., BBC, CNN, Reuters, Euronews, Al Jazeera)

Trustworthiness	
Works in library databases typically have been written by qualified authors.	Anyone can publish information on the Internet regardless of the quality and validity.
All works contained in library databases have been reviewed by knowledgeable reviewers, editors, and/or publishers.	Much of the information published on the Internet has not been evaluated by subject experts and, thus, you should be extra careful when using and citing Internet sources.
Authors typically are required to provide findings that are transparent and warranted (i.e., evidence-based).	The freedom to write anything allows authors not to be overly concerned about providing politically correct language that might yield more meaningful and richer information than can be obtained from works extracted from library subscription databases.
Databases are updated regularly.	Assessment of works is easily made due to being available worldwide in real time.
	Websites might not be updated regularly and, thus, can become outdated quickly; however, websites that are updated regularly might contain the most current information available.

Stability	
Published works in library databases are permanently stored.	The website address containing information of interest can be removed without notice.
The same published work can be retrieved from the same database for a significant length of time.	Information contained in a webpage can be moved to another webpage with no forwarding website address.
	Links to webpages can become inadvertently broken for a variety of reasons.

Searchability	
Library databases allow users to search for, to identify, to retrieve, and to download information.	Internet search engines allow users to search for, to identify, to retrieve, and to download information. However, you will need to wade through irrelevant information.
Library databases allow users to use Boolean operators, as well as filetype-, language-, time-, and subject-restricted tools to conduct focused searches.	

Citing	
Library databases typically contain full citations with management options	The citation of a significant number of works often is incomplete.
A list of other authors citing a particular retrieved work often is not available.	Much information retrieved from the web represents secondary sources, making it more subject to inaccuracies.
Information from a database typically can be combined/merged with information from other databases in a systematic manner via reference management software packages (e.g., RefWorks, ProCite, EndNotes, RefMan).	A list of other authors citing a particular retrieved work often is available (see, e.g., Google Scholar).

Figure 5.4   Differences between library subscription databases and Internet search engines

TOOL: ELECTRONIC SOURCES IN SOCIAL AND HEALTH SCIENCES

Table 5.2 presents a list of library subscription databases across several fields. Although this list is by no means exhaustive, it does include many of the most commonly used subscription databases.

Whatever choices are made regarding the databases, as indicated in Figure 5.1, it is important to create the audit trail by making a list of all selected library subscription databases and any search engines used, alongside the website address, and your rationale for selecting each source. The audit trail information can begin as handwritten notes, but should eventually be stored electronically, using a word processing software program (e.g., Microsoft Word), a spreadsheet application (e.g., Microsoft Excel), or one of the other information storage systems and techniques that we describe in Chapter 6.

Table 5.2 Electronic bibliographic databases representing the most widely used electronic sources in the fields of social and health sciences

Database (Host)	Description	Internet Address
Academic Search Premier (EBSCOhost)	Multidisciplinary full-text database	Connect through your university library
African Journal of Legal Studies (ProQuest)	Legal collection of journals specific to African countries	http://www.africalawinstitute.org/ajls/ or connect through your university library
Business Source Premier (EBSCOhost)	Scholarly business database	http://ebscohost.com/thisTopic.php?marketID=1&topicID=2
CINAHL (EBSCOhost)	Comprehensive source of full text for nursing and allied health journals	http://www.ebscohost.com/cinahl/
EconLit (EBSCOhost)	Covers areas related to economics	http://www.aeaweb.org/econlit/index.php or connect through your university library
Education: A SAGE Full-Text Collection (CSA Illumina)	Scholarly educational database	http://online.sagepub.com/ or connect through your university library
Education Full Text (WilsonWeb)	Scholarly educational database	http://hwwilson.com/Databases/educat.cfm
ERIC (EBSCOhost)	Education resource information center	www.eric.ed.gov or connect through your university library
European Constitutional Law Review (Academic Search Premier)	Legal collection of journals specific to European countries	http://journals.cambridge.org/action/displayJournal?jid=ECL or connect through your university library
Health Reference Center (Gale InfoTrac)	Leading journals covering health sciences and psychosocial sciences	Connect through your university library
Health Source: Nursing/Academic Edition (EBSCOhost)	Full-text journals focusing on many medical disciplines	http://www.ebscohost.com/thisTopic.php?marketID=1&topicID=83 or connect through your university library

Database (Host)	Description	Internet Address
MEDLINE	Medical information on medicine, nursing, dentistry, veterinary medicine, the healthcare system	http://www.ncbi.nlm.nih.gov/pubmed or connect through your university library
PAIS International (SilverPlatter)	Major areas include administration of justice, agriculture, forestry and fishing, banking and finance, business and service sector, culture, and religion	http://www.csa.com/factsheets/supplements/pais.php or connect through your university library
PsycARTICLES (EBSCOhost)	Definitive source of full-text, peer-reviewed scholarly and scientific articles in psychology	http://www.apa.org/pubs/databases/psycarticles/index.aspx or connect through your university library
PsycINFO (EBSCOhost)	Resource for abstracts of scholarly journal articles, book chapters, books, and dissertations	http://www.apa.org/pubs/databases/psycinfo/index.aspx or connect through your university library
SocINDEX with full text	Comprehensive and highest quality sociology research database	Connect through your university library
Social Services Abstracts (CSA Illumina)	Abstracts and indexes the international literature in sociology and related disciplines in the social and behavioral sciences	http://www.csa.com/factsheets/socioabs-set-c.php or connect through your university library

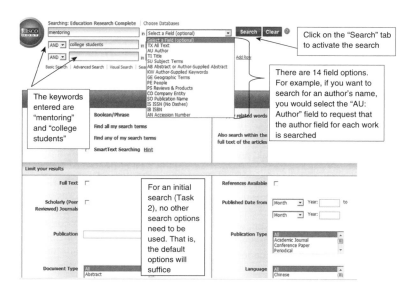

Figure 5.5 Screenshot of initial search on Educational Research Complete (EBSCOhost) database using the keywords "mentoring" and "college students" and 14 field options

EXAMPLE: SELECTING KEYWORDS IN A SEARCH

An appropriate database for the topic of *mentoring of college students* would be the Education Research Complete database because of its comprehensiveness as a database for education research, dating back to 1880. Keywords for a search might include "mentoring" and "college students," as displayed in Figure 5.5. By clicking "Search," hits are provided by using one of the following 14 field options: All text, Author, Title, Subject Terms, Abstract or Author-Supplied Abstract, Author-Supplied Keywords, Geographic Terms, People, Reviews & Products, Company Entity, Publication Name, ISSN (No Dashes), ISBN, and Accession Numbers.

Using this example, to search for a particular author, the author's name would be typed into the keyword box (i.e., left uppermost box) and the Author field option could be selected. This would make the electronic search more efficient because only the **author field of works** (e.g., journal articles, books) would be searched, instead of searching the whole document. Alternatively, to search for a particular title, a title (if already known) would be typed in the keyword box and then the Title field option would be selected. However, for an initial search, it suffices not to check any of the 14 field options but to leave the tab showing "Select a Field (optional)"—which is the default option. Other defaults worth using are:

- the "Boolean/Phrase" option of the "Search Modes" option, which allows the use of the Boolean operators "and," "or," and "not" (we will discuss the idea of Boolean operators when we outline Task 5)
- the "All" option of the "Document Type" option, which means that the following types of documents will be searched: abstract, article, bibliography, book review, case study, directory, editorial, entertainment review, erratum, interview, letter, obituary, poem, poetry review, proceeding, product review, recipe, short story, and speech
- the "All" option of the "Publication Type" option, which means that the following types of published works will be searched: academic journal, conference paper, periodical, reference book, and trade publication
- the "All" option of the "Language" option, which means that the following languages will be searched: Chinese, Croatian, Dutch/Flemish, English, Estonian, French, German, Icelandic, Italian, Latin, Lithuanian, Macedonian, Norwegian, Portuguese, Russian, Slovak, Spanish, and Turkish
- the "All" option of the "Number of Pages" option, which means that all pages will be searched. Further, you can limit the hits to full-text articles or scholarly (peer reviewed) journals

Also, the number of hits to works published can be limited to any month and/or year (e.g., 1990; when one of the first e-mentoring programs was developed in Canada) to any year (e.g., 2013). For an initial search, it makes sense not to select any month or year, which would result in the default option of searching all years to occur.

EXAMPLE: TRACKING THE NUMBER OF HITS

At the time of writing this chapter, using the keywords "mentoring" and "college students" and retaining the aforementioned defaults yielded 752 hits that are partially presented (i.e., part of the first webpage) in Figure 5.6. The initial searches for any other relevant databases would be identical to this search, and notes should be made to notate the **number of hits**, which are the results of each search strand of each case. As decisions are made in the initial search, as noted previously, topic guiding criteria establish which results become significant, or potentially useful for the CLR.

EXAMPLE: USING A SEARCH OF BOOKS

Although articles published in journals represent the most common type of printed or digital document used by literature reviewers, many other types of documents exist that inform literature reviews, including the following: books, theses, dissertations, monographs, encyclopedias, Internet websites, government documents, popular magazines, trade catalogues, interview transcripts, company reports, congressional/parliamentary bills, and advertisements. Of these, books can be especially useful. Thus, we suggest that in addition to searching library subscription databases, and perhaps Internet search engines, online bookstores such as Amazon.com (www.amazon.com) be utilized.

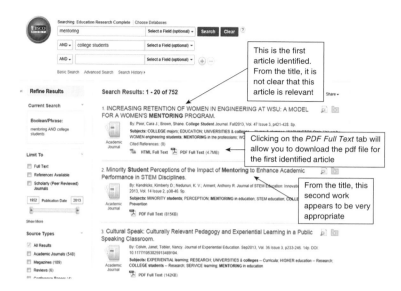

Figure 5.6 Screenshot of initial search on Educational Research Complete (EBSCOhost) database using the keywords "mentoring" and "college students," yielding 752 hits

Figure 5.7 Screenshot showing partial list of books identified via an initial search on the Amazon.com website using the keywords "mentoring" and "college students"

EXAMPLE: A TABLE OF CONTENTS OF A BOOK IN A SEARCH

Using our same keywords (i.e., "mentoring and college students"), a search of the Amazon.com website identified 188 hits, and of these books, the 15th listed book by

Goodlad Sinclair (1998) appeared to have particular potential, demonstrated in Figure 5.7. A very useful feature of the Amazon.com website is that users can look inside large parts of some of the books. Although no part of these books can be electronically copied, electronically saved, or printed, the user is able to read a large part of the book contents on the screen, as well as search for keywords or phrases within the book. Figure 5.8 provides a partial display of the table of contents of Sinclair's (1998) book.

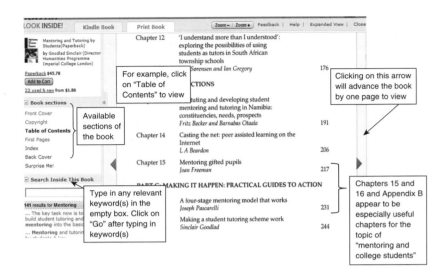

Figure 5.8 Screenshot of the table of contents of the book entitled *Mentoring and Tutoring by Students* that was identified via an initial search on the Amazon.com website using the keywords "mentoring" and "college students"

Another method of viewing books online is the service called Google Books (http://books.google.com/), which came to the fore in 2004. Figure 5.9 shows the Google Books search initiated by typing into the homepage search box the title of Sinclair's (1998) book. With more than 20 million scanned books in its library, Google Books contains approximately 15% of the unique books in the world. Other free Internet repositories (i.e., digital libraries) that might be worth exploring include HathiTrust (circa 2008; http://www.hathitrust.org/), Internet Archive (circa 1996; http://archive.org/index.php), Wikibooks (circa 2003; http://www.wikibooks.org/), Project Gutenberg (circa 1971; http://www.manufacturersdirectory.com/results1.aspx?keywords=project+gutenberg), and Wikisource (circa 2003; https://www.wikisource.org). All in all, many options exist that might be utilized in the initial search, in particular, library subscription databases, Internet search engines, and online book stores/digital libraries. Whatever tools selected for use should be documented as part of the topic guiding criteria and the Step 2 audit trail.

TASK 3: EXPLORING INFORMATION

After the initial search (Task 2), the next task is to obtain information about the selected topic (Task 3). At this point, you might be asking, "If my initial search leads to the identification of many works, how can I possibly read all of them?" If so, this is an excellent question! However, the good news is that you do not have to read the whole of each work that you identify. In fact, for books that you identify, it is usually sufficient for you to peruse the table of contents and to browse any relevant chapters. For articles, which likely will represent the bulk of the works that you identify from your initial search, at this stage of the literature review process, typically, it is sufficient to read the abstracts.

Yet, it is possible to extract dozens of articles, which might lead you to ask further, "If my initial search identifies many articles, am I supposed to read all of the abstracts?" If so, this is another excellent question. The answer is, "You should read a representative number of abstracts." Another excellent question would be, "How do I obtain a representative number of abstracts?" Remembering that the CLR involves mixed research techniques, we can obtain this representative number by using from the quantitative research tradition what is known as ***sampling theory*** in the field of statistics. Now, sampling theory is involved with the collection, analysis, and interpretation of data that are collected

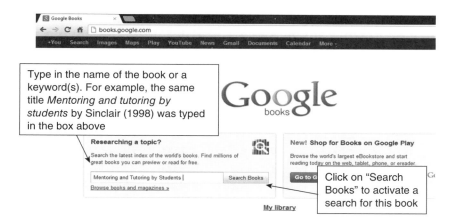

Figure 5.9 Screenshot showing how to conduct a search for a title (in this case the title *Mentoring and tutoring by students*) in Google Books

from random samples of a population of interest—in this case, the population is the total set of abstracts that are identified when a search term or search phrase is entered into a database.

Table 5.3, which utilizes sampling theory, presents the minimum number of abstracts needed to be read to obtain a representative number as a function of the total number of abstracts identified via your search. Thus, for example, in order to read a representative number of abstracts for the 665 articles identified earlier via the keywords "mentoring" and "college students," a reviewer would need to read between 242 ($N = 650$) and 248 ($N = 700$) articles—with interpolation suggesting that approximately 244 abstracts (which is a little closer to 242 than to 248, in the same way that 665 abstracts is a little closer to 650 than to 700) would be representative of the population of 665 abstracts. Thus, it would make sense to read the first 244 abstracts because, in most databases, they are listed in order of relevance.

You might think that 244 abstracts is a lot of abstracts to read! However, bearing in mind that abstracts typically range between 50 and 400 words (cf. Hahs-Vaughn & Onwuegbuzie, 2010; Hahs-Vaughn, Onwuegbuzie, Slate, & Frels, 2009), and bearing in mind that college students read at a rate of 300 words per minute, even the longest abstracts can be read within 90 seconds. So, 244 abstracts could be read within 6 hours. As such, by using a little sampling theory, as seen in Table 5.3, you can read a representative number of abstracts that

should provide you with synthesized information about your topic.

TASK 4: IDENTIFYING KEY TERMS

In addition to reading a representative number of abstracts and using these abstracts to glean information about the topic, abstracts can be used to select the articles that appear to be the most pertinent to your topic and to read these articles in their entirety. When conducting the initial search, we suggest reading at least six articles fully, as well as (at least) parts of printed or digital versions of any relevant books or any other material (e.g., theses, dissertations, monographs, encyclopedias, government documents) because a minimum of six articles stems from the findings of Guest, Bunce, and Johnson (2006), who demonstrated that examining six documents (i.e., interview transcripts) might be "sufficient to enable development of meaningful themes and useful interpretations" (p. 78). By reading these sources, preferably in their entirety, information can be ***contextualized***, which is critical for understanding critical elements that are important for interpreting information presented. Contextualizing also brings awareness of placing the topic in its historical context. Further, by reading at least six sources in their entirety during the initial search, additional keywords and phrases can be identified and lead to a more focused search (i.e., Task 4).

TOOL: TABLE OF SAMPLE NEEDED FOR A SEARCH USING SAMPLING THEORY

Table 5.3 Minimum number of abstracts needed to be read to obtain a representative number as a function of the total number of abstracts in the database(s)

N	n	N	n
10	10	2,000	322
50	44	3,000	341
100	80	4,000	351
150	108	5,000	357
200	132	6,000	361
250	152	7,000	364
300	169	8,000	367
350	183	9,000	368
400	196	10,000	370
450	207	15,000	375
500	217	20,000	377
550	226	30,000	379
600	234	40,000	380
650	242	50,000	381
700	248	75,000	382
750	254	100,000	384
800	260	250,000	384
850	265	500,000	384
900	269	1,000,000	384
950	274	10,000,000	384
1,000	278	500,000,000	384

N stands for size of the population of articles identified; *n* stands for the minimum number of abstracts to be read to obtain a representative number of abstracts. Adapted from "Determining sample size for research activities," by R. V. Krejecie and D. W. Morgan, 1970, *Educational and Psychological Measurement, 30*, pp. 607–610.

EXAMPLE: USING MICROSOFT EXCEL TO TRACK THE SEARCH

For the example of a literature review on "mentoring and college students," appropriate keywords would include "mentoring," "mentors," mentor," "mentorship," "college students," "undergraduate students," "freshmen," "sophomores," "juniors," "seniors," "graduate students," "master's students," "doctoral students," and "Ph.D. students." As is the case for the previous two tasks, it is essential to maintain an audit trail by documenting any new keywords and phrases. An Excel spreadsheet is depicted in Figure 5.10 for Task 3, which

Figure 5.10 Example of leaving an audit trail during Task 4 via an Excel spreadsheet

is useful to assist in the ongoing nature of maintaining an audit trail.

TASK 5: FOCUSING THE SEARCH

The task of focusing the search reminds us that the CLR is a continuous, dynamic process and uses mixed research techniques, because it is much like qualitative inquiry and data collection—involving ways to bracket, to make decisions, and to focus on particular data that make meaning. Further, the task of focusing the search depends upon ongoing decisions, reflections, and interpretations. The final collection of information sources, inclusive of all likely information, is sifted through, sorted, sifted again, categorized, reflected upon, and stored and organized (Step 3). Throughout this process, the culturally progressive lens of the reviewer helps to ensure that equity is reflected by the information selected, and that the topic is represented fairly.

The final task of initiating the search can be accomplished in three major ways. The first way is by using the list of keywords and phrases that you

identified during completion of Task 4. Using this list, synonyms and other words that can be associated with a topic can be explored. As noted previously, articles, books, and other sources help to generate additional keywords, or *operational keywords*. In addition, the use of an encyclopedia or a thesaurus can generate keywords, or **constitutive keywords**.

EXAMPLE: USING SYNONYMS FOR NEW KEYWORDS

In researching mentoring in colleges, as can be seen in Figure 5.11, the Microsoft Word program was used to identify keywords. For the word "mentor," right-click on any part of the word, and select "look up" from the dropdown option, as seen in the second part of this figure. Next, select the thesaurus options. Next, this figure displays the thesaurus versions which include "Thesaurus: English (United States)," "Thesaurus: English (United Kingdom)," and "Thesaurus: French (France)." For the literature review of mentoring and college students, we selected "Thesaurus: English (United States)," which yielded the following keywords that appear on the right-hand side of the second part of Figure 5.11: advisor, counselor, guide, tutor,

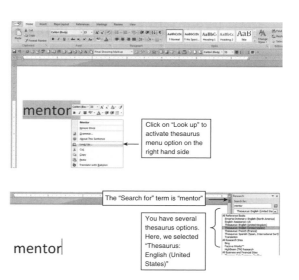

Figure 5.11 Screenshots of two steps showing the Microsoft Word program to identify constitutive keywords (i.e., synonyms) from the word "mentor"

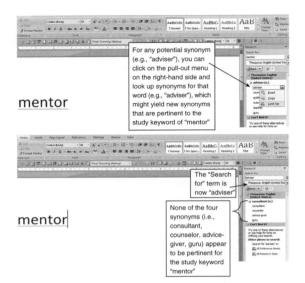

Figure 5.12 Two screenshots showing the final steps of how to use the Microsoft Word program to identify constitutive keywords (i.e., synonyms) from the word "mentor"

teacher, and guru. Of these words, *adviser* (or its variant *advisor*) and *tutor* appear to have potential as keywords for this topic. Whatever strategy is used to obtain your keywords and phrases, it is important to realize that keywords are the means to search library subscription databases, Internet search engines/meta-search engines, and online book stores/digital libraries. In the subsequent figure, Figure 5.12, the three steps were expanded for possible new search terms. Be sure to keep a running list of all keywords for the audit trail!

EXAMPLE: USING BOOLEAN OPERATORS

Figure 5.13 shows the results of a search in which three rows of keywords were used. In the first row, the keyword "mentor*" was used, in which the wildcard symbol (an asterisk [*]) leads to searches for variations in the word "mentor" (i.e., mentor, mentors, mentoring, mentorship). In the second row, the keywords "college students" is used with the Boolean operator "AND"—which, alongside "mentor*," leads to searches for all documents in the database that contain any variants of both "mentor" and "college students" (i.e., "mentor" and "college students"; "mentors" and "college students"; "mentoring" and "college students"; "mentorship" and "college students"). In the third row, the keyword "K-12" is used with the

TOOL: BASIC AND ADVANCED BOOLEAN SEARCH STRATEGIES

The second method of focusing the search is by using what are called ***Boolean operations.*** Table 5.4 presents a list of 6 basic and 11 advanced Boolean operations. It should be noted that whereas the six basic Boolean operations (i.e., AND, OR, AND NOT, asterisks, quotation marks, parentheses) are recognized by virtually every document search tool, the 11 advanced Boolean operations are not recognized by some document search tools. Therefore, the six basic Boolean operations are described to function as tools to focus the search. The first three basic Boolean operations (i.e., AND, OR, AND NOT) can be used directly via the Education Research Complete database that we described earlier.

As displayed in the last column of Table 5.4, use of the OR Boolean operator greatly increased the number of hits relative to the use of the AND Boolean operator. This is always the case. Thus, the OR operator expands a search, whereas the AND operator narrows a search. In Table 5.4, use of the NOT operator also greatly increased the number of hits; however, whether the AND NOT operator expands or narrows a search depends on the word or phrase that is being excluded from the search. Use of an asterisk expands the search, whereas use of quotation marks narrows a search—in this case, to only one hit. Finally, use of parentheses tends to narrow a search, especially when it is combined with the use of the OR operator on at least one occasion within the search string—as is the case in Table 5.4. In any case, a combination of these Boolean operators should be used to focus a search.

Table 5.4 Basic and advanced Boolean search strategies

Boolean Operation	Explanation of Boolean Strategy	Example of Boolean Strategy	Explanation of Example of Boolean Strategy	Number of hits (Education Research Complete)
		Basic Strategies		
AND	Searches for all documents in the database that contain words/phrases that lie either side of the "and"	mentoring AND college students	Searches all documents in the database that contain both the words "mentoring" and "college students"	665
OR	Searches for all documents in the database that contain at least one of the words/phrases that lie either side of the "OR"; useful for linking search words that are synonyms, antonyms, alternative spellings, or abbreviations	mentoring OR college students	Searches all documents in the database that contain either the word(s) "mentoring" or "college students" or both	88,897
NOT	Searches for all documents in which a search word or phrase is to be excluded	mentoring and NOT college students	Searches for all documents that contain the word "mentoring" but do not contain the phrase "college students"	8,024
*	Searches for word variations using the asterisk (*) as a wildcard symbol; it replaces letters that appear after the string, can be used more than once in a word, and can be used anywhere	mentor* AND college students	Searches for all documents that contain the phrase "college students" and any word that begins with "mentor" (e.g., "mentors", "mentoring")	11,728
""	Searches for all documents that contain the string of words in quotation marks	"mentoring and college students"	Searches for all documents that contain the phrase "mentoring and college students"	1
()	Searches for all documents using a combination of two or more Boolean operations	(mentoring OR tutoring) AND college students	Searches for all documents that contain the words "mentoring and college students" or the words "tutoring and college students" (but not "mentoring and tutoring and college students")	1,512

(Continued)

(Continued)

Boolean Operation	Explanation of Boolean Strategy	Example of Boolean Strategy	Explanation of Example of Boolean Strategy	Number of hits (Education Research Complete)
		Advanced Strategies		
W/n	Searches documents in databases with search words that appear within "n" words of each other; joins words and phrases that express parts of a single idea or joins closely associated ideas	mentoring W/3 "college students"	Searches for all documents that contain the words "mentoring" and "college students" within 3 or fewer words of each other; includes phrases such as "mentoring and college students"; "mentoring among college students"; but not "mentoring in the area of college"	N/R
PRE/N	Searches documents in databases in which the first search word precedes the second by not more than the stated number of words; primarily useful in situations where a different word order significantly alters meaning (e.g., "summary judgment" vs. "judgment summary")	mentoring and college* PRE/3 students	Searches for all documents that contain the words "mentoring" and a string in which a word beginning with "college" precedes the word "students" by 3 or fewer words; this string includes phrases such as "college students"; "colleges containing students"	N/R
W/p	Searches documents in databases with search words that appear within the same paragraph	mentoring OR tutoring W/p "college students"	Searches for all documents that contain the words "mentoring" or "tutoring" within the same paragraph as "college students"	N/R
W/SEG	Searches documents in databases in which both search words appear within the same segment (e.g., within the same title)	mentoring W/SEG "college students"	Searches for all documents in which the words "mentoring" and string "college students" appear within the same segment	N/R
W/s	Searches documents in databases in which both search words appear within the same sentence	mentoring W/s "college students"	Searches for all documents in which the words "mentoring" and string "college students" appear within the same sentence	N/R

Boolean Operation	Explanation of Boolean Strategy	Example of Boolean Strategy	Explanation of Example of Boolean Strategy	Number of hits (Education Research Complete)
ALLCAPS	Searches words in which all letters of the search word or phrase are capitalized	mentoring and ALLCAPS (GPA) and "college students"	Searches for all documents in which the words "mentoring" and the capitalized nickname academic achievement in the United States (i.e., GPA: grade point average) appears alongside "college students"	N/R
ATLEAST	Searches documents in databases in which a word or phrase appears at least a specified number of times; use ATLEAST when you want only documents that contain an in-depth discussion on a topic rather than just a mention	mentoring and ATLEAST10 (college students)	Searches documents in databases in which the word "mentoring" appears and the string "college student" appears at least 10 times	N/R
CAPS	Searches documents in databases in which capital letters appear anywhere in the word	mentoring and CAPS (college students)	Searches documents in databases in which the word "mentoring" appears and the string "college students" can have a capital letter anywhere	N/R
NOCAPS	Searches documents in databases in which capital letters do not appear anywhere in the word	mentoring and college students and NOCAPS (achieve*)	Searches documents in databases in which the words "mentoring" and "college students" appear alongside words such as "achieve" and "achievement" but not the disease ACHIEVE	N/R
PLURAL	Searches documents in databases in which only the plural form of the word appears	PLURAL (mentor) and college students	Searches documents in databases in which the plural word "mentors" and phrase "college student" appear	N/R
SINGULAR	Searches documents in databases in which only the singular form of the word appears	SINGULAR (mentor) and college students	Searches documents in databases in which the singular word "mentor" and phrase "college students" appear	N/R

N/R = This Boolean operation is not recognized by this database.

Boolean operator "NOT"—which, alongside "mentor*" AND "college students" leads to searches for all documents that contain any variant of the words "mentor" and "college students" but does not contain the phrase "K-12."

From Figure 5.14, it can be recognized that this route led to 823 hits, which is fewer than the 11,728 hits obtained when the search string "mentor*" AND "college students" was used (cf. Table 5.4). Conveniently, searches become even more focused by adding extra keyword rows. For instance, in Figure 5.15, a fourth row was added that contains the keyword "tutor*" (i.e., the word "tutor" alongside the asterisk) with the Boolean operator "NOT"—which, alongside "mentor*" AND "college students" and NOT "K-12", leads to searches for all documents that contain any variant of the words "mentor" and "college students" but does not contain the phrase "K-12" and does not contain any variant of the word "tutor" (e.g., "tutor", "tutors", "tutoring"). It can be recognized that this route led to 736 hits, which is fewer than

the 823 hits obtained when the search string "mentor*" AND "college students" and NOT "K-12" was used.

The third way of focusing the search is by using *limiters*, which are options that users have for reducing the scope (i.e., focus) of a search. Each search tool (i.e., library subscription databases, Internet search engines, and online book stores/digital libraries) has its own set of limiters. For example, as noted earlier, the Education Research Complete database contains the following limiters that can be seen after clicking the "Advanced Search" link (see Figure 5.16), which are partially displayed in Figure 5.17. Options are presented in the form of: Search modes (i.e., Boolean/phrase, "Find all my search terms", "Find any of my search terms", SmartText searching); the option to "Apply related words"; an option to "Also search within the full text of the articles"; an option to check "Full Text" (which would lead to a search of only full-text works); an option to check "Scholarly (Peer Reviewed) Journals" (which would lead to a search of only

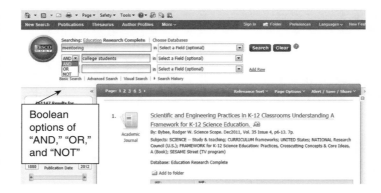

Figure 5.13 Screenshot of focused search on Education Research Complete database using the keywords "mentoring" and "college students"—illustrating the Boolean options of "AND," "OR," and "NOT"

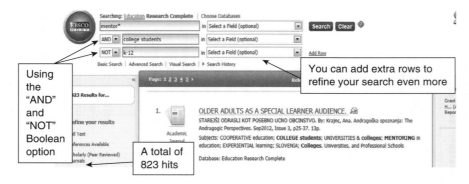

Figure 5.14 Screenshot of focused search on Education Research Complete database using the keywords "mentoring" AND "college students" and NOT "K-12"

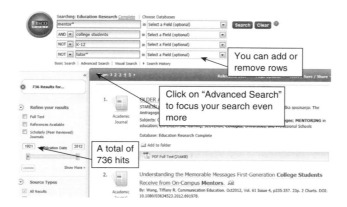

Figure 5.15 Screenshot of an even more focused search on Education Research Complete database using the keywords "mentoring" AND "college students" and NOT "K-12" and NOT "tutor*"

scholarly journals); an option to enter a publication outlet of interest (e.g., the nationally/internationally refereed journal entitled *Research in the Schools* wherein we serve as editors) in the blank field labeled as "Publication"; an option to check "References Available" (which would lead to a search of the available references); document type (i.e., abstract, article, bibliography, book review, case study, directory, editorial, entertainment review, erratum, interview, letter, obituary, poem, poetry review, proceeding, product review, recipe, short story, and speech); number of pages (i.e., equal to, less than, greater than), which allows the user to specify the page range; an option to enter "Image Quick View Types" (i.e., black and white photograph, color photograph, graph, map, chart, diagram, illustration); an option to enter "Published Date from" (i.e., month, year) and "Published Date to" (i.e., month, year); an option to enter the "Publication Type" (i.e., academic journal, conference paper, periodical, reference book, and trade publication); an option to enter the "Language" (i.e., ALL, Chinese, Croatian, Dutch/Flemish, English, Estonian, French, German, Icelandic, Italian, Latin, Lithuanian, Macedonian, Norwegian, Portuguese, Russian, Slovak, Spanish, and Turkish); an option to check "Cover Story"; an option to check "Image Quick View"; and an option to check "PDF Full Text" (which would lead to a search of only pdf full-text works).

EXAMPLE: LIMITING THE SEARCH

The scope of the search can be limited, or further focused, by using one or more of these limiters. The most common

limiter across search tools pertains to the year of publication. For instance, in the aforementioned literature search on "mentoring and college students," as mentioned earlier, it would make sense to limit sources to the post e-mentoring era that begun in 1990. Thus, as illustrated in Figure 5.16, a search could be limited to between 1990 and latest complete year at the time of writing—in this case 2013. This search yielded 531 hits (see Figure 5.17), which is 205 hits fewer than the 736 hits documented earlier when no limiters were used—suggesting that 205 works were published in the area of mentoring and college students (but not K-12 or a variant of the word "tutoring") up until the end of 1989. As is the case for the previous three tasks, it is essential to document the various routes established in this task as part of the audit trail.

CONCLUSIONS

For Step 2 (and for all of the steps in fact), remember the saying: "Fools rush in where angels fear to tread," which refers to people who lack knowledge hastily doing something that more informed people would avoid. This is the same when it comes to conducting a comprehensive literature review, wherein it is inadvisable to conduct it hastily. Rather, a comprehensive literature review should occur systematically and in small incremental steps. Such is the case for being detail-oriented in the documentation that takes place in the Exploration Phase of the CLR, especially in Step 2: Initiating the Search. A deliberate, conscientious, reflective, culturally progressive, and ethical approach will yield the most credible, relevant final product.

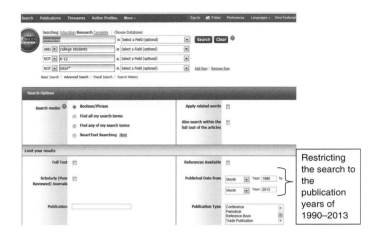

Figure 5.16 Screenshot of an even more focused search on Education Research Complete database using the "Advanced Search" option and the publication dates of 1990–2013

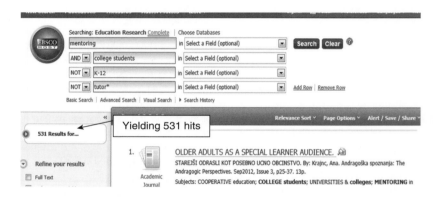

Figure 5.17 Screenshot of an even more focused search on Education Research Complete database using the "Advanced Search" option and the publication dates of 1990–2013—yielding 531 hits

In Chapter 4, we outlined Step 1 of the CLR which included a philosophical exploration of how a person sees and understands the world and human condition, and how you select a topic based on many assumptions (e.g., values, experiences, interests, and beliefs about how knowledge is acquired). It is important to realize that as a result of completing Step 2, it is likely that some of your belief systems discerned in Step 1 have shifted slightly. When exploring documents, it is likely that belief systems and philosophies will be influenced. If utilizing the reflective process of journaling at the end of each step, as awareness of culture and context

of information increases, the tentative topic that was initially selected also might shift.

In short, Step 2 involves multiple tasks and documentation of these tasks to identify potential literature databases, to perform an initial search, to explore information about the selected topic, to identify key terms associated with a topic, and to focus the search—based on topic guiding criteria. These tasks result in the initial set of information sources to store and to organize (Step 3). These sources will be examined closely in Step 4—the selection/deselection phase—with the goal of deciding which documents to retain and which documents to discard, based on relevance and evaluative criteria so that only trusted information is used. Next, the initial searches become an expanded search utilizing MODES to examine multiple perspectives, added insight, alternative explanations, and more. Also, keep in mind that the tasks and topic guiding criteria involved in initiating the search speak to the ethical approach within the methodology of the CLR.

The following concepts are important in review of Chapter 5:

- Initiating the search involves several tasks. First, it begins with identifying potential literature databases. Next, the initial search using initial keywords will yield some information sources (Task 2), and the number of sources yielded, or hits, should be documented.
- The use of topic guiding criteria provides a rationale as to the direction that an initial search takes and reveals some tentative beliefs about a topic, field, and/or discipline before initiating the search.
- Fields and disciplines can be identified in potential literature databases. Some databases are multidisciplinary, interdisciplinary, and transdisciplinary.
- Subject directories via the Internet are useful for browsing a topic when a clear idea of the information is not present. Many subject directories include a keyword search option that often eradicates the need for you to work through multiple levels of topics and subtopics.
- Because of the overall advantages of using library subscription databases compared to Internet sources, library subscription databases are a good starting point for the literature search.
- As decisions are made in the initial search, as noted previously, topic guiding criteria establish which results become significant, or potentially useful for the CLR.
- When conducting the initial search, reading at least six articles fully helps to develop meaningful themes and interpretations.
- As a search is focused, information sources should be contextualized so that they are not misinterpreted. Contextualizing also brings awareness of placing the topic in its historical context.
- The CLR is a continuous, dynamic process and uses mixed research techniques in the data collection (information sources) process. Identifying keywords, using Boolean operators, and using limiters help to focus, or to reduce the scope of, a search and should be documented as part of the audit trail.

CHAPTER 5 EVALUATION CHECKLIST

CORE	Guiding Questions and Tasks
Critical Examination	Did you consider how other fields might regard your topic?
	What are the initial trends and/or biases that you might have identified for information sources in databases on your topic? Are you falling into any traps for complacent thinking patterns?
Organization	To what extent did you document each search strand, database(s) used, and results for each time you searched?
	Did you store the notes of your initial search in at least two locations?
Reflections	What additional ideas have come to the fore as a result of your search? Are you finding enough literature on your topic area, and if not, why not?
	Think about your worldview and belief systems that guided your initial search. How might you succinctly articulate your topic guiding criteria? Are you considering the culturally progressive stance of the CLR so that you do not neglect particular sources?
Evaluation	Have you used sampling theory to substantiate your initial search? Were you careful to create notes that reflect the context of your information sources?

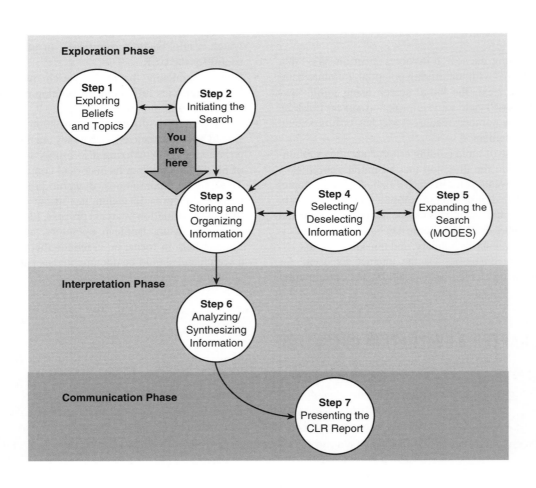

Exploration Phase

Step 1
Exploring
Beliefs
and Topics

Step 2
Initiating the
Search

You
are
here

Step 3
Storing and
Organizing
Information

Step 4
Selecting/
Deselecting
Information

Step 5
Expanding the
Search
(MODES)

Interpretation Phase

Step 6
Analyzing/
Synthesizing
Information

Communication Phase

Step 7
Presenting the
CLR Report

6

STEP 3: STORING AND ORGANIZING INFORMATION

CHAPTER 6 ROADMAP

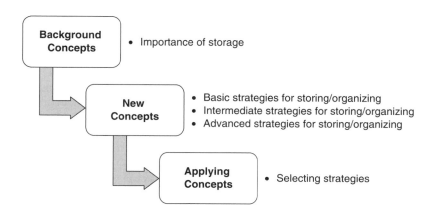

IMPORTANCE OF STORAGE

In terms of a single CLR, as can be seen from the Seven-Step Model representation at the beginning of this chapter, in addition to facilitating Step 2, the step of storing and organizing information facilitates each step in the Exploration Phase. Another important role of storing and organizing information is that it represents the most permanent way of leaving an audit trail, allowing reviewers or those conducting an audit (e.g., chairs/supervisors of dissertation committees) to keep track of both the CLR process and products, which, as we noted in Chapter 1, include the following:

- *raw data* (e.g., all selected literature, written field notes)
- *data reduction* and analysis products (e.g., summaries such as condensed notes, quantitative summaries, qualitative summaries, and theoretical notes)
- *process notes* that include methodological notes (e.g., procedures, strategies, rationales, designs) and trustworthiness notes (i.e., relating to credibility, validity, and appropriateness of the information collected)
- materials relating to intentions and dispositions that include *personal notes* (e.g., reflexive notes whereby the literature reviewers document their ideas, thoughts, experiences, concerns, challenges, and motivations) and expectations (e.g., predictions and intentions)

To facilitate a CLR, a reviewer should store and organize information in as *systematic* a way as possible. In the following sections, and because we have written this book simultaneously for beginning reviewers/researchers, emergent reviewers/researchers, and experienced reviewers/researchers, we will outline how

to store and to organize information at three different levels of complexity: basic, intermediate, or advanced strategies. In addition, we will describe how to store and to organize information using various forms of technology and different levels of collaboration.

NEW CONCEPTS

BASIC STRATEGIES FOR STORING AND ORGANIZING

A device for storing information can range from manual-based strategies to technology-based strategies. Such a device may store information, process information, or both. **Manual devices** provide a basic medium for storing information. Of these devices, those that involve the use of handwritten note-taking represent the most elementary media. The use of index cards is one such low-level storage device. Specifically, index cards may be used to document the information about a work, including author(s), year of publication, genre of work (e.g., book, book chapter, article), genre of narrative (e.g., empirical, conceptual, theoretical, methodological), genre of empirical report (e.g., quantitative research, qualitative research, mixed methods research), summary of content, major findings/conclusion, and full reference. Typically, each index card would represent no more than one work that you selected as part of the CLR process. However, multiple index cards can be used to store information regarding any single work, and then this set of index cards can be attached (e.g., stapled) together as a means of keeping the set intact. Figure 6.1 presents a sample of the index cards used for the Dyadic Mentoring Study after the initial search, which later was transferred to digital form.

Figure 6.1   A sample of the index cards used in the Dyadic Mentoring Study after the initial CLR search

Keep in mind that when writing your summary of works on the index cards, it is important to provide this summary using your own words in order to avoid *plagiarism*. For example, according to authors of the sixth edition of the *Publication Manual* (APA, 2010), writers should not claim the words and ideas of another author as their own and must "give credit where credit is due" (p. 15). Consequently, any content contained in a work that is summarized for the index card should be paraphrased and should be in words that are different from the verbiage or the statement(s) of the author(s) as much as possible. This way, when the information is transferred from index cards to the CLR report, the possibility of plagiarizing the original work is eliminated. Alongside each summary statement presented in the index card, the page number from the work from where the information was extracted also should be documented on the index card so that the original information might be retrieved quickly.

EXAMPLE: USING INDEX CARDS TO CODE

Index cards also can be used to organize by *color coding*, which provides a system for displaying information via

the use of different colors to indicate different information. For instance, with respect to the genre of the empirical report, the reviewer could use blue to indicate quantitative research studies, green to indicate qualitative research studies, and yellow to indicate mixed methods research.

STRENGTHS OF USING INDEX CARDS. The use of index cards to store and to organize information offers several advantages. First and foremost, index cards are a useful strategy for reviewers who do not have access to a computer. Indeed, a significant proportion of people worldwide do not have access to a computer or lack the computer skills to use computers—yielding a global digital divide (see, e.g., Kshetri & Dholakia, 2009). Another population that often does not have access to computers—even in developed nations— and that could benefit from the use of index cards is schoolchildren. Such index cards could be used by schoolchildren when conducting a literature review for a classroom project. Further, index cards may be used at times when computers cannot be easily accessed, because they are relatively small and portable. Also, these index cards can serve as reference cards that provide a concise set of notes (students in the United States might refer to this as a *cheat sheet* or *crib sheet*) that are used for quick reference by reviewers while they prepare to present their CLR findings in some oral manner such as during the defense of their thesis/dissertation or a conference presentation.

Another benefit of index cards is that they are compatible with some types of qualitative data analysis approaches and, thus, can facilitate Step 6 of the CLR, namely, the step wherein reviewers analyze and synthesize information. In fact, index cards are particularly suited for a qualitative data analysis approach known as *constant comparison analysis* (Glaser, 1965). In the context of a literature review, **constant comparison analysis** involves systematically reducing information extracted from the CLR process to codes, then developing themes from these codes (Onwuegbuzie, Leech, et al., 2011).

In the Dyadic Mentoring Study, the 47 sources were each written on a separate card. First, reading the information on each set of index cards multiple times is important, to become completely familiar with the information. Next, the information on each card is compared with other cards and assigned a label, which was written in this example on the top right-hand side of each index card. Therefore, similar chunks would be labeled with the same code, and after coding all the data, the codes are grouped by similarity by sorting the index cards into piles, with each pile containing index cards that have similar codes. If the reviewer deemed that an index card needed to be coded with more than one code (e.g., **double coding**), then he/she would duplicate that index card with duplicate information except that it would be provided with a different code (e.g., on the top right-hand side of each index card). In such instances, this would allow the same work to be placed in more than one pile, thereby contributing to multiple themes.

TOOL: STEP-BY-STEP GUIDE FOR MANUALLY CODING

Box 6.1 presents a four-step guide outlined by Onwuegbuzie and Frels (2012) for using index cards to conduct a constant comparison analysis of selected information extracted via a CLR search. We discuss this analysis in more detail in Chapter 9 and Step 6.

BOX 6.1

A FOUR-STEP GUIDE FOR USING INDEX CARDS TO CONDUCT A CONSTANT COMPARISON ANALYSIS OF SELECTED INFORMATION EXTRACTED VIA A COMPREHENSIVE LITERATURE REVIEW SEARCH

- First, use one color marker (e.g., blue) to highlight (i.e., hand code) particular text (e.g., words, phrases, sentences, or paragraphs) that you classify as belonging to one particular topic in your area (i.e., the first code) across all of your sources. Use a second color marker (e.g., green) to highlight text belonging to the second topic area (i.e., the second code) and so forth, until text belonging to all particular topics (your codes) has been highlighted in various colors.
- Second, paraphrase each phrase or sentence that is coded from the first color from each source that you coded (e.g., your first document, second document, and so forth) and write each of the colored sentences using your own words on an index card. The first color and card becomes code #1.

- Third, repeat this process using the second color from every source and transfer your paraphrased sentences from the second color onto a second index card. This information on the different and new index card becomes your data for your code #2.
- Fourth, repeat this process until you have compiled all of the sentences of each color from every selected source onto separate index cards.

Now you have multiple piles of index cards, one pile for each colour. Re-read the text belonging to the first pile and determine what this group of text (i.e., group of codes) has in common such that you can give this pile a name. This name is that of the first theme. Repeat this process until every pile has a theme name. Each theme and the text contained within it then are used to inform the literature review write-up. You will not need to provide the complete references of all articles on these cards, but you will need to refer back to your organized lists of literature and other sources in your write-up.

Adapted from "Writing a literature review," by A. J. Onwuegbuzie and R. K. Frels, 2012c, in C. Wagner, B. Kawulich, & M. Garner (Eds.), *Doing social research: A global context*, Maidenhead, England: McGraw-Hill, pp. 43–44. Copyright 2012 by McGraw-Hill.

LIMITATIONS OF USING INDEX CARDS. As useful as index cards are for storing and organizing information, and as superior as they are compared with relying on one's memory, they involve a number of limitations. One limitation is that it is difficult to store information from a particular source without having to use numerous index cards, which can become cumbersome very quickly. Also, compared to typing up summary information, it is more time-consuming to handwrite summary information as well as to correct or to revise information. Also, because of the relatively small size of index cards, only a limited amount of information can be presented on each index card. Another limitation is that if two or more reviewers are co-conducting the CLR, it is unwieldy for the reviewers to compare notes unless a complete, identical set of index cards is created for each reviewer. Yet another limitation is that it is not impossible to lose one or more of the index cards. An extremely important restriction pertains to the organization of information. Unfortunately, manually searching for words, phrases, sentences, numbers, and the like that are contained in index cards can be very time-consuming, especially when a lot of index cards are involved.

WORD PROCESSING SOFTWARE PROGRAMS

Although considered a basic strategy, the use of word processing software programs—representing a computer software application—signifies an upgrade from using index cards because reviewers are able to type up their notes for each work instead of handwriting them. Thus, compared to index cards, the use of word processing software programs is further along the continua of level of technology and level of collaboration. Table 6.1 provides a comprehensive—although not exhaustive—list of word processing software programs. The word processing software programs in this table are subdivided into commercial word processing software programs and free/open source word processing software programs. Using virtually any of these word processing software programs would allow reviewers electronically to edit, to format (e.g., change font and font size), to check spellings, to check grammar, to utilize a built-in thesaurus (which is very useful for paraphrasing text in order to avoid plagiarism), to print, and to save, among other tasks.

STRENGTHS OF USING WORD PROCESSING SOFTWARE PROGRAMS. The use of word processing software programs provides several advantages, especially over using index cards. First and foremost, word processing software programs are available to everyone who has access to a computer. As can be seen in Table 6.1, even if a reviewer cannot afford to buy a commercial word processing software program (e.g., Microsoft Word, WordPerfect), he/she can use one of the freeware/open source word processing software programs. In addition to being able electronically to edit, to format, to check

TOOL: A LIST OF WORD PROCESSING SOFTWARE PROGRAMS

When using word processing software programs, reviewers should summarize no more than one selected work on a page; however, multiple pages can be used to store information regarding any single work, and then these pages can be attached (e.g., stapled) together, after printing them out, as a means of keeping them intact. Interestingly, word processing software programs can be used to print out the information on each source to resemble an index-card format. For example, Microsoft Word can print out information in postcard form (called "Double Japan Postcard Rotated").

Table 6.1 Commercial and freeware/open source word processing software programs listed in chronological order

Name of Word Processor	Internet Address	Year of Initial Release
Commercial		
WordPerfect	http://www.wordperfect.com/gb/product/office-suite/?&mapcounter=1&pid=prod5200107	1979
Nota Bene	http://www.notabene.com/	1982
Microsoft Word	http://office.microsoft.com/en-gb/word/	1983 for MS-DOS 1985 for Mac OS/ Mac OS X 1989 for Windows
Applixware	https://www.vistasource.com/wp/	1986
FrameMaker	http://www.adobe.com/products/framemaker.html	1986
Lotus Word Pro	http://www-01.ibm.com/software/info/app/ecatalog/index.html	1989
Nisus Writer	http://www.nisus.com/	1989
CopyDesk	http://www.quark.com/Products/QuarkCopyDesk/	1991
WordPad	http://windows.microsoft.com/en-us/windows/using-wordpad#1TC=windows-7	1995
GNU TeXmacs	http://www.texmacs.org/tmweb/home/welcome.en.html	1996
Mariner Write	http://marinersoftware.com/	1996
PolyEdit	http://polyedit.com/	1998
InCopy	https://creative.adobe.com/products/incopy	1999
WordFile4ME	http://www.byronsoftware.org.uk/School/WordFile/index.htm	1999
Atlantis Word Processor	http://www.atlantiswordprocessor.com/en/	2000
ThinkFree Office	http://www.thinkfree.com/main.jsp	2001
Mellel	http://www.mellel.com/	2002
OpenOffice Writer	https://web.archive.org/web/20110428102539/http://www.openoffice.org/	2002
Apple Pages	http://www.iworkcommunity.com/	2005

Name of Word Processor	Internet Address	Year of Initial Release
Free and Open Source Software		
TextMaker	http://www.softmaker.com/english/ofwtm_en.htm	1987
Kingsoft Writer	http://www.wps.com/	1989
Groff	https://www.gnu.org/software/groff/	1990
TextEdit	https://developer.apple.com/library/mac/samplecode/TextEdit/Introduction/Intro.html	1990s
LyX	http://www.lyx.org/	1995
Calligra Words	https://www.calligra.org/	1998
AbiWord	http://abisource.com/	1999
Ted	http://www.nllgg.nl/Ted/	1999
Atlantis Nova	http://www.atlantiswordprocessor.com/en/	2000
Jarte	http://www.jarte.com/	2001
NeoOffice Writer	http://www.neooffice.org/neojava/en/index.php	2003
Lotus Symphony	http://www-03.ibm.com/software/products/en/lotusymp	2007
GNU TeXmacs	http://www.texmacs.org/tmweb/home/welcome.en.html	2010
LibreOffice Writer	https://www.libreoffice.org/discover/writer/	2011
Apache OpenOffice	http://www.openoffice.org/	2012
Polaris Office	https://www.polarisoffice.com/view/login	2013

spellings, to check grammar, to utilize a built-in thesaurus, to print, and to save, word processing software programs allow reviewers to copy and paste text (and images) from a document extracted from a CLR search to a document that the reviewer creates via a word processing software program for the purpose of storing and organizing information. However, in copying and pasting material, you should be careful *not* (a) to plagiarize any material in the final CLR report and (b) to violate any copyright laws by pasting images or long quotations into your CLR report without securing the necessary copyright permission.

Perhaps most usefully, word processing software programs allow reviewers to search for text (i.e., words or strings of words) extremely quickly (in seconds) to find each instance or all instances. Also, when needed, text can be searched and replaced by other text. Another useful tool associated with word processing software programs is the ability to track changes that reviewers make as they continue their journey of storing and organizing information. For example, Microsoft Word uses balloons to display deletions, formatting changes, comments, and content that the writer has moved from one section of the document to another section. As is the case when using index cards, reviewers can use colors to distinguish genres of information sources (e.g., quantitative research-based vs. qualitative research-based vs. mixed methods research-based). For instance, Microsoft Word has 20 predefined color schemes. Reviewers also can use the italics, bold, and underline features of word processing software programs to highlight text more easily than can be undertaken by hand when using index cards.

An additional advantage that word processing software programs have over index cards is that each document automatically is date-stamped and time-stamped, which is an important organizational feature for helping reviewers monitor the sequence of their CLR searches. Also, different word processing documents can be used for each iteration of the CLR search. Further, relative to index cards, it is much more difficult to lose the information that the reviewer has stored and organized because all word processing documents can easily be saved for future use or consultation on a computer's hard drive or portable data storage devices (e.g., USB flash drive); or, for even more security, these word processing documents can be saved to the cloud, which provides access to reviewers to access them from anywhere. Also, because documents produced by word processing software programs are in digital form, they can be sent electronically across the Internet (e.g., via email) or other computer networks to co-reviewers.

LIMITATIONS OF USING WORD PROCESSING SOFTWARE PROGRAMS. As useful as word processing software programs are for storing and organizing information, and as superior as they are over the use of index cards, they contain some limitations. However, perhaps the greatest limitation is that reviewers cannot use word processing software programs to group or to sort the summary information pertaining to the different works in an automated manner. Rather, they must sort the set of summary information manually via the *copy-and-paste* option of word processing software programs by copying a section of interest and moving it (i.e., pasting it) immediately before or after another section that falls into the same category, as defined by the reviewer, such that all summary information falling into the same categories are presented in consecutive pages.

Unfortunately, such manual organizing of summary information can be very time-consuming, especially when summary information pertaining to numerous works has been documented.

INTERMEDIATE STRATEGIES FOR STORING AND ORGANIZING

The use of spreadsheets (i.e., spreadsheet programs), which we consider to represent an intermediate strategy, signifies an upgrade both from using index cards and from using word processing software programs. Indeed, compared to index cards and word processing software programs, the use of spreadsheets is further along the continua of level of complexity (i.e., intermediate level) and level of technology. Broadly speaking, a *spreadsheet* program (circa 1962) is an interactive computer application program for storing, organizing, and analyzing information (i.e., data) that is presented in tabular form such that the data are organized in rows and columns, with each combination of row and column representing a cell. The utility of spreadsheet programs is that each cell can contain either numeric or text data. Further, the user can utilize formulas that are either in-built or created by them to calculate and to display automatically a value in a new cell that is based on the data contained in one or more other cells. By making changes to the data contained in one or more of these other cells, the value in this new cell automatically will be updated accordingly. With respect to built-in functions, spreadsheet programs contain arithmetic, mathematical, statistical, and financial functions. These spreadsheet programs also provide functions that convert between text and numbers, as well as functions that operate on strings of text.

TOOL: A LIST OF SPREADSHEET PROGRAMS

Table 6.2 provides a comprehensive—although not exhaustive—list of spreadsheet programs. The spreadsheet programs in this table are subdivided into commercial spreadsheet programs and free/open source spreadsheet programs. Using virtually any of these spreadsheet programs would allow reviewers electronically to store and to organize information extracted from a CLR. Of these spreadsheet programs, Microsoft Excel is the most commonly used (Power, 2004).

Table 6.2 Commercial and freeware/open source spreadsheet programs listed in chronological order

Name of Spreadsheet	Internet Address	Year of Initial Release
Commercial		
Framework	http://www.framework.com/	1984
Microsoft Excel	http://office.microsoft.com/en-us/excel	1985
StarOffice	http://web.archive.org/web/20101206170712/http://www.oracle.com/us/products/applications/open-office/index.html	1985
Corel Quattro Pro	http://www2.corel.com/us/	1988
Mariner Calc	http://marinersoftware.com/	1989
Quantrix	http://www.quantrix.com/	Early 1990s
Mesa	http://download.cnet.com/Mesa/3000-20411_4-3325.html	1991
PlanMaker	http://download.cnet.com/Plan-Maker/3000-18494_4-76016264.html	1994
SSuite Accel	http://www.ssuitesoft.com/accelspreadsheet.htm	1999
ThinkFree Office	http://www.thinkfree.com/main.jsp	2001
NeoOffice	http://www.neooffice.org/neojava/en/index.php	2003
wikiCalc	http://www.softwaregarden.com/products/wikicalc/	2005
Sheetster	http://sourceforge.net/projects/sheetster/	2007
Numbers	https://www.apple.com/mac/numbers/	2007
Resolver One	http://download.cnet.com/Resolver-One/3000-2077_4-10797708.html	2008
Free and Open Source Software		
3D-Calc	http://www.medcalc.org/legacysoftware/atari/	1989
OpenOffice Calc	https://web.archive.org/web/20110429120308/http://download.openoffice.org/index.html	2000
Gnumeric	http://www.gnumeric.org/	2001
Tiki Wiki CMS Groupware	http://info.tiki.org/tiki-index.php	2002
Simple Groupware	http://www.simple-groupware.de/cms/	2004
ZCubes	http://home.zcubes.com/	2006
Siag	http://siag.nu/	2006
IBM Lotus Symphony	http://www-03.ibm.com/software/products/en/lotusymp	2007
Pyspread	http://manns.github.io/pyspread/download.html	2008
CellPro	http://www.download366.com/cellpro?utm_source=google&utm_medium=cpc&utm_campaign=366_USA_en_longtail_Productividad&utm_content=CellPro&utm_term=cellpro&gclid=COXmwsG3zcACFZTm7AodGzwAQw	2008
LibreOffice Calc	https://www.libreoffice.org/discover/calc/	2010
Calligra Sheets	https://www.calligra.org/sheets/	2013
Kingsoft Office/ WPS Office	http://www.wps.com/	1997

STRENGTHS OF USING SPREADSHEET PROGRAMS. The use of spreadsheet programs provides several advantages over using index cards and word processing software programs. First and foremost, spreadsheet programs—at least the freeware/open source programs—are accessible to everyone who has access to a computer. Interestingly, according to Softpedia (2012), more than 1 billion users—representing more than 14% of the world's total population—have access to Microsoft Office, which is an office suite of applications for Microsoft Windows and OS X (i.e., designed to run on Mac computers) operating systems that include Microsoft Excel (alongside Microsoft Word and Microsoft PowerPoint). According to Softpedia (2012), one person purchases Microsoft Office worldwide every second. As such, for the remainder of this section on spreadsheet programs, we will focus our attention on Microsoft Excel.

EXAMPLE: A SUMMARY TABLE OF LITERATURE

Figure 6.2 presents a screenshot of a partial summary table of the literature review of the Dyadic Mentoring Study stored in a Microsoft Excel spreadsheet.

As is the case with Microsoft Word, Microsoft Excel allow reviewers electronically to edit, to format (e.g., change font and font size; bold or italicize text; underline all or selected text; apply a bottom border to cells or rows; or draw a line to underline cells), to check spellings (see Figure 6.3), to utilize a built-in thesaurus, to print, and to save. Further, the Microsoft Office Clipboard allows reviewers to copy multiple text and graphics from other programs (e.g., Microsoft Word, pdf files, HTML documents, webpages, email messages) and to paste them into the Microsoft Excel file that they are using to store and to organize CLR information. In turn, CLR information stored in the Microsoft Excel file can be copied and pasted onto the word processing software program (e.g., Microsoft Word) that the reviewer is using to write the CLR report. As such, again, we would like to caution you to paraphrase information extracted from the CLR before copying and pasting it into the CLR report, in order to guarantee that plagiarism and copyright violations are avoided. As can be seen in Figure 6.4, the Track Changes menu allows reviewers to track, to maintain, and to display information about changes that are made to an Excel workbook that is shared among two or more reviewers. Other reviewers then can decide to accept or to reject the tracked changes.

Another useful tool is the Translate menu tab that appears under the *REVIEW* option (see Figure 6.3). This feature allows reviewers to translate text (e.g., a word, a phrase, a paragraph) written in a different language (e.g., French) to a target language (e.g., English). Using the Translate menu tab helps reviewers to expand their

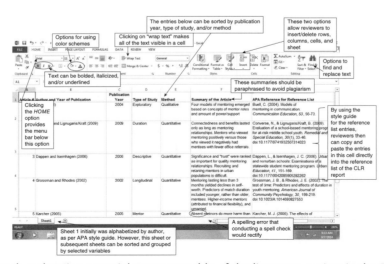

Figure 6.2 Screenshot showing a partial summary table of the literature review in the Dyadic Mentoring Study stored in a Microsoft Excel spreadsheet using the *HOME* option

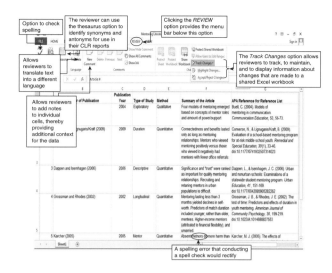

Figure 6.3 Screenshot showing the *REVIEW* option available to a Microsoft Excel spreadsheet, which includes spelling check, thesaurus, translate, comment insertion, and tracking

searches (i.e., Step 5) by including information from sources written in different languages.

EXAMPLE: SORTING SOURCES BY A VARIABLE

Earlier, we noted that when using either index cards or a word processing software program, any sorting or grouping of works has to be undertaken manually. However, when using Microsoft Excel, this sorting or grouping can occur in an automated manner. Figures 6.4 and 6.5 illustrate how to sort rows (i.e., sources) by one or more variables. Sorting sources is a very effective way of analyzing and synthesizing information because it can lead to the identification of important patterns. For instance, by sorting the sources by publication year, reviewers can identify publishing trends related to the underlying topic, as well as gaps in the body of knowledge.

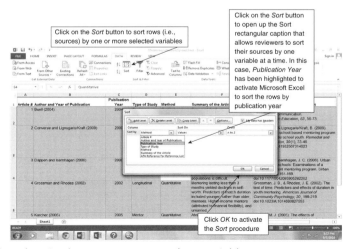

Figure 6.4 Screenshot showing how to sort sources by a variable

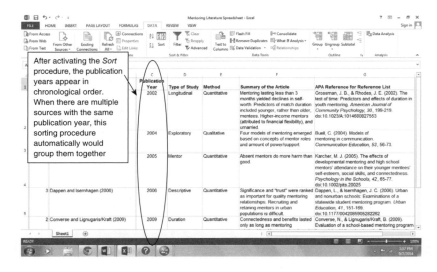

After activating the *Sort* procedure, the publication years appear in chronological order. When there are multiple sources with the same publication year, this sorting procedure automatically would group them together

Figure 6.5 Screenshot showing the sources sorted by publication year (i.e., in chronological order)

EXAMPLE: FILTERING DATA

Yet another strength of Microsoft Excel is that not only can reviewers search for text (e.g., a letter, a word, string of words) and find cells that contain text or blank cells (i.e., via the *Go To* command) and that meet a condition (e.g., contain the string "mentor"), but also they can find and replace text using wildcards (e.g., the wildcard "mentor*" could be used to find any word that starts with *mentor*, including "mentor," "mentors," "mentored," "mentoring," and "mentorship") or question marks (i.e., "gr?y" finds both "gray" and "grey"). Figure 6.6 presents a screenshot showing the options available from the *Find & Select* menu. A particular useful feature of the *Find & Select* menu is the AutoFilter option that allows reviewers to find text in one or more columns of data, and to filter these data by showing or hiding the data containing this text. When data are filtered, entire rows are hidden if

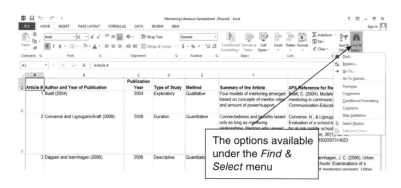

The options available under the *Find & Select* menu

Figure 6.6 Screenshot showing the *Find & Select* option available to a Microsoft Excel spreadsheet, which includes find and replace

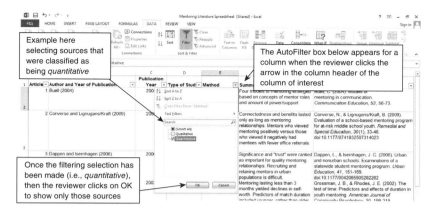

Figure 6.7 Screenshot showing the AutoFilter option used to find text in one or more columns of data, and to filter these data by showing or hiding the data containing this text

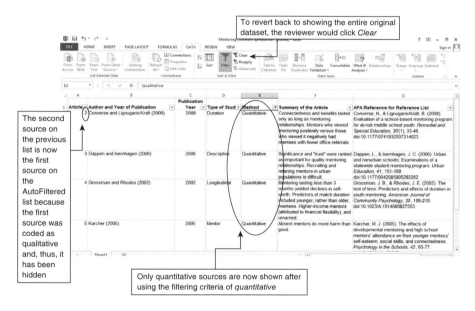

Figure 6.8 Screenshot showing only the quantitative sources after using the filtering criteria of *quantitative*

the text in one or more columns do not meet the filtering (i.e., selection) criteria.

Figure 6.7 shows a screenshot of this AutoFilter option. Figure 6.8 represents a screenshot that shows only the quantitative sources after using the filtering criteria of *quantitative*. This AutoFiltering option increases exponentially in utility as the number of sources contained in the Microsoft Excel file increases.

As is the case when using index cards and word processing software programs, reviewers can use colors to sort and to filter information contained in Microsoft Excel files. Using color coding can help reviewers explore and analyze information that has been stored in Microsoft Excel files. Reviewers also can use the italics, bold, and underline features of Microsoft Excel to highlight text. As for word processing software programs, Microsoft Excel files are automatically date-stamped and time-stamped. Further, because Microsoft Excel files are in digital form, they can be sent electronically across the Internet (e.g., via email) or other computer networks to co-reviewers.

Microsoft Excel, as do many other spreadsheet software programs, can have multiple interacting spreadsheets, often called *worksheets* or simply *sheets*, which are compiled together to produce a *workbook*. Specifically, a workbook, which represents a file, contains all the information that is stored in the various worksheets, with these worksheets typically being distinguished by tabs that flip between pages, with each tab containing one of the worksheets. Thus, in the context of storing and organizing CLR information, reviewers could use different worksheets for different components of the CLR process. In particular, the first worksheet could contain all the works selected at any stage of the CLR process. Then, subsequent worksheets could contain smaller subsets of the first worksheet that reflect the selection/deselection process of the CLR process (i.e., Step 4). For example, in the Dyadic Mentoring Study, Rebecca determined the final 47 works for her CLR report using the following criteria: (a) the research or concept illuminated or extended her understanding of the phenomenon of mentoring (i.e., provided meaning); and (b) the research design was rigorous and included vividness, creativity, thoroughness, congruence, and sensitivity.

Indubitably, the biggest difference between spreadsheets and word processing software programs and index cards is that the former actually can be used to *analyze* and to *synthesize* information going beyond *storing* and *organizing* information. In particular, descriptive statistics can be used to *analyze* and to *synthesize* CLR information. Indeed, frequency counts and proportions/percentages can be especially useful here. For instance, reviewers could determine the total number or proportion of quantitative-, qualitative-, and mixed methods-based studies that are contained in their spreadsheet databases and then report this information in their CLR write-ups. As an example, in the Dyadic Mentoring Study, Rebecca used this analysis to determine that of the 23 empirical articles on mentoring programs that she identified via her CLR search, 18 articles represented quantitative research studies and only five articles represented qualitative research studies; she used this finding to justify further her decision to conduct a qualitative research study.

If you are feeling more adventurous, you could use your spreadsheet to conduct one or more **inferential analyses** (e.g., univariate analysis, multivariate analysis) to analyze CLR information. For example, reviewers can conduct a chi-square analysis to examine the relationship between the method used in empirical studies (i.e., quantitative vs. qualitative vs. mixed methods) and another variable such as, in the context of the Dyadic Mentoring Study, whether the study was conducted on primary school students or secondary school students. Interestingly, Microsoft Excel has an Analysis ToolPak that allows reviewers to conduct an array of statistical analyses.

TOOL: INSTALLING THE ANALYSIS TOOLPAK FOR STATISTICAL ANALYSES

In order to access this arsenal of statistical analyses, you will have to load the Analysis ToolPak add-in, which, using Microsoft Excel Version 2013, involves the following steps:

1. Click the *FILE* tab at the top left of the menu bar, click *Options*, and then click the *Add-Ins* category.
2. Within the *Manage* box, select *Excel Add-Ins* and then click *Go*.
3. Within the *Add-Ins* dialog box, select the *Analysis ToolPak* check box, and then click *OK*.
4. If *Analysis ToolPak* check is not listed in the *Add-Ins available* box, click *Browse* to locate it.
5. If you are prompted that the Analysis ToolPak is not currently installed on your computer, you should click *Yes* to install it.

Following these steps will allow you to install and to activate the Analysis ToolPak more quickly than you can say "Comprehensive Literature Review" 20 times. If you are sleep deprived, it might take you a little longer! Figure 6.9 provides a screenshot showing how to obtain the Data Analysis menu that is available in Microsoft Excel via the Analysis ToolPak. Figure 6.10 displays the analysis tools that are available in Microsoft Excel.

In addition to statistical analyses, reviewers can use Microsoft Excel to create graphic representations (i.e., charts). For example, frequency counts and proportions/percentages can be transformed into bar charts or pie charts.

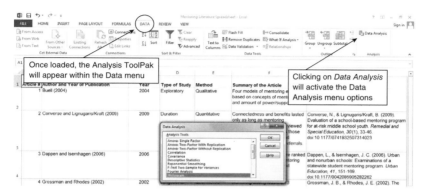

Figure 6.9 Screenshot showing how to obtain the Data Analysis menu

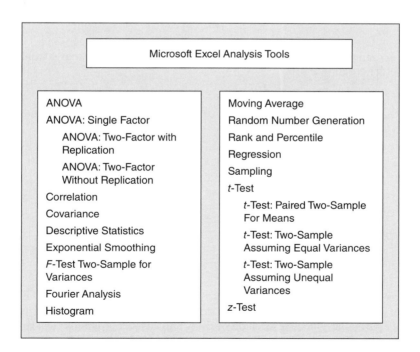

Microsoft Excel Analysis Tools

ANOVA
ANOVA: Single Factor
    ANOVA: Two-Factor with Replication
    ANOVA: Two-Factor Without Replication
Correlation
Covariance
Descriptive Statistics
Exponential Smoothing
F-Test Two-Sample for Variances
Fourier Analysis
Histogram

Moving Average
Random Number Generation
Rank and Percentile
Regression
Sampling
t-Test
    t-Test: Paired Two-Sample For Means
    t-Test: Two-Sample Assuming Equal Variances
    t-Test: Two-Sample Assuming Unequal Variances
z-Test

Figure 6.10 Analysis tools available in Microsoft Excel via the Analysis ToolPak

TOOL: AVAILABLE CHART TOOLS FOR CREATING VISUAL DISPLAYS

Figure 6.11 shows a screenshot showing how to obtain the Insert Chart menu that is available in Microsoft Excel for creating charts. Figure 6.12 presents the available tools for creating charts in Microsoft Excel. In Chapter 9, we discuss further the types of statistical analyses that can be used to analyze and to synthesize CLR information. In Chapter 10, we discuss how charts can be used to create a citation map that shows the evolution of published works on a topic over time.

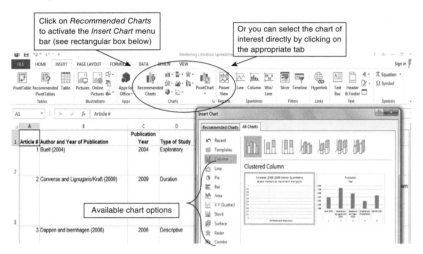

Figure 6.11 Screenshot showing how to obtain the Insert Chart menu that is available in Microsoft Excel for creating charts

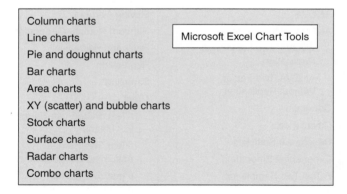

Figure 6.12 Available tools for creating charts in Microsoft Excel

Finally, another particularly notable strength of using spreadsheet programs such as Microsoft Excel is that the file that ensues can be imported to specialized analytical software for more advanced analysis. For example, Microsoft Excel can be exported to many computer-assisted qualitative data analysis software (CAQDAS) programs (e.g., QDA Miner, MAXQDA, NVivo), which can be used subsequently to inform the analysis and synthesis of CLR information, for example, by helping to identify emergent themes. We discuss the use of CAQDAS later in this chapter. Similarly, reviewers can export spreadsheets like Microsoft Excel to many statistical software programs such as SPSS to conduct more advanced analyses. One common advanced analysis that reviewers might consider conducting is meta-analysis, which, as defined in Chapter 2, represents the reviewer combining (i.e., aggregating) quantitative findings from as many available individual quantitative research studies as possible that address a set of related research hypotheses, with the goal of integrating the results. Conveniently, Microsoft Excel files can be imported to several meta-analysis software programs such as Comprehensive Meta-Analysis (CMA). In Chapter 8 and Chapter 9, we outline how to conduct meta-analyses and, in Chapter 9, we discuss several of these meta-analysis software programs.

LIMITATIONS OF USING SPREADSHEET PROGRAMS. As useful as spreadsheet programs are for storing and organizing information, and as superior as they are over the basic techniques of using index cards and word processing software programs, they contain one major limitation. Specifically, spreadsheet programs cannot actually store the works selected (i.e., Steps 2 and 4) of the CLR process within any worksheet file. That is, although reviewers can copy and paste information from digital files that are not copy protected for copyright purposes, they cannot store the whole work within a cell. However, as a next best operation, reviewers can insert a hyperlink (i.e., a word, phrase, picture, icon, symbol, or other element in a computer document or webpage on which a user may click to move to another part of the document or webpage or to open another document, webpage, or file) in a Microsoft Excel worksheet cell, specific chart components, or images.

WEB-BASED APPLICATIONS

Although considered an intermediate strategy, the use of *web-based applications* signifies an upgrade from merely using spreadsheets because reviewers are able to share the digital files that they use to store and to organize information. As such, compared to spreadsheets, the use of web-based applications is further along the continua of level of technology and level of collaboration.

The greatest appeal of these web-based applications is that often they are free to use, to an important degree. And we all like being able to use, a tool for free—correct? A highly popularized web-based (i.e., cloud-based computing) application that, to date, has been underutilized by reviewers is Google Drive. Broadly speaking, Google Drive represents a file storage and synchronization service that is hosted by Google. Because it was released on April 24, 2012

TOOL: CREATING A HYPERLINK

Box 6.2 presents the seven steps for creating a hyperlink to an existing file or webpage. Figure 6.13 presents a screenshot showing an example of a column that contains the *hyperlinks* to each work selected from the CLR search. The useful aspect of these hyperlinks is that if you click any of them, it will immediately open up the work. However, it should be noted that if you send (e.g., via email) your Microsoft Excel file that contains these hyperlinks to another person (e.g., co-reviewer), this person will be unable to activate these hyperlinks and open up the works unless the directory where these works have been saved uses some form of cloud storage. It is to this cloud storage that we now turn.

BOX 6.2

STEPS FOR CREATING A HYPERLINK TO AN EXISTING FILE OR WEBPAGE

1. On a worksheet, right click the cell or graphic where you want to create a hyperlink to any available electronic file (e.g., article, picture, website).
2. Click on Hyperlink.
3. Under Link to, click Existing File or Web Page.
4. Perform one of the following actions:

   o To enter the name and location of a known file or webpage to which you want to link, type that information in the **Address** box.

   o To locate a webpage, click **Browse the Web,** open the webpage to which you want to link, and then switch back to Excel without closing your browser. Or, to use recently linked pages, click **Browsed Pages** and then click the web.

   o To select a file, click **Current Folder**, and then click the file (e.g., journal article saved on your hard drive) to which you want to link, or, to use recently used files, click **Recent Files**, and then click the file. You can change the current folder by selecting a different folder in the **Look in** list.

5. If you want to create a hyperlink to a specific location in the file or on the webpage, click **Bookmark**, and then double-click the bookmark that you want to use. The file or webpage that you are linking to must have a bookmark.
6. In the **Text to Display** box, type the text that you want to use to label the hyperlink.
7. To display useful information when you rest the pointer on the hyperlink, click **ScreenTip**, type the text that you want in the **ScreenTip** text box, and then click **OK**.

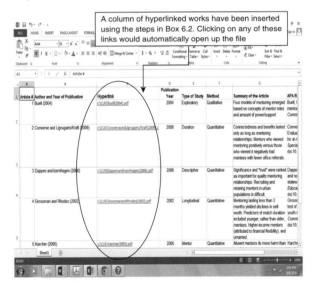

A column of hyperlinked works have been inserted using the steps in Box 6.2. Clicking on any of these links would automatically open up the file

Figure 6.13 Screenshot showing an example of a column that contains the hyperlinks to each work selected from the CLR search

(Mossberg, 2012), it is a relatively new service. Yet, in this short space of time, Google Drive already boasts more than 190 million monthly active users (Sambit Satpathy, 2014). Its popularity stems from the fact that it incorporates cloud storage, file sharing, and shared editing on documents (via Google Docs), spreadsheets (via Google Sheets), presentations (via Google Slides), and other electronic formats. Also, files that are shared publicly on Google Drive can be searched via web search engines. Google Drive users are offered an initial 5 GB of free online storage space and have to pay for more storage space.

GOOGLE DOCS. In a previous section on the use of word processing software programs, we outlined how programs like Microsoft Word can be used to store and to organize information. Well, if you were interested in using a word processing software program to store and to organize information in a collaborative, cloud-based computing manner, then Google Docs (www.google.com/enterprise/apps/business/products/docs/) could be used. In particular, Google Docs is a free, web-based word processing software program that is integrated with Google Drive, which allows multiple reviewers to share documents in real time by simultaneously creating, opening, and editing documents online. More specifically, reviewers are able to see character-by-character changes made by other reviewers as they unfold via a visible reviewer-specific color/cursor. Unfortunately, reviewers cannot receive notification of any changes made; however, Google Docs can notify reviewers when another reviewer makes or replies to a comment via a sidebar chat option. Another weakness of Google Docs is that it cannot highlight editing changes made by a particular reviewer in real time during a writing session; also, reviewers cannot jump straight to the editing changes made. However, reviewers can see the additions made to a document, with each reviewer distinguished by color, although, inconveniently, the entire document must be manually examined to locate these changes. Also, it should be noted that the revision history application only displays one edit at a time.

Documents created with Google Docs can be imported through the web interface or sent via email. Importantly, documents created via Google Docs can be saved to a reviewer's computer (i.e., hard drive or removable/rewritable storage device [e.g., USB flash drive]) using a variety of formats (e.g., pdf, RTF, text, HTML). These documents also are automatically saved to Google Drive. Each time the Microsoft Office Word document is saved, the online copy is automatically updated. Microsoft Office Word documents can be viewed and edited offline and synchronized later when online. Conveniently, while being saved to Google Drive, a revision history is automatically retained so that previous edits can be viewed. Documents can be labeled and archived to enhance organization of information.

Google Docs has a basic find-and-replace tool. Further, Google Docs provides a web-based clipboard tool that allows reviewers to copy and to paste information (e.g., text, images) among Google documents, spreadsheets, presentations, and drawings. This web-based clipboard also can be used to copy and to paste information among different computers. Information that is copied is stored on Google's servers for up to 30 days. Although Google Docs is not as comprehensive as is Microsoft Word, its simplicity makes it potentially appealing for many reviewers.

EXAMPLE: USE OF GOOGLE DOCS

Figure 6.14 presents a screenshot that shows part of a page of the literature review of the Dyadic Mentoring Study as a Google Docs file. You can see that Google Docs is similar to word processing software programs inasmuch as it includes the following tabs: *File, Edit, View, Insert, Format, Tools, Tables, Add-ons,* and *Help.*

GOOGLE SHEETS. In a previous section on the use of spreadsheets, we outlined how programs like Microsoft Excel can be used to store and to organize information. Well, if you were interested in using a spreadsheet to store and to organize information in a collaborative, cloud-based computing manner, then Google Sheets could be used. In particular, Google Sheets is a free, web-based spreadsheet that is integrated with Google Drive, which allows multiple reviewers to share documents in real time by simultaneously creating, opening, and editing documents online.

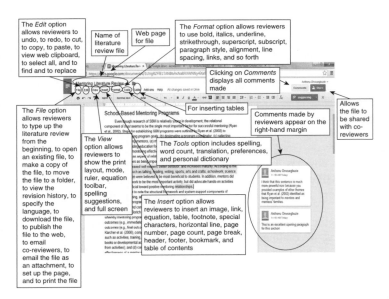

The *Edit* option allows reviewers to undo, to redo, to cut, to copy, to paste, to view web clipboard, to select all, and to find and to replace

Name of literature review file

Web page for file

The *Format* option allows reviewers to use bold, italics, underline, strikethrough, superscript, subscript, paragraph style, alignment, line spacing, links, and so forth

Clicking on *Comments* displays all comments made

The *File* option allows reviewers to type up the literature review from the beginning, to open an existing file, to make a copy of the file, to move the file to a folder, to view the revision history, to specify the language, to download the file, to publish the file to the web, to email co-reviewers, to email the file as an attachment, to set up the page, and to print the file

The *View* option allows reviewers to show the print layout, mode, ruler, equation toolbar, spelling suggestions, and full screen

For inserting tables

Comments made by reviewers appear on the right-hand margin

Allows the file to be shared with co-reviewers

The *Tools* option includes spelling, word count, translation, preferences, and personal dictionary

The *Insert* option allows reviewers to insert an image, link, equation, table, footnote, special characters, horizontal line, page number, page count, page break, header, footer, bookmark, and table of contents

Figure 6.14 Screenshot showing part of a page of the literature review in the Dyadic Mentoring Study as a Google Docs file

EXAMPLE: A SUMMARY TABLE IN MICROSOFT EXCEL

Figure 6.15 presents a screenshot showing a partial summary table of the Dyadic Mentoring Study literature review stored as a Google Sheets file. This file was created by uploading the Dyadic Mentoring Study's Microsoft Excel file that we presented earlier (see, for e.g., Figure 6.2). Consequently, you can see that Google offers an extension for Google Chrome Office editing for Google Sheets (and Google Docs) that enables reviewers to view and to edit Microsoft Excel (and Microsoft Word) on Google Chrome, via the Sheets (and Docs) apps. Further, Microsoft Office files that are available on the web (e.g., via web sites, email attachments) can be opened without having to download them.

From Figure 6.15, you can see that Google Sheets is similar to word processing software programs inasmuch as it includes the following tabs: *File*, *Edit*, *View*, *Insert*, *Format*, *Data*, *Tools*, *Add-ons*, and *Help*. These tabs are similar to the tabs provided by **Google Docs**, except that Google Sheets has a *Data* tab instead of a *Tables* tab. The *Data* tab allows reviewers to sort the Google worksheet by any column (either from A to Z or from Z to A); to specify the sort range; to filter data; to pivot table report; and to validate data (e.g., by providing the cell range, which would lead to invalid data being

identified). Conveniently, reviewers can use Google Drive on their mobile devices. For example, the Safari browser on iPhones and iPads allows reviewers to view documents and spreadsheets and to create and to edit Google Docs documents and spreadsheets. Most other mobile devices can be used to view and to edit Google Docs documents and spreadsheets via a mobile browser. These mobile apps also allow reviewers to work offline.

DROPBOX. Another tool that can be used to store and to organize information is Dropbox (circa 2008), which is a file hosting service that provides reviewers with cloud storage, file synchronization, personal cloud, and software. Owned and operated by Dropbox, Inc., whose headquarters are in San Francisco, California, Dropbox enables reviewers to create a file folder on each of their computers (i.e., both desktops and laptops/notebooks). Dropbox subsequently synchronizes each file so that they all show the same folder with identical contents regardless of the computer that the reviewer uses to view it. All files that are contained in this folder can be accessed via both the Internet and mobile phone applications. Dropbox provides software for several companies such as Microsoft Windows, Mac OS X, Android, Linux, iOS, BackBerry OS, and various web browsers.

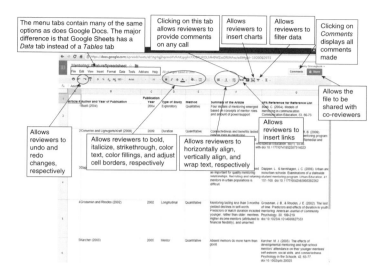

Figure 6.15   Screenshot showing a partial summary table of the literature review in the Dyadic Mentoring Study stored as a Google Sheets file

Conveniently, reviewers can *drop* (i.e., upload) any file into a desired folder. Also, reviewers can upload files manually via the Dropbox web feature. This file then is automatically uploaded to Dropbox's cloud-based service and made available to any of the reviewer's other computers and devices for which the Dropbox software has been installed, as well as to any other person whom the reviewer provides access to the Dropbox folder. Further, other people with access to the reviewer's Dropbox folder automatically are notified of any changes made to the Dropbox folder (e.g., addition or deletion of one or more files) via a real-time message that is displayed on their computers.

EXAMPLE: USE OF DROPBOX FOLDERS

Figure 6.16 presents a screenshot that shows the Dropbox folder for the Dyadic Mentoring Study. The most appealing feature of Dropbox is its synchronization and sharing of files among users. In addition, Dropbox contains a revision history application, with files that have been deleted from the Dropbox folder being able

to be recovered from any of the synced computers or devices. Also, multiple users can edit and re-post files without overwriting versions. The version history is kept for 30 days; however, reviewers can pay for the version history to be kept indefinitely. Dropbox users are offered an initial 2 GB of free online storage space. If more storage space is needed, then users would have to pay for it. Also, reviewers can gain extra free storage space by completing tasks such as sharing folders with other reviewers and inviting other people to join Dropbox. In any case, 2 GB of online storage space will allow reviewers to store and to organize information from several CLRs!

INTERNET-BASED SOCIAL BOOKMARKING SERVICES

The use of Internet-based social bookmarking services, which, per se, we consider to represent an intermediate strategy, signifies an upgrade from using both spreadsheets and web-based applications. Indeed, compared to spreadsheets and web-based applications, the use of Internet-based social bookmarking services is further along the continua of level of technology and level of collaboration. In general, an Internet-based social ***bookmarking service*** is a centralized web-based service that enables reviewers to add, to annotate, to edit,

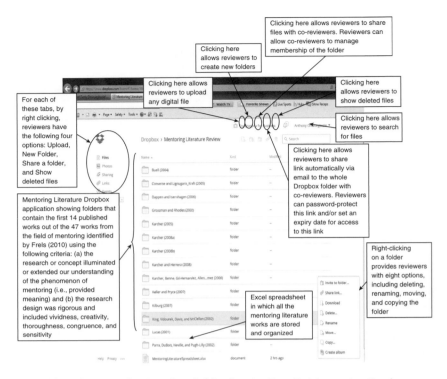

Figure 6.16   Screenshot showing the Dropbox folder for the Dyadic Mentoring Study

TOOL: COMPARISON CHART BETWEEN GOOGLE DRIVE AND DROPBOX

You might be asking: both Google Drive and Dropbox are useful tools to use to store and to organize information, as well as to share information, so which one should I use? Well, to help you decide which application to use to store and to organize information extracted from your CLR, we have provided Table 6.3, which presents a comparison of Google Drive and Dropbox. When you get the chance—hopefully sooner rather than later—experiment with both of these applications and see which one best suits your CLR needs.

Table 6.3   Comparison between Google Drive and Dropbox

Google Drive	Dropbox
Primarily is a web-based document editing and file storage system	Primarily is a synchronization program
Excels when used as a document editing and storage application; allows for simultaneous online editing of documents by users within a group; documents can be locked from further editing by the administrator	Excels when used as a synchronization application

Google Drive	Dropbox
Particularly useful for storing a few files for a long period of time and having the ability to download them at a later date	Particularly useful for updating files regularly and have the changes reproduced throughout each device
Does not allow for sharing via the desktop client	Allows file sharing directly through the desktop application via a link or by creating a shared folder with other reviewers; users within the same shared folder group can see everything placed in the folder by another user
Cannot automatically upload new files and synchronize changes unless all the files are documents that are being edited from the Google Docs website, which is not realistic for CLRs, which contain numerous non-Google Docs (e.g., published works as pdf files)	Can upload individual files from the Dropbox website
Contains a powerful search tool that performs highly specified searches of file names and text, as well as using optical character recognition to search images for context	Does not contain a powerful search tool
Provides 15 GB of free storage space	Provides 2 GB of free storage space
Only non-Google Docs files (e.g., images, videos) count toward the 15 GB limit	Every file that is uploaded to the Dropbox account counts towards the 2 GB limit
Does not offer any additional free storage space	Offers additional free storage space to reviewers who complete tasks such as referring friends to Dropbox
Online document editing is available	Online document editing is not available; files have to be downloaded to a computer before editing
Does not support file sharing through its desktop version	Supports file sharing through its desktop version
Provides version history to allow modifications to be reversed, selective folder syncing to manage content, events tracking, and customized sharing permissions	Provides version history to allow modifications to be reversed, selective folder syncing to manage content, events tracking, and customized sharing permissions

and to share bookmarks of web-based documents. For example, this tool can be used to build a community of experts and fellow reviewers from the field of mentoring who can share, annotate, discuss, and critique works (e.g., journal articles, books, book chapters, videos, photographs, websites) representing this area. In particular, these mentoring community members can co-organize their bookmarks (i.e., *tagging*) and co-construct vocabularies (i.e., *folksonomies*). In Chapter 8, we present several of the most popular Internet-based social bookmarking services.

Similarly, reviewers can use Internet-based social networking website services for academics and research. A popular free social networking website

service is ResearchGate (http://www.researchgate.net/) (circa 2008), which is a website for scientists and researchers to share works and to ask and to answer questions. ResearchGate contains many of the features that can be found among social network sites, including user profiles that are used to identify other users who share similar research interests. Reviewers can use ResearchGate to *follow* individual researchers/authors or even a research topic such as mentoring. Also, they can use the blogging tool to write (short) reviews of a work(s) or a researcher(s)/author(s). Reviewers can post questions that automatically are sent to researchers/authors who have declared on their user profile that they have expertise in that area, who subsequently are given a score that leads to a ranking of their scientific reputation. Also, reviewers can use private chat rooms where they can share data with other reviewers, and edit and discuss these shared documents. (Of course, reviewers should never upload works to the ResearchGate website that infringe the copyright of the publisher.) With more than 10,000 users registering every day and adding to its network of 4.5 million researchers (Taylor, 2014), ResearchGate is fast becoming what we call a *Facebook for reviewers*!

Another potentially useful social networking website for reviewers is Academia.edu (circa 2008). In particular, Academia.edu is a website that reviewers can use to track the works of researchers/authors who they follow. At the time of writing, more than 13 million researchers/academics are registered with Academia.edu, contributing more than 3 million works and 1 million research interests, attracting more than 15 million unique visitors each month.

EXAMPLE: USE OF SOCIAL NETWORKING

Figure 6.17 presents a screenshot of the Academia.edu social networking website.

ADVANCED STRATEGIES FOR STORING/ ORGANIZING INFORMATION

The use of reference management software programs, which we consider to represent an advanced strategy, signifies an upgrade from using spreadsheets, web-based applications, and Internet-based social bookmarking services—all of which represent an intermediate level for storing and organizing information. Indeed, compared to these intermediate strategies, the use of reference management software programs is further along the continua of level of complexity and level of technology. Broadly speaking, a *reference management software program* (circa 1984) is used to store and to organize scholarly works. In general, these software packages contain a database wherein full bibliographic references can be recorded. Further, with many of these reference management software programs, reviewers can use a web browser to search and to download references directly into their own programs. Also, they include a mechanism for generating many of the most common reference formats (e.g., American Psychological Association's *Publication Manual*, *The Chicago Manual of Style*, Modern Language Association's *MLA Handbook*) so that reference lists can be compiled automatically by the reference management software program in a manner that complies with the requirements of many publishers of scholarly works.

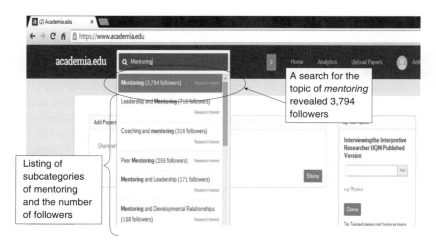

Figure 6.17 Screenshot showing the Academia.edu social networking website

Most of the reference management software programs can be integrated with word processing software programs. When this occurs, a reference list in the appropriate format will be produced automatically as the work (e.g., article, chapter) is being written (although reference management software programs do not produce 100% error-free reference lists and, thus, always should be double-checked for correct formatting; Onwuegbuzie, Hwang, Frels, & Slate, 2011), thereby minimizing the chance that a citation made in the body of the work is not presented in full in the reference list (i.e., bibliography), an error that is called a *citation error*. We discuss more about citation errors in Chapter 11. In addition, most reference management software programs enable reviewers to search references from online libraries.

Reference management software programs also can import summary information about published works directly from bibliographic databases. Unlike a ***bibliographic database***, which contains a list of all (or nearly all) works published with the field(s) or discipline(s) characterized by the database (e.g., the PsycINFO database that contains works representing the field of psychology), reference management software programs represent the reviewer's personal selection of relevant works published in a particular discipline or across disciplines. This reviewer's selection of published works, then, is a much smaller subset of the database(s) from which the works were selected—small enough to be accommodated easily on the reviewer's personal computer! The most appealing aspect of reference management software programs is that once a citation has been recorded, it can be used as many times as is needed to generate future reference lists.

TOOL: LIST OF SOURCE REFERENCE MANAGEMENT PROGRAMS

Currently, there are numerous reference management software programs available. Table 6.4 presents 31 commercial and freeware/open source reference management software programs listed in chronological order at the time of writing. You can see that references management software programs have a little more than 30-year history, with *Reference Manager* being the first of its kind, coming to the fore in 1982. A unique feature of Reference Manager is that reviewers can specify whether other reviewers are allowed to make edits to the database.

Table 6.4 Commercial and freeware/open source reference management software programs listed in chronological order

Name of Reference Management Software Program (Operating System)	Internet Address	Year of Initial Release	Major Citation Style
Commercial			
Reference Manager (Windows)	http://www.refman.com/	1984	APA/Chicago/ Turabian/ Harvard/MLA
EndNote (Windows; Mac OS X)	http://endnote.com/	1988	APA/Chicago/ Turabian/ Harvard/MLA

(Continued)

(Continued)

Name of Reference Management Software Program (Operating System)	Internet Address	Year of Initial Release	Major Citation Style
Bookends (Mac OS X)	http://www.sonnysoftware.com/bookends/bookends.html	1988	APA/Chicago/Turabian/Harvard/MLA
Biblioscape (Windows)	http://www.biblioscape.com/	1997	APA/Chicago/Turabian/Harvard/MLA
RefWorks (web-based, OS-independent)	http://www.proquest.com/products-services/refworks.html	2001	APA/Chicago/Turabian/Harvard/MLA
RefDB (cross-platform)	http://refdb.sourceforge.net/	2001	APA/Chicago/Turabian/Harvard/MLA
Sente (Mac OS X)	http://www.thirdstreetsoftware.com/site/Sente.html	2004	APA/Chicago/Turabian/Harvard/MLA
Citavi (Windows)	http://www.citavi.com/	2006	APA/Chicago/Turabian/Harvard/MLA
Papers (Windows; Mac)	http://www.papersapp.com/	2007	APA/Chicago/Turabian/Harvard/MLA
WizFolio (cross-platform)	http://wizfolio.com/	2008	APA/Chicago/Turabian/Harvard/MLA
SciRef (Windows)	http://sci-progs.com/	2012	APA/Chicago/Turabian/Harvard/MLA
Paperpile (cross-platform)	https://paperpile.com/	2013	APA/Chicago/Turabian/Harvard/MLA
Free and Open Source Software			
Pybliographer (Linux)	http://www.pybliographer.org/	1998	APA
BibDesk (Mac OS X)	http://bibdesk.sourceforge.net/	2002	APA
JabRef (cross-platform)	http://jabref.sourceforge.net/	2003	APA/Chicago/Turabian/Harvard/MLA

Name of Reference Management Software Program (Operating System)	Internet Address	Year of Initial Release	Major Citation Style
refbase (cross-platform)	http://www.refbase.net/index.php/Web_Reference_Database	2003	APA/Chicago/Turabian/Harvard/MLA
Bibus (Windows; Mac OS X)	http://bibus-biblio.sourceforge.net/wiki/index.php/Main_Page	2004	APA
CiteULike (centrally hosted website)	http://www.citeulike.org/	2004	APA/Chicago/Turabian/Harvard/MLA
Wikindx (portable)	http://wikindx.sourceforge.net/	2004	APA/Chicago/Turabian/Harvard/MLA
Algaion (cross-platform)	http://sourceforge.net/projects/aigaion/	2005	APA/Chicago/Turabian/Harvard/MLA
BibBase (centrally hosted website)	http://bibbase.org/	2005	APA
KBibTeX (cross-platform)	http://home.gna.org/kbibtex/	2005	APA/Chicago/Turabian/Harvard/MLA
BibSonomy (centrally hosted website)	http://www.bibsonomy.org/	2006	APA/Harvard
Zotero (Windows; Mac OS X; Linus)	https://www.zotero.org/	2006	APA/Chicago/Turabian/Harvard/MLA
Bebop	http://people.alari.ch/derino/Software/Bebop/index.php	2007	None
Mendeley (free up to 2 GB; cross-platform)	http://www.mendeley.com/	2008	APA/Chicago/Turabian/Harvard/MLA
Referencer (Linux)	https://launchpad.net/referencer/	2008	Unclear
Docear (cross-platform)	http://www.docear.org/	2009	APA/Chicago/Turabian/Harvard/MLA
Qiqqa (Windows; Android)	http://www.qiqqa.com/	2010	APA/Chicago/Turabian/Harvard/MLA
colwiz (free up to 3 GB; Windows; Mac OS X; Linus)	http://www.colwiz.com/	2011	APA/Chicago/Turabian/Harvard/MLA
ReadCube (Windows; Mac OS; IOS)	https://www.readcube.com/	2011	APA/Chicago/Turabian/Harvard/MLA

COMMERCIAL REFERENCE MANAGEMENT SOFTWARE PROGRAM: ENDNOTE. Of the purely commercial reference management software programs, EndNote—representing the second-earliest program—has been one of the most popularized. EndNote clusters citations into *libraries*. Reviewers can add a reference to a library via one of the following ways: manually, importing, exporting, copying from another EndNote library, and connecting from EndNote. When using EndNote, reviewers have available a window that contains a dropdown menu to select the type of reference that they require (e.g., journal article, book, newspaper article, film). Also, reviewers can select both general (e.g., author, publication year, title) and specific (e.g., ISBN, abstract) fields.

EXAMPLE: USE OF ENDNOTE FOR CITATIONS

Figure 6.18 presents a screenshot that shows EndNote X7 installed onto Microsoft Word 2013. Because of its popularity, many bibliographic databases allow reviewers to export references directly to their EndNote libraries. This saves reviewers time by enabling them to select multiple citations from these databases without having manually to type the citation information and abstract. (This time saved means time gained with respect to your social life!) However, what is extremely useful about EndNote is that right from within EndNote, reviewers can search hundreds of online resources to add references and pdf files. Reviewers also can build their EndNote libraries by importing pdf files that already reside on their computers or a portable data storage device such as a USB flash drive. In this way, EndNote can organize these pdf files. Further, reviewers can import one or more pdf files at a time, or they can let EndNote automatically upload any new files added. Additionally, it is easy for reviewers to rename pdf files during the importation process. EndNote also searches bibliographic databases to which reviewers subscribe (e.g., through their university libraries) and free full-text works that are available online, and then automatically downloads and attaches the pdf files to their EndNote libraries. Another useful feature is that reviewers can annotate their pdf files to help them find references later. More specifically, reviewers can save a single document, Excel spreadsheet, image, or other digital file type to each reference in an EndNote library. Furthermore, reviewers can sync their references across platforms to gain access to their attachments.

EndNote automatically locates and updates information, which means that you do not have to spend countless hours searching through individual records—again helping to improve your social life! Another set of social-life-enhancing features is the targeted and advanced search

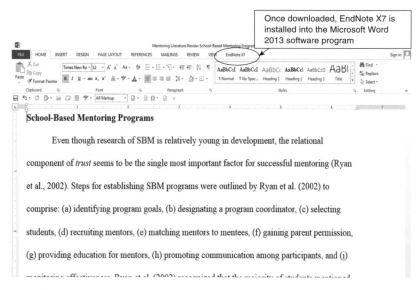

Figure 6.18 Screenshot showing EndNote X7 installed onto Microsoft Word 2013

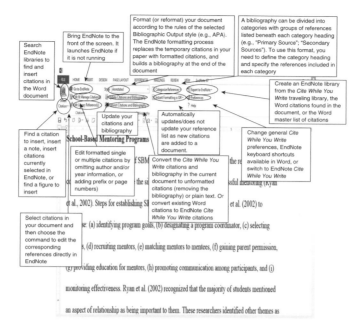

Figure 6.19 Screenshot showing the options available in EndNote X7

capabilities that allow reviewers to search through their entire libraries in seconds, including their pdf files and annotations, as well as to locate specific references or groups of references. Most usefully for the numerous authors who are not adept at compiling reference lists manually (Onwuegbuzie & Hwang, 2012, 2013; Onwuegbuzie, Hwang, Combs, & Slate, 2012; Onwuegbuzie, Hwang, et al., 2011), EndNote can automatically format the citation into numerous bibliographic output styles (e.g., APA, Chicago, Turabian, Harvard/MLA). Figure 6.19 presents a screenshot showing the options available in EndNote X7.

PARTLY FREE REFERENCE MANAGEMENT SOFTWARE PROGRAM: MENDELEY. For those of you who cannot or do not want to invest in a purely commercial reference management software program, you might consider using one of the 19 partially or fully free reference management software programs in Table 6.4 or another such program. One partially or fully free reference management software program that we recommend is Mendeley. Interested? (We were very interested when this tool was first brought to our attention.) Well, *Mendeley* is a desktop and web program for storing and organizing works, identifying the most current works, and

collaborating with other reviewers online. That is, Mendeley combines Mendeley Desktop—a pdf and reference management software programs that is available for Windows, OS X, and Linux—with Mendeley Web, which is an online social networking website service for reviewers and researchers. Mendeley requires reviewers to store all basic citation data on its servers.

EXAMPLE: USE OF MENDELEY TO STORE AND ORGANIZE

Like EndNote, Mendeley enables reviewers to store and to organize references and pdf files, to automatically extract metadata from pdf files, to annotate pdf files, to import references from online sources, to insert citations in Microsoft Word, to create a bibliography automatically, to import/export to and from other reference management software programs, to share references with other reviewers, to conduct a full-text search across all works in the database, to tag pdf files, to rename pdf files, and to provide readership statistics about authors and works. Figures 6.20–6.25 provide six screenshots pertaining to Mendeley.

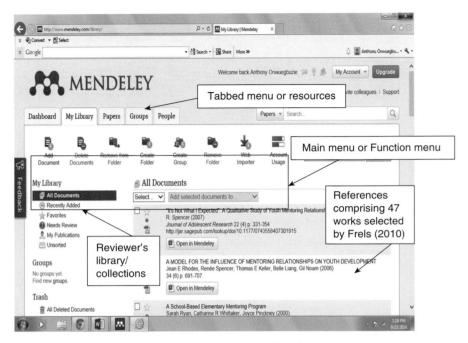

Figure 6.20 Screenshot showing the web version of Mendeley that reviewers can use to store and to organize online works that they extract from their CLRs

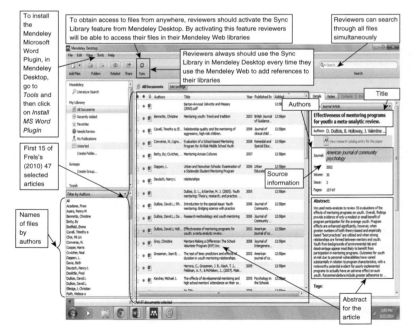

Figure 6.21 Screenshot showing the desktop version of Mendeley that reviewers can use to store and to organize online works that they extract from their CLRs

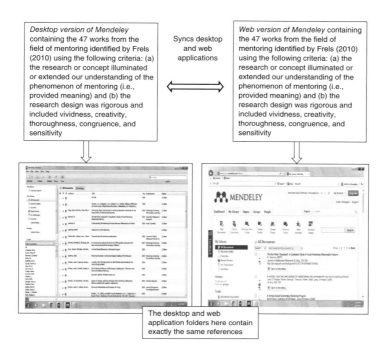

Desktop version of Mendeley containing the 47 works from the field of mentoring identified by Frels (2010) using the following criteria: (a) the research or concept illuminated or extended our understanding of the phenomenon of mentoring (i.e., provided meaning) and (b) the research design was rigorous and included vividness, creativity, thoroughness, congruence, and sensitivity

Syncs desktop and web applications

Web version of Mendeley containing the 47 works from the field of mentoring identified by Frels (2010) using the following criteria: (a) the research or concept illuminated or extended our understanding of the phenomenon of mentoring (i.e., provided meaning) and (b) the research design was rigorous and included vividness, creativity, thoroughness, congruence, and sensitivity

The desktop and web application folders here contain exactly the same references

Figure 6.22   Screenshot showing how Mendeley synchronizes files in both desktop and web applications

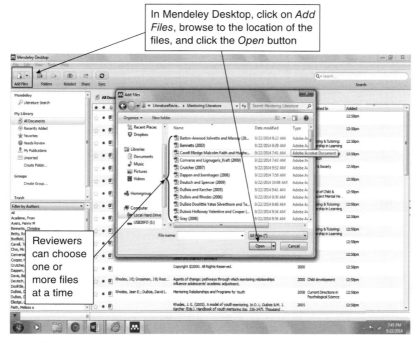

In Mendeley Desktop, click on *Add Files*, browse to the location of the files, and click the *Open* button

Reviewers can choose one or more files at a time

Figure 6.23   Screenshot showing how to store CLR information by adding files within the desktop application

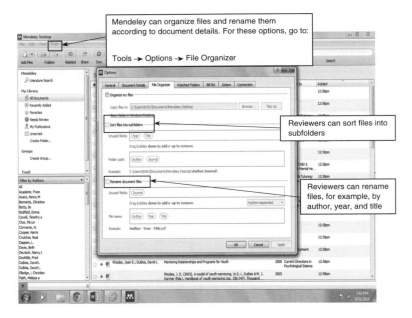

Figure 6.24　Screenshot showing how to organize CLR files

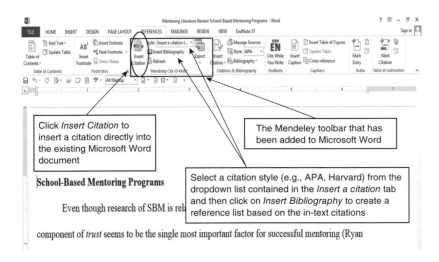

Figure 6.25　Screenshot showing Mendeley installed onto Microsoft Word 2013

A very useful feature of Mendeley is that there are free iPhone and iPad apps that are associated with it. However, the nicest aspect of Mendeley is that it provides reviewers with 2 GB of free web storage space. All you have to do to obtain this free space is to register at the Mendeley website (http://www.mendeley.com).

COMPUTER-ASSISTED QUALITATIVE DATA ANALYSIS SOFTWARE

The use of computer-assisted *qualitative data analysis software (CAQDAS)* programs—considered an advanced strategy—signifies an upgrade from using reference management software programs because not

TOOL: LIST OF CAQDAS POTENTIAL PROGRAMS

Table 6.5 provides a comprehensive—although not exhaustive—list of commercial and freeware/open source CAQDAS programs. Whereas most of these CAQDAS programs are purely qualitative software, a few of them (e.g., QDA Miner, WordStat, MAXQDA, Dedoose) represent mixed methods software wherein qualitative data (e.g., text, images) can be analyzed qualitatively *and* quantitatively within the same software program, thereby making them also a computer-assisted mixed methods data analysis software (CAMMDAS) program. Of these CAMMDAS programs, we particularly recommend QDA Miner for storing and organizing CLR information.

Table 6.5 Commercial and freeware/open source computer-assisted qualitative data analysis software programs listed in chronological order

Name of CAQDAS Program (Operating System)	Internet Address	Year of Initial Release
Commercial Software		
HyperRESEARCH (Windows; Mac OS)	http://www.researchware.com/	1991
ATLAS.ti (Windows; Mac OS)	http://www.atlasti.com/index.html	1993
f4analyse (Windows; Mac OS; Linux)	http://www.audiotranskription.de/english/f4-analyse	
MAXQDA (Windows; Mac OS)	http://www.maxqda.com/	1995
WordStat (Windows)	http://provalisresearch.com/	1998
NVivo (Windows; Mac OS)	http://www.qsrinternational.com/products_nvivo.aspx	1999
Transana (Windows; Mac OS)	http://www.transana.org/	2001
QDA Miner (Windows)	http://provalisresearch.com/	2004
XSight (Windows)	http://www.qsrinternational.com/products_xsight.aspx/	2006
Dedoose (Windows; Mac; Linux)	http://www.dedoose.com/	2009
Qiqqa (Windows; Android)	http://www.qiqqa.com/	2010
QCAmap (web browser)	http://www.qcamap.org/	

(Continued)

(Continued)

Name of CAQDAS Program (Operating System)	Internet Address	Year of Initial Release
webQDA (web browser)	https://www.webqda.com/	
Qualrus (Windows; Mac OS; Linux)	http://www.qualrus.com/	
Free and Open Source Software		
Aquad (Windows)	http://www.aquad.de/en/	1987
ELAN (Java-based for Windows; Mac OS; Linux)	https://tla.mpi.nl/tools/tla-tools/elan/	2002
Coding Analysis Toolkit (web-based)	http://cat.ucsur.pitt.edu/	2008
RQDA (Windows; Mac OS; Linux)	http://rqda.r-forge.r-project.org/	2008
Compendium (Java-based)	http://compendium.open.ac.uk/institute/	2009
FreeQDA (Java-based)	https://github.com/produnis/FreeQDA/downloads	2012
QDA Miner Lite (Windows)	http://provalisresearch.com/	2012
TAMS Analyzer (open source; Mac OS)	http://tamsys.sourceforge.net/	2002

only do they allow reviewers to store and to organize information but also they facilitate the formal analysis of this information. Thus, compared to reference management software programs, the use of CAQDAS is further along the continuum of level of technology.

EXAMPLE: USING CAQDAS FOR STORING, CODING, AND ANALYZING

QDA MINER. QDA Miner is an outstanding tool for storing, organizing, and analyzing CLR information. Figure 6.26 presents three screenshots that show how to create a new CLR project in QDA Miner that contains 47 works selected for the literature review of the Dyadic Mentoring Study. Once all the works extracted from the CLR process have been imported into QDA Miner (see Figure 6.27), any or all documents can be edited, coded,

and annotated manually, allowing reviewers to conduct one or more sets of qualitative analysis, quantitative analysis, and/or mixed analysis by ignoring irrelevant information and focusing on relevant information. For example, by coding the method section of each empirical research article in the set, reviewers could ascertain the evolution of research methods (e.g., quantitative vs. qualitative vs. mixed research) over time or compare research methods used by different authors.

As another example, by manually tagging the sections of each work (e.g., author, title, abstract, reference section), reviewers can conduct what is known as scientometrics and bibliometrics, which are analytical approaches in which the CLR information itself is subjected to an analysis (Péladeau, 2014). Scientometrics and bibliometrics may involve the assessment of the scientific contribution of authors or specific works (Péladeau, 2014). A particular appealing aspect of CAQDAS programs like QDA

Miner is that they allow the importation of CLR information extracted via all five MODES (i.e., Step 5 of the CLR process) that we discuss in Chapter 8. This includes the importation of media (e.g., audio, visual) and secondary data (e.g., saved as Excel files), as well as from interviews that reviewers conduct on experts. Another useful feature about using a program like QDA Miner is that it can be used as an (oral) presentation tool. We discuss the formal oral presentation of CLR reports in Chapter 10.

So, we suspect that many of you are thinking: I cannot wait to try out a CAQDAS or CAMMDAS program. Well, the good news is that many of these CAQDAS/CAMMDAS programs allow reviewers to download and to use a full free version for a period of 30 days or so. And we have even better news for you. If you cannot afford to purchase a copy of QDA Miner, we are sure that you will be pleased to know that Provalis Research, the developer of QDA Miner, recently has

developed a companion software program to QDA Miner, namely, QDA Miner Lite, that you can use to store and to organize CLR information. Because it is free, you will not be able to utilize some of the more advanced operations—especially those operations that pertain to analyzing information. However, QDA Miner Lite provides basic operations such as importing data from plain text, RTF, HTML, pdf, Excel, Microsoft Access, CSV, and tab-delimited text files.

EXAMPLE: CREATING A NEW FILE IN QDA MINER

Reviewers even can use QDA Miner Lite to import data from other CAQDAS programs such as ATLAS.ti, Hyper-RESEARCH, and Transana (see Table 6.5), as well as from

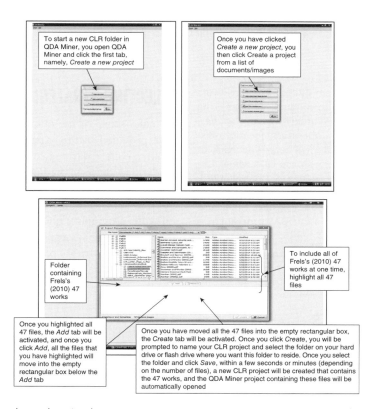

Figure 6.26 Screenshots showing how to create a new CLR project in QDA Miner that contains the Dyadic Mentoring Study's 47 works

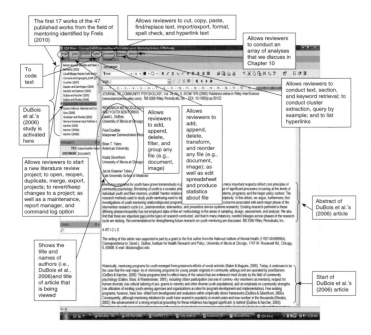

The first 17 works of the 47 published works from the field of mentoring identified by Frels (2010)

Allows reviewers to cut, copy, paste, find/replace text, import/export, format, spell check, and hyperlink text

Allows reviewers to conduct an array of analyses that we discuss in Chapter 10

To code text

Allows reviewers to conduct text, section, and keyword retrieval; to conduct cluster extraction, query by example; and to list hyperlinks

DuBois et al.'s (2006) study is activated here

Allows reviewers to add, append, delete, filter, and group any file (e.g., document, image)

Allows reviewers to add, append, delete, transform, and reorder any file (e.g., document, image); as well as edit spreadsheet and produce statistics about file

Allows reviewers to start a new literature review project; to open, reopen, duplicate, merge, export, projects; to revert/keep changes to a project; as well as a maintenance, report manager, and command log option

Abstract of DuBois et al.'s (2006) article

Shows the title and names of authors (i.e., DuBois et al., 2006)and title of article that is being viewed

Start of DuBois et al.'s (2006) article

Figure 6.27 Screenshot showing QDA Miner being used to store and to organize 47 works from the Dyadic Mentoring Study

Reference Information System (RIS) files. Reviewers also can use QDA Miner Lite to conduct searches using Boolean (i.e., *and, or, not*) and proximity (i.e., *includes, enclosed, near, before, after*) operators (for more discussion on Boolean operators, we refer you back to Chapter 5). Further, reviewers can use QDA Miner Lite to export tables that they create to XLS, tab-delimited, and CSV formats, as well as to export graphs to JPEG, BMP, PNG, and WMF formats. So, you have no excuse for not (at least) playing with a CAQDAS program as a CLR tool!

SELECTING STRATEGIES

To make sense of the numerous strategies that we have provided in this chapter, we presented them within a coherent framework. Specifically, first, we subdivided these strategies as a function of level of complexity; that is, we subdivided these strategies as representing basic (e.g., word processing software programs), intermediate (e.g., web-based applications), or advanced strategies (e.g., reference management software programs).

APPLYING CONCEPTS

Storing and organizing information—representing Step 3 in the CLR process—is a pivotal step in the process because without storing and organizing CLR information, analysis and synthesis cannot ensue. In this chapter, we have presented an array of strategies for storing and organizing CLR information that can be used by beginning, emergent, and experienced reviewers/researchers. These strategies range from using index cards to using CAQDAS/CAMMDAS programs.

TOOL: CATEGORIZING STRATEGIES FOR STORING AND ORGANIZING INFORMATION

You can see the aforementioned strategies for storing and organizing information in Figure 6.28. Second, we subdivided these strategies according to level of technology use. In Figure 6.28, these strategies not only increase in complexity level from top to bottom (i.e., across the level of complexity) but also from left to right (i.e., within each complexity level). Third, and finally, we subdivided these strategies as a function of their potential for promoting collaboration among reviewers/researchers. Again, in Figure 6.28, these strategies not only increase in collaboration level from top to bottom (i.e., across the level of complexity) but also from left to right (i.e., within each complexity level).

Also shown in Figure 6.28 are the steps of the CLR process that each strategy negotiates. You can see that all these strategies negotiate Step 2 (i.e., searching databases/documents) and Step 4 (i.e., selecting/ deselecting information). You can see too from Figure 6.28 that only two sets of strategies help reviewers to negotiate steps that go beyond Step 2 and Step 4. Specifically, Internet-based social bookmarking services also help reviewers to negotiate Step 5 fully, expanding the search to include one or more of the five MODES because these bookmarking services routinely are used to share works. Thus, any information extracted from the expanded search could be shared with others, as long as it does not violate any copyright laws or confidentiality agreements. Such information would include videos, audio, images, and secondary datasets saved as spreadsheets (e.g., Microsoft Excel).

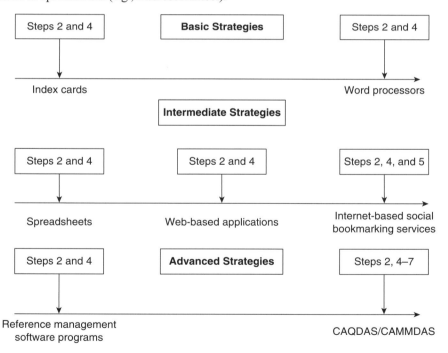

Figure 6.28 A typology for categorizing strategies for storing and organizing information extracted from the CLR process, and the steps that each strategy involves

TOOL: MODEL OF DIMENSIONS FOR STORING/ORGANIZING

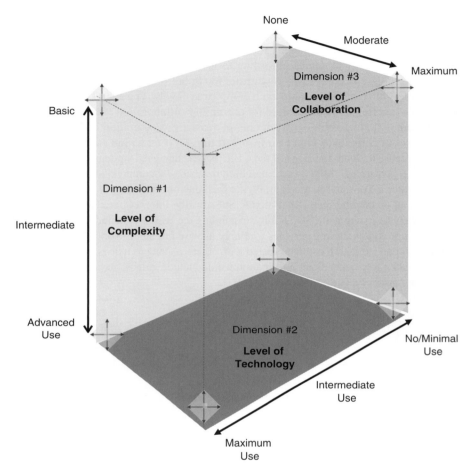

Figure 6.29 A three-dimensional model for categorizing strategies for storing and organizing information extracted from the CLR process[*]

[*] Diamond shapes represent eight possible combinations of the extreme points on the three dimensions of complexity, level of technology, and level of collaboration

CAQDAS/CAMMDAS programs are even more far-reaching because not only do they allow reviewers to store and to organize information extracted via the initial search (Step 2) and expanded search (i.e., Step 5), but also they allow reviewers to analyze and to synthesize the information, as well as even presenting the final report. Figure 6.29 presents our three-dimensional model for categorizing strategies for storing and organizing information extracted from the CLR process.

As can be seen from Figure 6.29, the model comprises the three aforementioned dimensions—levels of complexity (Dimension 1), technology (Dimension 2), and collaboration (Dimension 3)—with each dimension positioned at 90-degree angles to the other two. Using the model, any strategy used to store and to organize information extracted from any CLR can be positioned within the three-dimensional space as a way of indicating the multidimensional sophistication of the strategy used.

CONCLUSIONS

Interestingly, with the exception of reference management software programs, none of the tools presented in this chapter was designed originally to store and to organize CLR information. Yet, as we have demonstrated, their use has logical appeal, especially the higher up we go with respect to levels of complexity, technology, and/or collaboration. Currently, what we deem as representing the *gold standard* for storing and organizing literature is the use of CAMMDAS programs (e.g., QDA Miner) in a collaborative manner because they can play an important role in every step of the CLR process. However, we will leave it up to you to decide what strategy you will use to store and to organize CRL information. Whatever strategy you choose, we hope that you enjoy using it and that it helps you maximize the quality of your CLR. Remember that throughout the CLR process, you will come back to any system that you chose and make changes to some of the ways that you organized the sources collected.

These are some concepts in summary presented as a review for Step 3.

- Index cards may be used to document the information about a work, including author(s), year of publication, genre of work (e.g., book, book chapter, article), genre of narrative (e.g., empirical, conceptual, theoretical, methodological), genre of empirical report (e.g., quantitative research, qualitative research, mixed methods research), summary of content, major findings/conclusion, and full reference.
- Compared to index cards, the use of word processing software programs is further along the continua of level of technology and level of

collaboration, allowing reviewers electronically to edit, to format, to check spellings, to check grammar, to utilize a built-in thesaurus, to print, and to save, as well as to copy and paste text (and images) from a document extracted from a CLR search to a document that the reviewer creates via a word processing software program for the purpose of storing and organizing information.
- Spreadsheet programs allow reviewers electronically to store and to organize information extracted from a CLR. Of these spreadsheet programs, Microsoft Excel is the most commonly used (Power, 2004).
- Reviewers can use Microsoft Excel to create graphic representations (e.g., charts). For example, frequency counts and proportions/percentages can be transformed into bar charts or pie charts.
- Both Google Drive and Dropbox have a very important characteristic in common: each of them, effectively and at no additional financial cost, allows you to store your CLR files online in the cloud and to access them from any computer or mobile device from anywhere.
- A popular free social networking website service is ResearchGate (http://www.researchgate.net/) (circa 2008), which is a website for scientists and researchers to share works and to ask and to answer questions.
- When using EndNote, reviewers can select both general (e.g., author, publication year, title) and specific (e.g., ISBN, abstract) fields.
- The use of computer-assisted qualitative data analysis software (CAQDAS) programs—considered an advanced strategy—signifies an upgrade from using reference management software programs

because not only do they allow reviewers to store and to organize information but also they facilitate the formal analysis of this information.

- The use of computer-assisted qualitative data analysis software (CAMMDAS) programs (e.g., QDA Miner) in a collaborative manner represents the gold standard for storing and organizing literature because it can play an important role in every step of the CLR process.

CHAPTER 6 EVALUATION CHECKLIST

CORE	Guiding Questions and Tasks
Critical Examination	Which type of storage unit appears to be most functional? If a type of software represents acquiring new information in order to learn more about it, how confident are you that you will take a risk and try?
Organization	To what extent did you organize your information in the process? How did you name and/or organize files for easiest retrieval?
	Now that you have initiated a process for identifying "selected sources," consider different types of flowcharts and ways that your journey might be documented.
Reflections	What surprises you as most helpful to organize and to create your own system for finding information?
	Think about your collection of works. If you were to give them identity—both to the author and to the participants in the study—what cultural pieces might be missing? Note some of the surprises or wonderings that you have about this question so that you might address it in the limitations of your report.
Evaluation	What new ideas do you have as a result of storing documents? What computer technology help might benefit your growth in this area?

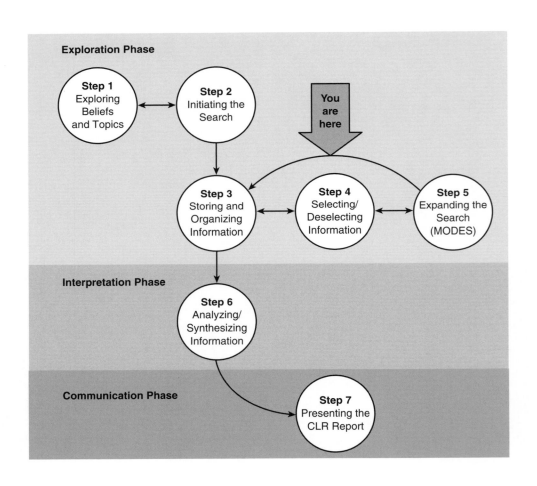

7

STEP 4: SELECTING/ DESELECTING INFORMATION

CHAPTER 7 ROADMAP

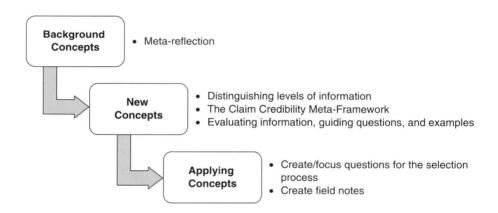

BACKGROUND CONCEPTS

Much like qualitative inquiry, the analysis process of the CLR begins the moment that a researcher initiates questions or wonderings related to phenomena. For example, a qualitative interview question focuses on words that are spoken by a participant, which oftentimes results in new questions. Therefore, qualitative researchers often remark that the analysis phase of a study begins at the point of data collection. Likewise, when a reviewer embarks on the selecting/deselecting process, analysis of sources is inevitable, due to the nature of examining, categorizing, and evaluating. First, a reviewer begins to sift through the initially stored documents and categories with the intention of selecting a sample of works to analyze and to synthesize. This process involves the focused, intentional act of categorizing information, critiquing the usefulness of information, and developing the foundation for establishing new evidence on the selected topic. The sorting and intentional efforts of selecting/deselecting represent a quality, or qualitative, *initial analysis* that might be regarded as an implicit or embedded type of analysis.

The Exploration Phase of the CLR process (i.e., Steps 1 through 5), at the very heart, is a direct result of the identity of the reviewer (as original thinker, critical thinker, and reflexive person), philosophical and topic beliefs, ethical awareness, and culturally progressive practices. These attributes and cultural awareness facilitate *how much weight t*o place on information based on the source itself (e.g., via its credibility, reliability, reputation) and the information extracted from the source—based on the goal of your literature review—which later helps you determine how each piece of information is positioned in the CLR. For example, one article might resonate with many aspects of what a reviewer wants to know and, further, the reviewer might also find that the context of this article, or where the research took place, sheds light on implications for the audience that he/she is seeking to address. Therefore, it is important that the selecting/deselecting process itself is warranted and transparent. Just because an information source offers some support for resulting ideas, the source should not automatically be selected; rather, the source should be subjected to the same scrutiny that other sources undergo. By keeping the end picture in mind, the final CLR report will be based on sound argument, trusted and credible sources, and well-thought-out consequences and implications.

META-REFLECTION

The essence of maintaining ethical and transparent practices entails reflection, organization, and documentation—a process that we call **meta-reflection**. This way, when another reviewer evaluates the CLR finished product, it will withstand the evaluative selection process for future researchers. All the way through the selection/deselection process, field notes should be taken about the sources, ideas associated with the sources, and any limitations associated with the sources for the audit trail. As always, the reviewer should provide sufficient detail such that he/she can retrace the steps at a much later point in time. Such an audit trail will be extremely helpful to the reviewer not only in the current CLR, but also in future CLRs that he/she conducts in the same research area. Also, an audit trail will be vital when the CLR involves more than one reviewer, as is often the case

when CLRs inform research studies that contain multiple researchers. And the use of multiple researchers in research studies is very common, occurring more than two-thirds of the time (Onwuegbuzie, 2014f). These criteria involve assessing claims made in the collection of sources. Step 4: Selecting/Deselecting involves establishing a set of criteria for choosing to use a source. It also integrates the ethics that we described in Chapter 2: non-maleficence (i.e., not causing harm); beneficence (i.e., providing benefit to others); justice (i.e., making decisions that are impartial, warranted, fair, and equitable); fidelity (i.e., involving loyalty, faithfulness, and fulfilling commitment); professional competence (i.e., recognizing limits of skills and knowledge); integrity (i.e., being respectful and honest); scholarly responsibility (i.e., knowing reporting standards); and respecting rights, dignity, and diversity (i.e., not misrepresenting others' scholarship). To this end, selecting/deselecting involves critical thinking and reflexive practices for assessing *worthiness* of information. These guidelines provide a pathway for meta-reflection, helping a reviewer decide whether to include or to exclude information based on claims reported by the author(s) (i.e., whether or not the claims are credible and salient to a topic)—inclusive of information sources that provide alternative explanations and/or multiple perspectives.

NEW CONCEPTS

Before scrutinizing information, it is helpful to view the initial search of databases as representing a *sample*, which is a set of cases (e.g., participants), selected from a *population*, or the larger set of sources. In the CLR, sampling is subject to judgment and, therefore, represents a *purposive sample*, identified by the topic-focused questions and other distinguishing criteria. As such, the reviewer defines the criteria and/or attributes for inclusion in the sample, which we term *Evaluation Criteria*, which are pre-established standards of rigor based on sound research practices. These practices and Evaluation Criteria are explained in detail in parts of this section, with additional resources provided in Appendix B of the book.

DISTINGUISHING LEVELS OF INFORMATION

The selecting/deselecting information step (much like other steps) represents an ongoing process because, as can be seen from the Seven-Step Model representation at the beginning of this chapter, information obtained via MODES (Step 5) should be sorted, categorized, and stored (Step 3), and subjected to the selection/deselection process (Step 4). Some of the evaluation process will occur without even knowing it. If you consider the CLR as a research study that stands alone or informs primary research, the information sources must be credible.

Therefore, each reviewer should create his/her own Evaluation Criteria with respect to a topic area, based on (a) the goal for the CLR and (b) the problem statement and focus questions created in the initial search (Step 2). These criteria guide the selection of the CLR. Next, for each source, a reviewer needs to be able to distinguish whether the source is to be trusted based on three areas: the Evaluation Criteria will evolve in that each source provides (a) sound argument, (b) evidence, and (c) consequences.

TOOL: FLOWCHART FOR SAMPLING

Figure 7.1 provides a preview for Step 4, which can lead to three major categories: (a) selected information that is categorized and stored for foundational and supplemental use; (b) deselected information that is stored and organized for *possible* use; and (c) deselected information that is not usable.

The major differences among the three categories is that the first category contains information sources that are considered "must-use sources" due to providing some type of meaningful information. The second category contains information sources that are considered "possibly needed sources" such that a reviewer would not need to reinvent the wheel by re-identifying this information in future database searches should this discarded information turn out to be pertinent. The final category includes the information sources that (a) present irrelevant information for your topic, (b) are of no use for either the

(Continued)

foundational or supplemental component of your own CLR report, (c) contain some type of apparently flawed claim or reasoning, (d) contain a major flaw in the research process (e.g., sampling-based flaw such as the study involving too small a sample size for its findings to be generalizable; instruments-based flaw such as the quantitative instrument used lacking sufficient score reliability or score validity), and/or a flaw in the interpretations (e.g., lacking validity/credibility of evidence).

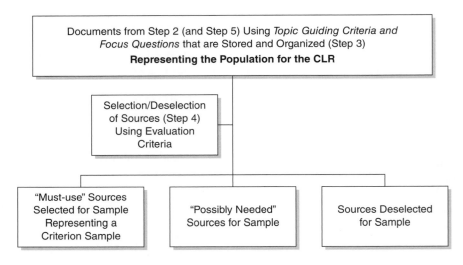

Figure 7.1   Initial organizational framework for the purposeful sample

EXAMPLE: VISUAL DISPLAY OF THE AUDIT TRAIL

Keep in mind that the same ideas used in the initial search and organization of sources become the Evaluation Criteria for a topic. Figure 7.2 provides one way of tracking the selecting/deselecting of sources based on the guiding criteria and focus questions created in Step 2 and expanded to serve as Evaluation Criteria in Step 4. This example from the Dyadic Mentoring Study also demonstrates the concept of the audit trail and the tracking of the initial search to the sample of sources used for data analysis/synthesis. By examining the figure, you might also discover how the search was extended and how the steps involved in the exploratory phase of the CLR work in an iterative fashion to inform each other.

FOUNDATIONAL AND SUPPLEMENTAL INFORMATION SOURCES

A reviewer in Step 4 is similar to a juror who has to decide *what evidence to select and what evidence to deselect* in making a determination of the guilt or non-guilt of the defendant, who might be a person, group, or organization against whom a claim or charge is being brought in court. One consideration for the juror would be *how much weight to place* on each selected piece of evidence. In the sorting process, it is likely that you gravitated toward an article that explains some important methodological concept, or a theoretical concept either relating to your topic or providing some background to establish your topic—in which case, it would be suitable as a supplemental source. However, it might not be suitable to be selected as a foundational source because it does not address directly the topic area for

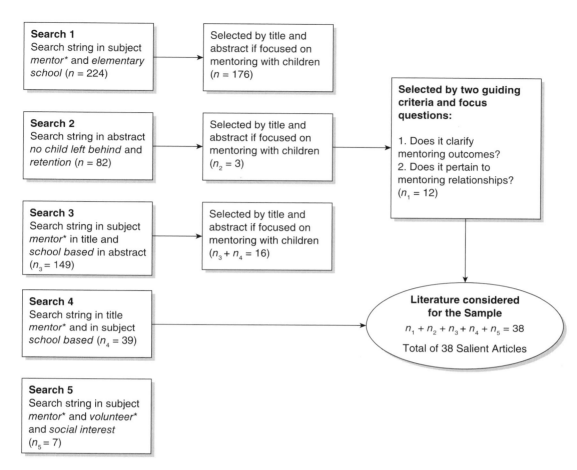

Figure 7.2 The audit trail and use of Evaluation Criteria for the sample in the Dyadic Mentoring Study

your CLR. Conversely, if a source reveals some ideas and/or findings that are directly relevant to your topic, then it would be selected as a foundational source. At this point, it is helpful to regard the CLR as a research study itself, and if it is to inform primary research, the CLR is a type of study embedded within a study.

ASSESSING SOURCES BASED ON CLAIMS

Understanding how sources are used is the first area to consider in the Evaluation Criteria. Communicating in the world of academe and scholarly writing is dependent upon the ability to **establish claim**. That is, a statement spoken or written is backed up by a justification, or reference. However, and discussed in more detail in the communication phase of the CLR, the premise for the claim must be solid. For this reason, the end product of your own CLR is dependent upon distinguishing each claim as being reputable, valid, credible, and legitimate—regardless of whether the claim is liked or disliked by the reviewer. By evaluating claims that lead to argument, you will be forming some initial impressions, which will lead to hunches and/or analysis questions that will be addressed in the interpretation phase of the CLR, namely, Step 6: Analyzing/Synthesizing Information.

At this point, you might be asking yourself: How do I determine which information sources are credible and/or pertinent based on claims? Consider the overall point for collecting information sources—to

TOOL: THE 12 COMPONENTS OF A PRIMARY RESEARCH REPORT

Figure 7.3 depicts 12 components of a report and how sources selected (the sample) are sorted into supplemental sources that inform any of the components of the CLR as a stand-alone study or extended to inform primary research. Both the foundational sources and supplemental sources are used separately in Step 6: Analyzing/Synthesizing Information. Also, referring back to Figure 7.1, the efforts for finding some "likely" sources will result in further organization of files that was initiated in Step 3. Taking some time to recognize the content of potential sources for use in the CLR is a critical component of Step 4. Therefore, the next sections provide further background to understand the selecting/deselecting process based on the claims made by the authors of each source.

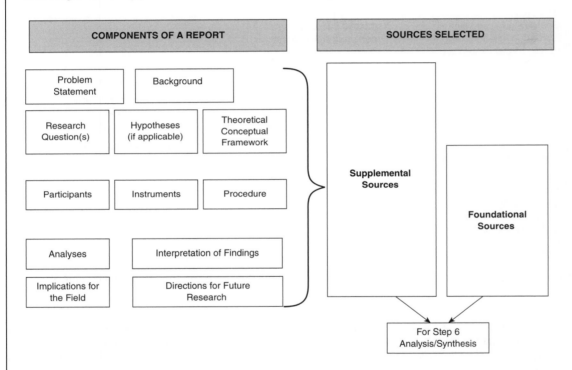

Figure 7.3 The 12 components of a report informed by supplemental and foundational sources to inform components of a report

establish one or more ideas, or claims, and to build some type of case for these claims. In fact, as you sort the information sources, you should evaluate the type of claim within each information source and how the claim was established, and you should evaluate the information for the claims that you anticipate making by collecting that source. Hart (2005) identified the following five types of claims

established for communicating ideas: (a) claims of fact, (b) claims of value, (c) claims of policy, (d) claims of concept, and (e) claims of interpretation.

Claims of fact are statements that can be demonstrated as being either true or false by confirmation or refutation, respectively. For example, a researcher might claim that the concept of mentor originated from Greek mythology, which can be verified or refuted using an authoritative source such as an encyclopedia. The difference between a claim based on facts and other forms of claim is that other claims necessitate additional evidence for enhanced credibility.

Conversely, *claims of value* are subjective judgments about the worth of something. As such, value claims cannot be demonstrated as being true or false. For example, an author might claim that mentoring is valuable for both mentees (e.g., students) and mentors to express themselves. To assess the credibility of such claims, the reviewer might assess the extent to which the claimant provided an adequate justification for his/her value claim. *Claims of policy* are normative statements about what *ought to be* undertaken rather than what *is* undertaken. For example, a researcher might claim that some form of a mentoring program should be required in secondary schools to increase achievement levels among low-achieving students. This type of statement can be much like claims of value and can launch a conversation about the pros and cons for such policy.

Claims of concept concern distinguished definitions and the way someone uses language or any particular term. For example, how a mentor defines *mentoring* likely would affect this person's style of mentoring. For a mentor who believes that her/his role is to provide explicit encouragement to mentees, the term mentor could be synonymous with the word encourager. In contrast, a mentor who believes that her/his role is to provide activities and to teach skills might regard the term mentor as representing a type of role model. Each claim of concept is based on specific definitions that are limiting, due to the specific nature of the experience, and, therefore, result in an emotional response. As described by Hart (2005), the use of words does not stem from dictionary definitions, but rather represents the interpretation of the user. Likewise, *claims of interpretation* represent assertions and can be in the form of assumptions, ideas, beliefs, propositions, theories, schemas, models, hypotheses, or the like. A claim of interpretation delineates the intended meaning attached to some reality or evidence. Reality and evidence necessitate interpretations, and interpretations can differ among individuals or groups.

In addition to Hart's (2005) list of claims, an often-overlooked but important type of claim used by authors of empirical research studies is a claim that we have identified as resulting from observation. *Claims of observation* are statements that emerge from empirical research studies, that are situated within the set of findings, and that address some of the same research questions. Unless a finding stems from population data, it cannot be demonstrated as being either true or false but rather as providing support or refutation for a knowledge claim. A reviewer then can assess the credibility of an observation claim partly by situating the set of findings underlying the observation claim within the set of extant findings addressing the same research question(s). By so doing, the reviewer can determine the extent to which the observation claim represents a preponderance of the evidence or lack thereof. Similar to other claims, claims based on observation differ from claims based on facts because, unlike claims based on facts, claims of observations necessitate additional evidence for enhanced credibility.

DETERMINING PRIMARY CLAIMS FROM SECONDARY CLAIMS

Virtually every piece of information extracted from Step 2: Initiating the Search, as well as Step 5: Expanding the Search, can be identified as representing one or more of these six claims. Before a reviewer can select or deselect an information source, she/he needs to determine the purpose and direction for the claim(s) and how claims might build on each other. Therefore, claims can be either primary or secondary in nature. *Primary claims* (i.e., primary source) are claims made directly by the author of the source (e.g., article, book, book chapter)—for example, based on the author's own primary research study. In contrast, *secondary claims* (i.e., secondary source) are claims contained in a source that are not made directly by the author of the source, but are inferred by the person (i.e., original owner of the claim) whom the author of the source is citing. This person might be a researcher, theorist, methodologist, or a reviewer.

EXAMPLE: WRITING A CLAIM

Looking at some practical examples of some claims that you might identify in your sample information helps, and after some practice with purposeful reading, validating claims becomes easier. First, it is critical that when reading a report, decide who the original owner of the claim is. Also, if the author of an information source makes a statement such as "According to Santos (2010)...," then this author is being ***non-factive***, which means that the author is being non-committal inasmuch as he/she is not expressing an opinion regarding the claim being made by Santos (2010). On the other hand, if the author of an information source uses a phrase such as "As theorized by Kapernick (2012)," then this author is being ***factive*** in that the author is making it clear that he/she agrees with the claim made by Kapernick (2012). Here, the claim made is shared between the author of the information source and Kapernick (2012) (whom the author is citing). Conversely, if the author of an information source makes a phrase such as "The defunct theory of Williams (2013)," then this author is being ***counter-factive***, in that the author is making it clear that he/she disagrees with the claim made by Williams (2013). In this case, the author of the information source is making a ***counter-claim***, which represents the opposing view of the claim made by Williams (2013), and if the author of the information source provides citations for this counter-claim, then he/she is sharing ownership of this counter-claim with those being cited. We discuss more about the stance and voice of authors in Chapter 11 for helping you in writing your own CLR.

EXAMPLE: OVERVIEW OF TYPES OF CLAIMS

To understand better the scrutiny process for evaluating claims, we provide an extract from the Dyadic Mentoring Study and types of claims in Figure 7.4. Each of these claims is established on information that is deemed as believable and credible in the selection/deselection process.

After viewing this figure, consider a time that someone told you something that you did not believe, such as "elephants can fly." If this person utilized any one or more types of claims (e.g., claim of fact, claim of observation), and if one of the claims were to lack credibility, you likely would dismiss the idea completely. Likewise, in the example from the Dyadic Mentoring Study provided in Figure 7.4, if any one of the referenced information sources used in this example lacked credibility, then the ideas might be discarded completely—based on unreliable information. On the other hand, if the claims made by the author are examined without identifying any false or unbelievable statements of claim, you might trust her/his ideas and retain her/his information for your own literature review. In fact, if a great deal of weight is placed on one or more ideas within a source, then this source would be sorted into the

foundational sources folder with other collected works that would be analyzed/synthesized in Step 6 of the CLR process.

ASSESSING SOURCES BASED ON ARGUMENT

Once you have perused your information sources and the importance of claims, it is important to take a pause and to examine the credibility of your claims that you might plan for your own argument(s) in the CLR. In short, each selected source of information has resonated with you and can provide you with a path of argumentation. It is helpful in your selection process to become familiar with Toulmin's (1958) model of argumentation, whereby for each claim, you identify (a) ***evidence*** to support the claim; (b) ***warrant*** that links the claim and its evidence; and (c) ***backing***, which comprises the context and assumptions used to provide justification for the warrant and evidence.

As a reviewer evaluates each information source, the use of Hart's (2005) guiding questions can facilitate assessment of claims such as: Is this source claim justified? What about the evidence, warrant, and backing? Are they all justified as well? Do all of these elements justify the claim in this source in its entirety and verbatim, or do any of the claims from this source need to be modified in some way in light of other sources? What evidence am I extracting and is there warrant and/or backing for this evidence? The use of the elements of claim, evidence, warrant, and backing for building argument are the underlying foundation that you, as the reviewer, should establish as a natural reasoning process (i.e., path of argumentation).

EXAMPLE: INCORPORATING ARGUMENT

Figure 7.5 illustrates an example of how to incorporate Toulmin's (1958) model of argumentation. We present this figure as an illustration of how sources should be selected carefully and with intention. For instance, if you want to present the claim that mentoring programs should be implemented in U.S. elementary schools—which represents both a claim of policy and a claim of value—then the onus would be on you to present your own claim based on credible information sources. In the figure, the call for mentoring programs in U.S. schools is supported by the information established

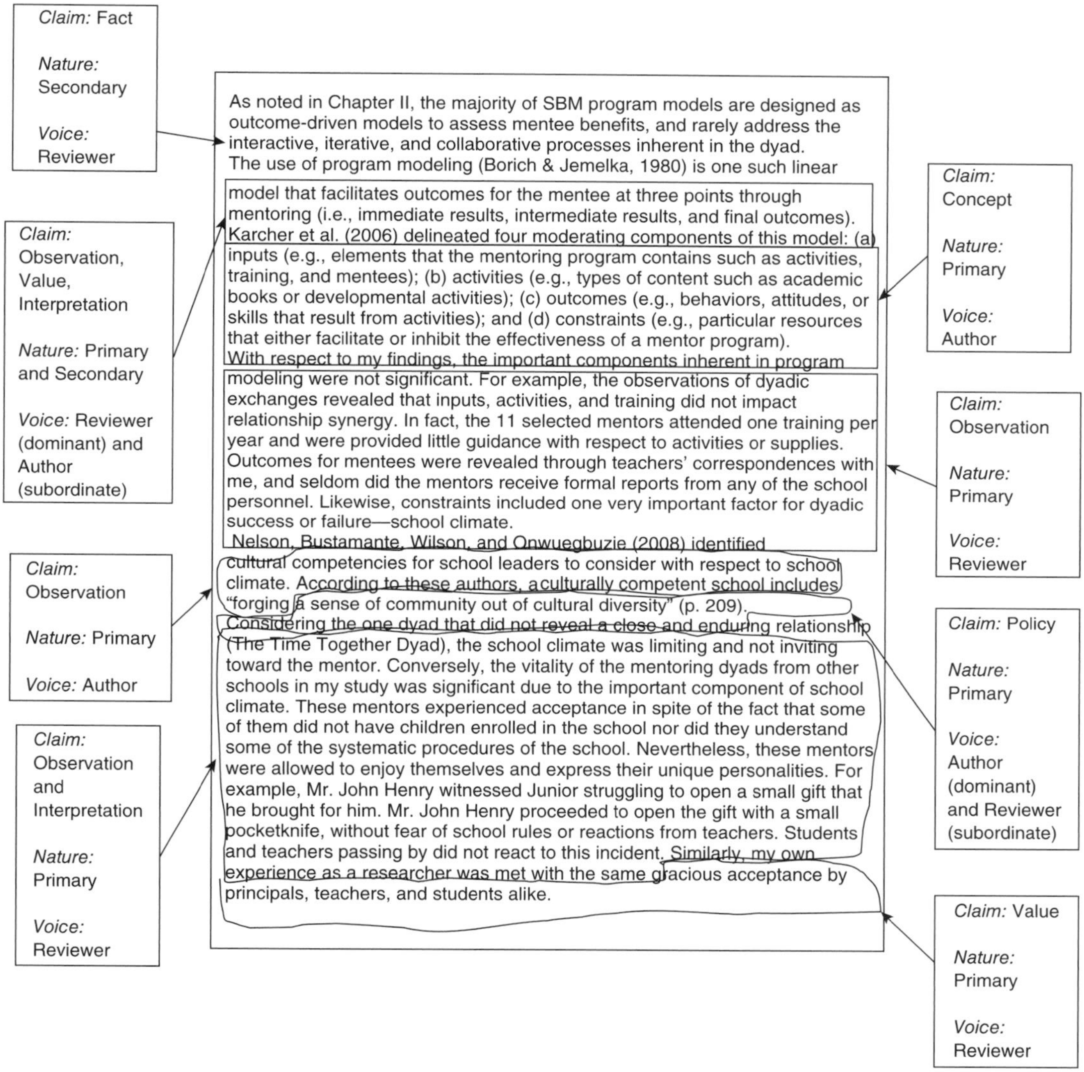
Claim: Fact
Nature: Secondary
Voice: Reviewer
Claim: Observation, Value, Interpretation
Nature: Primary and Secondary
Voice: Reviewer (dominant) and Author (subordinate)
Claim: Observation
Nature: Primary
Voice: Author
Claim: Observation and Interpretation
Nature: Primary
Voice: Reviewer
As noted in Chapter II, the majority of SBM program models are designed as outcome-driven models to assess mentee benefits, and rarely address the interactive, iterative, and collaborative processes inherent in the dyad.
The use of program modeling (Borich & Jemelka, 1980) is one such linear model that facilitates outcomes for the mentee at three points through mentoring (i.e., immediate results, intermediate results, and final outcomes).
Karcher et al. (2006) delineated four moderating components of this model: (a) inputs (e.g., elements that the mentoring program contains such as activities, training, and mentees); (b) activities (e.g., types of content such as academic books or developmental activities); (c) outcomes (e.g., behaviors, attitudes, or skills that result from activities); and (d) constraints (e.g., particular resources that either facilitate or inhibit the effectiveness of a mentor program).
With respect to my findings, the important components inherent in program modeling were not significant. For example, the observations of dyadic exchanges revealed that inputs, activities, and training did not impact relationship synergy. In fact, the 11 selected mentors attended one training per year and were provided little guidance with respect to activities or supplies. Outcomes for mentees were revealed through teachers' correspondences with me, and seldom did the mentors receive formal reports from any of the school personnel. Likewise, constraints included one very important factor for dyadic success or failure—school climate.
Nelson, Bustamante, Wilson, and Onwuegbuzie (2008) identified cultural competencies for school leaders to consider with respect to school climate. According to these authors, a culturally competent school includes "forging a sense of community out of cultural diversity" (p. 209).
Considering the one dyad that did not reveal a close and enduring relationship (The Time Together Dyad), the school climate was limiting and not inviting toward the mentor. Conversely, the vitality of the mentoring dyads from other schools in my study was significant due to the important component of school climate. These mentors experienced acceptance in spite of the fact that some of them did not have children enrolled in the school nor did they understand some of the systematic procedures of the school. Nevertheless, these mentors were allowed to enjoy themselves and express their unique personalities. For example, Mr. John Henry witnessed Junior struggling to open a small gift that he brought for him. Mr. John Henry proceeded to open the gift with a small pocketknife, without fear of school rules or reactions from teachers. Students and teachers passing by did not react to this incident. Similarly, my own experience as a researcher was met with the same gracious acceptance by principals, teachers, and students alike.
Claim: Concept
Nature: Primary
Voice: Author
Claim: Observation
Nature: Primary
Voice: Reviewer
Claim: Policy
Nature: Primary
Voice: Author (dominant) and Reviewer (subordinate)
Claim: Value
Nature: Primary
Voice: Reviewer

Figure 7.4 An extract from the Dyadic Mentoring Study showing all six claims

by King, Vidourek, Davis, and McClellan (2002) via their position that mentoring programs have been associated with increased levels of school connectedness, as well as self-esteem and academic achievement, among elementary school students. In this example, the link between the claim and evidence is established, namely, that "school connectedness is a powerful protective factor for students considered at risk for dropping out of school due to substance abuse, emotional distress, and deviant behavior" (Frels, 2010, p. 1).

Further, in this example, the backing (i.e., context and assumptions) is established using an information source, namely, Search Institute (2009b), which supports the argument that students excel developmentally to a greater extent when they are connected to an adult role model other than a parent. Importantly, Search Institute was deemed a credible source because it is a leading organization that "studies and works to strengthen the developmental relationships that help young people acquire the developmental assets that are reinforced by developmental committees where young people's success is everyone's top priority" (Search Institute, 2009a, ¶ 1).

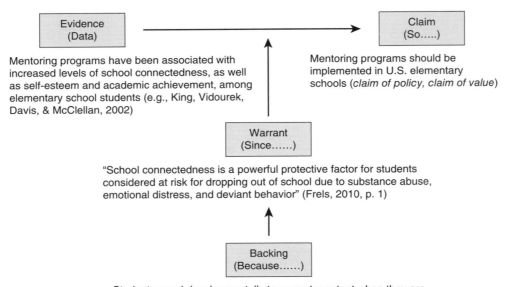

Mentoring programs have been associated with increased levels of school connectedness, as well as self-esteem and academic achievement, among elementary school students (e.g., King, Vidourek, Davis, & McClellan, 2002)

Mentoring programs should be implemented in U.S. elementary schools (*claim of policy, claim of value*)

"School connectedness is a powerful protective factor for students considered at risk for dropping out of school due to substance abuse, emotional distress, and deviant behavior" (Frels, 2010, p. 1)

Students excel developmentally to a greater extent when they are connected to a role adult model other than a parent (Search Institute, 2009a)

Figure 7.5 Toulmin's (1958) structure of an argument

Adapted from *Doing a literature review: Releasing the social science research imagination*, by C. Hart, 2005, London, England, p. 89. Copyright 2005 by Sage Publications.

Figure 7.5 illustrates how an argument results from information sources and the claim is based on evidence, warrant, and backing. In this example, it appears that the claim that *mentoring programs should be implemented in U.S. elementary schools* represents a sound argument. If, for example, the claim had been made instead that mentoring programs should be implemented in elementary schools—that is, the country "U.S." is removed—then, unless evidence, warrant, and backing can be found that reach beyond the United States, the country "U.S." would need to be inserted into the claim. As such, using Toulmin's (1958) model of argumentation provides a very useful method not only for assessing claims made by authors but also for assessing claims that they themselves make in their literature review reports. Moreover, it shows that your own line of reasoning plays a role in the information sources that you select and the argument that you plan to establish.

ASSESSING SOURCES BASED ON AUTHENTICITY AND MERIT

Another component of the Evaluation Criteria is recognizing the path of argumentation for authenticity and merit. **Authenticity** pertains to the trustworthiness of the person (e.g., author, educator, politician) providing the information that underlies the element. In contrast, **merit** includes the knowledge and competence of the person providing the information that underlies the element, the unbiased nature of the person, the relevance of the information, and the credibility of the information. For instance, in the path of argumentation in Figure 7.5, use of the source Search (2009a)—with its more-than-50-year history (Search Institute, 2009b)—provided both authenticity and merit to the backing element.

Both authenticity and merit can be evaluated to a greater extent in the quest to select information sources for a literature review. As we noted at the onset of this chapter, the selection process for information sources is much like the process used by a member of a jury who is examining information presented in a court case, some of which might be based on empirical information, such as claims of evidence and claims of observations. Other information might be based on inferences informed by empirical information, such as claims of interpretation, claims of policy, and claims of concepts. Some claims might be based on more abstract associations, which involve claims of value. In any case, it is useful to be cognizant of the type of claims that you are making in your own literature review for establishing an argument.

THE CLAIM CREDIBILITY META-FRAMEWORK

Figure 7.6—which we call the *Claim Credibility Meta-Framework*—provides an overview of how your Evaluation Criteria might change based on claims and arguments contained in each source. It can be seen from this figure that two of the claims (i.e., claim of fact, claim of observation) represent empirical information; three of the claims (i.e., claim of interpretation, claim of policy, claim of concept) are optimally informed by empirical information, and three of the claims (i.e., claim of policy, claim of concept, claim of value) represent abstract information. For claims that either represent empirical information or are optimally informed by empirical information, it is helpful to review the differences among quantitative, qualitative, or a combination of both quantitative and qualitative (i.e., mixed research).

The next step in the Evaluation Criteria also is presented in this figure: to examine and to critique **legitimation**, which is a term that encapsulates validity

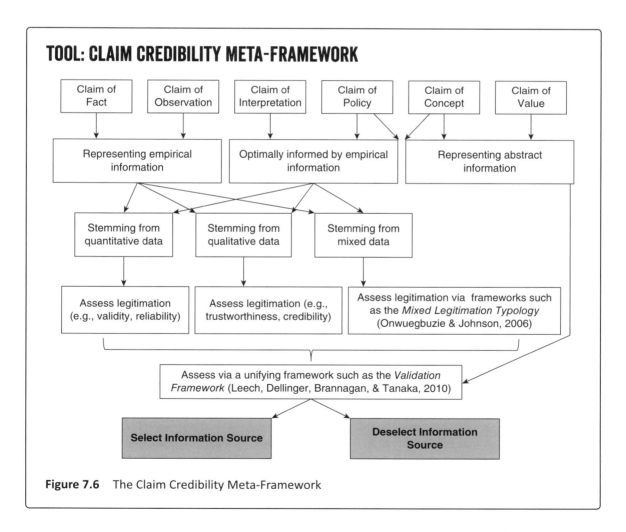

Figure 7.6 The Claim Credibility Meta-Framework

(in the quantitative research tradition) and credibility or trustworthiness (in the qualitative research tradition). Assessing sources based on legitimation is determining whether you have confidence that findings are in fact verifiable, warranted, and backed by evidence.

ASSESSING SOURCES BASED ON LEGITIMATION

After scrutinizing information underlying the claims and arguments made, it is easier to recognize whether the information sources are adequate for use. Next, in your systematic process, it is important to investigate each empirical research report to determine validity evidence (quantitative works), credibility evidence (qualitative works), and legitimation evidence (mixed research works)—or the extent to which the researcher(s) adequately addressed potential threats to the validity/credibility/legitimation of the findings. These items are in jeopardy, or *threat*, if the value in one or more areas of the research process (e.g., design, implementation, interpretation, dissemination) were compromised in some way. Threats include compromises to *validity*, or soundness of evidence (in quantitative research studies); *credibility*, or believability of evidence (in qualitative research studies); and *legitimation*, or trustworthiness of evidence (in mixed research studies). As you re-read and consider each empirical research report for your CLR, document the associated data or method: quantitative, qualitative, or mixed. Then, the legitimation of each research study should be evaluated so that you do not build your own claim with unreliable sources.

To this end, examine each quantitative research report, each qualitative research report, and each mixed research report with the intention of determining whether the researcher(s) used *rigorous research practices*. That is, you will need to determine the extent to which the research adheres to standards in the fields of social, behavioral, and health and beyond. If the researcher(s) do not report some of the important aspects associated with rigorous research practice, then it is apparent that the report is not transparent and, therefore, it might not be trusted. The following section reviews some best practices that should be addressed in the quantitative research studies that you have potentially selected. After examining each report using some of the best practices guidelines presented in the following sections, you might decide to select

the information, or to deselect the information. Or you might decide to select the information but note the reason for your hesitations, which are based on the threats to the validity/credibility/legitimation of the findings that you have identified.

SELECTING QUANTITATIVE RESEARCH

If the empirical information is quantitative, then there are several legitimation frameworks that can be used to assess the quality of the information and, hence, the claim(s) made by the authors of the study (i.e., claim of fact, claim of value, claim of policy, claim of concept, claim of interpretation, and/or claim of observation). When examining quantitative empirical research, it is important to determine how the author(s) of any study addressed the quality issues, which involve the internal validity and external validity of findings. Conceptualized by Campbell and Stanley (1963), *internal validity* can be defined as (a) "the ability to infer that a causal relationship exists between two variables" (Johnson & Christensen, 2010, p. 247). Further, internal validity is threatened or compromised when plausible rival explanations cannot be eradicated. Contrastingly, *external validity* is defined as "the extent to which the study results can be generalized to and across populations of persons, settings, times, outcomes, and treatment variations" (Johnson & Christensen, 2010, p. 585). It should be noted that high levels of one type of validity do not imply that the other type of validity also is high. For instance, even if a finding represents high internal validity, this characteristic does not necessarily imply that this finding has high external validity by being able to be generalized outside the study context.

Examining legitimation in quantitative research studies can be quite complex. As you begin to select potential empirical quantitative information sources, it is helpful to note the way in which legitimation was addressed by the researcher(s). For an overview of threats to external and internal validity, see Onwuegbuzie's (2003b) Quantitative Legitimation Model presented in Appendix B (also see the Meta-Validation Model of Onwuegbuzie, Daniel, & Collins, 2009). After examining the threats listed in Appendix B and how they can arise in various phases of the research process, consider the following scenario. If an author of a quantitative research study documented that mentoring programs increase school connectedness of elementary students, based on a very small sample size—say, a sample size of 10—then, even if this finding was high in internal validity (e.g., was generated via the use of an experimental research design such as a single-subject experimental design; see Appendix A), this sample size would pose a threat to generalizability via the external validity threat of *population validity*, which is the extent to which the author's finding can be generalized beyond the sample in his/her study to the population of elementary students. It also becomes problematic with respect to *ecological validity*, or the extent to which the author's finding can be generalized beyond the sample in his/her study to students in other schools in different locations (e.g., districts, cities, regions, and even countries). Therefore, either you would deselect this study—which is seriously flawed by the small sample size—or you would select the study, and after subjecting its findings to analysis and synthesis (i.e., Step 6), when presenting this finding in the CLR report (Step 7), you would ensure that this finding was adequately contextualized—for example, by noting the sample size limitation (e.g., "However, extreme caution should be exercised in generalizing these findings because of the small sample size…").

Similarly, in your examination of various quantitative information sources, you would deselect any seriously flawed study from your collection of works during the initial search (Step 2) or your expanded search (Step 5), based on whether the quantitative research findings are limited by important threats to internal validity and/or external validity. For quantitative research studies that involve the development or use of a (relatively) new quantitative instrument, it is helpful to understand how researchers validate an instrument. The following sections discuss three major types of validity (Onwuegbuzie, Daniel, et al., 2009): content-related validity, criterion-related validity, and construct-related validity. For more information about these three validity types, we refer you to the seminal works of Messick (1989, 1995).

Content-related validity is the extent to which the items on an instrument represent the content being measured. Evidence of content-related validity typically is not provided in numerical form; rather, this evidence is based on judgment, preferably by multiple experts who carefully, critically, and systematically examine the instrument to determine whether the content and objectives measured by the instrument items are adequately representative of those items that constitute the content domain.

EXAMPLE: EXAMINATION OF AN INSTRUMENT

An example of attending to content-related criteria can be seen in the Match Characteristics Questionnaire (MCQ), developed by Harris and Nakkula (2008), used in the Dyadic Mentoring Study. The MCQ, which measures match relationship quality, contains 62 items (15 subscales) that were developed for mentors of primary and secondary school students. Evidence of content-related validity of the MCQ could be gleaned by assessing the extent to which (a) every MCQ item appears to be relevant, important, and interesting to the respondents (i.e., face validity); (b) every MCQ item belongs in its respective subscale (i.e., item validity); and (c) the full set of MCQ items represents fully the total content area of match relationship quality (i.e., sampling validity). If in your own literature review, you were to discuss some of the Dyadic Mentoring Study's findings, you would look to determine whether some of the content-related criteria were described in the report.

Criterion-related validity, which necessitates the collection of logical and empirical evidence, is the extent to which scores on an instrument are related to an independent external/criterion variable that is believed to measure directly the underlying characteristic or behavior. Returning to our MCQ example, evidence of criterion-related validity of the MCQ could be obtained by assessing (a) the extent to which the MCQ scores are related to scores on another, already-established measure of match relationship quality that is available at the same point in time (i.e., *concurrent validity*); and (b) the extent to which MCQ scores are related to scores on another, already-established measure of match relationship quality administered in the future or to a measurement of some other criterion that is available at a future point in time (i.e., *predictive validity*). Again, when reviewing potential information sources that stem from the use of an instrument, you might be careful to note how the researcher(s) identified criterion-related validity.

Construct-related validity, which also necessitates the collection of logical and empirical evidence, is the extent to which an instrument can be interpreted as representing a meaningful measure of some characteristic or quality. Again, returning to our MCQ example, evidence of construct-related validity of the MCQ could be obtained by assessing how well the 15 MCQ subscales correspond to the construct domain of match relationship quality (i.e., structural validity), the meaning of scores and the intended and unintended consequences of using the MCQ (i.e., outcome validity), and the extent that meaning and use associated with a set of MCQ scores can be generalized to other populations (i.e., generalizability). If a researcher presents in a research report the use of an instrument, such as the MCQ, but does not describe the **psychometric properties** of the instrument appropriately—in this case, the construct-related validity—you might deselect that particular research report as an information source; or if you do select it, note for your own audience how this flaw limited your path of argumentation.

As you reflect upon each of your quantitative research information sources, decide the extent to which the authors described the instrument and psychometric properties (e.g., score reliability, score validity). Each quantitative research study selected at Step 2 and Step 5 that involves development or utilization of a (relatively) new instrument could be examined to determine whether the findings are limited or even invalidated by use of an instrument that lacks score validity (i.e., has low content-related, criterion-related, and/or construct-related validity). In either case, the reviewer would need to decide whether or not to deselect the study or information. If the study is still selected as part of the CLR report, remember that in your own report, you should point out the measurement limitations. An example of this would be: "Of the three selected quantitative information sources used to inform my literature review, the construct-related validity of one researcher's instrument is questionable because...". Also presented in Appendix B is a list of areas of validity and a description of each: content-related, criterion-related, and construct-related validity based on Onwuegbuzie, Daniel, et al.'s (2009) validity types.

SELECTING QUALITATIVE RESEARCH

If the empirical information is qualitative, then there are several potential threats to credibility. Much like examining quantitative research reports for possible selection, examining qualitative research studies also can be quite complex. Oftentimes, authors use various terms for this area, such as *credibility* and trustworthiness. Before examining each qualitative and mixed methods research report, it is helpful to review some of the threats to internal and external credibility to establish the trustworthiness of data results in any report.

In qualitative research and quantitative research alike, threats can occur at any phase of the research process: research design/data collection phase, data analysis phase, and data interpretation phase. According to Onwuegbuzie and Leech (2007b), *internal credibility* represents "the truth value, applicability, consistency, neutrality, dependability, and/or credibility of interpretations and conclusions within the underlying setting or group" (p. 234). In contrast, *external credibility* represents "the confirmability and transferability of findings and conclusions" (p. 235). Therefore, in effect, internal credibility in qualitative research is parallel to internal validity in quantitative research, whereas external credibility in qualitative research is parallel to external validity in quantitative research. Before examining your qualitative research information sources, or reports, understanding some best practices of ways that researchers might attend to threats to credibility will help you determine the value of evidence presented in each report. Again, much like we noted when examining a quantitative research article, an important point for you as a reviewer to keep in mind is the rigor and transparency of the research that you review. If the report reveals that credibility was compromised, then you might decide to deselect this work, or to select it with the awareness of the limitation.

As a case that parallels our earlier example on population validity, if in the Dyadic Mentoring Study the qualitative findings were generalized beyond the 11 sample members (i.e., selected members), then this sample size would pose a threat to external credibility via (a) the threat to **population generalizability** (i.e., the extent to which the findings can be generalized beyond the sample in the study [selected elementary level students and mentors] to the population [all elementary level students and mentors]); and (b) the threat to **ecological generalizability** (i.e., the extent to which the finding can be generalized beyond the sample in his/her study to students in other schools in different locations [e.g., districts, cities, regions, and even countries]). In the presence of such gross over-generalization, a reviewer either would deselect this study from the list of studies or the reviewer would select the study with the awareness of this limitation. If a study were to be selected that was characterized by one or more legitimation issues, after subjecting its findings to analysis and synthesis in Step 6, it would be important to document the limitation(s). Also, when presenting this finding in the CLR report (Step 7), a reviewer would ensure that this finding was adequately contextualized, for example, by noting the sample size limitation (e.g., "...However, extreme caution should be exercised in generalizing these findings because the goal of the study was to obtain an in-depth understanding of the phenomenon via a small sample of information-rich cases rather than to generalize the findings to the population…").

The systematic process for selecting and deselecting qualitative reports is much like the process of selecting quantitative reports. First, consider the claim being made. Next, align the qualitative research evidence to your argument. Then, take each qualitative research article in isolation and read it a second time, with the sole intention of examining the practices used and whether they did not step out of the boundaries for being trusted, or legitimate. Each qualitative research study selected in Step 2 (and later during Step 5) is examined to determine whether the qualitative research findings are limited by important threats to internal credibility and/or external credibility. Once these

TOOL: THE EVALUATION CRITERIA

Figure 7.7 presents a reference guide to add to your Evaluation Criteria in the area of legitimation.

Item	Definition	When a Threat Commonly Occurs	Question(s) to Ask When Examining a Research Report	Examples for How You Might Find Evidence of it in the Report
Descriptive validity	Factual accuracy of the account	Data collection as a result of design	Was the account accurately documented based on the transcript(s), interview(s), focus group(s)?	Was a recording device used? Were member-checking or other trustworthiness efforts explained?
Observational bias	Insufficient sample of words or behaviors to draw conclusions, or lacking of persistent observation	Data collection as a result of design Data analysis	Did the researcher(s) provide details, descriptions, rationales, and examples?	In the procedures, did the report explain duration/length and number of data collection points? In the data analysis, did the researchers address sufficient saturation?
Researcher bias Confirmation bias	A personal bias or prior assumption that cannot be suspended and is subconsciously transferred to participants and/ or data that are collected	Data collection as a result of design Data analysis and interpretation	Were initial hunches and/ or surprises of findings discussed?	In the procedures, did the researcher(s) provide examples of data collection interview questions and/or observation checklist items? In the discussion, did researcher(s) discuss addressing alternative and/or confirmatory evidence?
Reactivity	Participants responding/ changing as a result of being aware of the study	Data collection as a result of design	How did the researcher(s) present themselves and or the data collection tools? How did they recruit and interact with participants?	In the design, did the researcher(s) explain a logical sequence of steps for and type of sample? In the procedures, did they address the Institutional Review Board (IRB)? In the results or discussion, were limitations addressed?

Figure 7.7   Translating legitimation threats to questions and applications

threats have been identified, the reviewer would decide whether or not to deselect the qualitative research study or information. Threats can be *internal threats*, which occur as part of the design and/or process, or *external threats*, which occur when the researcher(s) explain and interpret the process. Further, for the purposes of scrutinizing qualitative research that might be considered as part of a literature review, we have created a guide (presented in Appendix B) based on some of the most common threats, in Onwuegbuzie and Leech's (2007b) work for interpreting inferences in qualitative research.

EVALUATING INFORMATION, GUIDING QUESTIONS, AND EXAMPLES

SELECTING MIXED RESEARCH

Before discussing mixed research (which would involve both validity and credibility threats), as a reviewer, you should keep in mind some of the reasons that researchers mix and how unique and complex mixed research can be. In fact, mixing might occur at varying degrees and in one or more ways:

- philosophical assumptions and stances, or the core beliefs about knowing
- collecting data (both numbers and words/actions)
- analyzing data by transforming either quantitative data to qualitative data, or vice versa
- interpreting data

Recognizing good mixed research requires background information about *why* a researcher might mix. Greene, Caracelli, and Graham (1989) distinguished rationales used for mixing quantitative and qualitative traditions. Greene et al. (1989) created a typology of these rationales that can be important to keep in mind when considering legitimation in mixed research studies. According to these authors, potential reasons to mix methods can be:

- *Complementarity*, which involves seeking to elaborate, to illustrate, to enhance, or to clarify understanding of the study by mixing or combining the quantitative and qualitative findings

- *Initiation*, which involves identifying paradoxes and contradictions that emerge when the quantitative findings and the qualitative findings are compared that might lead to a reframing of the research question
- *Triangulation*, which involves seeking consistency or convergence between the quantitative findings and the qualitative findings
- *Expansion*, which involves using quantitative findings and qualitative findings from different phases of the study to expand the breadth and range of a study
- *Development*, which involves using the quantitative findings to help inform the qualitative findings, or vice versa

Interestingly, and extremely appropriately for this chapter, the first letter of each of these five reasons yields the acronym CITED. This acronym makes it very easy for us to remember the five reasons when providing workshops and courses on mixed methods worldwide! If the empirical information represents a combination of qualitative and quantitative research traditions, then there are a few legitimation frameworks that can be used to assess the credibility of the information and, hence, one or more of the six aforementioned claims. In particular, Onwuegbuzie and Johnson (2006) provided nine legitimation types: sample integration legitimation, insider–outsider legitimation, weakness minimization legitimation, sequential legitimation, conversion legitimation, paradigmatic mixing legitimation, commensurability legitimation, multiple validities legitimation, and political legitimation. These nine mixed-methods legitimation types are presented in Appendix B with descriptions of each. Another framework for examining mixed research, which was developed by Teddlie and Tashakkori (2009), helps to recognize the *integration* threats of the research process using some guiding questions.

For instance, one mixed research legitimation type is *sample integration*, or the way that participant(s) or sample items are presented in relationship to each other. If, regarding information that emerged through a mixed research design, it was reported that mentoring programs increase school connectedness among U.S. public school students based on (a) a quantitative research study conducted on a large sample of elementary school students and (b) a qualitative research study conducted on a small sample of secondary school students, then the reviewer should assess the extent to which there is adequate sample integration legitimation to combine these quantitative and qualitative findings into a coherent inference—what Tashakkori and Teddlie (1998) call a *meta-inference*. If the reviewer concludes that there is not adequate sample integration legitimation for the author to make this claim (of interpretation), then he/she either would not include this author's claim in his/her literature review report, or the reviewer would report this author's inference using some form of counter-factive statement (e.g., "...However, this conclusion was problematic due to the threat to sample integration legitimation ..."). Whichever mixed legitimation framework is used, each mixed research study selected at Step 2 (and again in Step 5) could be examined to determine whether threats were minimized to *some extent*.

ASSESSING POINTS OF VALUE AND VALIDATION

Returning to the Claim Credibility Meta-Framework (Figure 7.6), it can be seen that all frameworks that we have discussed thus far for assessing claims can be applied to empirical information or are optimally informed by empirical information. Yet, when selecting/deselecting information sources, as an evaluator of information and information sources, you will basically need to recognize that some information is valuable, and the information stems from sources other than empirical research studies. To explain some of the important elements for any type of report, Leech, Dellinger, Brannagan, and Tanaka (2010) designed the framework "to organize information to assist in construct validation, or legitimation, of all types of data, including literature sources" (p. 19). Their intention was to facilitate a way to "evaluat[e]

individual study's inferences and to organize thoughts about a body of literature" (p. 327).

Some sources might not meet all of the standards that we have discussed but they might include areas of value, such as how the report is situated in history, or how the report provides meaningful consequences. Recognizing additional areas of value is applicable for quantitative, qualitative, or mixed research studies, as well as for conceptual, methodological, or other abstract sources. Noting some additional components outlined by Leech et al. (2010) can shed light on some significant reasons to select (or to deselect) an information source in addition to legitimation, in particular, the utilization/historical element and consequential element.

UTILIZATION/HISTORICAL ELEMENT. It is possible for the same inference to generate a different claim by different authors—what we refer to as a "*glass half full* versus *glass half empty*" scenario. As surmised by Dellinger and Leech (2007), "utilization or historical validity evidence accrues to a study's inferences, measures, or findings because of use (appropriate or not) in the extant literature or other applications, such as decision making or policy development" (p. 325). Therefore, the reviewer should seek to identify how a particular piece of information has been used elsewhere. In so doing, the reviewer should assess the validity of how that information was used. We provided an example of the potential pitfall of reviewers not examining historical evidence in Chapter 4 when we discussed the historical validity of Gibson and Dembo's (1984) Teacher Efficacy Scale (TES), and how many researchers still use the TES despite the bulk of evidence that has made extremely questionable its psychometric properties.

CONSEQUENTIAL ELEMENT. Whenever available, reviewers should examine the consequences of each

---

TOOL: VALIDATION OF SOURCES

Box 7.1 illustrates Leech et al.'s (2010) conceptualization of important areas to consider that address some type of value.

VALIDATION FRAMEWORK: ELEMENTS OF CONSTRUCT VALIDATION

Foundational Element

What pre-conceptions, pre-logic, biases, prior knowledge, and/or theories are (un)acknowledged by the researcher as relates to the meaning of the data?

Is the review of literature appropriate for the purpose of the study?

What is the quality of the review of literature (e.g., evaluation and synthesis of literature is appropriate, comprehensive, relevant, thorough, etc.)?

Does the review inform the purpose, design, measurement, analysis, and inferences?

Does the review confirm or disconfirm grounded theory?

Traditional QUAN	Traditional QUAL		Mixed Methods
Design-Related Elements	*Primary Criteria:*	*Secondary Criteria:*	Design Quality
Measurement-Related Elements	Credibility	Explicitness	Legitimation
Inference-Related Elements	Authenticity	Vividness	Interpretive
	Criticality	Creativity	Rigor
	Integrity	Thoroughness	
	Congruence	Sensitivity	

Translation Fidelity/Inferential Consistency Audit

Do the inferences follow from the links among the theories/lived experience, research literature, purpose, design, measurement, and analysis? Are meta-inferences consistent with these elements? How well does the chosen methodological approach maximize the available information necessary to achieve the purpose of the study? Is there a better approach given the theory, research literature, purpose, design, measurement, and analysis?

Utilization/Historical Element

How often, by whom, and in what ways have findings/measures been utilized, how appropriate were the uses of the findings/measures, and what, if anything, worthwhile does this contribute to the meaning of data?

Consequential Element

What are or have been the consequences of use of the findings/measures, are/were these consequences socially/politically acceptable, and what, if anything, worthwhile do these consequences contribute to the meaning of data?

Adapted from "Evaluating mixed research studies: A mixed methods approach," by N. L. Leech, A. B. Dellinger, K. B. Brannagan, and H. Tanaka, 2010, *Journal of Mixed Methods Research, 4*, p. 20. Copyright 2010 by Sage Publications.

of the four elements that characterize the path of argumentation. As noted by Leech et al. (2010), "The character of these consequences, social acceptability, and adequacy accrue validity evidence as to the meaning of the data and/or inferences from data" (pp. 21–22). As with all other components of the Validation Framework, the consequential element should be addressed continuously.

EXAMPLE: EXAMINATION OF CONSEQUENTIAL ELEMENTS

Figure 7.8 presents extracts from the Dyadic Mentoring Study that show how the validation framework hopes to recognize the aforementioned consequential elements for construct validation of sources.

In the Dyadic Mentoring Study, Frels (2010) utilized the validation framework (Leech et.al., 2010) to examine each source for shedding light on any consequences or particular social factors that might be inferred through the findings

Over the last decade, representatives of agencies and school district leaders throughout the country have endorsed mentoring programs by promoting the stated heartfelt lived experiences of both mentors and mentees (cf. BBBS, n.d.), noting the positive impact of mentoring on child and youth development when particular practices and components are in place (Cavell, Elledge, Malcolm, Faith, & Hughes, 2009; DuBois, Holloway, Valentine, & Cooper, 2002; Karcher, 2008b, Karcher& Herrera, 2008; Schmidt, McVaugh, & Jacobi, 2007). By 2002, the National Mentoring Database included more than 1,700 organizations advocating mentoring activities (DuBois, Holloway, et al., 2002). Whereas many mentoring relationships significantly impact children and youth (Converse &Lignugaris/Kraft, 2009; DuBois, Holloway, et al., 2002), some mentoring relationships have little or no impact and, moreover, can be detrimental for children and youth (Karcher, 2005; Karcher& Herrera, 2008; Rhodes, Reddy, & Grossman, 2005). According to Rhodes and DuBois (2008), mentoring programs "are likely to be effective to the extent that they are successful in establishing close, enduring connections that promote positive developmental change" (p. 257). Most importantly, Karcher (2005) ascertained that mentors who are frequently absent for weekly mentoring meetings might do more harm than good.

Thus, mentoring relationships appear to warrant particular, supportive characteristics on the part of the mentor, similar to characteristics of strong counseling relationships such as authenticity, empathy, collaboration, and companionship (Spencer, 2004).

…Spencer (2004) acknowledged that the field of youth mentoring is at the cusp of understanding the importance of devoting more serious efforts to explaining how relationships form. Most recently, researchers summoned for "clear and systematic efforts that examine mentoring critically" (Karcher et al., 2006, p. 710). In fact, assessing the quality of youth mentoring requires concerted attention to the dynamics of the dyadic relationship (student and mentor) to understand better the phenomenon of mentoring (Deutsch & Spencer, 2009).

Figure 7.8 An extract from the Dyadic Mentoring Study showing consequential elements

Adapted from *The experiences and perceptions of selected mentors: An exploratory study of the dyadic relationship in school-based mentoring*, by R. K. Frels, 2010, unpublished doctoral dissertation, Sam Houston State University, Huntsville, TX, pp. 3–4. Copyright 2010 by R. K. Frels.

CREATE FOCUS QUESTIONS FOR THE SELECTION PROCESS

Think about Step 4 and the selection process much like the process of collecting wardrobe items, or clothing, for your collection to wear. You would examine many aspects of an item for a good fit, which might include colors, stitching, durability of fabric, design, appropriateness for particular settings, and more. Yet, some questions will guide your selection process. The way you put together items from your collection can be an expression of your guiding belief system but now your focus is based on quality and value. The selection of information sources is a unique, individual process, based on quality, value, and good fit. The decision about whether to select and to deselect information often can be a complex one. Such a process of critique involves assessing, supporting, refuting, justifying, reifying, judging, discriminating, explaining, linking, concluding, and, finally, deciding. It is subject to your long-range plans for the goal of your CLR: to inform primary research or to stand alone. Regardless, in some way, it should contribute to the knowledge base or practices in your field or discipline and should be built on a strong foundation. For this reason, a critical eye to collect only quality sources is part of the ethical and responsible characteristics of a reviewer. For each work that was stored and categorized in Step 3, a new focused assessment takes placed based on the Claim Credibility Meta-Framework.

CREATE FIELD NOTES

Keep in mind that the selection/deselection process can be emotionally exhausting, due to how differently authors report their findings and ideas. One piece of advice is to keep focused on what it is that you exactly hope to outline in your argument. To this end, it is helpful to document in writing some of the important ideas that you have gleaned from your sources and which information sources tend to gravitate together. Then, re-examine some claims. In applying Step 4, be sure to recognize elements beyond claims and legitimation, such as the importance of validating sources based on foundation, historical, social, or other elements of value. By evaluating all aspects of potential sources, a reviewer will be in an optimal position possibly to include the information from a source.

The decisions might vary among reviewers and, of course, are based on Step 1: Exploring Beliefs and Topics. As such, it is essential to document some of the value elements as well as any threats that you identified for each source selected so that you can be transparent in your own work. This documentation might at this point include some items that you observe to expand the search. For example, you might notice that an author cited another interesting work in your topic area and you found the reference for this source in the reference list of the article. You should begin a spreadsheet of ideas as you come across them for expanding on your topic area. Documenting the examination, categorization, evaluation, and selection/deselection of information also will help with the composing of your own CLR because you will note ways to make an effective argument.

CONCLUSIONS

In this chapter, we provided multiple considerations for selecting/deselecting information sources. *It is essential that reviewers conduct this step with rigor in order to avoid promoting any fallacies made by authors that include arguments that are deceptive, misleading, unsound, or false* (in Chapter 11, we provide further discussion of fallacies). Indeed, only by evaluating information in such a rigorous way can reviewers assure consumers of their CLR reports that they have been and continue to be ethical and culturally progressive. As you move through the seven-step CLR, you will continue to discover sources that might contribute to your report in some way. Therefore, Evaluation Criteria become a more integrative process and, as a reviewer, you begin to develop a critical eye. The next chapter provides Step 5, the final step of the Exploration Phase of the CLR, which is extending the search. As you might note from the diagram that begins each chapter of the seven steps, the sources found in Step 5 also should be examined using Step 4 and stored using Step 3.

Before reading the next chapter and moving to Step 5: Expanding the Search Using MODES, the following concepts and key terms are important to keep in mind:

- The analysis process of the CLR begins at the moment a researcher initiates questions or wonderings related to phenomena.
- The selecting/deselecting involves the focused, intentional act of categorizing information, critiquing the usefulness of information, and developing the foundation for establishing new evidence on the selected topic.

- As an original thinker, critical thinker, and reflexive person, the reviewer refers back to philosophical and topic beliefs, ethical awareness, and culturally progressive practices.
- Selecting/deselecting involves critical thinking and reflexive practices using Evaluation Criteria, or the ethical guidelines for assessing *worthiness* of information.
- The following six types of claims for communicating ideas may be made: claims of fact, claims of value, claims of policy, claims of concept, claims of interpretation, and claims of observation.
- For each claim, you must identify (a) *evidence* to support the claim; (b) *warrant* that links the claim and its evidence; and (c) *backing*, which comprises the context and assumptions used to provide justification for the warrant and evidence.
- Evaluation Criteria facilitate selecting/deselecting information sources based on levels associated with: (a) justified claims; (b) sound argument; (c) legitimate results (validity/credibility); and (d) areas of the validation framework such as foundation, construct, historical/social merit, and consequences.
- Assessing sources based on legitimation is determining whether you have confidence that findings are in fact verifiable, warranted, and backed by evidence.
- Threats can be internal threats, which occur as part of the design and/or process, or external threats, which occur when the researcher(s) explain and interpret the process.

CHAPTER 7 EVALUATION CHECKLIST

CORE	Guiding Questions and Tasks
Critical Examination	How many sources will you analyze/synthesize? Is there more than one viewpoint? Are there both qualitative and quantitative studies represented? Conceptual works?
	Do you have a theoretical lens that might help you to understand the collection as a whole, such as social learning theory, ecological theory, and systems theory?
Organization	To what extent did you document both foundational works and supplemental works?
	How might you create groups within groups so that variables (author, context, and participant demographics) might be identified during the analysis?
Reflections	How prepared are you to discuss your topic area for interviewing an expert?
Evaluation	What new ideas do you have as a result of sorting through documents? How has your focus improved? Do you have a thorough understanding of a problem? Is the problem that you identified for your topic based on credible sources?

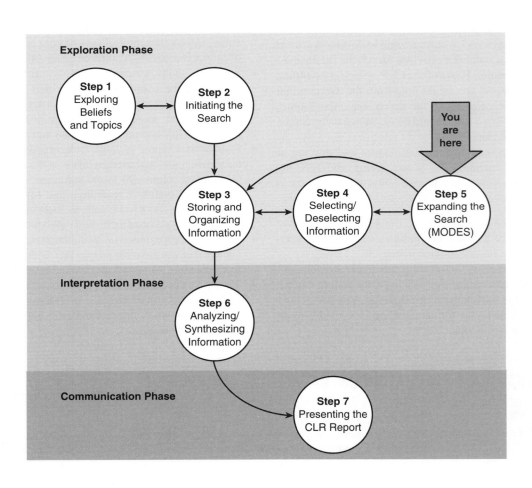

8

STEP 5: EXPANDING THE SEARCH—

MEDIA, OBSERVATION(S), DOCUMENTS, EXPERT(S), AND SECONDARY DATA

CHAPTER 8 ROADMAP

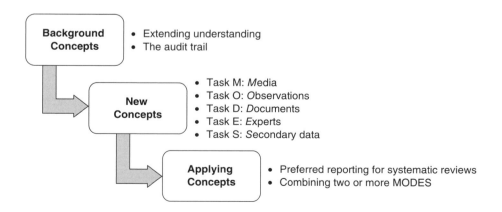

Background Concepts
- Extending understanding
- The audit trail

New Concepts
- Task M: *Media*
- Task O: *Observations*
- Task D: *Documents*
- Task E: *Experts*
- Task S: *Secondary data*

Applying Concepts
- Preferred reporting for systematic reviews
- Combining two or more MODES

EXTENDING UNDERSTANDING

Much like a detective, literature reviewers wanting to conduct comprehensive literature reviews should utilize these same five broad sources of data to inform their literature reviews, namely, **M**edia, **O**bservation(s), **D**ocuments, **E**xpert(s), and **S**econdary data. Interestingly, the first letter of each significant word labeling these five sources of information spells out the word *modes*. And we believe that the word *modes* is very appropriate because, as defined by dictionary.com (a free online dictionary), it represents "a manner of acting or doing" "a particular type or form of something" and "a designated condition or status, as for performing a task or responding to a problem" (http://dictionary.reference.com/browse/modes?s=t). And all of these definitions of the word modes are highly appropriate for the literature review context in that it is the manner of conducting the literature review.

Step 1 to Step 4 yielded a traditional review of the literature. And, after completing a traditional review of the literature using the guidelines and techniques outlined in Chapters 4–7, it is likely that you will have a useful body of information. However, it is unlikely that this body will be comprehensive or up-to-date. Consequently, to move toward a comprehensive review of the literature, a reviewer should go as far as possible beyond a traditional literature review by expanding her/his information search. In this chapter, we provide specific information to complete Step 5 using five broad tasks that involve collecting data via **M**edia, **O**bservation(s), **D**ocuments, **E**xpert(s), and **S**econdary data.

THE AUDIT TRAIL

Figure 8.1 illustrates the flow of Step 5 for (a) leaving an audit trail and (b) storing and organizing the literature, which both are positioned in the inner circles of the set of concentric ovals. This is because these two processes play a central role in the literature review expansion step (i.e., Step 5). You might recall that we discussed the importance of leaving an audit trail (cf. Halpern, 1983; Schwandt & Halpern, 1988) during all four previous steps of the CLR process.

TASK M: *MEDIA*

Conducting an expansion-based search via media involves searching for information using audio and/or visual tools. Each of these tools is listed and discussed below.

AUDIO TOOLS

One useful source with respect to audio tools is the use of audio books. An audio book is an audio recording of text that is read by one or more persons. Although the first audio recordings can be traced back to 1877, when Thomas Alva Edison invented the phonograph wherein sound was recorded on tinfoil cylinders via two needles (one needle for recording and one needle for playback), and although audio recordings have been available in schools and public libraries since the 1930s, it was not until the 1980s that book retailers began routinely to advertise and to display audio books on their shelves. Since the late 1990s, audio books can be downloaded directly from websites.

TOOL: VISUALIZING THE AUDIT TRAIL PROCESS

The audit trail should occur for each of the five expansion-based search tasks. As we have advised repeatedly in previous chapters, in leaving your audit trail, you should provide sufficient detail such that you can retrace your steps at a much later point in time. As part of the audit trail process, you should store and organize all information that you extract from each of the five expansion-based search tasks, using the techniques that we outlined in Step 3—representing the innermost oval.

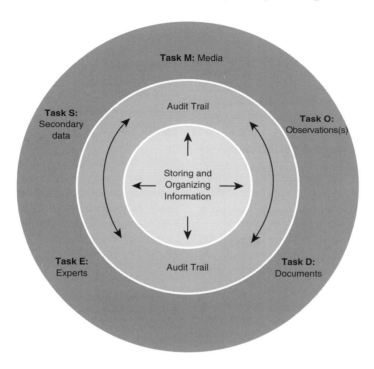

Figure 8.1 The literature review expansion cycle: Five-task process for expanding the literature review process

As can be seen in Figure 8.1, no arrows appear in the outermost oval where the five expansion-based search tasks reside. This is because these five expansion-based search tasks are not linear—indeed, these tasks can occur in any order. However, it should be noted that the sources of data representing these fives tasks are interactive and multidirectional, in much the same way as the sources of data extracted by a detective are interactive and multidirectional—for example, interviewing an expert witness might lead a detective to return to the scene of the crime and collect more observational data; in turn, collecting observational data from the scene of the crime might help the detective determine the most appropriate expert witnesses to interview, as well as the most appropriate questions to ask. In both the expansion-based search process and the crime investigation process, the process ends when *saturation* is reached—wherein it can be concluded that additional information will not yield any new insights for making inferences (Morse, 1995).

EXAMPLE: AUDIO BOOKS

A particularly useful online repository for downloading audio books is JustAudioBooks (i.e., https://www.justaudiobooks.com). This website contains more than 100,000 audio books that can be downloaded to several devices, including desktop computers, notebook/laptop computers, tablet computers (e.g., iPad line of computers), MP3 devices, iPods, and the like. Figure 8.2 shows the JustAudioBooks website with the keyword "mentoring" entered. Figure 8.3 shows some of the audio books that were generated using the "mentoring" keyword. A similar website is AudioBookStore (http://www.theaudiobookstore.com/).

VISUAL TOOLS

VIDEOS. With respect to visual tools, videos represent another way to expand a search. Videos can be accessed via both library subscription databases and public Internet sources. Regarding library subscription databases, a very comprehensive repository is Academic Video Online. Figure 8.4 shows the website page of Academic Video Online, and Figure 8.5

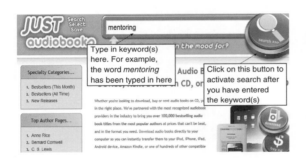

Figure 8.2   Screenshot showing the website page of JustAudioBooks

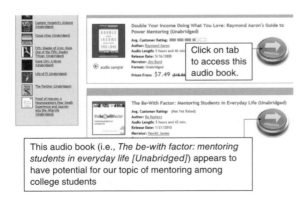

Figure 8.3   Screenshot showing some of the books generated by JustAudioBooks after entering the keyword "mentoring"

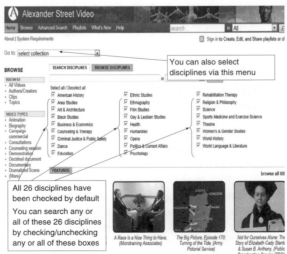

Figure 8.4   Screenshot showing the website page of the library subscription database Academic Video Online

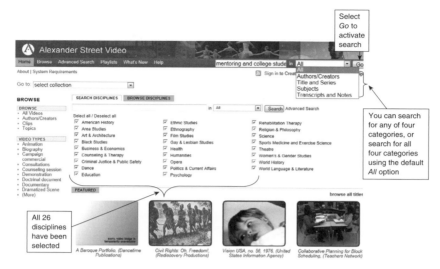

Figure 8.5 Screenshot showing the website page of the library subscription database Academic Video Online using the search string "mentoring and college students"

shows how you could conduct a search via Academic Video Online using the search string "mentoring and college students." You can search via any or all of 26 disciplines (e.g., art and architecture, counseling and therapy, education, ethnography, health, humanities, politics and current affairs, psychology, science, world history). Also, you can search the following categories: authors/creators, titles and series, subjects, and transcripts and notes; or you can select the default "all" option to search through all four categories.

EXAMPLE: VIDEO TOOLS

Figure 8.6 shows the result of this video search, which yielded 33 hits, with the video that is first listed representing

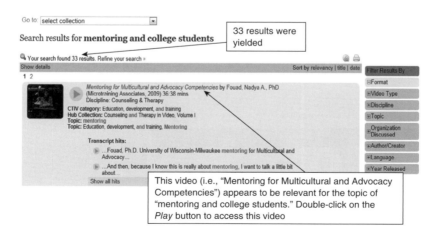

Figure 8.6 Screenshot showing the website page of the library subscription database Academic Video Online after using the search string "mentoring and college students"

Figure 8.7 Screenshot showing the advanced search options of the library subscription database Academic Video Online

a potentially useful video of length 36 minutes and 38 seconds, entitled "Mentoring for Multicultural and Advocacy Competencies" by Dr. Nadya Fouad. Figure 8.7 shows the advanced search options of Academic Video Online. These options allow users to specify the *title*, *series*, *author/creator*, *subject*, *publisher*, *discipline* (same 26 disciplines), *video type* (e.g., lecture/presentation, biography, documentary, editorial, interview), *language* (94 total languages; e.g., Arabic, English, French, Farsi, Swahili), *subtitle language* (11 languages: Arabic, Catalan, Dutch, English, Finnish, French, German, Hebrew, Italian, Russian, Spanish), *years released* (from and to), and *sort results by* (i.e., relevancy [default], title, date of recording).

EXAMPLE: YOUTUBE

Numerous databases of videos can be accessed via public Internet sources. However, the most popularized website is YouTube (circa 2005), which is a video sharing website wherein users can upload, view, download, and share videos. Figure 8.8 shows the YouTube homepage. Figure 8.9 shows the first page of approximately 12,000 results after entering the search string "mentoring and college students" via YouTube. As another example, if you were conducting a literature review on the topic of mixed (methods) research, then you might find useful one or both of two videos involving one of the authors of this literature review book: (http://www.youtube.com/watch?v=6DWe-9GuudJY) and (http://videolectures.net/ssmt09_onwueg-buzie_mmr/), which, at the time of writing, have had more than 10,000 and 6,000 views, respectively.

A useful video editing software application is iMovie (circa 1999). iMovie is a proprietary video editing software application owned by Apple Inc. that has been designed specifically for the Macintosh personal computer (i.e., Mac; circa 1984) and the mobile operating system, iOS (e.g., iPhone, iPad, iPad mini, iPod touch). iMovie imports video footage from digital video cameras to the Mac, as well as video and photo files from a hard drive. Users then can edit the video clips and photographs, for example, by inserting titles, music, sound

Figure 8.8 Screenshot showing the website page of the public Internet source YouTube

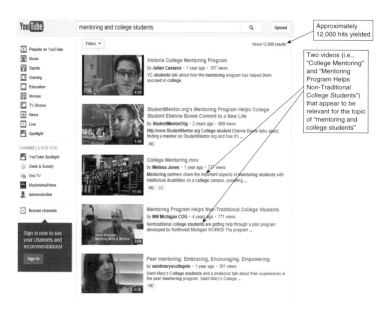

Figure 8.9 Screenshot showing first page of results after entering the search string "mentoring and college students" via YouTube

effects, images, video enhancement tools, transitions (e.g., fades), and the like.

iTunes (originally known as SoundJam MP), which was purchased and renamed by Apple Inc. in 2000, is another useful media-based tool that can expand a literature review. Specifically, iTunes simultaneously is a media player and a media library application that is used to play, to download, and to organize audio and video files (e.g., music, music videos, television shows, audio books, podcasts, movies) on personal computers that run the OS X operating system and the iOS-based mobile operating systems.

CRITERIA FOR OPEN SOURCES

In selecting videos to inform your literature review, it is important that you keep in mind the fact that "not all audios and videos are created equally." Thus, before selecting any audio or video, you should examine it for both authenticity (i.e., making certain that the video actually was created by the person who has been given credit for the video) and accuracy (i.e., assessing the factual accuracy of the video's content). Factors that help to establish authenticity include the inclusion of an author's face or voice on the video. A useful way of assessing

the authenticity of an audio or video is by contacting the author directly, for example, via an expert interview of some form (cf. section on expert interviews below). In establishing the accuracy of the video's content, the following three factors should be considered: (a) What is the knowledge and competence level of the audio's/video's author? (b) To what extent is the audio's/video's content dated? And (c) to what extent are the biases and motives of the audio's/video's author questionable? Further, in your quest for authenticity and accuracy, it is always better to use an audio/video that reflects a primary source (e.g., authored by a person who is considered by members of the academic community to be extremely knowledgeable about mentoring) than a secondary source (e.g., someone who is summarizing the ideas, theories, concepts, or the like of such a person).

PHOTOGRAPHS, DRAWINGS, AND PAINTINGS. Useful but extremely underutilized visual tools that can inform literature reviews are photographs, drawings, and paintings. Many people have stated, "A picture is worth a thousand words." However, rarely do literature reviewers include photographs, drawings, and

TOOL: LIST OF COMMON AUDIO AND VIDEO SHARING WEBSITES

Table 8.1 contains 60 of the most common audio and video hosting/sharing websites.

Table 8.1 Audio and video hosting/sharing search tools listed in alphabetical order

Hoster	Internet Address	Year of Conception	Notes
AcFun.tv	www.acfun.tv	2007	Chinese video sharing site
Afreeca	www.afreeca.com	2006	Based in South Korea, it is primarily for retransmitting TV channels, but it also allows users to upload their own videos and shows
Archive.org	www.archive.org	2001	Based in San Francisco, California, it offers permanent storage of and free public access to collections of digitized materials, including websites, videos, music, and approximately 3 million public-domain books
Bilibili.tv	www.Bilibili.tv	2010	Used in the People's Republic of China, where users can submit, view, and comment on videos
Blip.tv	http://blip.tv	2005	Founded in New York City, it creates a platform for producers of original web series to distribute and to monetize their productions
BlogTV	www.blogtv.com	2004	Began in Israel as a webcasting company to allow users to express their talents and ideas to the world
Break.com	www.break.com	1998	Humor website featuring comedy videos, flash games, and other material
Buzznet	www.buzznet.com	2005	Users participate in communities that are formed around ideas, events, and interests, most predominantly music, celebrities, and the media
Comedy.com	http://comedy.com	2006	Humor website
Crackle	www.crackle.com	2007	Owned by Sony Pictures Entertainment, its content consists primarily of Sony's library of films and television shows
Dailymotion	www.dailymotion.com/us	2005	With its headquarters in Paris, France, it is the third-largest video site in the world
EngageMedia	www.engagemedia.org	2006	Focuses on social justice and environmental issues in Australia, Southeast Asia, and the Pacific
ExpoTV	www.expotv.com	2004	Based in New York, it is a consumer-oriented video platform
Facebook	www.facebook.com	2004	Social networking service

Hoster	Internet Address	Year of Conception	Notes
Flickr	www.flickr.com	2004	Image hosting and video hosting website
Fotki	www.fotki.com/ us/en	1996	Digital photo sharing, video sharing, and media social network website and web service suite; it is one of the world's largest social networking websites
Funny or Die	www.funnyordie. com	2006	Comedy video website
Hulu	www.hulu.com	2008	On-demand streaming video of TV shows, movies, trailers, clips, and behind-the-scenes footage from many TV companies (e.g., NBC, Fox, ABC, CBS)
Lafango	http://lafango.com	2008	Allows users to create profiles, to upload and to share unlimited media (audio, video, images, and text), to communicate within user-developed communities, to compete in contests, and to blog
LiveLeak	www.liveleak.com	2006	Focuses on current events, politics, and reality-based footage such as war scenes from numerous parts of the world
Mail.Ru	http://mail.ru	1998	Most popular Russian website
MaYoMo	www.mayomo.com	2009	User-generated news site for mobile citizen journalism
Mefeedia	www.mefeedia.com	2004	Media search website
Metacafe	www.metacafe.com	2003	Based in San Francisco, California, it specializes in short-form video entertainment in the categories of movies, video games, sports, music, and TV
Mevio	www.mevio.com	2004	U.S.-based Internet entertainment network
Mobento	www.mobento.com	2011	Video streaming and search
Myspace	www.myspace.com	2003	Based in Beverly Hills, California, it is a social networking website
MyVideo	http://myvideo.ro	2006	Based in Bucharest, Romania, it is a video hosting service that is available in Romanian, German, and Dutch, with the German website being among the 1,000 most visited websites on the Internet
Nico Nico Douga	www.nicovideo.jp	2006	Fourteenth most visited website in Japan
OneWorldTV	http://oneworldgroup.org/tv	2001	Nonprofit internet video sharing and social networking website focusing on climate change, human rights, social justice, etc.

(Continued)

Hoster	Internet Address	Year of Conception	Notes
Openfilm	www.openfilm.com	2008	A website for finding and distributing independent films
Ourmedia	www.ourmedia.org	2005	Freely hosts any non-pornographic images, text, and video, or audio clips
Panopto	www.panopto.com	2007	Provides lecture recording, screencasting, video streaming, and video content management software, which is often used in e-learning environments
Photobucket	http://beta. photobucket.com	2003	An image hosting, video hosting, slideshow creation, and photo sharing website
Rambler Vision	www.rambler.ru	1996	Website for Russian speakers
ReelTime.com	www.reeltime.com	2004	An Internet-based video-on-demand provider located in Seattle, Washington
Rutube	http://rutube.ru	2006	A web video streaming service targeted to Russian speakers
SAPO Videos	www.sapo.pt	1995	Portuguese internet service provider
SchoolTube	www.schooltube. com	2006	Serves an elementary and secondary school community in the United States and worldwide
ScienceStage	http://sciencestage. com	2008	Global, science-oriented multimedia portal that specializes in online video streaming, to support communication among scientists, scholars, researchers in industry, and professionals; used by academics and students as a virtual educational tool
Sevenload	http://en.sevenload. com	2006	German-based video sharing website
SmugMug	www.smugmug.com	2002	Video game-oriented web service
Trilulilu	www.trilulilu.ro	2007	Biggest user-generated content (UGC) website in Romania
Tudou	www.tudou.com	2005	Video sharing website in the People's Republic of China
Twitvid	https://twitter.com	2006	Online social networking service and microblogging service that enables its users to send and to read text-based messages (i.e., "tweets") of up to 140 characters
VBOX7	http://vbox7.com	2006	Largest video sharing entertainment website in Bulgaria
Veoh	http://veoh.com	2007	Allows users to find and to watch major studio content, independent productions, and user-created material
Viddler	www.viddler.com	2005	Interactive online video platform (OVP) for uploading, sharing, enhancing, tagging, commenting on, and forming groups around videos

Hoster	Internet Address	Year of Conception	Notes
Videojug	www.videojug.com	2006	An instructional video website
Videolog	www.videolog.tv	2006	One of the main online video providers from Brazil
Vidoosh	www.vidoosh.tv	2007	Iranian video sharing, based in Brussels, Belgium
Vidyard	https://secure.vidyard.com	2011	Video marketing platform that hosts and analyzes video for businesses, consumer brands, and content producers
Vimeo	http://vimeo.com	2011	A U.S.-based video sharing website
Vuze	www.vuze.com	2003	Allows users to view, to publish, and to share original DVD and HD quality video content
vzaar	http://vzaar.com	2007	Online video for commerce
Wildscreen.tv	www.wildscreen.tv	2007	Allows users to upload self-generated video content; it is designed as an alternative to YouTube in that independent film makers, musicians, and other artists can monetize the content they produce
Yahoo! Screen	http://screen.yahoo.com	2006	A video sharing website on which users could upload and share videos
Youku	www.youku.com	2006	Chinese video hosting service based in the People's Republic of China; second-largest video site in the world
YouTube	www.youtube.com	2005	Video sharing website; largest video site in the world
Zoopy	www.zoopy.com	2006	Online and mobile social media community, hosting user-generated videos, photos, and audio

copies of paintings as part of their literature reviews. Social networking websites such as Facebook and Twitter are useful ways of extracting relevant photographs, as is Panoramio (circa 2005), which is an additional photo sharing tool. However, it is important always to keep in mind that if you want a photograph, drawing, or copy of a painting to appear in your final literature review report, then you should ensure that doing so does not violate any copyright laws, and obtain appropriate permissions.

TASK O: *OBSERVATIONS*

ON-SITE OBSERVATIONS

Although observations can be used in a primary qualitative inquiry, it is also informative for simply setting the stage in a literature review. It is important to note how observing concepts important for a topic might influence the very nature of providing a background in inquiry. We explained this section of a report in Figure 1.5 in Chapter 1. In fact, the observations lend understanding to a literature review and also might yield artifacts in the way of images for helping the reader understand areas relating to the topic. Therefore, a second way to expand the literature review is by collecting *observations* (Onwuegbuzie, Leech, et al., 2011). You might be wondering about this concept and how the use of observations for the CLR is differentiated from observations in primary research. Much like the other sources that inform the CLR, direct observations can justify or create the background for further or primary research.

EXAMPLE: INCORPORATING FIRST-HAND OBSERVATIONS

A reviewer who is conducting a literature review of mentoring in U.S. public schools could obtain more contextual information than from any research article by actually going to one or more school locations where mentoring programs take place. Once there, the reviewer could observe aspects of the school (e.g., size, location) and community that can be integrated with the extant literature. As a real-life example, we refer readers to Tony's literature review on the posttraumatic stress disorder, depression, anxiety, and coping among adolescents from the Gaza Strip (cf. Elbedour, Onwuegbuzie, Ghannam, Whitcome, & Abu Hein, 2007). Tony spent a few days in the Gaza Strip to observe first-hand for himself the conditions. While there, Tony also was able to speak with several children and adolescents who were victims of the Israeli–Palestinian conflict. These data were extremely useful not only in informing the subsequent literature review, but also for facilitating a type of *interrogation of the literature* (Onwuegbuzie, Collins, et al., 2010, p. 184) by identifying numerous reporting inaccuracies about the Gaza Strip context in the extant literature written by authors who had never been to the Gaza Strip. Through this direct observation, Tony was able obtain a balanced picture and address the perspectives of children and adolescents on both sides of the Israeli–Palestinian conflict in his CLR.

MAPPING OBSERVATIONS

Another technique for incorporating observation data into the literature review is by mapping information extracted from selected sources to examine trends of one or more types. For instance, in conducting a literature review of violence in U.S. public schools, a reviewer could map the locations where school shootings have taken place in an attempt to identify patterns or trends. This information then could be incorporated into the literature review.

For example, for a literature review pertaining to school violence, we examined school shootings that took place in the United States (Onwuegbuzie & Frels, 2013b), which spanned from 1927 (Bath School, Michigan; 45 died, 58 injured) to 2012 (Sandy Hook Elementary School in Newtown, Connecticut; 28 died, 2

injured) to 2015 (Umpqua College, Roseburg, Oregon; 9 died at the time of writing). After mapping the locations of these deadly incidents, we determined that most of these shootings took place in rural or suburban places with populations of fewer than 25,000—including Roseburg, Oregon— indicating that extreme violence at schools is not a problem restricted to urban areas.

GEOGRAPHIC INFORMATION SYSTEMS. Whenever possible, we recommend that you also consider mapping information that informs literature reviews using some form of geographic information systems (GIS). GIS applications allow users to collect and to analyze a structured database containing geographical elements that are spatially oriented to Earth (cf. Goodchild, Fu, & Rich, 2007; Institute, 2009). Using GIS applications, data can be represented via maps, charts, models, matrices, and other visual forms (Frels, Frels, & Onwuegbuzie, 2011). Thus, as noted by Onwuegbuzie, Leech, et al. (2011), "information from the extant literature can be integrated with GIS to enhance the reviewers' understanding of the underlying phenomenon by providing spatial and geographical contexts that facilitate the identification of patterns, trends, and relationships" (p. 197). Consequently, for example, a reviewer could use GIS, or other graphing applications, to map the location of school massacres in the United States to examine trends. This map then could be displayed in the final report as part of the literature review.

EXAMPLE: USE OF GIS TO MAP FINDINGS

Figure 8.10 provides an example of the world health rankings data being mapped onto the world map using GIS software—specifically a software tool called ArcGIS. You can see from this figure that, in general, countries from Western Europe (e.g., Germany, Italy, France) have the highest health care rankings. Such a GIS map surely would enhance the presentation of a literature review about the healthcare system worldwide by providing a reader-friendly visual display. Further, such visual displays could save space by helping to minimize the associated text, thereby lending support to the adage that "a picture is worth a thousand words."

Health System Attainment and Performance
Members of the World Health Organization

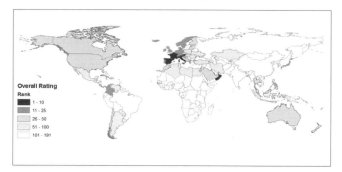

Figure 8.10 Each of the 191 countries as listed in the directory of the World Health Organization (2000) and which was retrieved via a spreadsheet from www.geographic.org. This information was depicted using a GIS software package (ArcGIS) to illustrate how a spatial representation of data might enhance literature reviews

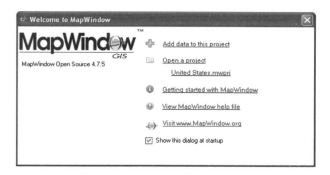

Figure 8.11 Screenshot showing the homepage of MapWindow GIS application

Figure 8.12 Screenshot of MapWindow GIS application displaying the U.S. map

ArcGIS (circa 1999), distributed by the Economic and Social Research Institute (ESRI; circa 1969), represents a popular suite of GIS software products (cf. http://www.arcgis.com/about/). These software products can be used to create and to utilize maps, to compile geographic data, to analyze mapped data, and to manage and to share geographic information in a database. ArcGIS products operate on desktop, server, and mobile platforms. Unfortunately, as might be expected, ArcGIS products are somewhat expensive for many single users. Figure 8.11 shows the screenshot of the homepage of MapWindow GIS, and Figure 8.12 shows a screenshot of a MapWindow GIS application displaying the U.S. map, which can be used to enhance a literature review whenever relevant data exist that can be mapped.

GROUND TRUTHING. Whenever possible, reviewers should seek to validate their GIS data via a technique known as ground truthing. Specifically, *ground truthing* involves actually visiting one or more of the places where the GIS data were collected in order to obtain a visual image of the data in person (Frels et al., 2011). When it is not possible to visit the location, the reviewer can ask a trusted associate (e.g., colleague, friend, family member) to visit the location. Alternatively, the reviewer could seek assistance from trustworthy local experts to ground truth the GIS data. If it is not possible for anyone to visit the location, then the reviewer should consider cross-validating the GIS data via tools such as current aerial photography or satellite images (Steinberg & Steinberg, 2006). As noted by Steinberg and Steinberg (2006), "ground truthing data is perhaps one of the most important steps of integrating GIS into social science research" (p. 82).

TASK D: *DOCUMENTS*

In Chapter 5 (i.e., Step 2: Initiating the Search), we described how to search the most common type of printed or digital sources that are used to inform literature reviews, namely, published articles. We demonstrated how to extract these articles from library subscription databases and public Internet sources.

EXAMPLE: JOURNAL SPECIAL ISSUES

Before leaving our discussion of journal articles, we will provide another useful tip for expanding your search. Specifically, whatever the topic of interest, we recommend that you always search to determine whether the topic has been the focus of any special issues published in journals. A useful format for searching for special issues in a certain area is as follows:

TOPIC NAME and JOURNAL and "SPECIAL ISSUE"

TOOL: LIST OF OPEN SOURCE GIS PRODUCTS

You might consider using an open source (i.e., free) GIS software product. Table 8.2 provides examples of free and open source GIS products. MapWindow GIS project, described above, is one such example.

Table 8.2 Open source GIS products

Product	Developer	Platform	Internet Address
GRASS GIS	U.S. Army	Multiple	http://grass.osgeo.org/
SAGA GIS	University of Göttingen	Multiple	http://www.saga-gis.org/en/about/software.html
Quantum GIS	Open Source Geospatial Foundation	Multiple	http://quantumgis.com/welcome-to-the-quantum-gis-project.html/
MapWindow GIS	Environmental Protection Agency	Windows	www.mapwindow.org

Note: Multiple platforms include Windows, Mac OS, and Linux.

The special issue is inserted within quotation marks because journal special issues are always called *special issues* and, as you might recall from Chapter 6, the use of quotation marks leads to a search for all documents that contain the string of words in quotation marks. Thus, for our mentoring and college students example, we used the following search string:

mentoring and college students and journal and "special issue"

This search revealed a few special issues, including the *Special Issue on Mentoring in Organizations* which was published in 1997 in the *Journal of Vocational Behavior* and a *Special Issue on Mentors and Mentoring* published in 1996 in the *Peabody Journal of Education*, wherein every article in these special issues was on the topic of mentoring. Thus, as can be seen, searching for special issues can be very fruitful. Although articles represent the most common type of printed or digital document used by reviewers, apart from books (which we discussed in Step 2), many other useful documents exist, including the following: dissertations and theses, monographs, encyclopedias, government documents, trade catalogues, and legal and public records information. We will discuss each of these document types in the subsequent sections.

DISSERTATIONS AND THESES

A dissertation or thesis is a document completed by students as a major and required part of their candidature for an academic degree or professional qualification. In some regions (e.g., United States, Slovenia, Slovakia), the word "thesis" typically is used for part of a bachelor's or master's degree program, whereas "dissertation" is normally applied to a doctorate program. In other regions (e.g., United Kingdom, Portugal, Brazil), the converse is true, with "dissertation" typically being applied to an undergraduate degree and/or a (taught) master's degree and "thesis" usually being applied to a doctorate degree.

Dissertations and theses typically represent an extended empirical research study, or an extended analysis or review of a chosen topic. Traditionally, these documents tend to contain a title page, a table of contents, an abstract, and multiple sections or chapters (e.g., introduction, literature review, methods,

results, discussion, bibliography/references section); however, they vary in structure in accordance with the field or discipline, as well as with the level of university (e.g., research university vs. [predominantly] teaching university) and region. A more recent form of a dissertation is called the *journal-ready dissertation*, which alongside a general introduction chapter, contains three journal-ready manuscripts. Sam Houston State University has clear guidelines for journal-ready dissertations(http://www.shsu.edu/dotAsset/e8038f71-a5d7-4b49-a74c-f119d279e8bd.pdf).

Regardless of the format, dissertations and theses tend to be much longer than are most journal articles. For example, an electronic search by Harmon, Howley, and Sanders (1996) of Dissertation Abstracts International (DAI)—a database for dissertations and theses—revealed 196 doctoral dissertations written between 1989 and 1993 that focused on rural education. These 196 doctoral dissertations, which were predominantly written by U.S. students, ranged in length from 74 to 923 pages, with the majority of them (80%) ranging between 100 and 300 pages. Thus, because of their overall length, dissertations and theses typically have longer literature review sections than do most published journal articles. As a result, not only do dissertations and theses often provide useful empirical findings that can inform a literature review, but also the literature review chapter/section of dissertations and theses—especially those that are the most current—because of their lack of strict space constraints, can help you expand your literature review, or at least help you validate your literature review by checking whether you have included all the most relevant literature.

Dissertation Abstracts International is a very popular library subscription database for obtaining dissertations and theses authored by U.S. students—as noted in the previous paragraph. Interestingly, most graduate students (i.e., 95%–98%) who graduate from U.S. institutions submit their dissertations and theses to ProQuest for publication or listing in DAI. These listings provide the following information: bibliographic citations that include title, author name, degree-granting institution, year awarded, number of pages, and ProQuest order number. Since 1988, most DAI entries also have included the name of the dissertation advisor/supervisor/chair. Also, since 1980, DAI entries have included 350-word dissertation/thesis abstracts too. These listings, which include approximately 5,000 new entries from the United States per month, are grouped by subject and printed in two separate sections: Section A, Humanities and Social Sciences, and Section B, Sciences and Engineering. Of all the printed sources for the ProQuest Dissertations and Theses database, DAI is the most current. Masters Abstracts International (MAI) is the source of the master's degree information in the ProQuest Dissertations and Theses database. More than 12,000 citations and abstracts of master's theses are published each year.

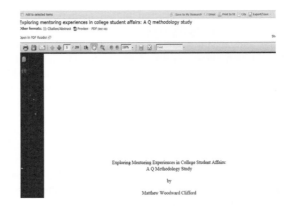

EXAMPLE: DISSERTATIONS AND THESES

Figure 8.13 shows how you could conduct a search via ProQuest Dissertations and Theses Full Text using the search string "mentoring and college students." This search yielded 75,891 hits. However, you can narrow the results by selecting options pertaining to the following elements: Full text, Subject, Index term (keyword), University/institution, University/institution location, Tags, Language, Database,

Figure 8.14 Screenshot showing the pdf file of the selected dissertation on the topic of "mentoring and college students" available for downloading from the library subscription database ProQuest Dissertations and Theses Full Text, assuming that the reviewer's institution subscribes to this database

and Publication date. Figure 8.14 shows a screenshot of the pdf file ready for downloading of the selected dissertation on the topic of "mentoring and college students" from the

Figure 8.13 Screenshot showing the website page of the library subscription database ProQuest Dissertations and Theses Full Text using the search string "mentoring and college students"

library subscription database ProQuest Dissertations and Theses Full Text, assuming that the reviewer's institution subscribes to this database.

Unfortunately, because the full text of dissertations and theses typically are only available via library subscription databases (as opposed to being available via public Internet sources), and free access to these full texts often depends on whether the institution to which the reviewer belongs subscribes to the database, many researchers do not include dissertations and theses as part of their literature reviews. However, because of their potentially rich nature, we encourage you to include them as part of your expanded literature review whenever possible.

RSS TECHNOLOGIES

As discussed in Chapter 2, RSS technologies notify a user when new dissertations and theses have been published. Depending on your institution, you might be able to create an RSS feed for dissertations and theses directly from your institution's website.

EXAMPLE: RSS FEEDS

Box 8.1 shows the steps for creating an RSS feed, as well as a website for obtaining an RSS reader to read the RSS feeds.

MONOGRAPHS

The word *monograph* (circa 1821) stems from the Greek words *mono* (single) and *grapho* (to write). Thus, a monograph, which also is called a scholarly treatise, is an extremely detailed essay

BOX 8.1

STEPS FOR CREATING AN RSS FEED FOR A RECENT SEARCH, AS WELL AS A WEBSITE FOR OBTAINING AN RSS READER

You can create an RSS feed, to automatically notify you of new documents matching your search. Follow these steps to create an RSS feed:

1. Click *Create RSS feed* on the Results page, or from a list of your Recent Searches.
2. A new window will open, showing details for your RSS feed.
3. Copy the URL displayed next to *Your RSS Feed.*
4. Add the URL to your RSS reader, or integrate it into your webpage.

The first time you access your RSS feed, no new documents will be available. However, as soon as new documents are available, your feed will be updated automatically with new information.

USING YOUR RSS FEED

Your RSS feed will be updated whenever new documents are available that match your search. You can link directly from a summary of the article to the full text in ProQuest, if available. You must log in to ProQuest to see the full text.

WHAT IS AN RSS READER?

RSS readers help you view the latest information from multiple sites at once. Many readers are freely available. There are many options; one web-based reader is available at http://www.bloglines.com.

Your RSS feed will expire after three months if it has not been viewed.

Adapted from the ProQuest website (http://proquest.umi.com/i-std/en/abi/rss/rss_search.htm).

or book covering a single subject or a component of a subject. The goal of a monograph is to present new and original information and scholarly research on a very specific topic that advances both the author's career and field. Typically, only one author is involved in writing a monograph; however, where necessary, multiple authors might be involved. Monographs are longer than are journal articles and may even be the length of a short book.

As such, publication of a monograph often provides evidence that the author has attained a high(er) level of recognition in her/his academic disciplines. In most instances, a monograph is written to serve as a standalone, non-serial document, although some monographs are published as part of a limited set of volumes. Thus, monographs differ from serial publications such as a magazine, journal, or newspaper. Monographs primarily are purchased by libraries, and generally published as individual volumes in a short print run.

EXAMPLE: MONOGRAPHS

Monographs are commonplace in many fields and disciplines. With respect to medical research, the International Agency for Research on Cancer, for example, published monographs to identify environmental factors that increase cancer risk for the purpose of justifying laws that prevent exposure to factors that cause cancer. As another example, the National Institute on Drug Abuse has a collection of monographs that monitor what works and does not work in drug abuse and addiction prevention for the purpose of using this information to determine best practices that improve drug abuse prevention, treatment, and policy.

Because monographs usually have a short print run, they are relatively expensive for publishers to print. Thus, the Internet is fast becoming a popular place to distribute monographs. Indeed, the Internet now contains millions of monographs—thereby making it easier to create an RSS feed for monographs. Interestingly, the Public Knowledge Project is developing the Open Monograph Press (http://pkp.sfu.ca/omp/), which is a workspace for monographs, with an archive and index that have been designed to make monographs accessible and retrievable (see Figure 8.15). Thus, a useful way of expanding a literature review is to search monograph databases that represent your field.

ENCYCLOPEDIAS

An *encyclopedia* (also spelled *encyclopaedia* or *encyclopædia*) is a type of reference work or compendium (e.g., a book, series of books, website, or CD-ROM) that contains a summary of information about many different subjects or a lot of information about a particular subject. Typically, encyclopedias consist of articles or entries that are arranged alphabetically by topic. Further, they are different from dictionaries; in particular, unlike dictionary entries, which focus as succinctly as possible on linguistic information about single words, encyclopedia entries contain factual information on the underlying topic. The earliest encyclopedia to have survived to modern times is *Naturalis Historia*, which was published around AD 77–79 by Pliny the Elder, a Roman statesman living in the 1st century AD. This encyclopedia contained 37 chapters that covered topics such as natural history, architecture, medicine, geography, and geology, and which included 20,000 facts from 2,000 works authored by more than 200 authors. In the Middle Ages, encyclopedias were written in English, Arabic, and Persian. Also, there were encyclopedias from China and India.

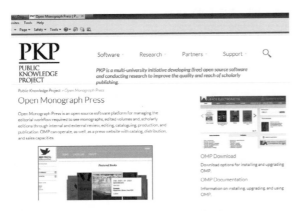

Figure 8.15 Screenshot showing the homepage of Open Monograph Press

EXAMPLE: ENCYCLOPEDIAS

Encyclopedias contain in-depth and relevant accumulated knowledge on numerous subjects, and it is common for them to include maps and illustrations, as well as statistics. Another appeal of encyclopedias is that their entries often contain citations and bibliographies. As such, encyclopedias represent an excellent source for expanding a literature review. However, most encyclopedias are expensive for single users. Fortunately, institutions of higher learning (e.g., universities) often subscribe to the most popularized encyclopedias. A very popular library subscription encyclopedia database is Encyclopædia Britannica / Britannica Academic Edition. Figure 8.16 is a screenshot of the Encyclopædia Britannica / Britannica Academic Edition database.

The year 1993 saw the introduction of the first free Internet-based online encyclopedia, via what was called the *Interpedia proposal*, which allowed anyone with Internet access to contribute to the encyclopedia by writing articles and uploading them onto the central catalogue of all Interpedia pages. However, it was not until 2000 that a stable, free Internet-based encyclopedia was established, namely, Nupedia (which only lasted until 2003). This encyclopedia was succeeded by English Wikipedia in 2001, which currently contains more than 4.3 million articles. Wikipedia, of which English Wikipedia represents the first and largest edition, is a multilingual, free Internet encyclopedia supported by the non-profit Wikimedia Foundation, which is collaboratively edited by anyone with access to the website. At the time of writing, it contains 30 million articles covering 287 languages. Thus, it is the largest and most popular general reference work on the Internet, ranking sixth worldwide among all websites on Alexa, and securing approximately 365 million readers worldwide. Compared to printed encyclopedias, Wikipedia and other online (i.e., digital) encyclopedias have the advantage that new information about a topic can be updated almost immediately, instead of waiting for the next release of the printed version. Further, digital encyclopedias make it easier to search for keywords or phrases than do printed versions.

Another advantage of digital encyclopedias is that they incorporate media that are difficult or even impossible to store in the printed format, such as audio and video, animations, hypertexting of words and phrases, and hyperlinking among items. However, despite its relative ease of accessing information, because this information is not subject to any peer review, the accuracy of information can be questionable. Thus, we ask you to exercise caution when using digital encyclopedias to expand your literature review. Indeed, many college-level teachers discourage or even prohibit their students from citing any information extracted from digital encyclopedias in general and Wikipedia in particular.

GOVERNMENT DOCUMENTS

Government documents involve the publications of documents by government agencies. Within the United States, government documents involve the publications of documents by both federal and local governments. These documents include statistical reports (e.g., U.S. Census), statutes, hearings, treaties, and periodicals. Documents also are published by international governmental organizations or intergovernmental organizations (IGOs) such as the United Nations and the World Health Organization (for a complete list of IGOs, see http://www.uia.org/yearbook), and non-governmental organizations (NGOs) such as the World Trade Organization.

Most academic libraries house government documents, which usually are shelved in a separate section and have their own classification schemes. For example, each U.S. federal document has its own unique Superintendent of Documents (SuDocs) number (cf. http://www.fdlp.gov/cataloging/856–sudoc-classification-scheme?start=1). Government documents are published in a variety of formats, including paper, microfiche, CD-ROM, and online.

A very popular library subscription database for government documents is the United States Government Printing Office (GPO), which is the world's largest publisher and which makes its publications available to the public through the Federal Documents Depository Program (circa 1813). The Federal Depository Library Program regularly distributes publications at no charge

Figure 8.16 Screenshot of the Encyclopædia Britannica / Britannica Academic Edition database

to approximately 1,400 Depository Libraries that are located in all 50 states, six territories and the District of Columbia, with slightly more than one half (52%) of these Depository Libraries represented by academic libraries and nearly one-fifth (19%) to public libraries. Figure 8.17 shows a screenshot of the GPO database.

EXAMPLE: GOVERNMENT DATABASES

Figure 8.18 displays a screenshot showing the results when the search strings "mentor*" and "college students" were used on the Government Printing Office database. In this instance, because none of the four titles appears to deal with mentoring *of* college students (only mentoring *by* college students), this database could not be used to expand the literature unless other related keywords can be used that are found to yield one or more relevant sources. However, it can happen—as was the case here—that a specific expanded search does not provide additional information to inform a literature review, in which case, you would search for alternative document types or conduct an expanded search via one or more of the other four MODES.

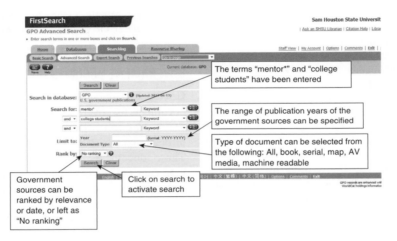

Figure 8.17 Screenshot of the Government Printing Office database

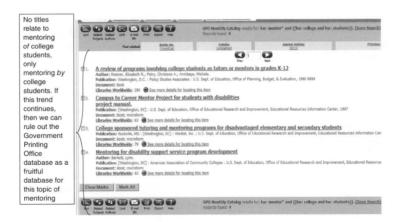

Figure 8.18 Screenshot showing the results when the search strings "mentor*" and "college students" were used on the Government Printing Office database

TRADE CATALOGUES

Broadly speaking, trade catalogues are printed documents that are published by manufacturers, wholesalers, and retailers. These documents promote sales by making advertising claims, including detailed descriptions of sale products, giving instructions for using products, and providing testimonials from satisfied customers. However, perhaps the most pertinent trade catalogue collection for reviewers is the Trade Literature Collection, which is known worldwide for providing an excellent source for the history of U.S. business, marketing, technology, design, and the like. An example of a trade catalogues collection is that of the National Art Library, which holds many examples of trade catalogues within its collections that are consistent with the research interests of the Victoria and Albert Museum in the United Kingdom.

LEGAL AND PUBLIC RECORDS INFORMATION

Outside the field of law, the use of legal information to enhance a literature review is not commonplace. Yet, many topics across numerous fields have a legal context. For instance, returning to our mentoring and college students example, although this topic might seem far removed from a legal context, we discovered the 2008 Higher Education Opportunity Act (Public Law 110–315), which encompasses a body of laws that relate to colleges and universities for students with intellectual disabilities to have a greater chance to obtain a degree. In this act, the word *mentor* is stated 42 times and the word *mentoring* is stated 62 times. As an example, in the amended Section 402E (20 U.S.C. 1070a–15), permissible services include "mentoring programs involving faculty members at institutions of higher education, students, or any combination of such persons" (p. 3203). Thus, using this Higher Education Opportunity Act, it is likely that a reviewer would have multiple opportunities to place a review regarding mentoring in higher education within a legal context.

EXAMPLE: LEGAL REVIEWS

Thus, legal reviews can be a helpful source in expanding the literature review. Conveniently, there are free legal research websites that facilitate legal reviews, such as Cornell Law School's Legal Information Institute, FindLaw .com, Martindale-Hubbell, Casetext, Lawyers.com, HG.org, and CanLII. A particularly useful database is LexisNexis (circa 1973), which represents the world's largest electronic database for legal and public-records related information.

Specifically, the LexisNexis database contains current U.S. statutes and laws and myriad published case opinions dating from the 1770s to the present. Further, it contains publicly available unpublished case opinions from 1980 to present day, as well as a library of briefs and motions and libraries of statutes, case judgments, and opinions for jurisdictions (e.g., France, Australia, Hong Kong, South Africa, United Kingdom). Also, the LexisNexis database contains law review and legal journal articles for countries for which materials are available. Figure 8.20 depicts a screenshot example of the LexisNexis Academic database.

It can be seen that this database allows the following searches:

- major world publications for current news from 1980 to current day via the following six sources: newspapers, magazines, wire services, broadcast transcripts, blogs, and all news; or the user can type in the name of the source (e.g., *New York Times*)
- legal cases by citation (e.g., 347 U.S. 483), parties (e.g., Mapp v. Ohio), or topic (e.g., mentoring)
- company information by name (e.g., Microsoft) or by ticker (e.g., MSFT)
- recent hot topics, with an advanced search option that allows the user to (a) search all available dates (default) or limit the search to current day or as far back as records allow by days, weeks, months, or years; (b) insert index terms related to a company, industry, subject, geography, or people; and (c) select the source of the major world publications: all news, foreign language news, broadcast transcripts, industry news publications, company information, federal and state cases, and U.S. law reviews
- people by last name and first name with respect to biographical references or recent news stories
- multiple kinds of content (a) for all available dates (default) or limiting the search to current day or as far back as records allow by weeks, months, or years; (b) by one or more of the following sources: major U.S. and world news, company profiles, U.S. Securities and Exchange Commission (SEC) filings, U.S. and state legal cases, or law reviews; (c) using the advanced search option that allows the user to:

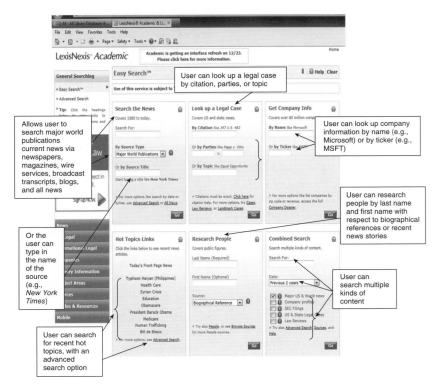

Figure 8.19 Screenshot of the LexisNexis Academic database

o search all available dates (default) or limit the search to current day or as far back as records allow by days, weeks, months, or years

o insert index terms related to a company, industry, subject, geography, or people

o select a segment (e.g., byline, city, country, edition)

Therefore, LexisNexis represents an extremely rich source of information that, in most instances, reviewers should consider using, regardless of their discipline or field.

GREY LITERATURE

So far, in this section, we have demonstrated ways to expand a literature review via searching for additional documents. For the most part, we have shown you numerous ways of searching for published documents whether in printed and/or digital form. However, as we noted in Chapter 1, many unpublished works, otherwise known as grey literature (or gray literature), can be a rich source of information. As a recap, Grey

Grey literature is a field in library and Information science that deals with the production, distribution, and access to *multiple document types* produced on all levels of government, academics, business, and organization in electronic and print formats not controlled by commercial publishing, i.e. where publishing is not the primary activity of the producing body. [emphasis added] (Grey Literature Network Service, 2012, ¶ 2)

literature can be in the form of reports (e.g., preprints, preliminary progress and advanced reports, technical reports from government agencies or scientific research groups, statistical reports, memoranda, state-of-the- art reports, market research reports, working papers from research groups or committees, white papers), conference proceedings, technical reports, technical specifications and standards, non-commercial translations, bibliographies, technical and commercial documentation, and official documents that have not been published commercially (e.g., government reports and documents) (Alberani et al., 1990).

CONFERENCE PAPERS. Of the numerous sources for grey literature, unpublished conference papers represent potentially a very fruitful avenue for expanding the literature review. Indeed, an increasing number of professional associations are setting up online repositories that contain previously presented conference papers. For example, with respect to the field of education, the American Educational Research Association (AERA; circa 1916)—with approximately 25,000 members—hosts an annual conference that is, arguably, the most prestigious conference in the field of education in the United States. The AERA's website provides a link to an online repository that contains previously presented conference papers.

EXAMPLE: CONFERENCE PAPERS

Figure 8.20 reveals a screenshot of the AERA online repository containing a selection of previous annual meeting papers (2010 onwards). This repository allows the user to conduct either a *simple search* or an *advanced search* (cf. Figure 8.21). A simple search uses a single criterion to search all metadata, which may be part of a word, full word, or multiple words. It is not case sensitive. In contrast, an advanced search uses multiple criteria to search select metadata or documents. It allows the selection of metadata to search (i.e., *paper title* vs. *session title* vs. *paper type* vs. *presented on* vs. *location* vs. *descriptors* vs. *methodology* vs. *byline* vs. *meeting unit* vs. *abstract* vs. *presentation notes* vs. *subsequent publication* vs. *URL link* vs. *DOI link*) and search method (i.e., *contains* vs. *doesn't contain* vs. *starts with* vs. *ends with*). It is also not case sensitive.

Figure 8.22 displays a screenshot showing the results of a search of the AERA's online repository for previous annual

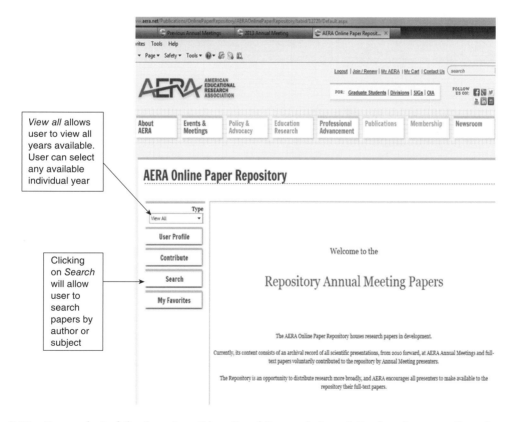

View all allows user to view all years available. User can select any available individual year

Clicking on *Search* will allow user to search papers by author or subject

Figure 8.20   Screenshot of the American Educational Research Association's online repository for previous annual meeting papers (2010 onwards)

Figure 8.21 Screenshot of the AERA online repository for previous annual meeting papers (2010 onwards) showing the option to conduct either a simple search or an advanced search

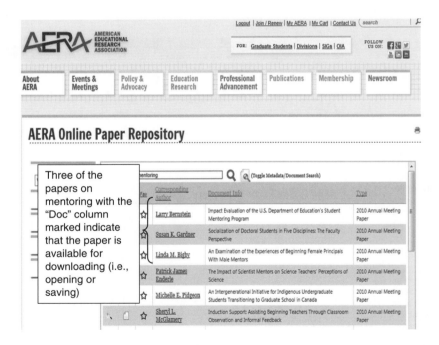

Three of the papers on mentoring with the "Doc" column marked indicate that the paper is available for downloading (i.e., opening or saving)

Figure 8.22 Screenshot showing search of the AERA online repository for previous annual meeting papers using the keyword "mentoring"

meeting papers using the keyword "mentoring." You can see that, at the time of writing, there are five available (i.e., downloadable, full-text) papers on the first web page. By perusing each of these available documents, it is likely that we would find at least one paper that is pertinent to our exemplar topic of *mentoring and college students*. We would like to remind you that these papers on mentoring are unpublished and might never be published—at least in their unpublished version. Also, we would like to point out that because of its prestige, the AERA attracts many of the most prolific educational researchers in the world. Thus, it is likely that at least some of these unpublished papers would be among the most cutting-edge papers, which means that failure to search this online depository might lead to one or more key current citations being omitted from the literature review on mentoring.

Thus, we recommend that, as part of conducting your expanded search via the MODES of documents, you determine whether any professional associations representing your field or discipline—especially the national- and international-level associations—host an online repository for unpublished conference papers. Keep in mind that even those professional associations that do not host online repositories usually list the title and perhaps even the abstract of each conference paper presented for the most recent years. By reading the titles and available abstracts, you can identify any potential papers for your CLR and contact the author(s) for either a digital or hard copy version of the paper. We will discuss the concept of contacting authors in more detail in parts of the next sections.

BLOGS. Blogs represent another useful type of grey literature. As we noted in Chapter 2, a blog is a type of website or part of a website that is updated with new content (e.g., commentary, description of events, pictures, videos) by one or more individuals as needed, with entries typically displayed in reverse-chronological order. A useful way to obtain blogs about grey literature is by subscribing to GreyNet's listserv (http://www.greynet.org/home/listserv.html). GreyNet's listserv is moderated to ensure that postings are relevant to the field of grey literature. The moderator organizes the blogs and posts them to the listserv subscribers.

EXAMPLE: BLOGS

Returning to our *mentoring and college students* example, a quick perusal of the Dogpile meta-search engine using the keywords "mentor" and "blog" led to several mentoring blog sites, including the site belonging to Dr. Lois Zachary called "Lois Zachary's Mentoring Expert Blog" (cf. http://mentoringexpert.wordpress.com/). At this site are tips, guidelines, and practical advice for both mentors and mentees, including anyone involved in the mentoring process or beginning the mentoring experience. Because Dr. Zachary is an internationally recognized mentoring and leadership expert, it makes sense at least to peruse this website for any information that might enrich the literature review. When we used the search string "mentoring blog and college students" on the Dogpile meta-search engine (www.dogpile.com), even more relevant sites emerged. For example, a College and Career Mentoring blog (cf. http://www.studentmentor.org/blog/) was revealed, as well as College Mentoring blog—Stu's Blog (cf. http://www.studentmentor.org/blog/)—to name just two blog sites. Another benefit of searching for blog sites pertaining to the topic of interest is that it often helps to identify experts in the topic area. This provides a nice segue to the next section, wherein we outline how you can involve the experts in your topic area who you have identified in helping you expand your literature review.

TASK E: *EXPERTS*
IDENTIFYING EXPERTS

While initializing the search (Step 2), storing and organizing information (Step 3), and selecting and deselecting documents (Step 4), you should have identified who are the most prolific authors/researchers regarding your chosen topic. We refer to these prolific authors and researchers as experts under the assumption that they have devoted a large proportion of their professional careers to researching and writing about this topic. These experts should have become apparent because they would have published multiple works in this area and would have been cited by many other authors writing on this topic. However, if, at this stage, you are still uncertain about who the most productive authors/researchers (i.e., experts) are, then one useful strategy to glean this information is by conducting a content analysis of the reference list of works that you have collected in Steps 2–5.

An extremely innovative way of identifying the most prolific authors/researchers in an area is to use computer-assisted qualitative data analysis software. For instance, Frels, Onwuegbuzie, and Slate (2010b) used the qualitative software QDA Miner (Provalis Research, 2009a) and WordStat (Provalis Research, 2009b) to conduct a content analysis and word count analysis, respectively, to determine the number of publications associated with every author (primary and secondary) publishing in the journal for which they served as editors, namely, *Research in the Schools*, over the last 15 years.

Another direct way to determine the experts in an area of interest is by using Harzing's (2009) Publish or

Perish software (www.harzing.com/pop.htm). Publish or Perish is a free software program (downloadable for Windows or Mac OS X) that retrieves and analyzes academic citations using Google Scholar. Returning once again to our mentoring example, we used Publish or Perish to determine the most cited authors in this area. Figure 8.23 displays a screenshot of the results showing the most cited works in the area of mentoring using the keyword "mentor*" via Harzing's (2009) Publish or Perish software and Google Scholar. The screenshot displays the 34 most cited authors in the area of mentoring that fit on the page at the time of writing. (The remaining authors can be obtained by scrolling down.) These authors are listed in the order of the number of citations. It can be seen from this figure that K. E. Kram had a book entitled *Mentoring at Work: Developmental Relationships in Organizational Life.* (Although not displayed in the screenshot, if you were to scroll the screen to the right, it will be specified that this was a book.) At the time of writing, this book, which was published in 1988, has been cited 3,208 times—more than any other work in this area.

EXAMPLE: ACTIVE AUTHORS

Interestingly, K. E. Kram also has the third most-cited work, entitled "Phases of the mentoring relationship," published in 1983 in the *Academy of Management Journal*, which, again at the time of writing, has been cited 1,635 times. You might already have been made aware of one or both of these works as part of your search in Step 2 or your expanded search in Step 5, and might even have stored and organized these references in Step 3. If not, then our next task is to determine whether these works are applicable for your literature review. If they pertain to college

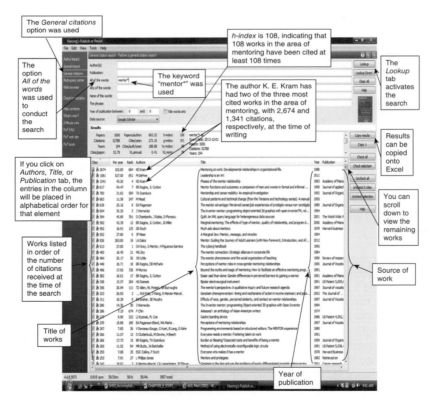

Figure 8.23 Screenshot showing the most cited works in the area of mentoring (in order of number of citations) using the keyword "mentor*" via Harzing's (2009) Publish or Perish software and Google Scholar

students, at least in part, then it is likely that these works are applicable. If they do not pertain to college students, then we should peruse these works to determine whether they can inform our literature review in any way. If we deem them applicable, then it is clear that K. E. Kram would be an expert of interest for us. Assuming that K. E. Kram is a person of interest, our next task is to determine whether K. E. Kram still is an active author—especially bearing in mind that K. E. Kram's most cited article was published more than 30 years ago. (Obviously, we only want to contact experts who are still active in the field.)

We can use Google Scholar to determine whether K. E. Kram is an active scholar. Figure 8.24 displays a screenshot showing results from Google Scholar using the search name "K E Kram." The advanced search option was used to limit the search to the years 2013 and beyond. It can be seen in this figure that K. E. Kram has had numerous works published in 2013. Thus, it appears that this author is still very much active. Also, by clicking on one or more of the open access links (e.g., articles that have a pdf or HTML hyperlink on the right-hand side of the screen), we were able to find out that K. E. Kram's first name is Karin, indicating that she is female. These open access articles also indicate that her affiliation is the Department of Microbiology and Immunology, College of Physicians and Surgeons, Columbia University, New York, NY, USA.

Some of these articles also contain her email address. Or we can go to her institution's website to obtain this information. So, if we decided to contact her, we would be in a position to do so. Using the information from our content analysis of the reference lists and/or the Publish or Perish results, we continue to identify the key experts in the topic area until we have a list of at least three experts of interest. Our recommendation of interviewing three experts is consistent with the recommendation of using three to five participants in case studies (Creswell, 2002), a minimum of three participants per subgroup for interviews (Onwuegbuzie & Leech, 2007a), and a minimum of three participants for mini-focus groups (Morgan, 1997).

EXAMPLE: PUBLISH OR PERISH SOFTWARE

Another benefit of using the Publish or Perish software is that, by examining the *Year* column (see Figure 8.24), you can determine publishing trends for your topic area (e.g., for which year(s) were the most works on mentoring published?). Also, by examining the *Publication* column, you can

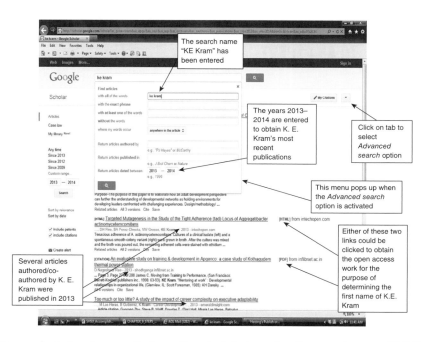

Figure 8.24   Screenshot showing results from Google Scholar using the search name "K E Kram"

determine trends in publishing outlets (e.g., which journal publishes the most works on mentoring?). However, even more importantly, the list of works yielded by the Publish or Perish software can be used to validate your search in Step 2 and your expanded search in Step 5 and to see whether you can identify any additional sources that you had missed up until this point. An interesting note is that Publish or Perish has revealed that the *h-index* for mentoring is 161. This number means that at least 161 works in the area of mentoring have been cited at least 161 times, which indicates that the topic of mentoring is very well established. To help put this number in perspective, using the search term "tutor*" using the Publish or Perish software revealed an *h-index* of 88.

INTERVIEWING EXPERTS

Once you have identified active experts of interest, you will be in a position to expand your search by interviewing them or talking directly with them, either formally or informally, as we noted in Chapter 2. The main goal of these interviews/talks is to attempt to obtain the experts' latest thinking on the topic of interest. The experts in the CLR process serve like an expert witness in a detective's investigation of a crime. The least intrusive way initially to contact these experts within the CLR process in general and the expanded search step (i.e., Step 5) in particular is to send them an email.

EXAMPLE: EMAIL/INTERVIEW

Box 8.2 provides an exemplar email to an expert. As can be seen, this email provides the expert with several options. First and foremost, the expert is given the option of declining the interview for the reason of being too busy. Hopefully, this will not occur. If the expert is interested and available for interview, then he/she can choose to be interviewed face-to-face or remotely (i.e., virtually or via phone call), or synchronously or asynchronously (i.e., via email). Further, you will notice the ethical statement about being prepared to obtain Institutional Review Board (IRB) approval to interview the expert—consistent with our description in Chapter 2 of the comprehensive literature reviewer as an ethical literature reviewer.

BOX 8.2

EXEMPLAR EMAIL TO AN EXPERT

Dear Dr. M. Entor

My name is A. Researcher. I am a graduate student at the University of Mentoring. I am currently conducting a study on mentoring in college. In conducting my literature review, I have come across many of your works, which I have read and have found to be extremely useful for understanding this topic. Your excellent works have answered a lot of my questions about mentoring. On a continued positive note, your works also have raised some very important questions. I read a textbook on conducting comprehensive literature reviews written by Onwuegbuzie and Frels, and they recommended that whenever possible, reviewers should interview prolific authors as part of conducting a comprehensive literature review. Therefore, although I realize you are extremely busy, I was wondering whether I can interview you to ask you a few questions about your valuable work. I should not need more than 30 minutes of your time. I live within driving distance of your institution. So, I will be happy to interview you face-to-face at a location of your choice (my first preference). Alternatively, I could interview you virtually (e.g., Skype, GoToMeeting, Google Hangout) or via the telephone. Please let me know what mode you prefer. As another alternative, I could email you my questions. If needed, I will seek Institutional Review Board (IRB) approval to interview you. Of course, I will acknowledge your assistance in my article.

I look forward to hearing from you at your convenience.

Warm regards,
A. Researcher

The advantage of conducting a prolific interview face-to-face is that you are more likely to obtain the full attention of the expert. Also, as recommended by Denham and Onwuegbuzie (2013) and Onwuegbuzie and Frels (2012a, 2012b), during face-to-face interviews, it is easier for you to observe the expert's non-verbal behaviors such as the following: kinesics (behaviors characterized by body displacements and postures), proxemics (behaviors reflecting special relationships of the interviewees/interviewers), chronemics (temporal speech markers such as gaps, silences, hesitations), and paralinguistics (behaviors indicating tenor, strength, or emotive color of the vocal expression). For a CLR, these non-verbal data can be integrated with verbal (i.e., interview) data for one or more of the following five purposes: (a) *corroborate* speech narrative (triangulation); (b) *capture* underlying messages (complementarity); (c) *discover* non-verbal behaviors that contradict the verbal communication (initiation); (d) *broaden* the scope of the understanding (expansion); and (e) *create new directions* based on additional insights (development) (Denham & Onwuegbuzie, 2013).

The advantages of virtual interviewing of experts compared to face-to-face interviewing are numerous. First, virtual interviewing reduces challenges associated with time, location, and space, as well as the cost of interviewing (e.g., travel). Also, a virtual interview allows a literature reviewer to contact experts who are difficult to reach (e.g., experts with limited mobility; experts who are extremely busy; experts who are traveling). By using a virtual interview, it is possible to increase participation of experts who routinely conduct research using computer-mediated communication (CMC) and Web 2.0 tools and who are comfortable in virtual environments (Biddix, 2008; Onwuegbuzie, Leech, et al., 2011). In our own experience, we have found that a high proportion of prolific authors agree to be interviewed in some form. For example, when conducting the Dyadic Mentoring Study, Rebecca expanded her study through the virtual interview of experts in search of information specific to understanding some background to documents that she located. By contacting an expert in the area of mentoring via email correspondence, she located a quantitative measure to use as part of the data collection process that

measured the quality of mentoring relationships. The author of the instrument provided it free of charge. This instrument was useful to support, or to triangulate the qualitative findings of her study (cf. Frels & Onwuegbuzie, 2013). In addition, Rebecca consulted via Skype one expert in research methodology for help in understanding some of the literature that she had selected. Thus, Rebecca was able to integrate the insights provided by each expert with her existing knowledge of the topic and to expand her understanding of the collected literature.

Interviewing experts as part of the CLR is beneficial for many reasons. First, by interviewing experts, reviewers can give the experts the opportunity to provide information that verifies, modifies, refutes, or updates the findings, interpretations, and/or concepts/ideas that the reviewers have gleaned from their literature reviews at that point. Second, these experts also can inform the reviewers of their latest unpublished works, ongoing works, and/or future works, as well as those of other co-authors/co-researchers or authors/researchers with whose work they are familiar. Indeed, it is not unusual for experts to provide reviewers with their unpublished works to add to their collections. These works would represent grey literature, as we discussed earlier. Indeed, such works can be of the utmost value to a reviewer because they would represent the most current thinking of these experts. As described by Onwuegbuzie, Leech, et al. (2011), an important limitation of using published works as the sole sources that inform a literature review—whether printed or digital works—is that there is always a time lag between when the findings, theories, or concepts emerged for the author and when the works in which they are delineated are published and made available to literature reviewers. We call this time lag the **emergence-to-publication time lag**. With the exception of a few fields (e.g., medicine, where results from clinical trials must be published as soon as possible), it is not unusual for this emergence-to-publication time lag to be at least 1 year.

Unfortunately, we have experienced time lags as long as 3 years such that by the time the work is published, the literature review is at least 3 years old—which is a long-enough time in some fields for a whole paradigm shift to have occurred (e.g., replacement of the term *mentally retarded* to *intellectually disabled* among educators and researchers). Book chapters and the sets of articles that form special issues published in journals are especially susceptible to lengthy emergence-to-publication time lags because the time that elapses between when the first set of authors and the last set of authors submit their works to journal/book editors can be long enough to render some of the information provided by the first set of authors as being outdated.

In a similar way, backlogs in journal issues and volumes could subject the publication of in-press manuscripts to significant delays, also outdating some of the information presented in these works. Thus, even if the reviewer obtains a work as soon as it is published (e.g., using an RSS feed), at least some of the information might be outdated. Further, even for a work that is published in a maximally timely manner, it is still possible that aspects of the authors' findings, concepts, or theories have changed over the relatively short passage of time. Unfortunately, in such cases, the authors' change of perspective is not reflected anywhere in the work that is examined by the literature reviewer.

A third way that experts can help reviewers expand their literature reviews via the interview process is by helping them select the most appropriate methods (e.g., most appropriate instruments, research design, procedures) to use for their current and/or future studies by providing an expert critique of the methods used in previous works. Experts might even directly critique reviewers' own methods that they have planned for their primary research.

EXAMPLE: SYNCHRONOUS INTERVIEWING

Interviewing experts offers much potential for expanding the literature review and, in turn, brings the reviewer closer to a rich, detailed CLR. In fact, as authors of this book, we have served as *experts* for other authors' literature reviews. For example, Tony recently participated in a 1-hour interview conducted by an author who was writing about legitimation in mixed research. It has been an excellent experience for us to have served both as interviewers of experts and experts being interviewed, because it has enabled us to arrive at some standard questions that a reviewer might consider asking, such as those questions in Box 8.3. Of course, these are just a few of the many questions that a reviewer can ask an expert. In fact, the questions shown are general questions, and it is likely that the reviewer also will ask questions that emerged directly from reading the expert's works.

BOX 8.3

EXAMPLES OF QUESTIONS TO ASK AN EXPERT DURING AN INTERVIEW

1. What is your view about the state of our knowledge of this topic?
2. Despite your own works, what do you characterize as the leading works in this area?
3. Who do you characterize as the leading authors in this area?
4. What do you believe are the gaps in our knowledge of this topic?
5. Has your thinking on this topic evolved since your last published work?
6. What is your latest thinking on this topic?
7. Are you working on any new work? If so, is it possible for you to share this work with me?
8. Do you know anyone else who is working on any new work? If so, is it possible for you to share with me what they are working on?
9. What other sources should I explore to find out more about this topic?
10. Where do you see this field going in the future?

For students who are conducting their literature reviews under the guidance of a supervisor/advisor, mentor, or experienced co-author, once they have interviewed one or more experts, they could undergo what Onwuegbuzie, Leech, and Collins (2008) conceptualized as a debriefing interview, wherein the reviewer is interviewed by her/his supervisor/advisor/mentor/co-author or another person who understands the underlying research topic. (Even experienced literature reviewers likely would benefit from undergoing a debriefing interview.) This debriefer would ask the reviewer questions that help him/her identify any hidden biases; evaluate his/her hunches or intuitions that come to the fore before, during, or after the reviewer's interview of a prolific author; and increase the reviewer's understanding of the information obtained from the prolific authors/researchers (Onwuegbuzie, Leech, and Collins, 2011). These debriefing interviews then can be audio- or videotaped, thereby providing an audit trail that the reviewer can analyze alongside all the literature review data collected in Steps 1–5.

TOOL: DEBRIEFING INTERVIEW QUESTIONS

Onwuegbuzie, Leech, and Collins (2008) provide a typology of interviewing questions that the debriefer could ask the reviewers regarding her/his bias stemming from the following eight concepts:

- the reviewer's experience with interviewing (e.g., "How would you characterize your training/experience conducting interviews?")
- the reviewer's perceptions of the prolific author(s) (e.g., "Which prolific author's responses did you feel were the most helpful?")
- the reviewer's depth of knowledge of non-verbal communication (e.g., "To what degree do you think the tonal quality [e.g., volume, pitch, quality of voice] or the dialogue between the prolific author and yourself impacted the dynamics of the interview?")
- the reviewer's interpretations of the information extracted from the interviews (e.g., "What information that was obtained from the prolific authors surprised you?")
- thoughts regarding how the interview(s) affected the reviewer (e.g., "Which part of the interview(s), if any, impacted you?")
- concerns regarding the impact of the interview(s) on the prolific author (e.g., "What other background variables might have influenced how the participant reacted?")
- ethical or political issues that might have arisen at any stage of the interview process (e.g., "What types of ethical issues did you encounter during the interview(s), if any?")
- the reviewer's identification of problems that stemmed from the interviews (e.g., "What dilemmas did you encounter during the study? How did you handle the dilemma?")

As additional ideas for debriefing experts for the CLR, a literature reviewer might turn to some questions that Onwuegbuzie et al. (2008) conceptualized based on Guba and Lincoln's (1989) five constructivist-based principles—termed *authenticity criteria*:

- fairness (i.e., "the extent to which different constructions and their underlying value structures are solicited and honored within the evaluation process"; Guba & Lincoln, 1989, pp. 246–247)
- ontological authenticity (i.e., the degree that the prolific authors' levels of awareness have been impacted by participating in the interviews)

(Continued)

(Continued)

- educative authenticity (i.e., the degree that the prolific authors are aware of, but not necessarily in agreement with, the constructions and values of other stakeholders [e.g., other prolific authors/researchers, consumers of their work])
- catalytic authenticity (i.e., the degree that the prolific authors' awareness of their new constructions or thoughts regarding other stakeholders' positions that emerge from the interviews evolves into decisions and actions [e.g., revising their own positions; producing follow-up work in the area])
- tactical authenticity (i.e., the degree that, as a result of their participation in the interviews, the prolific authors are empowered to act)

USE OF COMPUTER-MEDIATED COMMUNICATION (CMC) AND WEB 2.0 TOOLS. On a daily basis, many people all over the world use CMC and Web 2.0 tools to interact both professionally and socially with each other. Therefore, it is extremely surprising that, to date, no literature review textbook author has recommended the use of these tools as part of the literature review process. We plan to break this with introducing CMC and Web 2.0 tools for the CLR process—either asynchronously or synchronously. With respect to communicating synchronously with experts, a CMC tool with much potential is Twitter. Earlier in this chapter, we highlighted the mentoring blog site belonging to Dr. Lois Zachary—an internationally recognized mentoring and leadership expert—called "Lois Zachary's Mentoring Expert Blog" (cf. http://mentoringexpert.wordpress.com/), with tips, guidelines, and practical advice for both mentors and mentees. Interestingly, Dr. Zachary has a Twitter account (https://twitter.com/LoisZachary).

Therefore, as you begin to search for contact information of any expert of interest, you might first determine whether this expert has a Twitter account. For experts with Twitter accounts, you can ask questions such as those in Box 8.3 via a tweet (i.e., sending them a text-based question of up to 140 characters) via compatible external applications (e.g., smartphones), the Twitter website, or SMS (available in certain countries). Further, you might decide to *follow* (i.e., subscribe to) these experts' tweets. An advantage of using Twitter to expand the literature review is that, typically, an expert who has a Twitter account is accustomed to communicating using technology; consequently, asking a question about your topic of interest or their work via a tweet likely would be less invasive for them than using any other means of communication, and allows him/her the opportunity to delve into the topic of interest with other followers.

Twitter is not only useful for expanding the literature review via the expert component of MODES, but also it can be used to expand the literature review via the observation component of MODES. In particular, Twitter can be used to ***ground truth*** (i.e., validate) GIS data. Even the biggest news outlets in the world, such as the British Broadcasting Corporation (BBC) News (https://twitter.com/BBCNews), use Twitter to provide breaking news. In any case, with more than 500 million registered Twitter users worldwide, who post more than 340 million tweets per day (Lunden, 2012), time is ripe for reviewers to use it to expand their literature review and to help to move them toward a comprehensive literature review.

In addition to Twitter, other CMC tools for communicating with experts include professional network services. An example of such a service is LinkedIn (circa 2003), which has more than 259 million acquired users across more than 200 nations, more than 180 million monthly unique visitors worldwide, and is available in 20 languages—information that we obtained from a blog posted by Deep Nishar, the Vice President of Product at LinkedIn (cf. Nishar, 2013). Once identified, literature reviewers can maintain connections with experts in their topic areas. Indeed, reviewers should find that many potential experts are registered with professional network services like LinkedIn.

Another CMC-based avenue for communicating with experts is via Internet-based social bookmarking services, which represent an Internet method for organizing and managing hot-linked bookmarks of online resources. Here, reviewers can join a network of experts and, consequently, have access to experts' links to webpages. Although, unlike file sharing repositories such as Google Docs, the online resources themselves are not shared within these social bookmarking services, bookmarks provide references to these resources, with metadata providing tags (similar to keywords), descriptions of these resources, and short critiques or summaries of important information. These are just a few of the many CMC-based tools available that provide avenues to communicate with experts on their topics. And as time progresses, the capabilities of these tools only can increase. These are indeed exciting times for reviewers to expand their search!

INTERVIEWING MULTIPLE EXPERTS SIMULTANEOUSLY

Situations might arise where you are offered the opportunity to interview more than one expert at a time simultaneously. It might be the case that multiple experts who do not represent co-authors/co-researchers but who have a mutual respect for each other can be interviewed at the same time. In such instances, reviewers can conduct group-based interviews much like a focus group interview, either face-to-face or virtually. Unless all the experts reside and/or work in the same proximity, it is very likely that these focus groups will be conducted virtually, either synchronously or asynchronously. An online focus group particularly lends itself to interviewing multiple experts simultaneously (cf. Lobe, 2008). As is the case for individual expert interviews, questions such as those in Box 8.3 serve as a useful starting point. Whatever method is used, when conducting these focus groups, we recommend that reviewers utilize some of the best practices for conducting focus groups (cf. Morgan, 2008; Nicholas et al., 2010; Onwuegbuzie, Dickinson, Leech, & Zoran, 2009, 2010; Palmer, Larkin, de Visser, & Fadden, 2010; Stancanelli, 2010; Vicsek, 2010).

DELPHI-BASED INTERVIEW PROCEDURES. Another way that the reviewer can communicate with multiple experts is by using a variation of the Delphi method. Broadly speaking, the **Delphi method** is a technique for collecting data from experts for the purpose of obtaining a consensus about a given topic (Brewer, 2007).

BOX 8.4

EXAMPLES OF A VARIATION OF THE DELPHI METHOD

In an attempt to obtain an inclusive definition of the concept of mixed methods research, and as part of their literature review, Johnson, Onwuegbuzie, and Turner (2007) asked 31 leading mixed methods research methodologists to share their *current* definitions of mixed methods research. As reviewers, Johnson et al. (2007) could have used the definitions provided by many of these methodologists in their published works. However, because the mixed methods research field is evolving, even many of the published definitions that were less than 1-year old were considered to be in dire need of updating by their authors, indicating the time-lag limitations that we discussed previously. Using constant comparison analysis (Glaser & Strauss, 1967) to analyze the 19 definitions received from the selected mixed methodologists, Johnson et al. (2007) extracted themes, which they then used to conceptualize an inclusive definition (i.e., consensus) of mixed methods research that has become popularized. Thus, collecting data beyond the published literature ended up being very fruitful for these reviewers.

Adapted from "Innovative qualitative data collection techniques for conducting literature reviews," by A. J. Onwuegbuzie, N. L. Leech, and K. M. T. Collins, 2011, in M. Williams & W. P. Vogt (Eds.), *The Sage handbook of innovation in social research methods*, Thousand Oaks, CA: Sage, p. 194. Copyright 2011 by Sage.

EXAMPLE: DELPHI VARIATIONS

Box 8.4 presents an example of how Onwuegbuzie, Leech, and Collins (2011) utilized a variation of the Delphi method and interviews in order to obtain a consensus for a definition of mixed methods research.

INTERNET-BASED SOCIAL BOOKMARKING SERVICES. A very useful way of communicating with multiple experts simultaneously is by utilizing a social bookmarking service. A social bookmarking service with much potential is Delicious (see https://delicious.com/). This tool allows reviewers to build a community of experts and fellow reviewers who can share, annotate, discuss, and critique resources, such as journal articles, books, and websites. Another useful site is CiteULike (http://www.citeulike.org/), which is a free academic-based social bibliography site that allows a user to save articles and books online. In particular, reviewers can use this site to examine

other users' bibliographies and to view *tag* and *author clouds*, which is a cloudlike pictorial representation of the most frequent words by making them visually larger and bolder relative to less frequent words.

EXAMPLE: CITEULIKE

For example, Figure 8.25 displays a screenshot showing the results from CiteULike using the search string "mentoring and college students." Currently, there are more than 7 million articles in the system, with more than 1,000 articles being added daily. As users add articles or books to their online library collections, the individual citations in all bibliographies automatically update. Thus, all users can monitor who in the CiteULike community has added new material, as indicated by a number and user ID that are presented at the end of each reference.

Similarly, Zotero (http://www.zotero.org) is a freeware academic bibliography program that, once installed, resides in the computer's web browser. This tool allows users not only to compile academic citations from library

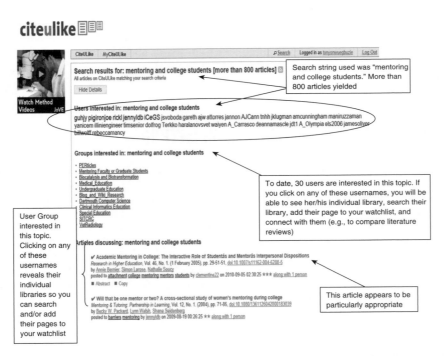

Figure 8.25 Screenshot showing results from CiteULike using the search string "mentoring and college students"

databases but also to archive any sources extracted on the Internet, such as websites, blog posts, Wiki entries, and grey literature. Zotero also can be used to save a copy of the full-text work. Users then can add tags, attachments, comments, and the like. At the time of writing, other bookmarking services include StumbleUpon (http://www.stumbleupon.com/), Diigo (https://www.diigo.com/), Digg (http://digg.com/), and reddit (http://www.reddit.com/).

In terms of research methodology, a useful site is Methodspace (http://www.methodspace.com/), where a reviewer can communicate with multiple expert research methodologists from all over the world. Alternatively, reviewers can form their own literature review groups and forums by using free software, such as Ning (http://ning.com) or Elgg (http://elgg.org/), to support special interest groups. By using bookmarking services and social network software, reviewers will become aware of new information and can evaluate the importance of this new information, as well as build relationships with other reviewers who cite similar works (Greenhow, Robelia, & Hughes, 2009). Further, as surmised by Greenhow et al. (2009), "as a supplement to traditional peer review of print-based journal manuscripts, these technologies allow each online reader to rate or rank, tag, and annotate materials" (p. 253). All in all, by communicating with experts during the (expanded) literature review process, as well as fellow reviewers, the emphasis on obtaining literature is shifted toward an emphasis on creating and nurturing, as well as maintaining human interaction, human cooperation, and, hence, human capital.

Even more importantly, communicating with experts in the field through formal or informal interviews helps the reviewer to capture to a much greater extent their voices—which is consistent with the critical dialectical pluralist research philosophy promoted by Onwuegbuzie and Frels (2013a). The goal of critical dialectical pluralism, which represents a social justice paradigm, is to give voice and to empower participants (Onwuegbuzie & Frels, 2013a)—in this case, the experts whose works the reviewer is citing—by allowing them to be maximally involved as *researchers* (i.e., co-reviewers) throughout the literature review process, especially with respect to the construction of knowledge.

TASK S: *SECONDARY DATA*

The fifth way that a reviewer can expand the literature review is by using available secondary data, analyzing these data, and then incorporating the results from these analyses into the literature review

report. As described in Chapter 2, *secondary data* (e.g., surveys, censuses, and records) represent information that is collected by someone other than the literature reviewer. There are three major ways of incorporating secondary data into the literature review process: (a) using already-analyzed secondary data, (b) using raw secondary data, and (c) collecting and analyzing secondary data.

USING ALREADY-ANALYZED SECONDARY DATA

When secondary data already have been analyzed, the reviewer should save the maximum amount of time in incorporating secondary data into the literature review process. Also, such secondary data, typically, have a pre-established degree of validity/legitimation and reliability/dependability that do not need to be re-examined by the reviewer. As an example, you might recall that in Chapter 2, when we used the search string *National Data and England* on the Google search engine, we identified the United Kingdom (UK) National Statistics Publication (UKNSP) homepage that contained secondary data centered around several themes. Let's now return to our mentoring and college students example. Suppose that in order to determine whether mentoring is important in UK higher education institutions, we wanted to find out what proportion of students drop out of college in their first year. Well, of the 11 themes available in the UKNSP database (e.g., economics), the most relevant theme for collecting performance data is *Children, Education and Skills*.

EXAMPLE: DATABASES

Figure 8.26 presents a screenshot showing the UKNSP database under this theme. It can be seen from this figure that the most relevant link is *Higher Education and Adult Learning Providers*. Figure 8.27 presents a screenshot from the Higher Education and Adult Learning Providers database showing two relevant links that contain performance indicators in higher education in the United Kingdom. For instance, clicking on the *Higher Education Performance indicator for Wales* link led to a pdf file (http://wales.gov.uk/docs/statistics/2013/130418–higher-education-performance-indicators-2011–12–en.pdf), which provided several population-level statistics such as that "22 per cent of

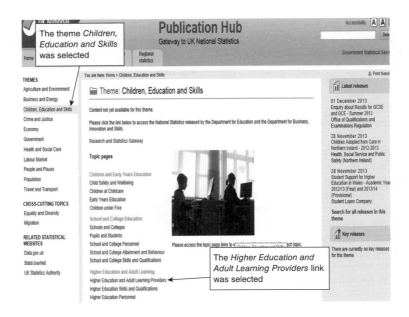

Figure 8.26 Screenshot showing the UK National Statistics Publication Database under the theme *Children, Education and Skills*

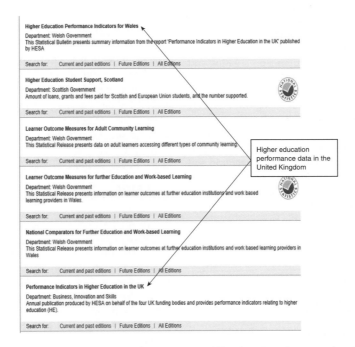

Figure 8.27 Screenshot from the UK National Statistics Publication Database under the theme *Children, Education and Skills* showing two relevant links that contain performance indicators in higher education in the United Kingdom

young full-time other undergraduate entrants to Welsh HEIs [Higher Education Institutions] in 2010–2011 did not continue before their first year" (p. 2). Thus, a secondary data finding such as this easily could be incorporated into the literature review. Indeed, such data—alongside any findings from Step 2 (searching databases) to Step 5 (expanding the search) of the literature review process that link mentoring to increased odds of graduation—could be used to build a case for the importance of mentoring.

USING RAW SECONDARY DATA

When secondary data already have been collected but not (fully) analyzed, then the reviewer could analyze part or all of the data and incorporate the findings into the literature review write-up. There are myriad databases across numerous fields and disciplines that reviewers can consider using. Let's turn, once again, to our mentoring and college students example. Let's say that, for the purpose of determining the need for mentoring in the United States, we wanted to determine the rate of graduation (i.e., completion rate) of undergraduate students. To obtain the most up-to-date data, we could locate a national database such as from the National Center for Education Statistics database (http://nces.ed.gov/). Alternatively, or in addition, we could obtain education databases compiled on one or more of the 50 states (including the District of Columbia) in the United States. One state that might justify the use of an education database is

Texas for the following reasons: (a) it is the second most populous state in the United States (U.S. Census Bureau, 2012); (b) it has a large percentage of underserved minority students (College Board, 2013); and (c) by 2040, the number of students in Texas public schools and universities will increase, and the majority of the students will be non-Anglos (Murdock et al., 2002). We would like to point out that, with respect to the first reason (i.e., second most populous state), we obtained this information using secondary data from the U.S. Census Bureau (Population Estimates) database (http://www.census.gov/popest/data/national/totals/2012/index.html)—which led to us downloading an Excel spreadsheet provided freely by the U.S. Census Bureau (see Figure 8.28).

Anyway, we have now built a case for using a Texas database to expand our literature review. Conveniently, there are several free education databases at our disposal. A particularly useful database is the Texas Higher Education Accountability System (http://www.txhighereddata.org/Interactive/Accountability/) (see Figure 8.29). Clicking on *Go* will provide the website in Figure 8.29, from which Excel files can be downloaded that contain numerous variables (i.e., key measures, contextual measures) that fall under the following categories: *Participation*, *Success*, *Excellence*, *Research*, or *Institutional Efficiency and Effectiveness*.

Once the appropriate Excel file has been downloaded (depending on the information of interest

Figure 8.28   Screenshot from the U.S. Census Bureau (Population Estimates) Database

and the reviewer's level of statistical understanding), because these secondary data typically involve large sample sizes, the reviewer often can conduct an array of statistical analyses that range from descriptive analyses (measures of central tendency [e.g., mean, median]; measures of variability/dispersion [e.g., variance, standard deviation]; measures of position [e.g., percentile rank, z score]) to exploratory analyses (e.g., exploratory factor analysis, cluster analysis) to inferential analyses (e.g., multiple regression, analysis of variance). (For a review of 58 statistical techniques and a typology, see Onwuegbuzie & Hitchcock, 2015.) For example, recently, researchers have investigated factors (e.g., percentage of tenure-track faculty) that are associated with graduation rates (cf. Smith et al., 2013; Wilcox-Pereira, Valle, Gonzales, Venzant, & Paitson, 2014).

COLLECTING AND ANALYZING SECONDARY DATA

The first two strategies for expanding the literature review via secondary sources involve the use of archival data that have been collected by other parties, with the first strategy involving the use of data from these sources that have already been analyzed by other parties, and the second strategy involving the reviewers analyzing these archival data. A third strategy that the reviewer has for expanding the literature review via secondary sources is collecting and analyzing secondary data. This strategy involves collecting the same information from a selected set of works identified in Steps 2–4, and then analyzing this information to identify trends.

In particular, reviewers can collect and compare information across works. As we discussed in Chapter 7, information pertaining to the 12 components of a primary research report provides a supplemental set of information. A common way of identifying trends is by determining the prevalence rates of aspects of one of more of these 12 supplemental components. For example, a reviewer could examine the prevalence rate across studies examining the same or similar research question of one or more elements of the introduction section of a report such as the prevalence of the use of a specific citation, theoretical/conceptual framework, research question, and/or hypothesis. Alternatively, a reviewer might be

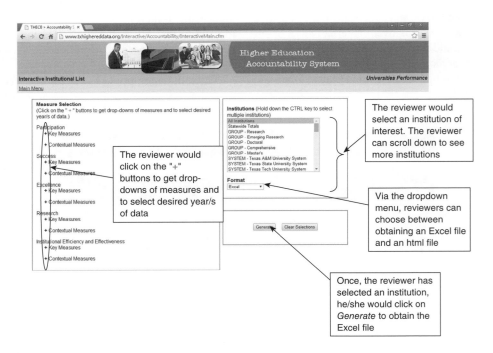

Figure 8.29 Texas Higher Education Accountability System database

interested in obtaining statistics across studies examining the same or a similar research question of one or more elements of the method section of a report such as the mean sample size, the distribution of sampling schemes (e.g., random sampling vs. non-random [purposive] sampling), the frequency of each region where studies have taken place, the frequency of each instrument used, the frequency of each intervention used, or the frequency of each analysis technique used. Collecting and analyzing such information can inform a literature review in important ways.

We should point out that much of the data needed to conduct these prevalence rate analyses can be collected in Step 3 of the CLR, namely, when the reviewer is storing and organizing the information. In particular, in addition to inserting information about each work (e.g., author, title, publication year, source) onto the spreadsheet, reviewers can collect information regarding one or more of these 12 components of a primary research report. You are likely asking at this stage: Why is it worth taking time to collect these data? If you are asking this, then, great question! Well, by collecting these data, reviewers can identify what

has worked and what has not worked with respect to extant works, which, in turn, can help them in their own primary studies at the research conceptualization, planning, and/or implementation phases of their empirical studies.

Also, it is worthwhile to track information about the participants used in the extant works. This mapping of information is not only useful for examining trends associated with participants in the selected research studies, but also very useful in mapping findings across studies. In particular, with respect to quantitative research studies, using information regarding where the study took place, effect sizes can be mapped to examine whether regional, nationwide, or even global trends prevail. Similarly, themes and other qualitative findings that address the same research question could be mapped. Thus, such mapping could enhance interpretations stemming from (quantitative) meta-analyses and (qualitative) meta-syntheses (Onwuegbuzie, Leech, and Collins, 2011). This would expand the literature review into a spatially integrated literature review.

APPLYING CONCEPTS

The collection of information of a work helps to provide what we may call the DNA of that work. Indeed, collecting this information can help reviewers improve the literature review write-up. In particular, collecting and analyzing DNA information of works help to expand and to enhance all four common types of narrative reviews that we described in Chapter 2, namely, *general reviews, theoretical reviews, methodological reviews*, and *historical reviews*. In Chapter 2, we also described the systematic literature review—representing one of the two major branches of traditional literature reviews—as a critical assessment and evaluation of all research studies that address a particular research question on a research topic. Further, the systematic literature review involves the transparent use of an organized method of identifying, collecting, and evaluating a body of literature on this topic using a predetermined set of specific criteria.

PREFERRED REPORTING FOR SYSTEMATIC REVIEWS

A set of specific criteria has been standardized by guidelines for reporting such as the *Preferred Reporting Items for Systematic Reviews and Meta-Analyses*, or PRISMA (Moher et al., 2009). As declared on the PRISMA Statement website (http://

www.prisma-statement.org/), PRISMA represents an evidence-based, standardized, minimum set of items for the purpose of helping literature reviewers improve the reporting of systematic reviews and meta-analyses that assess the benefits and risks of health care interventions.

The goal of using PRISMA is to help authors provide a transparent and complete literature review. According to the PRISMA Statement website,

TOOL: REPORTING STANDARDS FOR SYSTEMATIC REVIEWS IN HEALTHCARE

Another standard for reporting literature searches is STARLITE, which stands for (Sampling strategy, Type of study, Approaches, Range of years, Limits, Inclusions and exclusions, Terms used, Electronic sources) (Booth, 2006). STARLITE focuses on reporting of qualitative systematic reviews in healthcare. Other standards for reporting literature searches include the CONSORT Statement in randomized controlled trials (CONSORT Group, 2010), STARD Statement for reporting studies of diagnostic accuracy, MOOSE Statement for reporting meta-analyses of observational studies in epidemiology, and the STROBE Statement for observational studies in epidemiology (STROBE Group, 2010). Each of the most common standards for reporting studies is presented in Table 8.3.

Table 8.3 Most common standards for reporting studies in literature reviews

Standard	Website/Citation	Statement
PRISMA Statement	www.prisma-statement.org Moher et al. (2009)	PRISMA stands for **P**referred **R**eporting **I**tems for **S**ystematic Reviews and **M**eta-**A**nalyses. The aim of the PRISMA Statement is to help authors report a wide array of systematic reviews to assess the benefits and harms of a healthcare intervention. PRISMA focuses on ways in which authors can ensure the transparent and complete reporting of systematic reviews and meta-analyses.
STARLITE Statement	www.ncbi.nlm.nih.gov/pmc/articles/PMC1629442 Booth (2006)	The mnemonic STARLITE (**S**ampling strategy, **T**ype of study, **A**pproaches, **R**ange of years, **L**imits, **I**nclusions and exclusions, **T**erms used, **E**lectronic sources) can be used to convey the important elements for reporting literature searches.
MOOSE Statement	www.consort-statement.org/mod_product/uploads/MOOSE%20Statement%202000.pdf Stroup et al. (2000)	MOOSE stands for **M**eta-analysis **of** **O**bservational **S**tudies in **E**pidemiology. It provides guidelines for improving the usefulness of meta-analyses for authors, reviewers, editors, readers, and stakeholders.
STROBE Statement	www.strobe-statement.org/index.php?id=strobe-home von Elm, Altman, Gøtzsche, Vanderbroucke, and the STROBE Initiative (2007)	STROBE is an international, collaborative initiative of epidemiologists, methodologists, statisticians, researchers, and journal editors involved in the conduct and dissemination of observational studies, with the common aim of **ST**rengthening the **R**eporting of **OB**servational studies in **E**pidemiology.
CONSORT Statement	www.consort-statement.org Schulz, Altman, Moher, and the CONSORT Group (2010)	The CONSORT Statement is intended to improve the reporting of a randomized controlled trial (RCT), enabling readers to understand a trial's design, to conduct analysis and interpretation, and to assess the validity of its results. It offers a standard way for reviewers to prepare reports of trial findings, facilitating their complete and transparent reporting, and aiding their critical appraisal and interpretation. CONSORT stands for **Con**solidated **S**tandards **of** **R**eporting **T**rials.

Standard	Website/Citation	Statement
STARD Statement	www.stard-statement.org Bossuyt et al. (2003)	The objective of the STARD initiative is to improve the accuracy and completeness of reporting of studies of diagnostic accuracy, to allow readers to assess the potential for bias in the study (internal validity), and to evaluate its generalizability (external validity). The STARD Statement consists of a checklist of 25 items and recommends the use of a flow diagram that describes the design of the study and the flow of patients. STARD stands for **STA**ndards for the **R**eporting of **D**iagnostic accuracy studies.
COREQ Statement	intqhc.oxfordjournals.org/content/19/6/349.long Tong, Sainsbury, and Craig (2007)	COREQ stands for **CO**nsolidated criteria for **RE**porting **Q**ualitative research. The COREQ Statement consists of a 32-item checklist for interviews and focus groups.
ENTREQ Statement	www.equator-network.org/reporting-guidelines/enhancing-transparency-in-reporting-the-synthesis-of-qualitative-research-entreq Tong, Flemming, McInnes, Oliver, and Craig (2012)	ENTREQ stands for **EN**hancing **T**ransparency in **RE**porting the synthesis of **Q**ualitative research.
SQUIRE Statement	squire-statement.org/guidelines Davidoff, Batalden, Stevens, Ogrinc, Mooney, and the SQUIRE Development Group (2008)	SQUIRE stands for **S**tandards for **Qu**ality **I**mprovement **R**eporting **E**xcellence. It provides a framework for reporting formal, planned studies designed to assess the nature and effectiveness of interventions to improve the quality and safety of care.
CHEERS Statement	www.ispor.org/taskforces/EconomicPubGuidelines.asp Husereau et al. (2013)	CHEERS stands for **C**onsolidated **H**ealth **E**conomic **E**valuation **R**eporting **S**tandards. It provides guidelines available to authors and reviewers in order to support the quality, consistency, and transparency of health economic and outcomes research reporting in the biomedical literature.
CARE Statement	www.care-statement.org Gagnier et al. (2013)	The CARE guidelines provide a framework to support the need for completeness, transparency, and data analysis in case reports and data from the point of care. The acronym CARE was created from the first two letters in **ca**se and the first two letters in **re**ports.
SAMPL Statement	www.equator-network.org/wp-content/uploads/2013/07/SAMPL-Guidelines-6-27-13.pdf Lang and Altman (2013)	SAMPL stands for **S**tatistical **A**nalyses and **M**ethods in the **P**ublished **L**iterature. It provides guidelines for basic statistical reporting for articles published in biomedical journals.

although PRISMA has focused primarily on systematic reviews and meta-analyses of randomized trials, it can also be used as a basis for reporting reviews of other types of research (e.g., diagnostic studies, observational studies). PRISMA also can be used to evaluate studies during the literature review process. Currently, the PRISMA Statement contains a 27-item checklist and a four-phase flowchart (to obtain both of these items, see http://www.prisma-statement.org/statement.htm). In particular, the flowchart presents the flow of information via the different phases of a systematic review, mapping out information about the number of records identified in the literature searches, the number of studies included and excluded, and the reasons for exclusions. Presently, more than 170 journals representing the health sciences endorse the PRISMA Statement. An example of the item that is most pertinent for our current MODES chapter is Item 7, falling under *Methods*, which specifies that literature reviewers "Describe all information sources (e.g., databases with dates of coverage, contact with study authors to identify additional studies) in the search and date last searched." You will notice that the phrase "contact with study authors to identify additional studies" is consistent with our idea of using experts (i.e., MOD<u>E</u>S) in the expanded information search.

COMBINING TWO OR MORE MODES

Up until this point in this chapter, we have outlined how reviewers can move toward a comprehensive review of the literature—that is, move beyond a traditional literature review—by expanding their information searches by *separately* collecting data via the following five MODES: Media, Observation(s), Documents, Expert(s), and Secondary data. However, before we end this chapter, we should point out that information can be collected via two or more of these modes simultaneously. For instance, secondary data can be collected concurrently with one or more of the remaining four modes. As an example, after mapping the location of school massacres in the United States, a reviewer could link the findings that have been extracted via the five MODES to qualitative-based sociological data (e.g., overall crime rate, overall prevalence of

violent crimes in the community, overall prevalence of gun crimes in the community, poverty, education, health, religion). Of particular interest to the reviewer might be to use GIS to map the prevalence of gun sales across the United States so that he/she could examine the relationship between gun sales and school massacres (i.e., secondary data analysis).

CONCLUSIONS

Since the 1960s, the term *information explosion* has been used to describe the rapid increase in the amount of available information, and consequences of this profusion. Although this abundance of information has been used to good effect in many fields (e.g., criminology, forensic psychology, homeland security), when conducting literature reviews, reviewers underutilize much of this information. Unfortunately, none of the existing works on conducting literature reviews goes much beyond showing how to conduct *traditional* literature reviews (i.e., via the collection of literature that already exists either in printed or digital forms). Although many of these works adequately show how to conduct *traditional* literature reviews, these guides have not kept pace with this information explosion. Thus, in this chapter, we have provided a framework for extracting more information relevant to any research topic. Specifically, we outlined how to move toward a comprehensive review of the literature by expanding information searches via the separate or simultaneous use of the following five MODES: **M**edia, **O**bservation(s), **D**ocuments, **E**xpert(s), and **S**econdary data. Consequently, whereas traditional literature reviews are one-dimensional, the use of MODES transforms the literature review process to a comprehensive literature review that is multidimensional, interactive, emergent, iterative, dynamic, holistic, and synergistic!

As contended by Onwuegbuzie, Leech, et al. (2011), we believe that the use of MODES enhances both *representation* and *legitimation* in the literature review process. By enhancing *representation*, we mean that the reviewer is able to extract the most pertinent and up-to-date knowledge that informs the literature review process, which, in turn, would increase the possibility that knowledge saturation is reached, thereby yielding richer interpretations and increased understanding (i.e., *Verstehen*). Contrastingly, enhancing *legitimation* refers to increasing the validity of interpretations that evolve from the literature review process (e.g., by asking the prolific authors directly). Further, collecting data via the MODES gives further credence to our contention in Chapter 3 that the comprehensive literature review process represents not only a data collection tool and a method but also a study— and even a methodology. As such, collecting data via MODES has additional ethical implications. Indeed, when expanding the search, reviewers should not only adopt a multimodal approach via use of the MODES, but also adopt both a culturally progressive approach and ethical research approach, as discussed in Chapter 2. Ethical implications include seeking IRB approval whenever appropriate. Although seeking such IRB approval would require additional work on the part of the reviewer, as illustrated by the additional information extracted by Frels (2010) and Johnson et al. (2007), we believe that the end justifies the means. Moreover, through the use of MODES, the literature review process is not seen as a static process whereby information is extracted passively at one point in time—specifically, before the underlying study is conducted. Instead, the literature review process is conducted actively and proactively such that it is transformed into "a meaning-making process that takes place before, during, and after the study" (Onwuegbuzie, Leech, et al., 2011, p. 200).

As part of demonstrating how to expand the literature via the use of MODES, we have provided numerous links/websites. Some of these links/websites might be changed or removed by the time you read this chapter; however, what is important is not any specific website but the idea that reviewers increasingly have many CMC and Web 2.0 tools at their disposal to expand their literature search. One could only wonder how much more the MODES could be expanded when Web 3.0 tools—and which are just around the corner—become a reality! (These are predicted to be "more connected, open, and intelligent, with semantic Web technologies, distributed databases, natural language processing, machine learning, machine reasoning, and autonomous agents" Spivack, 2013, p. 17.)

In the next chapter, we describe Step 6, which is analyzing and synthesizing some of the sources selected. Before you move on to Step 6, revisit again Step 3, which is storing and organizing your information sources so that you begin to sort those sources that will be analyzed and synthesized. Keep in mind that some of your information sources do not need to be grouped into the foundational sources but can serve as supplemental sources which can be analyzed and synthesized separately from the foundation sources. We also suggest that you review these concepts for Step 5:

- Going beyond a traditional literature review involves expanding the search using additional sources including media, documents beyond journal articles, experts on the topic, and secondary data.
- Media are information sources that include audio books, video repositories, and visual tools.
- Observations can justify or create the background for understanding the CLR as a stand-alone report or to inform primary research.
- Geographic Information Systems (GIS) are a mapping tool for creating a display to understand background and for ground truthing a phenomenon.
- Documents beyond journal articles lend support for your topic and include journal special issues, dissertation or thesis studies, monographs, government papers, blogs, grey papers, and numerous others.
- Experts can be prolific authors and researchers who have devoted a large proportion of their professional careers to researching and writing about a topic.
- Virtual, synchronous interviews include both product (information) and process items, such as proxemics (behaviors reflecting special relationships of the interviewees/interviewers), chronemics (temporal speech markers such as gaps, silences, hesitations), and paralinguistics (behaviors indicating tenor, strength, or emotive color of the vocal expression).
- The Delphi method is a technique for collecting data from experts for the purpose of obtaining a consensus about a given topic.
- Communication with experts and use of Internet-based social bookmarking services help a reviewer capture their voices to a much greater extent.

- Book chapters and the sets of articles that form special issues published in journals are especially susceptible to lengthy emergence-to-publication time lags and, as a consequence, contain some outdated information.
- Debriefing interviews help to identify any hidden biases and to evaluate hunches or intuitions about the dialogue/interview so that greater awareness and understanding occur.

- Secondary data can be obtained in forms such as surveys, censuses, and records and can be used in a literature review if they are in raw or analyzed form.
- Overall, the use of MODES enhances both *representation* and *legitimation* in that a literature reviewer is able to extract the most pertinent and up-to-date knowledge that informs the literature review process toward greater saturation and legitimation.

CHAPTER 8 EVALUATION CHECKLIST

CORE	Guiding Questions and Tasks
Critical Examination	To what extent did you identify ways to expand the search?
Organization	To what extent did you document MODES pathways in writing? How did you store this information so that you can easily retrieve it?
	How prepared do you feel in your topic area if you were to contact an expert? What are some areas that you want to explore and how might you phrase your questions?
Reflections	Oftentimes, things we don't know that we don't know can limit our understanding of a topic. How might you address your knowledge gaps using MODES?
Evaluation	What technology skills might you acquire to facilitate your CLR? How can increasing your technology skills aid you as a literature reviewer/researcher?

PART THREE

INTEGRATION

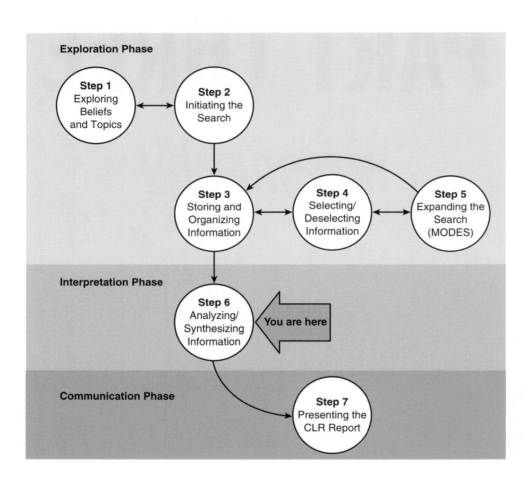

Exploration Phase

Step 1
Exploring
Beliefs
and Topics

Step 2
Initiating the
Search

Step 3
Storing and
Organizing
Information

Step 4
Selecting/
Deselecting
Information

Step 5
Expanding the
Search
(MODES)

Interpretation Phase

Step 6
Analyzing/
Synthesizing
Information

You are here

Communication Phase

Step 7
Presenting the
CLR Report

STEP 6: ANALYZING AND SYNTHESIZING INFORMATION

CHAPTER 9 ROADMAP

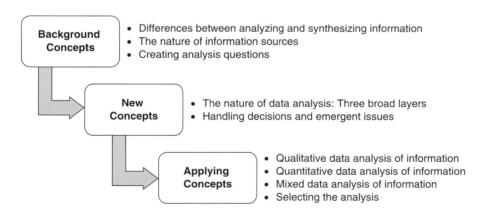

Background Concepts
- Differences between analyzing and synthesizing information
- The nature of information sources
- Creating analysis questions

New Concepts
- The nature of data analysis: Three broad layers
- Handling decisions and emergent issues

Applying Concepts
- Qualitative data analysis of information
- Quantitative data analysis of information
- Mixed data analysis of information
- Selecting the analysis

BACKGROUND CONCEPTS

You might recall that in order to select/deselect information (i.e., Step 4), reviewers have to conduct an *initial* analysis of each set of information. The major function of this initial analysis is to help reviewers use their identities as culturally progressive, multimodal, ethical, and reflexive researchers to determine whether the information that is selected for the final sample should be situated within (a) the foundational set of information or (b) one or more of the 12 components that characterize the supplemental set of information. As a reminder, the Dyadic Mentoring Study in our example of the CLR involved the use of only 47 works of the final sample of 209. Each of the remaining 162 works was categorized as one or more of the 12 supplemental components. Once the final sample of information has been categorized, reviewers are ready to conduct a *formal* analysis. Whether the literature review is conducted as a stand-alone work or to inform primary research, Step 6: Analyzing/Synthesizing Information always involves some type of formal analysis and synthesis for selected works.

Recently, several authors have attempted to make the literature review process more transparent by providing a step-by-step guide to conducting literature reviews (i.e., Bettany-Saltikov, 2012; Combs, Bustamante, & Onwuegbuzie, 2010a, 2010b; Cronin, Ryan, & Coughlan, 2008; Dellinger & Leech, 2007; Fink, 2009; Garrard, 2009; Hart, 2005; Jesson, Matheson, & Lacey, 2011; Leech et al., 2010; Machi & McEvoy, 2009; Onwuegbuzie et al., 2010; Onwuegbuzie & Frels, 2012c; Onwuegbuzie, Leech, & Collins, 2012; Ridley, 2012). However, although these works are informative, none of these textbooks include explicit instructions as how both to analyze and to interpret information extracted during the literature process using current data analytic techniques. Thus, our goal in this chapter is to begin to fill this extremely important void.

DIFFERENCES BETWEEN ANALYZING AND SYNTHESIZING INFORMATION

Whereas *analysis* of information involves systematically breaking down the information into its constituent parts, *synthesis* involves making connections among the parts that were identified via the analysis. Therefore, synthesizing involves much more than summarizing and occurs after the analysis for "recasting the information into a new or different arrangement. That arrangement should show connections and patterns that have not been produced previously" (Hart, 2005, p. 110). When you selected/deselected information sources (Step 4) and expanded your search (Step 5), it is likely that you continued making decisions as to what sources to include or not to include for analysis, or coding. At this point, you might have recognized some sources that were not suitable for coding but might be used to justify a particular position or to define a concept. For example, in the introduction paragraphs of the Dyadic Mentoring Study, background and context were presented to introduce the topic. Yet, most of these references were not used in the formal analysis, or thematic coding of selected sources. The point is: all of your sources can be used in the narrative of the CLR but only some of them will be coded and synthesized. Therefore, after reading this chapter for understanding the array of analyzing options available, it is important to establish one or more central, or guiding, questions about your topic so that your analysis strategies will remain focused. For example, the conceptual map created as part of the Dyadic Mentoring Study served initially as an audit trail. Next, it helped to establish which information sources were to be analyzed.

THE NATURE OF INFORMATION SOURCES

At this point, you might be asking yourself: Which analysis might I decide to use? We hope to facilitate this process by helping you to recognize that information you collected for the CLR has now become your data. Regardless as to whether you gravitate toward quantitative, qualitative, or mixed research, due to the nature of the CLR as involving the collection of words, observations, and images (e.g., drawings/photographs/video) via the MODES, at some level, there is always a qualitative component to the analysis/synthesis. Indeed, as we noted in Chapter 3, at the very least, the following elements of each empirical source that informs the CLR—whether representing quantitative, qualitative, or mixed research studies—contain qualitative information:

- information about the sample characteristics pertaining to *every* qualitative, quantitative, and mixed methods research study extracted for the CLR
- findings (e.g., themes, meta-themes, metaphors, quotations, narrative) pertaining to each qualitative research study presented in the literature review section of each source extracted for the CLR
- findings (e.g., themes, meta-themes, metaphors, quotations, narrative) presented in the results section of each qualitative research study extracted for the CLR
- information from the discussion/conclusion section of *every* quantitative, qualitative, and mixed research study extracted for the CLR

Also, the following elements of the qualitative, quantitative, and mixed methods research studies yield quantitative information:

- sample size(s) pertaining to *every* quantitative, qualitative, and mixed research study extracted for the CLR
- findings (e.g., descriptive statistics, score reliability, *p*-values, effect sizes, confidence interval, meta-analysis information) pertaining to each quantitative research study extracted for the CLR
- findings (e.g., descriptive statistics, score reliability, *p*-values, effect sizes, confidence interval, meta-analysis information) presented in the results section of each quantitative research study extracted for the CLR

As such, because there are numerous sources of both qualitative and quantitative data that can be obtained from sources extracted during the CLR process, reviewers have plenty of opportunity to use qualitative analytic approaches, methods, and techniques and/or quantitative analytic approaches, methods, and techniques to analyze CLR information. And when both qualitative *and* quantitative analytic approaches, methods, and techniques are used when analyzing/synthesizing CLR information, then the reviewer is conducting what can be referred to as a mixed analysis/synthesis.

CREATING ANALYSIS QUESTIONS

Two guiding criteria were presented for selecting topic information sources for CLR foundational information in the Dyadic Mentoring Study: (a) the source illuminated Rebecca's understanding of mentoring, and (b) the source helped her to understand the relationship aspect of mentoring. Based on these two criteria, it was important to create guiding question(s) before initiating the analysis/synthesis—what we call **analysis questions**. For this literature review, the analysis questions were: In what ways have researchers addressed mentoring relationships in a school setting? What factors have been effective and ineffective for establishing and promoting strong mentoring relationships? It is important to recognize that if the CLR is to inform primary research, the guiding questions for the CLR are created to explore topics relating to your overall primary research questions of the study.

As explained in Chapter 3, the array of quantitative and qualitative data that are potentially inherent in each work lends itself simultaneously to the analysis of some quantitative and some qualitative information. Remember that the CLR represents a mixed research study and that a literature reviewer might use quantitative research approaches and qualitative research approaches to synthesize both quantitative- and qualitative-based works. Much like the systematic process of Steps 1–5, the purpose of Step 6 is to conduct a *systematic* analysis of select information sources. Therefore, in the following sections, we begin by explaining the overall nature of data analysis on three broad levels using the terms *approach*, *method*, and *technique*. Next, we provide an overview of some of the ways of conducting analyses associated with these levels using qualitative, quantitative, and mixed method research traditions to be used to frame your own approach to your CLR data.

THE NATURE OF DATA ANALYSIS: THREE BROAD LAYERS

On the broadest layer, **analytic approach** refers to any one or more ways to conduct data analyses that represent whole systems, which in the case of information extracted for a CLR would be the information as a whole collection. In contrast, a less broad layer is *analytic method*, which is data analyses that represent *part* of a system, or a more in-depth examination of one or more information sources via analyses. In this case, the information that you extracted for the CLR might be grouped and analyzed for meaning. Finally, by *analytic technique*, we refer to a single step in the data analysis process. Typically, an analytic technique is a component that you might use regardless of whether you analyze the collection of information as a whole or in subsets. Thus, with regard to qualitative data analysis, as is the case for quantitative analyses, techniques are nested within methods, which are nested within approaches.

QUALITATIVE DATA

Hart (2005) recognized the importance for a literature reviewer systematically to extract "key ideas, theories, concepts, and methodological assumptions from the literature" (p. 110). Yet, it was his contention that techniques such as discourse analysis, conversation analysis, content analysis, and semiological analysis are not in the scope of analysis. Although we agree with Hart (2005) about the systematic nature of the information analysis process, we believe that *information extracted serves as data* and that the analyses to be conducted depend upon the skill of the researcher. Therefore, the information that you categorized to be analyzed and synthesized when you collected and sorted your sources serves as your dataset. As such, it would be difficult to analyze the CLR information either on a whole level or on a case (part of the collection) level without

some understanding of qualitative data analysis approaches, methods, and techniques.

Data analysis approaches in the qualitative tradition are directly linked to research design. (For a discussion of the nature and history of the 34 qualitative data analysis approaches that were identified via a CLR, we refer you to Onwuegbuzie & Denham, 2014a, 2014b.) For the purpose of analysis for the information collected as a whole system, the literature reviewer might select one guiding approach described in Chapter 1 and Chapter 3. As an example, you might decide to utilize components of grounded theory design (Glaser & Strauss, 1967), which entails coding via constant comparison analysis (Glaser, 1965). Analytical methods in the qualitative tradition can be integrated into most approaches and might include Miles and Huberman's (1994) array of within-case analyses and cross-case analyses, which are discussed later in this chapter. In addition, one or more qualitative analysis techniques can be used with any qualitative data analysis approach without compromising the integrity of the approach. For example, values coding can be used as part of a constant comparison analysis without preventing the analyst from claiming that constant comparison analysis was undertaken. Conversely, if any one qualitative data analysis approach—which, again, represents a whole system (e.g., constant comparison analysis)—was used as part of another qualitative data analysis approach (e.g., domain analysis), then the integrity of this dominant qualitative data analysis approach would be compromised, at least to a degree. For example, if a domain analysis approach was incorporated into a constant comparison analysis approach, then the overall analysis no longer could be called a constant comparison analysis approach.

QUANTITATIVE DATA

A quantitative data analysis approach for a whole system of information includes analyses such as descriptive analyses, exploratory analyses, confirmatory analyses, and inferential analyses. It could be likely that the information collected for a CLR is completely in numeric form. In this case, a quantitative approach to analyzing data would be to apply the analysis to the collected information across the board. Contrastingly, as previously defined, the term *data analysis* method refers to analyses that represent part of a system, which, for the CLR, would be to apply these statistics to groupings of information that contains numerical data. Quantitative data analysis methods include measures of central tendency, dispersion/variability, distribution shape, analysis-of-variance, regression, factor analysis, and spatial analysis. Finally, the term *techniques* refers to data analyses that represent a single step in the analysis process, which, in the quantitative tradition, include the calculation of a mean, median, standard deviation, independent samples *t*-test, repeated measures analysis of variance, exploratory factor analysis, descriptive discriminant analysis, path analysis, and so on. Typically, one or more quantitative analysis techniques and methods are essential components of a quantitative data analysis approach. For example, the quantitative analysis techniques of the mean (i.e., representing a central tendency method) and the standard deviation (i.e., representing a dispersion/variability method) are components of descriptive analysis approaches.

HANDLING DECISIONS AND EMERGENT ISSUES

Before proceeding with analyzing any of the information collected, much like a researcher, it is important to revisit the overall goal of the CLR. Consider your foundational information as a whole system and any inherent parts that it might have. Next, revisit the guiding questions that you established for analysis,

---

TOOL: VISUALIZING THE LEVEL OF MIXED METHODS INTEGRATION

Figure 9.1 illustrates a continuum which shows that the ways that qualitative and quantitative approaches, methods, and techniques can be integrated range from no integration to full integration. No integration occurs when the reviewer uses only qualitative approaches, methods, and/or techniques such as a meta-synthesis (which we describe later in this chapter); or only quantitative approaches, methods, and/or techniques such as a meta-analysis (which we also describe later in this chapter). In contrast, full integration occurs when the reviewer uses a mixed analysis in which qualitative and quantitative approaches, methods, and/or techniques are fully mixed. In between no integration and full integration are combinations of qualitative and quantitative approaches, methods, and/or techniques that represent partial integration. Our preference is that reviewers strive for a full integration of qualitative and quantitative approaches, methods, and/or techniques whenever possible. However, we recognize that the extent to which full integration takes place, would, at least in part, depend on the reviewer's philosophical belief system.

In the remainder of this chapter, we hope to facilitate the many decisions that are part of Step 6 in analyzing/synthesizing information. First, we outline some considerations for decisions and emergent issues—regardless of the approach and methods/techniques selected. Next, we present an overview of various approaches and methods pertaining to the research traditions—qualitative, quantitative, and mixed methods—that provide appropriate and functional avenues in making meaning of the information that was designated as the foundation information for the CLR.

(Continued)

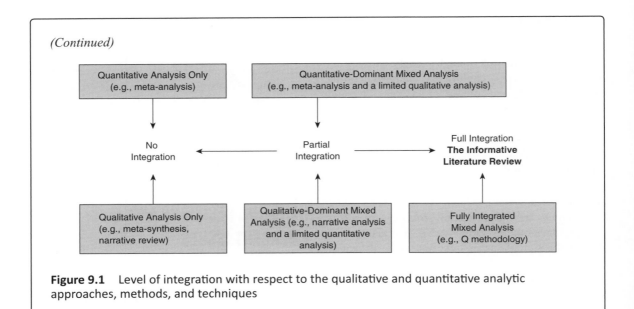

(Continued)

Quantitative Analysis Only
(e.g., meta-analysis)

Quantitative-Dominant Mixed Analysis
(e.g., meta-analysis and a limited qualitative analysis)

No
Integration

Partial
Integration

Full Integration
**The Informative
Literature Review**

Qualitative Analysis Only
(e.g., meta-synthesis,
narrative review)

Qualitative-Dominant Mixed
Analysis (e.g., narrative analysis
and a limited quantitative
analysis)

Fully Integrated
Mixed Analysis
(e.g., Q methodology)

Figure 9.1 Level of integration with respect to the qualitative and quantitative analytic approaches, methods, and techniques

and the meanings that you seek to delineate in the analysis/synthesis as they relate to your overall goal. Analyzing data is not just about coding and finding themes that go together; it is about reflecting on data for the subsequent synthesis that you will present in the communicating phase (Step 7). The guiding questions for the CLR will help to provide some boundaries in the analysis process. Yet, this process is flexible. The analysis/synthesis also includes making connections, categories, and memos—all of which stem from your philosophical stance and selection of (qualitative, quantitative, and/or mixed) approaches, methods, and techniques. As previously noted, data analysis is a product of research method, which connects directly to a research approach. Analysis techniques are strategies for optimizing interpretations from various perspectives. This process can include getting feedback on ideas, identifying codes, reducing information, counting frequencies, relating categories, and creating and examining data displays. One decision is to determine whether codes will be developed in a deductive way (i.e., making conclusions from general information: confirmatory) or an inductive way (i.e., making observations from information: drawing conclusions). Some coding strategies are more systematic than are others, depending on the selected research

approach. With any approach, coding is unique and is typically acquired *by doing*.

Another decision is to determine what constructs are most important to consider, based on your philosophical and theoretical frame. A type of mind mapping, or documented process, will help you to determine directions for coding and also gaps that might exist in your data. When unexpected ideas come to the surface and as you code, you can go back to your concept map and make decisions—based on your design—regarding how to handle them. (For more information about conceptual maps, see Maxwell, 2005.) A third decision to make is whether or not you will use computer-assisted qualitative data analysis software (CAQDAS) programs for coding. Before you begin working with any CAQDAS, distinguish the difference between a code and a theme. A ***code*** is a highlighted particular portion of text (or other data via MODES). Code names can change and are not necessarily emergent themes, and, typically, a code is a unit of analysis. The term ***categories*** typically refers to codes that are grouped into broader ideas, and the term ***theme*** refers to the codes that are in some way linked and integrated.

Finally, the analyses that you consider also depend on your own level of expertise in data analysis. To help facilitate the decisions of Step 6, and aligned with the array of quantitative and qualitative data that are potentially inherent in each work, the next sections present some common approaches, methods, and techniques (at an elementary, intermediate, and advanced degree of difficulty) in the qualitative, quantitative, and mixed research traditions which are helpful to review before mapping an analysis design. The other decisions, such as which particular analysis to use, are left up to you!

APPLYING CONCEPTS

QUALITATIVE DATA ANALYSIS OF INFORMATION

Onwuegbuzie, Leech, et al. (2012) identified 17 qualitative data analysis approaches that are optimal for analyzing information extracted from the literature review that yields the synthesis.

TOOL: LIST OF QUALITATIVE ANALYSES AND POSSIBLE MODES

Table 9.1 presents a portion of the data analysis approaches along with short descriptions. It can be seen from this table that reviewers have numerous design decisions to make before analyzing information extracted via each of the five MODES.

Table 9.1   Some possible qualitative analyses for MODES based on Onwuegbuzie, Leech, et al. (2012)

Type of Analysis	Short Description of Analysis	Use Associated with MODES
Constant comparison analysis	Systematically reducing source(s) to codes inductively, then developing themes from the codes. These themes may become headings and subheadings in the literature review section	All five MODES: **M**edia, **O**bservation(s), **D**ocuments, **E**xpert(s), and **S**econdary data
Classical content analysis	Systematically reducing source(s) to codes deductively or inductively, then counting the number of codes, under the assumption that the frequency of codes yields meaning	All five MODES: **M**edia, **O**bservation(s), **D**ocuments, **E**xpert(s), and **S**econdary data
Word count	Counting the total number of (key)words used or the number of times a particular word is used either during a within-study or between-study literature analysis	All five MODES: **M**edia, **O**bservation(s), **D**ocuments, **E**xpert(s), and **S**econdary data
Keywords-in-context	Identifying keywords and utilizing the surrounding words to understand the underlying meaning of the keyword in a source or across sources	All five MODES: **M**edia, **O**bservation(s), **D**ocuments, **E**xpert(s), and **S**econdary data
Domain analysis	Utilizing the relationships between symbols and referents to identify domains in a source(s)	All five MODES: **M**edia, **O**bservation(s), **D**ocuments, **E**xpert(s), and **S**econdary data
Taxonomic analysis	Creating a classification system that categorizes the domains in a pictorial representation (e.g., flowchart) to help understand the relationships among the domains	All five MODES: **M**edia, **O**bservation(s), **D**ocuments, **E**xpert(s), and **S**econdary data

(Continued)

(Continued)

Type of Analysis	Short Description of Analysis	Use Associated with MODES
Componential analysis	Using matrices and/or tables to discover the differences among the subcomponents of domains	All five MODES: **M**edia, **O**bservation(s), **D**ocuments, **E**xpert(s), and **S**econdary data
Theme analysis	Searching for relationships among domains, as well as a search for how these relationships are linked to the overall cultural context	All five MODES: **M**edia, **O**bservation(s), **D**ocuments, **E**xpert(s), and **S**econdary data
Discourse analysis	Selecting representative or unique segments of language use, such as several lines of an interview transcript involving a researcher, and then examining the selected lines in detail for rhetorical organization, variability, accountability, and positioning. Particularly useful for empirical articles, literature review articles, theoretical/conceptual articles, and methodological articles.	All five MODES: **M**edia, **O**bservation(s), **D**ocuments, **E**xpert(s), and **S**econdary data
Membership categorization analysis	Examining how authors/researchers communicate research terms, concepts, findings, and categories in their works	Three of five MODES: **M**edia, **E**xpert(s), and **S**econdary data
Semiotics	Using talk and text as systems of signs under the assumption that no meaning can be attached to a single term. This form of analysis shows how signs are inter-related for the purpose of creating and excluding specific meanings	Four of five MODES: **M**edia, **D**ocuments, **E**xpert(s), and **S**econdary data
Manifest content analysis	Describing observed (i.e., manifest) aspects of communication via objective, systematic, and empirical means	All five MODES: **M**edia, **O**bservation(s), **D**ocuments, **E**xpert(s), and **S**econdary data
Qualitative comparative analysis	Systematically analyzing similarities and differences across sources, typically being used as a theory-building approach, allowing the reviewer to make connections among previously built categories, as well as to test and to develop the categories further; this analysis is particularly useful for assessing causality in findings across sources	All five MODES: **M**edia, **O**bservation(s), **D**ocuments, **E**xpert(s), and **S**econdary data
Narrative analysis	Considering the potential of stories to give meaning to research findings, and treating data as stories, enabling reviewers to reduce data to a summary	One of five MODES: **E**xpert(s)
Text mining	Analyzing naturally occurring text within multiple sources in order to discover and to capture semantic information	Two of five MODES: **D**ocuments and **S**econdary data
Micro-interlocutor analysis	Analyzing information stemming from one or more focus groups of researchers, scholars, or practitioners about which participant(s) respond to each question, the order that each participant responds, the characteristics of the response, the non-verbal communication used, and the like	One of five MODES: **E**xpert(s)

Adapted from "Qualitative analysis techniques for the review of the literature," by A. J. Onwuegbuzie, N. L. Leech, and K. M. T. Collins, 2012, *The Qualitative Report, 17*(Art. 56), p. 12. Copyright 2012 by Anthony J. Onwuegbuzie, Nancy L. Leech, Kathleen M. T. Collins and Nova Southeastern University, Florida.

Due to the nature of information from MODES most often representing qualitative data such as words, pictures, observations, and primarily other articles (e.g., words of a primary researcher explaining a study and results), we provide a more in-depth description for qualitative data analyses beginning with some of the most commonly used qualitative data analyses on an elementary level and concluding with more difficult analyses on the intermediate and advanced levels, as follows:

- constant comparison analysis
- the four analyses comprising ethnographic analysis (i.e., domain analysis, taxonomic analysis, componential analysis, and theme analysis)
- discourse analysis
- qualitative comparative analysis

ELEMENTARY-LEVEL ANALYSIS

CONSTANT COMPARISON ANALYSIS. Constant comparison analysis was developed by Glaser and Strauss (Glaser, 1965, 1978, 1992; Glaser & Strauss, 1967; Strauss, 1987) as a core element for the grounded theory design (Glaser & Strauss, 1967). Strauss and Corbin (1998) posited that constant comparison analysis has five major characteristics: (a) to build theory—rather than to test theory; (b) to provide researchers with analytic tools to facilitate the analysis of data; (c) to help researchers extract multiple meanings from data; (d) to provide researchers with a systematic and creative framework for analyzing data; and (e) to help researchers identify, create, and observe relationships among components of the data when constructing a theme.

In grounded theory research, data that have been collected are analyzed through the following series of stages: an *open coding* stage (whereby data are grouped into smaller segments that are all given a descriptor, or code), an *axial coding* stage (whereby codes are grouped into similar categories), and a *selective coding* stage (wherein the emergent theory is integrated and refined), respectively, in order to "create theory out of data" (Strauss & Corbin, 1998, p. 56). Interestingly, according to Leech and Onwuegbuzie (2007), "constant comparison analysis since has been modified to be used to analyze data collected in one round (e.g., single round of interviews)" (p. 565), and even can be used to analyze a single document from a single case (i.e., within-in-case analysis). Further, Leech and Onwuegbuzie

(2007) outlined how constant comparison analysis "can be utilized with talk, observations, drawings/photographs/video, and documents" (Leech & Onwuegbuzie, 2008, p. 594). Thus, constant comparison analysis can be used to analyze all five MODES, as follows:

MEDIA. To perform a constant comparison analysis of information stemming from media, namely, audio or video, each audio segment or image/frame, respectively, is examined and coded; these codes are chunked, the chunks clustered, and the chunks labeled as themes until some form of saturation is reached, namely, data saturation (i.e., occurring when information occurs so repeatedly [across the audio or video] that the reviewer can anticipate it and whereby the collection of more information appears to have no additional interpretive worth; Sandelowski, 2008; Saumure & Given, 2008), or theoretical saturation (i.e., occurring when it can be assumed that the emergent themes adequately explain any future data collected; Sandelowski, 2008). As noted by Onwuegbuzie, Leech, et al. (2012), some CAQDAS programs (e.g., Transana, ATLAS.ti) can be used to enhance the coding of audio and video data.

OBSERVATIONS. Constant comparison analysis also could be used to analyze observational data by coding and chunking the observations collected by the reviewer for themes, which could be extracted for the purpose of generating new theory or, more importantly, to support or to refute initial codes that have been extracted via the other four MODES. The literature reviewer needs to write vivid descriptions of the observations before the analysis stage. Then, the process of coding and chunking can be systematic, based on the narrative of the observation. Again, several CAQDAS programs (e.g., QDA Miner, MAXQDA, NVivo) can be used to facilitate the analysis of observational data that inform the synthesis.

DOCUMENTS. Constant comparison analysis also can be used to analyze documents, that is, text in printed or digital form. To conduct this analysis, first, the reviewer reads through the complete set of information (whole works: preferred strategy) or subset of the information (e.g., results section of works: non-optimal strategy) one unit (e.g., work; section of work) at a time. Second, the reviewer chunks this information into smaller, meaningful components. Third, the reviewer labels each chunk with a descriptive label or a *code*. Fourth, the reviewer systematically compares each new chunk of data (e.g., work; section of work) with previous codes, such that similar chunks are labeled with the same code. After all the information has been coded and the codes clustered by similarity, themes are identified, labeled, and described based on each cluster. In writing the literature review section, the reviewer might use each theme to inform a paragraph or section, with the label given to each theme (or a variant of the label) providing the name of the section or subsection. Optimally, the constant comparison analysis ends when some form of saturation is reached (e.g., data saturation, theoretical saturation).

The point when the data tend to repeat ideas is called *saturation*, or no new themes emerge with respect to several components of a work. In particular, a reviewer can assess saturation of references by examining the reference list of each work (printed or digital) to determine the point at which each subsequent reference list reveals no new significant reference on the topic. With regard to the results section of works, saturation might be declared when no new findings emerge in subsequent results sections. In terms of the method section, saturation might be reached when no new instruments or procedures emerge in subsequent method sections. Finally, with respect to the introduction section, saturation might be reached when no new

theoretical frameworks or conceptual frameworks emerge in subsequent introduction sections. In any case, once saturation has been suggested, the reviewer is ready to conduct her/his synthesis.

As an example, the Dyadic Mentoring Study involved the use of constant comparison analysis to analyze the selected information for *themes* regarding school-based mentoring relationships, support for mentors, and contributions to the field of mentoring. For instance, incidences of direct support for both the mentor and the dyadic relationship, or ways in which effective programs outwardly supported dyadic mentoring relationships, emerged as a theme. In particular, constant comparison analysis revealed that the majority of effective school-based mentoring programs included elements of direct support for dyadic mentoring relationships. It was revealed that "the majority of directive (tangible) program inputs appear to be focused on supporting mentors, who might, in turn, be encouraged to undertake more effective mentoring" (Frels, 2010, p. 82).

EXPERT(S). After the interview of each expert has been transcribed, each expert's words can be coded and chunked, from which themes could be extracted. For example, at the onset of writing the CLR for the Dyadic Mentoring Study, Rebecca interviewed three prolific authors/researchers who were experts in the area of mentoring and a prolific author/researcher/ methodologist for insight pertaining to different aspects of the works that she selected. She analyzed the transcribed words using constant comparison analysis and was able to integrate each interviewee's expertise with information extracted from the other MODES that drove her ensuing synthesis.

SECONDARY DATA. Constant comparison analysis also could be used to analyze secondary data obtained by the reviewer (i.e., via already-analyzed secondary data, raw secondary data, or collecting and analyzing secondary data). In particular, these secondary data should be qualitative in nature. For example, if the reviewer generated qualitative-based secondary data by collecting all the critiques posted on the Delicious, Zotero, or another social bookmarking service, the reviewer then could conduct a constant comparison analysis of these critiques and allow any themes extracted to inform her/his synthesis.

INTERMEDIATE-LEVEL ANALYSIS

ETHNOGRAPHIC ANALYSIS. Ethnographic analysis, which was developed by Spradley (1979) to analyze interview data, comprises the following four analyses: (a) domain analysis, (b) taxonomic analysis, (c) componential analysis, and (d) theme analysis. Spradley developed these four sets of analyses to "have a single purpose: to uncover the system of cultural meanings that people use" (p. 94). Moreover, these ethnographic analyses were conceptualized by Spradley under the assumption that people have cultural knowledge, and by systematically examining people's words—what he called *folk terms*—and context, analysts can observe the relationships among the parts. It is by examining these parts that the researcher is able to understand the overall culture of the participant.

In Chapter 2, we demonstrated that culture—alongside ethics and multimodal components—are the driving influences of literature reviews in general and CLRs in particular. Indeed, all five MODES of the CLR process reflect the recognition that literature and other information sources are deeply embedded in culture. Thus, the CLR clearly lends itself to ethnographic analysis. Ethnographic analysis, in its complete form, comprises the aforementioned four qualitative data analysis approaches which are optimally conducted in the following order: domain analysis, taxonomic analysis, componential analysis, and theme analysis. Although each analysis can be used as a stand-alone analysis, when used in sequence with the other ethnographic analyses, each subsequent analysis is informed by the preceding analyses.

DOMAIN ANALYSIS. The first step in the ethnographic analysis process involves a search for the larger units of cultural knowledge, which Spradley (1979) refers to as *domains*. The primary goal of a domain analyst is to understand the domain, with the analyst first examining symbols under the assumption that symbols represent a pivotal way of communicating cultural meaning. Every culture—including the research culture and numerous research subcultures—has symbols or elements that represent other items. Symbols have three components (Spradley, 1979): (a) the symbol itself (cover term), (b) one or more referents (to what the symbol refers; included term), and (c) a relationship between the symbol and the referent (semantic relationship). Alternatively stated, domains are created from (a) cover terms (concepts; Y), (b) included terms (referents; X), and (c) a semantic relationship between the cover term (Y) and the included terms (X). In order to understand the symbol, it is essential for the researcher to analyze the relationship of the symbol to the referents, which is undertaken by examining semantics.

Spradley (1979) surmised that nine types of semantic relationships are particularly useful for analyzing semantic domains, which are displayed in Table 9.2. These semantic relationships represent the essence of domain analysis. The relationships might occur among information stemming from all five MODES.

TAXONOMIC ANALYSIS. Although domain analysis can be undertaken by itself, it can be combined with taxonomic analysis, which is the second step in the ethnographic analysis process. Once synthesis domains have been identified, taxonomic analysis can be used by selecting one domain and placing it into a taxonomy. Spradley (1979) defined a ***taxonomy*** as a classification system that inventories the domains into a flowchart or other visual representation to help the analyst understand the relationships among the domains. Thus, as is the case for domain analysis, a taxonomic analysis can be characterized as a set of categories that are organized on the basis of a single semantic relationship. However, in contrast to a domain analysis, via the construction of a taxonomy, a taxonomic analysis displays the relationships among all the terms that are contained in a domain.

Further, a taxonomic analysis displays the hierarchical structure of the terms representing a domain by identifying the subsets of terms and the relationship of these subsets to the domain as a whole (Spradley, 1979).

COMPONENTIAL ANALYSIS. Although componential analysis also can serve as a stand-alone analysis, it can be combined with domain analysis and taxonomic analysis, yielding the third step of the ethnographic analysis process. According to Spradley (1979), componential analysis is a "systematic search for attributes (components of meaning) associated with

TOOL: SIX STEPS OF A DOMAIN ANALYSIS AND DOMAIN RELATIONSHIP

Domain analysis (Spradley, 1979) involves six steps, some of which are repeated to understand the relationships:

1. Select a single semantic relationship (repeated).
2. Prepare a domain analysis worksheet (repeated).
3. Select a sample of informant statements (repeated).
4. Search for possible cover terms and included terms that fit the semantic relationship (repeated).
5. Formulate structural questions for each domain (repeated).
6. Make a list of all hypothesized domains.

Table 9.2   Spradley's (1979) types of relationships for domain analysis

Type	Relationship of X and Y
Strict inclusion	X is a kind of Y
Spatial	X is a place in Y, X is a part of Y
Cause–effect	X is a result/cause of Y
Rationale	X is a reason for doing Y
Location for action	X is a place for doing Y
Function	X is used for Y
Means–end	X is a way to do Y
Sequence	X is a step (stage) in Y
Attribution	X is an attribute of Y

Adapted from *The ethnographic interview*, by J. P. Spradley, 1979, Fort Worth, TX: Holt, Rinehart and Winston.

The types of relationships presented in Table 9.2 can be used, for example, to distinguish causal relationships (i.e., "X is a result/cause of Y") from other types of relationships or patterns. Step 5 of the domain analysis process is a particularly useful step because this step leads to additional structural questions (e.g., "How is X a cause of Y?"; "How is X an attribute of Y?"), which reviewers might address by re-examining sources that they already have extracted or by expanding the CLR via MODES. In particular, reviewers could interview experts to obtain their responses to the structural questions. For instance, returning to our mentoring and college students example, if a saturation-based conclusion emerged from the domain analysis that led the reviewer to conclude that mentoring is a cause of persistence among the *culture* of undergraduate students, in order to synthesize more effectively the CLR (even if it is to inform primary research that uses a different data collection technique), the reviewer could interview experts from the field of mentoring in an attempt to establish how this might be the case. Consequently, domain analysis provides a powerful analytic tool for analyzing information in a CLR that yields what we refer to as *synthesis domains* (i.e., representing the synthesis that pertains to each identified domain).

TOOL: EIGHT STEPS OF A TAXONOMIC ANALYSIS

Interestingly, as is the case for domain analysis, taxonomic analysis leads to further structural questions. After these questions are answered, the reviewer can refine the taxonomy and use it as part of her/his synthesis to help the reader understand the phenomenon of interest. The following list comprises eight steps in creating a taxonomy for analysis:

1. Select a domain for the taxonomic analysis.
2. Identify the appropriate substitution frame for analysis (a substitution frame [e.g., "is a result/cause of"] is similar to a semantic relationship, although it differs inasmuch as it helps to differentiate the included terms into subgroups).
3. Search for possible subsets among the included terms.
4. Search for larger, more inclusive domains that might include as a subset the one you are analyzing.
5. Construct a tentative taxonomy.
6. Formulate structural questions to verify taxonomic relationships.
7. Conduct additional structural interviews.
8. Construct a completed taxonomy.

Interestingly, as is the case for domain analysis, taxonomic analysis leads to further structural questions. After these questions are answered, the reviewer can refine the taxonomy and use it as part of her/his synthesis to help the reader understand the phenomenon of interest.

TOOL: EIGHT STEPS OF A COMPONENTIAL ANALYSIS

Componential analysis is particularly suited for the CLR if the reviewer wants to develop structural questions that they can ask experts to fill in gaps in understanding the contrast set. A componential analysis involves the following eight steps:

1. Select a contrast set for analysis.
2. Inventory all contrasts previously discovered.
3. Prepare a paradigm worksheet.
4. Identify dimensions of contrast that have binary values.
5. Combine closely related dimensions of contrast into ones that have multiple values.
6. Prepare contrast questions to elicit missing attributes and new dimensions of contrast.
7. Conduct an interview to elicit needed data.
8. Prepare a completed paradigm.

cultural symbols" (p. 174). When conducting this analysis, matrices and/or tables are created to determine the differences among the subcomponents of domains in order to "map as accurately as possible the psychological reality of our informant's cultural knowledge" (Spradley, 1979, p. 176). Generally speaking, at a minimum, the constructed tables have the following two dimensions: (a) *the contrast set* and (b) *dimensions of contrast*. The contrast set represents a set of attributes (i.e., components) of meaning for any term, whereas the dimensions of contrast represent questions that are formulated by the analyst for the purpose of differentiating the contrast set. Each question is constructed in such a way that the possible responses are either *yes* or *no*.

THEME ANALYSIS. The fourth and final analysis in the ethnographic process is theme analysis, which involves developing ideas or concepts that "go beyond such an inventory [of domains] to discover the conceptual themes that members of a society use to connect these domains" (Spradley, 1979, p. 185). Alternatively stated, a theme analysis involves a search for relationships among domains, as well as a search for how these relationships are linked to the overall cultural context. As is the case for constant comparison analysis, the reviewer might use each theme that is extracted from a theme analysis to inform a paragraph or even a (whole) section, with each theme label (or its variant) providing the name of the section or subsection.

DISCOURSE ANALYSIS. Discourse analysis is another intermediate technique that can be used to analyze the extracted information because it involves "examining the selected lines in detail for rhetorical organization, variability, accountability, and positioning" (Onwuegbuzie, Leech, et al., 2012, p. 12). Further, discourse analysis is particularly pertinent for analyzing information stemming from interviews of experts during the MODES process. Because the literature review typically involves the reviewer's account of information from multiple authors (e.g., procedures, findings, interpretations), discourse analysis can serve as a way of information meaning-making (Onwuegbuzie & Frels, 2014a)—a process we call a Discourse Analysis-Based Research Synthesis (DARS).

Specifically, DARS incorporates Gee's (2005, 2010) form of discourse analysis as a way to complete Step 6: Analyzing and Synthesizing Information by focusing on aspects of language used in the situation network and taking into consideration the verbal cues and clues that help listeners and readers interpret situations in particular ways and not other ways. Discourse analysis can be used to analyze information under the assumption that language is always reflexively related to situations, and that "all analyses are open to further discussion and dispute, and their status can go up or down with time as work goes on in the field" (Gee, 2005, p. 113).

Discourse analysis involves seven building tasks that are built on different grammatical devices (Gee, 2005): (a) significance: identifying how language makes particular ideas significant; (b) activities: noting what activity or activities in a piece of language is enacted; (c) identities: addressing how language is used to contextualize identity; (d) relationships: noting the sort of relationship of language that enacts with other people; (e) politics: identifying perspectives on social goods through language; (f) connections: addressing how a piece of language connects or disconnects; and (g) sign systems and knowledge: addressing how language privileges or disprivileges particular sign systems, beliefs, or ways of knowing. All of these building tasks have particular relevance for literature reviewers. (For detailed explanation of each building task, see Onwuegbuzie & Frels, 2014a.)

As revealed by DARS, discourse analysis can be extremely useful for the CLR process because any given source that is extracted from the initial literature review (i.e., Steps 2–4) or from the MODES process (i.e., Step 5) can represent a discourse. Thus, analysis of information represents an analysis of "the power of incomplete, ambiguous, and even contradictory discourses to produce a special reality that we experience as solid and real" (Phillips & Hardy, 2002, pp. 1–2). Simply put, discourse analysis can be a means to observe social reality via the extant information. More specifically, discourse analysis involves examining: how each source is meaningful in relation to other sources; the different discourses upon which the set of sources draw; and the antecedent and nature of their development, dissemination, and utilization by which they are made meaningful—as well as the role that they play in the formation of social reality via meaning-making (Onwuegbuzie & Frels, 2014a). By opting to use discourse analysis during the CLR process, a literature reviewer can examine the relationship between discourse and social reality. This process also highlights the importance of being cognizant of the social context in which these bodies of knowledge (i.e., sources) are situated.

EXAMPLE: USE OF CAQDAS FOR DISCOURSE ANALYSIS

Figure 9.2 depicts one page of the use of CAQDAS to analyze information via DARS (Onwuegbuzie & Frels, 2014a). In this picture, the use of a priori (i.e., predetermined categories/themes) coding was based on three of Gee's (2010) seven building tasks (i.e., identities, connections, and relationships) and one selected source. This particular discourse analysis revealed that the building tasks of *relationships* and *activities* were extremely prevalent.

ADVANCED-LEVEL ANALYSIS

QUALITATIVE COMPARATIVE ANALYSIS.
The final qualitative data analysis approach that we discuss to analyze information extracted during the CLR process is *qualitative comparative analysis*, developed by Ragin (1987) systematically to analyze similarities and differences across cases. Broadly speaking, qualitative comparative analysis is used as a theory-building approach, wherein the analyst makes connections among categories that have been identified

previously, as well as testing and developing these categories further (Miles & Weitzman, 1994). Historically, this form of qualitative analysis most commonly has been used in macrosocial studies to examine the conditions under which a state of affairs has come to the fore. In causal, macro-level contexts, qualitative comparative analysis often is utilized for reanalyzing secondary data collected by other researchers (e.g., Ragin, 1989, 1994). Thus, because the CLR, in the main, involves the collection and analysis of information that has been generated by other people (e.g., researchers), it is a natural extension to analyze literature in general (Onwuegbuzie & Frels, 2014b), and the five MODES in particular.

Qualitative comparative analysis begins with the construction of a ***truth table***, which is a list of all unique configurations of the study participants and situational variables that have been identified in the data, along with the corresponding type(s) of incidents, events, or the like that have been observed for each configuration (Miethe & Drass, 1999). The truth table delineates which configurations are unique to a category of the classification variable and which configurations are found in multiple categories. By comparing the numbers of configurations in these

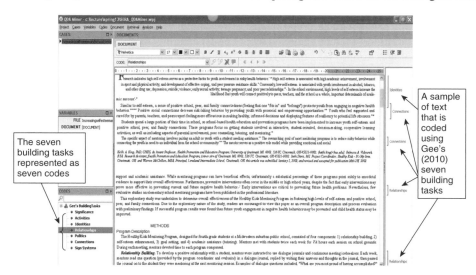

Figure 9.2 Screenshot showing a priori coding using Gee's (2010) seven building tasks

Adapted from "A framework for using discourse analysis for the review of the literature in counseling research," by A. J. Onwuegbuzie and R. K. Frels, 2014a, *Counseling Outcome Research and Evaluation*, 2, pp. 115–125.

groups, the analyst obtains an estimate of the extent to which types of events, experiences, or the like are similar or unique. The analyst then "compares the configurations within a group, looking for commonalities that allow configurations to be combined into simpler, yet more abstract, representations" (Miethe & Drass, 1999, p. 8). This step is undertaken by identifying and eliminating unnecessary variables from configurations. Specifically, variables are considered as being unnecessary if their presence or absence within a configuration has no impact on the outcome that is associated with the configuration. As such, qualitative comparative analysis represents a case-based analysis rather than a variable-based analysis (Ragin, 1989, 1994). The qualitative comparative analyst repeats these comparisons until no further reductions are possible. Next, redundancies among the remaining reduced configurations are eliminated, thereby leading to the final solution, specifically, a statement of the unique features of each category of the typology.

Qualitative comparative analysts treat each case holistically as representing a configuration of attributes. Moreover, qualitative comparative analysts assume that the effect of a variable may vary from one case to the next, depending upon the values of the other attributes of the case. Further, systematic and logical case comparisons are established from the rules of Boolean algebra to distinguish commonalities among these configurations, thereby reducing the complexity of the typology. Simply put, the goal of qualitative comparative analysis is to obtain a typology "that allows for heterogeneity within groups and that defines categories in terms of configurations of attributes" (Miethe & Drass, 1999, p. 10).

An important goal of qualitative comparative analysis is to distinguish between the idea of necessary cause and sufficient cause. According to Ragin (1987, 1989, 1994):

- A cause is defined as necessary if it must be present for an outcome to occur.
- A cause is defined as sufficient if by itself it can produce a certain outcome.
- This distinction is meaningful only in the context of theoretical perspectives.
- No cause is necessary if it is independent of a theory that specifies it as a relevant cause.

- Neither necessity nor sufficiency exists independently of theories that propose causes.
- Necessity and sufficiency are usually considered jointly because all combinations of the two are meaningful.
- A cause is both necessary and sufficient if it is the only cause that produces an outcome and it is singular (that is, not a combination of causes).
- A cause is sufficient but not necessary if it is capable of producing the outcome but is not the only cause with this capability.
- A cause is necessary but not sufficient if it is capable of producing an outcome in combination with other causes and appears in all such combinations.
- A cause is neither necessary nor sufficient if it appears only in a subset of the combinations of conditions that produce an outcome.
- In all, there are four categories of causes (formed from the cross-tabulation of the presence/absence of sufficiency against the presence/absence of necessity).

Qualitative comparative analysis can be used to analyze selected sources for the CLR by using themes extracted from another analysis (e.g., one of the remaining 15 qualitative data analysis approaches presented in Table 9.1) to create a truth table for understanding these themes. A particular appeal of qualitative comparative analysis is that it can be used for a large number of cases, "which generally cripples most qualitative research" (Soulliere, 2005, p. 424). In fact, in certain circumstances, qualitative comparative analysis can be used to inform causal statements about variables and phenomena that have been studied or identified by researchers.

EXAMPLE: CREATING A QUALITATIVE COMPARATIVE ANALYSIS

As an illustration, we summarize Onwuegbuzie and Frels's (2015b) conceptualization. These authors used the work of DuBois, Holloway, Valentine, and Cooper (2002) to visualize this approach. DuBois et al. (2002)

conducted a meta-analytic review of 55 articles regarding the effectiveness of mentoring programs for youth. From this review, these researchers developed an index of the characteristics of the 11 best practices for mentoring programs. Let us suppose that, as reviewers, we are especially interested in the following three characteristics of best practices: mentoring relationship monitoring, mentor training, and structured activities. Let us suppose further that we are interested in knowing which mentoring programs of these 55 articles were effective in retaining mentors and/or mentees, so that we could conduct a qualitative comparative analysis to determine which of these three characteristics is a necessary and/or sufficient cause of mentoring program effectiveness.

According to Ragin (1987), one of the initial tasks in qualitative comparative analysis is the preliminary coding of all variables selected for the analysis. Because Boolean algebra involves the use of dichotomous values (i.e., 0 and 1), when conducting qualitative comparative analysis, all variables (i.e., conditions) and all outcomes must be dichotomous. This assignment is accomplished by coding the conditions and outcomes using categories such as presence/absence or high/low. In Onwuegbuzie and Frels's (2015b) example, the presence of each of the characteristics (mentoring relationship monitoring, mentor training, and structured activities) is indicated by "1," whereas absence is indicted by "0." Similarly, the presence of an effective mentoring program is indicated by "1," whereas absence is indicted by "0." This coding led to a data matrix that contains 1s and 0s for each of the 55 articles. From the matrix, a truth table can be constructed that might resemble Table 9.3. This truth table summarizes the pattern of outcomes (i.e., whether or not the mentoring program was effective) associated with different configurations of causal conditions (i.e., characteristics of best practices). Fundamentally, a truth table presents the different combinations of causal conditions and the value of the outcome variable for the cases (i.e., articles) conforming to each combination.

Table 9.3 indicates some contradictory outcomes. However, what is clear is that when none of the three characteristics (i.e., mentoring relationship monitoring [MRM], mentor training [MT], and structured activities [SA]) is present, none of the mentoring programs is effective (MPE). At the opposite end of the spectrum, when all three characteristics are present, then 20 of the mentoring programs are effective. An interesting observation is that more mentoring programs are effective when mentoring relationship monitoring is present than when it is not present.

Using the free qualitative comparative software called fsQCA (http://www.u.arizona.edu/~cragin/fsQCA/) to analyze the truth table in Table 9.3 (i.e., standard analyses)

Onwuegbuzie and Frels (2015b) identified two combinations of conditions linked to the outcome of the mentoring program being effective, which yielded the following two logical equations:

1. MPE = MRM
2. MPE = MT and SA

The first solution (i.e., Equation 1) indicates that mentoring relationship monitoring is a necessary and sufficient condition for a mentoring program to be effective. That is, the first solution indicates that mentoring relationship monitoring must be present for a mentoring program to be effective, regardless of whether mentor training or structured activities are present. The fsQCA software program revealed a *consistency* score of 1.0 for the first solution, which indicates that this condition did not include any case (i.e., work) that did not display the outcome (i.e., effective mentoring program).

The second solution indicates that neither mentored training nor structured activities are necessary for the mentoring program to be effective. (A cause is both necessary and sufficient if it is the only cause that produces an outcome and it is singular.) However, either one is sufficient for the mentoring program to be effective. (A cause is sufficient but not necessary if it is capable of producing the outcome but is not the only cause with this capability.) The fsQCA output revealed a *consistency* score of 1.0 for the first condition (i.e., Equation 1), which indicates that this condition did not include any case (i.e., article) that did not display the outcome (i.e., effective mentoring program). *Raw coverage* measures the proportion of memberships in the outcome explained by each term of the solution. The finding from the fsQCA output that the raw coverage for the first solution (.94) is higher than is the raw coverage (.43) for the second solution indicates that the first solution covers more cases (i.e., more of the 55 articles) in the data set.

Solution consistency of qualitative comparison analysis indicates the combined consistency of the causal conditions. That is, solution consistency measures the degree to which membership in the solution (the set of solution terms) is a subset of membership in the outcome. The fsQCA output revealed a solution consistency of 1.0, which indicates that the membership in the solution (the set of solution terms) is a subset of membership in the outcome (i.e., effective mentoring program). ***Solution coverage*** indicates the proportion of membership in the outcome that can be explained by membership in the causal recipes. The fsQCA output also revealed a solution coverage of 1.0, which indicates that all the articles for which the outcome is present (i.e., effective mentoring program) are a member of either of the solutions and, thus, are explained by the model. That both the solution consistency and solution coverage are 1.0 (i.e., greater than .75; Ragin, 2008) indicates a correctly specified model.

In summary, the qualitative comparative analysis of the truth table in Table 9.3 suggests, in particular, the importance of mentoring relationship monitoring in securing an effective mentoring program. Thus, as can be seen, qualitative comparative analysis, "with its holistic combinatorial logic and emphasis on causal heterogeneity" (Soulliere, 2005, p. 434), lends itself to information extracted during the CLR process.

The example used here involves the use of a conventional (i.e., crisp) set. A **crisp set** is dichotomous such that a case—in this case, an information source—is either *in* or *out* of a set. Thus, in the example above, for the set of characteristics, a conventional set is comparable to a binary variable with two values: 1 (*in*; i.e., present) and 0 (*out*; i.e., absent). In contrast, a **fuzzy set** allows membership anywhere in the interval between 0 and 1 while retaining the two qualitative states of full membership and full non-membership. Therefore, the fuzzy set of risk characteristics could include factors that are *fully in* the set (fuzzy membership = 1.0), some that are *almost fully in* the set (membership = .90), some that are neither *more in* nor *more out* of the set (membership = .50, also known as the *crossover point*), some that are "barely more out than in" the set (membership = .45), and so on, down to those that are *fully out* of the set (membership = 0). The onus is on the reviewer to specify procedures for assigning fuzzy membership scores to cases, and these procedures must be both open and explicit (i.e., leaving an audit trail) so that they can be evaluated by other reviewers and researchers.

Table 9.3 Truth table for selected characteristics of best practices for mentoring programs among the 55 articles: fictitious data

Conditions			Outcome
Mentoring Relationship Monitoring (MRM)	Mentor Training (MT)	Structured Activities (SA)	Mentoring Program Effective (MPE)?
0	0	0	0
0	0	1	0
0	1	0	1
0	1	1	3
1	0	0	10
1	0	1	9
1	1	0	12
1	1	1	20
		Total	55

QUALITATIVE DATA ANALYSIS METHODS

As we stated earlier, qualitative data analysis methods are data analyses that represent part of a system. Thus, these methods can serve as either a standalone analysis or in combination with a qualitative data analysis approach. They might even encompass some data analysis techniques.

QUALITATIVE DATA ANALYSIS TECHNIQUES

As stated earlier, qualitative data analysis techniques are data analyses that represent a single step in the qualitative data analysis process. As such, these techniques represent a more micro type of analysis that usually operates at the level of coding. Techniques can be integrated into most approaches for coding the CLR.

SALDAÑA'S 32 CODING TECHNIQUES. In his seminal book, Saldaña (2012) identified 32 coding techniques to represent what he established as either the first cycle or second cycle, with one hybrid method lying in between them. According to Saldaña (2012), *first cycle* techniques are coding strategies that occur during the initial coding of data, and which are

TOOL: WITHIN-CASE AND CROSS-CASE DISPLAYS MAPPED ONTO THE CLR PROCESS

Analysis methods for the CLR can include Miles and Huberman's (1994) array of within-case analyses and cross-case analyses. Specifically, all 19 within-case analyses and 18 cross-case analyses conceptualized by Miles and Huberman (1994) can be mapped onto the CLR process. These analyses are presented in Table 9.4 and Table 9.5.

Table 9.4 Miles and Huberman's (1994) within-case displays mapped onto the CLR process

Type of Display	Description
Partially ordered:	
Poem	Analyzing information using poetry; also known as interpretive poem, found poetry (e.g., Prendergast, 2006), research experience poem, poem from the field, or data poem (see Lahman et al., 2010)
Context chart	Using networks that map in graphic form the inter-relationships among groups studied by researchers and roles that underlie the context of individual behavior
Checklist matrix	Analyzing/displaying one major concept, variable, or domain that includes several unordered components
Time-ordered:	
Event listing	Using a matrix or flowchart to organize a series of concrete events by chronological time periods and to sort them into multiple categories
Critical incident chart	Mapping a few critical events across the literature
Event-state network	Mapping general states that are not as time-limited as events, and that might represent moderators or mediators that link specific events of interest
Activity record	Displaying a specific recurring activity across the literature that is limited narrowly in time and space
Decision modeling flowchart	Mapping thoughts, plans, and decisions made during a flow of activity that is bounded by specific conditions
Growth gradient	Using a network to map events that are conceptualized as being linked to an underlying variable that changes over time
Time-ordered matrix	Mapping when particular phenomena occurred
Role-ordered:	
Role-ordered matrix	Mapping the "roles" of each selected work by sorting data in rows and columns that have been collected from or are about a set of data that reflect the views, beliefs, expectations, and/or behaviors of the authors/researchers
Role-by-time matrix	Mapping the "roles" of each selected work and preserving chronological order
Conceptually ordered:	
Conceptually clustered matrix	Creating a text table with rows and columns arranged to cluster items that are related theoretically, thematically, or empirically

(Continued)

(Continued)

Type of Display	Description
Thematic conceptual matrix	Using a display that reflects the ordering of themes
Folk taxonomy	Typically representing a hierarchical tree diagram that displays how a researcher/author classifies important phenomena
Cognitive map	Displaying the researcher's/author's representation of concepts pertaining to a particular domain
Effects matrix	Displaying data yielding one or more outcomes in a differentiated manner, focusing on the outcome/dependent variable of interest
Case dynamics matrix	Displaying a set of elements for change and tracing the consequential processes and outcomes for the purpose of initial explanation
Causal network	Displaying the most important independent and dependent variables across the information sources and their inter-relationships

Adapted from *Mapping Miles and Huberman's within-case and cross-case analyses onto the literature review process*, by A. J. Onwuegbuzie and Rebecca K. Frels, 2014c, unpublished manuscript, Sam Houston state University, Huntsville, TX, p. x. Copyright 2014 by A. J. Onwuegbuzie and Rebecca K. Frels.

Table 9.5 Miles and Huberman's (1994) cross-case displays mapped onto the CLR process

Type of Display	Description
Partially ordered:	
Partially ordered meta-matrices	Displaying descriptive data for each of the selected information sources simultaneously
Case-ordered:	
Case-ordered descriptive meta-matrix	Including descriptive data from all information sources but the information sources are ordered by the main variable of interest
Two-variable case-ordered matrix	Displaying descriptive data from all information sources but the information sources are ordered by two main variables of interest that are represented by the rows and columns
Contrast table	Displaying a few exemplary information sources wherein the variable occurs in low or high form, and contrasting several attributes of the basic variable
Scatterplot	Plotting all information sources on two or more axes to determine how close from each other the information sources are
Case-ordered effects matrix	Sorting information sources by degrees of the major cause of interest, and showing the diverse effects for each information source
Case-ordered predictor-outcome matrix	Arranging information sources with respect to a main outcome variable, and providing data for each information source on the main antecedent variables
Predictor-outcome consequences matrix	Linking a chain of predictors to some intermediate outcome, and then illustrating the consequence of that outcome

Type of Display	Description
Time-ordered:	
Time-ordered meta-matrix	Creating a table in which columns are organized sequentially by time period and the rows are not necessarily ordered
Time-ordered scatterplot	Displaying similar variables across information sources over two or more time periods
Composite sequence analysis	Allowing extraction of typical stories that several information sources share, without eliminating meaningful sequences
Conceptually ordered:	
Content-analytic summary table	Allowing the reviewer to focus on the content of a meta-matrix without reference to the underlying information source
Substructing	Allowing the identification of underlying dimensions
Decision tree modeling	Displaying decisions and actions that are made across several information sources
Variable-by-variable matrix	Creating a table that displays two major variables in its rows and columns ordered by intensity, with the cell entries representing the information sources
Causal models	Creating a network of variables with causal connections among them in order to provide a testable set of propositions or hunches about the complete network of variables and their inter-relationships
Causal networks	Conducting a comparative analysis of all information sources using variables deemed to be the most influential in explaining the outcome or criterion
Antecedents matrix	Creating a display that is ordered by the outcome variable, and displaying all of the variables that appear to change the outcome variable

Adapted from *Mapping Miles and Huberman's within-case and cross-case analyses onto the literature review process*, by A. J. Onwuegbuzie and Rebecca K. Frels, 2014c, unpublished manuscript, Sam Houston state University, Huntsville, TX, p. x. Copyright 2014 by A. J. Onwuegbuzie and Rebecca K. Frels.

As needed, a reviewer can use one or more of these displays to analyze and to display results of a synthesis.

subdivided into the following seven subcategories (with their methods in parentheses): *grammatical methods* (attribute coding, magnitude coding, sub-coding, simultaneous coding); *elemental methods* (structural coding, descriptive coding, in vivo coding, process coding, initial coding); *affective methods* (emotion coding, values coding, versus coding, evaluation coding); *literary and language methods* (dramaturgical coding, motif coding, narrative coding, verbal exchange coding); *exploratory methods* (holistic coding, provisional coding, hypothesis coding); and *procedural methods* (protocol coding, outline of cultural materials coding, domain and taxonomic coding, causation coding). Conversely, the *second cycle* methods are coding strategies that "require such analytic skills as classifying, prioritizing, integrating, synthesizing, abstracting, conceptualizing, and theory building" (p. 58), as follows: *pattern coding, focused coding, axial coding, theoretical coding, elaborative coding,* and *longitudinal coding*. Finally, *theming data* (eclectic coding) lies in between the first and second cycles.

EXAMPLE: SUMMARY OF CODING TECHNIQUES

Table 9.6 presents a summary of how each of Saldaña's (2012) 32 coding techniques can be applied to analyzing information that is extracted from literature based on Onwuegbuzie, Hwang, and Frels's (2014) six stages: *Stage 1*: Conduct a CLR using the five MODES to identify the relevant literature. *Stage 2*: Store and organize the information extracted from the CLR—optimally, upload all of the sources into a CAQDAS program (e.g., QDA Miner). *Stage 3*: Decide whether to code all information sources that have been identified or whether to code one or more subsets of these sources, and decide, for each source, whether to code the whole source or one or more segments of the source (say the section of the source [e.g., results section of an empirical research article] that contains the findings). *Stage 4*: Set up all or a subset of Saldaña's (2012) codes a priori. *Stage 5*: Code each source using Saldaña's (2012) a priori codes. *Stage 6*: Conduct a cross-case analysis (Miles & Huberman, 1994) in order to compare and to contrast the coding of the selected a priori codes across the selected research studies, with each article representing a case.

Onwuegbuzie et al. (2014) used Saldaña's (2012) 32 a priori codes to analyze seven mentoring-based qualitative research studies that informed Frels's (2010) literature review. In Stage 5, after reading the results and discussion sections of each article multiple times, they identified words, phrases, sentences, or paragraphs that indicated one or more of Saldaña's 32 codes. They noted that of Saldaña's 32 codes, 11 were relevant for the seven qualitative research articles. Figure 9.3 illustrates a priori coding on one page of one article using several of Saldaña's codes and the use of the CAQDAS software QDA Miner (Provalis Research, 2011). In Step 6, they conducted a cross-case analysis by comparing and contrasting the coding of Saldaña's 32 codes across the seven mentoring-based qualitative research studies (i.e., seven cases). In particular, they used QDA Miner to subject the 11 codes to a correspondence analysis, which is a multivariate analysis and graphical technique (Michailidis, 2007) that allows researchers to conduct a cross-case analysis of Saldaña's codes—namely, a form of case-ordered display.

EXAMPLE: MAP OF A CORRESPONDENCE ANALYSIS

Figure 9.4 illustrates the seven qualitative research articles mapped, via a correspondence analysis, onto the space that displays the Saldaña codes that were used to code one or more of these articles. This figure maps the articles related to each other with regard to these Saldaña codes. For instance, it can be seen from Figure 9.4 that the qualitative research study conducted by Spencer (2006), which is located close to the origin, clustered around the following three subcategories of affective methods: values coding,

Table 9.6 Summary of Saldaña's (2012) 32 coding techniques mapped onto the CLR process

	Coding Method	How to Apply to Literature Review
1	Attribute coding	Apply attribute codes to log information about the literature (e.g., empirical/theoretical paper, qualitative/quantitative research/academic disciplines). By utilizing attribute codes, previous studies can be sorted out by year, methodology (quantitative or qualitative), or journals. For example, a reviewer can identify the gap between years in terms of the number of conducted studies by organizing literature by attribute codes.
2	Axial coding	Like focused coding, axial coding involves determining which codes stemming from the literature are dominant or less dominant, to organize them systematically or thematically (e.g., crossing out, getting rid of redundant codes). Also, axial coding can be utilized to specify the dimension of categories generated by focused coding of the literature. Axial codes can be utilized to identify different dimensions of constructs.
3	Causation coding	Causation coding can be utilized to analyze causality between variables, mediate variables, and outcomes in empirical reports. Causation coding can be employed for both within- and between-literature analysis. Causation codes can be developed into a causation model.

	Coding Method	How to Apply to Literature Review
4	Descriptive coding	Descriptive coding is applied with descriptive nouns, after the reviewer generates descriptive codes. Also, descriptive codes can be utilized for visual data. After generating descriptive codes, a reviewer can determine the frequency of descriptive codes by utilizing tools such as Word Cloud, a graphical representation of content analysis software programs (e.g., WordStat), or qualitative data analysis software programs (e.g., QDA Miner, NVivo, MAXQDA) that facilitate the counting of words or codes. Examining descriptive codes might help a reviewer to identify "keywords" to explore the topic.
5	Domain and taxonomic coding	Domain and taxonomic coding can be employed to analyze and to synthesize research findings by distinguishing relationships or patterns among terms used in the literature and by organizing them into a taxonomy.
6	Dramaturgical coding	Dramaturgical coding involves items such as objectives, conflicts or obstacles, strategies to deal with conflicts or obstacles, attitude, emotions, and subtexts. Dramaturgical coding can be utilized to analyze text or talk data that inform a literature review and might be useful for understanding power relationship among constituencies.
7	Eclectic coding	Eclectic coding can be employed to generate themes. For example, codes previously generated through various coding methods such as initial coding can be selected and synthesized into themes or categories.
8	Elaborative coding	Elaborative coding can be applied at the stage of reflecting or evaluating the literature review process or product in order to refine theoretical constructs or themes.
9	Emotion coding	Similarly to in vivo codes, emotion codes can be utilized to analyze an author's feelings or mood about his/her research findings. For example, the emotion code "surprising" can imply that the finding in the article was unexpected or new.
10	Evaluation coding	Evaluation codes can be generated to provide recommendations for further research and practice stemming from findings. By examining evaluation codes, a reviewer can identify the gap between previous and current studies and generate a research question(s).
11	Focused coding	Focused coding involves searching for the most frequent codes appearing in a body of works to develop the most prominent category or categories.
12	Holistic coding	Holistic codes can be utilized to grasp basic themes or issues as a whole. Holistic codes can be generated by scanning the abstract or whole works and can be used to determine the relevancy of literature to the specific topic or searching criteria.
13	Hypothesis coding	Hypothesis codes can be applied to generate hypotheses in the current studies from a between-literature analysis. A reviewer can analyze literature and find a relationship between two or more variables and generate hypothesis codes (e.g., significant/non-significant). By examining generated codes, hypotheses can be generated for the current study.
14	In vivo coding	In vivo codes can be applied to analyze the authors' opinions, usually found in the discussion section by using words verbatim with "quotation marks." They can be interpreted to determine how authors reflect on their research findings.
15	Initial coding	Initial coding, referred to as "open coding," can be employed when analyzing literature data with an open-ended approach and different coding methods, if necessary. Open coding can be utilized in both within- and across-literature data analysis.
16	Longitudinal coding	Longitudinal codes can be used to categorize previous articles and to organize them across time. By utilizing longitudinal coding, a reviewer can identify how research paradigms or trends in the specific topic area have changed across time.

(Continued)

Table 9.6   (Continued)

	Coding Method	How to Apply to Literature Review
17	Magnitude coding	Findings, especially from quantitative studies, can be summarized by using supplemental alphanumeric or symbolic codes indicating frequency, direction, presence, intensity, and so on. For example, information from qualitative and quantitative data can be coded by magnitude codes (e.g., 1 or 0, +/−, positive/neutral/negative) for a meta-analysis or a meta-summary.
18	Motif coding	Motif coding involves repeated terms/words/phrases or characteristics throughout literature. Motif coding can be patterned and analyzed possibly to determine the significant elements/events that can influence research findings.
19	Narrative coding	Narrative coding is especially relevant in qualitative research studies in general and narrative inquiries in particular. The form of coding involves developing codes that represent the participants' narratives from a literary perspective.
20	Outline of cultural materials coding (OCM)	Outline of cultural materials coding (OCM) is especially pertinent for literature representing the field of anthropology and archeology. OCM provides coding for ethnographic studies.
21	Pattern coding	Pattern coding can be employed to find patterns or relationships among previously generated codes by analyzing commonalities and grouping them by similarities.
22	Process coding	Process codes, referred to as "action codes," can be utilized to represent research procedures that authors employed in their studies, yielding a within-study literature analysis.
23	Protocol coding	Protocol coding involves using a priori codes or categories to code the literature.
24	Provisional coding	Provisional codes, referred to as "preset codes," which emerged from a preliminary investigation or a literature review(s), can be used to analyze literature, with the expectation that these codes will be modified, revised, or deleted during the data analysis.
25	Simultaneous coding	When exploring a new topic, multiple codes can be applied to the same datum to add multidimensional perspectives.
26	Structural coding	Structural coding can be utilized to label literature so that a reviewer can access the literature review data quickly. For example, structural codes such as "theory" and "methods," or "Stage 1" or "Stage 2" representing research components or research stage, can be used to sort out literature. Categorizing literature by structural codes will make a reviewer access literature more easily at each stage of the research process.
27	Subcoding	Researching findings can be summarized by using subcodes in the taxonomy and hierarchy format if needed.
28	Theoretical coding	Theoretical coding can be utilized to integrate or to synthesize themes or categories by linking all categories and subcategories and reorganizing them. Theoretical codes can be core themes or constructs for the literature review.
29	Values coding	Values coding can be utilized to reflect an author's value system, comprising three elements: value, attitude, and belief. These codes can be interpreted to evaluate the research findings, for example, by assessing the degree to which the author's value system impacted the research findings and interpretations, especially in the topic areas such as gender and ethnic studies.

	Coding Method	How to Apply to Literature Review
30	Verbal exchange coding	Verbal exchange coding involves interpreting data through the researcher's experience and reflection to explore cultural practices of the researcher. Typically, this coding involves extensive written reflection.
31	Versus coding	Versus coding can be applied to identify different patterns or perspectives by dichotomous groups, individuals, or concepts. They can be applied within- or across-literature. For example, when reviewing articles about the topic "Barriers to doctoral student completion," a versus code, "Professor vs. Student," can be generated because professors and students might have different perspectives in perceiving barriers to doctoral student completion.
32	Theming the data	Theming the data involves selecting/deselecting codes to generate a theme. Theming the data can be utilized for between-literature analysis.

Adapted from *Mapping Saldaña's coding methods onto the literature review process*, by A. J. Onwuegbuzie, E. Hwang, and Rebecca K. Frels, 2014, pp. 19–22. Copyright 2014 by A. J. Onwuegbuzie, E. Hwang, and Rebecca K. Frels.

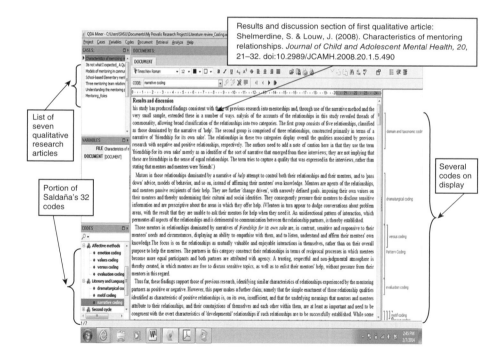

Figure 9.3   Screenshot showing a priori codes represented by Saldaña's 32 codes

Adapted from *Mapping Saldaña's coding methods onto the literature review process*, by A. J. Onwuegbuzie, E. Hwang, and Rebecca K. Frels, 2014, p. 32. Copyright 2014 by A. J. Onwuegbuzie, E. Hwang, and Rebecca K. Frels.

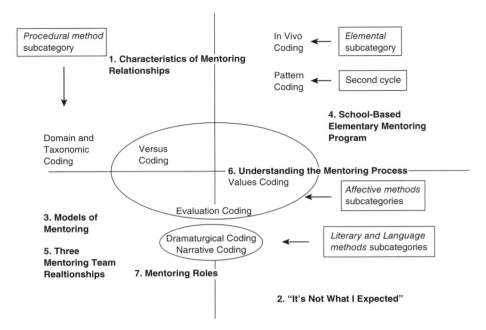

Figure 9.4 Correspondence analysis plot of 8 out of the 11 Saldaña codes on the 7 mentoring-based qualitative research articles that informed The Dyadic Mentoring Study

Adapted from *Mapping Saldaña's coding methods onto the literature review process*, by A. J. Onwuegbuzie, E. Hwang, and Rebecca K. Frels, 2014, p. 35. Copyright 2014 by A. J. Onwuegbuzie, E. Hwang, and Rebecca K. Frels.

versus coding, and evaluation coding. Contrastingly, the qualitative research studies conducted by Lucas (2001) and Spencer (2007) clustered closer to two literary and language methods: dramaturgical coding and narrative coding. In addition, the qualitative research studies by Buell (2004) and Kilburg (2007) clustered around both the affective methods and literary and language subcategories, as well as the procedural method subcategory of domain and taxonomic coding. Onwuegbuzie et al.'s (2014) coding led them to conclude, among other aspects, that the affective needs of mentees is central (see, e.g., the central role that affective methods played in the correspondence plot in Figure 9.4)—which highlighted the importance of the mentoring relationship with Karcher's (2005) findings.

QUALITATIVE SYNTHESIS

By qualitative synthesis, we are referring to systems that involve the use of qualitative approaches to yield a synthesis of select components of (a) the foundational set of information and/or (b) one or more of the 12 components that characterize the supplemental set of information. The most popularized qualitative approach for synthesizing information is a meta-synthesis, which we have grouped with advanced-level analysis.

META-SYNTHESIS. In Chapter 2, we described a meta-synthesis as a way of merging or bringing together findings from qualitative research studies. A qualitative meta-synthesis is appropriate whenever a reviewer is interested in synthesizing two or more qualitative research studies that address a similar research question—especially when these studies involve the use of the same qualitative research design. As such, the meta-synthesis is a functional data analysis system that might add meaning if integrated with other extracted data for the CLR. We also introduced meta-ethnography, which is an interpretive methodology that synthesizes multiple ethnographic studies, introduced by Noblit and Hare (1988).

TOOL: STEPS FOR A META-ETHNOGRAPHY

According to Noblit and Hare (1988) (see also Lee, Hart, Watson, & Rapley, 2014), meta-ethnography involves the following seven steps:

1. Getting started (i.e., determining the research question(s) that would be addressed by the meta-ethnography)
2. Deciding what is relevant to the initial interest (i.e., defining the focus of the meta-ethnography; identifying relevant studies; developing inclusion criteria to make decisions about what studies to include; critically appraising each study via quality criteria)
3. Reading and re-reading the studies (i.e., becoming as familiar as possible with every included study; beginning the process of identifying emergent themes)
4. Determining how the studies are related (i.e., comparing and contrasting the metaphors, concepts, and themes that emerged from each included study [e.g., via tables or grids] to identify commonalities)
5. Translating the studies into one another (i.e., for each pair of works, distinguishing *reciprocal translations* [i.e., metaphors, concepts, and themes that the pair of studies have in common] from *refutational translations* [i.e., contradictions of metaphors, concepts, and themes between each pair of studies] from *overlapping translations* [i.e., studies that overlap without being substitutional])
6. Synthesizing translations (i.e., moving from the three translations [e.g., reciprocal translation] to a higher-order interpretation that integrates the translations into more than the parts alone imply—a "line of argument" synthesis)
7. Expressing the synthesis (i.e., disseminating the synthesis in an appropriate manner to interested audience members)

As a final point regarding meta-syntheses, because it can be assumed that the inclusion of meta-synthesis findings has the potential to enhance the analysis and interpretation of information extracted from a CLR, reviewers should search databases (see Chapter 8) to determine whether any reviewer previously has conducted a meta-synthesis pertaining to the underlying topic. This search can be obtained by using the following search string for all the selected databases:

"Name of topic" and meta-synthesis

The more recent the meta-synthesis identified by the reviewer, the less likely that the reviewer has to conduct a meta-synthesis himself/herself. Of course, the reviewer should evaluate any identified meta-synthesis studies using some of the techniques for evaluating the quality of information sources discussed in Chapter 8 to assess whether any identified and selected meta-synthesis study needs to be deselected (i.e., not included as part of the final CLR report) due to poor quality. Further, for any meta-synthesis studies that are selected for inclusion as part of the CLR, as discussed in Chapters 8, it is important that the reviewer considers using one of the common standards for reporting qualitative research studies/syntheses such as COREQ or ENTREQ (see Table 8.3).

QUANTITATIVE DATA ANALYSIS OF INFORMATION

The analysis of information extracted from the CLR process usually can benefit from the use of descriptive analyses (quantitative approach). In particular, literature reviewers can use measures of central tendency and dispersion in general (i.e., quantitative methods) and means, proportions, and standard deviations in particular (i.e., quantitative techniques) to analyze information extracted from the CLR process. For example, the literature reviewer could analyze and interpret means that have been reported by authors of primary quantitative research studies, as well as report how these means vary from each other across these studies. Due to the fact that most of the data of a CLR tend to be qualitatively collected (even though it might be a quantitative study), we provide a brief overview of quantitative data analysis approaches and quantitative syntheses for consideration to complete Step 6.

ELEMENTARY-LEVEL ANALYSIS

In Chapter 8, we outlined how a reviewer can expand the literature review by using available *secondary data*—the "S" in MODES. In that chapter, we provided examples of the kinds of information that can be extracted via secondary data. As a quick recap, these data could be incorporated into the literature review process via the following three ways: (a) using already-analyzed secondary data, (b) using raw secondary data, and (c) collecting and analyzing secondary data. Descriptive statistics can play an important role for all three ways. Whereas the first way would involve merely reporting and interpreting descriptive statistics that already have been presented by the authors, the second and third ways would involve the reviewer actually computing the descriptive statistics.

Most importantly, descriptive analyses can be used to analyze information from any or all of the 12 components of a primary research report: problem statement, literature review, theoretical/conceptual framework research question(s), hypotheses, participants, instruments, procedures, analyses, interpretation of the findings, directions for future research, and implications for the field. Frequency counts and proportions/percentages can be especially useful here. For example, as part of the CLR, a reviewer could determine the total number or proportion of studies in which a particular theoretical/conceptual framework has been used. Alternatively, a reviewer could determine the total number or proportion of studies in which a certain research question has been addressed or a certain hypothesis tested. Providing findings from such descriptive analyses results in the reviewer presenting much richer CLR findings than merely using words such as "few," "some," "many," or "most" to describe a trend.

INTERMEDIATE-LEVEL ANALYSIS

Building on the use of description statistics with respect to the method section of empirical studies, a reviewer could assess the distribution of the demographic characteristics of participants across studies investigating the same research question. Or the reviewer could determine the total number or proportion of studies in which a particular instrument, research design, or analytical technique has been used to investigate a research question of interest. With regard to the results section of an empirical report, the reviewer could determine the total number or proportion of studies in which a particular finding or interpretation has been documented. Whenever descriptive analyses are used, literature reviewers also should consider using visual displays, such as pie charts and bar diagrams, to supplement their analyses (cf. Onwuegbuzie & Dickinson, 2008).

ADVANCED-LEVEL ANALYSIS

The analysis of information extracted from the CLR process usually also can benefit from the use of inferential analyses (quantitative approach). In particular, literature reviewers can use univariate analyses or multivariate analyses (i.e., quantitative methods) to analyze information extracted from the CLR process. Assuming that descriptive statistics for a certain variable have been provided by authors, one example involves an independent samples *t*-test to compare the means derived for a variable of interest in two studies, an analysis of variance (ANOVA) to compare the means derived for a variable of interest in three or more studies, or a multiple analysis of variance (MANOVA) to compare two or more means simultaneously across multiple studies. As another example, reviewers can conduct a chi-square analysis to compare frequency data reported for the same variable across two or more studies.

The information extracted from the secondary data phase of the CLR process particularly lends itself to the use of inferential analyses. This is particularly the case when the reviewer collects secondary data himself/herself. Further, as is the case for descriptive analyses, inferential analyses can be used to analyze information from any or all of the 12 components of a primary research report.

QUANTITATIVE SYNTHESIS

By quantitative synthesis, we are referring to systems that involve the use of quantitative approaches to yield a synthesis of select components of (a) the foundational set of information and/or (b) one or more of the 12 components that characterize the supplemental set of information. The most popularized quantitative approach for synthesizing information is a meta-analysis.

META-ANALYSIS. As noted in Chapter 2, a meta-analysis represents a quantitative data analysis system (i.e., representing a set of quantitative research approaches, methods, and techniques) wherein the literature reviewer combines (i.e., aggregates) quantitative findings—that are deemed valid—from as many available individual quantitative research studies as possible that address a set of related research hypotheses for the purpose of integrating the results. There are two major goals in meta-analysis: (a) to estimate the mean effect size (i.e., weighted average) across the selected studies; and (b) to examine the variability of effect sizes across studies as a function of study design effects (e.g., randomized designs vs. non-randomized designs; called *homogeneity analysis*) (Glass, 1976). Although meta-analyses have been popularized primarily as a systems analysis for randomized control designs, they are also appropriate for synthesizing results stemming from other quantitative research designs such as correlational research designs. (For a review of quantitative research designs, see Appendix A.)

We identified also in Chapter 2 that the meta-analysis is endorsed by the Cochrane Collaboration (Cochrane Collaboration, 2012), but due to the complexities, it is beyond the scope of this book to present a full description of the analyses involved in meta-analysis (for an excellent review, see Rosenthal, 1991, or Lipsey & Wilson, 2001). However, we hope to highlight some of the major analytical features of meta-analyses. Before we begin, it should be noted that a meta-analysis is optimal when the underlying studies address similar (i.e., homogeneity) research questions via comparable populations, interventions, research design, instruments, comparisons, and outcomes. Thus, it is essential that meta-analysts assess heterogeneity.

If all the studies were equally accurate in estimating the effect size (i.e., homogeneous), then all the reviewer would have to do to estimate the overall or combined (i.e., aggregate) effect would be to compute the mean of the effect sizes. But if some studies in the set are more accurate than are the other studies in estimating the effect size (i.e., heterogeneous), then, instead of computing the simple mean of the effect sizes, the reviewer would have to compute a weighted mean wherein studies that yield the more accurate effect-size estimates are given more weight than are the other studies. Thus, the reviewer must determine how the weights should be assigned. Specifically, the reviewer has two choices for weight assignment: the fixed effects model (yielding a fixed effects analysis) and a random effects model (yielding a random effects analysis). These two models operate under two different assumptions about the nature of the underlying effect sizes that necessitate different procedures for assigning weights.

The assumption underlying the *fixed effects model* is that one true effect size exists that characterizes all the selected studies. In other words, it is assumed that any observed differences in the effect sizes across studies are due to chance alone (i.e., sampling error within each study). As such, the combined effect provides the estimate of the common effect size. Conversely, the assumption underlying the random effects model is that the effect size varies from one study to the next (e.g., the effect size is larger for studies in which the effects were measured more reliably or the intervention had more integrity). Moreover, the effect sizes reported in the selected studies are assumed to represent a random sample of the distribution of effect sizes, and the combined effect size estimates the mean effect size in the distribution.

As explained by Borenstein, Hedges, and Rothstein (2007), when using a fixed effects model, the same effect size is being estimated in all studies, and so weights are assigned to all studies based solely on how much information each study captures. Therefore, studies with the largest sample sizes are given the most weight, whereas studies with the smallest sample sizes are given the least weight. Contrastingly, because when using a random effects model the reviewer is attempting to estimate the mean of the distribution of true effects, each study is estimating a different effect size under the assumption that effect size represents a sample from the population of effect sizes whose mean is to be estimated. As a result, compared to the fixed effects model, in the random effects model, weights are assigned that are more balanced, with the differential in weights given between studies with the largest and smallest sample sizes not being as great. In other words, compared with the fixed effects model, the random effects model weights studies with the smaller sample sizes more heavily in the ensuing pooled effect-size estimate. It should be noted that the fixed effects model and random effects model are equivalent when there is no heterogeneity of the effect size across the studies.

The results of meta-analyses are presented using frequencies, percentages, odds ratios, risk ratios, confidence intervals, and other statistical indices. Tables and graphs (e.g., funnel plots) typically are used to display meta-analytic results. The Cochrane Collaboration expects meta-analysts to include a sensitivity analysis. Specifically, a *sensitivity analysis* allows the reviewer to assess the robustness (i.e., the degree of unbiased estimates) of the pooled effect-size estimate that stems from a meta-analysis by assessing the extent to which the pooled effect-size estimate varies as a function of the change in a certain parameter (e.g., change in inclusion criteria for selecting studies). This sensitivity analysis is conducted by comparing the results of two or more meta-analyses of the same dataset (e.g., the pooled effect-size estimate from the full dataset vs. a dataset containing only published studies; the pooled effect-size estimate from the earlier published studies vs. the later published studies). For an excellent step-by-step guide to conducting meta-analyses using both the fixed effects model and the random effects model, we refer the reader to Borenstein et al. (2007). There are some critics of meta-analyses who note the inherent limitations. However, many of these criticisms can be addressed as long as the meta-analyst applies the best practices (see, e.g., Cochrane Collaboration, 2012).

TOOL: LIST OF THE LIMITATIONS AND STRENGTHS OF META-ANALYSES

Critics of meta-analyses cite one or more of the following limitations of meta-analyses:

- they necessitate much effort to conduct—yielding a "time-consuming" criticism
- they require competence in quantitative research (e.g., knowledge of sampling theory, statistical techniques)—yielding a "novice meta-analyst" criticism
- the quantitative components do not allow the reviewer to identify the more qualitative distinctions among studies—yielding a "lack of context" criticism
- they might involve the combining of effect sizes from studies that are distinctly different (e.g., based on different sampling procedures, cultural and historical configurations, operationalizations, and statistical analyses)—yielding an "apples and oranges" criticism
- most meta-analyses include flawed studies to some degree (e.g., small sample size; non-randomized design)—yielding a "garbage in, garbage out" criticism

- aggregate effect sizes are distorted by selection bias that results from studies reporting negative and null findings that were not located by the reviewer, for example, due to the fact that they were not published—yielding a "file drawer problem" criticism
- integration of multiple dependent results from the same study—yielding a "violation of independence" criticism
- analysis of between-study differences being essentially correlational—yielding a "correlation-does-not-equal-causation" criticism
- tests of homogeneity are unduly affected by low statistical power, and homogeneity statistics can become unreliable (e.g., depend somewhat on the choice of effect-size metric) and difficult to interpret when the reviewer wishes to test more than one moderator of effect sizes at a time—yielding a "Type I and Type II error" problem
- interaction effects being ignored in favor of main effects—yielding a "non-interaction seeking bias" criticism
- small number of effect sizes included—yielding a "sample size" criticism
- a false sense of *objectivity*, *precision*, and *scientism*—yielding a "lack of integrity" criticism

Advocates of meta-analyses cite one or more of the following strengths of meta-analyses in that they:

- represent a more systematic way of conducting a literature review than do other types of literature reviews (i.e., narrative literature reviews)
- impose a discipline on the part of the reviewer whose goal is to be maximally inclusive (i.e., comprehensive) in analyzing and synthesizing (appropriate) quantitative research studies
- represent quantitative findings in a more differentiated and sophisticated manner than do narrative reviews
- are capable of finding relationships across studies that might be obscured via narrative reviews
- reduce the possibility of a reviewer over-interpreting effects across studies
- can handle an unlimited number of studies; they facilitate appropriate weighting of studies
- facilitate appropriate interpretation of findings
- facilitate the examination of characteristics of studies as potential explanations for consistent/ inconsistent findings across studies
- take into account moderating variables when summarizing findings
- facilitate the resolution of controversial findings
- examine consistency of findings across variables that cannot be undertaken at the level of a single primary study (e.g., demographic characteristics; integrity of the intervention)
- identify interactional relationships or trends that are either too subtle to identify or cannot be hypothesized and tested in individual studies
- facilitate synthesis of findings

Further, as stated by Fink (2009):

> Supporters point out that despite its flaws, meta-analysis is a systematic method for dealing with important issues when results from several studies disagree, when sample sizes of individual studies are relatively small, or when a larger study is unlikely to be performed in time to answer a pressing question. Even detractors agree that a meta-analysis can be viewed as a way to present the results of disparate research studies on a common scale. (p. 225)

There are several commercial statistical software programs that greatly facilitate the conduct of a meta-analysis. Bax, Yu, Ikeda, and Moons (2007) noted that "the most suitable meta-analysis software for a user depends on his or her demands; no single program may be best for everybody" (¶ 38). However, the most common commercial statistical software programs include the following: Comprehensive Meta-Analysis (CMA), MetAnalysis, MetaWin, and WEasyMA. Of these, Bax et al. (2007) found CMA to be the most versatile, especially with respect to the range of data that this software could analyze. (For example, MetAnalysis and WEasyMA can analyze data only from two-by-two tables.) CMA can be downloaded and used for a free trial period from the following website: www.Meta-Analysis.com.

A few meta-analysis software programs are free for academic use, including MIX and RevMan.

According to Bax et al. (2007), RevMan (currently version 5.2 at the time of writing) was developed by and for the Cochrane Collaboration. Because copy-and-paste and import options are limited, getting started necessitates more preparation than is the case for most other software programs (Bax et al., 2007). However, once data have been placed into the analysis module, the meta-analysis is straightforward, yielding detailed output, although the display of graphs is limited. The help resources in RevMan are extremely comprehensive (Bax et al., 2007).

MIXED ANALYSIS OF INFORMATION

It is helpful to remember that at the heart of the CLR is methodology, and the CLR is a mixed research study. However, the meta-framework of the CLR recognizes that "mixing" occurs by meaning-making from any

TOOL: SOFTWARE FOR META-ANALYSIS

Figure 9.5 shows a screenshot of the RevMan software program. It can be seen from this figure that this software program allows the user to open an existing review from a file, to create a new review, to use the tutorial, to view help, and to read the handbook. Of the new reviews, RevMan allows the user to conduct an intervention review, diagnostic test accuracy review, methodology review, or overview of reviews. Encouragingly, Bax et al. (2007) found no discrepancies in the meta-analysis results yielded by RevMan and CMA. For an excellent review of the most common meta-analysis software program, we refer readers to Bax et al. (2007). As a final point regarding meta-analyses, because it can be assumed that the inclusion of meta-analysis findings has the potential to enhance the analysis and interpretation of information extracted from a CLR, reviewers should search databases (see Chapter 8) to determine whether any reviewer previously has conducted a meta-analysis pertaining to the underlying topic. This search can be obtained by using the following search string for all the selected databases:

"Name of topic" and meta-analysis

The more recent the meta-analysis identified by the reviewer, the less likely that the reviewer has to conduct a meta-analysis himself/herself. Of course, the reviewer should evaluate any identified meta-analysis studies using some of the techniques for evaluating the quality of information sources discussed in Chapter 8 to assess whether any identified and selected meta-analysis study needs to be deselected (i.e., not included as part of the final CLR report) due to poor quality. Further, for any meta-analysis studies that are selected for inclusion as part of the CLR, it is important that the reviewer considers using one of the common standards for reporting quantitative research studies such as PRISMA.

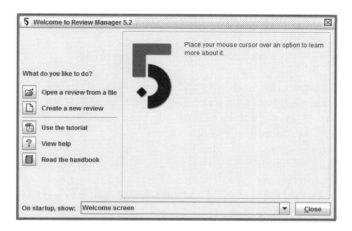

Figure 9.5   Screenshot showing the RevMan meta-analysis software

aspect of a work (e.g., research article, book chapter, book), including the title, abstract, literature review section, theoretical or conceptual framework, purpose statement(s), research question(s), hypotheses, statement of the educational significance, method section, results section, and discussion section. Therefore, selecting a mixed methods approach to *analysis*, per se, is not essential to the CLR. However, it is a good idea to understand the nature of analysis from a mixed research approach and, optimally, to utilize these concepts on some layer of integration.

Onwuegbuzie and Combs (2010) have provided an evidence-based definition of a mixed analysis that includes integration of one or more qualitative analyses with one or more quantitative analyses, including an analysis "within the same framework that is guided either a priori, a posteriori, or iteratively (representing analytical decisions that occur both prior to the study and during the study)" (p. 425).

ELEMENTARY-LEVEL MIXED ANALYSIS

When qualitative analyses of qualitative-based information and quantitative analyses of quantitative-based information are combined within the same literature review, then this combination yields a mixed analysis. This combination represents a powerful way to analyze and to synthesize CLR information and is the smallest

level of integration of qualitative and quantitative analytical approaches, known as a *non-crossover mixed analysis* (Onwuegbuzie & Combs, 2010) or a *within-tradition mixed analysis*—which stem from the assumptions that:

- quantitative and qualitative analyses are unique and distinguishable from each other
- quantitative and qualitative analyses are different and thus should be conducted separately
- quantitative data require exclusively quantitative analyses
- qualitative data require exclusively qualitative analyses
- syntheses stemming from the quantitative data stem from the quantitative analysis
- syntheses stemming from the qualitative data stem from the qualitative analysis

Thus, only after syntheses from the quantitative analyses and syntheses from the qualitative analyses have been obtained can a combined synthesis be obtained.

INTERMEDIATE-LEVEL ANALYSIS

Reviewers can conduct an even more integrated mixed analysis of CLR information, namely, via the

TOOL: COMMON MIXED (METHODS) ANALYSIS APPROACHES

The following list presents some common mixed analysis approaches:

- *concurrent mixed analyses*: the qualitative and quantitative analyses are conducted independently but interpretations stemming from each set of analyses yield combined inferences or meta-inferences
- *sequential mixed analyses*: the mixing of qualitative and quantitative analyses occurs in chronological order and they are dependent on each other
- *parallel mixed analyses*: the mixing of qualitative and quantitative analyses occurs independently and the interpretations stemming from each set of analyses are not combined into a coherent whole
- *conversion mixed analyses*: one type of data is transformed to two types of data that can be analyzed using both in a way that the original and transformed data between them can be subjected to both qualitative and quantitative analyses
- *multilevel mixed analysis*: qualitative and quantitative analyses are conducted at different levels of aggregation to address inter-related research questions
- *fully integrated mixed analyses*: mixing of qualitative and quantitative analyses occurs in an interactive manner (Teddlie & Tashakkori, 2009)
- *crossover mixed analyses*: one or more analysis types associated with one tradition (e.g., quantitative analysis) are used to analyze data associated with a different tradition (e.g., qualitative data) (Onwuegbuzie & Combs, 2010)

In contrast, as previously defined, the term *methods* refers to mixed analyses that represent part of a system, such as *quantitizing* (i.e., converting qualitative data into numerical codes that can be analyzed statistically; Miles & Huberman, 1994; Sandelowski, Voils, & Knafl, 2009; Tashakkori & Teddlie, 1998) and *qualitizing* (i.e., converting numerical data into narrative data that can be analyzed qualitatively; Tashakkori & Teddlie, 1998). Finally, the term *techniques* refers to mixed analyses that represent a single step in the mixed analysis process, which include frequency analysis of themes (Miles & Huberman, 1994; Sandelowski et al., 2009; Tashakkori & Teddlie, 1998) and *profile formation* (Tashakkori & Teddlie, 1998).

Typically, one or more mixed analysis techniques and methods are essential components of a mixed analysis approach. For example, the mixed analysis method of quantitizing and qualitizing are components of conversion mixed analysis approaches. Thus, with regard to mixed analysis, as is the case for qualitative and quantitative analyses, techniques are nested within methods, which are nested within approaches.

To date, very few literature reviewers integrate both qualitative analysis and quantitative analyses of information within the same literature review. Yet, to do so would not only culminate in a CLR but, even more importantly, would increase the likelihood of the reviewer reaching *Verstehen* after conducting Step 6 of the CLR.

use of a *crossover mixed analysis*. Thus, in the following sections, we will outline some ways of conducting a crossover mixed analysis of CLR information. The most introductory level of crossover analysis would include the use of the most basic forms of quantitizing and qualitizing. With respect to quantitizing, reviewers could convert emergent themes that are reported by authors of qualitative research studies into a quantitative form that allows them to analyze the transformed themes quantitatively—for example, by determining the prevalence of these transformed themes across the selected qualitative studies.

For instance, the seven mentoring-based qualitative research studies that informed the Dyadic Mentoring Study could be subjected to a qualitative analysis using a qualitative approach, method, or technique (see our earlier discussion of qualitative analyses). Each theme that emerged from this analysis then could be quantitized, for example, by creating an *inter-respondent matrix* (i.e., Article × Theme Matrix) (Onwuegbuzie, 2003a; Onwuegbuzie & Teddlie, 2003) wherein if an article contained that theme, then a score of 1 would be given to the theme for that article; otherwise a score of 0 would be given. This dichotomization would yield a matrix that consists only of 0s and 1s.

EXAMPLE: AN INTER-RESPONDENT MATRIX

Table 9.7 provides an example of the seven mentoring-based qualitative research studies that informed the Dyadic Mentoring Study and how the inter-respondent matrix can be used to compute various effect sizes (e.g., prevalence rates of themes). Looking at the row totals and percentages,

it can be seen from this table that the fourth article (i.e., ID 04) contributed to the most themes (i.e., 5/6 = 83.3%), with the third article (i.e., ID 03) contributing to the fewest themes (i.e., 1/6 = 16.7%). Examining the column totals reveals that Theme 4 is the most endorsed theme, with five of the seven articles being coded with this theme. Thus, the manifest effect size (i.e., effect sizes that pertain to observable content; Onwuegbuzie & Teddlie, 2003) for Theme 4 is 71.4%. Conversely, the manifest effect size for Theme 3, the least endorsed theme, is 28.6%.

Note that if an article contained information pertaining to inputs for direct support for mentoring programs that was eventually categorized under a particular theme, then a score of 1 would be given to the theme for that article; a score of 0 would be given otherwise. Quantitizing information contained in articles is not only restricted to information from qualitative articles. Qualitative information from quantitative research articles and mixed research articles also could be quantitized. Such qualitative information includes the literature review, conceptual framework, theoretical framework, procedures used, and interpretation of findings.

With regard to qualitizing, reviewers could convert quantitative data that are reported by authors of quantitative research studies into qualitative form that allows them to analyze the transformed themes qualitatively. For example, the reviewer could use the quantitative findings

Table 9.7   Example of how to use the inter-respondent matrix to compute effect sizes for six selected themes pertaining to inputs for direct support for mentoring programs extracted from the seven qualitative research articles on mentoring relationships identified in the Dyadic Mentoring Study

Article ID	Theme 1	Theme 2	Theme 3	Theme 4	Theme 5	Theme 6	Total	%
01	1	0	1	1	1	0	4	66.7
02	0	1	0	1	0	1	3	50.0
03	0	0	0	1	0	0	1	16.7
04	0	1	1	1	1	1	5	83.3
05	1	0	0	0	1	0	2	33.3
06	0	0	0	0	1	1	2	33.3
07	1	1	0	1	0	1	4	66.7
Total	3	3	2	5	4	4	21	
%	42.9	42.9	28.6	71.4	57.1	57.1		

Theme 1 = Use of parental and peer influences
Theme 2 = Length of relationship
Theme 3 = Appropriate mentee characteristics (e.g., at risk, but not emotionally disturbed)
Theme 4 = Promoting positive perceptions in mentors
Theme 5 = Treating mentees as equals
Theme 6 = Supporting collaboration

across studies for **narrative profile** formation, constructing one or more of the following narrative profiles: *modal profiles* (i.e., detailed narrative descriptions of a group of people based on the most frequently occurring attributes in the group), *average profiles* (i.e., profiles based on the average of a number of attributes of the individuals or situations), *holistic profiles* (i.e., overall impressions of the investigator regarding the unit of investigation), *comparative profiles* (i.e., obtained by comparing one unit of analysis with another, and includes possible similarities/differences between them), and *normative profiles* (i.e., similar to narrative profiles but are based on the comparison of an individual or group with a standard, such as a normative group; see Tashakkori & Teddlie, 1998).

As an illustration, a reviewer might use narrative profiles to synthesize ideas gleaned via a methodological literature review of quantitative research articles. A reviewer can create a narrative profile for the quantitative methods used across the set of quantitative research studies addressing a particular research question or examining a phenomenon that is based on the sample size, sampling scheme, instrumentation (e.g., score reliability, score validity), procedures, and analysis. This narrative profile could help the reviewer identify the strengths and weaknesses of the methods used and provide future

directions. As is the case for quantitizing, qualitizing information is not only restricted to information from quantitative articles. Quantitative information from qualitative research articles and mixed research articles also could be qualitized. Such quantitative information includes sample size, age of the participants, and number of emergent themes.

Another way of conducting a mixed analysis of CLR information is by comparing the findings of qualitative research articles and quantitative research articles that examine the same phenomenon. This is a crossover mixed analysis technique known as *data comparison* (Onwuegbuzie & Combs, 2010).

EXAMPLE: RESULTS OF SYNTHESIZING LITERATURE IN A DATA COMPARISON

A data comparison of literature can be seen in Figure 9.6 in the Dyadic Mentoring Study whereby the seven qualitative research studies on school-based mentoring and 16 quantitative research studies on school-based mentoring yielded two categories of support elements (direct and indirect).

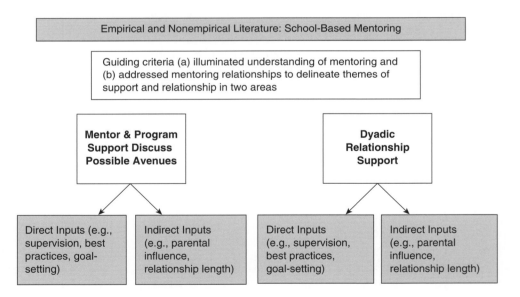

Figure 9.6 A conceptual map for the Dyadic Mentoring Study for direct and indirect inputs for mentoring revealed through the literature

Adapted from *The experiences and perceptions of selected mentors: An exploratory study of the dyadic relationship in school-based mentoring*, by R. K. Frels, 2010, unpublished doctoral dissertation, Sam Houston State University, Huntsville, TX, p. 78. Copyright 2010 by R. K. Frels.

As seen in Figure 9.6, the two sets of articles were sorted in terms of mentoring programs into two major themes using the following criteria: (a) program components emphasize mentor or program support (i.e., literature highlighting activities for mentoring as a primary element for positive outcomes); or (b) program components emphasize dyadic relationship support (i.e., literature highlighting relationships as a primary element for positive outcomes). This figure also shows that these articles yielded two different approaches for such support: (a) school-based mentoring programs that emphasize direct inputs, which refer to the manner in which mentoring program components emphasize tangible program elements (e.g., advocating developmental activities with dyads); and (b) school-based mentoring program components that emphasize indirect support, which refer to the manner in which mentoring program administrators might support mentoring through non-tangible elements such as ongoing mentor training.

Intermediate approaches to conducting a crossover analysis of the CLR information can occur via use of the inter-respondent matrix discussed earlier. In particular, via the

inter-respondent matrix, descriptive or univariate analyses might be conducted. For example, with respect to quantitizing, had the sample of articles been much larger (i.e., containing at least between 30 and 60 articles, which would represent from 5 articles per theme as the bare minimum to at least 10 articles per theme; Cattell, 1978; Gorsuch, 1983; Hatcher, 1994; Onwuegbuzie & Daniel, 2003), the inter-respondent matrix could have been subjected to an exploratory factor analysis. With a larger sample size, other analyses could have been conducted, such as a series of chi-square analyses to examine differences in the prevalence of themes generated between the qualitative research articles and quantitative research articles.

EXAMPLE: LATENT CLASS ANALYSIS

With regard to qualitizing, a latent class analysis could be used to form a narrative profile. As an example,

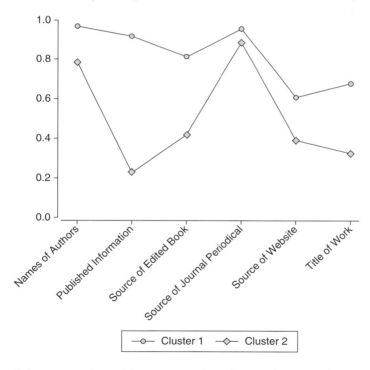

Figure 9.7 Profiles of the manuscripts with respect to the reference list error themes

Adapted from "Editorial: Evidence-based guidelines for avoiding reference list errors in manuscripts submitted to journals for review for publication," by A. J. Onwuegbuzie, A. E. Hwang, R. K. Frels, & J. R. Slate, 2011, *Research in the Schools*, 18(2), pp. i–xli, xii. Copyright 2011 by Mid-South Educational Research Association.

Onwuegbuzie, Hwang, et al. (2011) conducted a review of grey literature—namely, 131 manuscripts submitted to *Research in the Schools*, a nationally/internationally refereed journal—over a 6-year period to determine the nature and prevalence of American Psychological Association (2010) style errors made in the reference lists of these manuscripts. A total of 466 unique reference list errors were identified, which yielded 14 reference list error themes. A latent class analysis—a multivariate technique—of the six most common reference list error themes revealed a two-cluster solution, with Cluster 1 (comprising 57.1% of manuscripts) being relatively high with respect to all six reference list error themes, and Cluster 2 (comprising 42.9% of manuscripts) being high on two of the reference list themes (i.e., Names of authors and Source of journals/periodicals) but relatively low on the remaining four reference list error themes. That is, the latent class analysis revealed two profiles of authors with respect to the commission of reference list errors. Figure 9.7 displays these two distinct groups of manuscripts.

ADVANCED-LEVEL ANALYSIS

Building on Onwuegbuzie and Hitchcock's (2014, 2015) framework for conducting advanced-level mixed analysis approaches, we include correspondence analysis, Bayesian meta-analysis, Q methodology, and a mixed synthesis to provide an overview of advanced-level analyses for the CLR. Although these mixed analyses are complex, a literature reviewer might seek consultation or mentorship to accomplish their use for interpreting works collected via MODES.

CORRESPONDENCE ANALYSIS. Correspondence analysis is a descriptive and exploratory multivariate analysis and graphic technique wherein categorical (i.e., nominal level) variables are factored and mapped in a space that displays their relationships in two or more dimensions (Greenacre, 1984; Michailidis, 2007). Simply put, a correspondence analysis allows a researcher to examine graphically the relationship between categorical variables and subgroups. In the context of the literature review, a correspondence analysis allows a reviewer to examine graphically relationships (a) among selected works with respect to the themes contained with them, (b) among emergent themes contained in

selected works, and/or (c) between the emergent themes and the selected works. Conveniently, the CAQDAS program QDA Miner allows the analyst to conduct a correspondence analysis of the emergent themes. An example of the power of the use of correspondence analysis can be seen in Figure 9.4, which shows how this form of advanced crossover mixed analysis helps reviewers get much more out of their analysis of CLR information.

BAYESIAN META-ANALYSIS. Previously in this chapter, we outlined the conventional meta-analysis system. In recent years, a Bayesian form of meta-analysis has emerged. Broadly speaking, Bayesian methods are used when researchers are hoping to predict an outcome or event (O'Hagan & Luce, 2003). In particular, the Bayesian approach requires the establishment of a prior probability distribution, which is often informed, in part, by the subjective judgment of the researcher. This prior probability distribution forms the basis for calculating a posterior probability distribution. Together, the prior and posterior are used to ascertain the likelihood of a parameter (i.e., a population value) given the observed evidence. Thus, prior data and knowledge of context are important considerations when using Bayesian approaches. Newman, Hitchcock, and Onwuegbuzie (2013) outlined how Bayesian analysis can be enhanced by incorporating qualitative data. In the context of a literature review, information from qualitative and quantitative works can be combined to produce a posterior distribution. This is what occurs in a Bayesian meta-analysis. Specifically, as surmised by Booth, Papaioannou, and Sutton (2012), Bayesian meta-analysis can be used "to explore the likelihood of something happening through one type of research evidence and then to establish it more reliably via another type of research (usually qualitative followed by quantitative)" (p. 157).

An excellent resource for the use of Bayesian meta-analysis is that provided by Voils et al. (2009). These researchers investigated whether people are less likely to continue taking their medicines if their medication schedule is complicated than if their medication schedule is straightforward. They identified 11 qualitative research studies and six quantitative research studies that informed their

Bayesian meta-analysis. In particular, they used information from the qualitative research studies to determine an a priori likelihood that the complexity of the medication schedule was a factor. Then, these researchers used the results of the quantitative research studies to confirm this likelihood. As noted by Voils et al. (2009), Bayesian meta-analysis is an infrequently used approach for synthesizing qualitative and quantitative research findings. Thus, we encourage more reviewers to use this approach.

Q METHODOLOGY. Q methodology (developed in the mid-1930s by William Stephenson after he received a Ph.D. in both Physics and Psychology) involves examining correlations among participants across a sample of variables that results in a reduction of the participants' many viewpoints to a few *factors*, which are assumed to represent shared feelings, opinions, beliefs, perspectives, or preferences (Newman & Ramlo, 2010). Because Q methodology involves the use of factor analysis, historically, it has been considered as being a quantitative approach. However, because the study of subjectivity is identified more with the qualitative tradition, and because Q methodology typically involves the use of small samples, in recent years, Q methodology has been reframed as a mixed methodology (Ernest, 2011; Newman & Ramlo, 2010) that involves "a successful combination of the two differing styles of research" (Ray & Montgomery, 2006, p. 3).

In Chapter 8, we discussed the utility of expanding the literature review by talking to experts (e.g., via interviews, focus groups). Once these experts have been identified, they could be asked to participate in a Q methodology study.

TOOL: STEPS FOR CONDUCTING A Q METHODOLOGY STUDY

As conceptualized by Onwuegbuzie and Frels (2015a), the steps of the Q methodology study could be as follows:

The first step of the Q (methodology) study would involve the development of a set of, say, 40 items (i.e., statements)—called the *concourse*—that evolve from the analysis of the CLR information on the underlying topic using techniques that have been described heretofore in this chapter. (Typically, the number of items range from 30 to 60.) The reviewer randomly assigns each of the 40 statements a number from 1 to 40. The Q participants (the selected experts) then are asked to sort (subjectively) each statement relative to the other statements along a continuum anchored by opposite ratings such as "most agree" to "most disagree", "most like me" to "most unlike me," or "most like my view" to "least like my view." During this process of sorting, the reviewer places these 40 statements into a distribution that approximates the normal curve that is represented by a grid (e.g., sorting the statements along a nine-point quasi-normal distribution from –4 to +4). The Q participants can sort these statements either face-to-face (if convenient for them) or via an online sorting format that utilizes the free FlashQ program (www.hackert.biz/flashq).

At this stage, qualitative techniques (e.g., interviews) can be used to understand the participants' rationales for sorting the statements to facilitate the quality of inferences that the reviewer can derive from the Q study. Once the statements are sorted by the participants, the reviewer then subjects the Q sorts to a factor analysis that involves factor extraction and factor rotation, which lead to the identification (i.e., *flagging*) of the experts who are represented by each factor, and which generate factor descriptions and analyses for each factor that only involve the experts who are flagged on that factor.

(Continued)

(Continued)

The reviewer can create one or more of the following four types of tables associated with Q methodology: (a) factor scores, (b) rank-ordered list of Q items (i.e., statements) alongside z scores to create a representative sort for each emergent factor, (c) the list of statements that distinguish each factor from other factors, and (d) the list of consensus statements that depict agreement among all the factors (Newman & Ramlo, 2010). Conveniently, the reviewer can use software programs that have been developed specifically to facilitate the Q sort analysis (e.g., PQMethod; Schmolck, 2002). These software programs allow the integration of qualitative and quantitative data (Newman & Ramlo, 2010). As such, Q methodology involves using a mixed research approach to interpret the statistics generated by the factor analysis informed by qualitative data of the inter-relationships among the statements, involving the search for themes (i.e., factors). The goal of this Q methodology systematically is to identify categories, to connect them, and to search for disconfirming evidence (Ernest, 2011).

The use of Q methodology involves both quantitizing (e.g., converting statements to a quasi-normal distribution that subsequently is factor analyzed) and qualitizing (e.g., forming narrative profiles for each emergent factor) within the same analysis. Interestingly, Q methodology can be transformed to a mixed analysis to a greater degree by conducting follow-up quantitative analyses (e.g., correlating the experts' views with other variables of interest [e.g., demographic variables]) and qualitative analyses (e.g., conducting and analyzing follow-up interviews to confirm or to disconfirm inferences that emerge from the factor analysis).

MIXED SYNTHESIS

By mixed synthesis, we are referring to systems that involve the use of mixed research approaches to yield a synthesis of select components of (a) the foundational set of information and/or (b) one or more of the 12 components that characterize the supplemental set of information. The most popularized quantitative approach for synthesizing information is a meta-summary.

META-SUMMARY. According to Sandelowski and Barroso (2003), a *meta-summary* is "a form of systematic review or integration of qualitative findings in a target domain that are themselves topical or thematic summaries or surveys of data" (p. 227). As described in Chapter 2, a meta-summary results in the computation of what Onwuegbuzie (2003a) termed an effect size pertaining to qualitative findings. These effect sizes are a "quantitative transformation of qualitative data in the service of extracting more meaning from those data and verifying the presence of a pattern or theme" (Sandelowski & Barroso, 2003, p. 231)—and, thus, represent a crossover mixed analysis (Onwuegbuzie & Combs, 2010). Martsolf, Cook,

Ross, Warner Stidham, and Mweemba (2010) provide an example of a meta-summary whereby they used 31 published qualitative research studies on adults' responses to sexual violence, with a particular focus on survivors' use of professional services. The combined samples consisted of 46 men, 984 women, and six couples who had experienced sexual violence at some point in the past. These authors extracted a total of 271 findings on this topic, which they edited into complete sentences that could be understood by readers who had not read the original report. These 271 findings subsequently were consolidated into 16 more abstract statements by eliminating redundant statements and combining similar statements. Martsolf et al. (2010) computed a frequency effect size for each of these 16 statements by dividing the number of articles containing that finding by the total number of articles ($n = 31$). Using a cutoff of 15% recommended by Sandelowski, Lambe, and Barroso (2004), Martsolf et al. documented eight findings with effect sizes greater than 15%. These findings indicated that qualities of professional service providers and outcomes of professional services were perceived either positively or negatively—as opposed to neutrally—by survivors, regardless of the provider's professional discipline. Most importantly, the authors concluded that "professionals who work with sexual violence survivors can use these findings to improve their practices" (p. 489). This study shows the utility of meta-summaries for analyzing and synthesizing qualitative findings.

As a final point regarding meta-summaries, because it can be assumed that the inclusion of meta-summary findings has the potential to enhance the analysis and interpretation of CLR information, reviewers should search databases (see Chapter 8) to determine whether any reviewer previously has conducted a meta-summary pertaining to the underlying topic. This search can be obtained by using the following search string for all the selected databases:

"Name of topic" and meta-summary

The more recent the meta-summary identified by a literature reviewer, the less likely that the reviewer has to conduct a meta-summary himself/herself. Of course, the reviewer should evaluate any identified meta-summary studies using some of the techniques for evaluating the quality of information sources discussed in Chapter 7 to assess whether any identified and selected meta-summary study needs to be deselected (i.e., not included as part of the final CLR report) due to poor quality. Further, for any meta-summary studies that are selected for inclusion as part of the CLR, as discussed in Chapter 8, it is important that the reviewer considers using one of the common standards for reporting qualitative research studies/syntheses such as COREQ or ENTREQ (see Table 8.3).

SCIENTOMETRICS AND BIBLIOMETRICS. Scientometrics, which was developed in 1978, involves using quantitative and qualitative techniques to study the development and mechanism of science and technology. Of particular research interest is the assessment of scientific output and the impact of scientific findings. Thus, reviewers from the field of scientometrics also often examine the reference list sections of works to assess the impact of journals and authors, to identify trends in scientific citations, and to study the production of scientific indicators and their implications for policy.

Indices that have emerged from scientometrics include the impact factor and the *h-index*. The ***impact factor*** is an indicator used to assess the relative importance or significance of an academic journal such that journals with higher impact factors are considered to be more important than are those with lower impact factors. In turn, impact factors are used to assess the quality of a scholar's works. For any given year, the impact factor of a journal is the average number of citations received per article published in that journal during the two preceding years. Thus, if a journal has an impact factor of 2 in 2013, it means that articles published in this journal in 2011 and 2012, on average, each received two citations in 2013. Journals within a field or discipline then can be ranked by the size of their impact factor. Impact factors and their rankings are indexed in *Journal Citation Reports*, which is an annual publication by the Science and Scholarly Research Division of Thomas Reuters. As we described in Chapter 8, the ***h-index*** represents an attempt to measure both the productivity and impact of the published works of a scholar or a group of scholars based on the number of citations that they have received across other works.

In contrast, bibliometrics (circa 1969) is a technique used to analyze academic literature. These techniques include citation analyses and content analyses, which means that there is overlap between scientometrics and bibliometrics. Bibliometrics studies also may involve creating thesauri, measuring usage of works by readers, and assessing the structures (e.g., grammatical, syntactical) of texts in published works, as well as conducting "a content analysis of words in titles, abstracts, the full text of books, journal articles or conference proceedings, or keywords assigned to published articles by editors or librarians" (Péladeau, 2014, ¶ 1).

EXAMPLE: SCIENTOMETRICS AND BIBLIOMETRICS

Returning, once again, to our mentoring example, scientometrics and bibliometrics could be used to conduct analyses such as the following:

- analyzing words in the titles of all articles published in one or more journals (e.g., journals representing the field of mentoring; journals representing the field of education) over a selected period of time (e.g., last 20 years) via a co-word analysis and clustering techniques to identify relationships among concepts and changes in mentoring topics over time
- analyzing words in the abstracts of all mentoring articles published in one or more journals (as above) over a selected period of time (as above) to investigate and to map their content
- analyzing keywords of all mentoring articles published in one or more journals (as above) over a selected period of time (as above) to track changes in the influence of sub-disciplines over time
- analyzing all full-text mentoring articles published in one or more journals (as above) over a selected period of time (as above) to ascertain the evolution of theoretical frameworks, research methods (e.g., quantitative vs. qualitative vs. mixed research), analysis techniques, or the like over time or to compare how these elements have been used by different authors or in different journals
- analyzing all mentoring articles published in one or more journals (as above) over a selected period of time (as above) by conducting a co-citation analysis to identify which scholars and well-known works in the field of mentoring have been the most influential
- analyzing all mentoring articles published in one or more journals (as above) over a selected period of time (as above) to identify similarities and differences in definitions of words and phrases such as "mentoring" and "mentoring relationships" over time

QDA Miner and WordStat are two computer-assisted qualitative data analysis software (CAQDAS)/computer-assisted mixed methods data analysis (CAMMDAS) programs that are especially useful for conducting scientometrics and bibliometrics studies.

TOOL: ATTRIBUTES OF CAQDAS FOR MIXED (METHODS) ANALYSES

As documented by Péladeau (2014), these software programs can conduct analyses that include the following:

- *Data Importation*: Importing articles as Microsoft Word, pdf, RTF, and HTML files, and associating metadata (e.g., dates, numerical and categorical data) with these articles, which allows reviewers to create a body of full-text articles with relevant variables. Importing RIS data files via QDA Miner allows information to be imported directly from journal databases (e.g., ProQuest, EBSCO) and reference management software programs (e.g., EndNote, Mendeley; cf. Chapter 6). Also, QDA Miner's Document Conversion Wizard can be used to split single documents into multiple documents, or to extract variables from structured listings or reports.
- *Editing, Tagging, and Annotating*: Once reviewers import documents into QDA Miner, they can be edited, coded, and annotated manually and then transferred to WordStat to conduct a content analysis of text. Manually tagging the reference sections of journal articles enables reviewers to perform a co-citation analysis; manually coding selected sections of journal articles allows reviewers to compare and to contrast these sections over time or across journals.
- *Text Preprocessing*: Reviewers can use WordStat to *transform* words into stems (e.g., *mentor* as a stem for *mentor, mentors, mentoring, mentorship*), to *lemmatize* (i.e., to sort words in a set, in an attempt to ascertain the headword, under which all other words in the set subsequently are listed),

and to *remove* words that have little or no semantic value (e.g., conjunctions, pronouns, prepositions), which allows them to focus on more relevant words and phrases.

- *Words and Phrases Extraction*: WordStat can process up to 300,000 words per second; thus, within a few seconds, reviewers can obtain frequency counts of significant words, extract common phrases, and create visual displays (e.g., bar charts, dendrograms, word clouds).
- *Analysis of Co-occurrence*: Reviewers can conduct an analysis of co-occurrences via statistical techniques such as hierarchical clustering, multidimensional scaling, and proximity plots, in order to identify topics and themes in a discipline.
- *Comparative Analysis*: Reviewers can compare the frequencies of words, phrases, or content categories across different sources (e.g., journals, countries) over time to identify the evolution of a scientific discipline or specific concepts (e.g., mentoring), or to map the geo-spatial distribution of selected variables. In making these comparisons, reviewers can compute descriptive statistics (e.g., frequencies, percentages), inferential statistics (e.g., chi-square tests, correlations, *F*-tests), and visual displays (e.g., bar charts, line charts, bubble charts, heatmaps, correspondence analysis plots).
- *Application of Content Analysis Dictionaries*: Reviewers can use WordStat to build dictionaries of keywords and key phrases, as well as to use these dictionaries to cluster these keywords/phrases into broader concepts that are subjected to a frequency analysis. Reviewers also can build a dictionary of authors or journals and perform a co-citation pattern analysis.
- *Keyword-in-Context*: Reviewers can use the Keyword-in-Context (KWIC) feature to test the validity of existing or user-built dictionaries by ensuring that words or phrases that are flagged by the dictionary capture the intended meaning.

EXAMPLE: ANALYSIS USING WORDSTAT

In Figure 9.8, we illustrate the use of the WordStat program and the considerable potential that this program provides for conducting scientometrics and bibliometrics studies.

SELECTING THE ANALYSIS

We opened this chapter by differentiating a literature analysis from a literature synthesis in that, technically speaking, the analysis occurs before the synthesis and the latter is a type of connection-making of the many relevant parts that were deconstructed, or analyzed. Also, earlier, we stated that alongside a formal analysis of the foundational set of information, reviewers can conduct a formal analysis of one or more of the 12 components that characterize the supplemental set of information (i.e., problem statement, background, theoretical/conceptual framework, research question[s], hypotheses, participants, instruments, procedures, analyses, interpretation of the findings, directions for future research, and implications for the field). Thus, potentially, reviewers can conduct up to 13 rounds of formal analyses of information when the goal of the CLR is to inform primary research. However, typically, the analysis of the foundational set of information typically comes first because this is the set that will most inform the actual literature review section. And it should be noted that reviewers can use different analyses for the different rounds of formal analyses.

Before you begin to analyze formally any set of information and select the best type(s) of analysis, it is helpful to create a roadmap, which is a conceptual

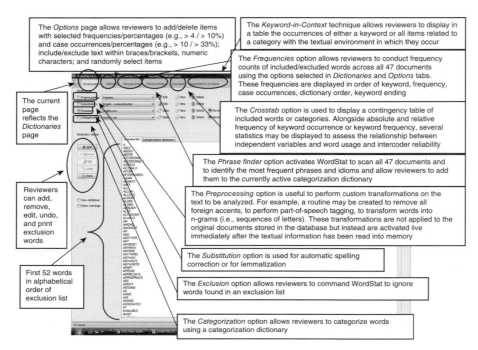

The *Options* page allows reviewers to add/delete items with selected frequencies/percentages (e.g., > 4 / > 10%) and case occurrences/percentages (e.g., > 10 / > 33%); include/exclude text within braces/brackets, numeric characters; and randomly select items

The *Keyword-in-Context* technique allows reviewers to display in a table the occurrences of either a keyword or all items related to a category with the textual environment in which they occur

The *Frequencies* option allows reviewers to conduct frequency counts of included/excluded words across all 47 documents using the options selected in *Dictionaries* and *Options* tabs. These frequencies are displayed in order of keyword, frequency, case occurrences, dictionary order, keyword ending

The current page reflects the *Dictionaries* page

The *Crosstab* option is used to display a contingency table of included words or categories. Alongside absolute and relative frequency of keyword occurrence or keyword frequency, several statistics may be displayed to assess the relationship between independent variables and word usage and intercoder reliability

The *Phrase finder* option activates WordStat to scan all 47 documents and to identify the most frequent phrases and idioms and allow reviewers to add them to the currently active categorization dictionary

Reviewers can add, remove, edit, undo, and print exclusion words

The *Preprocessing* option is useful to perform custom transformations on the text to be analyzed. For example, a routine may be created to remove all foreign accents, to perform part-of-speech tagging, to transform words into n-grams (i.e., sequences of letters). These transformations are not applied to the original documents stored in the database but instead are activated live immediately after the textual information has been read into memory

The *Substitution* option is used for automatic spelling correction or for lemmatization

First 52 words in alphabetical order of exclusion list

The *Exclusion* option allows reviewers to command WordStat to ignore words found in an exclusion list

The *Categorization* option allows reviewers to categorize words using a categorization dictionary

Figure 9.8   Screenshot showing WordStat being used to analyze the Dyadic Mentoring Study of 47 works

map or matrix of your most relevant information sources, such as the one introduced in Figure 9.1. To begin to develop this map or matrix requires discerning not only salient sources but also a realistic completion point so that you can begin the analysis. In fact, you might recognize that at this point you have probably revisited Step 3: Storing and Organizing Information—where you conducted your initial analysis of information—and throughout the CLR process thus far, you have refined your ideas and reordered some of your files. Here, you will need to decide and to categorize each set of information into one of the 13 elements of information.

Next, consider the various qualitative and quantitative analytical approaches, analytical methods, and analytical techniques that we presented in this chapter and decide which of these, or combination of these (i.e., mixed methods), might be useful and practical to understand better some of the areas that surfaced in your search. For some of the technical aspects of analyzing your information sources and coding techniques, it might be feasible to learn more about your selected approach and/or

consult a colleague with specialty knowledge in the area for guidance. Nonetheless, your gravitation to one or more approaches likely will align with your experience of Step 1: Exploring Beliefs and Topics.

For instance, if a literature reviewer adopted a constructivist-based research philosophy, then he/she might not be (as) comfortable conducting any of the quantitative or mixed analysis approaches, methods, and techniques, and likely will prefer conducting one of the qualitative analysis approaches, methods, and/or techniques. In contrast, if a reviewer maintained a postpositivist research philosophy, then he/she might not be (as) comfortable conducting any of the qualitative or mixed analysis approaches, methods, and techniques, and likely will prefer conducting one of the quantitative analysis approaches, methods, and/or techniques.

Alternatively still, if a reviewer adopted a research philosophy that is associated more with the mixed research tradition (e.g., some form of pragmatism [say, pragmatism-of-the-middle], some form of dialectical pluralism [e.g., critical dialectical pluralism]), then he/she likely would be comfortable conducting one or more mixed analysis approach, method, and/or technique—either by combining one or more qualitative analysis approaches, methods, and/or techniques with one or more quantitative analysis approaches, methods, and/or techniques (i.e., conducting a non-crossover mixed analysis); or by conducting some form of crossover mixed analysis at the introductory, intermediate, or advanced level.

In any case, by analyzing your selected sources, new discoveries will come to the fore and new ideas might ensue that will influence the forthcoming synthesis, or combination of emergent concepts. Document this exploratory process by noting times that you wonder about particular attributes and characteristics of your topic and questions that arise—much like the qualitative researcher creates field notes. Your emergent ideas will constitute the next level of synthesis of information, which continues with the communication phase and the final CLR report.

CONCLUSIONS

As articulated throughout each step, the reflective process helps to facilitate each step of the CLR, and Step 6 is no exception. To complete this step, it is important to think about what you want to learn from the works via the analysis questions designed. If the CLR is a stand-alone project, these questions serve much like research questions. If the goal for the CLR is to inform primary research, then these questions seek some background for justifying the study. Thinking about Step 6, much like any research, you can analyze data on any level—a brief analysis using constant comparison analysis, or a more complex analysis using works that include secondary data and a mixed analysis. Therein lies the answers that you might have in making some important decisions associated with Step 6. You might also ask yourself: How much time do you have and what is your skill level? Simply put, the concept map (or design) for your foundational information also depends on your level of resources for analyzing data. We are confident that you will be able to find at least one analysis approach that meets your needs and that is consistent with your research philosophy. Of course, our preference is for reviewers, whenever possible and without compromising their research philosophies, at least to consider using mixed analysis procedures for analyzing CLR information. Also, we recommend that, whenever possible, reviewers should use computer software (e.g., QDA Miner, SPSS) to enhance their analyses of CLR information.

One goal for Step 6 as part of the interactive steps of the CLR is to increase rigor for the literature review process—that is, the importance of analyzing and synthesizing information in a maximally arduous manner. Traditionally, rigor has been viewed as a methodological issue. However, in addition to being a methodological issue, even more importantly, we view rigor as an *ethical* issue. Indeed, we contend that by analyzing CLR information in a rigorous manner, the final product is a synthesis that is both **warranted** and **transparent**—consistent with the American Educational Research Association's (2006) standards for reporting on empirical social science research. In turn, as a reviewer you will maintain the stance of an ethical reviewer—wherein the works of others are honored in a culturally progressive manner and not misrepresented.

Reviewing this summary of chapter concepts helps to distinguish some important qualities and considerations of Step 6:

- Establishing one or more central, or guiding, questions about your topic will keep you on focus in the analysis process.
- When analyzing qualitative and quantitative data, there are three broad levels: analytic approaches, analytic methods, and analytic techniques.
- Synthesizing information sources involves arranging, comparing, contrasting, translating, categorizing, interpreting, deriving, extrapolating, and producing, and cannot take place until the information is analyzed.
- In grounded theory research, constant comparison analysis is used through a series of stages—an *open coding* stage, an *axial coding* stage, and a *selective coding* stage—to create theory in regard to the topic.
- Ethnographic analysis comprises domain analysis, taxonomic analysis, componential analysis, and theme analysis for the purpose of understanding cultural meanings for groups of people.
- Discourse analysis may involve seven building tasks that guide the coding of data.

- Qualitative comparative analysis is an approach that is used to build theory whereby the analyst makes connections among categories identified previously for testing and developing them further.
- Qualitative methods for analyzing and synthesizing information sources include Miles and Huberman's 19 within-case analyses and 18 cross-case analyses.
- Qualitative techniques include Saldaña's 32 coding techniques.
- A meta-synthesis is a synthesis of two or more qualitative studies that address a similar research question with similar qualitative research designs.
- Quantitative methods include measures of central tendency, dispersion/variability, distribution shape, analysis of variance, regression, factor analysis, and spatial analysis
- Analysis of variance (ANOVA) is a comparison of means for a variable of interest in three or more studies. A multiple analysis of variance (MANOVA) is a comparison of means of two or more means simultaneously across multiple studies.
- A meta-analysis is a quantitative data analysis system that aggregates quantitative findings across research studies to estimate the mean effect size or to examine the variability of effect sizes across studies as a function of study design effects.
- Crossover mixed analysis is a basic form of quantitizing and qualitizing data, or converting/transforming data associated with one tradition to another tradition (e.g., qualitative to quantitative).
- A Bayesian meta-analysis can be used to ascertain the likelihood of something occurring through one type of research evidence (i.e., qualitative analysis) and then to establish it more reliably via another type of research evidence (i.e., qualitative analysis).
- Q methodology examines correlations among participants across a sample of variables, which results in a reduction of the participants' many viewpoints to a few factors, which are assumed to represent shared feelings, opinions, beliefs, perspectives, or preferences.
- A meta-summary is a type of systematic review that integrates qualitative findings in a target domain that are topical or thematic summaries or surveys of data.
- Before analyzing information sources as data, it is helpful to create a conceptual map or matrix of the information sources.

CHAPTER 9 EVALUATION CHECKLIST

CORE	Guiding Questions and Tasks
Critical Examination	To what extent did you identify the approach, method, and techniques that might apply to understanding your topic area?
Organization	To what extent did you notate the description and primary references to describe your selected analyses?
	To what extent did you document references to information sources that were not selected for the analyses but might be used in a narrative?
Reflections	To what extent did you list any limitations of your synthesis, such as differences in information source research questions and or methodologies?
	Who might you contact to be mentored for conducting an analysis or for conducting a mixed analysis? What concepts do you need to learn or review?
Evaluation	Discern your selection of way(s) to analyze the information you selected. What are some new areas of knowledge that you acquired and what do you need to learn to accomplish this step?

PART FOUR

COMMUNICATION

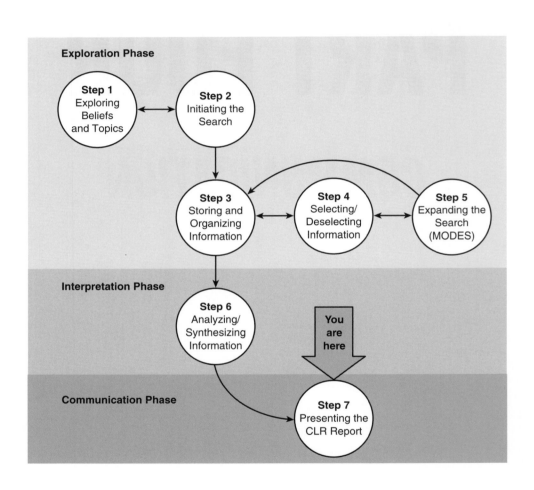

10

STEP 7: PRESENTING THE CLR REPORT— PLANNING PHASE

CHAPTER 10 ROADMAP

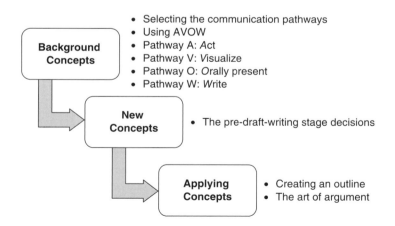

Background Concepts
- Selecting the communication pathways
- Using AVOW
- Pathway A: *Act*
- Pathway V: *Visualize*
- Pathway O: *Orally present*
- Pathway W: *Write*

New Concepts
- The pre-draft-writing stage decisions

Applying Concepts
- Creating an outline
- The art of argument

SELECTING THE COMMUNICATION PATHWAY(S)

Consider the way that all great leaders convey a humanistic, unique presentation of a speech. He/she might consider the delivery opportunity as a type of performance and it is likely that the leader will match the goals of this speech to audience needs and expectations. Likewise, literature reviewers might consider not only the use of a speech to perform ideas, but also all of the multiple venues associated with performance and communication. To this end, we describe four broad ways to present a CLR report: Act, Visualize, Orally present, and Write. Interestingly, the first letter of each significant word labeling these four pathways to communicating information spells out the word *AVOW*. And we believe that the word *avow* is highly appropriate because, as defined by dictionary.com (a free online dictionary) the word *avow* represents "to declare frankly or openly"; "own"; "acknowledge"; "confess"; "admit" (http://dictionary.reference.com/browse/avow?s=t). And all of these definitions of the word *avow* are highly appropriate for the synthesis reporting context. For example, in the context of literature reviews, the acronym AVOW reminds us to declare frankly or openly the results of a CLR.

USING AVOW

The use of AVOW—representing Step 7—is the final step of the CLR. It is the sole step of the communication phase that is a compilation of all of your efforts to provide a rigorous, transparent process and logical, relevant synthesis and conclusions. And, after completing Steps 1–6, the reviewer should have an important story to tell. Before beginning this step, it is helpful to reflect on the art of communication and the attributes of a highly skillful communicator. According to Myatt (2012), in a featured *Forbes* magazine article on communication secrets of great leaders, the most skilled communicators develop the ability to develop a sharp sense of situational and contextual awareness so that their ideas embrace their audiences on an emotional and aspirational level. Further, he explains that one secret that receives little attention by most communicators is that their messages must be framed so that they meet the needs and expectations of the audience. Thus, in the following sections, we outline how to present the CLR synthesis effectively (and creatively) .

PATHWAY A: ACT

Although, traditionally, a literature review report might have been limited to the written findings, Pathway A of AVOW involves a performance or acting-out of the CLR. Performing a synthesis resembles ***performance ethnography***, which "is concerned with embodying aspects of ethnographic description" and "focuses on the important transformative process of becoming" (Alexander, 2005, p. 412). There are numerous ways that syntheses might be acted on or performed, including the following:

- poetry
- music
- movement and dance
- dramatization

Regardless of the performance modality, these pathways can be a powerful tool to convey key findings or critical points that words alone might not communicate. We elaborate on each of these areas in the following sections to spark imagination and creativity for developing an interesting and compelling report/presentation of your synthesis.

THE USE OF POETRY

Poetry involves using rhythmical composition (i.e., in metric form) to report a synthesis. As posited by Hirshfield (1997), poetry has the potential to clarify and to accentuate our human existence. Faulkner (2009) stated, "These observations about poetry as a means to enlarge understanding, resist clear undemanding interpretations, and move closer to what it means to be human elucidates the reason some researchers use poetry as a means of representing research" (p. 16). Moreover, Furman, Langer, Davis, Gallardo, and Kulkami (2007) concluded that research poetry provides an avenue for a researcher to access universality, with poets using their personal experiences to create a product that is universal or generalizable because the readers identify with the work.

Prendergast (2009) identified 40 different labels that researchers used to describe their use of poems in qualitative research, including the following: *found poetry* (e.g., Prendergast, 2006), *research experience poetry*, *poetry from the field*, *data poetry* (cf. Lahman et al., 2010), *investigative poetry* (Hartnett, 2003), *interpretive poetry*, and *research poetry* (Faulkner, 2009). However, we use the term **synthesis poem** to distinguish it from other uses of poems in research. A synthesis poem particularly is useful when the reviewer believes that the other modes of presentation (i.e., visualize, orally present, and write) will not adequately capture the synthesis (Faulkner, 2005, 2009), when he/she has had direct experience with the phenomenon under study (Behar, 2008), to write with more passion (Richardson, 1997), and to reach more diverse audiences (Richardson, 2002).

EXAMPLE: USING POETRY

Box 10.1 presents an example of a synthesis poem that was created by Onwuegbuzie (2012) after he conducted a

CLR regarding arguments between researchers who conduct purely quantitative research and researchers who conduct purely qualitative research—commonly referred to as the *paradigm war*—which has taken place between purists of both traditions since the 1980s.

THE USE OF MUSIC

Music can play a direct or indirect role in presenting the literature. A direct role implies that the story of the CLR is told in a straightforward way through music. An example of this would be converting Tony's poem about mixed research (Onwuegbuzie, 2012) into a song that represents a particular genre (e.g., rap, rock, classical, jazz, soul, country, hip hop). In fact, this communication tool might be offered by posting the MP3 recording using a link on the Internet and including a brief component that explains the methodological considerations (i.e., the audit trail) and intended audience. Music also might play an indirect role whereby the story is spoken (e.g., orally) with appropriate music being played in the background. In most western cultures, the written word has been privileged over other forms of communication—including music. Yet, in many cultures, music has played an important role in the historical research tradition. For example, in many African countries, drums have been instrumental (excuse our pun!) in transmitting history from one generation to the next (Finnen, 2004). Interestingly, Frels (2012) compared mixed methods research education to the romantic composer Gustav Mahler, stating the following:

> I recently renewed my appreciation for the musical work of Gustav Mahler through reflecting on the complexities and humanistic characteristics of MMR [mixed methods research], and I echo the sentiments of the conductor Marin Alsop as he described walking onstage to conduct Mahler's Fifth Symphony: 'It's a large-scale journey, guaranteed to provide surprises and new discoveries along the way' (Alsop, 2005, para 2). Likewise, educational researchers might recognize the value of this large-scale journey through effective MMR planning, implementation, and dissemination—all of which entail unexpected juxtapositions and times of dissonance. (p. 191)

BOX 10.1

FIRST SEVEN VERSES OF A SYNTHESIS POEM WRITTEN BY ONWUEGBUZIE (2012) THAT PROVIDED A SYNTHESIS OF THE DEBATES THAT HAVE OCCURRED BETWEEN PURISTS REPRESENTING THE QUANTITATIVE AND QUALITATIVE RESEARCH TRADITIONS SINCE THE 1980S

GENERATION Q: A DREAM FOR MIXED RESEARCHERS IN THE RADICAL MIDDLE

QUAN researchers on one side;
QUAL researchers on the other;
Anyone in-between
Ends up being smothered.

A discipline built on division,
turmoil and tears.
Much blood has been spilt
throughout the years.

QUAN and QUAL researchers
claim the other paradigm is flawed;
But when it comes to methodological tolerance
good practices are ignored.

QUAN and QUAL researchers
often have been segregated
And for those wanting unity,
this has been ill-fated.

Scholars from other fields
are extremely surprised;
for many can see through
this paradigmatic disguise.

All educational researchers
I think you will find,
compared to other disciplines
are many years behind.

Mixed research in some journals
has been virtually forbidden;
to publish in these journals,
mixed research identities must be hidden.

Adapted from "Introduction: Putting the *mixed* back into quantitative and qualitative research in educational research and beyond: Moving towards the *radical middle*," by A. J. Onwuegbuzie, 2012, *International Journal of Multiple Research Approaches*, 6, p. 212. Copyright 2012 by eContent Management Pty Ltd.

Oftentimes, music and other creative arts bring to the fore a heightened awareness of polarities for people and provide an avenue for the audience to approach feelings and thoughts at a symbolic and metaphoric level (Rogers, 1993). In short, music adds an emotional level to the CLR presentation. In 2013, researcher and neuroscientist Antonio Damasio discussed with world-renowned cellist Yo-Yo Ma how music helps to convey emotion for addressing humanistic problems at a deeper level. Johnson (2013) described their dialogue:

> Ma also explained the edge effect—the point when two different adjoining ecological communities meet and create greater species diversity and new life forms. The edge effect became a metaphor throughout the event, when Damasio and Ma talked about blending disciplines in order to make new discoveries. (¶ 17)

For the CLR, when music is carefully selected and/or created to communicate findings, it can help tap into a transformative experience that is sensitive to culture and contextual considerations that might be difficult to express using the written word.

THE USE OF MOVEMENT AND DANCE

In much the same way as can music, movement in general and dance in particular can be used to present CLR findings, either directly or indirectly. For instance, Cancienne and Snowber (2003) deem dance "as a place of inquiry and the body as a site for knowledge" (p. 237) and outline how this awareness influences interpretation of research. In her qualitative research book, Janesick (2010) uses the metaphor of dance and yoga to serve "as a continuous lens from which to understand qualitative research methods" (p. xiii).

THE USE OF DRAMATIZATION

Oftentimes in teaching, dramatization is used to engage students through interactive activities. Likewise, the use of drama for the CLR might include points of improvisation, storytelling, role playing, and so forth.

EXAMPLE: USING DRAMATIZATION

When Rebecca presented (i.e., *defended*) her dissertation (i.e., Frels, 2010) to her dissertation committee, rather than present it in a conventional way, she performed her dissertation by having audience members play the roles of the participants in her qualitative research study. As another example, when Tony presented findings from an extensive critical review of the literature on effect sizes (i.e., Onwuegbuzie & Levin, 2003), in an attempt to minimize any tensions in the room emanating from staunch effect-size proponents, as part of his presentation, he outlined the limitations of effect sizes via a skit wherein he played two roles: (a) Tony (his true self) and (b) Tony (his alter ego who served as a devil's advocate by asking critical questions that he predicted some of the staunch effect-size proponents would ask). Next, he alternated chairs to distinguish which persona was talking on each occasion. This performance appeared to be extremely successful in that it generated a lot of laughter in the room and minimized any tensions that might have ensued among the audience members.

As a third example, prior to the publication of the written version of debriefing interviews in research, the authors (Collins, Onwuegbuzie, Johnson, & Frels, 2013) undertook an unrehearsed demonstration showing the power of conducting debriefing interviews rather than providing a traditional presentation (e.g., using PowerPoint slides). This demonstration appeared to be very effective due to the fact that audience members actually experienced the debriefing interview synchronously. Indeed, almost 1 year after this presentation, one of the audience members communicated via an email: "I am still impressed with your demonstration of the peer debriefing process at the AERA [American Educational Research Association] session."

PATHWAY V: *VISUALIZE*

Keeping in mind the saying that "a picture is worth a thousand words," another array of communication tools that might enhance audience engagement involves visualization, which can be drawings, paintings, photographs, videos, and multimedia. The literature reviewer would be intentional with the selection of visual tools, keeping in mind the intended audience, cultural context, and accessibility. Thus, representing CLR syntheses visually has much intuitive appeal.

EXAMPLE: CREATING A VIDEO LECTURE

The CLR synthesis could lead to a YouTube video. Or, even more appropriately, a video of the CLR synthesis could be posted on an online video repository such as VideoLectures.net, hosted by the Jozef Stefan Institute in Slovenia, which is the world's biggest academic online video repository; it is peer reviewed and contains more than 18,000 videos delivered by nearly 12,000 authors. At the most advanced level, a CLR synthesis could be made into a documentary film. Broadly speaking, a documentary film is a nonfictional motion picture that is primarily written for instructional or historical purposes. Once made, these documentaries can be posted on online repositories such as All Documentaries, which is a free international documentary database.

Figure 10.1 presents an example of an online video lecture to disseminate a report.

PATHWAY 0: *O*RALLY PRESENT

One of the most common ways of disseminating the CLR synthesis is via an oral presentation. To evidence this point, Skidmore, Slate, and Onwuegbuzie (2010)

determined that at least 300,000 presentations are given each year in education and education-related conferences alone. And because the overwhelming majority of empirical, conceptual, theoretical, and methodological conference papers involve the citation of one or more extant works, a literature review plays some role in virtually all conference presentations. Here, the literature reviewer might communicate the CLR using the forms that we described in Chapter 2, namely, (a) one of the four common narrative reviews (i.e., general reviews, theoretical reviews, methodological reviews, and historical reviews); (b) one of the four common systematic reviews (i.e., meta-analysis, rapid review, meta-synthesis, and meta-summary); or (c) an integrative review (i.e., involving some combination of narrative review and systematic literature review).

Presenting at a conference has many benefits beyond simply making known the findings of a CLR or primary study, including the following: (a) providing reviewers with the ability to share the most up-to-date information on a given topic to an interested audience in a relatively short amount of time; (b) obtaining feedback from a conference audience that reviewers can use to provide an even more comprehensive literature review; (c) providing a unique opportunity for reviewers to connect with other reviewers of the same body of knowledge to develop professional networks; and (d) providing an opportunity to build an academic reputation on

Figure 10.1   Screenshot of VideoLectures.net online video repository

the topic (Skidmore et al., 2010). In short, a professional conference is a networking opportunity that can provide growth for the identity of a literature reviewer as well as growth for the knowledge base in the topic area.

Conference presentations vary and, depending on the conference, they can take many forms, including paper presentations, roundtable discussions, poster sessions, panel sessions, symposia, and performances/demonstrations. Across these oral presentation formats, it is very common for literature reviewers to use some type of presentation software program such as, respectively, Hewlett-Packard Bruno (circa 1979), Microsoft PowerPoint (circa 1990), Corel Presentations (circa 1996), Kingsoft Presentation (circa 1997), CustomShow (circa 1998), OpenOffice.org Impress (circa 2000),

Apple Keynote (circa 2003), SlideRocket (circa 2006), Google Docs (circa 2007), GNOME Ease (circa 2009), emaze (circa 2009), Prezi (circa 2009), LibreOffice Impress (circa 2010), PowToon (circa 2012), and SlideWiki (circa 2013). Of these software programs, Microsoft PowerPoint is the most widely used, with 95% share of the presentation software market share, which has been installed on more than 1 billion computers that provide approximately 350 PowerPoint presentations every second worldwide (Parks, 2012). Thus, Microsoft PowerPoint can be a useful medium for reviewers to present their CLRs, as long as appropriate practices are followed regarding design elements such as the text, the background used for the text, the pace that the information is presented, the visual information used, how data are displayed, and delivery.

TOOL: POINTS TO REMEMBER IN AN ORAL PRESENTATION

If you would like to investigate more information about communicating an effective presentation, we refer you to our reference list (which is an excellent source for information) and Box 10.2, which provides an overview of points to remember in an oral presentation (Skidmore et al., 2010).

BOX 10.2

CHECKLIST FOR A PROFESSIONAL PRESENTATION

Preparation

❏ Unambiguous purpose
❏ Organized content
❏ Two or three key take-home points
❏ Back-up plan

Conference and Presentation Type Norms to Know

❏ Time allotted per presenter?
❏ Space and equipment availability?
❏ Handout?

(Continued)

(Continued)

- ❏ Type?
- ❏ Quantity?
- ❏ Distribution time (beginning or end?)

Presentation Points to Remember

- ❏ The presentation is not the paper!
- ❏ Minimize extraneous cognitive load

  - ❏ Simplify background
  - ❏ Text

    - ❏ Display only relevant text
    - ❏ Minimize text on slide
    - ❏ Consistent fonts throughout

  - ❏ Visuals

    - ❏ Enhance understanding of key points
    - ❏ Focus attention using color, size, or shapes
    - ❏ Narrate graphics instead of providing on-screen text
    - ❏ Related words and visuals are within close proximity
    - ❏ Animation and narration occur concurrently

  - ❏ Data

    - ❏ Appropriate level of detail or complexity
    - ❏ Focus attention on most salient feature

Delivery

- ❏ Building rapport and exuding confidence

  - ❏ Demeanor

    - ❏ Purposeful movements
    - ❏ Straight but relaxed posture
    - ❏ Eye contact

  - ❏ Voice
  - ❏ Varying pitch and loudness

    - ❏ Pace

  - ❏ Professional dress

- ❏ Contextual flexibility – be responsive to your audience
- ❏ Grand entrance and exit

Adapted from " Editorial: Developing effective presentation skills: Evidence-based guidelines," by S. Skidmore, J. R. Slate, and A. J. Onwuegbuzie, 2010, *Research in the Schools, 17*(2), pp. xxv–xxxvii. Reprinted with kind permission of the Mid-South Educational Research Association and the Editors of *Research in the Schools*.

Prezi, which is an increasingly popular competitor to Microsoft PowerPoint, is a cloud-based presentation software and storytelling tool that can aid reviewers in presenting their CLRs on a virtual canvas (Gunelius, 2012). This tool incorporates what is called a zooming user interface (ZUI), which allows reviewers to zoom in and out of their CLR presentations, as well as to display and to navigate (to size, to rotate, or to edit) through information (e.g., texts, videos, and images) within a multidimensional (e.g., parallax 3D; a type of glasses-free 3D technology that separates the image into columns of left and right pixels and includes a non-transparent and non-translucent barrier layer containing vertical slits to [re]direct the user's eyes appropriately) space. Specifically, the reviewer places objects (i.e., information extracted via MODES) on a canvas and navigates among these objects. Frames allow presentation media to be grouped together as a single presentation object. Paths are used to represent navigational sequences that link all the presentation objects with the goal of providing a coherent CLR presentation. A particular appeal of Prezi is that an app (Prezi Viewer) has been developed for the iPad for viewing Prezis (Watters, 2011). However, as with Microsoft PowerPoint and all other presentation software programs, reviewers should design their Prezis in such a way as to minimize cognitive overload during their CLR presentations (Skidmore et al., 2010).

Although conference presentations and other venues for orally presenting the CLR synthesis tend to occur face to face, reviewers also can orally present their CLR syntheses virtually. In particular, reviewers can present CLR syntheses via video telecommunications technologies that facilitate communication between persons at two or more locations by simultaneous multi-way video and audio transmissions. Of these video telecommunications technologies, **videoconferencing** is particularly common. Two types of videoconferencing exist. There are self-contained systems such as a console that includes all electrical interfaces, the control computer, the appropriate software or hardware, omnidirectional microphones, a high-quality remote controlled video camera, and a TV monitor with loudspeakers and/or a video projector; these systems comprise devices that are either non-portable (typically used for large meetings) or portable (e.g., have fixed cameras, and microphones and loudspeakers that are integrated into the console). And there are desktop systems that include add-ons to personal computers that transform them into videoconferencing devices and that generate **e-meetings**. Popular videoconferencing software includes Skype (circa 2003), Google Hangouts (circa 2013), Adobe Connect (circa 2006), WebEx (circa 1996), ooVoo (circa 2006), and GoToMeeting (circa, 2004). These and other videoconferencing-based presentations also can be made via many mobile devices (e.g., iOS, Android, BlackBerry, iPhone, iPad). Some videoconferencing software is free to use, at least to some degree (e.g., Skype, ooVoo, Google Hangouts). Alternatively, reviewers can use **web conferencing**—most often called **webinars**—which facilitate virtual presentations that occur over the Internet. A major difference between videoconferencing and web conferences is that, although videoconferences always are interactive, web conferences are not necessarily interactive. As a result of videoconferencing and web conferencing, reviewers can disseminate their CLR syntheses to interested audiences from many parts of the world, including those from geographically isolated locations.

PATHWAY W: *W*RITE

The most common way of disseminating the CLR synthesis is by producing a written account. The planning phase for writing is much like the planning of an effective speech. It takes into account the relationship with the audience so that points are communicated in a meaningful, relevant, and useful way. Often, an oral presentation at professional conferences is referenced by other authors using the phrase "Paper presented at..." In fact, when such oral presentations are to be referenced, according to the sixth edition of the *Publication Manual* of the American Psychological Association (APA, 2010), they are referenced using the following template:

> Presenter, A. A. (Year, Month). *Title of paper.* Paper presented at the meeting of Organization Name, Location.

Communicating the CLR via writing is unique because it represents a dialogue; yet, different from other communication modalities that occur synchronously, the written report is read well after it is written. That is, of all the pathways to communicate the CLR, the communication venues of *visualize* and *write* require the ability to anticipate the audience's reactions. It requires the skills of writing ideas without immediate verbal or non-verbal feedback. Therefore, in the planning of a written report, it is important to consider multiple ways to address any anticipated reactions, expectations, and needs for your intended audience. It is a good idea for literature reviewers informally to present some major points to a trusted peer or colleague and attempt to explain them in a succinct fashion before a formal presentation. This and other recommendations that we make for the written pathway, or CLR report, also can be applied to the other three AVOW ways of presenting syntheses—**A**cting, **V**isualizing, and **O**rally presenting. Regardless of the communication path that is selected, the literature reviewer should tailor the message in a way that will establish credibility, trust, rapport, and value. Before these relational components of communication can be addressed, the message must be planned. For the writing process, organization of the report occurs at three levels: the pre-draft-writing stage, the draft-writing stage, and the draft-audit stage. Each of these stages is discussed in turn, with the pre-draft-writing stage discussed in this chapter and the other two stages (i.e., draft-writing stage and the draft-audit stage) being presented in the next chapter (i.e., Chapter 11).

NEW CONCEPTS

In the previous chapter, we explained the meta-framework of the CLR analysis and synthesis, containing an array of qualitative, quantitative, and mixed analysis approaches, methods, and techniques for analyzing and synthesizing works at three levels of complexity: introductory, intermediate, and advanced. After the reviewer has selected which analytical techniques to use, he/she should continue analyzing and synthesizing information extracted via the five MODES (i.e., Step 6) until data saturation and/or theoretical saturation is reached. Once saturation has been reached, the reviewer is now in a position to begin writing the CLR. However, before the first draft is written, it is a good idea for the reviewer to plan how to write this draft. We call this the *pre-draft-writing phase*.

THE PRE-DRAFT-WRITING STAGE DECISIONS

The pre-draft-writing phase is one of great reflexivity. During the pre-draft-writing phase, there are several decisions to be made—which, in turn, will facilitate the narrative report. It is likely that you have made some of the decisions that are listed below already. Also, it should be noted that although these decisions have been presented in somewhat of a logical order, this order is far from being a strict one.

DECISION 1: DETERMINE THE GOAL

As explained in Chapter 1, one of two major goals drive the literature review: (a) a stand-alone review, or an end in itself (i.e., independent work) and (b) an informative review for primary research at one or more phases of the research process (i.e., research conceptualization phase, research planning phase, research implementation phase, and research dissemination phase). Thus, in this pre-draft-writing stage, the reviewer should revisit the CLR goal. This decision is important because each goal leads to different genres of reports. For example, with respect to journal articles, literature reviews that stem from the first goal (i.e., a stand-alone review) tend to lead to longer articles than do literature reviews that stem from the second goal (i.e., primary research), wherein the literature review section for the latter goal typically represents only one major section of the body of the article—with the other major sections being the method section, results section, and discussion section.

DECISION 2: DETERMINE THE INTENDED OUTLET

Alongside revisiting the goal of the CLR, reviewers should confirm their intended outlets for their CLR report. In particular, will the literature review be written wholly or in part of a dissertation/thesis, journal article, technical report, book, book chapter, or the like? As is the case for the goal of the CLR, the choice of outlet will determine the length of the CLR report. For example, a dissertation or a thesis would afford the reviewer much more signature space (i.e., maximum number of pages allowed by the editor or publisher) for the CLR report than would a book chapter, which, in turn, would afford the reviewer more signature space than would a journal article.

DECISION 3: DETERMINE THE INTENDED AUDIENCE

Deciding on the intended audience is important because it would help the reviewers determine how to frame their CLR reports, which determines the language that they might use, how much explanation of terms and concepts that they should include, and so forth. For example, returning to our mentoring and college students example, a reviewer likely would not need to provide as much explanation of mentoring terms and concepts if he/she submitted the report to a mentoring journal such as *Mentoring & Tutoring: Partnership in Learning*—whose readers mostly will be familiar with the standard mentoring terms and concepts—than if he/she submitted the report to another type of journal.

DECISION 4: REVISIT BELIEF SYSTEMS

In Step 1, presented in Chapter 4, we discussed the important role that research philosophical beliefs, discipline-specific beliefs, and topic-specific beliefs play in the CLR process. At this stage, reviewers should revisit these beliefs. Indeed, as we discussed previously, these beliefs influence virtually every decision made—and now they influence decisions made during the CLR writing process (e.g., what analysis and synthesis findings to include and to exclude). Reviewers are in an extremely powerful position, having the goal of capturing the voices of other authors of extant works without exploiting or distorting these voices. That is, at all times, the writing should reflect a culturally progressive, ethical, and multimodal stance, as well as promoting a communitarian view of power

that might occur between the CLR writer and a reader who may be evaluating the writing. This reader might be an instructor, or a reviewer for a potential journal; and by adopting a communitarian view of power, the reviewer demonstrates that he/she is respectful of alternate views and belief systems that are represented by reciprocity among reviewers and between reviewers and authors of the works being reviewed.

Consequently, in preparing to write the first CLR draft, literature reviewers should revisit their beliefs, stances, views, and practices via reflexivity—looking for tensions, paradoxes, complicity, and undue bias. Whenever possible, at this pre-draft-writing stage, reviewers should undergo some form of debriefing (Collins et al., 2013; Combs et al., 2010a, 2010b; Frels & Onwuegbuzie, 2012a; Nelson, Onwuegbuzie, Wines, & Frels, 2013; Onwuegbuzie et al., 2008) because, oftentimes, saying something in a conversation uncovers new discoveries and awareness of "how something might sound" to another.

DECISION 5: CREATE AN OUTLINE

As part of our micro definition of a comprehensive literature review in Chapter 1, we defined the CLR as representing "a logical argument of an interpretation of relevant published and/or unpublished information on the selected topic from multimodal texts and settings." Consequently, as an important part of outlining their CLR write-ups, and bearing in mind the previous decisions made, reviewers should establish the path of argumentation that they will use. This path, which stems from the analysis and synthesis step of the CLR process (i.e., Step 6), must be both *transparent* for "mak[ing] explicit the logic of inquiry and activities that led from the development of the initial interest, topic, problem, or research question" (AERA, 2006, p. 33) and *warranted* (i.e., sufficient evidence is provided to justify the synthesis; AERA, 2006, p. 33). Thus, in order to facilitate the pre-decisions for writing, we suggest that, prior to writing the first draft of their CLR reports, reviewers create an outline or road map of the decisions throughout the CLR and decide where to present the criteria for making each decision. It might be that you could decide to present the methodology of your review in a short section just before your synthesis or interwoven into the results of your synthesis. This roadmap might change as you begin to write but it is a good starting place so that you will begin to write with a focus.

Whatever the genre of the work that contains the CLR report, all reports should be organized so that the writing is focused on your overall CLR goal and guiding questions. Logically, we compare the draft-writing stage to a greeting and conversation with your audience. This stage will ease the reader into the topic and lay the groundwork for your writer/reader relationship. The greeting might be considered your introduction section. As you begin to provide further details and uncover the heart of your CLR, it is much like the interactive dialogue or conversation with your readers, even though they will be reading your ideas after you complete your end of the conversation via the report. Finally, just as human interaction logically ends with communicating what might come about after your interaction concludes, the written report also leaves the reading audience with something changed—whether it be a perspective, belief, understanding, or action.

Much like the aforementioned greeting and conversation, the CLR written report contains at least three major sections, namely: (a) the introduction, (b) the body, and (c) the summation (Machi & McEvoy, 2009). There are also some personal considerations to which you might attend so that you organize your draft-writing times for when you might be most productive. As explained by Johnson and Mullen (2007), productive scholarship is conducive to a writer's biological rhythm, and being in the "writer's flow" (p. 49), which is the state of focus, clarity, and inspiration resulting in breakthrough moments for momentum in writing goals.

AN OVERVIEW OF ORGANIZING WRITING

THE INTRODUCTION SECTION

This section provides a preview of your topic and allows the reader to begin to read with some expectations. According to Machi and McEvoy (2009),

the introduction section can be framed using six basic subsections that are general statements presented in one or more sentences: introduction statement, topic statement, context statement, significance statement, problem statement, and organization statement. Each of these subsections is discussed in turn.

The *introduction statement* refers to a set of sentences or often one sentence that focuses the reader immediately on the topic. It is the *narrative hook* that captures the attention (i.e., "hooks") of readers. The narrative hook is engaging and entices readers to a sense of wondering about the topic—by inducing emotions, feelings, or beliefs. For example, in their study examining the mentoring experiences across grade span among principals, mentors, and mentees, Frels, Zientek, and Onwuegbuzie (2013, p. 29) presented their opening sentence as follows:

> The current teacher shortage across the USA substantiates the imminent need for teachers to be effective and engaging, with a "growth-oriented mentoring mindset" (Mullen, 2010, p. 1) that focuses on their own learning and nurtures the learning of others (Dweck, 2006).

This sentence contains two powerful but substantiated claims. By using phrases/words such as "imminent need," "effective and engaging," "growth-oriented mentoring mindset," and "learning," the authors sought to induce an emotional response and a sense of curiosity to continue reading. Hopefully, you will agree that this sentence is enticing for readers—at least those interested in the topic of school-based mentoring.

The *topic statement* is one or more sentences that represent the general ideas or concepts underlying the research topic. It delineates the focus and perspective of the report and outlines the key ideas pertaining to the topic. This section typically should be only between one and three paragraphs in length. It builds on the narrative hook and establishes a rationale for investigating the topic. Next, the *context statement* contains one or more sentences that provide a backdrop for the topic. These sentences both build on the study topic statement and expand on issues or problems that might have contributed to the topic. The context section describes any background information so that the audience can place the topic within relationships, major players, or time variables. This statement tends to convince the reader that the topic should be explored further. In this section, the reviewer's belief systems (i.e., overall worldview, research philosophy, and discipline-specific philosophy) should become apparent.

So far, we have described three of the six introduction statements that might be regarded as a type of welcome to your CLR. After the introduction statement, topic statement, and context statement, the introduction section would continue the greeting by establishing a significance statement. Using one or more sentences, the *significance statement* is a declaration of need. Although it is written for a general audience, it should be appealing to a reader so that he/she interacts on a cognitive and emotional level with your vision, or for what changes might occur as a result of synthesizing the selected information sources. The more transparent (i.e., explicit) and warranted (i.e., defensible) the significance statement is, the more persuasive it will be to readers that studying the underlying topic has important value.

Just after the significance statement, the introduction moves to the *problem statement*. These sentences describe the current state of affairs of what problems surround the topic that prompted your CLR and the challenges that warranted your investigation that might be better understood using the theoretical and/or conceptual stance that you selected. Finally, the introduction section concludes with the *organization statement*. These sentences will be an advanced organizer, or list of upcoming sections of the CLR. The organization statement allows the reader to feel comfortable with what to expect so that upon further reading, he/she can better integrate the new information with her/his own understanding of the topic. Continuing with the metaphor of a conversation and how a conversation builds just after the topic is introduced, reflect on ways in which you process information and some of the

rhetorical devices that helped you to connect with the writing. This introduction section and its six parts (i.e., introduction statement, topic statement, context statement, significance statement, problem statement, and organization statement) can include questions, humor, personal stories, metaphors, analogies, and literary devices to help connect your introduction of the topic with ideas important to the reader/audience so that they will trust what they read and engage in your dialogue.

To help you feel comfortable as a reader and as an advance organizer of our own writing, the next few sentences present our own short organization statement. You might now begin to recognize how we transition into a new section by linking one idea to the next idea. Here it is. In the following sections, we describe and provide examples for building on the introduction section, much like a conversation builds just after meeting someone. As such, the next sections explain the purposes of the body and summary sections of the CLR. By outlining these sections as part of Decision 5, you will be well on your way to your next decision for planning your draft.

THE BODY SECTION

Machi and McEvoy (2009) described the heart of a report as the body section. This section can be conceptualized in two parts: the *discovery argument* and the *advocacy argument*. The discovery argument component provides details pertaining to the circumstances, or relationships, inherent that formed the background for the situation or phenomenon. It is a type of unearthing of salient information and a journey for the reader. After undergoing Step 6 of the CLR process—that is, after analyzing and synthesizing selected works—the literature sets the stage to advocate for one or more points by establishing a sequence of points that stem from the themes and codes extracted in Step 6. This discovery argument is presented as if the reviewer were to tell a story that is well reasoned, logical, and substantiated by the works synthesized.

As noted by Machi and McEvoy (2009), the discovery argument also includes "document[ing] and catalog[ing] the claim statements, supporting evidence, suitable citations, and warrant justification necessary to build the argument for what is known" (p. 137). The outline created in the pre-draft-writing phase should yield a logical, consistent, and clear pattern of discoveries/concepts that formed a point of view or synthesis, which essentially is the reviewer's reasoning pattern or the premises for an upcoming conclusion. Some common key words of premise arguments are: *because, rather than, since, due to, for the purposes of, given that, whereby, if*, and *as a result.*

The advocacy argument is built on the discovery argument and creates implications to address the discovery or premise argument. It is a logical response to what was revealed and is based on the synthesis data. It is communicating, or advocating for, your conclusions, which are the thematic groupings of codes toward what is often referred to through the idiom *the bottom line*, or the most important part of something. Here, the codes provide the evidence to justify a position. Literature reviewers also should present a critique of key sources by referring back to the validation framework (i.e., Step 4; Leech et al., 2010) such that diverse perspectives can be promoted for

additional understanding. Reviewers should use the conclusions of the background statement to outline what is known about the topic.

THE SUMMATION SECTION

This section of your outline, which is expanded during the first writing of your draft, is the last major section of the report. The *summation section* is a chain presentation of the following items: (a) restatement of the thesis statement (i.e., premise), (b) revisiting the thesis analysis, and (c) relating implications of the report and practical challenges and/or limitations to consider. Machi and McEvoy (2009) defined the thesis statement as "express[ing] a conclusion based on a case developed using existing knowledge, sound evidence, and reasoned argument" (p. 157). As such, reviewers begin the summation section by restating the thesis statement from the opening section of the literature review. By referring back to the codes and themes that were generated at Step 6 of the CLR process, interpreting what these codes and themes mean, the reviewer would have addressed what is regarded as a thesis analysis, wherein the reviewer explores the thesis from multiple

---

APPLYING CONCEPTS

Thinking of an outline as a type of roadmap for an upcoming journey, the literature reviewer/writer should recognize that even the best of plans are subject to change. The outline might be considered as the major points of interest that are planned in advance of taking a vacation or trip.

---

perspectives. Finally, the reviewer, who is now transformed into a communicator through writing, should state the implications so that practical everyday issues might be addressed or academic questions might be a renewed motivation for the audience. The summation should include ways in which the thesis addressed the problems revealed in the introduction sections.

CREATING AN OUTLINE

Once you arrive at any particular point during your travels—the writing process—it is reasonable that you might discover some new points of interest. Therefore, remember to be flexible and curious during the pre-writing phase as you outline your intentions.

EXAMPLE: WRITING AND SECTIONS OF A REPORT

Figure 10.2 provides an example from Chapter 2 of the Dyadic Mentoring Study. In this outline, we overlayed Machi and McEvoy's (2009) three-element typology for the major sections of a CLR report. To address transparency in her CLR process, Rebecca described the methodological framework—developed by Combs et al. (2010a, 2010b)—that she used to conduct her literature review (i.e., Outline Section I). This section is followed by an introduction, which provides context to the reader for the general field of mentoring. Next, in Outline Sections II–V, she used an iterative process to code themes in the school-based mentoring literature to reveal best practices with respect to mentoring models as revealed through her synthesis. Then, Outline Sections VI–VIII provide what she learned through the CLR and the practical applications as a result. Rebecca's CLR chapter concludes with a concise summary of the literature presented—alongside a figure that provides a conceptual framework that represents

the literature presented in her chapter—implications, and a discussion of how her dissertation study adds to the body of knowledge. The headings for Outline Sections II–VIII either represented or were inspired by themes that emerged from her constant comparison analysis (see Chapter 9) of the information that she extracted via the five MODES (see Chapter 8). The subheadings under these sections represented or were inspired by the codes that emerged through constant comparison analysis and discourse analysis. These headings and subheadings provided the pathway for writing the argument. Of course, none of these headings were at any point necessarily final, and all of them were subject to modification, removal, or replacement during the first draft of writing. Consider the headings as the roadmap, which is important to compile, before embarking on the journey of writing the first draft.

DECISION 6: DETERMINE INFORMATION, SOURCES, AND MODES

Once the (tentative) section and subsection headings have been determined and documented in outline form, other decisions during the pre-draft-writing

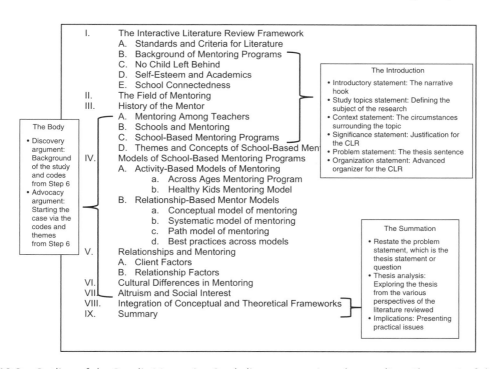

Figure 10.2 Outline of the Dyadic Mentoring Study literature review chapter (i.e., Chapter 2 of the dissertation)

stage can be added. The next decision is to determine the information (e.g., theory, method, finding, interpretation, quotation), sources (e.g., article, chapter, book, blog, video, observation, secondary data set), and MODES (i.e., Step 5) that should represent each section and subsection. It is possible that at the time you created the outline, this decision also was visited. In fact, in Step 3, at the time when organizing information, it might be possible that the outline was already in progress. The better a reviewer stores and organizes information, the easier the decisions will be relating to how to illustrate theoretical/methodological information, sources, and modes. For this reason, CAQDAS and CAMMDAS programs (see Chapter 9) are particularly useful. For example, if QDA Miner had been used during Step 6 to analyze information, then much of the synthesis would have been addressed because the software combines themes/ideas coded by the literature reviewer as one of its many features.

EXAMPLE: USE OF CAQDAS/CAMMDAS RESULTS FOR MAJOR HEADINGS

A CAQDAS/CAMMDAS program example is presented in Figure 10.3 using a screenshot whereby 47 information sources were selected for the Dyadic Mentoring Study, and then coded by Rebecca using an a posteriori coding process, namely, constant comparison analysis. The codes were aggregated by the software and prompted her to distinguish and to generate themes and subthemes. The synthesis was the ongoing process of integrating the theoretical and conceptual frameworks with her introduction section, which, in turn, informed her thesis sentence, which then was added to her outline. By viewing the right-hand side of the screenshot, the pathway for writing the results of the CLR was established and based on the general codes throughout the 47 articles.

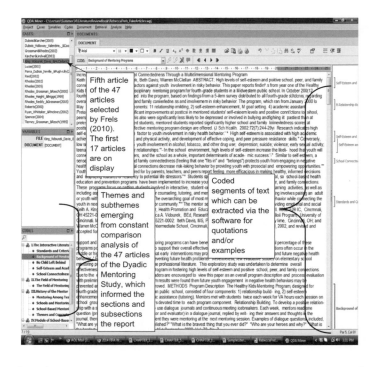

Figure 10.3 Screenshot showing a posteriori coding using constant comparison analysis, which generated themes and subthemes, which, in turn, informed the sections and subsections of Frels's (2010) literature review chapter (i.e., Chapter 2)

DECISION 7: DECIDE THE EMPHASIS OF INFORMATION, SOURCES, AND MODES

As one of your many decisions in the pre-draft phase, the decision to place focus on one or more guiding ideas is made. To assist in this decision, literature reviewers should refer back to the validation framework (Leech et al., 2010) presented in Step 4 to determine which information might be emphasized. Revisiting the historical, contextual, social, methodological, and other trusted elements of information might reveal ways in which one or more works strongly influenced your overall CLR process including your topic-specific beliefs and worldview. Moreover, one or more information sources might be a strong impetus for the way that you conceptualized the CLR. This decision is not often easy; yet, by revisiting these steps in the Exploration and Interpretation Phases of the Seven-Step Model, the literature reviewer might recognize and re-evaluate characteristics and sources that initially prompted his/her passion to undertake a particular topic.

EXAMPLE: WRITING THE PURPOSE STATEMENT

We illustrate the decision for emphasis and the rationale that accompanied it by leaning again on the example of the Dyadic Mentoring Study review and synthesis of 47 works. During her CLR process, Rebecca located an author who reported that he measured (quantitatively) school-based mentoring relationships. Upon contacting and dialoging (to her surprise) with this author, she was led to a qualitative research study (Spencer, 2004). Using the reference list, she expanded her search and located a work by the same author and a colleague (Deutsch & Spencer, 2009) that validated and sparked a new understanding for her of her CLR synthesis—prompting her to add a second purpose to her own primary research. She added a second purpose to her dissertation study built on the CLR that emphasized three articles, and presented this emphasis by stating:

> A second purpose [of this study] was to build on the qualitative body of research (Spencer, 2004, 2007) for understanding roles, purposes, approaches, and

experiences of the relationship process with mentees (the dyadic relationship) and the relationship as a setting "which can be measured and assessed independently from the characteristics of its individual members or the surrounding program" (Deutsch & Spencer, 2009, p. 49). (Frels, 2010, p. 23)

DECISION 8: COMPARE AND CONTRAST INFORMATION SOURCES

The next decision is to compare and to contrast information from each source so that alternate views are honored and given voice. In this decision, the literature reviewer should act as a type of external evaluator so that each of the sections and subsections provide at least one alternate view or idea (in contrast) as well as what has become consensus. For this step, it might be helpful to think of the ethical guidelines for using focus groups as a data collection tool. When a researcher utilizes one or more focus groups, the facilitator negotiates multiple voices and documents expressions, words, and stories from these multiple voices. In data analysis, the researcher strives to understand each voice individually and in the context of the group, as well as the data that emerged from the group that helped to address the research question(s). Information from each source might be considered much like the researcher considers voices in a focus group—individually and collectively (Onwuegbuzie, Dickinson, et al., 2010). If one voice adds an idea or disagrees with an idea, it is important for this voice to be included (Onwuegbuzie, Dickinson, et al., 2010).

Greene et al.'s (1989) typology for providing a rationale for mixing data (quantitative and qualitative) in research methodology helps to distinguish why a literature reviewer might compare and contrast information sources and the themes that emerged to form each section/subsection. These rationales capture the important concepts that were distinguished when we discussed the CLR as methodology in Chapter 1. Building on these rationales in research, a literature reviewer might plan to address some new ideas in writing whereby one theme in an outline is cross-walked with another, which yields new information. When each section/subsection is compared and contrasted, it is clear to see that a final report might reveal added meaning.

TOOL: CROSS-WALKING SECTIONS OF A REPORT

The following ideas for generating interesting sections of a report are based on Greene et al.'s (1989) typology (i.e., *CITED*) to expand meaning and new knowledge by examining one theme or set of findings of the CLR with other themes using ***Complementarity*** (i.e., seek elaboration, illustration, enhancement, and clarification of the information from one source with results from one or more other sources), ***Initiation*** (i.e., discover paradoxes and contradictions that emerge when information from two or more sources are compared that might lead to a reframing of the path of argument that drives the CLR), ***Triangulation*** (i.e., compare information from one source with information from one or more other sources), ***Expansion*** (i.e., expand breadth and range of a CLR by using information from multiple sources within a section for different subsections), and ***Development*** (i.e., use the information from one source to help inform the one or more other sources).

Comparing and contrasting information from different sources allows reviewers to consider additional groupings for added significance or meanings. It is important to remember that these groupings are subject to change, just as your outline will possibly be changed as you begin the first draft. Where differences are found between sets of information, it is helpful to evaluate critically the reasons for the differences such as the setting, the theoretical stance, or the methodology used to generate the information (e.g., qualitative vs. quantitative vs. mixed methodology).

DECISION 9: IDENTIFY GAPS IN THE KNOWLEDGE BASE

When comparing and contrasting multiple sources and themes that emerged from sources, literature reviewers should be cognizant to notice the ideas, concepts, and/or practices that are not discussed. In qualitative research, this concept was described by Charmaz (2005) for addressing the times that participants (individually or collectively) are silent in particular categories. When working to see any areas that were not considered, discussed, or regarded by authors of the works in your topic area or discipline, the critical evaluator begins to document gaps in the knowledge base. In particular, for CLRs that inform primary studies, identifying gaps in the literature often provides the literature reviewer/researcher with a stronger rationale for undertaking a particular study.

EXAMPLE: USING GAPS IN LITERATURE FOR ADDITIONAL MEANING

For example, while comparing and contrasting information in school-based mentoring, Rebecca noticed that few studies delineated cultural nuances or differences. Therefore, she added a section in her CLR entitled "Cultural Differences in Mentoring" (see Figure 10.2, Outline Section VI). She opened the discussion of this section stating that "scant research appears to exist with respect to the role of gender and ethnicity in mentoring relationships" (Frels, 2010, p. 93). The lack of cultural considerations in the information that she reviewed revealed a gap in the literature—which provided a stronger justification for her study and the foundation for her research questions: (a) "What are the differences and similarities in perceptions and experiences of selected school-based mentors as a function of the gender of the mentor?" (b) "What are the differences and similarities in perceptions and experiences of selected school-based mentors as a function of the ethnicity of the mentor?" (c) "What are the differences and similarities in perceptions and experiences of selected school-based mentors in same-gender mentee/mentor pairings versus different-gender mentee/mentor pairings?" and (d) "What are the differences and similarities in perceptions and experiences of selected school-based mentors in same-ethnic mentee/mentor pairings versus different-ethnic mentee/mentor pairings?"

DECISION 10: DETERMINE THE SUMMARY POINTS

When reflecting on the content of each section and subsection, you should explore the possibility of whether a summary is needed. Such a summary would involve restating the inferences and conclusions made in this section/subsection. The longer and more complex the section/subsection is—as often is the case in dissertations where there are little or no page restrictions—the more likely that a summary is needed. Just as the advance organizer allows a reader to become interested and curious about the upcoming points to be made, the summaries of points at key locations provide an additional opportunity for what Kolb (1984) described as reflective observation of a new experience, which lends itself to new ideas, or to modification of existing ideas. Providing a summary also helps readers cognitively to sort and to remember what the reviewer has presented before moving on to the next section/subsection. In the pre-draft-writing phase, or the planning of the written report, this decision might be simply noted by the literature reviewer by reading the outline and noticing the amount of content to be presented in each section/subsection as if he/she had little prior knowledge of what is being written. The literature reviewer might place a note after difficult concepts and/or numerous items presented within a concept as a reminder to "summarize this section" when creating the first draft.

DECISION 11: DETERMINE THE CONCLUSION AND/OR IMPLICATION POINTS

At the same time the reviewer reflects on whether a summary is needed for a section/subsection, he/she should reflect on whether conclusions and/or implications are needed. As is the case for a summary, the longer and more complex the section/subsection is, the more likely that conclusions and/or implications are needed. A conclusion and implication point, however, involves interpretations on the part of the literature reviewer. The *interpretation*, or extension of emergent themes, is similar to what is regarded in the language arts as literary criticism, or the intersecting worlds of the writer and the text and the text and the reader—situated in the premise that no particular view is singly correct.

Mellor and Patterson (2000) introduced the concept of literary interpretation through the works of William Shakespeare to provide insight into the way that knowledge is conveyed and received as an experience within particular places and particular times—all of which indicate and endorse particular values and beliefs about the world. Even though an interpretation is presented as a type of argument for a conclusion and/or implication, as warranted by Mellor and Patterson (2000), it is helpful for both writers and readers to: (a) determine how and for what purpose the interpretation was constructed, and (b) discriminate what makes the interpretation credible for any particular context. If the goal of the CLR was to inform primary research, the conclusions and/or implications that become critical points in the CLR report also might be compared and contrasted to the conclusions and/or implications that stem from the primary research study.

DECISION 12: THEORETICAL, CONCEPTUAL, AND PRACTICAL FRAMEWORKS

Eisenhart (1991) advanced the concept of molding research using theoretical, conceptual, and practical points, or frameworks. Each framework has a unique role to play in the CLR report. Specifically, a *theoretical framework* guides the research process via the use of formal theory "developed by using an established, coherent explanation of certain sorts of phenomena and relationships" (Lester, 2005, p. 458). In contrast, the *conceptual framework* represents "an argument that the concepts chosen for investigation, and any anticipated relationships among them, will be appropriate and useful given the research problem under investigation" (Lester, 2005, p. 460). In contrast still, a *practical framework* "guides research by using 'what works' in the experience of doing something by those directly involved in it" (Lester, 2005, p. 459). Using these definitions, in empirical research studies, theoretical frameworks tend to be most appropriately used in quantitative research studies and mixed research studies when one or more hypotheses are being tested. Contrastingly, conceptual frameworks tend to appear more in qualitative research studies and mixed research studies that are of a more exploratory nature, although conceptual frameworks also can be used in quantitative research studies. Finally, practical frameworks are much less common than are theoretical and conceptual frameworks; however, they can be used in studies representing all three genres. Yet, to establish critical interpretations, conclusions, and/or implications resulting from the CLR, any one of these frameworks is applicable.

EXAMPLE: COMMUNICATING FRAMEWORKS IN THE REPORT

By revisiting the CLR that Rebecca undertook to inform her dissertation research, we distinguish how the literature reviewer might communicate the CLR via guiding frameworks. To inform her interpretations of the CLR on the topic of adult–child school-based mentoring relationships, she utilized a theoretical framework based on Bronfenbrenner's (1979) ecological theory to communicate results on four levels of interaction: (a) the microsystem (Level 1): the immediate environment or setting with which the child or adolescent closely interacts (e.g., classroom, playground, home, recreation center, religious institution); (b) the mesosystem (Level 2): the other systems wherein the child or adolescent spends time, such as family and school; (c) the exosystem (Level 3): the systems by which the child or adolescent might be influenced but of which he/she is not directly a member, including relationships among school teachers, school administrators, and the child/adolescent's parents or other close family members; and (d) the macrosystem (Level 4): the larger cultural milieu surrounding the child or adolescent such as the society or community at large that includes societal worldviews, cultural norms, ideologies, policies, or laws that indirectly impact the child or adolescent. Based on Bronfenbrenner's (1979) theory, conclusions of the CLR could be communicated on a practical level for stakeholders and revealed that:

> Therefore, children who are mentored by adults are affected through each level of environment or system: (a) the immediate environment of classroom, peer group, and family; (b) the connections through mentoring events and other events (i.e., family, classroom, peer group); (c) the impact of the larger environment experienced by families, mentors, school policies, and the community; and (d) the indirect influences of cultures, laws, and belief systems that accompany a child's many environments. (Frels, 2010, p. 7)

EXAMPLE: WRITING/DISPLAYING THE CONCEPTUAL FRAMEWORK

In addition to linking the Dyadic Mentoring Study's CLR results to theory, Rebecca incorporated a conceptual framework so that readers could recognize how her interpretations of information were formed. In the report, she defined her conceptual framework based on Mullen's (2000) concept of comentoring—which accentuates personal experiences, negotiated understanding, and cooperative interactions between a mentor and a mentee as an adaptable, interactive process. Rebecca provided a visual representation of her conceptual framework, which we provide in Figure 10.4 as an example of how to depict complicated concepts, such as a theoretical or conceptual framework, through illustrations. In describing this figure, Rebecca explained to the reader(s):

> As seen [in this figure], the prerequisites of willingness and abilities promote the dyadic exchange between mentee and mentor. Next, interaction and appreciative understanding become overlapping strategies that integrate so that mentoring relationships might create new ideas. This effort, as synergy, increases insight and growth for separate members of the dyad (Conner, 1993). Researchers in the field of SBM [school-based mentoring] have explored changes for mentees, with little focus on changes for mentors, and how dyadic interactions possibly motivate mentors toward *good mentoring*. Through a synergetic comentoring framework, mentoring is viewed as a form of coengagement, reeducation, productivity, and innovation (Mullen, 1999). (Frels, 2010, p. 9)

Conveying the theoretical and/or conceptual framework in visual form is commonplace in literature reviews of the highest quality and is a hallmark of CLRs that contain conceptual frameworks. Indeed, Ravitch and Riggan (2012) provided multiple definitions of a conceptual framework that included the following: "A purely visual representation of a study's organization or major theoretical tenets. Such a representation is usually included within one's literature review, generally as a stand-alone figure" (p. 6). So, as can be seen, in primary research studies, theoretical and/or conceptual frameworks are a very useful "way of linking all of the elements of the research process: researcher disposition, interest, and positionality; literature; and theory and methods" (Ravitch & Riggan, 2012, p. 6). When CLRs serve as stand-alone accounts (i.e., are not used for primary research studies), theoretical and conceptual frameworks often end up being one of the end products of the report. However, both types of frameworks also can drive the CLR write-up. We provide several examples of this type of framing in our final chapter entitled, "Postscript: Theory-Driven and Model-Driven Literature Reviews."

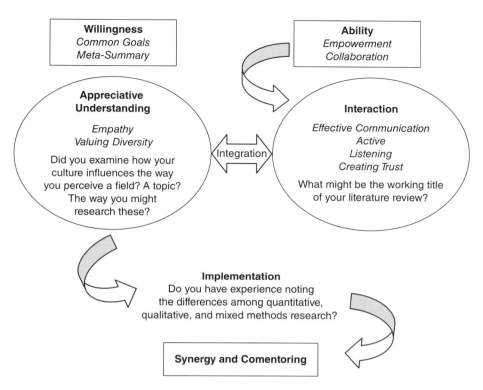

Figure 10.4 A synergetic, comentoring framework for mentoring relationships (Mullen, 1999) interpreted by Frels (2010) for the purpose of her study

Adapted from *The experiences and perceptions of selected mentors: An exploratory study of the dyadic relationship in school-based mentoring*, by R. K. Frels, 2010, unpublished doctoral dissertation, Sam Houston State University, Huntsville, TX, p. 10. Copyright 2010 by R. K. Frels.

Lester's (2005) description of frameworks is further detailed by an examination of theoretical framing in the field of literacy and Dressman's (2007) four schools, or levels of integration: theoretical frame as *foundational platform*, theoretical frame as *focal apparatus*, theoretical frame as *discursive scaffold*, and theoretical frame as *dialectical scaffold*. Consider the description words selected to accentuate the purpose of theory: foundational platform, focal apparatus, discursive scaffold, and dialectical scaffold. Of these four levels and through the use of semantics, it can be reasoned that of the four, the final level—dialectical scaffold—is the most interactive (dialectical) scaffold (supportive instrument for high levels). When using a theoretical frame as solely a foundational platform, theory acts primarily as the basis or justification for initiating the research study itself, as well as to orient readers to the researcher's overall perspective. In such studies, any theory that is discussed in the introductory sections of the report is not presented in the methods sections and only scantily appears—if at all—in the results, discussion, and concluding sections of the report. Such use of theory gives the overall impression that research (or the CLR) is based on, or informed by, theory—thereby indicating that theory played an important role in understanding the plan for the investigation but the theory was not the driving force with respect to the design, analysis, or interpretation and implications of the findings.

In contrast, using a theoretical frame as focal apparatus involves theory as a way of drawing the reader's attention to specific aspects of the study. Typically, in the introduction/literature review section, the description of the framing theory appears in a separate section from the review of the extant literature. The methods and findings sections of the report usually contain little or no reference to the underlying theory. However, the discussion section contains reference to the theory in a meaningful manner so that the reader might be drawn into a new understanding or implication. Such use of theory gives the overall impression that theory also framed the findings; yet, it remains separate from procedural sections in the report.

Conversely, when using a theoretical frame as a discursive (expanding) scaffold, there is extensive reference to theory/theorists, which generally appears throughout most sections of the report. Here, a specific theory is used as the framework not only for the conceptualization of the study but usually for the research design, as well as the report, interpretations, and implications of the findings. Thus, essentially, the theoretical frame is intertwined with the findings and their interpretations. For reports that use a discursive scaffold frame, the findings provide support for the supporting theory. In turn, the theory is used to provide evidence of the generalizability of the results and their interpretations. Such use of theory gives the reader(s) an overall impression of "a unified and well-constructed whole, in which theory and the report's empirical findings exist in symmetry, balance, and harmony" (Dressman, 2007, p. 345).

In stark contrast to other levels of theoretical framing, when using a dialectical scaffold, not only is the theoretical framework explicitly and often extensively delineated, but also it is the driving motivation/explanation for the method, results, and discussion sections of the report. However, rather than the study being characterized by a reciprocal relationship between theory and the data—as is the case for discursive scaffold theoretical frames—"the relationship between the empirical aspects of the report and its theoretical framework is agonistic" (Dressman, 2007, p. 345). This positioning of theory reveals discourse and contradictions, and can seem at times combative to delineating findings. Yet, similar to the way that music must have highs and lows, sound reasoning must avoid using the premise rhetoric for justifying the argument.

This notion of circular thinking is referred to as *petitio principii*, or begging of the question, whereby the argument takes for granted the very same premise that it seeks to demonstrate. Barker (1989) used the example of how a person who wants to become more skillful at playing chess should study both the shrewd moves of experts and also the poor moves of novice players. By recognizing times of poor reasoning, it is more likely that a literature reviewer can avoid the mistake of fallacy, or the logical mistake in reasoning, that is tempting to make. Likewise, a dialectical scaffold level of theoretical framework in presenting the CLR also can address critical thinking skills, or constructive criticism for embracing disagreement, debate, dissonance, difference, divergence, and dialogue, as outlined by Onwuegbuzie (2012) as effective mixed methods thinking. Further, it is not unusual for a study, including a CLR, to include two or more theoretical frames that compete against each other and the findings. Alternatively, the theory is used to challenge existing interpretations of empirical phenomena; alternatively still, the data are used to challenge theoretical tenets. Such use of theory gives the overall impression to the reader not of certainty and coherence, but of uncertainty and tension. Although all four levels of theory are viable ways to frame empirical research studies, the discursive scaffold and dialectical scaffold levels represent the two most extensive ways to integrate theory throughout the report. As such, we recommend aligning strongly a theoretical framework in one of these two ways when planning the CLR report, whenever possible.

DECISION 13: LINKING INFORMATION AND FRAMEWORKS

Once the guiding theoretical, conceptual, and/or practical framework has been created and noted in sections/subsections of the report—assuming that at least one of these frameworks is relevant for the CLR report—reviewers should identify the relationships among works that relate to and promote the selected framework, as well as those that do not. Relating the collected and synthesized information to the selected framework would clarify the argument and conclusions of the literature reviewer and highlight some other ways of thinking about emerging ideas and concepts. Moreover, consider the theoretical and/or conceptual framework as a potential pathway for defining ambiguous terms. The outline such as the one illustrated in Figure 10.4 should be revisited after deciding how the information sheds light on the guiding framework(s) and how the frameworks clarify and juxtapose concepts revealed in the synthesis and individual works. By reflecting on some of the questions that arose when undertaking the challenge of "using theory-colored glasses" and re-examining your efforts, the outline might be amended so that the selected framework becomes more transparent and warranted for a holistic interpretation and argument.

DECISION 14: ENDING THE REPORT

Another important decision to make is how effectively to conclude the CLR report. The metaphor of a conversation between two people in the case can be helpful. When ending an important conversation, both parties have integrated new learning, and depending on a person's own life experiences and values, each person processes and accommodates former thoughts and feelings with new thoughts and feelings—to some degree. Yet, because a writer/reader relationship is asynchronous, the role of the writer is to provide transparency of guiding frameworks and perspective so that the reader might experience somewhat the same process of learning. Therefore, before ending this imaginary conversation with another person, consider what you want to stand out most in that person's mind as a result of the entire experience. This final ending beckons the question: What is different as a result of this experience/review?

As such, the literature reviewer might revisit the initial goal for the CLR (i.e., to stand alone or to inform primary research). Next, the literature reviewer should consider the original message and frameworks that center this message for creating the *thesis sentence*, or the message of intent that was originally composed. It is important to revisit continually the thesis and use it as a guiding force for subsequent writing. We offer some potential endings for the CLR report that pertain to a stand-alone literature review and which inform primary research.

REPORTS THAT INFORM PRIMARY RESEARCH. For literature reviews written as part of a primary research report, an effective and very common way of ending is by critically identifying the gap in the body of knowledge that most closely relates to the reviewer's primary research study. This gap would provide the overall rationale for the primary research study. As surmised by Onwuegbuzie and Daniel (2005), the most common rationale is that few or no researchers have undertaken the study that the review will undertake (if the CLR is part of a some type of research proposal such as a dissertation research proposal or a grant proposal) or has undertaken (if the study has been completed)—providing one or more citations, if possible.

The second most common rationale is that although several/many researchers have conducted the study, few or no researchers have studied the topic using the (proposed) population, instrument, setting, site, or the like. The third most common rationale is that although several/many researchers have undertaken the study, the findings have been mixed (Onwuegbuzie & Daniel, 2005). In providing the rationale of the study, reviewers should be cognizant to reveal whether any studies exist that have addressed the same issue as they intend to address. If not, or if only a few studies exist, then this would make their statement of the rationale even more powerful. An alternative way of ending the CLR report is by delineating the educational significance of the primary research study. The educational significance statement(s) makes clear to readers the "So what?" question for the primary research study.

EXAMPLE: COMPOSING A SIGNIFICANCE STATEMENT

In the Dyadic Mentoring Study and within Rebecca's summary section, the following statement was included to link the report to educational significance:

> In conclusion, my study is important for schools participating in mentoring programs because greater understanding of mentors should reveal ways to implement quality mentor training with respect to mentors' motives, sense of empowerment, and

identities. Research and emphasis on the relational aspect of mentoring resonates with the call for a paradigm shift toward the relational processes of mentoring, taking into account ethnicity factors, cultural differences, and gender roles of mentors. Indeed, by understanding the interactions of mentors and mentees within the dyadic relationship, schools might implement programs that both encourage mentors and support mentoring goals for student success. (Frels, 2010, p. 102)

WHEN THE GOAL OF THE CLR IS TO STAND ALONE. For literature reviews written as stand-alone reports, a common method is to provide directions for future research. Much like the CLR endings for informing primary research, the stand-alone CLR might critically examine gaps and contradictions in the state of research for a topic or discipline that warrants a new positioning or approach. It might be helpful to re-examine the conclusions and/or implications with any overall persuasive or clarifying points that extend your position. In fact, similar to ways in which primary research targets evidence-based practices for stakeholder wants and needs, the CLR can likewise address best practices as translational research "aimed at enhancing the adoption of best practices in the community" (National Institutes of Mental Health, 2007, subsection 1). Remember, when deciding on the ending for the CLR report, clarity of reasoning is key. It is not sufficient merely to declare that "more research is needed." Rather, the CLR should reveal specific directions for future research—directions that, if pursued, would advance the body of knowledge on the topic.

THE ART OF ARGUMENT

Before beginning to write the first draft of a report, it is helpful to review how effective writers create an effective or **valid argument**. Salmon (1973) provided insight into the scope of logic in reasoning and advocated that "when we attempt to complete the arguments we encounter, we bring to light the assumptions that would be required to make them logically correct" (p. 48). He offers three preliminary steps to avoid contradiction and to accept beliefs that can be adequately defended in discourse:

1. Arguments should be recognized so that unsupported statements must be distinguished from conclusions of arguments.
2. When an argument is disclosed, the premises and conclusions must be identified.
3. If an argument is incomplete, the missing premises must be supplied.

Before writing the sections that are outlined in this planning phase of Step 7, a literature reviewer should take some time (but not too much time) for incubation on the plan sketched out. Oftentimes in research, this time allows for you to detach emotionally from the ideas and formatting of ideas so that when you come back to them, you might see them as if you are seeing them for the first time.

Effective writers begin the creative process of putting ideas into words by outlining the content of each chapter and section. Before tackling the first draft, writers might create a short paragraph describing each section/subsection so that they might envision the final picture and how this one picture might move to the next. After creating this outline and verbally describing each section, a writer is "free to move around the pieces until all of the parts fit together" (Johnson & Mullen, 2007, p. 100). As an outline or plan for the report is considered, it is important to remember that the qualities of **parsimony**: economy of words that should be used so that this practice extends to every level—words, ideas, assumptions, key points—enabling writing to be clear, concise, and spare without sacrificing thoroughness and completeness (especially when providing a rationale or premise for stated propositions, positions, or arguments). With this sentence, we decided to end with "enough said."

CONCLUSIONS

Much like good research, the planning of a literature review report requires forethought and intention—keeping the overall goal and intended audience in mind. The communication phase of the literature review also involves anticipating reactions, questions, and potential responses. In fact, the pre-draft-writing stage also might serve as a way to perform a type of self-check of belief

TOOL: A CHECKLIST FOR DECISIONS (BEFORE WRITING)

Table 10.1 presents a summary of the decisions outlined in the pre-draft-writing stage of Step 7 for communicating the CLR.

Table 10.1   Summary table of decisions made at the pre-draft-writing stage for communicating the CLR

Decision	Label
1	Determine the goal
2	Determine the intended outlet
3	Determine the intended audience
4	Revisit belief systems
5	Create an outline
6	Determine information, sources, and MODES
7	Decide the emphasis of information, sources, and MODES
8	Compare and contrast information sources
9	Identify gaps in the knowledge base
10	Determine the summary points
11	Determine the conclusion and/or implication points
12	Disclose the theoretical, conceptual, and/or practical framework
13	Determine relationships between information and frameworks
14	Determine the report ending

systems. This self-check occurs by examining how you might emphasize more strongly particular findings and the way in which you situate alternate views. Some findings and ideas can be difficult to describe, and the AVOW pathways (i.e., **A**ct/perform, **V**isualize, **O**rally present, **W**rite) provide creative alternatives for meaningful ways to communicate some complex findings. As we have mentioned throughout the seven steps, the CLR is a mixed research approach, and like mixed research, decisions at the planning stage begin with the end goal in mind. Other decisions such as intended outlet, audience, negotiating belief systems, and personal communication style impact *the way* we organize and report the CLR. Like mixed research,

any two literature reviewers might approach the CLR process differently. Yet, by clearly communicating each of the seven steps, each pathway for communicating is warranted and transparent. By remembering Greene et al.'s (1989) typology of rationales for conducting mixed research, such as triangulation (i.e., comparing information among sources) and initiation (i.e., recognizing contradictions among sources), a reviewer can create a report that honors multiple perspectives and critical interpretations.

In the planning of the report, it is important to stay focused on your main point, or argument, and how you plan to present this case. You will be sharing both some of the methodological decisions and criteria that led you to particular results as well as the topic's most useful points. You should organize yourself by talking out loud the main points of your ideas, justified by the steps that you took to arrive at them and the evidence that you synthesized.

In this chapter, the following important concepts are presented as an overview of the planning phase of Step 7 for disseminating the findings of the CLR:

- Literature reviewers might consider not only the use of a speech to perform ideas, but also multiple venues associated with communicating a CLR report using the acronym AVOW: Act, Visualize, Orally present, and Write.
- The CLR should be communicated so that it is focused on overall goal(s) and guiding question(s).
- The literature reviewer should communicate in a way that establishes credibility, trust, rapport, and value.
- The outline created in the planning phase should yield a logical, consistent, and clear pattern of discoveries/concepts that form a point of view or synthesis, which essentially is the reviewer's reasoning pattern or the premises for an upcoming conclusion.
- Before writing the CLR report, the literature reviewer should revisit the initial goal for the CLR (i.e., to inform primary research or to stand alone) because each goal leads to different elements in the report.
- Literature reviewers should confirm their intended outlets for their CLR report and how best to convey results to stakeholders.
- The outline created in the pre-draft-writing phase should yield a logical, consistent, and clear pattern of discoveries/concepts that form a point of view or synthesis.
- A theoretical, conceptual, and/or practical framework should guide the writing process.

Next, in Chapter 11: Presenting the CLR Written Report, we move your well-thought-out and documented plan into the active writing process.

CHAPTER 10 EVALUATION CHECKLIST

CORE	Guiding Questions and Tasks
Critical Examination	To what extent did you identify the audience and relevant needs relating to the topic area?
Organization	To what extent did you respond to the decisions for planning an effective presentation?
	To what extent did you create the outline and to what extent did you include the audit trail pieces of your process?
Reflections	To what extent did you base your outline and section paragraphs on one or more frameworks?
	To what extent did you come to any new understandings of how your argument might evolve?
Evaluation	Present your ideas to a peer or colleague in a structured talk using your outline. Ask your listener to restate some of your points so that you might evaluate if what you stated is the same point(s) that were received.

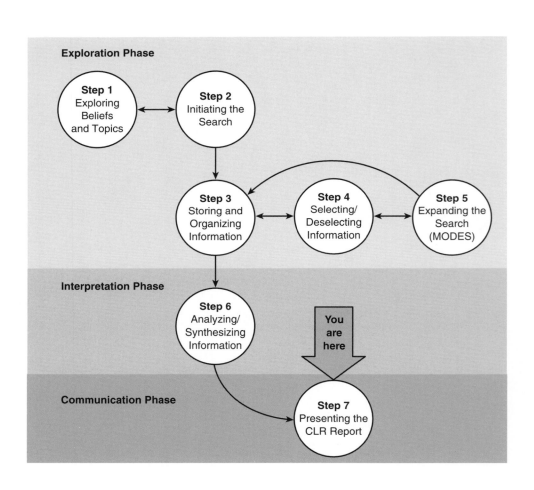

11

STEP 7: PRESENTING THE CLR WRITTEN REPORT

CHAPTER 11 ROADMAP

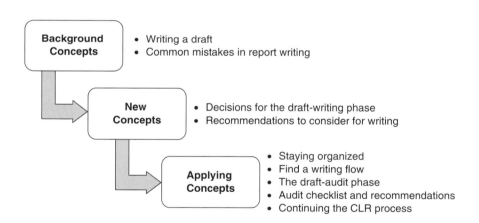

Background Concepts
- Writing a draft
- Common mistakes in report writing

New Concepts
- Decisions for the draft-writing phase
- Recommendations to consider for writing

Applying Concepts
- Staying organized
- Find a writing flow
- The draft-audit phase
- Audit checklist and recommendations
- Continuing the CLR process

BACKGROUND CONCEPTS

Consider the quest of an investigative reporter or journalist who conducts a thorough investigation of a story. First, a journalist might select a story based on knowledge and beliefs; yet, the story must be of interest to the community. Often, without knowing, the journalist uses personal hunches that related directly to a worldview (Step 1). He/she investigates the background on the story, which is much like the way a literature reviewer searches databases (Step 2), and then logically organizes and stores artifacts and information in some way, which is much like Step 3. As an ethical journalist, sources and information are checked for credibility of facts so that only reliable sources are used, which parallels Step 4 of the CLR, selecting/deselecting documents.

When a journalist follows any additional leads after an initial investigation, he/she is expanding sources (Step 5) in a way that is inclusive of the MODES (Media, Observation[s], Documents, Expert[s], Secondary data). Much like Step 6 of the CLR, a journalist analyzes and synthesizes information in a logical manner to be reported to an interested audience. Finally, a journalist has a professional and ethical responsibility to report the story by disclosing one or more perspectives so that the audience might have the opportunity to integrate knowledge of the issue without unwarranted bias (parallel to CLR Step 7: Presenting the CLR Report).

Of all these steps, reporting with credibility is the most important step with respect to a journalist's integrity, trustworthiness, and career. No matter how credible and important the story might be, if the journalist does not communicate clearly, then the journalist's efforts are wasted, as is the important findings. The acts of technical writing and systematic evaluation of the writing are the focus of the remainder of this chapter.

WRITING A DRAFT

The writing process requires both skill and practice. Acquiring the skills to write, much like learning a musical instrument, requires motivation, time, and patience. Hopefully, throughout the first six steps of your CLR process, if you adhered to the reflective journaling at the end of each step, you have recognized some growth within yourself for putting your thoughts onto paper. As you begin to shift into the technical writing process of Step 7, you should expect that you will create many drafts of your report. That is, you will write a draft and rework it several times, oftentimes making a decision to accept one version of a section as a finished product and moving to the next section to meet a deadline for completion.

COMMON MISTAKES IN REPORT WRITING

The characteristics noted earlier, much like characteristics involved in any art, must be used in balance with each other. Writers of the CLR report might make some of the traditional mistakes that are made by inexperienced writers. For example, a writer might make the mistake of providing too many details of a concept, which could lead the reader to a new thought, or to become off task. Details are important for painting a picture; yet, in technical writing, *parsimony*, or the concept of *economy with words*, should be foremost in a writer's mind. For situations where the CLR writer believes that more background information might be needed for readers who are new to the topic or concept, in lieu of a detailed and potentially distracting description in the CLR report, he/she could provide them with one or more relevant citations/references obtained from her/his set of supplemental sources established at Step 4 which they could consult if they are interested. We expand this point in a future section entitled "Refer to Additional Sources."

Balancing just how many details are needed to keep a description from being static lends itself to expanding your vocabulary, and comes about by revisiting what you write (editing) often. Yet, the flow of writing and the editing of writing must maintain a type of balance so that this creative endeavor might evolve. It is also quite common to experience the dreaded concept known as *writer's block*, which, in western societies, is the term used to describe not knowing either where to begin or how to proceed in the creative effort of communicating through the written words. It is defined in Merriam-Webster (n.d.) as a "psychological inhibition preventing a writer from proceeding with a piece" (http://www.merriam-webster.com/dictionary/writer's block). Common blocks might be due to a lack of confidence, motivation, or inspiration, or distractive thoughts. Another common mistake made by inexperienced writers is failing to recognize the degree of authority that they have on the topic or subject area. We recommend that you begin with many details, and edit some of them as you revise or rework the first draft.

Another common mistake of inexperienced writers is failing to risk rephrasing ideas in their own words. This mistake leads to many shifts of voice, tone, and movement in writing and a poor flow of words. Too often, inexperienced writers will provide paraphrase after paraphrase, yielding lack of argument and position. In the attempt to provide details, inexperienced writers default to the use of many quotations, which make the report choppy and incoherent. Inexperienced writers might use quotations due to a lack of understanding of exactly what an author might mean, or due to a lack of confidence that it can be restated accurately. We discuss recommendations relating to auditing each draft to avoid overusing quotations later in this chapter.

Also, we provide recommendations later in this chapter to address the writing error of *plagiarism*, or the failure to restate *originally* an author's idea. Some inexperienced writers believe that if they use a thesaurus and replace one or two words, then they have avoided plagiarism. Yet, plagiarism also applies to the original author's sentence structure. Confidence for the act of writing might be more present for some writers than for others, due either to past learning experiences or to cognitive verbal skills in vocabulary, syntax, persuasive style, or communication elements. Yet, allowing the words to flow freely with rich descriptions will be the foundation for which the form, structure, order, focus, coherence, and rhythm will emerge. Later in this chapter, we discuss other pitfalls that lead to plagiarism, with recommendations for avoiding it in the draft-audit phase.

In academic writing, it is common for inexperienced writers to wonder which sentences require a reference, or to credit to the original source and/or other relevant sources. Some concepts might seem to be generally known in a field; yet, these general concepts also should be evaluated for reference(s). A general rule is that most statements should be justified by one or more references to provide context and credit for the fact that is being presented. Exceptions to the rule would be if the statement were your own opinion or a principle that is generally agreed upon regardless of field or culture, such as that the earth rotates around the sun or that people are cognitive, emotional, and social beings. We will expand on other common mistakes of inexperienced writers throughout this chapter.

DECISIONS FOR THE DRAFT-WRITING PHASE

Much like the multiple decisions that a literature reviewer makes as a researcher of literature, the draft-writing phase requires critical decisions for moving from abstract ideas to articulating these ideas through writing. We refer to the writing process as the draft-writing phase (doing the writing) and the draft-audit phase (systematic evaluation of what you do).

NEW CONCEPTS

So that we do not lose sight of our own purpose and focus of Step 7 (as explained above), we move you into the decisions to consider as you begin the first and subsequent drafts of the CLR report. We provide some recommendations too for the draft-writing process that should help you with *good writing*. Also, throughout the remainder of this chapter, we provide examples, tools, and some common mistakes made in composing a report, with recommendations for addressing them.

TOOL: ESTABLISHING THE FOCUS FOR THE REPORT

As previously mentioned, and as each draft becomes an improved and more focused product, these phases become a seamless process. The writing *process* involves development and progression of the ***pre-draft outline***, which was a focus for Chapter 10, and moves from the form of an abstract picture into a final, focused snapshot of the CLR, which is presented in Figure 11.1.

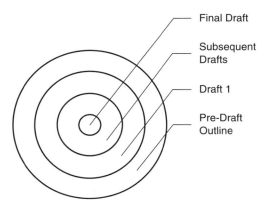

Figure 11.1 The draft writing process toward a focused, polished final report

Each draft version is a result of the decisions made by the reviewer, reflecting on these decisions, and evaluating these decisions. We begin the draft-writing phase with a list of critical decisions, or considerations, and some related recommendations for launching the writing process.

RECOMMENDATIONS TO CONSIDER FOR WRITING

RECOMMENDATION 1: BEGIN WITH BROAD KNOWLEDGE

An extremely effective way of writing the CLR is using what is called a funnel shape approach, more commonly known as the **V-shape approach** (Onwuegbuzie & Frels, 2012c). This approach involves reviewers organizing their CLR reports such that the references to sources that are least related to the topic are discussed first, and the most related references are discussed last. This V-shape approach would almost guarantee that the CLR report flows logically.

EXAMPLE: USING A V-SHAPE APPROACH

In examining the purposes and approaches of selected mentors in school-based mentoring, Frels, Onwuegbuzie, et al. (2013) began their CLR by discussing the importance of connectedness for promoting positive youth development. Next, these authors noted that the importance of connectedness has led to school-based mentoring programs being established that match students with community mentors; however, they point out that, often, mentoring programs have been created too quickly and, thus, do not include many of the components that are effective for mentors in establishing longer-lasting mentoring relationships. In the closing paragraph of the

CLR, Frels, Onwuegbuzie, et al. (2013) cite three studies conducted by Dr. Renee Spencer (Boston University) (Spencer, 2004, 2006, 2007) examining the outcomes of relationships between mentors and mentees, which represent studies that were the closest to their study, and highlight the gap that they had identified during their CLR, leading to the major rationale of their study: "Even though mentoring programs have been examined with respect to positive or negative outcomes, researchers have not addressed adequately *how* mentors contribute toward the dyadic exchange for successful or unsuccessful relationships" (p. 618).

RECOMMENDATION 2: SPECIFY DATABASES AND HITS

Surprisingly, very few reviewers specify the databases used in the search (e.g., library subscription databases, Internet sources). Further, very few reviewers specify the number of hits. Yet, such information is very useful not only for contextualizing the underlying topic but also for explicating the gap in the literature and, hence, establishing the path of argumentation regarding the rationale of the study.

EXAMPLE: HOW TO DISCLOSE SEARCH ITEMS

Frels, Onwuegbuzie, et al.'s (2013) statement below provides an example of the utility of this information:

> Even though mentoring programs have been examined with respect to positive or negative outcomes, researchers have not addressed adequately *how* mentors contribute toward the dyadic exchange for successful or unsuccessful relationships. In addition, qualitative inquiry in the field of mentoring research is scant—as noted by R. K. Frels (2010) in a review of literature specifically focused in the area of youth/ adult mentoring relationships—with only seven articles including a qualitative component of a total of 47 SBM articles discovered across several bibliographic databases: Academic Search Premier (EBSCOhost),

Education Full-Text (WilsonWeb), ERIC (EBSCOhost), and PsycINFO (EBSCOhost). (pp. 618–619)

RECOMMENDATION 3: SPECIFY THE ANALYSIS USED

As noted previously, in Chapter 9, we provided a meta-framework containing an array of qualitative, quantitative, and mixed analysis approaches, methods, and techniques for analyzing and synthesizing CLR information. We recommend that reviewers delineate the analysis that they used.

EXAMPLE: HOW TO DISCLOSE THE ANALYSIS

Even if the reviewer has a relatively small signature space to provide the CLR write-up, he/she can provide this information in one sentence, as did Frels and Onwuegbuzie (2012b):

> Specifically, we coded each work using constant comparison analysis and determined that supportive components of mentoring models could be direct or indirect and dyads were influenced mostly through indirect support such as: the length of the relationship; mentors recognizing social, emotional, cognitive, and behavioral factors of mentees; mentors promoting positive perceptions with mentees; mentoring time that was process-based and not results based; mentors treating mentees as equals; and collaboration in the dyad. (p. 184)

RECOMMENDATION 4: COMPARE DEFINITIONS

A ***constitutive definition*** is a formal definition (e.g., dictionary definition) wherein a term is defined by using other terms. This form of definition involves the defining of concepts in abstract terms. In contrast, an operational definition provides a definition of a concept that is very specific in meaning in terms of the operations by which it is measured or assessed. Further, an ***operational definition*** ascribes meaning to a concept by specifying the operations that must be performed in order to measure or to manipulate the concept. The overall purpose of an operational definition is to delimit a term, to ensure that everyone concerned understands the particular way in which a term is being used. Moreover, providing an operational definition allows researchers to move from the level of concepts, constructs, and theory to the level of observation, upon which science is based.

By comparing constitutive definitions and operational definitions, some misperceptions can be averted. For example, in attempting to argue that some form of generalization occurs in *all* qualitative research studies—contrary to some qualitative researchers (cf. Williams, 2000) who claim that generalization is not an issue in qualitative research—Onwuegbuzie and Collins (2014) provided a constitutive definition of the word *generalization*, as follows:

> According to the American Heritage College Dictionary (1993, p. 567), to generalize is "to reduce to a general form, class, or law" and "to draw inferences or a general conclusion from." As such, a generalization represents "an act or an instance of generalizing" (the American Heritage College Dictionary, 1993, p. 567). Thus, the terms *generalize*, *generalization*, and *generalizations* transcend research in general and research traditions in particular. These terms do not represent either quantitative terms or qualitative terms. Indeed, generalizations have occurred since ancient times. (p. 652)

RECOMMENDATION 5: DISTINGUISH NOTABLE WORKS

Another important practice that helps reviewers to establish the path of argumentation is by distinguishing or making clear the ***notable works*** — classic or landmark works—from regular ones. This can be accomplished by using terms like *seminal, landmark, groundbreaking, pivotal, pioneering, classic, influential, prominent, far-reaching, innovative, cutting edge, original, leading*, and *well-cited* when describing these works. Also, reviewers should make it clear what their unique contributions are.

RECOMMENDATION 6: PROVIDE A TOPIC TIMELINE

Another useful strategy is to provide a timeline for the topic. That is, it is useful for reviewers to specify the onset of the topic, problem, or concept. Unfortunately, this information is not always readily available. Therefore, one way to obtain this historical information is by adding words like *history*, *origin*, and *onset* to the search string.

EXAMPLE: CREATING A HISTORY TIMELINE

For example, to obtain information about the history of mentoring, a reviewer can use a search string such as the following:

> mentor and (history or origin or onset)

When this search string was used via the Dogpile metasearch engine, the following link (of many useful links) was revealed: http://www.behindthename.com/name/mentor. This link provided a brief history of the concept of *mentor*. Interestingly, Frels (2010) described this history as follows:

> *Mentor* was a major figure in the legendary Homeric epic (Homer, 1969) of the Trojan War when Ulysses (Odysseus), King of Ithaca, departed to declare war on the Trojans. Ulysses left his infant son (Telemachus) in the hands of his friend Mentor. Hence, Mentor was responsible not only for the boy's education, but also for the shaping of his character, the wisdom of his decisions, and the clarity and steadfastness of his purpose in life. When Ulysses's son grew into manhood, he began searching for his father, and Mentor went with him. Mentor's role was embellished by the fact that Athena, the supreme goddess of the Greeks, also intermittently transformed into the form of Mentor, especially when Telemachas appeared confused or needed to make a decision. Hence, mentoring appeared to be a gift from the gods. (p. 61) [emphasis in original]

Knowing the origin of a concept helps the reviewer appropriately to provide a timeline and historical context for it.

RECOMMENDATION 7: PROVIDE SPECIFICS FOR THE TIMELINE(S)

A CLR write-up becomes more transparent and warranted as the reviewer provides more specificity. This specificity is even more important when providing a timeframe. For instance, it was much more informative in the dyadic mentoring study to state "Since the 1980s, nomenclature of mentoring programs has contained many dimensions across various disciplines" (p. 60)—than to make a statement such as the following: "For many years, nomenclature of mentoring programs has contained many dimensions across various disciplines." The latter statement likely would lead readers to ask: How long is *many years*?; and What years are being referenced? Clearly, reviewers should avoid invoking these types of questions on the part of the readers.

RECOMMENDATION 8: DOCUMENT THE EVOLUTION OF IDEAS

When citing a leading author in a field that has a long history, it is essential that reviewers provide information about the development of the thinking and the ideas of authors in the topic area.

EXAMPLE: EXAMINING AUTHOR DEVELOPMENT OF IDEAS

For instance, returning to our mentoring example, if a reviewer was interested in writing a section on self-efficacy of mentees, then it would make sense to cite Albert Bandura, who conceptualized both social learning theory and the construct of self-efficacy—and who is among the 10 most influential psychologists ever (Cherry, 2010) and the fourth most-frequently cited psychologist of all time (Haggbloom, 2002), with approximately 340,000 citations at the time of writing. Bandura has spent more than 63 years authoring works (i.e., since 1952). And naturally, his theory of self-efficacy (and social learning theory) has evolved over these years. Thus, before citing any of Bandura's works, reviewers should familiarize themselves with his major publications, comparing and contrasting his earlier works on self-efficacy (e.g., Bandura, 1962) to his later works (e.g., Bandura, 1997; Benight & Bandura, 2004), while considering questions such as: What are the similarities? What are the differences? And how has Bandura's original theory evolved over time? Making such a comparison is an important feature of a CLR report!

RECOMMENDATION 9: REFERENCE DISSENTING WORKS

It is essential that reviewers search thoroughly for authors who criticize ideas, conceptualizations, theories, findings, or interpretations of source authors, however popular they are and how much historical validity exists.

EXAMPLE: PROVIDING ALTERNATIVE VIEWS

For example, has any author criticized Bandura's (1962, 1997) self-efficacy theory? Box 11.1 provides an example of citing *dissenting works* and documenting the argument over time, which was presented by Onwuegbuzie and Levin (2005, p. 11). As ethical researchers, it is essential to present dissenting works that are identified as such in order to prevent readers from assuming that there is unanimity among authors/researchers regarding the underlying idea, conceptualization, theory, finding, interpretation, or the like. Moreover, citing dissenting works can help to strengthen the rationale of the reviewer's primary research study. In such cases, the reviewer should point out this rationale in the CLR report, further specifying the (emergent) educational significance such as that "it was hoped that the findings that emanated from the primary study would help to settle the debate."

RECOMMENDATION 10: REFER TO ADDITIONAL SOURCES

There are times when reviewers can only mention an issue that is related but not central to the underlying

BOX 11.1

EXCERPT FROM ONWUEGBUZIE AND LEVIN'S (2005) ARTICLE PROVIDING AN EXAMPLE OF CONTRASTING PERSPECTIVES BETWEEN AUTHORS

Criticizing Robinson and Levin's (1997) two-step model, Cahan (2000) argued that the inferential statistical test and the corresponding effect size are technically unrelated procedures. According to Cahan, the two-step approach is valid only if the statistical significance or nonsignificance of observed effects provides information about the amount of error included. Cahan noted that: (a) statistically nonsignificant effects do not necessarily consist entirely or mostly of noise, and can be error-free; and (b) statistically significant effects are not necessarily error-free, nor do they necessarily contain a trivial amount of random error. Thus, statistically significant effects are not necessarily "real" and can be due mostly to error. As such, Cahan concluded that the logic of the two-step approach, which assumes a negative relationship between the statistical significance of observed effects and the amount of random error contained, is flawed.

Levin and Robinson (2000) countered Cahan's (2000) criticism of their two-step model by arguing that null hypothesis significance testing and effect-size estimation *are* both "conceptually and functionally related" (p. 35). Levin and Robinson further contended that if researchers maintain a logical connection between hypothesis-testing and effect-size estimation at the analytical and interpretational stages of quantitative studies, they would be fostering what they call "conclusion coherence" (p. 35), or consistency between researchers' formal statistical analyses and their verbal conclusions based on those analyses. According to Levin and Robinson (1999), many examples exist wherein researchers who analyze data with small sample sizes in the absence of *p*-values over-interpret their effect sizes. Indeed, Levin (1998a) stated:

> In its extreme form, [such action] degenerates to strong conclusions about differential treatment efficacy that are based on comparing a single score of one participant in one treatment condition with that of another participant in a different condition. (p. 45)

In support of Robinson and Levin's assertions (i.e., Levin, 1998a; Levin & Robinson, 1999, 2003; Robinson & Levin, 1997; Wainer & Robinson, 2003), Fan (2001) demonstrated through Monte Carlo sampling that an observed finding that appears to have substantive significance (i.e., a large effect size) actually could be the result of sampling error, thereby making any resultant conclusions unreliable and potentially misleading. Based on his findings, Fan recommended that information about both statistical significance and effect sizes be reported for observed findings:

> Statistical significance testing and effect size are two related sides that together make a coin; they complement each other but do not substitute for one another. Good research practice requires that, for making sound quantitative decisions in educational research, both sides should be considered. (p. 275)

Adapted from "Strategies for aggregating the statistical nonsignificant outcomes of a single study," by A. J. Onwuegbuzie and J. R. Levin, 2005, *Research in the Schools, 12*(1), p. 11. Copyright 2005 by Mid-South Educational Research Association.

topic. Reasons for only a brief mention of an issue might be due to space constraints or not to distract readers unduly. In such cases, reviewers should refer readers to other works that they believe might be of interest to them—including works that are classic, seminal, influential, and well-cited and *pass* the Evaluation Criteria presented in Step 4 of the Seven-Step Model.

EXAMPLE: HOW TO LEAD READERS TO ADDITIONAL INFORMATION

A common way of referring readers is by using statements such as "For a more detailed discussion, see, for example, Author (20xx)…"

Alternatively, the statements can be made in parentheses either as a stand-alone sentence (to minimize distraction), or at the end of a sentence as part of sentence, as follows: "Whenever possible, mentors should be familiar with mentoring best practices (see, e.g., Frels, 2010)."

However, the most efficient way to refer readers to one or more works is via, in parentheses, inserting the Latin abbreviation "cf." which means "compare." For example, in the last sentence of their opening paragraph, Frels, Onwuegbuzie, et al. (2013) stated the following: "Often, mentoring programs are created hastily without a full understanding of the program components that are effective for mentors and those components that increase the likelihood that mentors dedicate themselves for longer-lasting mentoring relationships (cf. Spencer, 2007)" (p. 618). These authors used **the abbreviation "cf."** because the creation of mentoring programs was not a central aspect of their CLR, although it was pertinent to their research topic. The "cf." was an encouragement for interested readers to consult Spencer (2007) to obtain more information.

RECOMMENDATION 11: PROVIDE ONE OR MORE CITATION MAPS

Citation maps represent a useful way to document the relationship among authors' ideas, conceptualizations, theories, findings, and interpretations at different times and across different disciplines, as well as to identify covert linkages among the origins of an idea, its development, claims associated with the idea, evidence generated to support the claims, warrant that links the evidence claim and evidence, and context and assumptions used to provide justification (i.e., validity/legitimation) for the warrant and evidence (Hart, 2005). These maps can be expressed as a narrative or visually depicted (e.g., table, figure, graph, matrices, charts, networks, lists, and Venn diagrams). Creating citation maps forces reviewers to be even more reflexive about the works that they have extracted via MODES, as well as providing "the geography of research and thinking that have been done on a topic" (Hart, 2005, p. 144). As surmised by Hart, these citation maps help reviewers to identify what is known, when it was known, what methods were used, and by whom. As such, citation mapping represents a useful method for presenting an overview of the topic.

EXAMPLE: CITATION MAPS

Table 11.1 presents the example of a citation map presented in the Dyadic Mentoring Study. Using a spreadsheet like Microsoft Excel, such information can be converted to a chart, as in Figure 11.2.

Table 11.1 Partial chronologically ordered citation map of the first 18 of the 47 works (Frels, 2010)

	Author(s)	Date of Publication
1	Tierney, Grossman, & Resch	1995
2	Rhodes, Haight, &. Briggs	1999
3	Barton-Arwood, Jolivette, & Massey	2000
4	Rhodes, Grossman, & Resch	2000
5	Roberts	2000
6	Lucas	2001
7	DuBois, Holloway, Valentine, & Cooper	2002
8	Grossman & Rhodes	2002
9	King, Vidourek, Davis, & McClellan	2002
10	Parra, DuBois, Neville, & Pugh-Lilly	2002
11	Reid	2002
12	Rhodes	2002
13	Ryan, Whittaker, & Pinckney	2002
14	Bennetts	2003
15	Karcher & Lindwall	2003
16	Spencer	2004
17	DuBois & Karcher	2005
18	Karcher	2005

Adapted from *The experiences and perceptions of selected mentors: An exploratory study of the dyadic relationship in school-based mentoring*, by R. K. Frels, 2010, unpublished doctoral dissertation, Sam Houston State University, Huntsville, TX, p. 53. Copyright 2010 by R. K. Frels.

In addition to citation maps, a literature reviewer should consider using one or more of the following *displays* to communicate results in the report: feature maps, tree diagrams, summary record sheets, worksheets, linear relationship maps, content maps, taxonomic maps, compositional characteristic maps, concept maps, and

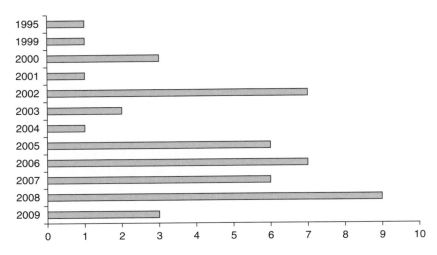

Figure 11.2 Number of articles that met Frels's (2010) guiding criteria and years published. The year 2009 was incomplete due to the time gap from submission to publication and accessibility of articles

Adapted from *The experiences and perceptions of selected mentors: An exploratory study of the dyadic relationship in school-based mentoring*, by R. K. Frels, 2010, unpublished doctoral dissertation, Sam Houston State University, Huntsville, TX, p. 53. Copyright 2010 by R. K. Frels.

semantic maps. As is the case for Miles and Huberman's (1994) displays that were mapped onto the CLR process (see Chapter 9), the use of a visual concept map simultaneously provides a method of analysis and the display. Specifically, in feature maps, the content of as many works as possible are analyzed and displayed in a systematic manner.

EXAMPLE: CREATING VISUAL DISPLAYS

One goal of a feature map display is to compare and to contrast findings among studies examining the same topic. A worksheet represents a visual display in the form of a matrix, and can be used to make comparisons among authors with respect to the same topic or concept. Oftentimes, worksheets, per se, are not presented as part of the final CLR report but are used in the analysis and synthesis step (i.e., Step 6) of the CLR process. If a CAQDAS/CAMMDAS program already had been used in Step 3 and/or Step 6, then it is extremely straightforward to produce a worksheet for a visual display in the final report. For example,

the "Coding Retrieval" option (under the "Retrieval" menu) of QDA Miner can be used to produce a worksheet. Figure 11.3 shows a screenshot of a worksheet generated via QDA Miner by Denham and Onwuegbuzie (2013). These authors analyzed all 687 articles published in *The Qualitative Report* between 1990 and 2012. The articles in the worksheet were those articles in which the concept of triangulation was discussed explicitly. These articles then were coded with respect to how triangulation was enhanced (i.e., reflexivity vs. thick description).

Summary record sheets provide a display in the form of a matrix of selected bibliographic information and coded information for a literature review (Hart, 2005). As is the case for worksheets, summary record sheets typically are not presented as part of a literature review but can be used, for example, to identify trends in the literature. **Relationship maps** explicitly illustrate the relationships among variables identified in the literature. Linear relationship maps represent special cases of relationship maps, showing the linear relationships among variables. Similarly, **content maps** illustrate the content of underlying topics that are hierarchically arranged. **Taxonomic maps** illustrate how a range of elements can be placed into a general class or typology. Taxonomic maps can be displayed via a table or other diagram (e.g., box diagram, lines and nodes).

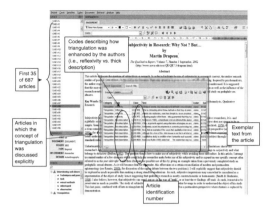

Figure 11.3   Screenshot of a worksheet generated via QDA Miner by Denham and Onwuegbuzie (2013)

EXAMPLE: ILLUSTRATING SUMMARY RECORDS

Figure 11.4 illustrates a relationship map developed by Wao (2008), who examined factors related to time to attainment of the doctorate degree in education—a study that has important implications for mentoring.

EXAMPLE: USING CONTENT MAPS

Table 11.2 provides an example of a content map developed by Collier (2013), who studied the effects of a comprehensive, multiple, high-risk behaviors prevention program on high school students—another inquiry that has important implications for mentoring. In contrast, concept maps portray linkages among concepts and processes. Figure 11.5 shows the display map in the Dyadic Mentoring Study for direct and indirect inputs for mentoring (revealed through the analysis of sources).

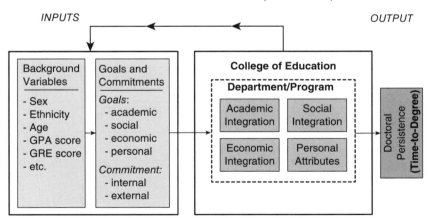

Figure 11.4   Relationship map created by Wao (2008) showing variables identified from the literature that are associated with persistence of students in doctoral programs

Adapted from *A mixed methods approach to examining factors related to time to attainment of the doctorate in education*, by H. O. Wao, 2008, unpublished doctoral dissertation, University of South Florida, Tampa, FL, p. 26. Copyright 2008 by H. O. Wao.

Table 11.2 Partial conceptual map presented by Collier (2013): rank order and prevalence rates of current adolescent high-risk behaviors

High-Risk Behavior	Prevalence Rates	Study Author & Year
1. Alcohol use	Almost 75% have drunk	NCASACU, 2011
	41.8% currently drink	CDC, 2009b
2. Binge drinking	24% currently binge drink	CDC, 2009b
3. Pornography	42%–72.8% of youth Internet users had seen online pornography	Sabina, Wolak, & Finkelhor, 2008; Wolak, Mitchell, & Finkelhor, 2007
	20% engage in sexting	National Campaign to Prevent Teen and Unplanned Pregnancy, 2008
4. Marijuana use	36.8% currently use	
5. Illegal drugs	22.6% currently use	NIDA, 2010
6. Sex/oral sex	34.2% currently sexually active and 13.8% had sexual intercourse with four or more persons during their lives	CDC, 2009b
7. Driving under the influence	28.3% currently engage in behavior	CDC, 2009b
8. Tobacco use	19.5% current users and 46.3% ever tried cigarettes	CDC, 2009b
9. Bullying	19.9%–28.1% at school	CDC, 2009b; NCASACU, 2011
Cyberbullying	11%–13.8% online	Agatston, Kowalski, & Limber, 2007; Williams & Guerra, 2007

Adapted from *Effects of comprehensive, multiple high-risk behaviors prevention program on high school students,* by C. Collier, 2013, unpublished doctoral dissertation, Sam Houston State University, Huntsville, TX, p. 64. Copyright 2010 by C. Collier.

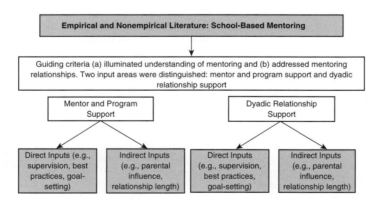

Figure 11.5 A concept map developed by Frels (2010) showing direct and indirect inputs for mentoring revealed through the literature

Adapted from *The experiences and perceptions of selected mentors: An exploratory study of the dyadic relationship in school-based mentoring*, by R. K. Frels, 2010, unpublished doctoral dissertation, Sam Houston State University, Huntsville, TX, p. 78. Copyright 2010 by R. K. Frels.

EXAMPLE: USING TAXONOMY MAPS

We include, as a visual display, part of the map created by Onwuegbuzie and Corrigan (2014) to represent a taxonomy of the mixed research process (which can be applied to a literature review). Box 11.2 presents this visual display as a summary of the multiple points for reference.

Finally, *semantic maps* are used in the field of literacy and can be helpful in a CLR report to represent words and their logical aspects of meaning in a graphic form. These maps are semantic in nature when these concepts denote words or other symbols similar in meaning.

EXAMPLE: USING SEMANTIC MAPS

Figure 11.6 provides one example of a semantic map that was developed by Frels, Onwuegbuzie, and Slate (2010a) to display for the reader their research about writers using appropriate verbs. We included an example of a semantic map for selecting a verb in the writing process so that, as a literature reviewer, you might see a display that is helpful and also recognize ways to grow as a writer.

		Weakest Level	Intermediate Level	Strongest Level
Representing Statement	*Explicit Verbs*	indicated, mentioned	stated	declared pronounced
	Implicit Verbs	speculated		assumed
	Inclusive Verbs	included	characterized	contained, comprised
Representing Cognition	*Comparison Verbs*	compared, contrasted		discriminated
	Verification Verbs	triangulated		confirmed, verified
	Interpretation Verbs	inferred	realized	concluded
	Cognitive Process Verbs	thought	believed	noticed
	Reference Verbs	consulted	summarized	expected
	Perception Verbs	(no obvious hierarchy)		
	Proposition Verbs	speculated	hypothesized	established
Representing Knowledge	*Evidence-Based/Data-Driven Verbs*	noted	observed found	documented experienced
	Procedural Verbs	reviewed	consulted	scrutinized
	Visual Verbs	(no obvious hierarchy)		
	Direct Object Verbs (Stages in Research Process)	sampled		provided
	Creation Verbs	crafted, originated		developed

Figure 11.6 Semantic map developed by Frels, Onwuegbuzie, and Slate (2010a) showing the strength of verbs and their variation of meaning

BOX 11.2

PARTIAL GUIDELINES FOR CONDUCTING AND REPORTING MIXED RESEARCH FOR RESEARCHERS PRESENTED BY ONWUEGBUZIE AND CORRIGAN (2014) THAT BUILDS ON LEECH AND ONWUEGBUZIE (2010)

Steps and Guidelines
Formulate

1. *Determine the Goal of the Study*

1.1. Identify philosophical assumptions and stances (e.g., pragmatism-of-the-middle, pragmatism-of-the-right, pragmatism-of-the-left, anti-conflationist, critical realist orientation, dialectical stance, complementary strengths, transformative-emancipatory, a-paradigmatic stance, substantive theory, communities of practice stance, dialectical pluralism, critical dialectical pluralism; Onwuegbuzie, Johnson, & Collins, 2009).

1.2. Identify the conceptual stance (a-paradigmatic, substantive theory, complementary strengths, multiple paradigms, dialectic, alternative paradigm; Teddlie & Tashakkori, 2010).

1.3. Determine generalization goal (i.e., external [statistical] generalization, internal [statistical] generalization, analytic generalization, case-to-case transfer, naturalistic generalization; Onwuegbuzie, Slate, Leech, & Collins, 2009).

1.4. Treat each relevant article as data that generate both qualitative (e.g., qualitative findings, literature review of source article, source article author's conclusion) and quantitative (e.g., p values, effect sizes, sample size score reliability, quantitative results) information that yields a mixed research synthesis (Onwuegbuzie & Frels, in press).

1.5. Subject each document selected as part of the literature review to summarization, analysis, evaluation, and synthesis (Onwuegbuzie & Frels, in press).

1.6. Provide literature reviews that are comprehensive, current, and rigorous; that have been compared and contrasted adequately; and that contain primary sources that are relevant to the research problem under investigation, with clear connections being made between the sources presented and the present study (Onwuegbuzie & Frels, in press).

1.7. Present clearly the theoretical/conceptual/practical framework (Lester, 2005).

1.8. Assess the findings stemming from each individual study and the emergent synthesis for trustworthiness, credibility, dependability, legitimation, validity, plausibility, applicability, consistency, neutrality, reliability, objectivity, confirmability, and/or transferability (cf. Dellinger & Leech, 2007; Leech, Dellinger, Brannagan, & Tanaka, 2010).

1.9. Present the goal of the study (i.e., predict; add to the knowledge base; have a personal, social, institutional, and/or organizational impact; measure change; understand complex phenomena; test new ideas; generate new ideas; inform constituencies; and examine the past; Newman, Ridenour, Newman, & DeMarco, 2003).

2. **Formulate Research Objectives**

   2.1. Specify the objective(s) of the study (i.e., exploration, description, explanation, prediction, and influence) for the different (i.e., quantitative, qualitative, mixed) phases of the study (Johnson & Christensen, 2013).

   2.2. Specify the rationale for each objective.

   2.3. Present clearly how these objectives relate to each other.

3. **Determine the Research/Mixing Rationale**

   3.1. Specify the rationale of the study (Onwuegbuzie & Daniel, 2005).

   3.2. Specify the rationale for combining qualitative and quantitative approaches (i.e., participant enrichment, instrument fidelity, treatment integrity, and significance enhancement; Collins, Onwuegbuzie, & Sutton, 2006).

4. **Determine Research/Mixing Purpose(s)**

   4.1. Specify the purpose of the study (Onwuegbuzie & Daniel, 2005).

   4.2. Specify the purpose for combining qualitative and quantitative approaches (e.g., identify representative sample members, conduct member check, validate individual scores on outcome measures, develop items for an instrument, identify barriers and/or facilitators within intervention condition, evaluate the fidelity of implementing the intervention and how it worked, enhance findings that are not significant, compare results from the quantitative data with the qualitative findings; Collins, Onwuegbuzie, & Sutton, 2006).

Adapted from "Guidelines for conducting and reporting mixed research in the field of counseling and beyond," by N. L. Leech and A. J. Onwuegbuzie, 2010, *Journal of Counseling and Development, 45*, pp. 68–69. Copyright 2010 by the American Counseling Association.

RECOMMENDATION 12: DOCUMENT EVOLUTION OF METHODOLOGY AND METHOD(S)

As described in Chapter 3, the terms *methodology* and *method* are very different, with methodology representing a broad approach to scientific inquiry with general preferences for certain types of designs, sampling logic, analytical strategies, and so forth; and *method* representing specific strategies and procedures for research design, sampling, data collection, analysis, interpretation, and the like. For constructs that have a long history, it is essential for reviewers to document the evolution of the methodologies and methods used to study them. With respect to methodologies, reviewers should consider examining selected empirical research studies to determine the trends in the use of quantitative, qualitative, and mixed research approaches. If, for example, a predominance is found in one kind of approach, and the reviewer intends to conduct his/her primary research study using the other approach, then this will provide another strong rationale for his/her study.

EXAMPLE: WRITING A RATIONALE FOR SEARCH CRITERIA

Table 11.3 presents a partial feature map from the literature review section of the Dyadic Mentoring Study whereby the majority of studies had involved the use of quantitative research approaches; yet, this study was a qualitative research study—thereby adding an additional strong rationale for the research, as follows:

> Of the 23 (empirical only) articles that met my standards and criteria for the literature review, 18 of these articles represent quantitative studies and fewer of these articles represent qualitative studies. As such, there appears to be a general lack of qualitative research on mentoring programs, especially regarding the role and approach of mentors (Rhodes, 2005). Furthermore, it is clear from this review of literature that more research is needed to understand mentors' experiences of the dyadic relationship regarding their role and approach, and intimate exchanges that might include struggles and challenges with a mentee. (Frels, 2010, p. 100)

In addition to comparing across research traditions, reviewers should compare within research traditions. For example,

Table 11.3 Partial feature map presented in the Dyadic Mentoring Study, displaying empirical research and contributions to mentoring practices

Study and Author	Input or Evaluative Component	Methodological Paradigm	Results/Contribution to Mentoring Practices
Buell (2004)	Exploratory	Qualitative	Four models of mentoring emerged based on concepts of mentor roles and amount of power/support.
Cavell, Elledge, Malcolm, Faith, & Hughes (2009)	Frequency of meeting	Quantitative	Outcomes documented for aggressive children over a period of 2 years regarding externalized behavior problems. The use of a program with more frequent mentoring yielded more supportive relationships than that of a shorter-termed program.
Converse & Lignugaris/Kraft (2009)	Duration	Quantitative	Connectedness and benefits lasted only as long as mentoring relationships. Mentors who viewed mentoring positively versus those who viewed it negatively had mentees with fewer office referrals.
Dappen & Isernhagen (2006)	Descriptive	Quantitative	Significance and "trust" were ranked as important for quality mentoring relationships. Recruiting and retaining mentors in urban populations is difficult.

Adapted from *The experiences and perceptions of selected mentors: An exploratory study of the dyadic relationship in school-based mentoring*, by R. K. Frels, 2010, unpublished doctoral dissertation, Sam Houston State University, Huntsville, TX, p. 72. Copyright 2010 by R. K. Frels.

reviewers can compare the following elements across studies: sampling scheme (e.g., random vs. purposive sampling); sample size; characteristics of the participants (e.g., gender composition, ethnic composition); instruments used (e.g., quantitative research studies: standardized tests vs. teacher-made tests; qualitative research studies: interviews vs. observations); research design (e.g., quantitative research studies: experimental research designs vs. nonexperimental research designs [say correlational research, action research]; qualitative research studies: phenomenological research designs vs. ethnographic research); and procedures (e.g., length of time of studies). This is consistent with our statement in Chapter 3 that, for empirical studies, the CLR should be applied to all

12 components of a primary research report, including the participants, instruments, procedures, and analyses. In so doing, reviewers should utilize quality frameworks such as Leech et al.'s (2010) Validation Framework, Onwuegbuzie's (2003b) Quantitative Legitimation Model, Onwuegbuzie and Leech's (2007b) Qualitative Legitimation Model, and Onwuegbuzie and Johnson's (2006) Mixed Legitimation Typology. Such comparisons would help reviewers to identify from the literature the best research practices used by researchers, as well as the weakest research practices—and to avoid errors such as those committed by researchers who have used the Teacher Efficacy Scale (Gibson & Dembo, 1984), as we described in Chapter 3.

RECOMMENDATION 13: REFERENCE ANY META-ANALYSIS, META-SYNTHESIS, AND META-SUMMARY FINDINGS

As noted in Chapter 9, reviewers always should search to determine whether meta-analysis, meta-synthesis, and/or meta-summary studies on a topic exist. Meta-analysis studies, if undertaken appropriately, make the work of the reviewer much easier. If no meta-analysis/meta-synthesis/meta-summary studies exist, the reviewer should consider conducting such a study (i.e., the secondary data component of MODES; cf. Chapter 8)—even if it only involves a limited sample of works. An example of citing a meta-analysis study that generated quantitative findings can be gleaned

from the Dyadic Mentoring Study (p. 89), as presented in Box 11.3. Because Rebecca identified only five qualitative research studies on mentoring programs, it is not surprising that she could not locate any meta-synthesis or meta-summary studies conducted in this area.

EXAMPLE: CITING A META-SYNTHESIS

An example of citing a meta-synthesis study that generated qualitative findings discussed by Pease (2013, pp. 10–11) is presented in Box 11.4. Finally, an example of citing a meta-summary study discussed by Hickey (2010, p. 37) is presented in Box 11.5.

RECOMMENDATION 14: REFERENCE RELIABILITY GENERALIZATION FINDINGS

Reliability generalization (RG) studies involve exploring variance in measurement error affecting score reliability across studies (Vacha-Haase & Thompson, 2000). Although very informative, few RG studies exist because they are time-consuming. Thus, the results of such studies should be presented in the literature review when found.

BOX 11.3

EXAMPLE OF CITING A META-ANALYSIS STUDY THAT GENERATED QUANTITATIVE FINDINGS PRESENTED BY FRELS (2010, p. 89)

DuBois, Holloway, et al. (2002) identified moderators of program effectiveness through a meta-analysis of 55 evaluations of the effects of mentoring programs on youth. Their findings provided evidence of only small effect sizes to modest effect sizes, ranging from $d = .15$ to $d = .45$ across nine independent samples. Thus, specific program features for increasing desired results for stronger mentee outcomes were identified and comprised: (a) monitoring the program, (b) providing ongoing training for mentors, (c) involving parents, (d) structuring activities, and (e) clarifying expectations about attendance.

BOX 11.4

EXAMPLE OF CITING A META-SYNTHESIS STUDY THAT GENERATED QUALITATIVE FINDINGS PRESENTED BY PEASE (2013, pp. 10–11)

To gain a more integrated understanding of the psychosocial nature of women's experiences of PPD [postpartum depression], Beck (2002) conducted a "meta-synthesis" of the findings from 18 qualitative studies of women with PPD. Meta-synthesis is a method that considers "the theories, grand narratives, generalizations, or interpretive translations produced from the integration or comparison of findings from qualitative studies" (Sandelowski, Docherty, & Emden, 1997, p. 366). These studies, conducted in Canada, the USA, the United Kingdom, and Australia, were published between 1990 and 1999 and included data from 309 mothers. This meta-synthesis revealed four major themes underlying women's experiences of PPD, namely "(a) incongruity between expectations and reality of motherhood, (b) spiraling downward, (c) pervasive loss, and (d) making gains" (Beck, 2002, p. 3).

BOX 11.5

EXAMPLE OF CITING A META-SUMMARY STUDY PRESENTED BY HICKEY (2010, P. 37)

O'Connor's (2006) meta-summary of the literature on students' perceptions identified the following themes: fear of harming patients, a desire to help people, a need to integrate theory and clinical practice, and a desire to master psychomotor skills. Students also reported a need to focus on skill mastery before encountering more complex patient situations. Clinical environments that allowed them to learn and practice not only psychomotor skills but also communication, time management, and organizational skills were reported as more important (Hartigan-Rogers et al., 2007).

EXAMPLE: PROVIDING RELIABILITY GENERALIZATION

Box 11.6 provides an example of citing an RG study that was presented by Onwuegbuzie, Roberts, and Daniel (2005, p. 230).

RECOMMENDATION 15: CITE VALIDITY META-ANALYSIS FINDINGS AND LEGITIMATION META-SYNTHESIS FINDINGS

A *validity meta-analysis* involves the reviewer conducting a study to determine the most prevalent threats to internal and external validity of quantitative

findings. Similarly, a *legitimation meta-synthesis* involves the reviewer conducting a study to determine the most prevalent threats to internal and external credibility of qualitative findings. Both of these reviewer-conducted studies are consistent with the secondary data component of MODES (cf. Chapter 8).

EXAMPLE: CITING VALIDITY META-ANALYSIS

Box 11.7 provides an example of citing a validity meta-analysis study presented by Onwuegbuzie (2000c, pp. 7–8).

BOX 11.6

EXAMPLE OF CITING A RELIABILITY GENERALIZABILITY STUDY PRESENTED BY ONWUEGBUZIE, ROBERTS, AND DANIEL (2005, p. 230)

In a more recent study in which a large variety of reliability generalization meta-analyses across an array of articles and journals were summarized, Vacha-Haase, Henson, and Caruso (2002) reported that is "in most empirical studies authors failed to report the reliability of their own scores (M = 75.6%, SD = 17.0%) or even mention reliability at all (M = 56.3%, SD = 18.4%)" (p. 563). Hence, many researchers are not in a position to determine the extent to which measurement error has affected the observed findings in their studies.

BOX 11.7

EXAMPLE OF CITING A VALIDITY META-ANALYSIS STUDY PRESENTED BY ONWUEGBUZIE (2000c, pp. 7–8)

Once discussion of rival hypotheses becomes commonplace in literature reviews, *validity meta-analyses* could be conducted to determine the most prevalent threats to internal and external validity for a given research hypothesis (Onwuegbuzie, 2000a). These *validity meta-analyses* would provide an effective supplement to traditional meta-analyses. In fact, the *validity meta-analyses* could lead to *thematic* effect sizes being computed for the percentage of occasions in which a particular threat to internal or external validity is identified in replication studies (Onwuegbuzie, 2000b). For example, a narrative that combines traditional meta-analyses and *validity meta-analyses* could take the following form:

> Across studies, students who received Treatment A performed on standardized achievement tests, on average, nearly two-thirds of a standard deviation (Cohen's (1988) *Mean d* = .65) higher than did those who received Treatment B. This represents a large effect. However, these findings are tempered by the fact that in these investigations, several rival hypotheses were noted. Specifically, across these studies, *statistical regression* was the most frequently identified threat to internal validity (prevalence rate/effect size = 33%), followed by *mortality* (effect size = 22%). With respect to external validity, *population validity* was the most frequently cited threat (effect size = 42%), followed by reactive arrangements (effect size = 15%).

Such *validity meta-analyses* would help to bolster further the importance of external replications, which are the essence of science (Onwuegbuzie & Daniel, 1999; Thompson, 1994).

Adapted from *Revisioning rival hypotheses for the 21st century: Collaborative design of a web-based tool for learning about the validity of empirical studies*, by A. J. Onwuegbuzie, 2000c, unpublished manuscript, Sam Houston State University, Huntsville, TX, pp. 7–8. Copyright 2010 by A. J. Onwuegbuzie.

STAYING ORGANIZED

In the writing phase of Step 7, organization is the key for keeping you from becoming overwhelmed with the many decisions that you need to make about the important process and product components to include in the report. Therefore, as an ethical (and systematic) literature reviewer, the use of audit checklists creates the organization needed for creating the CLR report.

FIND A WRITING FLOW

In addition to the items listed above, consider particular styles of communication as well as the possibilities of AVOW and any creative outlets to consider for the report. Consider the writing styles of the authors of some of the documents that you reviewed. For the most part, if adhering to technical writing, the style was organized, succinct, and focused. Yet, as a reader, you might have engaged yourself more so in one or more articles due to the ability of the researcher to write with voice and depth.

TOOL: SUMMARY TABLE OF RECOMMENDATIONS FOR WRITING

We summarize the aforementioned decisions and recommendations in the form of a checklist in Table 11.4 as an audit point for establishing the focus for the draft-writing process.

Table 11.4   Summary table of decisions made at the draft-writing stage

Item	Draft-Writing Stage Recommendation
1	Use V-shape for writing the CLR report
2	Specify databases used for the CLR and number of *hits*
3	Specify the analysis used to analyze information that was presented in the CLR report
4	Compare constitutive definitions and operational definitions
5	Distinguish notable works from regular works
6	Provide a timeline for the topic
7	When providing a timeframe, be as specific as possible
8	Document evolution of author's thinking
9	Cite dissenting works
10	Refer the reader to other works on issues that are not discussed in detail
11	Provide one or more citation maps
12	Document evolution of methodologies and methods used to study the underlying construct
13	Cite meta-analysis, meta-synthesis, and meta-summary findings
14	Cite reliability generalization findings
15	Cite validity meta-analysis findings and legitimation meta-synthesis findings

Writers of fiction novels regard highly the concept of ***writer's voice***, which involves the way that an author conveys a message: putting together words using a unique sensibility and distinctive outlook that enriches the author's niche (Maass, 2004). The written report, as a synthesis of information based on methodology, includes specific rhetoric, which is language that is used; the emphasis made to either individuals as a complex entity or to people in general; and the words used to persuade the reader that the findings/evidence, interpretations, ideas, conceptualizations, theories, and the like can be trusted (Chilisa & Kawulich, 2010).

TOOL: POINTS TO CONSIDER FOR INTERESTING WRITING

Kirby and Liner (1988) specified 10 working criteria for discerning rhetoric and writer's voice, which we connect to the CLR report in Figure 11.7. This figure highlights the importance of writing characteristics that result in interesting and skillful writing.

Making Writing Interesting		
Voice	Makes writing believable	Creates an imprint of the writer
Movement	Creates a sense of order	Moves a reader along
Informative	Reveals important information	Adds to the reader's experience
Inventive	Presents something new, or something old in a new way	Is a unique experience
Making Writing Technically Skillful		
Sense of audience	Anticipates readers' needs	Compliments a reader with meaningful interpretations
Detail	Concrete, selective words	Creates a real-life image
Rhythm	Words sounding effortless	Allows the reader to find pattern
Form	The way words are organized	How sections of words appear on a page
Mechanics	Conventions of spelling, punctuation, usage	Informed control of writing rules

Figure 11.7   Characteristics of interesting and technically skillful writing skills adapted from Kirby and Liner (1988)

THE DRAFT-AUDIT PHASE

Once the literature reviewer has written the first full draft of the CLR report, he/she is ready for the ***audit phase of writing***, which is the careful, systematic process of inspection. Each inspection helps the reviewer to determine areas to revise and/or to rework. In so doing, it is helpful to keep in mind the fact that no writer—however experienced—can write a first draft as her/his final draft! This misperception occurs with many students—both undergraduate and graduate students alike—and results in them becoming discouraged when they receive (extensive) feedback and editorial suggestions on their literature review drafts. The goal for the reviewer is to maximize the clarity, structure, coherence, and precision of the narrative.

Ideally, reviewers should allow at least 2 or 3 days to elapse after completing the first draft and before auditing this draft. This would allow time for *incubation*.

By allowing sufficient time before revising or reworking each draft, the literature reviewer might expunge as much as possible the mental picture formed of their drafts and to be able to audit from a fresh perspective. To this end, there are several items to which the literature reviewer might attend when auditing the first and each subsequent draft. These audit items are listed in the following section so that you might utilize them as both a guide for writing and as a checklist to review your drafts. After each audit item is presented, a brief description is provided to guide how you might determine whether it was adequately addressed. Next, to help you to apply some of the concepts of the seven steps in your report, we outline some tools that might be useful for each audit.

The authors of the American Psychological Association's *Publication Manual* (sixth edition) provide specific ways to write clearly and concisely at the onset of Chapter 2, and noted that "sound organization structure is the key to clear, precise, and logical communication" (APA, 2010, p. 62), which is best accomplished through the use of leveled headings. They advise against having only one subsection heading and subsection within a section, much like a good outline. In addition to organizational elements, *continuity of ideas* refers to the use of punctuation marks to cue the reader(s) to "pauses, inflections, subordination, and pacing normally heard in speech" (APA, 2010, p. 65).

With respect to tone, the authors of the *Publication Manual* recognized that although technical writing is quite different from literary writing, it does not and should not lack style or be dull. Rather, your writing should present ideas in an interesting, compelling manner and tone so that the report reflects your position and involvement with the problem. Other elements of writing for attending to precision and clarity include avoiding:

- *colloquial expression*, which is the linguistic way of communicating that is interpreted differently by different readers (e.g., "put up with" instead of "tolerated")

- *jargon*, which is substituting a euphemistic phrase for a familiar word (e.g., "taking care of one's body" instead of "physical wellness")

- *attribution error*, which is the way a writer might inappropriately attribute action in order to appear to be objective. Attribution errors include the use of anthropomorphism, or attributing human characteristics to inanimate sources, such as "the mentoring program recommended that mentors increased time at the school" instead of "mentoring program coordinators recommended time increases"

Another common attribution error is what the authors of the *Publication Manual* refer to as abusing the *editorial we*, or the broad usage of the pronoun as all inclusive (e.g., "In the field of mentoring, we work to establish strong connections"). Often throughout this chapter and book, we (Tony and Rebecca) use the pronoun appropriately, which refers to the two of us as co-researchers, co-authors, or co-editors. In addition to many more style and organization considerations for your CLR report, consider the overall quality of the report that you are presenting, or the details that impact the physical appearance of your efforts. These details include the typeface that you select, the page headings, and the use of a word-processing program spell check.

AUDIT CHECKLIST AND RECOMMENDATIONS

At the onset of this chapter, we explained the writing process as being reflective and evaluative. Next, we discussed a few of the common errors delineated in some writing style guides. The following section presents a list of checkpoints so that you can use a systematic process to audit your first and subsequent drafts. Although these checkpoints are numbered from 1 to 18, rather than being linear they are recursive, with most, if not all, of these checkpoints optimally being revisited as needed at multiple times during the draft-audit phase. Further, these checkpoints are not exhaustive and no one checkpoint is more important than another. In fact, we expect that this list will expand for you as you add your own items. Within these checkpoints, we offer some additional tools and examples to facilitate the audit process.

CHECKPOINT 1: COMPARE THE DRAFT WITH THE PRE-DRAFT OUTLINE

In Chapter 10, we recommended that before writing the first draft of the CLR report, reviewers should create an outline. Assuming that an outline was created, reviewers should compare the draft with the outline to ensure that the path of argumentation in the outline has been fully realized.

CHECKPOINT 2: PROVIDE A SUFFICIENT NUMBER OF HEADINGS AND SUBHEADINGS

As previously mentioned, the headings of a CLR report should either represent or be inspired by themes that emerged from the analysis and synthesis of selected works (cf. Chapter 9), whereas the subheadings should either represent or be inspired by the codes that fit into these general headings. As a general rule, the longer the CLR report, the more headings/subheadings are needed. By dividing the CLR report into major sections (i.e., via headings that contain more general information) and subdividing those sections into subsections (i.e., via subheadings that contain more specific information), each heading/subheading should be constructed in such a way as to help readers to locate information relatively quickly, as well as help to reduce cognitive load. Further, headings and subheadings should help readers by not only previewing the subject and purpose of the discussion that is contained within it but also delineating its structure and scope. Even more importantly, headings/subheadings should help readers follow the path of argument by creating a hierarchy of information. Thus, after writing the first draft, reviewers should assess both the quantity and quality of headings and subheadings. Further, we recommend that all sections contain at least two or three paragraphs, because a one-paragraph section typically does not justify having its own heading.

CHECKPOINT 3: ENSURE THAT RESEARCH FINDINGS ARE DIFFERENTIATED FROM OTHER INFORMATION

CLR reports contain an array of information, including ideas, conceptualizations, theories, findings, interpretations of source authors, and the like. Of these, findings represent the ***best evidence*** that support or refute a reviewer's logic of argumentation. As such, reviewers should distinguish clearly between research findings and other types of information. One of the most effect ways of accomplishing this distinction is by careful choice of verb usage. In our experience as editors and guest editors of journals, as well as reviewers for and editorial board members of numerous journals, we have observed that many authors use inappropriate verbs in their literature reviews. In particular, we have noticed that many authors overuse the verb *found*. For example, in a review of all mixed research articles that were published either in *Reading Research Quarterly* ($n = 21$) or *Journal of Literacy Research* ($n = 12$) between 2003 and 2008, Onwuegbuzie and Frels (2010) reported that, on average, authors of these articles used the word *found* more than 13 times. Moreover, on closer examination, these authors noticed that many authors, on at least one occasion, used the verb *found* when discussing nonempirical findings such as theories. This led to Frels et al. (2010a) developing a framework to help authors select verbs appropriately. These authors provided several visual representations for displaying their verb typologies.

TOOL: SELECTING APPROPRIATE VERBS

To help writers recognize appropriate verbs for contextual meaning, they categorized verbs representing statements— explicit, implicit, or inclusive. Figure 11.8 features this list.

(Continued)

(Continued)

Explicit Verbs		Implicit Verbs	Inclusive Verbs
remarked	stated	speculated	comprised
noted	defined	assumed	consisted of
commented	indicated	explained	contained
mentioned	ascertained	argued	included
documented	bracketed	associated	characterized
affirmed	outlined	reinforced	categorized
pronounced	advised	suggested	labeled
asserted	cautioned	interpreted	
declared	admonished	implied	
reported	delineated		
discussed	operationalized		
addressed			
summed			
acquiesced			
conceded			

Note: The list of verbs in this table is by no means exhaustive.

Figure 11.8   Typology of verbs representing statement for scholarly writing

Adapted from "Editorial: A typology of verbs for scholarly writing," by R. K. Frels, A. J. Onwuegbuzie, and J. R. Slate, 2010a, *Research in the Schools*, *17*(1), p. xxv. Copyright 2010 by Mid-South Educational Research Association.

To help you further with verb selection, the next figure, Figure 11.9, presents verbs categorized as representing cognition—namely, comparison verbs, verification verbs, interpretation verbs, cognitive process verbs, reference verbs, perception verbs, and proposition verbs. In this figure, we have pointed out the classes of verbs that are useful for: comparing and contrasting authors or works; delineating findings/evidence; delineating interpretations; and discussing ideas, conceptualizations, theories, and so forth.

Table 11.5 depicts verbs categorized as representing knowledge or action—namely, evidence-based/data-driven verbs, procedural verbs, visual verbs, direct object verbs, and creation verbs—and the four major sections of empirical research reports and examples of the primary and secondary verb categories that could be used accordingly. Finally, to help you to identify which verbs in academic discourse might be more suitable for particular sections of a report, Table 11.6 presents verbs, sorted by the sections of a report. Of particular interest for writing the CLR report are the verbs categorized under the introduction/literature review section.

We hope that after viewing these particular lists, you will strive to avoid evidence-based/data-driven verbs such as *found* when describing authors' propositions (e.g., theories, conceptualizations)—as some authors mistakenly do. As you rework your drafts, consider the importance of clarity in writing and select the most appropriate verb in each and every case.

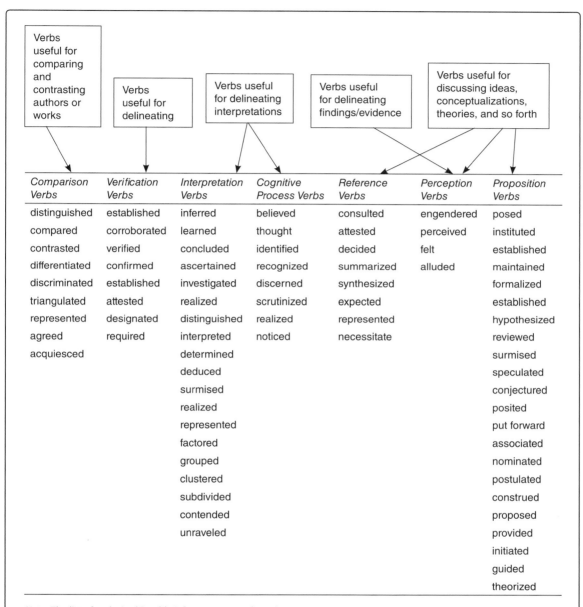

Comparison Verbs	Verification Verbs	Interpretation Verbs	Cognitive Process Verbs	Reference Verbs	Perception Verbs	Proposition Verbs
distinguished	established	inferred	believed	consulted	engendered	posed
compared	corroborated	learned	thought	attested	perceived	instituted
contrasted	verified	concluded	identified	decided	felt	established
differentiated	confirmed	ascertained	recognized	summarized	alluded	maintained
discriminated	established	investigated	discerned	synthesized		formalized
triangulated	attested	realized	scrutinized	expected		established
represented	designated	distinguished	realized	represented		hypothesized
agreed	required	interpreted	noticed	necessitate		reviewed
acquiesced		determined				surmised
		deduced				speculated
		surmised				conjectured
		realized				posited
		represented				put forward
		factored				associated
		grouped				nominated
		clustered				postulated
		subdivided				construed
		contended				proposed
		unraveled				provided
						initiated
						guided
						theorized

Note: The list of verbs in this table is by no means exhaustive.

Figure 11.9   Typology of verbs representing cognition for scholarly writing

Adapted from "Editorial: A typology of verbs for scholarly writing," by R. K. Frels, A. J. Onwuegbuzie, and J. R. Slate, 2010, *Research in the Schools*, *17*(1), p. xxvi. Copyright 2010 by Mid-South Educational Research Association.

(Continued)

(Continued)

Table 11.5 Typology of verbs representing knowledge or action for scholarly writing

Evidence-Based/ Data-Driven Verbs	Procedural Verbs	Visual Verbs	Direct Object Verbs	Creation Verbs
found	analyzed	displayed	gathered	crafted
embarked	examined	graphed	collected	originated
encountered	performed	illustrated	composed	generated
noted	conducted	presented	sampled	synthesized
revealed	undertook	mapped	randomized	engendered
detected	consulted	depicted	chose	stimulated
tested	scrutinized	represented	selected	instituted
discovered	consented		elected	constituted
traced	originated		developed	theorized
observed	composed		contrived	established
documented	produced		modeled	developed
experienced	conceptualized		provided	maintained
uncovered	consulted		procured	devised
extracted	reviewed		preferred	invented
	evaluated		adopted	
	contrived			
	investigated			

Note: The list of verbs in this table is by no means exhaustive.

Adapted from "Editorial: A typology of verbs for scholarly writing," by R. K. Frels, A. J. Onwuegbuzie, and J. R. Slate, 2010, *Research in the Schools*, *17*(1), p. xxvii. Copyright 2010 by Mid-South Educational Research Association.

Table 11.6 Examples of the categorical use of verbs (primary and secondary) for academic discourse

Section of Article	Category of Verb
Introduction/Literature review section	*Verbs representing statement*
	Explicit verbs (primary)
	Implicit verbs (primary)
	Inclusive verbs (secondary)
	Verbs representing cognition
	Proposition verbs (secondary)
	Reference verbs (primary)
	Cognitive Process verbs (secondary)

Section of Article	Category of Verb
Method section	*Verbs representing knowledge or action*
	Creation verbs (primary)
	Procedural verbs (primary)
	Direct Object verbs (primary)
	Visual verbs (secondary)
	Verbs representing cognition
	Comparison verbs (secondary)
Results section	*Verbs representing knowledge or action*
	Evidence-Based/Data-Driven verbs (primary)
	Procedural verbs (primary)
	Visual verbs (secondary)
	Direct Object verbs (secondary)
	Verbs representing cognition
	Perception verbs (primary)
	Verification verbs (primary)
	Comparative verbs (secondary)
Discussion section	*Verbs representing cognition*
	Proposition verbs (secondary)
	Interpretation verbs (primary)
	Reference verbs (primary)
	Cognitive Process verbs (secondary)

Adapted from "Editorial: A typology of verbs for scholarly writing," by R. K. Frels, A. J. Onwuegbuzie, and J. R. Slate, 2010, *Research in the Schools*, *17*(1), p. xxix. Copyright 2010 by Mid-South Educational Research Association.

CHECKPOINT 4: ENSURE THAT REVIEWER'S VOICE/STANCE IS DISTINGUISHED FROM EACH AUTHOR'S VOICE/STANCE

As noted previously, CLR reports provide a path of argumentation. Consistent with our assertion here, in Chapter 1, as part of our micro definition, we stated that *a CLR is a logical argument of an interpretation of relevant published and/or unpublished information on the selected topic*. That is, reviewers cannot maintain a fully neutral position in a CLR; rather, their ethical and cultural lens serves as a bi-directional filter that is shaped by, and shapes, their CLRs. As such, even though CLRs represent summarization, analysis, evaluation, and synthesis of the relationship among authors' ideas, conceptualizations, theories, findings, and interpretations, these elements are cohered via the reviewer's voice, reflecting the series of decisions made by the reviewer such as what information is included and excluded and what information is emphasized or criticized. Simply put, all CLR reports comprise a combination of the reviewer's voice and the selected (i.e., cited/referenced) authors' voices, and it is imperative that a literature reviewer distinguishes each selected author's voice/stance from his/her own.

TOOL: DISTINGUISHING VOICE

As an example, the statement "According to Watson (2014), this theory has implications for mentors" is ***non-factive***, inasmuch as, by stating it, the reviewer does not express an opinion of the author's conclusion. Conversely, the statement "As stated by Watson (2014), this theory has implications for mentors" is ***factive***, implying that the reviewer presupposes that the author is correct. Consequently, whereas the first statement presents the author's stance, the second statement reflects the reviewer's stance. These and other examples of author/reviewer stances are presented in Box 11.8.

BOX 11.8

EXAMPLES OF STATEMENTS THAT INDICATE THE AUTHOR'S STANCE AND THE REVIEWER'S STANCE

REPORTING THE AUTHOR'S STANCE

Positive (the author has a positive reaction)—*Selected verbs: agreed, accepted, emphasized, noted, pointed out, believed, supported, endorsed, subscribed to*

Examples:

- Benge (2013) agreed that this theory best explained the phenomenon

- Borg (2010) accepted this explanation

- Kohler (2012) endorsed this claim

- Collier (2011) subscribed to this theory

Negative (the author has a negative reaction)—*Selected verbs: disagreed, questioned, criticized, refuted, dismissed, disputed, opposed, rejected*

Examples:

- Benge (2013) disagreed that this theory best explained the phenomenon

- Borg (2010) criticized this explanation

- Kohler (2012) refuted this claim

- Collier (2011) rejected this theory

REPORTING THE REVIEWER'S STANCE

Factive (the reviewer presupposes that the author is correct)—*Selected verbs: acknowledged, recognized, demonstrated, shed light on, identified*

Examples:

- Benge (2013) acknowledged that this theory best explained the phenomenon
- Borg (2010) recognized this explanation
- Kohler (2012) demonstrated that this claim was warranted
- Collier (2011) shed light on this theory
- As stated by Watson (2014), this theory has implications for mentors

Counter-factive (the reviewer presupposes that the author is incorrect)—*Selected verbs: disregarded, misunderstood, confused, ignored, misrepresented*

Examples:

- Benge (2013) disregarded the fact that this theory best explained the phenomenon
- Borg (2010) misunderstood this explanation
- Kohler (2012) ignored this claim
- Collier (2011) misrepresented this theory

Non-factive (the reviewer does not express an opinion of the author's information)—*Selected verbs: regarded, advanced, discussed, posited, believed, proposed, theorized, used*

Examples:

- Benge (2013) regarded this theory as the best explanation of the phenomenon
- Borg (2010) advanced this explanation
- Kohler (2012) discussed this claim
- Collier (2011) used this theory
- According to Watson (2014), this theory has implications for mentors

Depending on the field involved and the style guide associated with the field, the literature reviewer can make his/her voice explicit via the use of personal pronouns. Doing so can be very effective for showing the *logic of argumentation*.

EXAMPLE: APPROPRIATE USE OF PRONOUNS

The quotation below from the Dyadic Mentoring Study provides an example of the use of the personal pronoun *my*:

Oftentimes, the term *model* is synonymous with the term *program*. Indeed, both programs and models include mentoring practices to facilitate desired outcomes for mentored students. Thus, my use of both of these terms in the following sections reflects this inconsistent use across the literature. (Frels, 2010, p. 81)

However, it should be noted that in manuscripts submitted for blind review for consideration for publication in a peer-reviewed source such as a journal, personal pronouns should never be followed by a self-citation (e.g., "The present theory represents an extension of my previous theory [Jones, 2010]") because this reveals the author of the manuscript containing the CLR report. In fact, as noted by the authors of the *Publication Manual* (APA, 2010) guidelines, "In masked review, the identity of the author of a manuscript is concealed from reviewers during the review process.... Authors are responsible for concealing their identities in manuscripts that are to receive masked review" (p. 226). Also, in the section entitled "Blinding" within the *Manuscript Submission* guidelines for the American Educational Research Association flagship journal, *Educational Researcher* (cf. https://us.sagepub.com/en-us/nam/educational-researcher/journal201856#submission-guidelines), the following statement appears:

> *Information in text that would identify the [sic] those references as belonging to the author should be deleted from the manuscript* (e.g., text citations of "my previous work," especially when accompanied by a self-citation; a preponderance of the author's own work in the reference list). *These may be reinserted in the final draft.* [emphasis added] (p. 18)

That is, once the manuscript has been accepted for publication and the blind review process has been completed, the literature reviewer can insert or unblind any self-citations that accompanied personal pronouns. An additional way of making the writer's (i.e., reviewer's) voice clear is via the use of adjectives or adverbs. For example, these elements can make explicit the extent to which the reviewer agrees or disagrees with the idea, concept, theory, finding, or interpretation. Examples of adjectives that emphasize the reviewer's commitment to the author's statement and show endorsement and non-endorsement, respectively, include the following: "Mallette's (2003) popularized theory..." and "Peterson's defunct theory..." Examples of adverbs include starting a sentence with a word like *undoubtedly* or *surprisingly*.

A summary at the end of the CLR report also can clarify the writer's (i.e., reviewer's) voice and emphasize statements using qualifying phrases (e.g., "this theory has logical appeal"), words (e.g., "promising"), and sentences at the end of a section or subsection. Depending on the length of the summary, it can appear in a separate section using an appropriate heading/subheading that includes the word "summary." Alternatively, a shorter summary can be appended to the final paragraph(s) in the section/subsection or be embedded within the last paragraph of that section/subsection providing that doing so does not make this paragraph overly long. When a summary is appended or embedded, the writer (i.e., reviewer) should provide an introductory phrase such as "In summary..."

TOOL: SUMMARY LIST FOR AUDITING CLAIMS

Table 11.7 presents a summary of how the relationship between the voice of the writer (i.e., reviewer) and the cited author varies as a function of the citation pattern. You can see from this table that the left-hand column provides examples of a claim that can be classified either as a claim of observation or a claim of interpretation, varied according to citation pattern. Indeed, the citation patterns in this table represent the most common citation patterns that writers (i.e., reviewers) use in their literature review reports. The middle two columns provide the consequence of each citation pattern in terms of the role of the writer's (i.e., reviewer's) voice and the author's voice, respectively. The last column specifies who (between the writer and author) is responsible for the claim made.

You can see from this table that, in the first row, because the writer (i.e., reviewer) does not provide any citation for the claim made, the writer is solely responsible for the claim made, and the voice of the author (who actually made this claim in her/his work but was not cited by the writer) is not at all present. In the second row, the writer is making a factive claim, and by providing the citation at the end of the claim, the writer is taking the lead responsibility for this claim, although the claim is being shared between the writer and the cited author. Ridley (2012) refers to the citing of an author's name in parentheses outside the structure of the sentence (as is the case in row 2) as a *non-integral reference* (p. 124). As noted by Ridley (2012)—yes, we (i.e., Rebecca and Tony) are using a factive statement here!—using a non-integral reference represents a way of emphasizing the idea, conceptualization, theory, finding, or interpretation instead of the author who is being attributed with the claim named and, hence, being cited. That is, the "the source information is brought into the foreground rather than the cited author" (Ridley, 2012, p. 127). Contrastingly, when the author being cited has a function in the claim made, such as serving as the subject of the claim (as in rows 4 and 6 in Table 11.7) or serving as the agent of the verb in a passive sentence (as in row 5 in Table 11.7), then the writer (i.e., reviewer) is using the citation as an *integral reference*. In using integral references, the writer typically has decided to emphasize the cited author rather than the idea, conceptualization, theory, finding, or interpretation.

The third row in Table 11.7 represents another factive claim; however, because both the citation and the indication that the writer agrees with this statement appear in the first clause, this claim is being shared equally. The fourth row also represents a factive claim, although this claim is not stated as strongly by the writer as in the second and third rows. And by providing the citation at the beginning of the claim, the writer is taking secondary responsibility for this claim, although the claim is

Table 11.7 Relationships among the claim, writer's voice, and cited author's voice

Example	Writer's (i.e., Reviewer's) Voice	Author's Voice	Responsibility for the Claim
Schools across the United States eagerly have implemented school-based mentoring (SBM) programs to promote student success	Sole	None	Writer (i.e., reviewer)
Schools across the United States eagerly have implemented SBM programs to promote student success (Spencer, 2007)	Dominant	Secondary	Shared
As Spencer (2007) stated, schools across the United States eagerly have implemented SBM programs to promote student success	Equal	Equal	Shared
Spencer (2007) noted that schools across the United States eagerly have implemented SBM programs...	Secondary	Dominant	Shared
Schools across the United States eagerly have implemented SBM programs to promote student success has been noted by Spencer (2007)	Secondary	Dominant	Shared
Spencer (2007) contended that schools across the United States eagerly have implemented SBM programs...	Background	Sole	Author
According to Spencer (2007), schools across the United States eagerly have implemented SBM programs...	Background	Sole	Author

Adapted from "Attribution and averral revisited: Three perspectives on manifest intertextuality in academic writing," by N. Groom, 2000, in P. Thomas (Ed.), *Patterns and perspectives: Insights into EAP writing practice,* p. 22. Copyright 2000 by the Centre for Applied Language Studies, University of Reading, England.

(Continued)

(Continued)

being shared between the writer and the cited author. The fifth row represents another weaker factive claim; however, the cited author is the agent of the verb within a passive statement. Finally, the last two rows represent a non-factive claim because the writer at this stage is not making it clear whether he/she agrees (i.e., factive) or disagrees (i.e., counter-factive) with the claim, although there might be a hint (hence the designation of *background* in the table) that the writer will make her/his position clear somewhere later in the CLR report as part of her/his path of argumentation. Table 11.7 demonstrates that CLR writers have a lot of control over who is (most) responsible (i.e., writer vs. cited author) for the claim being made. That is, CLR writers have control over the ***positionality*** of their voices within the report. The two major components that determine the extent to which the writer's voice is foregrounded (i.e., made dominant) in the CLR report are level of factivity (i.e., factive vs. counter-factive vs. non-factive) and the citation style (i.e., integral reference vs. non-integral reference)—both of which writers tend to have control over.

CHECKPOINT 5: AVOID USING ANNOTATIONS

A very common mistake made by beginning reviewers is the use of annotations in the literature review reports. That is, rather than write a literature review as a coherent essay that makes clear their logic of argumentation, inexperienced writers might structure the report using a series of brief summaries (i.e., annotations). This style of annotating findings restricts the flow of the writer and makes for an uninteresting report. An example of overusing annotations is:

> "Alias (2012) found xxxx… Smith (2014) found xxx…Jones (2014) found xxx…"

This use of annotations likely stems, at least in part, from one of the myths perpetuated by textbook authors that we identified in Chapter 1, namely, that the literature review represents only a *summary* of the extant literature. Tying together a series of annotations in a literature review report might provide a *summary* of the extant literature; however, it does not educate readers as to how these bodies of information relate to each other. Nor does it enlighten readers as to the legitimacy of each author's claims. Thus, reviewers should check that their CLR draft does not contain annotations, but rather, as we defined in Chapter 1, represents a systematic, holistic, synergistic, and cyclical process of exploring, interpreting, synthesizing, and communicating published and/or unpublished information.

EXAMPLE: COMBINING MULTIPLE REFERENCES

Box 11.9 provides an example of a paragraph that contains multiple sources that are combined in an efficient and coherent manner and which indicates clearly the author's stance in a non-factive manner (Checkpoint 4). In particular, we refer you to the final paragraph where the reviewer, Collier (2013), presented 10 findings of 10 sets of studies examining 10 high-risk behavior variables (i.e., driving while drinking, gambling, pornography, self-injury, bullying and cyberbullying, eating disorders, video game addiction, suicide, dating violence, sex) within the same sentence. Many novice researchers likely would have presented these findings in a rote manner using at least 10 sentences (i.e., one or more sentences for each of the 10 high-risk behaviors)—often using a verb like *found* multiple times—in a way such as the following:

> Researchers have found that adolescents struggle with driving while drinking (CDC, 2009b). Further, researchers have found that adolescents struggle with gambling (Powell et al., 1999). Pornography also has been found to be a source of struggle for adolescents (Braun-Courville & Rojas, 2009)…

Or the following:

> CDC (2009b) found that adolescents struggle with driving while drinking. Further, Powell et al. (1999) found that adolescents struggle with gambling. Also,

Braun-Courville and Rojas (2009) found pornography to be a source of struggle for adolescents...

In contrast, by citing numerous studies within the same sentence, Collier (2013) has structured the paragraph around the topic instead of around the findings of individual authors. Apart from making the narrative more coherent, it also represents a much more efficient style of writing, being especially useful when the literature review has to be written within a few pages. Next, Figure 11.10 provides an example of a paragraph that contains multiple sources that are compared and contrasted in a coherent manner (Checkpoint 5), and which indicates clearly the author's stance in a non-factive manner (Checkpoint 4).

BOX 11.9

EXAMPLE OF A PARAGRAPH THAT CONTAINS MULTIPLE SOURCES THAT ARE COMBINED IN AN EFFICIENT AND COHERENT MANNER AND WHICH INDICATES CLEARLY THE AUTHOR'S STANCE IN A NON-FACTIVE MANNER

In the United States, the average age of first use of alcohol and marijuana is between 15 and 17 (CDC, 2008, 2009b; SAMHSA, 2007). One in eight high-school students have a diagnosable clinical substance use disorder involving nicotine, alcohol, or other drugs (NCASACU, 2011). However, nicotine, alcohol, and drugs are not the only choice among the growing variety of high-risk behaviors (Sussman, Lisha, & Griffiths, 2010). Today, adolescents struggle with driving while drinking (CDC, 2009b), gambling (Powell et al., 1999), pornography (Braun-Courville & Rojas, 2009), self-injury (Alfonso & Dedrick, 2010; Hilt et al., 2008), bullying and cyberbullying (Agatston et al., 2007), eating disorders (Pisetsky et al., 2008), video game addiction (Griisser et al., 2007), suicide (Pelkonen & Marttunen, 2003), dating violence (Hickman et al., 2004; Spencer & Bryant, 2000), and sex (CDC, 2009b; NCASACU, 2011; SAMSHA, 2007).

Adapted from *Effects of comprehensive, multiple high-risk behaviors prevention program on high school students*, by C. Collier, 2013, Unpublished doctoral dissertation, Sam Houston State University, Huntsville, TX, p. 63. Copyright 2010 by C. Collier.

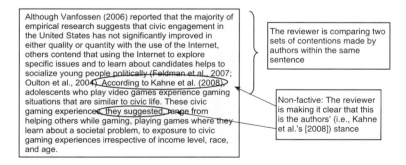

Figure 11.10 Example of a paragraph that contains multiple sources that are compared and contrasted in a coherent manner (Checkpoint 5), and which indicates clearly the author's stance in a non-factive manner (Checkpoint 4)

Adapted from "The impact of icivics on students' core civic knowledge," by K. LeCompte, B. Moore, and B. Blevins, 2011, *Research in the Schools, 18*(2), p. 59. Copyright 2011 by Mid-South Educational Research Association.

CHECKPOINT 6: WHENEVER POSSIBLE, PROVIDE METHODOLOGICAL AND/OR PROCEDURAL INFORMATION ALONGSIDE FINDINGS

Part of avoiding the use of annotations is contextualizing at least some of the studies cited. And an effective way of contextualizing a study is by presenting *methodological* (e.g., research approach [i.e., quantitative vs. qualitative vs. mixed]; research philosophy [e.g., postpositivism, social constructionism]) and/or *procedural* (e.g., sampling scheme, sample size, characteristics of the sample, method of data collection, research design, data analysis technique) information about the study. Apart from contextualizing studies, providing methodological/procedural information can be used as a form of the reviewer's critique of the study, making clearer the reviewer's logic of argumentation. Unfortunately, novice researchers typically do not contextualize the studies that they cite.

EXAMPLE: CONTEXTUALIZING FINDINGS

Figure 11.11 presents an example of a paragraph wherein procedural information is provided by the reviewer, namely, Benge (2012).

More recently, Mol, Bus, and de Jong's (2009) meta-analysis examining the impact of interactive storybook reading on vocabulary and print knowledge provided additional evidence supporting the use of read-alouds as a method to foster vocabulary growth in young children. The analysis, a result of an examination of 31 quasi-experimental studies conducted between 1986 and 2007, revealed significant growth in students' oral language skills, including their expressive vocabulary, when students were exposed to frequent and interactive storybook read-alouds.

The reviewer has provided useful procedural information that allows readers to assess the quality of Mol, Bus, and de Jong's (2009) finding. Although, as discussed in Chapter 9, meta-analyses are highly regarded by quantitative researchers, the quality of this study would have been even greater if at least some of the 31 studies examined by Mol et al. (2009) had represented true experiments

Figure 11.11 Example of a paragraph wherein procedural information is provided by the reviewer (Checkpoint 5)

Adapted from *Effect of cartoon mnemonics and revised definitions on the acquisition of tier-two vocabulary words among selected fifth-grade students*, by C. L. Benge, 2012, unpublished doctoral dissertation, Sam Houston State University, Huntsville, TX, pp. 6–7. Copyright 2012 by C. L. Benge.

CHECKPOINT 7: MINIMIZE THE USE OF QUOTATIONS, ESPECIALLY LONG QUOTATIONS

A very common mistake made by novice reviewers is that they tend to overuse quotations. However, every time a reviewer inserts a quotation, he/she is adding another author's voice with a different writing style to the reviewer's voice. And the longer the quotation, the more the author's voice would interfere with the reviewer's voice, thereby interrupting the flow of the CLR report. Further, when quotations are used out of context, they likely will not fully convey the reviewer's meaning, thereby masking the path of argumentation. And any attempt by the reviewer to explain out-of-place quotations might obfuscate the reviewer's path even further because this explanation might include irrelevant details that are not related to the underlying topic, which would distract readers.

CHECKPOINT 8: USE METAPHORS WHENEVER POSSIBLE TO ENHANCE MEANING

According to Lackoff and Johnson (1980), *metaphors* transmit meaning from one conceptual domain to

TOOL: GUIDELINES FOR QUOTATIONS

Quotations should be used sparingly, especially long quotations. Whenever possible, quotations should be paraphrased carefully to avoid any hint of plagiarism. An important benefit in paraphrasing quotations is that the reviewer will be in total control as to the text that is selected for the CLR report, thereby ensuring that all non-essential information is removed, and at the same time ensuring that the flow of the CLR report is not interrupted. Box 11.10 provides several guidelines for using quotations.

BOX 11.10

GUIDELINES FOR USING QUOTATIONS

1. Use a quotation if it supports the reviewer's stance or the selected author's stance.

2. Use a quotation if it supports a knowledge claim.

3. Use a quotation if it illuminates the reviewer's path of argumentation.

4. Use a quotation only if it is difficult to paraphrase accurately and doing so would lead to a loss of meaning.

5. Use a quotation if its authority is essential to the reviewer's logic of argumentation.

6. Use a quotation if the language being quoted is appropriate.

7. Use the exact quotation (i.e., verbatim) and double-check for any errors of omission or commission.

8. Select quotations that minimize the interruption of the flow of the CLR narrative.

9. When using quotations the following three steps are important.

    a. Introduce the quotation.
    b. Provide the quotation:

        i. For any word or phrase that is grammatically incorrect, point this out to the reader by inserting a bracket that contains the letter "sic," which originates from the Latin phrase *sic erat scriptum* (i.e., "thus it is written").
        ii. To shorten (long) quotations, use ellipses [...], or use only portions of the quotation that is relevant.

    c. Discuss the quotation:

        i. Clarify how the quotation is consistent with the logic of argumentation.
        ii. Explain any technical terms or ambiguous words.

10. Although using the word "quote" instead of quotation is rampant, strictly speaking, "quote" is a verb and "quotation" is a noun. Thus, essentially, you "quote a quotation."

(Continued)

(Continued)

11. See, for example, the following links:

    http://quotations.about.com/cs/quotations101/a/bl_quotquotn.htm

    http://grammar.about.com/od/words/a/quotationgloss.htm

12. Do not begin a sentence with a quotation. Rather, quotations should be introduced using a format such as "According to Smith (2007, p. 5),"

13. Also, you should never have a quotation standing alone as a complete sentence (cf. http://www2.ivcc.edu/rambo/eng1001/quotes.htm; http://ww2.sjc.edu/archandouts/usingquotations.pdf)

14. For many style guides, shorter quotations should be embedded within the paragraph; longer quotations should appear as an indented block; e.g., for APA style:

    a. If the quotation has fewer than 40 words, the quotation should be embedded within the paragraph via the use of quotation marks (cf. APA, 2010, pp. 92, 171).

    b. An indented block format (with no quotation marks) should be used for quotations containing more than 39 words (cf. APA, 2010, p. 171).

---

another domain, from which theory often emerges. Moreover, metaphors create mental images that facilitate communication of concepts, thereby enhancing meaning by helping readers to connect new or difficult concepts to familiar entities such as food or entertainment. By creating new literacies, metaphors represent more than the literal meaning. As surmised by Coffey and Atkinson (1996), metaphors are "a device of representation through which new meaning can be learned" (p. 85). We encourage reviewers to use metaphors whenever possible to enhance meaning extracted from the CLR.

EXAMPLE: USING METAPHORS

We have used metaphors on several occasions in this book. For example, in Chapter 2, we used the metaphor of distinguishing a type of bird for *birdwatchers* to help readers identify similarities among types of literature reviews and classify them by distinguishing characteristics. In Chapter 3, we used the metaphor of *music genre* as methodology. In Chapter 4, we used the metaphor of

cuisine and a buffet serving line in a restaurant to represent mixed methods research. Figure 11.12 provides an example of a paragraph in which a metaphor is used and which indicates clearly the reviewer's stance.

CHECKPOINT 9: CHECK TO ENSURE THAT THE APPROPRIATE TYPE OF CLAIM HAS BEEN MADE THROUGHOUT THE CLR REPORT

In Chapter 7, we outlined five types of claims that Hart (2005) conceptualized, and added a sixth claim as follows: (a) claims of fact, (b) claims of value, (c) claims of policy, (d) claims of concept, (e) claims of interpretation (representing Hart's [2005] five claims), and (f) claims of observation (representing our additional claim).

CHECKPOINT 10: USE LINK WORDS/PHRASES TO MAXIMIZE TRANSITIONS BETWEEN SENTENCES AND BETWEEN PARAGRAPHS

Another common weakness of literature reviews written by novice reviewers is the lack of appropriate

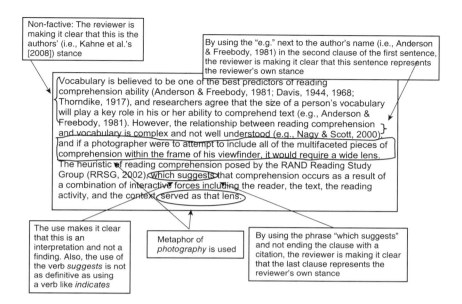

Figure 11.12 Example of a paragraph that contains multiple sources that are compared and contrasted in a coherent manner (Checkpoint 4), in which a metaphor is used (Checkpoint 8), and which indicates clearly the reviewer's stance (Checkpoint 3)

Adapted from *Effect of cartoon mnemonics and revised definitions on the acquisition of tier-two vocabulary words among selected fifth-grade students,* by C. L. Benge, 2012, unpublished doctoral dissertation, Sam Houston State University, Huntsville, TX, pp. 6–7. Copyright 2012 by C. L. Benge.

transitions between sentences and between paragraphs. Unfortunately, this lack of transition prevents a literature review from being maximally coherent, thereby making it more difficult for readers to follow the reviewer's logic of argumentation. ***Link words/ phrases*** are very useful for connecting ideas and, hence, for connecting sentences and paragraphs. Interestingly, analyzing manuscripts that were submitted over a 3-year period (2011–2014) to the journal *Research in the Schools* (*RITS*), for which they serve as editors, via the use of QDA Miner and WordStat, Onwuegbuzie and Frels (2015c) documented that the dimension labeled as *Add information/provide similarity* was the most commonly used (by 71.6% of authors), followed by the dimension labeled *narration* (by 60.8% of authors), and then the dimension labeled *sequence previous ideas* (also 60.8% frequency). The remaining nine dimensions were used by less than 50% of the authors. The two most common link words, respectively, were *Finally* (52.7%) and *Additionally*

(51.4%). All other link words/phrases were used by one-third of the authors or less. Even more compelling was Onwuegbuzie and Frels's (2015c) finding that the following dimensions statistically significantly and practically significantly predicted whether or not a manuscript was rejected by the editor: *Add information/provide similarity, Narration,* and *Provide an emphasis.* More specifically, manuscripts that contained one or more link words/phrases that were classified as *Add information/provide similarity* were 1.75 (95% confidence interval [CI] = 1.09, 2.79) times less likely to be rejected than were their counterparts; manuscripts that contained one or more link words/phrases that were classified as *Narration* were 1.32 (95% CI = 1.01, 2.31) times less likely to be rejected than were their counterparts; and manuscripts that contained one or more link words/phrases that were classified as *Provide an emphasis* were 1.75 (95% CI = 1.07, 2.86) times less likely to be rejected than were their counterparts. This is the very first

TOOL: CHECKING CLAIMS

Table 11.8 presents a description of each of these six claims. It is important that reviewers check to ensure that they have made the appropriate type of claim throughout their CLR drafts, and that, for each claim, they provide evidence (i.e., by using data to support the claim that they are making), warrant (i.e., by providing an expectation that links the claim and its evidence), and backing (i.e., comprising the context and assumptions used to provide justification for the warrant and evidence) (cf. Toulmin, 1958).

Table 11.8 Different types of claims

Type of Claim	Description
Claims of fact	Statements that can be demonstrated as being true or false. For example, statements such as *London is the capital of England* or *There are four universities in Manchester* are either true or false: they can be verified or refuted using evidence such as an authoritative reference (e.g., encyclopedia). The difference between a claim based on facts and other forms of claim is that others require additional warrants and backing for their acceptance.
Claims of value	These cannot be demonstrated as being true or false: they are judgments about the worth of something. For example, someone might make the statement that watching *Coronation Street* (a British soap opera) is a waste of time; this is a judgmental statement. To back it up, they might add a qualifying standard, such as *Watching soap operas does nothing to improve the mind or enhance understanding of the world around us*. One might agree with the value claim or make a challenge through the counter-claim that modern living is stressful, that people need relaxation, and that watching *Coronation Street* is a form of relaxation and, therefore, is good for people.
Claims of policy	Normative statements about what ought to be done rather than what is done. For example, someone might claim that public libraries are an essential part of the culture of a civilized country and should, therefore, be protected from budget cuts. In this case, we see a claim of policy combined with a claim of value.
Claims of concept	These are about definitions and the recognizability of the language used. For example, when comparing views on abortion or euthanasia, the way the claim is worded would be important. Some organizations, such as *Life*, would claim that abortion is murder of an unborn child. The claim employs particular definitions that are not only restrictive but also emotive. The use of words is not, therefore, as given in dictionary definitions, but is a matter of interpretive use.
Claims of interpretation	These are about proposals on how some data or evidence are to be understood. Facts mean nothing without interpretations, and interpretations can and often do differ.
Claims of observation	Statements that emerge from empirical research studies, that are situated within the set of findings, and that address some of the same research questions. Unless a finding stems from population data, they cannot be demonstrated as being either true or false but rather as providing support or refutation for a knowledge claim.

Adapted from *Doing a literature review: Releasing the social science research imagination*, by C. Hart, 2005, London, England, p. 90. Copyright 2005 by Sage Publications.

TOOL: POTENTIAL LINKING WORDS

Figure 11.13 presents a sample of Onwuegbuzie's (2014a) typology of transition words and phrases.

Add information/provide similarity:	Narration:	Provide an emphasis:	Contrast ideas:
And	At first	Naturally	But
In addition	Initially	Especially	Unfortunately
As well as	In the beginning	Specifically	However
Also	At the beginning	Particularly	Although/Even though
Too	At the end	In particular	Despite/Despite the fact that
Furthermore/further	In the end	Moreover	In spite of/In spite of the fact
Moreover	Immediately	Whatever	that
Apart from	Suddenly	Whenever	Nevertheless
In addition to	As soon as	The more	Nonetheless
Besides	Then	Above all	While
Not only… but also	Next	Exactly because	Whereas
In the same way/vein	Finally	In fact	Unlike
In the same manner	At last	Indeed	In theory… in practice…
Equally important	Eventually	In particular	In contrast/Contrastingly
By the same token	Before	Certainly	Conversely
Again	After	Notably	On the one hand… Neither…
Equally	Afterwards	To be sure/To be certain	nor
Identically	Until	Surely	On the contrary
As well as	When	Markedly	At the same time
Together with	While	Surprisingly	Even so
Likewise	During	Alarmingly	Then again
Correspondingly	Soon	Significantly	Above all
Similarly	Prior to	Frequently	In reality
Additionally	Once	Infrequently	After all
Another key point	No sooner than	Oftentimes	Yet
	To begin with	Typically	Still
		Usually	Or
		Obviously	Albeit
			Besides
Summarize previous information:	**Provide a result:**	**Express purpose:**	As much as
			Instead
In short	Therefore	In order to	Otherwise
In brief	Thus	To	Rather
In summary	Consequently	So that	Regardless
To summarize	This means that	In the event that	Notwithstanding
In a nutshell	As a result	For the purpose of	Aside from
To conclude	As such	With this in mind	Uniquely
In conclusion	Thereby	In the hope that	Comparatively
As a whole	This is why	To the extent that	In the long run
Simply put	For this reason	In the hope that	As has been noted
In other words	Under those	To this end	In a word
Overall	circumstances	In view of	For the most part
All in all	In that case	If… then	Given these points
Generally	In effect	Unless	In essence
On the whole	Hence/henceforth	When	Eventually
In the main	Thereupon	Whenever	In any event
To sum up	Accordingly	While	In either case
To put it differently	Forthwith		Ultimately

Figure 11.13 A typology of link words

study in which the potential importance of using link words/phrases has been empirically demonstrated. Thus, we encourage reviewers to assess their use/nonuse of link words/phrases.

CHECKPOINT 11: ASSESS THE READABILITY OF THE CLR DRAFT

Another component of writing that helps to maximize the coherency of a CLR report is readability. Broadly speaking, *readability* is the ease with which a text can be read and understood. Over the past century, readability has been studied by numerous researchers, yielding more than 1,000 items in the literature (Harris & Hodges, 1995). Since the development of the first readability formula in 1923 (Lively & Pressey, 1923), numerous reading formulas have been developed. Of these formulas, the two most popular have been the Flesch Reading Ease and the Flesch–Kincaid Grade Level. According to Flesch (1946), the highest (i.e., easiest) Flesch Reading Ease score is approximately 100, with a Flesch Reading Ease score between 90 and 100 indicating that the text potentially can be understood by fifth-grade students; a Flesch Reading Ease score between 60 and 70 indicating that the text potentially can be understood by eighth- to ninth-grade students; and a Flesch Reading Ease score between 0 and 30 indicating that the text potentially can be understood by college graduate students. In contrast, the formula for the Flesch–Kincaid Grade Level, in effect, converts the Flesch Reading Ease score to a U.S. grade level in order for users (e.g., administrators, educators, parents, students) to assess the readability level of text using a common metric.

Conveniently, both the Flesch Reading Ease score and the Flesch–Kincaid Grade Level can be obtained in seconds via Microsoft Office Word's *readability statistics*. In order to extract these two indices via Microsoft Office Word's 2013 readability program, the user should click on *FILE*, then *Options*, then *Proofing*, and then check *Show readability statistics*. These steps will lead to readability statistics being displayed whenever the user conducts a spell-check of her/his document. (However, unfortunately, the Mac version of Microsoft Office Word for the Flesch–Kincaid Grade Level has presently been artificially capped at grade-level 12.) Using

Microsoft Office Word's 2013 readability program, and selecting one of the chapters of our CLR book at random—namely, Chapter 2—yielded a Flesch Reading Ease score of 9.6 and a Flesch–Kincaid Grade Level of 18.5. Therefore, we can assume that Chapter 2 represents text that is appropriate for the readers of our book!

EXAMPLE: CHECKING READABILITY

Onwuegbuzie, Mallette, Hwang, and Slate (2013) examined whether the readability of manuscripts submitted to a journal for consideration for publication predicted their eventual disposition (i.e., accept/revise-and-resubmit vs. reject). These researchers found that manuscripts with Flesch Reading Ease scores between 0 and 30 were 1.64 more times less likely to be rejected than were manuscripts with Flesch Reading Ease scores greater than 30; and manuscripts with Flesch–Kincaid Grade Level scores of 16 and above were 4.55 times less likely to be rejected than were manuscripts with Flesch–Kincaid Grade Level scores less than 16. Thus, Onwuegbuzie, Mallette, et al. (2013) provided compelling evidence that the readability of the text warrants important consideration. More specifically, what is important is not producing a text that is as easy as possible but rather matching the text to the reading level of the readers.

Consistent with their findings, Gazni (2011)—who examined 260,000 abstracts spanning 22 disciplines of articles published between 2000 and 2009 from the five institutions (e.g., Harvard) that receive the largest number of citations—documented a statistically significant, negative relationship between text difficulty and citation rates: in particular, the more difficult the text, the more it was cited. Further, the Flesch Reading Ease scores of *all* abstracts fell within the most difficult range (i.e., 0–30), with scores ranging from an average of 12 to an average of 25.

Similarly, Metoyer-Duran (1993)—who examined whether readability estimates differed significantly among abstracts of published, accepted, and rejected manuscripts submitted to *College and Research Libraries* during the 1990–1991 period—discovered that the readability estimates of manuscripts accepted for publication were significantly different from the readability estimates of manuscripts rejected for publication. Specifically, manuscripts that were accepted for publication contained text that was more difficult than was the text in manuscripts that were rejected, with the mean Flesch Reading Ease score being 28.04—again, in the 0–30 range—for accepted manuscripts and 30.77 (i.e., outside the 0–30 range) for rejected manuscripts.

Therefore, based on the only three studies in which the predictability of readability indices with respect to manuscript disposition has been examined, and which yielded consistent findings (i.e., Gazni, 2011; Metoyer-Duran, 1993; Onwuegbuzie, Mallette, et al., 2013), we encourage reviewers to use readability indices to assess the appropriateness and flow of their CLR drafts, deeming CLR drafts with Flesch Reading Ease scores between 0 and 30 and Flesch–Kincaid Grade Level scores of 16 and above as being appropriate. As noted by Macdonald-Ross (1978), reviewers can engage in a writing–rewriting cycle, as follows:

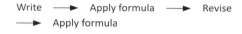

Write ⟶ Apply formula ⟶ Revise ⟶ Apply formula

CHECKPOINT 12: ASSESS THE STRUCTURE OF THE CLR DRAFT FOR PARALLELISM

Another useful check for reviewers to conduct is assessing the structure of the CLR draft for *parallelism*, or the way in which two or more ideas are presented equally. Often, the CLR drafts that have the clearest logic of argumentation are those that have parallel structure. Ways that CLR drafts can be checked for parallelism include the following: (a) for any sections that contain findings, both positive and negative findings are presented; (b) any discussion of strengths of an entity is accompanied by a discussion of weaknesses, and vice versa; (c) authors who both agree and disagree with a viewpoint are cited; and (d) available quantitative research and qualitative research findings (as well as mixed research findings) are reported. In so doing, for any unavoidable lack of parallelism, such as a lack of qualitative research findings, reviewers might consider pointing out to readers this discrepancy, to avoid any reader assuming that the reviewer is responsible for this lack of parallelism. It should be noted that parallelism does not imply balance. That is, reviewers do not have to find an (approximately) equal number of quantitative and qualitative findings, an equal number of positive and negative findings, or

an equal balance between the reviewer's voice and the authors' voices to attain parallelism. Indeed, in most cases, such a balance does not exist. In fact, noting to readers an imbalance likely would help to clarify further the reviewer's logic of argument. However, by at least presenting ideas, conceptualizations, theories, findings, and interpretations at both ends of the spectrum whenever available, however unevenly presented, increases the ethicalness of the CLR.

CHECKPOINT 13: CHECK CLR DRAFT FOR GRAMMATICAL ERRORS

Onwuegbuzie and Daniel (2005) documented that authors who submit manuscripts that contain poorly written literature reviews are more than six times more likely to have their manuscripts rejected than are their counterparts. Thus, reviewers always should take steps to ensure that their CLR drafts are as error free as possible with respect to grammar. Indeed, grammatical errors not only can be very distracting to readers, but also they can make it more difficult for readers to follow the reviewer's logic of argumentation.

CHECKPOINT 14: CHECK CLR DRAFT FOR STYLE GUIDE/MANUAL ERRORS

Each field and discipline has its own professional writing conventions. The most common conventions include the following: *American Psychological Association Publication Manual* (primarily used for the social sciences), *The Chicago Manual of Style* (primarily used in the United States), *The Modern Language Association Style Manual* (primarily used for the humanities), *American Medical Association Manual of Style* (primarily used in medicine), *American Sociological Association Style Guide* (primarily used for sociology), and *American Chemical Society Style Guide* (primarily used for chemistry). It is essential that reviewers follow the writing conventions associated with their fields/disciplines as closely as possible. In fact, Onwuegbuzie, Combs, Slate, and Frels (2010) documented that manuscripts which contained nine or more different APA errors were 3.00 times more likely to be rejected than were manuscripts containing fewer than nine different APA errors.

TOOL: CHECKLIST FOR GRAMMATICAL ERRORS

Figure 11.14 presents a list of the most common grammatical errors committed by authors that were identified by Onwuegbuzie (2014e). Reviewers who experience difficulties avoiding grammatical errors might consider obtaining help. For example, most universities offer writing classes. Also, many universities contain writing centers that provide a variety of services for students free of charge. International reviewers with writing difficulties might consider hiring proof-readers.

Grammatical Error	Example of Error	Corrected Version
Non-use of possessive case	These authors findings These author's findings Each authors' findings Frels' (2014) study…	These authors' findings These authors' findings Each author's findings Frels's (2014) study…
Mismatch between possessive pronouns and nouns	Several researchers have developed their own instrument	Several researchers have developed their own instruments
Mismatch between indefinite article and noun	Some researchers have reported a higher scores	Some researchers have reported higher scores
Colloquial expressions	The researcher ran her analysis	The researcher conducted her analysis
Using *may* instead of *might*	These findings may have implications for teachers	These findings might have implications for teachers
Contractions	The findings didn't support the theory	The findings did not support the theory
Anthropomorphism	The study found	The study revealed The researcher found
Split infinitives unnecessarily being used	The number of mixed research studies in this area has continued to steadily increase	The number of mixed research studies in this area steadily has continued to increase
The word *if* often is mistakenly used as a substitute for the word *whether*	Researchers have not decided if this interpretation represents the most viable explanation	Researchers have not decided whether this interpretation represents the most viable explanation
Between being used when more than two elements are involved	Debates have emerged between quantitative, qualitative, and mixed researchers	Debates have emerged among quantitative, qualitative, and mixed researchers
The words *feel*, *think*, and *believe* being used interchangeably	The researcher feels that this is an important finding	The researcher thinks that this is an important finding

Using the phrase *comprised of*	The sample comprised of both teachers and students	The sample contained/consisted of both teachers and students
Subject–verb disagreement	Data is	Data are
The word *include(s)* or *included* being used when the list involved is exhaustive	The sample included 100 males and 100 females	The sample comprised 100 males and 100 females
Not recognizing that words such as *Thus* and *Therefore* indicate a conditional action, whereas the word *Thereby* represents a process	Two participants dropped out of the study, therefore reducing the sample size to 98 Two participants dropped out of the study; thereby, the sample size was reduced to 98	Two participants dropped out of the study, thereby reducing the sample size to 98 Two participants dropped out of the study; therefore, the sample size was reduced to 98
While not only being used to link events occurring simultaneously	While these findings are unusual, they are not unique The experimental group members were mostly male, while the control group members were mostly female	Although these findings are unusual, they are not unique The experimental group members were mostly male, whereas the control group members were mostly female
The word *since* not referring strictly to time	Causality could not be assumed since the research design was correlational	Causality could not be assumed because the research design was correlational
The word *that* not only being used for restrictive clauses and the word *which* not only being used for nonrestrictive clauses (set off with commas)	The findings which were the most compelling arose from the qualitative phase The findings, that were collected during the qualitative phase, were very compelling	The findings that were the most compelling arose from the qualitative phase The findings, which were collected during the qualitative phase, were very compelling
The word *who* not being used for human beings	The researchers that used this technique were in the majority	The researchers who used this technique were in the majority
The word *Caucasian* being used	The sample comprised 250 Caucasian students	The sample comprised 250 White students
Mismatch between the subject and plural pronoun used	The researcher must ask themselves	Researchers must ask themselves
The words *This* and *These* being used as stand-alone pronouns	This demands attention These have implications for doctors	This gap in the literature demands attention These findings have implications for doctors

Figure 11.14 The most common grammatical errors and words/phrases that reduce clarity

Adapted from *Prevalence of grammatical errors in journal article submissions*, by A. J. Onwuegbuzie, 2014e, unpublished manuscript, Sam Houston State University, Huntsville, TX. Copyright 2014 by A. J. Onwuegbuzie.

TOOL: CHECKLIST FOR APA STYLE GUIDELINES

Figure 11.15 contains 25 of the 60 most prevalent APA errors, which are presented in order of prevalence, alongside the prevalence rate (i.e., percentage), the description of the APA error as stated in the *Publication Manual*, and their associated page numbers. Rather than attempting to learn the APA style guide by reading the *Publication Manual*—a likely overwhelming process—we recommend that beginning reviewers, and even experienced reviewers who are required to follow the APA style guide, use this figure to help them focus their efforts. Moreover, reviewers can use this list to rule out APA stipulations and guidelines with which they are familiar and, therefore, focus on the APA errors that they commit. As such, this figure could serve as a personalized checklist for reviewers to use when editing their CLR drafts.

No.	APA Error Code	%	Description of Error and Reference to Sixth Edition APA Rule Page No.
1	Numbers	57.3	Not using figures (e.g., all numbers 10 and above; p. 122); not using numbers to represent time, dates, ages, sample, subsample, or population size or in a numbered series (p. 112)
2	Hyphenation	55.5	Not hyphenating a compound with a participle when it precedes the term it modifies (p. 97)
3	Use of *et al.*	44.5	Not citing all authors the first time; in subsequent citations, not including only the surname of the first author followed by "et al." (not italicized and with a period after "al"; p. 175)
4	Headings: Punctuation	44.5	Not capitalizing the words in headings appropriately; incorrectly using capitalization or punctuation with Level 4 headings (pp. 101–102)
5	Use of *since*	41.8	Using *since* instead of *because* (p. 83)
6	Tables and figures	40.0	Not presenting tables in tabular form and repeating information in the text; not formatting figures according to APA (e.g., not copied, SPSS outputs; p. 141)
7	Use of commas between elements	40.0	Not using commas between elements (including before *and* and *or*) in a series of three or more items (p. 88)
8	Use of abbreviations/ acronyms	37.3	Not spelling out acronyms on the first occasion used (p. 104)
9	Spacing	30.0	Not consistently using double spacing between lines, including use of direct quotations (p. 229)
10	Usage of & as opposed to the word *and*	33.6	Incorrectly using the ampersand in the text or the word *and* in the citation (p. 177)
11	Use of past tense	32.7	Not using past tense to describe previous findings (p. 78)
12	Use of italics for symbols	30.9	Not italicizing symbols (e.g., *n*) (p. 118)

13	Misuse of *while*	29.1	Using the word *while* instead of the word *whereas* or *although* (p. 83)
14	Formatting	29.1	Not formatting correctly (e.g., incorrect indentations, use of italicizing or bold, title too long, title not being on the first page, header font not matching body of paper; p. 62)
15	Misuse of *which*	28.2	Using the word *which* instead of the word *that* when the clause is restrictive (p. 83)
16	Anthropomorphism	27.3	Giving human characteristics to inanimate sources (p. 68)
17	Alphabetizing citations and references	26.4	Not placing all references in alphabetical order; not placing citations in text in alphabetical order (p. 178)
18	Capitalization of titles	24.5	Not capitalizing nouns followed by numerals or letters that denote a specific place in a numbered series (e.g., *year 1* instead of *Year 1*; p. 101)
19	Misuse of the word *data*	24.5	Misusing the word *data* as singular as opposed to plural (p. 79)
20	Elements and seriation	23.6	Incorrectly using *1, 2, 3*, instead of (*a*), (*b*), (*c*) (p. 64)
21	Misuse of superscript with numerals	22.7	Incorrectly using superscript (e.g., *4th* as opposed to *4th*; p. 113)
22	Citations: Commas and authors	22.7	Not placing a comma to separate the last two authors in a list of three or more authors (p. 184)
23	Boldface and italicized type	22.7	Misusing bold or italicized text (p. 106)
24	Citations: Direct quotes and page numbers	19.1	Neglecting to state a page number when direct quotations are used; a page number is not needed when direct quotations are not used; incorrectly using a capital *P* instead of a lowercase *p* (p. 170)
25	Misuse of the term *subjects*	17.3	Incorrectly using the term *subjects* instead of the correct term: *participants* (p. 73)

Figure 11.15 Errors and percentages of occurrence with references to the sixth edition of the *Publication Manual* (APA, 2010)

Adapted from "Editorial: Evidence-based guidelines for avoiding the 25 most common APA errors in journal article submissions," by A. J. Onwuegbuzie, J. P. Combs, J. R. Slate, and R. K. Frels, 2010, *Research in the Schools*, *16*(2), pp. xii–xiv. Copyright 2010 by Mid-South Educational Research Association.

CHECKPOINT 15: CHECK CLR DRAFT FOR PRESENTATION OF AN ADEQUATE NUMBER OF CITATIONS/REFERENCES

An important check for reviewers to include is whether their CLR drafts contain an adequate number of citations. Although the number of citations vary as a function of the goal of the CLR (e.g., stand-alone review vs. an end in itself) and the type of review (i.e., narrative review [i.e., general reviews, theoretical reviews, methodological reviews, and historical reviews] vs. systematic review [i.e., meta-analysis, rapid review, meta-synthesis, meta-summary] vs. integrative review), there are general citation trends that have been identified by researchers (Beile, Boote, & Killingsworth, 2004; Haycock, 2004; Onwuegbuzie, 2014b, 2014c), which provide guidelines for reviewers as to how many citations are adequate in journal articles and dissertations. Most notably, Onwuegbuzie, Frels, Hwang, and Slate (2013) examined the number of citations—as measured by the number of references used and the number of references per manuscript/article page—used in manuscripts submitted to two flagship journals for review for publication, namely: *Research in the Schools* (*RITS*) and *Educational Researcher* (*ER*). Also, these researchers examined the number of citations used in articles published in the following two flagship journals: *Research in the Schools* (*RITS*) and the *Journal of Mixed Methods Research* (*JMMR*). They observed that (unpublished) manuscripts that were submitted to *RITS* for review with fewer than 45 references were 2.52 times more likely to be rejected than were (unpublished) *RITS* manuscripts with 45 references or more. Further, (unpublished) manuscripts submitted to *ER* for review with fewer than 61 references were 1.73 times more likely to be rejected than were (unpublished) *ER* manuscripts with 61 or more references.

With respect to articles ($n = 66$) actually published in *RITS* over a 6-year period (2008–2013), Onwuegbuzie, Frels, et al. (2013) reported that the mean number of references was 48.39 (*SD* = 21.83), with the number of references ranging from 11 to 108. Further, approximately 90% of the articles contained 21 references or more, approximately 75% of the articles contained 34 references or more, approximately 67% of the articles contained 37 references or more, approximately 50% of the articles contained 46 references or more, approximately 33% of the articles contained 55 references or more, approximately 25% of the articles contained 62 references or more, and approximately 10% of the articles contained 79 references or more. With regard to articles ($n = 146$) actually published in *JMMR* over an 8-year period (2007–2014), Onwuegbuzie, Frels, et al. (2013) reported that the mean number of references was 50.88 (*SD* = 21.50), with the number of

references ranging from 9 to 139. Interestingly, approximately 90% of the articles contained 25 references or more, approximately 75% of the articles contained 36 references or more, approximately 67% of the articles contained 40 references or more, approximately 50% of the articles contained 48 references or more, approximately 33% of the articles contained 58 references or more, approximately 25% of the articles contained 63 references or more, and approximately 10% of the articles contained 77 references or more. These findings combined suggest that approximately 50 articles is the norm for these three journals (i.e., *RITS*, *ER*, *JMMR*). With respect to dissertations representing the field of education, on average, reference lists have been documented as containing between 159 (Beile et al., 2004) and 295 (Haycock, 2004) cited works. However, as admonished by Onwuegbuzie, Frels, et al. (2013),

> merely adding references is, by no means, not sufficient to improve the quality of a manuscript. Rather, authors should include only the most relevant citations that render a manuscript as being both warranted and transparent—as advocated by AERA (2006). These citations should be used to conduct operations such as to summarize, to frame, to support, to refute, to develop, and to expand assumptions, ideas, beliefs, propositions, theories, schemas, models, hypotheses, procedures, methodologies, findings, interpretations, conclusions, or the like that are made by the author(s) himself/herself/themselves, by the author(s) that is being cited, and/or by stakeholders. (p. xiii)

Further, for empirical reports, reviewers not only should provide an adequate number of citations in their literature review sections, but also they should provide relevant citations for as many of the 12 components of a primary research report as appropriate. In fact, it is only by providing an adequate number of relevant references in their CLR drafts that reviewers can effectively situate the works that they cite within the extant literature. Thus, reviewers should check that their CLR drafts contain a sufficient number of citations.

CHECKPOINT 16: CHECK THE CLR DRAFT FOR CITATION ERRORS AND REFERENCE LIST ERRORS

Alongside checking for style guide errors in the body of your CLR draft, reviewers also should examine their reference lists/bibliographies extremely carefully and check for citation errors and reference list errors. Both types of errors are strictly to be avoided regardless of the style guide that the reviewer is following. *Citation errors* represent inconsistencies between sources that are provided in the body of the text and how they are referenced in the reference list. For example, according to the authors of APA (2010), citation errors occur when authors fail "to make certain that each source referenced appears in both places [text and reference list] and that the text citation and reference list entry are identical in spelling of author names and year" (p. 174).

Citation errors fall into one of five areas: (a) work that is cited in text does not appear in the reference list; (b) work that appears in the text is not consistent with the corresponding work that is presented in the reference list; (c) work that is cited in the reference list does not appear in the text; (d) work that appears in the text is incomplete or inaccurate; and (e) work that appears in the reference list is incomplete or inaccurate (Onwuegbuzie, Frels, & Slate, 2010). Surprisingly, more than 90% of authors commit one or more of these five types of citation errors (Onwuegbuzie, Combs, Frels, & Slate, 2011; Onwuegbuzie, Frels, & Slate, 2010). As such, the citation error represents the most prevalent style guide error among authors (Onwuegbuzie, Combs, et al., 2011; Onwuegbuzie, Frels, & Slate, 2010). And to make matters worse, a citation error typically cannot be rectified directly by readers or even copyeditors—thereby making it the most serious style guide error. Interestingly, manuscripts with citation errors are significantly less likely to be accepted for publication in journals (Onwuegbuzie, Frels, & Slate, 2010). Thus, every reviewer should work as hard as possible to avoid citation errors when compiling reference lists because these errors not only adversely affect the trustworthiness of the CLR report, they also cast doubts about the credibility and integrity of the reviewer.

Reference list errors are style guide errors that appear in the reference list. Unfortunately, like citation errors, reference list errors are rampant, not only among authors who follow the APA style guide (Onwuegbuzie, Hwang, et al., 2012; Onwuegbuzie, Hwang, et al., 2011), but also among authors who follow other style guides (Onwuegbuzie, 2014d), with manuscripts containing the most reference list errors being significantly more likely to be rejected for publication (Onwuegbuzie, Hwang, et al., 2011).

CHECKPOINT 17: CHECK FOR FALLACIES IN ARGUMENTS IN THE CLR DRAFT

When constructing an argument, reviewers should check to ensure that they have not made any fallacies. In general, *fallacies* are arguments that are deceptive, misleading, unsound, or false. Thouless and Thouless (1990, 2011) identified 37 fallacies

TOOL: CHECKLIST FOR APA STYLE ERRORS

Box 11.11 contains the 50 most prevalent APA-based reference list errors, which are presented in order of prevalence. As before, this figure can be used by reviewers to help them focus their efforts in learning how to create error-free APA-based reference lists, thereby serving as a personalized checklist for reviewers to use when editing the reference lists associated with their CLR drafts. For those reviewers looking for a practice exercise for reducing reference list errors, we refer you to Onwuegbuzie, Hwang, et al. (2011). Committing citation and reference list errors represents a serious ethical issue. Indeed such errors prevent reviewers who commit them from declaring that they have conducted an *ethical* review.

BOX 11.11

THE 50 MOST PREVALENT REFERENCE LIST ERRORS PRESENTED IN DESCENDING ORDER OF FREQUENCY

Reference List Error

Serial (issue) numbers presented when the page numbers in each volume are continuous

Comma not presented to separate two authors

Superscripts inappropriately used when providing edition number

Space not presented between initials of each author

Period not presented after the author's name (when the author does not represent a person but an organization) and before the publication year

Website inappropriately underlined

Month not given for a paper presentation

"Publications" or "Publications Inc" inappropriately presented when listing the publisher

Reference list not double spaced

Citations not presented in alphabetical order

Title of journal article inappropriately capitalized

Comma not presented after retrieval year of internal source

Volume number not italicized

"Inc" inappropriately presented when listing the publisher

Title of book inappropriately capitalized

"&" not used to separate the last two authors

Reference heading is bolded

Retrieval date not provided for web-based citations

First letter of the second part of the title not capitalized

Title of edited books inappropriately capitalized

Title of journal not italicized

Space not presented to separate initials of each editor of an edited book

"And" instead of "&" to separate the last two authors

City, state, and/or publisher not always provided

Title of book not always italicized

Period inappropriately appears after the numbers of ERIC

Page number of book chapters not presented after the title of the book

Space not presented between "pp." and the page number

Page number of journal articles not presented

Initials of all authors not presented

State pertaining to the publisher not abbreviated

made by authors, and Hart (2005) extended their concept for 19 fallacies that are pertinent for reviewers. Further, reviewers should check their CLR drafts to ensure that any criticisms contained within it are effective. As stated by Hart (2005), the following characteristics are elements of ***effective criticism*** that reviewers should embrace: (a) evaluating the strengths and weaknesses of a position before agreeing on it and defending it; (b) acknowledging that a particular perspective has some utility, whereas other perspectives need to be refuted; (c) focusing on ideas, conceptualizations, theories, findings, and interpretations and not on the author of these elements (i.e., criticizing the message and not the messenger); (d)

being cognizant of one's own critical stance, providing a defensible rationale for selecting each work for criticism, and looking out for flaws in the critique; (e) selecting elements from existing arguments and reframing them to yield a synthesis, which represents a new perspective; (f) identifying weaknesses in an argument by identifying fallacies, circular reasoning, lack of plausibility, or lack of evidence; and (g) identifying flaws in a criticism made by another person of some perspective (e.g., idea, conceptualization, theory, finding, or interpretation), thereby resulting in a rejection of the criticism made, and, in the absence of any meritorious criticisms, acknowledging the usefulness of the original perspective.

TOOL: CHECKLIST FOR FALLACIES IN ARGUMENT

To facilitate effective criticism, Table 11.9 presents a personalized checklist for avoiding fallacies.

Table 11.9 Fallacies in arguments

Fallacy	What it is and How to Avoid it
Implied definition	Referring to something without clearly defining it; always define what you refer to, especially concepts
Inaccurate definition	Closing down alternatives by giving a restrictive definition
Changing meanings	Defining something as A, then using A, in a different way, B
Emotional language	Using value-loaded or ethically loaded terms
Use of all rather than some	Using bland generalization to incorporate all variables and, therefore, to minimize contradictory examples
Ignoring alternatives	Giving one interpretation or example as if all others could be treated and categorized in the same way
Selected instances	Picking out unusual or unrepresentative examples
Forced analogy	Using an analogy without recognizing the applicability of other contradictory analogies
Similarity	Claiming there is no real difference between two things even when there is
Mere analogy	Use of analogy with no recourse to examples from the real world
False credentials	Exaggerating your credentials or experience to convince others of your authority
Technical language	Deliberate use of jargon intended to impress the reader and/or hide the lack of a foundation to an argument
Special pleading	Claiming a special case to raise your argument above other similar portions. This is often associated with the use of emotive language
Playing on the reader	Telling readers what they want to hear rather than challenging their thinking and assumptions
Claiming prejudice	Attributing prejudice to an opponent in order to discredit them
Appealing to others for authority	Claiming that someone else in authority has made the same argument as yourself in order to strengthen your own position
False context	Giving examples out of context or using nothing but hypothetical scenarios
Extremities	Ignoring center ground positions by focusing only on the extreme ends of a spectrum of alternatives
Tautology	Use of language structures to get acceptance of your argument from others. This is often in the form of "too much of X is bad"; therefore, X itself is not good.

Adapted from *Doing a literature review: Releasing the social science research imagination*, by C. Hart, 2005, p. 98. Copyright 2005 by Sage Publications.

CHECKPOINT 18: CHECK FOR ETHICAL PRACTICES IN THE CLR DRAFT

Although all the previous recommendations that we have provided represent important elements of the CLF draft audit, indubitably the most essential pertains to the ethicalness of the CLR draft. The absence of particular details in the report results in ethical consequences. These ***ethical issues*** include the following: falsification, fabrication, nepotism, copyright violations, and plagiarism. The first three ethical issues are the most serious because they represent deliberate actions. For example, a literature reviewer cannot falsify a researcher's finding by accident. However, the latter ethical issues are worthy of discussion because they easily could occur by accident. We will discuss each of these ethical issues, in turn.

Copyright violation. A copyright violation represents the use of information that is protected by copyright law without permission. Such an action infringes specific exclusive rights that legally have been bestowed on the copyright holder. These rights include the right to distribute, to reproduce, and/or to exhibit the copyrighted work, or to produce derivative works (i.e., one or more works that are based in part or in whole on the original copyrighted work). In the context of academic publishing, the copyright holder typically is the publisher of the work; however, the author of the work can be a copyright holder, especially when the work has been published in an open source outlet (e.g., journal). Or the copyright might be shared between the author(s) and the publisher—as is the case for the excellent journal entitled *The Qualitative Report*.

To comply with copyright laws, the literature reviewer *always* must acknowledge the copyright owner(s), give full credit to the copyright owner(s), and obtain written permission—in both print and electronic form—to adapt or to reproduce the information. This acknowledgment often appears in footnotes. The most common copyrighted elements that you should acknowledge are lengthy quotations, tables, and figures that are being adapted or reproduced for your report. The requirements for obtaining permission to use copyrighted material vary from one copyright owner to the next. For this reason, reviewers must determine from the publisher or copyright owner the specific requirements to adapt or to reproduce copyrighted information. It is the reviewer's responsibility to do this and no one else's responsibility! Typically, the best place to secure information pertaining to reproducing or to adapting copyrighted information is via the publisher's website. If no information is available, then we advise contacting the author(s) of the information, who likely will have contact information of the publisher because, at some point, a copyright transfer of ownership was signed. Permissions requests should specify the source material (e.g., title of work that contains the copyrighted material to be adapted or reproduced, author[s], year of publication, page number) and the nature of the reuse (e.g., adaptation or reproduction in a dissertation).

Obtaining permission might take a few weeks, and once permission is granted, reviewers should follow the stipulations for displaying the copyrighted material given by the publisher. Some copyright holders have specific wording that they require copyright seekers to use in their manuscripts as a condition for granting permission. It should be noted that if you plan to publish your CLR report, most publishers will not move forward with your publication if it contains adapted and/or reproduced material for which copyright permission has not been obtained. You might have noticed that this chapter contains numerous tables and figures, which are notated with an acknowledgment that we have adapted or reproduced them from other sources. In addition, on numerous occasions throughout the chapter we refer to the concept of plagiarism. According to the Committee on Academic Conduct (1994), there are six types of plagiarism:

1. using another author's words without (properly) citing the author
2. using another author's ideas without (properly) citing the author
3. citing the source using the words of the author verbatim without using quotation marks
4. borrowing the structure of another author's phrases, sentences, or paragraphs without (properly) citing the author of this information

5. borrowing all or part of another student's paper or using someone else's outline or draft to write your own paper; and
6. using a manuscript-writing service or someone else to write the paper for you

One type of plagiarism that oftentimes is difficult to recognize is when a writer presents any previously published work created by her/him as new work. This is called self-plagiarism. Although a limited amount of duplication of a reviewer's own previously published work is acceptable (i.e., information that is necessary to understand that contribution, such as an explanation of a reviewer's previously published theory), the resultant CLR report must signify an original contribution to knowledge.

In order to avoid any accusation of plagiarism or self-plagiarism, the literature reviewer should take copious notes at every stage of the CLR process, keeping track of every source and crediting sources of any information that they use. As you audit each draft, remember that changing a few words or phrases or reversing the order of phrases or sentences typically is not sufficient to avoid any charge of plagiarism; rather, the entire extract must be paraphrased in your own words. An effective way of avoiding plagiarism is by attempting to write a summary of the author's words without looking at the source. Then, carefully and critically compare the summary to the original work, not only checking the summary for accuracy and completeness, but also checking for duplication of wording. If you find that you have used more than two consecutive words from the original—not including articles and prepositions—you should place these duplicated words in quotation marks (Campbell, Ballou, & Slade, 1989) and cite the source. This check for plagiarism ultimately is the responsibility of the literature reviewer.

Another way of checking for plagiarism is via the use of computer-assisted plagiarism detection (CaPD) devices that are referred to as plagiarism detection systems (PDS). Because CaPDs facilitate the comparison of sizable collections of documents, they are more reliable than is manual checking. Specifically, PDS checks for plagiarism either are intrinsic or external (Stein, Koppel, & Stamatatos,

2007). Intrinsic PDS checks involve the analysis of a document without comparing it to other documents. This technique involves the software program identifying fluctuations in the writing style of the author across the document as an indicator for potential plagiarism. In contrast, external PDS checks involve the software program comparing a target document to a set of other documents. Then, using similarity criteria (e.g., verbatim text overlap), the software program retrieves all documents that contain text that is similar in some degree to the target document (Stein, Meyer zu Eissen, & Potthast, 2007). It should be noted that PDS cannot reliably detect plagiarism without human judgment. Indeed, PDS can generate false positives (Culwin & Lancaster, 2001).

Several PDS exist. Open source (i.e., free) PDS include eTBLAST (http://etest.vbi.vt.edu/etblast3/). Closed source (i.e., commercial) PDS include Turnitin (http://www.turnitin.com/), Copyscape (http://www.copyscape.com/), Grammarly (http://www.grammarly.com/?alt1051=2), iThenticate (http://www.ithenticate.com/), and PlagTracker (http://www.plagtracker.com/). An increasing number of universities and other institutions subscribe to PDS. In this case, reviewers who belong to such an institution likely will be able to use a PDS free of charge. Because it is very possible to plagiarize another author's work inadvertently, we recommend that reviewers use a PDS before they declare their CLR report as being in final form.

CONTINUING THE CLR PROCESS

As we stated in Chapter 1, one of the myths perpetuated by textbook authors is that the literature review represents only one phase of the research process. Yet, as we outlined in Chapter 3 and emphasized earlier in this chapter, the CLR can be applied to any or all of the 12 components of a primary research report. Specifically, whereas the CLR can be applied to nine of these components prior to conducting the primary research study (i.e., problem statement, literature review, theoretical/conceptual framework, research question(s), hypotheses, participants, instruments, procedures, analyses)—which we call a *pre-data collection/analysis CLR*—the

TOOL: SUMMARY TABLE OF CHECKPOINTS

Table 11.10 presents a summary table of the draft-audit checkpoints and contains all 18 of our recommendations for each draft audit. Once these checkpoints have been addressed and the first draft is revised accordingly, you will have your second draft, which will be a marked improvement from the first draft. Then, you should check the second draft in a systematic way, using the same 18 checkpoints, which yields the third draft. With each systematic audit, the time spent in the reworking/revising process becomes considerably less and the report becomes considerably closer to a finished product. This process of creating drafts should continue until no further revisions are required for a draft after addressing these checkpoints. At this point, we would like to point out to beginning writers that even the most experienced scholars write multiple drafts before declaring their CLR reports as being in final form. As an example, several chapters in our book resulted in more than 10 drafts being written before we (Rebecca and Tony) declared these chapters as being in final form.

Table 11.10 Summary checklist for auditing the first and subsequent writing drafts

	Checkpoint
1	Compare the draft with the pre-draft outline
2	Provide a sufficient number of headings and subheadings
3	Ensure that research findings are differentiated from other types of information
4	Ensure that reviewer's voice/stance is distinguished from each author's voice/stance
5	Avoid using annotations
6	Whenever possible, provide methodological and/or procedural information alongside findings
7	Minimize the use of quotations, especially long quotations
8	Use metaphors whenever possible to enhance meaning extracted from the CLR
9	Check to ensure that an appropriate type of claim has been made throughout the CLR report
10	Use link words/phrases to maximize transitions between sentences and between paragraphs
11	Assess the readability of the CLR draft
12	Assess the structure of the CLR draft for parallelism
13	Check the CLR draft for grammatical errors
14	Check the CLR draft for style guide/manual errors
15	Check the CLR draft for presentation of an adequate number of citations/references
16	Check the CLR draft for citation errors and reference list errors
17	Check for fallacies in arguments in the CLR draft
18	Check for ethical practices in the CLR draft

CLR is applied to the remaining three components once the data for the primary research study have been collected and analyzed (i.e., interpretation of the findings, directions for future research, and implications for the field)—which we call a *post-data collection/analysis CLR*.

The post-data collection/analysis of the CLR involves your discussion section of the report and the way findings are grounded in credible sources and contribute to the knowledge base. That is, reviewers should contextualize their findings when interpreting the findings, providing directions for future research, and providing implications for the field. As part of interpreting the research findings, reviewers should compare and contrast their findings with the information provided in their CLR report section. In particular, reviewers should delineate how and the extent to which their findings support or refute previous findings presented in their CLR report section. Also, reviewers should interpret their findings in the context of their frameworks (i.e., theoretical framework, conceptual framework, and/or practical framework). For example, to what extent do the findings *support* the framework(s)? To what extent do the findings *extend* the framework(s)? To what extent do the findings *modify* framework(s)? Examples of the post-data collection/analysis CLR conducted by Frels (2010) in the Dyadic Mentoring Study are provided below.

EXAMPLE: COMPARING/ CONTRASTING RESULTS TO OTHER INFORMATION

Box 11.12 provides an example of comparing and contrasting findings to previously cited literature; Box 11.13 offers an example of interpreting findings in the context of a conceptual framework. Box 11.14 provides an example of interpreting findings in the context of a theoretical framework, which was stated in the Dyadic Mentoring Study as Bronfenbrenner's (1979) ecology of human development model; Figure 11.16 portrays an example of a visual representation of interpreted findings within a theoretical framework; Box 11.15 presents interpreted findings in the context of the philosophical lens; and Box 11.16 provides an excerpt from the Dyadic Mentoring Study providing implications for the field. As this chapter for writing the CLR report comes to a close, it is our hope that these examples will help you to incorporate our recommendations in practice.

BOX 11.12

EXAMPLE OF COMPARING AND CONTRASTING FINDINGS TO THE PREVIOUSLY CITED LITERATURE

With respect to African American mentors, for both male and female, results were mixed. Through the observations, bantering language was noted within the dyads of similar ethnicity and explicit encouragement with goal-setting was observed in the one dyad of different ethnicity. Thus, the tone of dyads regarding language and non-verbal communicators was high and active in African American/African American mentoring matches. Consistent with this finding, Mitchell-Kernan (1972) attributed loud-talking as being one linguistic tool in the African American community. Further, she explained that a folk conversation is "a fluent and lively way of talking characterized by a high degree of personal style, which may be used when its function is referential or directive—to get something from someone or get someone to do something" (p. 318). The *Enlightening for Me Dyad* of Mr. John Henry and Junior represented this style of language as effective for a close and enduring relationship. As stated by Mr. John Henry, mentoring will continue into high school if Junior (presently in Grade 1) is willing.

Adapted from *The experiences and perceptions of selected mentors: An exploratory study of the dyadic relationship in school-based mentoring*, by R. K. Frels, 2010, unpublished doctoral dissertation, Sam Houston State University, Huntsville, TX, pp. 310–311. Copyright 2010 by R. K. Frels. [Emphasis added.]

BOX 11.13

EXAMPLE OF INTERPRETING FINDINGS IN THE CONTEXT OF A CONCEPTUAL FRAMEWORK

Results of my study lend support for Mullen's (1999) concept of synergetic comentoring as an integration of appreciative understanding and interaction. In dyads, empathy and valuing diversity were present and these characteristics were partnered with effective communication, active listening, and trust. Conversely, in the one case whereby the mentor did not want to continue mentoring after 1 year, she expressed that due to an inconsistent interaction with her mentee, she felt ineffective. Hence, the efforts on the part of the mentor (e.g., asking too many questions to engage) established a strained tone to the session whereby the mentor in the dyad worked harder than did the mentee for attempting communication. Furthermore, my study brings to the foreground salient characteristics such as implicit encouragement, bantering language, a relaxed here-and-now presence, and the natural use of humor to Mullen's (1999) four-step process of interaction (i.e., appropriately expressing meaningful ideas), appreciative understanding (i.e., each member learning to appreciate conflict, utilize empathy, and value diversity), integration (i.e., creativity in the approach), and implementation (i.e., the dyad moving toward change). Further, Mullen (1999) explained that a type of willingness for common goals underscores appreciative understanding and interaction. Taking into account that, oftentimes, mentees do not know why they have been selected to participate in SBM [school-based mentoring], their goals in mentoring might differ from the goals of the mentor. Thus, if mentors set goals too far beyond the dyadic exchange, the goal might not be common.

The findings of my study, viewed through the lens of synergetic comentoring, validate the importance for mentors to be aware of their own sense of fulfillment in mentoring beyond the quest for altruism or lofty goals. Considering the Mutual Comfort Dyad and the words of Amaya, it was apparent that she felt honored that her mentee, an 11-year-old African American male, would be so willing to spend time with "an old Hispanic lady like me." Thus, a type of comradeship existed in the dyad that moved the mentor beyond the role of tutor or friend. Furthermore, a synergetic comentoring exchange occurs through both respects to impact a type of *life space*, described by Lewin (1951) to include the objective world and subjective or perceived aspects of imagination. In keeping with a dialectical pragmatic research philosophy that incorporates social constructionism, it can be concluded that perceived closeness on the part of mentors is a true and realistic experience impacting the immediate world of both the mentee and mentor and the synergetic exchange in the dyad.

Adapted from *The experiences and perceptions of selected mentors: An exploratory study of the dyadic relationship in school-based mentoring*, by R. K. Frels, 2010, unpublished doctoral dissertation, Sam Houston State University, Huntsville, TX, pp. 315–316. Copyright 2010 by R. K. Frels.

BOX 11.14

EXAMPLE OF INTERPRETING FINDINGS IN THE CONTEXT OF A THEORETICAL FRAMEWORK

The findings of my study interpreted through Bronfenbrenner's (1979) ecological theory yielded particularly noteworthy results. With regard to the microsystem, or Level 1, the factors of activity, role, and interpersonal

(Continued)

(Continued)

relations constitute the foundation of the experience (Bronfenbrenner, 1979). Thus, each mentoring dyad was a significant part of the mentee's immediate setting (i.e., Level 1). Further, as defined by Bronfenbrenner (1979), the dyad comprises "whenever two persons pay attention to or participate in one another's activities" (p. 56) and is important for development in two respects: (a) when one member is paying close and sustained attention to the activity of the other, and (b) when the two participants perceive themselves as doing something together.

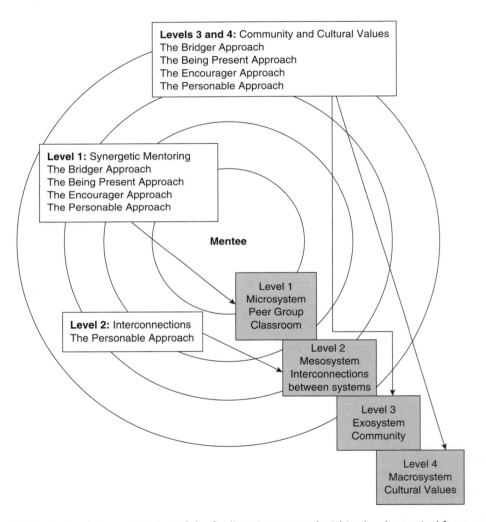

Figure 11.16 A visual representation of the findings interpreted within the theoretical framework: Bronfenbrenner's (1979) ecology of human development model and the four mentoring approaches

Adapted from *The experiences and perceptions of selected mentors: An exploratory study of the dyadic relationship in school-based mentoring*, by R. K. Frels, 2010, unpublished doctoral dissertation, Sam Houston State University, Huntsville, TX, pp. 316–318. Copyright 2010 by R. K. Frels.

Bronfenbrenner (1979) further delineated that reciprocity, with concomitant mutual feedback, generates a momentum of its own for motivation in the participants not only to persevere, but also to engage in increasingly more complex patterns of interaction. He described the phenomenological existence of a primary dyad whereby both participants exist for each other even when they are not together through each other's thoughts, strong emotional feelings, and influence on behavior when apart. In fact, not only do mentoring relationships exist on the microsystem level, the mentoring relationship can be a negotiator of other systems, acting on Level 2, the *mesosystem* (i.e., interconnections between systems)—especially in the case of the Personable Approach.

Bronfenbrenner (1979) suggested that interconnections among two or more settings in which a child participates lead to relationships that further negotiate development. In this system, Bronfenbrenner (1979) posited four general types: (a) multisetting participation, when the same person engages in activities in more than one setting; (b) indirect linkage, when the same person does not actively participate in both settings, but connection is through a third party who serves as an intermediate link; (c) intersetting communications, whereby messages transmitted from one setting to the other provide specific information to persons in the other setting; and (d) intersetting knowledge, whereby information or experiences that exist in one setting inform the other. In mentoring, when the mentor engages in discussions of family, peers, and school, the mentor acts as an indirect linkage, or the intermediate link that negotiates various events and settings through the four themes of encouragement, relating, time and presence, and language nuances. Considering ecological theory, each approach in mentoring (i.e., the Bridger Approach, the Being Present Approach, the Encourager Approach, and The Personable Approach) was influential to the microsystem, or Level 1, of a child's world.

BOX 11.15

EXAMPLE OF INTERPRETING FINDINGS IN THE CONTEXT OF A PHILOSOPHICAL LENS

The use of discourse analysis (Gee, 2005) was particularly helpful when considering my philosophical stance of dialectical pragmatism (Johnson, 2009) whereby I combined social constructionism (Longino, 1993) and a two-way interactive transformative-emancipatory (Mertens, 2007) stance to recognize how language, and the use of language, pertained to the dyadic relationship. Considering the stance of social construction-ism, the social processes and interactions of dyad members in my study provide examples that knowledge is in part the product of social negotiation and people come to share an intersubjective understanding (Schwandt, 2007).

To interpret the characteristics of mentoring dyads via a social context (i.e., Level 1; Bronfenbrenner, 1979), the subtheme profile characteristics (e.g., explicit vs. implicit; prescriptive vs. instrumental vs. developmental) were mapped on continua to relate to the social milieu of the mentee (i.e., Levels 2, 3, and 4; Bronfenbrenner, 1979). Figure 41 depicts the 13 profile characteristics within a social context. As seen in Figure 41, implicit encouragement (I) is considered to be highly social because it involves a nonverbal creativity on the part of the mentor and a strong receptor on the part of the mentee. Additionally, developmental activities (D) are collaborative in nature and, thus, are more social than are prescriptive activities. The exchange/process-oriented

(Continued)

(Eo) relating is highly social due to the way it invokes processing and a back-and-forth dialogue, as opposed to support-oriented relating, which is a comfortable and quiet type of *feeling felt* when active listening takes place. Likewise, a here-and-now presence (HaNP) is intent upon both members of the dyad recognizing the value of the moment and the social implications of sharing this moment. Finally, of the three language nuances, humor (H) is the highest in social nature due to the way that both the mentor and mentee experience the same laughter; self-disclosure (S) is the second-highest on the continuum due to the level of trust in the social dyad that takes place when sharing. Conversely, questions (Q) are low in social nature due to the one-way hierarchal interchange.

BOX 11.16

EXCERPT OF IMPLICATIONS FOR THE FIELD

In the fast-paced culture of community altruism, and for the future impact for our children, it is important for mentors to recognize that mentoring can be rich and rewarding in its own right. As noted in my study through the words of Margie, mentors should not expect that *pat-on-the-back*, and they may never recognize the difference they make. Thus, setting expectations or goals too high might lead to what Spencer (2007) so eloquently described of disappointed mentors: "It's not what I expected" (p. 47). Mentors who might be disappointed at times should draw inspiration from Savannah to stay steady and confident by using self-encouragement to complete the yearly commitment.

CONCLUSIONS

Step 7 of the Seven-Step Model is extensive, because it is the accumulation of all of the other steps, and is dependent upon some personal characteristics such as prior experience with academic writing, the ability to designate considerable time to developing ideas, and most of all—patience with the process. It might even be true that during the writing process, a literature reviewer might experience times of doubt about directions that the report takes and is tempted to change the initial questions that drove the CLR. The initial goal, objective(s), and rationale that initiated your literature review will reveal that the process itself likely resulted in some changes from your initial positions. It is important to remember that, much like the research process, the questions that you ask of the data, or information sources, yield answers specific to these questions.

For this reason, by revisiting some of your initial philosophical-, discipline-, and topic-specific stances in the course of completing your literature review, you might disclose to a higher degree, through particular rhetoric learned in the process, your biases toward confirmatory results. Ask yourself the question: What findings surprised you and why? This question can help you to highlight areas of disagreement pertaining to the topic for new learning and impact future directions for research. Also, the systematic evaluation of each draft yields a finished product that is consistent and unified. As you reflect on your final audit, consider the information sources that you stored, and reorganize the sources so that you might revisit and include them in any follow-up research. Take some time to celebrate arriving at this point in the CLR process, and reflect on your efforts in producing the final draft!

In this chapter, the following important concepts were presented:

- The way that an author conveys a message involves rhetoric (which is language that is used) and the emphasis that stems from philosophical stance and methodological choices.
- Economy with words, or parsimony, should guide choices for words.
- Originality is important when citing other authors' works to avoid plagiarism. Confidence for communicating original author ideas using your own voice helps a writer to avoid plagiarism.
- The V-shape (or funnel) approach involves organizing the CLR reports such that the references to sources that are least related to the topic are discussed first and the most related references are discussed last.
- It is important to include significant aspects of the search process in the report to contextualize the topic and to establish a path of argumentation.

- Clarifying notable works helps to establish some of the groundbreaking discoveries in a topic area. Other distinguishable steps in the decision process of the CLR are important to note, such as the evolution of ideas, points of disagreement in dissenting works, and additional sources for inquiry.
- Citation maps are useful for understanding and clarifying concepts, theories, findings, and interpretations. Meta-analyses, meta-syntheses, and meta-summaries can provide considerable advantages in the report, such as practical significance and usefulness of information.
- The time between writing drafts helps the literature reviewer to re-read and to rework the draft from a more objective state. With each new reading, the draft improves in clarity and focus. The use of the audit checklist facilitates a systematic evaluation of the ideas and technical writing elements of the report. The use of readability indices helps assess appropriateness and flow in the revision cycle.
- Ensuring that the reviewer's voice/stance is distinguished from each author's voice/stance adds clarity to the literature review report.
- Minimizing the use of annotations and quotations, providing a sufficient number of headings and subheadings, using metaphors and link words/phrases, contextualizing findings by providing methodological and/or procedural information, maximizing parallelism, avoiding fallacies in arguments, and checking for grammatical, style guide, citation, and reference list errors—all represent important steps in the quest to write with discipline.
- Ensuring that the literature review report is free from falsification, fabrication, nepotism, copyright violations, and plagiarism is paramount for an ethical and culturally progressive literature reviewer.
- The post-data collection/analysis of the CLR involves your discussion section of the report and the way that findings are grounded in credible sources and contribute to the knowledge base.

CHAPTER 11 EVALUATION CHECKLIST

CORE	Guiding Questions and Tasks
Critical Examination	To what extent did you identify the audience and relevant needs relating to the topic area?
Organization	To what extent did you respond to the many decisions for planning an effective presentation?
	To what extent did you create the outline and to what extent did you include the audit trail pieces of your process?
Reflections	To what extent did you base your outline and section paragraphs on one or more frameworks?
	To what extent did you come to any new understandings of how your argument might evolve?
Evaluation	Present your ideas to a peer or colleague in a structured talk using your outline. Ask your listener to restate some of your points so that you might evaluate if what you stated is the same point(s) that were received.

POSTSCRIPT: THEORY-DRIVEN AND MODEL-DRIVEN LITERATURE REVIEWS

In our book, we have provided in detail a Seven-Step Model for conducting a comprehensive literature review (CLR) that represents a methodology, method, tool, and multimodal (or new literacies) approach. At its optimum, the reviewer conducting the CLR is an original thinker, critical thinker, reflexive researcher, ethical researcher, and—above all—a culturally progressive researcher. In presenting our seven steps in Chapter 4 through Chapter 11, our goal was to show you how to conduct a CLR that will inform the knowledge base. Thus, with a few exceptions (e.g., the use of discourse analysis to analyze information extracted from the CLR process), we outlined methodologies, methods, and strategies that led to **a posteriori analyses** of information extracted from the CLR process. Moreover, we presented the CLR process as a thesis- or theory-generating process that, once some form of saturation has been reached (e.g., data saturation, theoretical saturation), yields "a conclusion based on a case developed using existing knowledge, sound evidence, and reasoned argument" (Machi & McEvoy, 2009, p. 157). Here, the CLR process can be conducted by someone with little or no knowledge of the topic of interest because the knowledge will emerge as the CLR process unfolds.

Although conducting a CLR for the purpose of thesis/theory generation is very much the norm, there are times when the CLR can be used as a theory-confirmation, theory-modification, or theory-expansion process. This process involves the use of a theory (i.e., broad proposed explanation of a phenomenon that is testable, verifiable, and falsifiable through evidence) or a model (i.e., [abstract] verbal, visual, physical, or mathematical representation or manifestation of a theory) to drive the CLR process in general and the CLR analysis and synthesis in particular. As appealing as these theory-driven and model-driven CLRs are, they are very rarely conducted. Thus, the purpose of the remainder of this postscript is to provide examples of theory-driven and model-driven CLRs.

THEORY-/MODEL-DRIVEN CLRs: EXEMPLAR 1

In 1956, educational psychologist Dr. Benjamin Bloom chaired a committee of educators whose goal was to promote forms of thinking in education that were higher than merely remembering facts (i.e., rote learning). Bloom's committee identified three domains of learning or educational objectives—namely, **cognitive**, which relates to mental skills; **affective**, which pertains to attitudes, feelings, and emotions; and **psychomotor**, which relates to manual or physical skills. From this committee emerged what is referred to as

Bloom's Taxonomy for the cognitive (Bloom et al., 1956) and affective (Krathwohl, Bloom, & Masia, 1964) domains. Bloom et al.'s (1956) taxonomy for the cognitive domain is used most often when designing instruction or learning processes. This domain involves knowledge and the development of intellectual skills that comprise six hierarchically ordered levels of cognitive operations or processes, which range from the lowest-order process (i.e., simplest) to the highest-order process (i.e., most complex)—yielding what might be deemed as *degrees of difficulty*, such that the preceding level should be mastered before the next level can be negotiated effectively. These six levels, in ascending order, are as follows:

1. Knowledge

2. Comprehension

3. Application

4. Analysis

5. Synthesis

6. Evaluation

Knowledge indicates exhibiting memory of learned information, including knowledge of specifics (e.g., facts, data, terminology, basic concepts), knowledge of ways of addressing specifics (e.g., guidelines, criteria, methodologies, procedures), and knowledge of the universals and abstractions (e.g., principles, laws, axioms, tenets, generalizations, theories). **Comprehension** signifies understanding the meaning of information by translating, organizing, comparing, contrasting, describing, interpreting, and summarizing the main ideas. **Application** demonstrates being able to use already acquired knowledge to solve problems that arise in new situations by applying this acquired knowledge in different ways. **Analysis** involves examining and subdividing information or concepts into component parts in order to understand the organizational structure and to generate inferences. **Synthesis** involves combining a (diverse) set of information in a unique way that yields the creation of new meaning that represents a coherent whole. Finally, **evaluation** involves making judgments about the quality and validity/credibility of information, ideas, or products that are based on evidence or criteria.

During the 1990s, Lorin Anderson, a former student of Benjamin Bloom's, and a Carolina Distinguished Professor Emeritus at the University of South Carolina (who was a professor at the same institution while Tony was pursuing his doctorate degree), led a new committee that met for 6 years for the purpose of updating Bloom et al.'s (1956) taxonomy. This committee led to the publication of Anderson, Krathwohl, Airasian, and Cruikshank's (2001) revised taxonomy. In particular, Anderson et al. (2001) changed the labeling of Bloom et al.'s (1956) six levels from noun to verb forms. Further, they renamed the lowest-level category, knowledge, as remembering. Here, **remembering** involves retrieving, recognizing, and recalling relevant information from long-term memory.

Additionally, the categories of comprehension and synthesis were renamed as understanding and creating, respectively. **Understanding** involves constructing meaning from oral, written, and visual messages via classifying, comparing, contrasting, summarizing, explaining, interpreting, inferring, and exemplifying (Anderson et al., 2001). **Creating** involves combining elements into a coherent whole by reorganizing elements into a new pattern or structure via planning, generating, or producing (Anderson et al., 2001). The remaining three categories (i.e., application, analysis, evaluation) remained the same; however, the evaluation category, renamed as evaluating, which represented Bloom et al.'s (1956) highest level, was now Anderson et al.'s (2001) second-highest level. Thus, Anderson et al.'s (2001) revised six levels, in ascending order, are as follows:

1. Remembering

2. Understanding

3. Applying

4. Analyzing

5. Evaluating

6. Creating

In Chapter 3, alongside describing the reviewer as a culturally progressive researcher, an ethical researcher, and a multimodal researcher, we described the reviewer as an original *thinker*, a critical *thinker*, and a reflexive researcher or *learner*. And because Anderson et al.'s (2001) taxonomy and Bloom et al.'s (1956) taxonomy involve the categorization of processes of *thinking* and *learning*, it makes sense that both of these taxonomies can be used to classify the CLR process in terms of level of cognitive complexity. Thus, building on the works of Granello (2001) and Levy and Ellis (2006), who mapped Bloom et al.'s (1956) taxonomy onto the literature review process, in the remainder of this section, we have used Anderson et al.'s (2001) taxonomy to categorize the CLR process.

1. REMEMBERING INFORMATION

Remembering information, the lowest level of the CLR process, is commonly accomplished by activities such as reading, identifying, retrieving, recognizing, and recalling relevant information. Writing CLR reports at this level is characterized by information that is regurgitated from other sources without demonstrating an understanding of this information or an ability to distinguish between main ideas and less important ideas, among the quality of information sources, and/or which information is most relevant to the underlying topic. Reviewers who write CLR reports at this level might report unnecessary statistical information (e.g., exact p values to several decimal places), use quotations excessively, or overuse verbs like *found* (as we discussed in Chapter 11). Further, reviewers at this stage tend to rely solely on the interpretations of the authors that they are citing; give more weight to works that support their premise; and write sections of their CLR reports that typically are organized by works read instead of by topic or theme, with each paragraph containing a presentation of the name and/or title of a specific work alongside a summary of the work (e.g., findings).

2. UNDERSTANDING INFORMATION

Understanding information, the second-lowest level of the CLR process, is commonly accomplished by remembering activities such as reading, identifying, retrieving, recognizing, and recalling relevant information, and additional activities such as summarizing, classifying, explaining, exemplifying, differentiating, interpreting, and meaning-making. Unlike reviewers who are at the remembering level of development, reviewers who write CLR reports at the understanding level are able to translate information from one source to another. Also, they are able to interpret information and to understand the meaning of the information underlying the source and, thus, are able to present the main ideas and not to overuse quotations. However, like their remembering-level counterparts, they still tend to focus solely on the introduction and discussion sections of empirical articles, rely on authors' own interpretations, give more weight to works that support their premise, and arrange paragraphs by selected works instead of by the main idea. Even more importantly, like their remembering-level counterparts, they are unable to differentiate between the quality of sources, and to determine which information is maximally relevant to the underlying topic.

3. APPLYING INFORMATION

Applying information, the third-lowest level of the CLR process, is commonly accomplished by remembering activities such as reading, identifying, retrieving, recognizing, and recalling relevant information, and understanding activities such as summarizing, classifying, explaining, exemplifying, differentiating, interpreting, and meaning-making; as well as breaking down information into constituent parts, and determining how these parts relate to each other and to the overall path of argumentation. Other applying-level activities include organizing, demonstrating, illustrating, solving, relating, attributing, and classifying. Unlike reviewers who are at the remembering or understanding levels of development, reviewers who write CLR reports at the applying level are able to use previously learned material in new situations, as well as to apply concepts, theories, axioms, principles, rules, tenets, procedures, and methodologies. Also, they are able to connect directly each work to the underlying topic. However, like their remembering-level and understanding-level counterparts, they still tend to focus solely on the introduction and discussion sections of empirical articles, rely on author's own interpretations, give more weight to works that support their premise, and arrange paragraphs by selected works instead of by the main idea. Most importantly, like their remembering-level and understanding-level counterparts, they are unable to differentiate between the quality of sources and which information is maximally relevant to the underlying topic.

4. ANALYZING INFORMATION

Analyzing information, the third-highest level of the CLR process, is commonly accomplished by remembering activities such as reading, identifying, retrieving, recognizing, and recalling relevant information; understanding activities such as summarizing, classifying, explaining, exemplifying, differentiating, interpreting, and meaning-making; and applying activities such as organizing, demonstrating, illustrating, solving, relating, attributing, classifying, breaking down information into constituent parts, and determining how these parts relate to each other and to the overall path of argumentation; as well as comparing, contrasting, separating, connecting, and selecting. Unlike reviewers who are at the remembering, understanding, or applying levels of development, reviewers who write CLR reports at the analyzing level are able to identify why the selected information is important. Also, not only can they link works to the main idea but also they can incorporate a layer of complexity by identifying the components of works that support their path of argumentation. Further, unlike their lower-level counterparts, they do not rely on authors' own interpretations, and their CLR reports contain more detailed description of information associated with the selected works (e.g., methodologies used by the cited researchers). Analyzing-level reviewers also are able to identify patterns that emerge and, importantly, can reach their own conclusions from their analysis of the set of information. However, like their lower-level counterparts, they still tend to give more weight to works that support their premise. In addition, they cannot resolve contradictory findings. Most importantly, although they are able to differentiate between the quality of sources to a limited degree, they do not use a systematic method for evaluating information.

5. EVALUATING INFORMATION

Evaluating information, the second-highest level of the CLR process, is commonly accomplished by remembering activities such as reading, identifying, retrieving, recognizing, and recalling relevant information; understanding activities such as summarizing, classifying, explaining, exemplifying, differentiating, interpreting, and meaning-making; applying activities such as organizing, demonstrating, illustrating, solving, relating, attributing, classifying, breaking down information into constituent parts, and determining how these parts relate to each other and to the overall path of argumentation; and analyzing activities such as comparing, contrasting, separating, connecting, selecting, linking, identifying, detailing, and concluding; as well as assessing, judging, discriminating, deciding, recommending, selecting, and supporting.

Unlike reviewers who are at the remembering, understanding, applying, or analyzing levels of development, reviewers who write CLR reports at the evaluating level are able to make judgments based on external criteria and standards and, thus, to make decisions about the quality of articles and validity of information using evaluation frameworks such as those discussed in Chapter 7. Also, they are able to distinguish among the six types of claims (i.e., claims of fact, claims of value, claims of policy, claims of concept, claims of interpretation, claims of observation), as well as among opinions, ideas, concepts, hypotheses, hunches, theories, and findings. Further, they have a high tolerance for ambiguous, contradictory, or vague findings and can evaluate such findings as a function of methodology used. Evaluating-level reviewers also can present different sides of the argument with a minimum of reviewer bias by outlining the strengths and limitations of each work. However, like their lower-level counterparts, they are unable both to present a logically synthesized discussion wherein the information from several sources is woven together coherently, and to synthesize the information into a whole that exceeds the sum of its parts.

6. CREATING INFORMATION

Creating information, the highest level of the CLR process, is commonly accomplished by remembering activities such as reading, identifying, retrieving, recognizing, and recalling relevant information; understanding activities such as summarizing, classifying, explaining, exemplifying, differentiating, interpreting, and meaning-making; applying activities such as organizing, demonstrating, illustrating, solving, relating, attributing, classifying, breaking down information into constituent parts, and determining how these parts relate to each other and to the overall path of argumentation; analyzing activities such as comparing, contrasting, separating, connecting, selecting, linking, identifying, detailing, and concluding; and evaluating activities such as assessing, judging, discriminating, deciding, recommending, selecting, and supporting; as well as combining, mixing, integrating, modifying, rearranging, designing, composing, inferencing, and generalizing. Unlike reviewers who are at the remembering, understanding, applying, analyzing, or evaluating levels of development, reviewers who write CLR reports at the creating level are able to organize the CLR thematically or conceptually by combining opinions, ideas, concepts, hypotheses, hunches, theories, and findings in a way that contains a warranted and transparent path of argumentation in which parts are integrated to form a logical and coherent whole that exceeds the sum of its parts and wherein conclusions are logically based on appropriate evaluative frameworks. Further, reviewers at this creating level are able to integrate the set of information into broader concepts or themes and to reorganize these elements into a new pattern or structure that yields value-added information.

IMPLICATIONS OF USING BLOOM'S REVISED TAXONOMY FOR CLRs

If a reviewer were interested in conducting a CLR on the topic of literature reviews, he/she could use Bloom's revised taxonomy—namely Anderson et al.'s (2001) taxonomy—in an a priori manner to frame his/her CLR report. For example, the reviewer could use the introduction section of the CLR report to introduce Anderson et al.'s (2001) taxonomy. Then, in the body of the CLR report, the reviewer could divide it into the six sections, one for each of the six taxonomy levels, onto which the literature review process would be mapped.

Throughout this book, we used the topic of mentoring to illustrate various steps and processes. In this case, the use of Anderson et al.'s (2001) taxonomy also might be regarded using the lens of mentoring. In particular, as outlined by Granello (2001), Anderson et al.'s (2001) taxonomy can increase the "cognitive complexity" (p. 301) of reviewers' CLR reports. For example, mentors could help reviewers to move their

CLR reports from: (a) the remembering level to the understanding level by teaching them how to paraphrase information accurately and adequately; (b) the understanding level to the applying level by taking their paraphrased text and connecting directly to the underlying topic; (c) the applying level to the analyzing level by developing a list of questions that they could ask themselves in order to analyze information (e.g., Do the author's interpretations stem directly from the findings? Are there alternative interpretations of the findings?); (d) the analyzing level to the evaluating level by identifying and using external criteria and standards to distinguish among the six types of claims made by cited authors and by making decisions about the quality of articles and validity of information; and (e) the evaluating level to the creating level by developing a detailed outline that we described under Decision 5 in Chapter 10 (cf. Granello, 2001).

THEORY-/MODEL-DRIVEN CLRs: EXEMPLAR 2

We have seen how a model from the field of educational psychology, namely, Bloom's revised taxonomy (Anderson et al., 2001), can be used to drive a CLR conducted on the topic of the literature review. Interestingly, we can also use a theory from the field of social psychology to frame a CLR on this same topic. Specifically, we can use Kelley's (1967, 1973) **theory of causal attribution**—also known as the Kelley **covariation model**—which relates to both self-perception and social perception. According to Kelley (1973), "an effect is attributed to the one of its possible causes with which, over time, it covaries" (p. 108). In other words, a specific behavior can be attributed to potential causes that occur simultaneously. Kelley (1973) posited that the causes of an outcome can be attributed to the person (i.e., internal attribution), the stimulus (i.e., external attribution), the circumstance, or some combination of these factors. Kelley (1967, 1973) theorized that people use three types of information when making judgments about the cause of the event, as follows:

- **Consensus information**: This information pertains to whether other people respond in a similar manner to a specific stimulus (i.e., covariation of behavior across different people). If many people (e.g., mentors) respond (e.g., give encouragement) in the same way to the stimulus (e.g., a mentee), then it can be concluded that consensus is high. In contrast, if only one person responds in a particular way to the stimulus (e.g., a mentee), then it can be concluded that consensus is low. High consensus is attributed to the stimulus (i.e., a mentee), whereas low consensus is attributed to the person providing the unique response (i.e., mentor).

- **Distinctiveness information**: This information relates to how unique the behavior is to a given situation. If a person (e.g., mentor) responds similarly (e.g., gives praise) to different circumstances (e.g., different CLR reports written by a mentee)—then it can be concluded that distinctiveness is low. Contrastingly, if a person responds uniquely (e.g., gives praise) to a specific circumstance (e.g., a particular CLR report written by a mentee), then it can be concluded that distinctiveness is high. If the distinctiveness is high, the behavior would be attributed more to the circumstance (i.e., the particular CLR report written by a mentee) than to the person (i.e., mentor); if the distinctiveness is low, the behavior would be attributed more to the person than to the circumstance.

- **Consistency information**: This information relates to how consistent the behavior is over time (i.e., covariation of behavior across time). If the person (e.g., mentor) responds similarly (e.g., gives encouragement) to a circumstance (e.g., a meeting with a mentee) on repeated occasions (e.g., at every meeting with the mentee), then it can be concluded that consistency is high. If, on the other hand, the person does not respond similarly (e.g., does not always give encouragement) to a specific circumstance (e.g., a meeting with a mentee) on repeated occasions (e.g., at every meeting with the mentee), then it can be concluded that consistency is low. High consistency is attributed to the person (i.e., mentor who consistently gives encouragement), whereas low consistency is attributed to the circumstance (i.e., meeting with the mentee).

KELLEY'S THEORY OF CAUSAL ATTRIBUTION USED AS A FRAME FOR THE CLR PROCESS

Kelley's theory is particularly viable when the person involved is able to observe the behavior of interest on multiple occasions. Thus, it lends itself to the literature review process in which, for many if not most topics, it is common for studies to be replicated on multiple occasions. In particular, Kelley's theory can be used to categorize decisions made by the reviewers in the CLR process with respect to the underlying hypothesis (i.e., quantitative) or hunch (i.e., qualitative). And so mapping Kelley's (1967, 1973) theory of causal attribution might yield the following:

- **Consensus information**: In the context of CLRs, if many other researchers interpret a given set of findings the same way as does the researcher who originally observed these findings and whom the reviewer wants to cite, then it can be concluded that consensus is high and the interpretation can be attributed to the finding. In contrast, if the other researchers interpret a given set of findings differently from the researcher who originally observed these findings, then it can be concluded that consensus is low and the interpretation can be attributed to the researcher who originally obtained and interpreted the finding. Thus, in citing this researcher, it is important that the reviewer cites this lack of consensus.

- **Distinctiveness information**: In the context of CLRs, if the reviewer provides the same interpretation for different findings, especially findings that (seemingly) contradict each other, then it can be concluded that distinctiveness is low, and the interpretation can be attributed to the reviewer. Contrastingly, if a reviewer provides different interpretations for different findings, then it can be concluded that distinctiveness is high, and the interpretation can be attributed to the specific finding. Thus, in making interpretations, the reviewer should check to ensure that the distinctiveness associated with this interpretation is high.

- **Consistency information**: In the context of CLRs, if the reviewer provides the same interpretation to a finding that is replicated in several studies (e.g., findings with similar effect sizes), then it can be concluded that consistency is high, and the interpretation can be attributed to the reviewer. If, on the other hand, the reviewer provides different interpretations to a finding that is replicated in several studies, then it can be concluded that consistency is low, and the interpretation can be attributed to the circumstance (e.g., methodology [e.g., characteristics of the sample] used to generate the finding). Thus, in making interpretations, the reviewer should be cognizant of her/his level of consistency.

Reviewers can use Hewstone and Jaspars's (1987) conceptualization to evaluate whether when making one of the six types of claims (i.e., claims of fact, claims of value, claims of policy, claims of concept, claims of interpretation, claims of observation), they are making a personal (i.e., internal), stimulus (i.e., external), or circumstantial attribution by assessing the levels of consensus, distinctiveness, and consistency underlying the claim, as follows:

> Low Consensus, Low Distinctiveness, High Consistency = Reviewer Attribution
>
> High Consensus, High Distinctiveness, High Consistency = Stimulus Attribution (e.g., data, evidence)
>
> High Consensus, Low Distinctiveness, Low Consistency = Circumstance Attribution (e.g., methodology)

Reviewers, then, can use Kelley's (1967, 1973) theory of causal attribution to ensure that each claim made by reviewers is valid/credible and appropriate; reviewers should focus on making stimulus attributions and/or circumstance attributions. Whenever reviewers feel the need to make a claim that reflects reviewer attribution, they should make this attribution source clear to their readers by using pronouns (e.g., *We believe*; *We predict*; *We postulate*) and appropriate adverbs (e.g., *perhaps*, *possibly*, *maybe*).

THEORY-/MODEL-DRIVEN CLRs: EXEMPLAR 3

We have seen how a model from the field of educational psychology (i.e., Bloom's revised taxonomy; Anderson et al., 2001) and social psychology (i.e., theory of causal attribution; Kelley, 1967, 1973) can be used to drive a CLR conducted on the topic of the literature review. As a third example, we use a theory from the field of counseling psychology to frame a CLR on this same topic. Specifically, we can use Marcia's (1966) theory of identity achievement. Building on Erikson's (1959, 1968) theoretical model of identity development, Marcia (1966) operationalized the identity formation process and defined four hierarchically ordered identity statuses, wherein members in each identity status are determined by the degree of personal exploration and commitment related to ideological and interpersonal issues. The four identity statuses are as follows:

- **Identity diffusion**: This is the least developmentally advanced identity status. Indeed, this is not a firm identity and there are no defined circumstances. An individual at this stage has not explored alternatives and has not made a commitment to any definite direction in her/his life.

- **Identity foreclosure**: An individual in the identity foreclosure phase has undergone little or no exploration and remains firmly committed to childhood values and assumptions. In this status, the individual's life issues have not been reformulated in her/his own terms.

- **Moratorium**: An individual in the moratorium status is in a state of active crisis or exploration. She/he is struggling to make commitments to a definite direction in her/his life, and has not yet found a direction. This individual is in the process of synthesizing internal structures to shape her/his identity.

- **Identity achievement**: This phase is the most developmentally advanced phase. An individual in this phase has undergone a period of exploration of alternatives and has made well-defined commitments to definite directions in her/his life. Such an individual has an identity that appears to represent an internalized (structurally mature mode of control) identity status.

MARCIA'S THEORY OF CAUSAL ATTRIBUTION USED AS A FRAME FOR THE CLR PROCESS

Marcia's (1966) theory lends itself to the process of writing the CLR report. In particular, using Marcia's theory, the level of the CLR report can be categorized as follows:

- **Identity diffusion**: CLR reports that represent identity diffusion are disorganized or incoherent. At best, reviewers who write CLRs at this level merely provide a listing of what others have found, with no summative discussion and no integration. Also, they tend to overuse quotations.

- **Identity foreclosure**: Reviewers whose CLR reports represent identity foreclosure tend to focus solely on summarizing the introduction and discussion sections of articles. Further, they rely solely on the interpretations of the authors whom they are citing. They are unable to differentiate among the quality of sources. Another characteristic of these reports is that the sections are organized by works read instead of by topic or theme. Any conclusions made by reviewers operating at this stage are premature.

- **Moratorium**: Reviewers whose CLR reports represent moratorium are able to distinguish main ideas from less important ideas and to determine which information is most relevant to the topic at hand. However, they tend to give more weight to works that support their premise. Also, they do not use a systematic method for evaluating information, cannot resolve contradictory findings, and cannot link material across works.

- **Identity achievement**: Reviewers whose CLR reports represent identity achievement are able: to integrate parts to form a coherent whole; to pool ideas and research findings across works into thematically or conceptually outlined literature reviews; to collate relevant information extracted from their analysis of the components and to integrate it into broader concepts or themes; to make decisions about the quality of works and validity of information using evaluation framework parts to form a coherent whole; to distinguish among conclusions stemming from findings, experience, opinion, or speculation; to evaluate contradictory findings as a function of methodology used; and to tolerate and to accept ambiguous, contradictory, or vague results. Further, literature reviews that represent identity achievement are organized thematically, contain well-organized arguments that are well grounded in the literature, and provide the strengths and limitations of works cited. Also, all sides of the argument are presented with a minimum of researcher bias, and logical, synthesized conclusions are made based on appropriate evaluative frameworks.

Simply put, the CLR report should have a clear identity.

THEORY-/MODEL-DRIVEN CLRs: EXEMPLAR 4

We have seen how a model from the field of educational psychology (i.e., Bloom's revised taxonomy; Anderson et al., 2001), social psychology (i.e., theory of causal attribution; Kelley, 1967, 1973), and counseling psychology (i.e., Marcia, 1966) can be used to drive a CLR conducted on the topic of the literature review. As a fourth example, we use a theory from the field of educational measurement to frame a CLR. Specifically, in Chapter 7 and Appendix B, we presented Onwuegbuzie, Daniel, and Collins's (2009) *Meta-Validation Model*, which was derived from Messick's (1989, 1995) theory of validity, wherein validity was conceptualized as a unitary concept. This Meta-Validation Model identifies three major types of validity: content-related validity, criterion-related validity, and construct-related validity; these are subdivided into several areas of validity evidence (cf. Figure A.3).

MESSICK'S THEORY OF VALIDITY USED AS A FRAME FOR THE CLR PROCESS

Onwuegbuzie et al. (2007) used the Meta-Validation Model vis-à-vis Messick's (1989, 1995) Theory of Validity to conduct a CLR on instruments that are used for students to evaluate the teaching of faculty members at most universities and colleges in the United States—namely *teacher evaluation forms* (TEFs). Onwuegbuzie, Daniel, and Collins (2009) contended that all of the areas of validity evidence in Figure A.3 in Appendix B are needed to assess fully the score validity of TEFs. Using the Meta-Validation Model, Onwuegbuzie et al. (2009) interpreted the quality of evidence regarding TEFs as presented in Box P.1.

THEORY-/MODEL-DRIVEN CLRs: EXEMPLAR 5

Thus far, we have applied the use of a model from the field of educational psychology (i.e., Bloom's revised taxonomy; Anderson et al., 2001), social psychology (i.e., theory of causal attribution; Kelley, 1967, 1973), counseling psychology (i.e., Marcia, 1966), and educational measurement (i.e., theory of validity, Messick, 1989, 1995; Meta-Validation Model, Onwuegbuzie, Daniel, and Collins, 2009) for interpreting the topic of the literature review. As a fifth and final example, we use a theory from the field of sociology to frame a CLR—specifically, Bronfenbrenner's (1979) ecological systems theory.

In Chapter 11, we discussed Bronfenbrenner's (1979) ecological systems model as utilized in the Dyadic Mentoring Study. As a recap, Bronfenbrenner's (1979) ecological systems model comprises the following four levels, or layers, of environment that impact the development of children or adolescents: (a) the microsystem (Level 1): the immediate environment with which the child or adolescent closely interacts

BOX P.1

Table P.1 Interpretation of quality of evidence regarding teaching evaluation forms (TEFs) using Messick's (1989, 1995) Theory of Validity and Onwuegbuzie, Daniel, and Collins's (2009) Meta-Validation Model

Validity Type	Evidence
Criterion-related:	
Concurrent validity	Strong
Predictive validity	Strong
Content-related:	
Face validity	Adequate
Item validity	Inadequate
Sampling validity	Inadequate
Construct-related:	
Substantive validity	Inadequate
Structural validity	Inadequate
Convergent validity	Adequate
Discriminant validity	Inadequate
Divergent validity	Inadequate
Outcome validity	Weak
Generalizability	Tentative

(e.g., classroom, playground, recreation center, home); (b) the mesosystem (Level 2): the other systems in which the child or adolescent spends time, such as the family and school; (c) the exosystem (Level 3): the systems by which the child or adolescent might be influenced but of which he/she is not explicitly a member, such as the relationships among school teachers, school administrators, and the child/adolescent's parents or other close family members; and (d) the macrosystem (Level 4): the larger cultural world surrounding the child/adolescent such as the social milieu that includes societal belief systems, cultural norms, ideologies, policies, or laws that indirectly affect the child/adolescent.

Onwuegbuzie, Collins, and Frels (2013) mapped Bronfenbrenner's (1979) ecological systems model onto the qualitative, quantitative, and mixed research process. Onwuegbuzie et al. (2013) posited that virtually all research studies representing the social, behavioral, and health fields involve research conducted at one or more of Bronfenbrenner's (1979) four levels that they coined as: *micro-research studies* (i.e., Level 1: research wherein one or more persons or groups are studied within his/her/their immediate environment[s]), *meso-research studies* (i.e., Level 2: research wherein one or more persons or groups are studied within other systems in which he/she/they spend time), *exo-research studies* (i.e., Level 3: research wherein one or more persons or groups are studied within systems by which he/she/they might be influenced but of which he/she/they are not explicitly a member), and *macro-research studies* (i.e., Level 4: research wherein one or more persons or groups are studied within the larger sociocultural world or society surrounding him/her/them).

Thus, for instance, returning to our example in Chapter 10, a reviewer could use Onwuegbuzie, Collins, and Frels's (2013) conceptualization of the mapped Bronfenbrenner (1979) ecological systems model to frame her/his CLR on the topic of mentoring and college students. For example, the works identified at Step 2 (Initiating the Search) and Step 5 (Expanding the Search), and selected and retained at Step 4 (Selecting/Deselecting Information) for the foundational set at Step 3 (Storing and Organizing Information), could categorize the selected foundational studies as micro-research studies, meso-research studies, exo-research studies, or macro-research studies.

CONCLUSIONS

In Chapter 10, we outlined Dressman's (2007) four levels of integration: theoretical frame as ***foundational platform*** (i.e., wherein theory acts primarily as the basis or justification for initiating the primary research study itself, as well as orienting readers to the researcher's overall perspective); theoretical frame as ***focal apparatus*** (i.e., wherein theory acts as a way of drawing the reader's attention to specific aspects of the study); theoretical frame as ***discursive scaffold*** (i.e., wherein the theory or model used to frame the literature review section also is used as a framework for the conceptualization of the study, as well as for the research design, interpretations, and implications of the findings); and theoretical frame as ***dialectical scaffold*** (i.e., wherein the theory or model used to frame the literature review section also is the driving motivation/explanation for the method, results, and discussion sections of the primary research report in such a way as to challenge existing interpretations of empirical phenomena and/or to challenge theoretical tenets). The five examples in this postscript provide compelling illustrations of how reviewers can use a relevant theory or model to frame the CLR. Alternatively stated using Dressman's (2007) typology, reviewers can use a relevant theory or model as a foundational platform or focal apparatus.

However, what is even more useful is that reviewers can use a theory or model as a discursive scaffold or dialectical scaffold. For instance, used as a discursive scaffold, in addition to using a relevant theory or model to frame the CLR, reviewers can use this theory or model to drive the sampling design used in the primary research study, as outlined by Onwuegbuzie and Collins (2013) (see also Onwuegbuzie & Collins, 2014). Reviewers also can use this theory or model to frame other procedures, including the data collection procedures that comprise what data are collected (e.g., quantitative vs. qualitative vs. both types of data), how they are collected (e.g., via [quantitative-based] surveys or [qualitative-based] interviews), and when they are collected (e.g., the sequence). Providing even more of a discursive scaffold, reviewers can analyze the data collected to reflect the theory or model selected to frame the CLR. And once data are analyzed via this theory or model, it is natural for the reviewer to interpret the findings in this manner, as well as to frame the results and discussion sections of the primary research report.

An illustration of the use of a theory as a discursive scaffold can be obtained from Cathy Beck-Cross's (2014) award-winning conference paper, for which Tony had the pleasure of serving as Distinguished Discussant for a State and Regional Research Associations' (SRERA) distinguished paper session during the 2014 AERA conference in Philadelphia, Pennsylvania, and which gave Tony the opportunity informally to interview Cathy and learn more about her discursive scaffolding process. Specifically, Beck-Cross (2014) used the 2010 Iowa Youth Survey Data to examine, via a quantitative research study, individual, family, school, and community predictors of high school (i.e., 11th grade) male suicidal behaviors. Apart from using Bronfenbrenner's (1979) ecological systems theory to frame her literature review, Beck-Cross (2014) used two of Bronfenbrenner's (1979) levels (macrosystem and microsystem) to select her variables from the 2010 Iowa Youth Survey Data such as race/ethnicity (macrosystem variable) and a measure of individual risky behaviors (i.e., microsystem variables).

Most creatively, Beck-Cross (2014) used hierarchical multiple regression analyses to examine the extent that variables selected at Bronfenbrenner's (1979) macrosystem and microsystem levels predicted 11th-grade males' likelihood of suicide intent or suicide attempt, with the variables divided into different blocks. The hierarchical multiple regression analyses led to several conclusions regarding the macrosystem and microsystem variables, including the following: (a) "The macrosystem variable of race/ethnicity was a statistically significant predictor of suicide attempt, indicating that youth who reported having an attempt were more likely to also report being nonwhite. However, the practical significance of this result may be small" (p. 20); and (b) "Each of the microsystem variables demonstrated prediction of male youth suicidal behaviors, and works interchangeably to strengthen youth interpersonally, and within their family, school, and community systems, and therefore decreases the likelihood of suicidal behaviors" (p. 22). Subsequently, she provided implications for policy and practice as a function of these variables—specifically, at the individual, family, school, and community levels.

FINAL THOUGHTS

As a final note, we view the use of a theory or model to frame CLRs as representing a complex way of conducting CLRs and writing up CLR reports, because the reviewer must be cognizant of the major theories and models in their fields or disciplines. Oftentimes, it is common practice for researchers to distinguish a theoretical, conceptual, or practical frame to guide primary research efforts. Likewise and as a comprehensive component of the literature review, the same practice holds true. Thus, reviewers should not conduct theory-driven and model-driven CLRs in an a priori manner until they are very familiar with the knowledge base on their selected topics. However, reviewers can conduct theory-driven and model-driven CLRs in an iterative manner as follows: After identifying works at Step 2 (Initiating the Search) and Step 5 (Expanding the Search), at the selection/deselection step (Step 4), the reviewer might discover a theory or a model that could be used to frame the CLR—in which case, the subsequent steps of the CLR process (Analyzing/Synthesizing Information [Step 6] and Presenting the CLR Report [Step 7]) are driven by this theory/model. In this way, the seven-step CLR process and theory-/model-driven CLR represent a great marriage!

We believe that this is one of the more exciting areas for the further development of CLRs. Our claim here is supported by the fact that the two papers that we cited earlier, in which Bronfenbrenner's (1979) ecological systems theory was used as a discursive scaffold (i.e., Beck-Cross, 2014; Onwuegbuzie & Collins, 2014), received outstanding paper awards. Thus, we encourage you to utilize theory-/model-driven CLRs whenever appropriate. And because the use of theory-/model-driven CLRs currently is extremely rare, if you conduct such a CLR, it is very likely that we would be interested in interviewing you (i.e., as an expert) as part of our MODES expansion to understand fully the process that you used, so that, hopefully, we can expand this emerging way of conducting CLRs for future iterations of this text and continue to represent a culturally progressive and multimodal approach.

APPENDICES

APPENDIX A: SUPPLEMENTAL TABLES OF QUANTITATIVE, QUALITATIVE, AND MIXED RESEARCH DESIGNS

Table A.1 Quantitative research designs

Class of Research Design	Research Design	Description
Non-experimental		
	Quantitative historical	The researcher uses statistical and computer software programs to analyze large databases that contain economic data, political data, social data, demographic data, and other forms of data. For example, a researcher might use census data, economic data (e.g., price information), and sales receipts to reconstruct the economic history of slavery or gender inequality.
	Descriptive	The researcher uses numbers to describe the current state of affairs of a person, group, situation, or phenomenon. For example, a researcher might administer a survey to graduate students to determine their levels of satisfaction after conducting a literature review.
	Correlational	The researcher uses numbers to determine the extent and direction of the relationship between two or more variables. For example, for a large sample of master's students enrolled in a research methodology course, a researcher might determine the relationship between the number of citations provided in a research report and the score given by the course instructor for the research report.
Pre-experimental		
	One-group posttest-only design (i.e., one-shot case study)	The researcher studies one group that is exposed to an intervention, treatment, or event and then is administered some form of quantitative-based post-measure. For example, a researcher might take the blood pressure of a group of doctoral students after (but not before) they have conducted a literature review.
	One-group posttest-only design using multiple substantive posttests	The researcher studies one group that is exposed to an intervention, treatment, or event and then is administered several relevant and substantive (in terms of theory) quantitative-based post-measures. For example, a researcher might measure several vital signs of a group of doctoral students after (but not before) they have conducted a literature review.

(Continued)

Table A.1 (Continued)

Class of Research Design	Research Design	Description
	One-group posttest-only design using internal controls	The researcher studies one group that is exposed to an intervention, treatment, or event and then is administered a quantitative-based post-measure. In addition, an internal control group that represents the same population is administered a post-measure, with no intervention, treatment, or event occurring before. For example, a researcher might measure the blood pressure level of a group of doctoral students after (but not before) they have conducted a literature review. Another group of doctoral students from the same institution is selected and their blood pressure is measured.
	One-group posttest-only design using multiple control groups	The researcher studies one group that is exposed to an intervention, treatment, or event and then is administered a quantitative-based post-measure. In addition, multiple non-equivalent control groups are administered a post-measure, with no intervention, treatment, or event occurring before. For example, a researcher might measure the blood pressure level of a group of doctoral students after (but not before) they have conducted a literature review. Several other groups of doctoral students representing various academic disciplines from the same or different institutions are selected and their blood pressures are measured.
	Regression extrapolation contrasts	The researcher studies one group that is exposed to an intervention, treatment, or event and then is administered a quantitative-based post-measure. The scores from this quantitative-based post-measure then are compared to scores that were predicted using other information. For example, a researcher might examine doctoral students' levels of performance on a literature review report among students who have read our literature review book. These post-measure scores then are compared to scores on a literature review report predicted by these students' level of reading comprehension using a regression equation that was determined from another group of doctoral students (who had not read our literature review book) in which level of reading comprehension was found to be an important (i.e., statistically significant and practically significant) predictor of performance on a literature review report.
	One-group pretest-posttest design	The researcher studies one group that is administered a quantitative-based pre-measure; then is exposed to an intervention, treatment, or event; and then is administered the same quantitative-based post-measure. For example, a researcher might take the blood pressure of a group of doctoral students before *and* after they have conducted a literature review.
	One-group pretest-posttest design using a double pretest	The researcher studies one group that is administered a quantitative-based pre-measure on two occasions; then is exposed to an intervention, treatment, or event; and then is administered the same quantitative-based post-measure. For example, a researcher might take the blood pressure of a group of doctoral students twice before *and* once after they have conducted a literature review. Thus, the

Class of Research Design	Research Design	Description
		researcher can assess whether an increase or decrease in blood pressure levels after conducting a literature review is over and above the increase or decrease that occurs between the two pre-measure administrations (i.e., over and above maturation).
	One-group pretest-posttest design using a non-equivalent dependent variable	The researcher studies one group that is administered two quantitative-based pre-measures, wherein one pre-measure is expected to change after the intervention/treatment/event and the other pre-measure is not expected to change; then is exposed to an intervention, treatment, or event; and then is administered the same two quantitative-based post-measures. For example, a researcher might take the blood pressure level (expected to change) and body temperature level (not expected to change) of a group of doctoral students before *and* after they have conducted a literature review. Thus, the researcher can assess whether an increase or decrease in blood pressure levels after conducting a literature review is over and above the increase or decrease that occurs in body temperature. A similar increase in both blood pressure and body temperature levels might indicate the onset of an illness that is not related to the conduct of the literature review.
	Normed comparison contrasts	The researcher studies one group that is administered a quantitative-based pre-measure; then is exposed to an intervention, treatment, or event; and then is administered the same quantitative-based post-measure. The scores from this quantitative-based post-measure then are compared to available normative data. For example, a researcher might examine doctoral students' levels of performance on a literature review report among students who have read our literature review book. These post-measure scores then are compared to normative scores on a literature review section of a research proposal or research report that are available from other sources.
	Secondary source contrasts	The researcher studies one group that is administered a quantitative-based pre-measure; then is exposed to an intervention, treatment, or event; and then is administered the same quantitative-based post-measure. The scores from this quantitative-based post-measure then are compared to other available data (e.g., local norms). For example, a researcher might examine doctoral students' levels of performance on a literature review report among students who have read our literature review book. These post-measure scores then are compared to normative scores on a literature review section of a research proposal or research report that are available from one or more other classes.
	Removed treatment design	The researcher studies one group that is administered a quantitative-based pre-measure; then is exposed to an intervention, treatment, or event; and then is administered the same quantitative-based post-measure on two or more occasions, with the

(Continued)

Class of Research Design	Research Design	Description
		intervention/treatment/event removed before the final post-measure occurs. For example, a researcher might administer a measure of anxiety toward the literature review process to a group of doctoral students and then expose these students to a mentoring-based literature review process such as the *interactive literature review process* (ILRP; cf. Combs, Bustamante, & Onwuegbuzie's [2010a, 2010b] nine-stage process), wherein they are mentored through the first three stages of the literature review process. Then, they are administered the same measure of anxiety. After this, the mentoring-based literature review process is stopped and the students continue conducting their literature reviews without mentoring, and the same measure of anxiety again is administered.
	Repeated-treatment design	The researcher studies one group that is administered a quantitative-based pre-measure; then is exposed to an intervention, treatment, or event; and then is administered the same quantitative-based post-measure on one or more occasions; then the intervention/treatment/event is removed, followed by the same quantitative-based post-measure being administered on one or more occasions; then the intervention/treatment/ event is reintroduced, followed by the same quantitative-based post-measure being administered on one or more occasions for the final time. For example, a researcher might administer a measure of anxiety toward the literature review process to a group of doctoral students and then expose these students to a mentoring-based literature review process such as the *interactive literature review process* (ILRP; cf. Combs et al., 2010a, 2010b), wherein they are mentored through the first three stages of the literature review process. Then, they are administered the same measure of anxiety. After this, the mentoring-based literature review process is stopped and the students continue conducting their literature reviews without mentoring, and the same measure of anxiety again is administered. After this post-measure is administered, the students undergo the final six stages of the mentoring-based literature review process, and the same measure of anxiety again is administered.
	Static-group comparison design	The researcher studies two or more non-randomly formed groups: one or more (experimental) groups that are exposed to a new or different intervention, treatment, or event; and one or more (control or comparison) groups that are exposed to the traditional intervention, treatment, or event; then, all groups are administered the same quantitative-based post-measure. For example, a researcher might examine the difference in doctoral students' levels of performance on a literature review report between students who have read our literature review book and students who have not read our literature review book.

Class of Research Design	Research Design	Description
Quasi-experimental		
	Non-equivalent control group design	The researcher studies two or more non-randomly formed groups: one or more (experimental) groups that are exposed to a new or different intervention, treatment, or event; and one or more (control or comparison) groups that are exposed to the traditional intervention, treatment, or event; all groups are administered a quantitative-based pre-measure and post-measure. For example, a researcher might compare pre- and post-measure differences in doctoral students' levels of performance on a literature review report between students who are assigned non-randomly to a group in which our literature review book is read and students who are assigned non-randomly to a group in which our literature review book is not read.
	Non-equivalent control group design using an independent pretest sample	The researcher studies a non-randomly formed group that is administered a pre-measure and then exposed to a new or different intervention, treatment, or event before being administered a post-measure; also, pre-measure information is collected from a randomly formed independent sample, representing a group with overlapping membership that is drawn randomly from the same population and then administered the same post-measure. For example, a researcher might compare pre- and post-measure differences in a group of doctoral students from a university who have read our literature review book with respect to levels of performance on a literature review report. Another group of doctoral students from the same university (i.e., comparison group) are randomly selected for whom scores on a literature review report are available. These students then are given the same post-measure of performance (without their reading our literature review book). Then, the post- and pre-measure differences of both the experimental group and comparison group are compared.
	Non-equivalent control group design using a double pretest	The researcher studies one group that is administered the same quantitative-based pre-measure twice; then is exposed to an intervention, treatment, or event; and then is administered the same quantitative-based post-measure on one occasion. The control group also is administered the same quantitative-based pre-measure twice, ideally with the same time delay between administrations. Then, the control group is exposed to a traditional (or no) intervention, treatment, or event and consequently receives the same post-measure. If no group biases were present, then any differences between the two pre-measure scores should be similar for both the experimental and control groups. For example, a researcher might administer a measure of anxiety toward the literature review process twice to a group of doctoral students and then expose these students fully to a mentoring-based literature review process such as the *interactive literature review process* (ILRP; cf. Combs et al., 2010a, 2010b). Then, they are administered the same measure of anxiety once. The control

(Continued)

Class of Research Design	Research Design	Description
		group, which is not exposed to the mentoring-based literature review process, is administered two pre-measures and one post-measure, with all measures being administered as closely as possible to the same time as is the experimental group.
	Non-equivalent control group design using switching replications	The researcher studies two non-randomly formed groups, in which both groups receive the pre-measure; then, the first group is exposed to the intervention/treatment/event and the second group is not exposed to the intervention/treatment/event. Following this, both groups receive the post-measure. The researcher then administers the intervention/treatment/event to the second group, whereas the first group does not receive the intervention/treatment/event. Then, both groups receive the post-measure. The second introduction of the intervention/treatment/event yields a modified replication of the first introduction. This design gives two opportunities to assess the efficacy of the intervention/treatment/event. For example, a researcher might assess the efficacy of a literature review workshop by introducing it to two groups at different time points, with the other group serving as the control whenever one group is exposed to the workshop.
	Non-equivalent control group design using a reversed-treatment control group	The researcher studies two non-randomly formed groups, in which both groups receive the pre-measure; then, the first group is exposed to the intervention/treatment/event whereas the second group is exposed to a conceptually opposite intervention/treatment/event. Following this, both groups receive the post-measure. For example, a researcher might assess the efficacy of two very different literature review workshops, wherein one group of doctoral students was exposed to a workshop in which the complexity of the literature review process was emphasized, whereas the other group was exposed to a workshop in which the simplicity of the literature review process was emphasized. Both groups received the same pre-measure and post-measure, namely, a measure of anxiety toward the literature review process.
	Case-control design (i.e., case-referent design, case-comparison design, case-history design, retrospective design)	The researcher studies two groups (i.e., cases and controls) that are formed based on some outcome of interest. Then, the cases and controls are compared using retrospective data to determine whether one group was exposed to the hypothetical cause more than was the other group. For example, a researcher might identify one group of people who completed their doctoral dissertations within a certain period of time (cases) and another group of doctoral students who did not complete their doctoral dissertations within the same period of time (controls). Then, all students representing both groups are asked (retrospectively) whether they read any books solely devoted to the literature review process. If significantly more cases had read one or more literature review books than had the controls, then the researcher might be justified in concluding that literature review books may play a role in helping doctoral students complete their dissertations.

Class of Research Design	Research Design	Description
	(Interrupted) Time series design	The researcher studies one group that is repeatedly administered a quantitative-based pre-measure; then is exposed to an intervention, treatment, or event; and then is repeatedly administered the same quantitative-based post-measure. For example, a researcher might take the blood pressure of a group of doctoral students repeatedly before *and* repeatedly after they have conducted a literature review.
	Multiple time series design	The researcher studies two or more non-randomly formed groups: one or more (experimental) groups, subjects, or setting that are exposed to a new or different intervention, treatment, or event; and one or more (control or comparison) groups, subjects, or setting that are exposed to the traditional intervention, treatment, or event; all groups are administered the same quantitative-based measure repeatedly at both pre- and post-intervention/treatment/event. For example, a researcher might compare repeatedly administered pre- and post-measure differences in doctoral students' levels of performance on a literature review report between students who have read our literature review book and students who have not read our literature review book.
	Regression discontinuity design	The researcher assesses the efficacy of an intervention, treatment, or event by correlating the pre-measure and post-measure of a targeted group above and below a cut point and then assesses the differences in trend (i.e., slope). For example, a researcher might administer a measure of anxiety toward the literature review process at the start and end of a research methodology course. Assuming the relationship between these pre-measure and post-measure scores is positive and significant, those scoring below the cut point of the pre-measure are provided with a literature review workshop—which represents the intervention—that emphasizes anxiety-reduction techniques. Assuming an intervention effect, the researcher should observe a clear shift upwards (i.e., an upward bump or *discontinuity*) in the regression line only for those in the intervention group. In other words, the regression line should illustrate a split or break around the cut point score, with the intervention group demonstrating a bump whereas the comparison group (i.e., those above the cut point score) remains constant. If the intervention was not efficacious, the regression line would remain continuous.
	Counterbalanced design	The researcher studies two or more non-randomly formed groups, in which: all groups are exposed to all interventions/treatments/events; each group is exposed to the interventions/treatments/events in an (optimally randomly) different order (called counterbalancing, to minimize what is called an order effect); the number of groups equals the number of interventions/treatments/events; and all groups are administered a quantitative-based post-measure after

(Continued)

Table A.1 (Continued)

Class of Research Design	Research Design	Description
		each intervention/treatment/event. For example, a researcher might compare post-measure differences in doctoral students' levels of performance on two literature review reports that were written after they have undergone each of two different literature review workshops in random order.

Experimental (randomized control design)

	Pretest-posttest control-group design	The researcher studies two or more randomly formed groups: one or more (experimental) groups that are exposed to a new or different intervention, treatment, or event; and one or more (control or comparison) groups that are exposed to the traditional intervention, treatment, or event; all groups are administered a quantitative-based pre-measure and post-measure. For example, a researcher might compare pre- and post-measure differences in doctoral students' levels of performance on a literature review report between students who have read our literature review book and students who have not read our literature review book. Here, the students are randomly assigned either to the book-reading condition or to the non-book-reading condition.
	Posttest-only control-group design	The researcher studies two or more randomly formed groups: one or more (experimental) groups that are exposed to a new or different intervention, treatment, or event; and one or more (control or comparison) groups that are exposed to the traditional intervention, treatment, or event; all groups are administered a quantitative-based post-measure (but no pre-measure). For example, a researcher might compare post-measure differences in doctoral students' levels of performance on a literature review report between students who have read our literature review book and students who have not read our literature review book. Here, the students are randomly assigned either to the book-reading condition or to the non-book-reading condition.
	Solomon four-group design	The researcher studies participants who are randomly assigned to one of four groups: two groups are administered a quantitative-based pre-measure and two groups are not administered the pre- quantitative-based measure. Of the two groups that are administered a pre-measure, one (experimental) group is exposed to the intervention, treatment, or event and one (control or comparison) group is exposed to the traditional intervention, treatment, or event; of the two groups that are *not* administered a pre-measure, one (experimental) group is exposed to the intervention, treatment, or event and one (control or comparison) group is exposed to the traditional intervention, treatment, or event; all groups are administered a quantitative-based post-measure. This design allows the researcher not only to compare the experimental (regardless

Class of Research Design	Research Design	Description
		of whether they were administered the pre-measure) and control/comparison groups (regardless of whether they were administered the pre-measure) to assess the effect of the intervention/treatment/event but also (a) to compare the groups that received the pre-measure (regardless of whether they are in the experimental or control/comparison group) to the groups that did not receive the pre-measure (regardless of whether they are in the experimental or control/comparison group) to assess the effect of the pre-measure on the outcome; and (b) to compare the experimental groups that received the pre-measure to the experimental group that did not receive the pre-measure to assess the extent to which the pre-measure interacts with the intervention/treatment/event. For example, a researcher might compare pre- and post-measure differences in doctoral students' levels of performance on a literature review report between students who have read our literature review book and students who have not read our literature review book. Here, the students are randomly assigned either to the book-reading condition (with or without a pre-measure) or to the non-book-reading condition (with or without a pre-measure). If the two experimental groups perform equally well on the literature review report and better than do both control groups, then the researcher can be even more confident about the efficacy of our literature review book.
	Crossover trial (i.e., crossover study)	The researcher conducts a longitudinal study in which participants are randomly exposed to a series of different treatments, interventions, or events—including at least two treatments/interventions/events, of which one condition represents the traditional treatment/intervention/event. In most cases, all the participants are exposed to all the treatments/interventions/events. Optimally, the treatments/interventions/events are counterbalanced to minimize any order effect. Also, an appropriate length of time (called a washout period) is provided to minimize the effect of one treatment/intervention/event carrying over to the next phase involving another treatment/intervention/event. For example, a researcher might compare post-measure differences in doctoral students' levels of performance on two literature review reports that were written after they have undergone each of two different literature review workshops in random order that took place several weeks apart.
	Single-case study (i.e., single-case experimental design; single-subject experimental design)	The researcher studies the change in some characteristic (e.g., behavior, performance) of a participant who is exposed to a treatment, intervention, or event. For example, a researcher might examine the change in the performance of a literature review report of a master's student before and after this student undergoes a literature review workshop. The student is administered both the pre-measure and post-measure on multiple occasions.

Table A.2 Major qualitative research designs

Research Design	Description
Grounded theory	The researcher uses a rigorous set of procedures to produce substantive theory of social phenomena.
Ethnography	The researcher describes and interprets cultural phenomena that reflect the knowledge, beliefs, behaviors, and/or system of meanings that represent the life of a cultural group.
Case study	The researcher conducts an in-depth study of a bounded individual unit (e.g., a person, group, or event) to generate knowledge of the particular; the researcher can seek understanding of issues that are intrinsic to the case itself (i.e., intrinsic case study) or can select and study cases because they are deemed to be instrumentally useful in enhancing understanding of or theorizing about a phenomenon (i.e., instrumental case study).
Phenomenological research	The researcher, by setting aside (i.e., bracketing) as much as possible all preconceived judgments and experiences (i.e., descriptive phenomenological research), or by not bracketing (i.e., interpretive phenomenological research), studies the everyday subjective conscious experience (i.e., lived experience) from the perspective of one or more individuals in order to understand the meaning of a phenomenon.
Ethnomethodology	The researcher, by setting aside (i.e., bracketing) as much as possible all preconceived judgments about how encounters are socially structured, studies how individuals negotiate everyday interactions and produce social order (i.e., study of social action).
Life history	The researcher provides an extensive account of an individual's life as told to the researcher by the individual, who describes what it is like to be this particular person.
Oral history	The researcher compiles historical information about individuals or families via video, audio, or written works of individuals who participated in or observed past events, and whose recollections are to be documented and preserved for historic purposes.
Narrative research	The researcher generates and analyzes stories of life experiences. In particular, the researcher studies the way that individuals make meaning of their lives as narratives.
Symbolic interactionist study	The researcher studies the symbols and meanings that individuals learn and attach to the actions and objects that permeate their everyday lives.
Microethnography	The researcher uses tools such as video and films in order to obtain a close, repeated look at what individuals do in real time as they interact.
Literary criticism	The researcher studies, evaluates, and interprets literature.

Table A.3 Major mixed research designs

Research Design	Description
Concurrent designs	The researcher implements the quantitative and qualitative phases of the mixed research study at approximately the same point in time. Moreover, the quantitative phase(s) are not dependent on the findings from the qualitative phase(s), and vice versa.
Sequential designs	The researcher implements the quantitative and qualitative phases of the mixed research study one after the other (i.e., sequentially) such that the quantitative phase(s) depend, to some degree, on the findings from the qualitative phase(s), or vice versa.
Equal status designs	The researcher implements the quantitative and qualitative phases of the mixed research study with approximately equal emphasis with respect to addressing the research question(s).
Dominant status designs	The researcher implements the quantitative and qualitative phases of the mixed research study such that one component (e.g., qualitative phase[s]) has significantly higher priority than does the other phase (e.g., quantitative phase[s]).
Partially mixed designs	The researcher implements the quantitative and qualitative phases of the mixed research study such that both the quantitative and qualitative phases are conducted either concurrently or sequentially in their entirety before being mixed at the data interpretation stage.
Fully mixed design/fully integrated design	The researcher implements the quantitative and qualitative phases of the mixed research study such that the quantitative and qualitative techniques are mixed within one or more of the following or across the following four components: (a) the research objective (e.g., the researcher uses research objectives from both quantitative and qualitative research, such as the objectives of both exploration and prediction); (b) type of data and procedures; (c) type of analysis; and (d) type of inference.
Triangulation design/convergent design	The researcher implements the quantitative and qualitative phases of the mixed research study in which (a) the quantitative and qualitative data are collected concurrently, (b) the quantitative and qualitative analyses occur separately, and (c) the findings stemming from the quantitative and qualitative analyses are compared. The goal is to assess levels of convergence or to use one set of findings to compare to the other set of findings.
Explanatory design	The researcher implements the quantitative and qualitative phases of the mixed research study in which the quantitative data collection and analysis (Phase 1) precedes the qualitative data collection and analysis (Phase 2) that build on Phase 1. The goal is to explain the quantitative findings.
Exploratory design	The researcher implements the quantitative and qualitative phases of the mixed research study in which the qualitative data collection and analysis (Phase 1) precedes the quantitative data collection and analysis (Phase 2) that build on Phase 1. The goal is to test the qualitative findings.
Embedded/nested design	The researcher implements the quantitative and qualitative phases of the mixed research study concurrently or sequentially, in which the qualitative sample represents a subset (i.e., subsample) of the quantitative sample, or vice versa. The goal here is to conduct a more in-depth study of the phenomenon using a smaller sample of participants in the second phase.
Transformative design	The researcher implements the quantitative and qualitative phases of the mixed research study concurrently or sequentially within a transformative theoretical framework that focuses directly on the perceptions, lives, and experiences of marginalized, underrepresented, or underserved persons or groups.
Multiphase design	The researcher implements the quantitative and qualitative phases of the mixed research study concurrently or sequentially over multiple phases of the study. The goal here typically is to study a phenomenon longitudinally.

(Continued)

Table A.3 (Continued)

Research Design	Description
Identical design	The researcher implements the quantitative and qualitative phases of the mixed research study concurrently or sequentially, in which the quantitative and qualitative phases involve the same sample members.
Parallel design	The researcher implements the quantitative and qualitative phases of the mixed research study concurrently or sequentially, in which the quantitative and qualitative phases involve samples that are different but are drawn from the same population of interest (e.g., administering a quantitative measure of attitudes toward the literature review process to one class of doctoral students for the quantitative phase, and conducting in-depth interviews and observations examining strategies used to conduct literature reviews on a small sample of doctoral students from another class within the same university, or from another university for the qualitative phase).
Multilevel design	The researcher implements the quantitative and qualitative phases of the mixed research study concurrently or sequentially, in which the quantitative and qualitative phases involve samples that are extracted from different levels of the study (e.g., students vs. teachers).
Conversion design	The researcher transforms one type of data and then analyzes both quantitatively and qualitatively. The goal here is to answer related aspects of the same research questions.
Holistic design	The researcher implements the quantitative and qualitative phases of the mixed research study concurrently or sequentially, in which the goal is to move toward one integrated explanation of the findings.
Iterative design	The researcher implements the quantitative and qualitative phases of the mixed research study sequentially, in which there is a fluid interplay of the findings stemming from each phase.

Note: This table was created based on the following sources: Creswell and Plano Clark (2010), Greene and Caracelli (1997), Leech and Onwuegbuzie (2009), Rallis and Rossman (2003), and Teddlie and Tashakkori (2009).

APPENDIX B: QUANTITATIVE, QUALITATIVE, AND MIXED LEGITIMATION FRAMEWORKS

QUANTITATIVE LEGITIMATION FRAMEWORKS

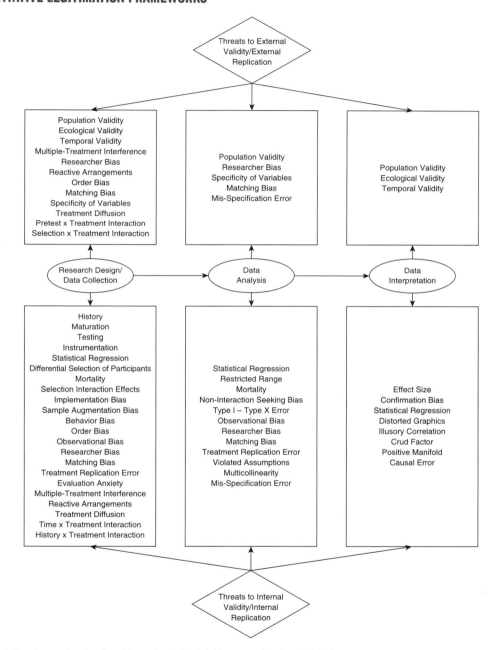

Figure A.1 Quantitative Legitimation Model (Onwuegbuzie, 2003b)

Adapted from "Expanding the framework of internal and external validity in quantitative research" by A. J. Onwuegbuzie, 2003b, *Research in the Schools*, 10(1), pp. 71–90. Reprinted with kind permission of the Mid-South Educational Research Association and the Editors of *Research in the Schools*.

Figure A.2 Threats throughout the quantitative research phases

Specific Validity Threat	Research Phase and Description
Internal Validity	**Design/Data Collection Phase of Research**
History	Occurrence of events or conditions that are not related to the intervention or independent variable but that occur at some point during the study to yield changes in the dependent variable (i.e., outcome) such that the longer a study lasts, the more likely that history will pose a threat to validity
Maturation	Processes that reside within a study participant due, at least in part, to the passage of time, which lead to physical, mental, emotional, and/or intellectual changes (e.g., aging, boredom, fatigue, motivation, learning) that can be incorrectly attributed to the independent variable
Testing	Changes that might occur in participants' scores obtained on the second administration or post-intervention measure arising, at least in part, from having taken the pre-intervention instrument
Instrumentation	Occurs when scores yielded from a quantitative measure lack the appropriate level of consistency (i.e., low reliability) and/or validity (i.e., inadequate content-, criterion-, and/or construct-related validity)
Statistical regression	Occurs when participants are selected because of their extremely low or extremely high scores on some pre-intervention/pre-study measure, wherein there is a tendency for extreme scores to regress, or to move toward, the mean on subsequent measures
Differential selection of participants	Substantive differences between two or more of the (typically intact) comparison groups prior to the implementation of the intervention or the study
Mortality/attrition	Wherein participants who have been selected to participate in a research study either fail to take part at all or do not participate in every phase of the study (i.e., drop out of the study)—resulting in the findings being biased
Selection interaction effects	One or more threats to internal validity interacting with the differential selection of participants to produce an effect that resembles the intervention effect. For example, a *selection by mortality* threat can occur if one group has a higher rate of mortality than do the other groups, such that any differences between the groups create factors unrelated to the intervention that are greater as a result of differential mortality than was the case prior to the start of the study. Other threats include selection by history and selection by maturation
Implementation bias	Stems from differences in the application of the treatment to the intervention groups as a result of differential motivation, time, training, or resources; inadequate knowledge or ability; poor self-efficacy; implementation anxiety; stubbornness; or poor attitudes among those administering the treatment
Sample augmentation bias	Being the opposite of mortality, it prevails when one or more individuals that were not selected by the researcher join the study
Behavior bias	Occurs when a participant has a strong personal bias in favor of or against the intervention prior to the beginning of the study. It is most often a threat when participants are exposed to all levels of a treatment
Order bias	When multiple interventions are being compared in a research study, such that all participants are exposed to and measured under each and every intervention condition, and the effect of the order of the intervention conditions cannot be distinguished from the effect of the intervention conditions

Specific Validity Threat	Research Phase and Description
Observational bias	Occurs when the data collectors have obtained an insufficient sampling of the behavior(s) of interest
Researcher bias	Occurs when the researcher has a personal bias in favor of one intervention or technique over another, which might be subconsciously transferred to the participants in such a way that their behavior is affected. In addition to affecting the behavior of participants, the researcher's bias could affect study procedures or even contaminate data collection techniques. It could be active or passive
Matching bias	Occurs when the matching is non-optimal after (a) the researcher uses matching techniques to select a series of groups of individuals (e.g., pairs) who are similar with respect to one or more characteristics, and then assigns each individual within each group to one of the intervention conditions; or (b) once participants have been selected for one of the intervention conditions, the researcher finds matches for each member of this condition and assigns these matched individuals to the other intervention group(s)
Treatment replication error	Occurs when researchers collect data that do not reflect the correct unit of analysis, with the most common form of treatment replication error being when an intervention is administered once to each group of participants or to two or more classes or other existing groups, yet only individual outcome data are collected—which seriously violates the assumption that each replication of the intervention for each and every participant is independent of the replications of the intervention for all other participants in the study
Evaluation anxiety	Occurs when the performance of one or more participants is affected unduly by debilitative levels of anxiety such that systematic error is introduced into the measurement
External Validity	
Multiple-treatment interference	Occurs when the same research participants are exposed to more than one intervention, leading to carryover effects from an earlier intervention making it difficult to assess the effectiveness of a later treatment
Reactive arrangements	Changes in a participant's response(s) that can occur as a direct result of being cognizant that he/she is participating in a research investigation, comprising the following five major components: (a) the Hawthorne effect (i.e., when participants interpret their receiving an intervention as being given special attention, confounding the effects of the intervention); (b) John Henry effect (i.e., when on being informed that they will be in the control group, participants selected for this condition decide to compete with the treatment or intervention by exerting extra effort during the study period); (c) resentful demoralization (i.e., participants in the control group become resentful about not receiving the intervention, interpreting this omission as a sign of being ignored or disregarded, and becoming demoralized, thereby leading to a reduction in normal levels of effort expended and ensuing decrements in performance or other outcomes); (d) the novelty effect (i.e., increased motivation, interest, or participation on the part of study participants merely because they are undertaking a different or novel task, thereby affecting their responses in a way that is not related to the independent variable); and (e) the placebo effect (i.e., participants in the control group attaining more favorable outcomes [e.g., more positive attitudes, higher performance levels] merely because they believed that they were in the intervention group)
Treatment diffusion	Occurs when members in different intervention groups communicate with each other, such that some of the treatment seeps out or diffuses into the control group—resulting in the study no longer having two or more distinctly different interventions, but overlapping interventions—thereby violating the assumption of independence

(Continued)

Figure A.2   (Continued)

Specific Validity Threat	Research Phase and Description
Time × treatment interaction	Occurs when (a) individuals in one group are exposed to an intervention for a longer period of time than are individuals receiving another intervention in such a way that this differentially affects group members' responses to the intervention; (b) participants in different groups receive their respective interventions for the same period of time, but one of these interventions needs a longer period of time for any positive effects to be realized; or (c) the post-measure for one of the intervention groups is delayed long enough for the effect of the intervention to have changed
History × treatment interaction	Occurs when the interventions being compared experience different history events that differentially affect group members' responses to the intervention
Population validity	From the sample of individuals on which a study was conducted, the extent to which findings are generalizable to the population from which the sample was drawn
Ecological validity	Extent to which findings from a study can be generalized across settings, conditions, variables, and contexts—thereby representing the extent to which findings from a study are independent of the setting or location in which the investigation took place
Temporal validity	Extent to which research findings can be generalized across time—or the extent that results are invariant across time
Multiple-treatment interference	See above. It is a threat to external validity inasmuch as it affects the order that the treatments or interventions are administered (i.e., sequencing effect) which reduces a researcher's ability to generalize findings to the population because generalization typically is limited to the particular sequence of interventions that was administered
Researcher bias	See above. The more unique the researcher's characteristics and values that influence the data collected, the less generalizable the findings
Reactive arrangements	See above. The five components of reactive arrangements adversely affect external validity because, in their presence, findings pertaining to the intervention are determined by which of these components prevail
Order bias	See above. The extent to which findings resulting from a particular order of administration of treatments or interventions cannot be generalized to situations in which the sequence of interventions is different
Matching bias	See above. Extent to which findings from the matched participants cannot be generalized to the results that would have occurred among individuals in the accessible population for whom a match could not be found (i.e., individuals in the sampling frame who were not selected for the study)
Specificity of variables	Occurs when one of the following seven variables are so unique to the study that the findings are not generalizable: type of participants, time, location, circumstance, operational definition of the independent variables, operational definition of the dependent variables, and types of instruments used
Treatment diffusion	See above. Extent to which the intervention is diffused to other treatment conditions in a unique (i.e., unreplicable) way that threatens the researcher's ability to generalize the findings
Pretest × treatment interaction	Situations in which the administration of a pretest increases or decreases the participants' responsiveness or sensitivity to the intervention or treatment, thereby making the observed findings pertaining to the pretested group unrepresentative of the effects of the independent variable for the unpretested population from which the study participants were selected—allowing the researcher to generalize the findings to pretested groups but not to unpretested groups

Specific Validity Threat	Research Phase and Description
Selection × treatment interaction	Stems from important pre-intervention differences between intervention groups that emerge because the intervention groups are not representative of the same underlying population—thereby making it unjustifiable for the researcher to generalize the results from one group to another group
Internal Validity	**Data Analysis Phase of Research**
Statistical regression	See above. Use of techniques that attempt to control statistically for pre-existing differences among the groups being studied, such as analysis of covariance (ANCOVA), that (a) are unlikely to produce unbiased estimates of the intervention effect and (b) might render the residual scores as uninterpretable
Restricted range	Inappropriately categorizing continuous variables in non-experimental designs, then using analysis of variance (ANOVA) in an attempt to justify making causal inferences, which, instead, leads to a discarding of relevant variance, in turn, leads to a loss of statistical power and reduced effect size
Mortality/ attrition	See above. The extent to which subsampling from a dataset (e.g., casewise deletion or listwise deletion strategies in the presence of missing data; reducing the size of the largest group(s) to resemble more closely the size of the smaller group(s) to undertake a balanced analysis) introduces or adds bias into the analysis
Non-interaction seeking bias	Neglecting to assess the presence of interactions when testing hypotheses, which leads to a statistical model that does not honor, in the optimal sense, the nature of reality that he/she wants to study
Type I to Type X error	Type I—falsely rejecting the null hypothesis
	Type II—incorrectly failing to reject the null hypothesis
	Type III—incorrect inferences about result directionality
	Type IV—incorrectly following up an interaction effect with a simple effects analysis
	Type V error—internal replication error measured via incidence of Type I or Type II errors detected during internal replication cycles when using methodologies such as the jackknife procedure
	Type VI error—reliability generalization error—measured via linkages of statistical results to characteristics of scores on the measures used to generate results (e.g., when researchers fail to consider differential reliability estimates for subsamples within a data set)
	Type VII error—heterogeneity of variance/regression—measured via the extent to which data treated via ANOVA/ANCOVA are not appropriately screened to determine whether they meet homogeneity assumptions prior to analysis of group comparison statistics
	Type VIII error—test directionality error—referring to the extent to which researchers express alternative hypotheses as directional yet assess results with two-tailed tests
	Type IX error—sampling bias error—assessed via disparities in results generated from numerous convenience samples across a multiplicity of similar studies
	Type X error—degrees of freedom error—representing the tendency of researchers using certain statistical procedures (e.g., stepwise procedures) to compute the degrees of freedom utilized in these procedures inaccurately (cf. Daniel & Onwuegbuzie, 2000)
Observational bias	See above. Occurs whenever inter-rater reliability or intra-rater reliability of the coding scheme is less than 100%

(Continued)

Figure A.2 (Continued)

Specific Validity Threat	Research Phase and Description
Researcher bias	See above. Occurs when a researcher is evaluating open-ended responses, or the like, and allows his/her prior knowledge of the participants to influence the scores given (i.e., halo effect), resulting in findings that are biased
Matching bias	See above. Occurs when the researcher matches groups after the data on the complete sample have been collected, which introduces bias as a result of omitting those who were not matched
Treatment replication error	See above. Occurs when the researchers use an inappropriate unit of analysis (even though data are available for them to engage in a more appropriate analysis), such as analyzing individual data to compare cooperative learning groups instead of analyzing group data, the former leading to the independence assumption being violated, resulting in the inflation of Type I error and effect-size estimates
Violating assumptions	Stems from a failure to check statistical model assumptions
Multicollinearity	Failure to assess multicollinearity in multiple regression models when multicollinearity is present
Mis-specification error	Failure to specify and to test an appropriate statistical model, including non-interaction seeking bias, discussed above
External Validity	
Population validity	See above. Occurs when a researcher analyzes a subset of her/his dataset such that there is a discrepancy between those sampled and those not sampled from the full dataset, leading to findings from the subset that are less generalizable than would have been the case if the total sample had been used
Researcher bias	See above. Occurs when the particular type of bias of the researcher is so unique that the findings are not generalizable
Specificity of variables	See above. Depends on the manner in which the independent and dependent variables are operationalized (e.g., use of local norms vs. national/standardized norms)
Matching bias	See above. Some researchers match individuals in the different intervention groups just prior to analyzing the data. Matching provides a threat to external validity at this stage if those not selected for matching from the dataset are in some important way different than those who are matched, such that the findings from the selected individuals might not be generalizable to the unselected persons
Mis-specification error	See above. Occurs when the researcher omits one or more important variables (e.g., interaction terms) from the analysis and it is not clear whether the findings would be the same if the omitted variable(s) had been included
Internal Validity	**Data Interpretation Phase of Research**
Effect size	Occurs when the researcher fails to report and to interpret confidence intervals and effect sizes, leading to under-interpretation of associated p values when sample sizes are small and the corresponding effect sizes are large, or an over-interpretation of p values when sample sizes are large and effect sizes are small
Confirmation bias	Occurs when interpretations and conclusions based on new data are overly consistent with preliminary hypotheses

Specific Validity Threat	Research Phase and Description
Statistical regression	See above. Occurs when a study involves extreme group selection, matching, statistical equating, change scores, time series studies, or longitudinal studies, and findings from this investigation reflect some degree of regression toward the mean
Distorted graphics	Occurs when the researcher uses only graphical means to inform interpretations instead of triangulating the graphical data with empirical evaluation
Illusory correlation	Occurs when the researcher overestimates the relationship among variables that are only slightly related or not related at all
Crud factor	Occurs when the sample size is so large that the researcher identifies and interprets relationships that are not real but represent statistical artifacts
Positive manifold	Occurs when the researcher misinterprets relationships between variables by failing to recognize that individuals who perform well on one ability or attitudinal measure tend to perform well on other measures in the same domain
Causal error	Occurs when the researcher infers causality from a correlation between variables
External Validity	
Population validity	See above. Occurs when researchers over-generalize their conclusions across populations
Ecological validity	See above. Occurs when researchers over-generalize their conclusions across settings or contexts
Temporal validity	See above. Occurs when researchers over-generalize their conclusions across time

Adapted from "A model for presenting threats to legitimation at the planning and interpretation phases in the quantitative, qualitative, and mixed research components of a dissertation," by C. L. Benge, A. J. Onwuegbuzie, and M. E. Robbins, 2012, *International Journal of Education, 4*, pp. 83–92. Copyright 2012 by C. L. Benge, A. J. Onwuegbuzie, and M. E. Robbins.

Validity Type	Description
Criterion-related	
Concurrent validity	Assesses the extent to which scores on an instrument are related to scores on another, already-established instrument administered approximately simultaneously or to a measurement of some other criterion that is available at the same point in time as the scores on the instrument of interest
Predictive validity	Assesses the extent to which scores on an instrument are related to scores on another, already-established instrument administered in the future or to a measurement of some other criterion that is available at a future point in time as the scores on the instrument of interest
Content-related	
Face validity	Assesses the extent to which the items appear relevant, important, and interesting to the respondent
Item validity	Assesses the extent to which the specific items represent measurement in the intended content area
Sampling Validity	Assesses the extent to which the full set of items sample the total content area
Construct-related	
Substantive validity	Assesses evidence regarding the theoretical and empirical analysis of the knowledge, skills, and processes hypothesized to underlie respondents' scores
Structural validity	Assesses how well the scoring structure of the instrument corresponds to the construct domain
Convergent validity	Assesses the extent to which scores yielded from the instrument of interest are highly correlated with scores from other instruments that measure the same construct
Discriminant validity	Assesses the extent to which scores generated from the instrument of interest are slightly but not significantly related to scores from instruments that measure concepts theoretically and empirically related to but not the same as the construct of interest
Divergent validity	Assesses the extent to which scores yielded from the instrument of interest are not correlated with measures of constructs antithetical to the construct of interest
Outcome validity	Assesses the meaning of scores and the intended and unintended consequences of using the instrument
Generalizability	Assesses the extent that meaning and use associated with a set of scores can be generalized to other populations

Figure A.3   Description of validity evidence based on Onwuegbuzie, Daniel, and Collins (2009)

Adapted from "A meta-validation model for assessing the score-validity of student teacher evaluations," by A. J. Onwuegbuzie, L. G. Daniel, and K. M. T. Collins, 2009, *Quality & Quantity: International Journal of Methodology, 43*, p. 202. Copyright 2009 by Springer.

QUALITATIVE LEGITIMATION FRAMEWORK

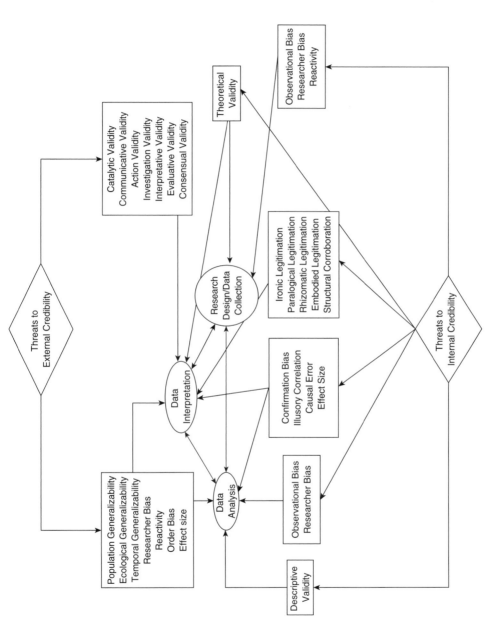

Figure A.4 Onwuegbuzie and Leech's (2007b) Qualitative Legitimation Model

Adapted from "Validity and qualitative research: An oxymoron," by A. J. Onwuegbuzie and N. L. Leech, 2007b, *Quality & Quantity: International Journal of Methodology, 41,* pp. 233–249. Reprinted with kind permission of Springer.

Figure A.5 Threats throughout the qualitative research phases

Type of Threat	Specific Validity Threat	Description
Internal credibility		**Research Design/Data Collection**
	Descriptive validity	The factual accuracy of the account (e.g., transcripts obtained via an interview, focus group) as documented by the researcher (see Maxwell, 1992, 2005)
	Observational bias	Occurs when the researchers have obtained an insufficient sampling of words or behaviors from the study participant(s)—stemming from a lack of persistent observation or prolonged engagement (Lincoln & Guba, 1985)
	Researcher bias	Occurs when the researcher has personal biases or a priori assumptions that he/she cannot bracket (i.e., suspend) which the researcher might subconsciously transfer to the participants in such a manner that their attitudes, behaviors, or experiences are affected; or the researcher could affect study procedures (e.g., ask leading questions in an interview) or even contaminate data collection techniques
	Reactivity	Involves changes in a participant's responses that arise from being aware that he/she is participating in a research investigation
External credibility		
	Observational bias	Occurs when the researcher uses an observational protocol that is unique
	Order bias	Occurs when the order of the questions that are posed in an interview or focus group, or the order in which observations are made, unduly affects the dependability and confirmability of the data
Internal credibility		**Data Analysis**
	Observational bias	Occurs if an insufficient sample of words or behaviors is analyzed from the underlying data
	Researcher bias	Occurs when the researcher has personal biases or a priori assumptions that he/she cannot bracket (i.e., suspend), which unduly affects his/her analysis of the data
External credibility		
	Catalytic validity	Degree to which a given research study empowers and liberates a research community (Lather, 1986)
	Communicative validity	Involves assessing the legitimation of knowledge claims in a discourse such that legitimation is agreed upon by the collection of researchers (Kvale, 1995)
	Action validity	Justification of the legitimation of the research findings is based on whether or not it works—that is, whether or not the research findings are used by decision makers and other stakeholders (Kvale, 1995)
	Investigation validity	Based on the quality of the researcher's skills, such that legitimation represents the researcher's quality control (e.g., ethicalness)

Type of Threat	Specific Validity Threat	Description
	Interpretive validity	Extent to which a researcher's interpretation of an account represents an understanding of the perspective of the individuals or group(s) under study and the meanings attached to their words and actions (Maxwell, 1992, 2005)
	Evaluative validity	Extent to which an evaluation framework can be applied to the objects of study, rather than a descriptive, interpretive, or explanatory one (Maxwell, 1992)
	Consensual validity	Based on the opinion of others, with "an agreement among competent others that the description, interpretation, and evaluation and thematics of an educational situation are right" (Eisner, 1991, p. 112)
Internal credibility		**Data Interpretation**
	Researcher bias	Occurs when the researcher has personal biases or a priori assumptions that he/she cannot bracket (i.e., suspend), which unduly affects his/her interpretations of the findings
	Confirmation bias	Occurs when interpretations and conclusions based on new data are overly congruent with a priori hypotheses, and when there is at least one plausible rival explanation to the underlying findings that might be demonstrated to be superior if the researcher maintained an open mind when interpreting data
	Illusory correlation	Occurs when the researcher identifies a relationship among events, people, and the like, when no such relationship actually exists
	Causal error	Occurs when the researcher provides causal explanations for phenomena without attempting to verify such interpretations
	Effect size	Occurs when the researcher uses quantitative-based terms such as *many*, *most*, *frequently*, and *several*, but does not justify these terms by using some form of quantitative analysis (i.e., effect size) such as counting
	Ironic legitimation	Based on the assumption that there are multiple realities of the same phenomenon such that the truth value of the research depends on its capacity to reveal coexisting opposites (Lather, 1993)
	Paralogical legitimation	Represents that aspect of legitimation that reveals paradoxes (Lather, 1993)
	Rhizomatic legitimation	Arises from mapping data and not only from describing data (Lather, 1993)
	Voluptuous/ embodied legitimation	Represents the extent to which the researcher's level of interpretation exceeds her/his knowledge base stemming from the data (Lather, 1993)
	Structural corroboration	The extent to which the researcher utilizes multiple types of data to support or to contradict the interpretation
External credibility		
	Population generalizability	Occurs when researchers over-generalize their findings across populations

(Continued)

Figure A.5 (Continued)

Type of Threat	Specific Validity Threat	Description
	Ecological generalizability	Occurs when researchers over-generalize their findings across settings or contexts
	Temporal generalizability	Occurs when researchers over-generalize their findings across time
	Reactivity	Involves changes in a participant's responses that arise from being aware that he/she is participating in a research investigation that is so unique that he/she affect the transferability of the findings
	Order bias	Occurs when the order of the questions that are posed in an interview or focus group schedule, or the order in which observations are made, unduly affects the transferability of the findings
	Effect size	Occurs when the researcher bases interpretations on quantitative-based terms such as *many*, *most*, *frequently*, and *several*, but does not justify these terms by using some form of quantitative analysis (i.e., effect size) such as counting

Adapted from "A model for presenting threats to legitimation at the planning and interpretation phases in the quantitative, qualitative, and mixed research components of a dissertation," by C. L. Benge, A. J. Onwuegbuzie, and M. E. Robbins, 2012, *International Journal of Education, 4*, pp. 94–97. Copyright 2012 by C. L. Benge, A. J. Onwuegbuzie, and M. E. Robbins.

MIXED RESEARCH LEGITIMATION FRAMEWORK

Legitimation Type	Description
Sample integration	The extent to which the relationship between the quantitative and qualitative sampling designs yields quality meta-inferences
Inside-outside	The extent to which the researcher accurately presents and appropriately utilizes the insider's view and the observer's view for purposes such as description and explanation
Weakness minimization	The extent to which the weakness from one approach is compensated by the strengths from the other approach
Sequential	The extent to which one has minimized the potential problem wherein the meta-inferences could be affected by reversing the sequence of the quantitative and qualitative phases
Conversion	The extent to which the quantitizing or qualitizing yields quality meta-inferences
Paradigmatic mixing	The extent to which the researcher's epistemological, ontological, axiological, methodological, and rhetorical beliefs that underlie the quantitative and qualitative approaches are successfully (a) combined or (b) blended into a usable package
Commensurability	The extent to which the meta-inferences made reflect a mixed worldview based on the cognitive process of *Gestalt* switching and integration
Multiple validities	The extent to which addressing legitimation of the quantitative and qualitative components of the study results from the use of quantitative, qualitative, *and* mixed validity types, yielding high-quality meta-inferences
Political	The extent to which the consumers of mixed methods research value the meta-inferences stemming from *both* the quantitative and qualitative components of a study

Figure A.6 Typology of mixed methods legitimation types

Adapted from "The validity issue in mixed research," by A. J. Onwuegbuzie and R. B. Johnson, 2006, *Research in the Schools, 13*(1), pp. 48–63. Reprinted with kind permission of the Mid-South Educational Research Association and the Editors of *Research in the Schools.*

REFERENCES

Abbott, A. D. (2001). *Chaos of disciplines*. Chicago, IL: University of Chicago Press.

Adler, L. (1996). Qualitative research of legal issues. In D. Schimmel (Ed.), *Research that makes a difference: Complementary methods for examining legal issues in education, NOLPE Monograph Series* (No. 56) (pp. 3–31). Topeka, KS: NOLPE.

Alberani, V., Pietrangeli, P. D. C., & Mazza, A. M. R. (1990). The use of grey literature in health sciences: A preliminary survey. *Bulletin of the Medical Library Association, 78*, 358–363.

Alexander, B. K. (2005). Performance ethnography: The reenacting and inciting of culture. In N. K. Denzin & Y. S. Lincoln (Eds.), *The Sage handbook of qualitative research* (pp. 411–441). Thousand Oaks, CA: Sage.

Alsop, M. (2005). *Mahler's fifth symphony: The Everest of music*. Retrieved from http://www.npr.org/templates/story/story.php?storyId=6925538

American Educational Research Association. (2006). Standards for reporting on empirical social science research in AERA publications. *Educational Researcher, 35*(6), 33–40.

American Evaluation Association. (2011). *American Evaluation Association statement on cultural competence in evaluation*. Retrieved from http://www.eval.org/p/cm/ld/fid=92

American Heritage College Dictionary. (1993). (3rd ed.). Boston, MA: Houghton Mifflin.

American Psychological Association. (2003). Guidelines on multicultural education, training, research, practice, and organizational change for psychologists. *American Psychologist, 58*, 377–402.

American Psychological Association. (2010). *Publication manual of the American Psychological Association* (6th ed.). Washington, DC: Author.

Anderson, L. W., Krathwohl, D. R., Airasian, P. W., & Cruikshank, K. A. (Eds.) (2001) *A taxonomy for learning, teaching, and assessing: A revision of Bloom's taxonomy of educational objectives*. Boston, MA: Pearson Education Group.

Anstey, M., & Bull, G. (2010). Helping teachers to explore multimodal texts. *Curriculum Leadership, 8*(16). Retrieved from http://www.curriculum.edu.au/leader/helping_teachers_to_explore_multimodal_texts,31522.html?issueID=12141

Astor, R. A., Meyer, H. A., & Behre, W. J. (1999). Unowned places and times: Maps and interviews about violence in high schools. *American Educational Research Journal, 36*, 3–42. doi:10.3102/00028312036001003

Augur, C. P. (1989). *Information sources in grey literature*. London, England: Bowker-Saur.

Ayer, A. J. (1956). *The problem of knowledge*. New York, NY: St Martin's Press.

Bandura, A. (1962). *Social learning through imitation*. Lincoln, NE: University of Nebraska Press.

Bandura, A. (1977). Self-efficacy: Toward a unifying theory of behavioral change. *Psychological Review, 84*, 191–215. doi:10.1037//0033–295X.84.2.191

Bandura, A. (1997). *Self-efficacy: The exercise of control*. New York, NY: Freeman.

Barker, S. F. (1989). *The elements of logic* (5th ed.) New York, NY: McGraw-Hill.

Bates, M. (1989). The design of browsing and berrypicking techniques for on-line search interface. *Online Review 13*, 407–431. Retrieved from http://www.gseis.ucla.edu/faculty/bates/berrypicking.html

Bax, L., Yu, L. M., Ikeda, N., & Moons, K. G. M. (2007). A systematic comparison of software dedicated to meta-analysis of causal studies. *BMC Medical Research Methodology, 7*, 40. doi:10.1186/1471–2288–7–40. Retrieved from http://www.biomedcentral.com/1471–2288/7/40

Beck-Cross, C. (2014, April). *Individual, family, school, and community predictors of high school male suicidal behaviors: An analysis of 2010 Iowa Youth Survey Data*. Invited outstanding paper presented at the annual meeting of the American Educational Research Association, Philadelphia, PA.

Behar, R. (2008). Between poetry and anthropology: Searching for languages of home. In M. Cahnmann-Taylor & R. Siegesmund (Eds.), *Arts-based research in education: Foundations for practice* (pp. 55–71). New York, NY: Routledge.

Beile, P. M., Boote, D. N., & Killingsworth, E. K. (2004). A microscope or a mirror? A question of study validity regarding the use of dissertation citation analysis for evaluating research collections. *Journal of Academic Librarianship, 30*, 347–353. doi:10.1016/j.acalib.2004.06.001

Benge, C. L. (2012). *Effect of cartoon mnemonics and revised definitions on the acquisition of tier-two vocabulary words among selected fifth-grade students*. Unpublished doctoral dissertation, Sam Houston State University, Huntsville, TX.

Benge, C. L., Onwuegbuzie, A. J., & Robbins, M. E. (2012). A model for presenting threats to legitimation at the planning and interpretation phases in the quantitative, qualitative, and mixed research components of a dissertation. *International Journal of Education*. 4, 65–124. doi:10.5296/ije.v4i4.2360. Retrieved from http://www.macrothink.org/journal/index.php/ije/article/view/2360/2316

Benight, C. C., & Bandura, A. (2004). Social cognitive theory of posttraumatic recovery: The role of perceived self-efficacy. *Behaviour Research and Therapy, 42*, 1129–1148. doi:10.1016/j.brat.2003.08.008

Bettany-Saltikov, J. (2012). *How to do a systematic literature review in nursing: A step-by-step guide*. New York, NY: Open University Press.

Biddix, J. P. (2008). Multitasking CMC to study connected organizations. In S. Kelsey & K. St.-Amant (Eds.), *Handbook of research on computer mediated communication* (Vol. 1, pp. 309–324). Hershey, NY: Information Science Reference.

Biesta, G. (2010). Pragmatism and the philosophical foundations of mixed methods research. In A. Tashakkori & C. Teddlie (Eds.), *Sage handbook of mixed methods in social and behavioral research* (2nd ed., pp. 95–117). Thousand Oaks, CA: Sage.

Bloom, B. S., Engelhart, M. D., Furst, E. J., Hill, W. H., & Krathwohl, D. R. (1956). *Taxonomy of educational objectives: Cognitive domain*. New York, NY: McKay.

Boote, D. N., & Beile, P. (2005). Scholars before researchers: On the centrality of the dissertation literature review in research preparation. *Educational Researcher, 34*(6), 3–15. doi:10.3102/0013189X034006003

Booth, A. (2006). "Brimful of STARLITE": Toward standards for reporting literature searches. *Journal of Medical Library Association, 94*, 421–429. Retrieved from http://www.ncbi.nlm.nih.gov/pmc/articles/PMC1629442/

Booth, A., Papaioannou, D., & Sutton, A. (2012). *Systematic approaches to a successful literature review*. Thousand Oaks, CA: Sage.

Borenstein, M., Hedges, L., & Rothstein, H. (2007). *Meta-analysis: Fixed effect vs. random effects*. Retrieved from http://www.meta-analysis.com/downloads/Meta-analysis fixed effect vs random effects.pdf

Bossuyt, P. M., Reitsma, J. B., Bruns, D. E., Gatsonis, C. A., Glasziou, P. P., Irwig, L. M.,... de Vet, H. C. W., and the STARD Group. (2003). Towards complete and accurate reporting of studies of diagnostic accuracy: The STARD Initiative. *Annals of Internal Medicine, 138*, 40–44. doi:10.7326/0003–4819–138–1–200301070–00010

Brewer, E. W. (2007). Delphi technique. In N. J. Salkind (Ed.), *Encyclopedia of measurement and statistics* (pp. 240–246). Thousand Oaks, CA: Sage.

Bronfenbrenner, U. (1979). *The ecology of human development: Experiments by nature and design*. Cambridge, MA: Harvard University Press.

Buell, C. (2004). Models of mentoring in communication. *Communication Education, 53*, 56–73.

Campbell, D. T., & Stanley, J. C. (1963). *Experimental and quasi-experimental designs for research*. Chicago, IL: Rand McNally.

Campbell, W. G., Ballou, S. V., & Slade, C. (1989). *Form and style: Theses, reports, term papers* (7th ed.). Boston, MA: Houghton.

Cancienne, M. B., & Snowber, C. N. (2003). Writing rhythm: Movement as method. *Qualitative Inquiry, 9*, 237–253. doi:10.1177/1077800402250956

Cattell, R. B. (1978). *The scientific use of factor analysis in behavioral and life sciences*. New York, NY: Plenum.

Charmaz, K. (2005). Grounded theory in the 21st century: Applications for advancing social justice studies. In N. K. Denzin & Y. S. Lincoln (Eds.), *Handbook of qualitative research* (3rd ed., pp. 507–536). Thousand Oaks, CA: Sage.

Cherry, K. (2010, December 30). *10 most influential psychologists*. Retrieved from http://psychology.about.com/od/historyofpsychology/tp/ten-influential-psychologists.htm

Chilisa, B., & Kawulich, B. B. (2010). Selecting a research approach: Paradigm, methodology and methods. In C. Wagner, B. Kawulich, & M. Garner (Eds.), *Practical social research*. Maidenhead, England: McGraw-Hill.

Cochrane Collaboration. (2012). Retrieved from http://www.cochrane.org

Cochrane Library. (2012). Retrieved from http://www.thecochranelibrary.com/view/0/index.html

Coffey, A., & Atkinson, P. (1996). *Making sense of qualitative data*. Thousand Oaks, CA: Sage.

Coladarci, T., & Fink, D. R. (1995, April). *Correlations among measures of teacher efficacy: Are they measuring the same thing?* Paper presented at the annual meeting of the American Educational Research Association, San Francisco, CA.

College Board. (2013). *Advanced placement report to the nation*. Retrieved from http://apcentral.collegeboard.com/home

Collier, C. (2013). *Effects of comprehensive, multiple high-risk behaviors prevention program on high school students*. Unpublished doctoral dissertation, Sam Houston State University, Huntsville, TX.

Collins, K. M. T., Onwuegbuzie, A. J., Johnson, R. B., & Frels, R. K. (2013). Practice note: Using debriefing interviews to promote authenticity and transparency in mixed research. *International Journal of Multiple Research Approaches, 7*, 271–283.

Collins, K. M. T., Onwuegbuzie, A. J., & Sutton, I. L. (2006). A model incorporating the rationale and purpose for conducting mixed methods research in special education and beyond. *Learning Disabilities: A Contemporary Journal, 4*, 67–100.

Combs, J. P., Bustamante, R. M., & Onwuegbuzie, A. J. (2010a). An interactive model for facilitating development of literature reviews. *International Journal of Multiple Research Approaches, 4*, 159–182. doi:10.5172/mra.2010.4.2.159

Combs, J. P., Bustamante, R. M., & Onwuegbuzie, A. J. (2010b). A mixed methods approach to conducting literature reviews for stress and coping researchers: An interactive literature review process framework. In G. S. Gates, W. H. Gmelch, & M. Wolverton (Series Eds.) & K. M. T. Collins, A. J. Onwuegbuzie, & Q. G. Jiao (Vol. Eds.), *Toward a broader understanding of stress and coping: Mixed methods approaches* (pp. 213–241). The Research on Stress and Coping in Education Series (Vol. 5). Charlotte, NC: Information Age.

Committee on Academic Conduct. (1994). *Bachelor's degree handbook*. Seattle, WA: University of Washington.

Conner, D. R. (1993). *Managing at the speed of change*. New York, NY: Villard.

CONSORT Group. (2010). *CONSORT statement*. Retrieved from http://www.consort-statement.org

Creswell, J. W. (2002). *Educational research: Planning, conducting, and evaluating quantitative and qualitative research*. Upper Saddle River, NJ: Pearson Education.

Creswell, J. W., & Plano Clark, V. L. (2010). *Designing and conducting mixed methods research* (2nd ed.). Thousand Oaks, CA: Sage.

Cronin, P., Ryan, F., & Coughlan, M. (2008). Undertaking a literature review: A step-by-step approach. *British Journal of Nursing, 17*, 38–43.

Culwin, F., & Lancaster, T. (2001). Plagiarism issues for higher education. *Vine, 31*, 36–41. doi:10.1108/03055720010804005

Curtis, S., Gesler, W., Smith, G., & Washburn, S. (2000). Approaches to sampling and case selection in qualitative research: Examples in the geography of health. *Social Science and Medicine, 50*, 1001–1014. doi:10.1016/S0277-9536(99)00350-0

Daniel, L. G., & Onwuegbuzie, A. J. (2000, November). *Toward an extended typology of research errors*. Paper presented at the annual meeting of the Mid-South Educational Research Association, Bowling Green, KY.

Davidoff, F., Batalden, P., Stevens, D., Ogrinc, G., Mooney, S., and the SQUIRE Development Group. (2008). Publication guidelines for quality improvement studies in health care: Evolution of the SQUIRE project. *Quality and Safety in Health Care, 17*(Suppl. 1), i3–i9. doi:10.1136/qshc.2008.029066

Debachere, M. C. (1995). Problems in obtaining grey literature. *IFLA Journal, 21*(2), 94–98. doi:10.1177/034003529502100205

Dellinger A. (2005). Validity and the review of the literature. *Research in the Schools, 12*(2), 41–54.

Dellinger, A., & Leech, N. L. (2007). A validity framework: A unified approach to evaluating validity of empirical research. *Journal of Mixed Methods Research, 1*, 309–332. doi:10.1177/1558689807306147

Denham, M., & Onwuegbuzie, A. J. (2013). Beyond words: Using nonverbal communication data in research to enhance thick description and interpretation. *International Journal of Qualitative Methods, 12*, 670–696.

Denzin, N. K., & Lincoln, Y. S. (1994). *The handbook of qualitative research*. Thousand Oaks, CA: Sage.

Deutsch, N. L., & Spencer, R. (2009). Capturing the magic: Assessing the quality of youth mentoring relationships. *New Directions for Youth Development, 121*, 47–70. doi:10.1002/yd.296

Di Castelnuovo, A., Rotondo, S., Iacoviello, L., Donati, M. B., & Gaetano, G. (2002). Meta-analysis of wine and beer consumption in relation to vascular risk. *Circulation, 105*, 2836–2844. doi:10.1161/01.CIR.0000018653.19696.01

Dressman, M. (2007). Theoretically framed: Argument and desire in the production of general knowledge about literacy. *Reading Research Quarterly, 42*, 332–363. doi:10.1598/RRQ.42.3.1

DuBois, D. L., Holloway, B. E., Valentine, J. C., & Cooper, H. (2002). Effectiveness of mentoring programs for youth: A meta-analytic review. *American Journal of Community Psychology, 30*, 157–197.

Dweck, C. S. (2006). *Mindset: The new psychology of success*. New York, NY: Random House.

Eisenhart, M. A. (1991). *Conceptual frameworks for research circa 1991: Ideas from a cultural anthropologist; implications for mathematics education researchers*. Proceedings of the 13th annual meeting of the North American Chapter of the International Group for the Psychology of Mathematics Education (Vol. 1, pp. 202–219), Blacksburg, VA.

Eisner, E. W. (1991). *The enlightened eye: Qualitative inquiry and the enhancement of educational practice*. New York, NY: Macmillan.

Elbedour, S., Onwuegbuzie, A. J., Ghannam, J., Whitcome, J. A., & Abu Hein, F. (2007). Posttraumatic stress disorder, depression, anxiety, and coping among adolescents from the Gaza Strip in the wake of the second uprising (Intifada): Psychosocial and political considerations. *Child Abuse & Neglect, 31*, 719–729. doi:10.1016/j.chiabu.2005.09.006

Encyclopædia Britannica. (2014). *Eidetic image*. Retrieved from http://www.britannica.com/EBchecked/topic/180955/eidetic-image

Erikson, E. H. (1959). *Identity and the life cycle*. New York, NY: International University Press.

Erikson, E. H. (1968). *Identity, youth and crisis*. New York, NY: W. W. Norton & Company.

Ernest, J. M. (2011). Using Q methodology as a mixed methods approach to study beliefs about early childhood education. *International Journal of Multiple Research Approaches, 5*, 223–237. doi:10.5172/mra.2011.5.2.223

Esri (2009). *Environmental Systems Research Institute*. Retrieved from http://www.gis.com/whatisgis/index.html

Farace, D. J., & Schöpfel, J. (2010). *Grey literature in library and information studies*. Berlin, Germany: De Grooter Saur.

Faulkner, S. L. (2005). Methods and poems. *Qualitative Inquiry, 11*, 941–949. doi:10.1177/1077800405276813

Faulkner, S. L. (2009). *Poetry as method: Reporting research through verse*. Walnut Creek, CA: Left Coast Press.

Fink, A. (2009). *Conducting research literature reviews: From the Internet to paper*. Thousand Oaks, CA: Sage.

Finnen, W. C. (2004). *Talking drums: Reading and writing with African American stories, spirituals, and multimedia resources*. Portsmouth, NH: Teacher Ideas Press.

Flesch, R. (1946). *The art of plain talk*. New York, NY: Harper & Row.

Frels, R. K. (2010). *The experiences and perceptions of selected mentors: An exploratory study of the dyadic relationship in school-based mentoring*. Unpublished doctoral dissertation, Sam Houston State University, Huntsville, TX.

Frels, R. K. (2012). Foreword: Moving from discourse to practice. *International Journal of Multiple Research Methods, 6*, 190–191.

Frels, J. G., Frels, R. K., & Onwuegbuzie, A. J. (2011). Geographic information systems: A mixed methods spatial approach in business and management research and beyond. *International Journal of Multiple Research Approaches, 5*, 367–386. doi:10.5172/mra.2011.5.3.367

Frels, R. K., & Onwuegbuzie, A. J. (2012a). Interviewing the interpretive researcher: An impressionist tale. *The Qualitative Report, 17*(Art. 60), 1–27. Retrieved from http://www.nova.edu/ssss/QR/QR17/frels.pdf

Frels, R. K., & Onwuegbuzie, A. J. (2012b). The experiences of selected mentors: A cross-cultural examination of the dyadic relationship in school-based mentoring. *Mentoring & Tutoring: Partnership in Learning, 20*, 181–206. doi:10.1080/13611267.2012.679122

Frels, R. K., & Onwuegbuzie, A. J. (2013). Administering quantitative instruments with qualitative interviews: A mixed research approach *Journal of Counseling and Development, 91*, 184–194. doi:10.1002/j.1556–6676.2013.00085.x

Frels, R. K., Onwuegbuzie, A. J., Bustamante, R. M., Garza, Y., Leggett, E. S., Nelson, J. A., & Nichter, M. (2013). Purposes and approaches of selected mentors in school-based mentoring: A collective case study. *Psychology in the Schools, 50*, 618–633. doi:10.1002/pits.21697

Frels, R. K., Onwuegbuzie, A. J., & Slate, J. R. (2010a). Editorial: A typology of verbs for scholarly writing. *Research in the Schools, 17*(1), xiv–xxv. Retrieved from http://www.msera.org/download/RITS_17_1_Verbs.pdf

Frels, R. K., Onwuegbuzie, A. J., & Slate, J. R. (2010b). Editorial: *Research in the Schools*: The flagship journal of the Mid-South Educational Research Association. *Research in the Schools, 17*(1), i–vii.

Frels, R. K., Zientek, L. R., & Onwuegbuzie, A. J. (2013). Differences of mentoring experiences across grade span among principals, mentors, and mentees. *Mentoring & Tutoring: Partnership in Learning, 21,* 28–58. doi:10.1080/13611267.2013.784058

Furman, R., Langer, C. L., Davis, C. S., Gallardo, H. P., & Kulkami, S. (2007). Expressive research and reflective poetry as qualitative inquiry: A study of adolescent identity. *Qualitative Research, 7,* 301–315. doi:10.1177/1468794107078511

Gaber, J. (2000). Meta-needs assessment. *Evaluation and Program Planning, 23,* 139–147. doi:10.1016/S0149–7189(00)00012–4

Gagnier, J. J., Kienle, G., Altman, D. A., Moher, D., Sox, H., Riley, D., and the CARE Group. (2013). The CARE guidelines: Consensus-based clinical case reporting guideline development. *Global Advances in Health and Medicine, 2*(5), 38. doi:10.7453/gahmj.2013.008

Gallegos, J. S., Tindall, C., & Gallegos, S. A. (2008). The need for advancement in the conceptualization of cultural competence. *Advances in Social Work, 9,* 51–62.

Ganann, R., Ciliska, D., & Thomas, H. (2010). Exploring systematic reviews: Methods and implications of rapid reviews. *Implementation Science, 5*(56), 1–10. Retrieved from http://www.implementationscience.com/content/5/1/56

Garrard, J. (2009). *Health sciences literature review made easy: The matrix method.* Sudbury, MA: Jones and Bartlett.

Gazni, A. (2011). Are the abstracts of high impact articles more readable? Investigating the evidence from top research institutions in the word. *Journal of Information Science, 37,* 273–281. doi:10.1177/0165551511401658

Gee, J. P. (2005). *An introduction to discourse analysis: Theory and method.* New York, NY: Routledge.

Gee, J. P. (2010). *An introduction to discourse analysis: Theory and method* (2nd ed.). New York, NY: Routledge.

Gibson, S., & Dembo, M. (1984). Teacher efficacy: Construct validation. *Journal of Educational Psychology, 76,* 569–582. doi:10.1037//0022–0663.76.4.569

Glaser, B. G. (1965). The constant comparative method of qualitative analysis. *Social Problems, 12,* 436–445. doi:10.1525/sp.1965.12.4.03a00070

Glaser, B. G. (1978). *Theoretical sensitivity.* Mill Valley, CA: Sociology.

Glaser, B. G. (1992). *Discovery of grounded theory.* Chicago, IL: Aldine.

Glaser, B. G., & Strauss, A. L. (1967). *The discovery of grounded theory: Strategies for qualitative research.* Chicago, IL: Aldine.

Glaser, B., & Strauss, A. (1971). *Status passage.* Chicago, IL: Aldine.

Glass, G. (1976). Primary, secondary, and meta-analysis of research. *Educational Researcher, 5*(10), 3–8. doi:10.3102/0013189X005010003

Goodchild, M. F., Fu, P., & Rich, P. (2007). Sharing geographic information: An assessment of the geo-spatial one-step. *Annals of the Association of American Geographers, 97,* 250–266. doi:10.1111/j.1467–8306.2007.00534.x

Gorsuch, R. L. (1983). *Factor analysis* (2nd ed.). Hillsdale, NJ: Erlbaum.

Granello, D. H. (2001). Promoting cognitive complexity in graduate written work: Using Bloom's taxonomy as a pedagogical tool to improve literature reviews. *Counselor Education and Supervision, 40,* 292–307.

Grant, M. J., & Booth, A. (2009). A typology of reviews: An analysis of 14 review types and associated methodologies. *Health Information and Libraries Journal, 26,* 91–108. doi:10.1111/j.1471–1842.2009.00848.x

Greenacre, M. (1984). *Theory and applications of correspondence analysis.* Orlando, FL: Academic Press.

Greene, J. C. (2006). Toward a methodology of mixed methods social inquiry. *Research in the Schools, 13*(1), 93–98.

Greene, J. C. (2008). Is mixed methods social inquiry a distinctive methodology? *Journal of Mixed Methods Research, 2,* 7–22. doi:10.1177/1558689807309969

Greene, J. C., & Caracelli, V. J. (1997). Defining and describing the paradigm issue in mixed-method evaluation. In J. C. Greene & V. J. Caracelli (Eds.), *New directions for evaluation: Number 74: Advances in mixed-method evaluation: The challenge and benefits of integrating diverse paradigms.* San Francisco, CA: Sage.

Greene, J. C., Caracelli, V. J., & Graham, W. F. (1989). Toward a conceptual framework for mixed-method evaluation designs. *Educational Evaluation and Policy Analysis, 11,* 255–274. doi:10.3102/01623737011003255

Greenhow, C. M., Robelia, E., & Hughes, J. (2009). Web 2.0 and classroom research: What path should we take now? *Educational Researcher, 38,* 246–259. doi:10.3102/0013189X09336671

Grey Literature Conference Program. (2004). *Sixth international conference on grey literature: Work on grey in progress.* Amsterdam, The Netherlands: GreyNet, Grey Literature Network Service.

Grey Literature Network Service. (2012). *Mission statement*. Amsterdam, The Netherlands: GreyNet, Grey Literature Network Service. Retrieved from http://www.greynet.org/greynethome.html

Guba, E. G., & Lincoln, Y. S. (1989). *Fourth generation evaluation*. Newbury Park, CA: Sage.

Guest, G., Bunce, A., & Johnson, L. (2006). How many interviews are enough? An experiment with data saturation and variability. *Field Methods, 18*, 59–82. doi:10.1177/1525822X05279903

Gunelius, S. (2012, April 18). *Stand out from competitors with Prezi presentations*. Retrieved from http://www.forbes.com/sites/work-in-progress/2011/03/23/stand-out-from-competitors-with-prezi-presentations/

Guskey, T. R., & Passaro, P. D. (1994). Teacher efficacy: A study of construct dimensions. *American Educational Research Journal, 31*, 627–643. doi:10.3102/00028312031003627

Haggbloom, S. J. (2002). The 100 most eminent psychologists of the 20th century. *Review of General Psychology, 6*, 139–152. doi:10.1037//1089–2680.6.2.139

Hahs-Vaughn, D. L., & Onwuegbuzie, A. J. (2010). Quality of abstracts in articles submitted to a scholarly journal: A mixed methods case study of the journal *Research in the Schools. Library and Information Science Research, 32*, 53–61. doi:10.1016/j.lisr.2009.08.004

Hahs-Vaughn, D. L., Onwuegbuzie, A. J., Slate, J. R., & Frels, R. K. (2009). Editorial: Bridging research-to-practice: Enhancing knowledge through abstracts. *Research in the Schools, 16*(2), xxxvii–xlv.

Hailey, D. M. (2007). Health technology assessment in Canada: Diversity and evolution. *Medical Journal of Australia, 187*, 286–288. Retrieved from http://www.mja.com.au/public/issues/187_05_030907/hai10766_fm.pdf

Hall, B., & Howard, K. (2008). A synergistic approach. *Journal of Mixed Methods Research, 2*, 248–269. doi: 10.1177/1558689808314622

Halpern, E. S. (1983). *Auditing naturalistic inquiries: The development and application of a model*. Unpublished doctoral dissertation, Indiana University.

Harden, A., & Thomas, J. (2010). Mixed methods and systematic reviews: Examples and emerging issues. In A. Tashakkori & C. Teddlie (Eds.), *Sage handbook of mixed methods in social and behavioral research* (2nd ed., pp. 749–774). Thousand Oaks, CA: Sage.

Harmon, H. L., Howley, C. B., & Sanders, J. R. (1996). Doctoral research in rural education and the rural R&D menu. *Journal of Research in Rural Education, 12*(2), 68–75.

Harris, J. T., & Nakkula, M. J. (2008). *Match Characteristic Questionnaire (MCQ)*. Unpublished measure, Harvard Graduate School of Education.

Harris, T. L., & Hodges, R. E. (Eds.). (1995). *The literacy dictionary: The vocabulary of reading and writing*. Newark, DE: The International Reading Association.

Hart, C. (2005). *Doing a literature review: Releasing the social science research imagination*. London, England: Sage.

Hartnett, S. J. (2003). *Incarceration nation: Investigative prison poems of hope and terror*. Walnut Creek, CA: AltaMira.

Hatcher, L. (1994). *A step-by-step approach to using the SAS® system for factor analysis and structural equation modeling*. Cary, NC: SAS Institute.

Harzing, A. W. K. (2009, January). *Publish or perish*. Retrieved from www.harzing.com/pop.htm

Haycock, L. A. (2004). Citation analysis of education dissertations for collection development. *Library Resources & Technical Services, 48*, 102–106.

Henson, R. K. (2002). From adolescent angst to adulthood: Substantive implications and measurement dilemmas in the development of teacher efficacy research. *Educational Psychologist, 37*, 137–150. doi:10.1207/S15326985EP3703_1

Henson, R. K. (2003). Relationships between preservice teachers' self-efficacy, task analysis, and classroom management beliefs. *Research in the Schools, 10*(1), 53–62.

Henson, R. K., Kogan, L. R., & Vache-Haase, T. (2001). A reliability generalization study of the Teacher Efficacy Scale and related instruments. *Educational and Psychological Measurement, 61*, 404–420. doi:10.1177/00131640121971284

Herrnstein, R. J., & Murray, C. (1994). *The bell curve: Intelligence and class structure in American life*. New York, NY: Free Press.

Hewstone, M., & Jaspars, J. (1987). Covariation and causal attribution: A logical model of the intuitive analysis of variance. *Journal of Personality and Social Psychology, 53*, 663–672. doi:10.1037//0022–3514.53.4.663

Heyvaert, M., Maes, B., & Onghena, P. (2011). Applying mixed methods research at the synthesis level: An overview. *Research in the Schools, 18*(1), 12–24.

Hickey, M. T. (2010). Baccalaureate nursing graduates' perceptions of their clinical instructional experiences and preparation for practice. *Journal of Professional Nursing, 26*, 35–41.

Hirshfield, J. (1997). *Nine gates: Entering the mind of poetry and craft.* Saint Paul, MN: Graywolf Press.

Homer (1969). *The Odyssey.* New York, NY: Simon and Schuster.

Husereau, D., Drummond, M., Petrou, S., Carswell, C., Moher, D., Greenberg, D.,… Loder, E. (2013). Consolidated Health Economic Evaluation Reporting Standards (CHEERS) statement. *European Journal of Health Economics, 14*, 367–372. doi:10.1007/s10198–013–0471–6

Janesick, V. J. (2010). *Stretching exercises for qualitative researchers* (3rd ed.). Thousand Oaks, CA: Sage.

Jesson, J. K., Matheson, L., & Lacey, F. M. (2011). *Doing your literature review: Traditional and systematic techniques.* London, England: Sage.

Jinha, A. (2010). Article 50 million: An estimate of the number of scholarly articles in existence. *Learned Publishing, 23*, 258–263. doi:10.1087/20100308

Johnson, P. J. (2013) *Edge effect.* University of Southern California Dornsife. Retrieved from http://dornsife.usc.edu/news/stories/1482/edge-effect/

Johnson, R. B. (2011, May). Dialectical pluralism: A metaparadigm to help us hear and "combine" our valued differences. In S. J. Hesse-Biber (Chair), *Addressing the credibility of evidence in mixed methods research: Questions, issues and research strategies.* Plenary conducted at the meeting of the Seventh International Congress of Qualitative Inquiry, University of Illinois at Urbana-Champaign.

Johnson, R. B., & Christensen, L. B. (2010). *Educational research: Quantitative, qualitative, and mixed approaches* (4th ed.). Thousand Oaks, CA: Sage.

Johnson, R. B., & Gray, R. (2010). *A history of philosophical and theoretical issues for mixed methods research.* In A. Tashakkori & C. Teddlie (Eds.), *Sage handbook of mixed methods in social and behavioral research* (2nd ed., pp. 69–94). Thousand Oaks, CA: Sage.

Johnson, R. B., & Onwuegbuzie, A. J. (2004). Mixed methods research: A research paradigm whose time has come. *Educational Researcher, 33*(7), 14–26. doi:10.3102/0013189X033007014

Johnson, R. B., Onwuegbuzie, A. J., & Turner, L. A. (2007). Toward a definition of mixed methods research. *Journal of Mixed Methods Research, 1*, 112–133. doi:10.1177/1558689806298224

Johnson, W. B., & Mullen, C. A. (2007). *Write to the top! How to become a prolific academic.* New York, NY: Palgrave Macmillan.

Karcher, M. J. (2005). The effects of developmental mentoring and high school mentors' attendance on their younger mentees' self-esteem, social skills, and connectedness. *Psychology in the Schools, 42*, 65–77. doi:10.1002/pits.20025

Karchmer-Klein, R., & Shinas, V. H. (2010). 21st century literacies in teacher education: Investigating multimodal texts in the context of an online graduate-level literacy and technology course. *Research in the Schools, 19*(1), 60–74.

Kelley, H. H. (1967). Attribution theory in social psychology. In D. Levine (Ed.), *Nebraska symposium on motivation* (Vol. 15). Lincoln, NE: University of Nebraska Press.

Kelley, H. H. (1973). The process of causal attribution. *American Psychologist, 28*, 107–128. doi:10.1037/h0034225

Kilburg, G. M. (2007). Three mentoring team relationships and obstacles encountered: A school-based study. *Mentoring & Tutoring: Partnership in Learning, 15*, 293–308. doi:10.1080/13611260701202099

King, K. A., Vidourek, R., Davis, B., & McClellan, W. (2002). Increasing self-esteem and school connectedness through a multidimensional mentoring program. *Journal of School Health, 72*, 294–299. doi:10.1111/j.1746–1561.2002.tb01336.x

Kirby, D., & Liner, T. (1988). *Inside out* (2nd ed.). Portsmouth, NH: Boynton/Cook.

Kolb, D. A. (1984). *Experiential learning experience as a source of learning and development.* Englewood Cliffs, NJ: Prentice-Hall.

Krathwohl, D. R. (2002). A revision of Bloom's taxonomy: An overview. *Theory into Practice, 41*, 212–218. doi:10.1207/s15430421tip4104_2

Krathwohl, D. R., Bloom, B. S., & Masia, B. B. (1964). *Taxonomy of educational objectives: The classification of educational goals. Handbook II: The affective domain.* New York, NY: McKay.

Krejecie, R. V., & Morgan, D. W. (1970). Determining sample size for research activities. *Educational and Psychological Measurement, 30*, 607–610.

Kress, G. (2003). *Literacy in the new media age.* London, England: Routledge.

Kress, G. (2010). *Multimodality: A social semiotic approach to contemporary communication.* New York, NY: Routledge.

Kshetri, N., & Dholakia, N. (2009). *Global digital divide*. Retrieved from http://ebooks.narotama.ac.id/files/Encyclopedia of Information Science and Technology (2nd Edition)/Global Digital Divide.pdf

Kvale, S. (1995). The social construction of validity. *Qualitative Inquiry, 1*, 19–40. doi:10.1177/107780049500100103

Lackoff, G., & Johnson, M. (1980). *Metaphors we live by*. Chicago, IL: University of Chicago Press.

Lahman, M. K. E., Geist, M. R., Rodriguez, K. L., Graglia, P. E., Richard, V. M., & Schendel, R. K. (2010). Poking around poetically: Research, poetry, and trustworthiness. *Qualitative Inquiry, 16*, 39–48. doi:10.1177/1077800409350061

Lang, T. A., & Altman, D. G. (2013). Basic statistical reporting for articles published in biomedical journals: The "Statistical Analyses and Methods in the Published Literature" or the SAMPL Guidelines. In P. Smart, H. Maisonneuve, & A. Polderman (Eds.), *Science editors' handbook* (pp. 1–9). European Association of Science Editors. Retrieved from http://www.equator-network.org/wp-content/uploads/2013/07/SAMPL-Guidelines-6–27–13.pdf

Lather, P. (1986). Issues of validity in openly ideological research: Between a rock and a soft place. *Interchange, 17*, 63–84. doi:10.1007/BF01807017

Lather, P. (1993). Fertile obsession: Validity after poststructuralism. *Sociological Quarterly, 34*, 673–693. doi:10.1111/j.1533-8525.1993.tb00112.x

Lee, R. P., Hart, R. I., Watson, R. M., & Rapley, T. (2014). Qualitative synthesis in practice: Some pragmatics of meta-ethnography. *Qualitative Research*. Advance online publication. doi:10.1177/1468794114524221

Leech, N. L., Dellinger, A. B., Brannagan, K. B., & Tanaka, H. (2010). Evaluating mixed research studies: A mixed methods approach. *Journal of Mixed Methods Research, 4*, 17–31. doi:10.1177/1558689809345262

Leech, N. L., & Onwuegbuzie, A. J. (2007). An array of qualitative analysis tools: A call for data analysis triangulation. *School Psychology Quarterly, 22*, 557–584. doi:10.1037/1045–3830.22.4.557

Leech, N. L., & Onwuegbuzie, A. J. (2008). Qualitative data analysis: A compendium of techniques and a framework for selection for school psychology research and beyond. *School Psychology Quarterly, 23*, 587–604. doi:10.1037/1045–3830.23.4.587

Leech, N. L., & Onwuegbuzie, A. J. (2009). A typology of mixed methods research designs. *Quality & Quantity: International Journal of Methodology, 43*, 265–275. doi:10.1007/s11135–007–9105–3

Leech, N. L., & Onwuegbuzie, A. J. (2010). Guidelines for conducting and reporting mixed research in the field of counseling and beyond. *Journal of Counseling and Development, 88*, 61–69. doi:10.1002/j.1556–6678.2010.tb00151.x

Lester, F. K. (2005). On the theoretical, conceptual, and philosophical foundations for research in mathematics education. *ZDM, 37*, 457–467. doi:10.1007/BF02655854

Levy, Y., & Ellis, T. J. (2006). A systems approach to conduct an effective literature review in support of information systems research. *Informing Science Journal, 9*, 181–212.

Lincoln, Y. S., & Guba, E. G. (1985). *Naturalistic inquiry*. Beverly Hills, CA: Sage.

Lipsey, M. W., & Wilson, D. B. (2001). *Practical meta-analysis*. Applied Social Research Methods series (Vol. 49). Thousand Oaks, CA: Sage.

Lively, B., & Pressey, S. (1923). A method for measuring the "vocabulary burden" of textbooks. *Educational Administration and Supervision, 99*, 389–398.

Lobe, B. (2008). *Integration of online research methods*. Ljubljana, Slovenia: Faculty of Social Sciences, University of Ljubljana.

Lucas, K. F. (2001). The social construction of mentoring roles. *Mentoring & Tutoring, 9*, 23–47. doi:10.1080/13611260120046665

Lunden, I. (2012, July 30). Twitter passed 500M users in June 2012, 140M of them in US; Jakarta 'biggest tweeting' city. *TechCrunch*. Retrieved from http://techcrunch.com/2012/07/30/analyst-twitter-passed-500m-users-in-june-2012–140m-of-them-in-us-jakarta-biggest-tweeting-city/

Maass, D. (2004). *Writing the breakout novel workbook*. Cincinnati, OH: Writer's Digest Books.

Macdonald-Ross, M. (1978). Language in texts. *Review of Research in Education, 6*, 229–275. doi:10.2307/1167247

Machi, L. A., & McEvoy, B. T. (2009). *The literature review: Six steps to success*. Thousand Oaks, CA: Corwin Press.

Marcia, J. E. (1966). Development and validation of ego identity status. *Journal of Personality and Social Psychology, 3*, 551–558. doi:10.1037/h0023281

Martsolf, D. S., Cook, C. B., Ross, R., Warner Stidham, A., & Mweemba, P. (2010). A meta-summary of qualitative findings about professional services for survivors of sexual violence. *The Qualitative Report, 15*, 489–506. Retrieved from http://www.nova.edu/ssss/QR/QR15–3/martsolf.pdf

Maxwell, J. A. (1992). Understanding and validity in qualitative research. *Harvard Educational Review, 62*, 279–299.

Maxwell, J. A. (2005). *Qualitative research design: An interactive approach* (2nd ed.). Newbury Park, CA: Sage.

McGhee, G., Marland, G. R., & Atkinson, J. M. (2007). Grounded theory research: Literature reviewing and reflexivity. *Journal of Advanced Nursing, 60*, 334–342. doi:10.1111/j.1365–2648.2007.04436.x

Medawar, P. B. (1964, August 1). Is the scientific paper fraudulent? *Saturday Review*, 42–43.

Mellor, B., & Patterson, A. (2000). Critical practice: Teaching Shakespeare. *Journal of Adolescent & Adult Literacy, 43*, 508–517.

Merriam-Webster. (n.d.). Writer's block. Retrieved from http://www.merriam-webster.com/dictionary/writer's block

Messick, S. (1989). Validity. In R. L. Linn (Ed.), *Educational measurement* (3rd ed., pp. 13–103). Old Tappan, NJ: Macmillan.

Messick, S. (1995). Validity of psychological assessment: Validation of inferences from persons' responses and performances as scientific inquiry into score meaning. *American Psychologist, 50*, 741–749.

Metoyer-Duran, C. (1993). The readability of published, accepted, and rejected papers appearing in *College & Research Libraries*. *College & Research Libraries, 54*, 517–526.

Michailidis, G. (2007). Correspondence analysis. In N. J. Salkind (Ed.), *Encyclopedia of measurement and statistics* (pp. 191–194). Thousand Oaks, CA: Sage.

Miethe, T. D., & Drass, K. A. (1999). Exploring the social context of instrumental and expressive homicides: An application of qualitative comparative analysis. *Journal of Quantitative Criminology, 15*, 1–21.

Miles, M., & Huberman, A. M. (Eds.). (1994). *Qualitative data analysis: An expanded sourcebook* (2nd ed.). Thousand Oaks, CA: Sage.

Miles, M. B., & Weitzman, E. A. (1994). Choosing computer programs for qualitative data analysis. In M. B. Miles & M. Huberman (Eds.), *Qualitative data analysis: An expanded sourcebook* (2nd ed., pp. 311–317). Thousand Oaks, CA: Sage.

Moher, D., Liberati, A., Tetzlaff, J., & Altman, D. G., and PRISMA Group. (2009). Preferred reporting items for systematic reviews and meta-analyses: The PRISMA Statement. *PLoS Med, 6*(6), e1000097. doi:10.1371/journal.pmed1000097

Morgan, D. L. (1997). *Focus groups as qualitative research* (2nd ed.). Qualitative Research Methods Series 16. Thousand Oaks, CA: Sage.

Morgan, D. L. (2007). Paradigms lost and pragmatism regained: Methodological implications of combining qualitative and quantitative methods. *Journal of Mixed Methods Research, 1*, 48–76. doi:10.1177/2345678906292462

Morgan, D. L. (2008). Focus groups. In L. M. Given (Ed.), *The Sage encyclopedia of qualitative methods* (Vol. 1, pp. 352–354). Thousand Oaks, CA: Sage.

Morse, J. M. (1995). The significance of saturation. *Qualitative Health Research, 5*, 147–149. doi:10.1177/104973239500500201

Mossberg, W. S. (2012, April 25). Google stores, syncs, edits in the cloud. *The Wall Street Journal*. Retrieved from http://online.wsj.com/news/articles/SB10001424052702303459004577362111867730108?mg=reno64–wsj&url=http%3A%2F%2Fonline.wsj.com%2Farticle%2FSB10001424052702303459004577362111867730108.html

Mullen, C. A. (1999). Introducing new directions for mentoring. In C. A. Mullen & D. W. Lick (Eds.), *New directions in mentoring: Creating a culture of synergy* (pp. 10–17). New York, NY: Routledge.

Mullen, C. A. (2000). Constructing co-mentoring partnerships: Walkways we must travel. *Theory Into Practice, 3*, 4–11. doi:10.1207/s15430421tip3901_2

Mullen, C. A. (2010). Editor's overview: Fostering a mentoring mindset across teaching and learning contexts. *Mentoring & Tutoring: Partnership in Learning, 18*, 1–4. doi:10.1080/13611260903448284

Murdock, S. H., White, S., Hogue, M. N., Pecotte, B., You, X., & Balkan, J. (2002). *A summary of The Texas Challenge in the Twenty-First Century: Implications of population change for the future of Texas*. College Station, TX: The Center for Demographic and Socioeconomic Research and Education in the Department of Rural Sociology at Texas A&M University.

Myatt, M. (2012). *10 communication secrets of great leaders*. Retrieved from http://www.forbes.com/sites/mikemyatt/2012/04/04/10–communication-secrets-of-great-leaders/

National Institutes of Mental Health. (2007). *Division of developmental translational research*. Retrieved from http://www.nimh.nih.gov/about/organization/ddtr/index.shtml

Nelson, J. A., Onwuegbuzie, A. J., Wines, L. A., & Frels, R. K. (2013). The therapeutic interview process in qualitative research studies. *The Qualitative Report, 18*(79), 1–17. Retrieved from http://www.nova.edu/ssss/QR/QR18/nelson79.pdf

Newman, I., Hitchcock, J. H., & Onwuegbuzie, A. J. (2013). *Bayes methodology: Mixed methods in drag*. Unpublished manuscript, Florida International University, Miami, FL.

Newman, I., & Ramlo, S. (2010). Using Q methodology and Q factor analysis in mixed methods research. In A. Tashakkori & C. Teddlie (Eds.), *Sage handbook of mixed methods in social and behavioral research* (2nd ed., pp. 505–530). Thousand Oaks, CA: Sage.

Nicholas, D. B., Lach, L., King, G., Scott, M., Boydell, K., Sawatzky, B. J.,... Young, N. L. (2010). Contrasting Internet and face-to-face focus groups for children with chronic health conditions: Outcomes and participant experiences. *International Journal of Qualitative Methods, 9*, 105–121.

Nishar, D. (2013, January 9). *200 million members!* [Web log post]. Retrieved from http://blog.linkedin.com/2013/01/09/linkedin-200–million/

Noblit, G., & Hare, R. (1988). *Meta-ethnography: Synthesizing qualitative studies*. Newbury Park, CA: Sage.

Nordenstreng, K. (2007). Discipline or field? Soul-searching in communication research. *Nordicom Review, Jubilee Issue*, 211–222.

O'Hagan, A., & Luce, B. R. (2003). *A primer on Bayesian statistics in health economics and outcomes research*. Bethesda, MD: MEDTAP International.

Onwuegbuzie, A. J. (1993). The interaction of statistics test anxiety and examination condition in statistics achievement of post-baccalaureate non-statistics majors. *Dissertation Abstracts International: Section A. Humanities and Social Sciences, 54*(12), 4371.

Onwuegbuzie, A. J. (1999). Defense or offense? Which is the better predictor of success for professional football teams? *Perceptual and Motor Skills, 89*, 151–159. doi:10.2466/pms.1999.89.1.151

Onwuegbuzie, A. J. (2000a). Factors associated with success among NBA teams. *The Sport Journal* [on-line serial], *3*(2). Retrieved from http://www.thesportjournal.org/VOL3NO2/Onwue.htm

Onwuegbuzie, A. J. (2000b). Is defense or offense more important for professional football teams? A replication study using data from the 1998–1999 regular football season. *Perceptual and Motor Skills, 90*, 640–648. doi:10.2466/pms.2000.90.2.640

Onwuegbuzie, A. J. (2000c, April). *Revisioning rival hypotheses for the 21st century: Collaborative design of a web-based tool for learning about the validity of empirical studies*. Interactive symposium presented at the annual meeting of the American Educational Research Association (AERA), New Orleans.

Onwuegbuzie, A. J. (2003a). Effect sizes in qualitative research: A prolegomenon. *Quality & Quantity: International Journal of Methodology, 37*, 393–409. doi:10.1023/A:1027379223537

Onwuegbuzie, A. J. (2003b). Expanding the framework of internal and external validity in quantitative research. *Research in the Schools, 10*(1), 71–90.

Onwuegbuzie, A. J. (2010). *Literature review taxonomy of objectives*. Unpublished manuscript, Sam Houston State University, Huntsville, TX.

Onwuegbuzie, A. J. (2012). Introduction: Putting the *mixed* back into quantitative and qualitative research in educational research and beyond: Moving towards the radical middle. *International Journal of Multiple Research Approaches, 6*, 192–219.

Onwuegbuzie, A. J. (2014a). *A typology of link words*. Unpublished manuscript, Sam Houston State University, Huntsville, TX.

Onwuegbuzie, A. J. (2014b). *How many works should I cite in my manuscript? A citation analysis of the Journal of Mixed Methods Research*. Manuscript submitted for publication.

Onwuegbuzie, A. J. (2014c). *How many works should I cite in my manuscript? A citation analysis of the Research in the Schools journal*. Unpublished manuscript, Sam Houston State University, Huntsville, TX.

Onwuegbuzie, A. J. (2014d). *Meta-analysis of studies of the accuracy of reference lists in published article*s. Unpublished manuscript, Sam Houston State University, Huntsville, TX.

Onwuegbuzie, A. J. (2014e). *Prevalence of grammatical errors in journal article submissions*. Unpublished manuscript, Sam Houston State University, Huntsville, TX.

Onwuegbuzie, A. J. (2014f). *The degree of collaboration in qualitative, quantitative, and mixed research studies.* Unpublished manuscript, Sam Houston State University, Huntsville, TX.

Onwuegbuzie, A. J., & Collins, K. M. T. (2013, February). *The role of Bronfenbrenner's ecological systems theory in enhancing interpretive consistency in mixed research.* Invited James E. McLean Outstanding Paper presented at the annual meeting of the American Educational Research Association, Philadelphia, PA.

Onwuegbuzie, A. J., & Collins, K. M. T. (2014). Using Bronfenbrenner's ecological systems theory to enhance interpretive consistency in mixed research. *International Journal of Research in Education Methodology, 5,* 651–661.

Onwuegbuzie, A. J., Collins, K. M. T., & Elbedour, S. (2003). Aptitude by treatment interactions and Matthew effects in graduate-level cooperative learning groups. *Journal of Educational Research, 96,* 217–230. doi: 10.1080/00220670309598811

Onwuegbuzie, A. J., Collins, K. M. T., & Frels, R. K. (2013). Foreword: Using Bronfenbrenner's ecological systems theory to frame quantitative, qualitative, and mixed research. *International Journal of Multiple Research Approaches, 7,* 2–8. doi:/10.5172/mra.2013.7.1.2

Onwuegbuzie, A. J., Collins, K. M. T., Leech, N. L., Dellinger, A. B., & Jiao, Q. G. (2010). A meta-framework for conducting mixed research syntheses for stress and coping researchers and beyond. In G. S. Gates, W. H. Gmelch, & M. Wolverton (Series Eds.) & K. M. T. Collins, A. J. Onwuegbuzie, & Q. G. Jiao (Eds.), *Toward a broader understanding of stress and coping: Mixed methods approaches* (pp. 169–211). The Research on Stress and Coping in Education Series (Vol. 5). Charlotte, NC: Information Age Publishing.

Onwuegbuzie, A. J., & Combs, J. P. (2010). Emergent data analysis techniques in mixed methods research: A synthesis. In A. Tashakkori & C. Teddlie (Eds.), *Sage handbook of mixed methods in social and behavioral research* (2nd ed., pp. 397–430). Thousand Oaks, CA: Sage.

Onwuegbuzie, A. J., Combs, J. P., Frels, R. K., & Slate, J. R. (2011). Editorial: Citation errors revisited: The case for *Educational Researcher. Research in the Schools, 18*(1), i–xxxv. Retrieved from http://www.msera.org/download/RITS_18_1_Complete.pdf

Onwuegbuzie, A. J., Combs, J. P., Slate, J. R., & Frels, R. K. (2010). Editorial: Evidence-based guidelines for avoiding the most common APA errors in journal article submissions. *Research in the Schools, 16*(2), ix–xxxvi. Retrieved from http://msera.org/download/RITS_16_2_APAErrors6th.pdf

Onwuegbuzie, A. J., & Corrigan, J. A. (2014). Improving the quality of mixed research reports in the field of human resource development and beyond: A call for rigor as an ethical practice. *Human Resource Development Quarterly, 25,* 273–299.

Onwuegbuzie, A. J., & Daniel, L. G. (2003, February 12). Typology of analytical and interpretational errors in quantitative and qualitative educational research. *Current Issues in Education* [Online], *6*(2). Retrieved from http://cie.ed.asu.edu/volume6/number2/

Onwuegbuzie, A. J., & Daniel, L. G. (2005). Editorial: Evidence-based guidelines for publishing articles in *Research in the Schools* and beyond. *Research in the Schools, 12*(2), 1–11. Retrieved from www.msera.org/download/Rits_editorial_12_2.pdf

Onwuegbuzie, A. J., Daniel, L. G., & Collins, K. M. T. (2009). A meta-validation model for assessing the score-validity of student teacher evaluations. *Quality & Quantity: International Journal of Methodology, 43,* 197–209. doi:10.1007/s11135–007–9112–4

Onwuegbuzie, A. J., & Denham, M. A. (2014a). Qualitative data analysis. In R. Warden (Ed.), *Oxford bibliographies.* Oxford, England: Oxford Bibliographies.

Onwuegbuzie, A. J., & Denham, M. A. (2014b). *Trends in the use of qualitative analysis approaches.* Unpublished manuscript, Sam Houston State University, Huntsville, TX.

Onwuegbuzie, A. J., & Dickinson, W. B. (2008). Mixed methods analysis and information visualization: Graphical display for effective communication of research results. *The Qualitative Report, 13,* 204–225. Retrieved from http://www.nova.edu/ssss/QR/QR13–2/onwuegbuzie.pdf

Onwuegbuzie, A. J., Dickinson, W. B., Leech, N. L., & Zoran, A. G. (2009). Toward more rigor in focus group research: A new framework for collecting and analyzing focus group data. *International Journal of Qualitative Methods, 8,* 1–21.

Onwuegbuzie, A. J., Dickinson, W. B., Leech, N. L., & Zoran, A. G. (2010). Toward more rigor in focus group research in stress and coping and beyond: A new mixed research framework for collecting and analyzing focus group data. In G. S. Gates, W. H. Gmelch, & M. Wolverton (Series Eds.) & K. M. T. Collins, A. J. Onwuegbuzie, & Q. G. Jiao (Eds.), *Toward a broader understanding of stress and coping: Mixed methods approaches* (pp. 243–285). The Research on Stress and Coping in Education Series (Vol. 5). Charlotte, NC: Information Age Publishing.

Onwuegbuzie, A. J., & Frels, R. K. (2010). *An examination of the frequency rate of the verb "found" throughout scholarly publications*. Unpublished manuscript, Sam Houston State University, Huntsville, TX.

Onwuegbuzie, A. J., & Frels, R. K. (2012a, June). *A mixed research framework for collecting and analyzing nonverbal communication data in interviews*. Paper presented at the International Mixed Methods Conference, Leeds, England.

Onwuegbuzie, A. J., & Frels, R. K. (2012b, May). *Mixed research techniques for collecting and analyzing nonverbal communication data in qualitative interviews*. Paper presented at the Eighth International Congress of Qualitative Inquiry, Urbana-Champaign, IL.

Onwuegbuzie, A. J., & Frels, R .K. (2012c). Writing a literature review. In C. Wagner, B. Kawulich, & M. Garner (Eds.), *Doing social research: A global context* (pp. 29–51). Maidenhead, England: McGraw-Hill.

Onwuegbuzie, A. J., & Frels, R. K. (2013a). Introduction: Towards a new research philosophy for addressing social justice issues: Critical dialectical pluralism 1.0. *International Journal of Multiple Research Approaches, 7*, 9–26.

Onwuegbuzie, A. J., & Frels, R. K. (2013b). *Trends in school massacres in the United States*. Manuscript submitted for publication.

Onwuegbuzie, A. J., & Frels, R. K. (2014a). A framework for using discourse analysis for the review of the literature in counseling research. *Counseling Outcome Research and Evaluation, 2*, 115–125. doi:10.1177/2150137811414873

Onwuegbuzie, A. J., & Frels, R. K. (2014b). *A framework for using qualitative comparative analysis for the review of the literature*. Unpublished manuscript, Sam Houston State University, Huntsville, TX.

Onwuegbuzie, A. J., & Frels, R. K. (2014c). *Mapping Miles and Huberman's within-case and cross-case analyses onto the literature review process*. Unpublished manuscript, Sam Houston State University, Huntsville, TX.

Onwuegbuzie, A. J., & Frels, R. K. (2015a, April). *A mixed research framework for using Q Methodology in the literature review process*. Paper presented at the annual meeting of the American Educational Research Association, Chicago, IL.

Onwuegbuzie, A. J., & Frels, R. K. (2015b). *The effectiveness of mentoring programs for youth: An analysis and synthesis of the literature*. Manuscript submitted for publication.

Onwuegbuzie, A. J., & Frels, R. K. (2015c). *The missing link: The use of link words and phrases as a link to manuscript quality*. Manuscript submitted for publication.

Onwuegbuzie, A. J., Frels, R. K., & Frels, J. G. (2010). *A rationale typology for mixing quantitative and qualitative GIS applications in mixed research*. Unpublished manuscript, Sam Houston State University, Huntsville, TX.

Onwuegbuzie, A. J., Frels, R. K., Hwang, E., & Slate, J. R. (2013). Editorial: Evidence-based guidelines regarding the number of citations used in manuscripts submitted to journals for review for publication and articles published in journals. *Research in the Schools, 20*(2), i–xiv.

Onwuegbuzie, A. J., Frels, R. K., & Slate, J. R. (2010). Editorial: Evidence-based guidelines for avoiding the most prevalent and serious APA error in journal article submissions—The citation error. *Research in the Schools, 17*(2), i–xxiv. Retrieved from http://www.msera.org/download/RITS_17_2_Citations.pdf

Onwuegbuzie, A. J., & Hitchcock, J. H. (2014). *Toward a framework for conducting advanced mixed analysis approaches*. Unpublished manuscript, Sam Houston State University, Huntsville, TX.

Onwuegbuzie, A. J., & Hitchcock, J. H. (2015). Advanced. In S. N. Hesse-Biber & R. B. Johnson (Eds.), *Oxford handbook of mixed and multimethod research* (pp. 275–295). New York, NY: Oxford University Press.

Onwuegbuzie, A. J., & Hwang, E. (2012). *Reference list errors in manuscripts submitted to a journal for review for publication*. Unpublished manuscript, Sam Houston State University, Huntsville, TX.

Onwuegbuzie, A. J., & Hwang, E. (2013). Reference list errors in manuscripts submitted to a journal for review for publication. *International Journal of Education, 5*(1), 1–14. doi:10.5296/ije.v5i2.2191. Retrieved from http://www.macrothink.org/journal/index.php/ije/article/view/2191

Onwuegbuzie, A. J., Hwang, E., Combs, J. C., & Slate, J. R. (2012). Editorial: Evidence-based guidelines for avoiding reference list errors in manuscripts submitted to journals for review for publication: A replication case study of *Educational Researcher*. *Research in the Schools, 19*(2), i–xvi.

Onwuegbuzie, A. J., Hwang, E., & Frels, R. K. (2014, April). *Mapping Saldaña's coding methods onto the literature review process*. Paper presented at the annual meeting of the American Educational Research Association, Philadelphia, PA.

Onwuegbuzie, A. J., Hwang, E., Frels, R. K., & Slate, J. R. (2011). Editorial: Evidence-based guidelines for avoiding reference list errors in manuscripts submitted to journals for review for publication. *Research in the Schools, 18*(2), i–xli. Retrieved from http://msera.org/rits.htm

Onwuegbuzie, A. J., & Johnson, R. B. (2006). The validity issue in mixed research. *Research in the Schools, 13*(1), 48–63.

Onwuegbuzie, A. J., Johnson, R. B., & Collins, K. M. T. (2009). A call for mixed analysis: A philosophical framework for combining qualitative and quantitative. *International Journal of Multiple Research Methods, 3*, 114–139. doi:10.5172/mra.3.2.114

Onwuegbuzie, A. J., & Leech, N. L. (2003, February). *Meta-analysis research: Cautions and limitations.* Paper presented at the annual meeting of the Eastern Educational Research Association, Hilton Head, SC.

Onwuegbuzie, A. J., & Leech, N. L. (2007a). Sampling designs in qualitative research: Making the sampling process more public. *The Qualitative Report, 12*, 238–254. Retrieved from http://www.nova.edu/ssss/QR/QR12–2/onwuegbuzie1.pdf

Onwuegbuzie, A. J., & Leech, N. L. (2007b). Validity and qualitative research: An oxymoron? *Quality & Quantity: International Journal of Methodology, 41*, 233–249. doi:10.1007/s11135–006–9000–3

Onwuegbuzie, A. J., Leech, N. L., & Collins, K. M. T. (2008). Interviewing the interpretive researcher: A method for addressing the crises of representation, legitimation, and praxis. *International Journal of Qualitative Methods, 7*(4), 1–17.

Onwuegbuzie, A. J., Leech, N. L., & Collins, K. M. T. (2011). Innovative qualitative data collection techniques for conducting literature reviews. In M. Williams & W. P. Vogt (Eds.), *The Sage handbook of innovation in social research methods* (pp. 182–204). Thousand Oaks, CA: Sage.

Onwuegbuzie, A. J., Leech, N. L., & Collins, K. M. T. (2012). Qualitative analysis techniques for the review of the literature. *The Qualitative Report, 17*(Art. 56), 1–28. Retrieved from http://www.nova.edu/ssss/QR/QR17/onwuegbuzie.pdf

Onwuegbuzie, A. J., & Levin, J. R. (2003, April). *Characteristics of effect sizes: The good, the bad, and the ugly.* Paper presented at the annual meeting of the American Educational Research Association, Chicago, IL.

Onwuegbuzie, A. J., & Levin, J. R. (2005). Strategies for aggregating the statistical nonsignificant outcomes of a single study. *Research in the Schools, 12*(1), 10–19.

Onwuegbuzie, A. J., Mallette, M. H., Hwang, E., & Slate, J. R. (2013). Editorial: Evidence-based guidelines for avoiding poor readability in manuscripts submitted to journals for review for publication. *Research in the Schools, 20*(1), i–xi.

Onwuegbuzie, A. J., Roberts, J. K., & Daniel, L. G. (2005). A proposed new "What If" reliability analysis for assessing the statistical significance of bivariate relationships. *Measurement and Evaluation in Counseling and Development, 37*, 228–239.

Onwuegbuzie, A. J., Slate, J. R., Leech, N. L., & Collins, K. M. T. (2009). Mixed data analysis: Advanced integration techniques. *International Journal of Multiple Research Approaches, 3*, 13–33.

Onwuegbuzie, A. J., & Teddlie, C. (2003). A framework for analyzing data in mixed methods research. In A. Tashakkori & C. Teddlie (Eds.), *Handbook of mixed methods in social and behavioral research* (pp. 351–383). Thousand Oaks, CA: Sage.

Onwuegbuzie, A. J., Witcher, A. E., Collins, K. M. T., Filer, J. D., Wiedmaier, C. D., & Moore, C. W. (2007). Students' perceptions of characteristics of effective college teachers: A validity study of a teaching evaluation form using a mixed-methods analysis. *American Educational Research Journal, 44*, 113–160. doi:10.3102/0002831206298169

Palmer, P., Larkin, M., de Visser, R., & Fadden, G. (2010). Developing an interpretative phenomenological approach to focus group data. *Qualitative Research in Psychology, 7*, 99–121.

Parks, B. (2012, August 30). Death to PowerPoint! *Bloomberg Businessweek.* Retrieved from http://www.businessweek.com/articles/2012–08–30/death-to-powerpoint

Paul, R., & Elder, L. (2006). *The art of Socratic questioning.* Dillon Beach, CA: Foundation for Critical Thinking.

Pawson, R., Greenhalgh, T., Harvey, G., & Walshe, K. (2005). Realist review: A new method of systematic review designed for complex policy interventions. *Journal of Health Services Research & Policy, 10*(Suppl. 1), 21–34. doi:10.1258/1355819054308530

Pease, L. (2013). *A qualitative study of fathers' experiences of depression after having or adopting a child.* Unpublished master's thesis, Carleton University, Ottawa, Canada. Retrieved from https://curve.carleton.ca/system/files/theses/27549.pdf

Péladeau, N. (2014). *What are scientometrics and bibliometrics?* Retrieved from http://provalisresearch.com/solutions/applications/scientometrics-bibliometrics-software/

Phillips, N., & Hardy, C. (2002). *Discourse analysis: Investigating processes of social construction.* Thousand Oaks, CA: Sage.

Pielstick, C. (1998). The transforming leader: A meta-ethnography analysis. *Community College Review, 26*(3), 15–34. doi:10.1177/009155219802600302

Pluye, P., Gagnon, M. P., Griffiths, F., & Johnson-Lafleur, J. (2009). A scoring system for appraising mixed methods research, and concomitantly appraising qualitative, quantitative, and mixed methods primary studies in mixed studies reviews. *International Journal of Nursing Studies, 46*, 529–546. doi:10.1016/j.ijnurstu.2009.01.009

Power, D. J. (2004). A brief history of spreadsheets. *DSSResources.COM.* Retrieved from http://dssresources.com/history/sshistory.html

Prendergast, M. (2006). Found poetry as literature review: Research poems on audience and performance. *Qualitative Inquiry, 12*, 369–388. doi:10.1177/1077800405284601

Prendergast, M. (2009). "Poem is what?" Poetic inquiry in qualitative social science research. *International Review of Qualitative Research, 1*, 541–568.

Provalis Research. (2009a). QDA Miner 3.2 [computer software]: *The mixed method solution for qualitative analysis.* Montreal, Quebec, Canada: Author. Retrieved from http://www.provalisresearch.com/QDAMiner/QDAMinerDesc.html

Provalis Research. (2009b). WordStat 5.0 [computer software]. Montreal, Quebec, Canada: Author. Retrieved from http://provalisresearch.com/products/content-analysis-software/

Provalis Research. (2011). QDA Miner (Version 4.0.3) [computer software]. Montreal, Quebec, Canada: Author.

Ragin, C. C. (1987). *The comparative method: Moving beyond qualitative and quantitative strategies.* Berkeley, CA: University of California Press.

Ragin, C. C. (1989). The logic of the comparative method and the algebra of logic. *Journal of Quantitative Anthropology, 1*, 373–398.

Ragin, C. C. (1994). Introduction to qualitative comparative analysis. In T. Janoski & A. M. Hicks (Eds.), *The comparative political economy of the welfare state: New methodologies and approaches* (pp. 299–319). New York, NY: Cambridge University Press.

Ragin, C. C. (2008). *Redesigning social inquiry: Set relations in social research.* Chicago, IL: University of Chicago Press.

Rallis, S. F., & Rossman, G. B. (2003). Mixed methods in evaluation contexts. In A. Tashakkori & C. Teddlie (Eds.), *Handbook of mixed methods in social and behavioral sciences* (pp. 491–512). Thousand Oaks, CA: Sage.

Ravitch, S. M., & Riggan, J. M. (2012). *Reason and rigor: How conceptual frameworks guide research.* Thousand Oaks, CA: Sage.

Ray, C. M., & Montgomery, D. M. (2006). Views in higher education toward methods and approaches for character development of college students. *Journal of College & Character, VII*(5), 1–15.

Review of Educational Research. (2011). Aims and scope. Retrieved from https://uk.sagepub.com/en-gb/eur/review-of-educational-research/journal201854#aims-and-scope

Richardson, L. (1997). Skirting a pleated text: De-disciplining an academic life. *Qualitative Inquiry, 3*, 295–304. doi:10.1177/107780049700300303

Richardson, L. (2002). Poetic representations of interviews. In J. F. Gulbrium & J. A. Holstein (Eds.), *Handbook of interview research: Context and method* (pp. 877–891). Thousand Oaks, CA: Sage.

Ridley, D. (2012). *The literature review: A step-by-step guide for students* (2nd ed.). Thousand Oaks, CA: Sage.

Rogers, N. (1993). *The creative connection.* Palo Alto, CA: Science & Behavior Books.

Rosenthal, R. (1991). *Meta-analytic procedures for social research* (Rev. ed.). Newbury Park, CA: Sage.

Saldaña, J. (2012). *The coding manual for qualitative researchers* (2nd ed.). Thousand Oaks, CA: Sage.

Salmon, W. C. (1973). *Logic* (2nd ed.). Upper Saddle River, NJ: Prentice-Hall.

Sandelowski, M. (2008). Theoretical saturation. In L. M. Given (Ed.), *The Sage encyclopedia of qualitative methods* (Vol. 1, pp. 875–876). Thousand Oaks, CA: Sage.

Sandelowski, M., & Barroso, J. (2003). Creating metasummaries of qualitative findings. *Nursing Research, 52*, 226–233. doi:10.1097/00006199–200307000–00004

Sandelowski, M., & Barroso, J. (2006). *Handbook for synthesizing qualitative research.* New York, NY: Springer.

Sandelowski, M., Docherty, S., & Emden, C. (1997). Qualitative metasynthesis: Issues and techniques. *Research in Nursing and Health, 20,* 365–371. doi:10.1002/(SICI)1098–240X(199708)20:4<365::AID-NUR9>3.3.CO;2–7

Sandelowski, M., Lambe, C., & Barroso, J. (2004). Stigma in HIV-positive women. *Journal of Nursing Scholarship, 36,* 122–128. doi:10.1111/j.1547–5069.2004.04024.x

Sandelowski, M., Voils, C. I., & Barroso, J. (2006). Defining and designing mixed research synthesis studies. *Research in the Schools, 13*(1), 29–40. doi:10.1016/j.bbi.2008.05.010

Sandelowski, M., Voils, C. I., & Knafl, G. (2009). On quantitizing. *Journal of Mixed Methods Research, 3,* 208–222. doi:10.1177/1558689809334210

Satpathy, S. (2014, June 25). Google drive has over 190 million 30-day active users. *BGR.* Retrieved from http://www.bgr.in/news/google-drive-has-over-190-million-30-day-active-users/

Saumure, K., & Given, L. M. (2008). Data saturation. In L. M. Given (Ed.), *The Sage encyclopedia of qualitative methods* (Vol. 1, pp. 195–196). Thousand Oaks, CA: Sage.

Schmolck, P. (2002). *PQMethod manual mirror.* Unpublished manuscript. Retrieved from http://www.rz.unibw-muenchen.de/~p41bsmk/qmethod/

Schulz, K. F., Altman, D. G., Moher, D., and the CONSORT Group. (2010). CONSORT 2010 Statement: Updated guidelines for reporting parallel group randomized trials. *Annals of Internal Medicine, 152,* 726–732. doi:10.7326/0003–4819–152–11–201006010–00232

Schwandt, T. A. (2007). *The Sage dictionary of qualitative inquiry* (3rd ed.). Thousand Oaks, CA: Sage.

Schwandt, T. A., & Halpern, E. (1988). *Linking auditing and metaevaluation: Enhancing quality in applied research.* Newbury Park, CA: Sage.

Search Institute. (2009a). *Search Institute.* Retrieved from http://www.search-institute.org

Search Institute. (2009b). *Search Institute history.* Retrieved from http://www.search-institute.org/about/history

Sherwood, G. (1997a). Meta-synthesis: Merging qualitative studies to develop nursing knowledge. *International Journal for Human Caring, 3*(1), 37–42.

Sherwood, G. (1997b). Meta-synthesis of qualitative analyses of caring: Defining a therapeutic model of nursing. *Advanced Practice Nursing Quarterly, 3*(1), 32–42.

Sinclair, G. (1998). *Mentoring and tutoring by students.* London, England: Kogan Page.

Skidmore, S., Slate, J. R., & Onwuegbuzie, A. J. (2010). Editorial: Developing effective presentation skills: Evidence-based guidelines. *Research in the Schools, 17*(2), xxv–xxxvii.

Smith, R. N., Byers, V. T., McAlister-Shields, L., Dickerson, S., Hwang, E., & Weller, K. (2013, February). *First-time college student success: Are adjuncts really the way to go?* Paper presented at the annual meeting of the Southwest Educational Research Association, San Antonio, TX.

Softpedia. (2012, July 10). *Microsoft's Office has over one billion users.* Retrieved from http://news.softpedia.com/news/Microsoft-s-Office-Has-Over-One-Billion-Users-280426.shtml

Sojka, R. E., & Maryland, H. F. (1993, February). *Driving science with one eye on the peer review mirror.* Paper presented at the forum proceedings of Ethics, Values, and the Promise of Science, San Francisco, CA.

Soulliere, D. M. (2005). Pathways to attrition: A qualitative comparative analysis of justifications for police designations of sexual assault complaints. *The Qualitative Report, 10,* 416–438. Retrieved from http://www.nova.edu/ssss/QR/QR10–3/soulliere.pdf

Spencer, R. (2004). Studying relationships in psychotherapy: An untapped resource for youth mentoring. *New Directions for Youth Development, 103,* 31–42. doi:10.1002/yd.89

Spencer, R. (2006). Understanding the mentoring process between adolescents and adults. *Youth & Society, 37,* 287–315. doi:10.1177/0743558405278263

Spencer, R. (2007). "It's not what I expected": A qualitative study of youth mentoring relationship failures. *Journal of Adolescent Research, 22,* 331–354. doi:10.1177/0743558407301915

Spivack, N. (2013). *Web 3.0: The third generation web is coming.* Retrieved from http://lifeboat.com/ex/web.3.0

Spradley, J. P. (1979). *The ethnographic interview.* Fort Worth, TX: Holt, Rinehart and Winston.

Stake, R. E. (2005). Qualitative case studies. In N. K. Denzin & Y. S. Lincoln (Eds.), *The Sage handbook of qualitative research* (3rd ed., pp. 443–466). Thousand Oaks, CA: Sage.

Stancanelli, J. (2010). Conducting an online focus group. *The Qualitative Report, 15*, 761–765. Retrieved from http://www.nova.edu/ssss/QR/QR15–3/ofg2.pdf

Stein, B., Koppel, M., & Stamatatos, E. (2007). Plagiarism analysis, authorship identification, and near-duplicate detection PAN'07. *SIGIR Forum, 41*(2), 68–71. doi:10.1145/1328964.1328976

Stein, B., Meyer zu Eissen, S., & Potthast, M. (2007). Strategies for retrieving plagiarized documents. *Proceedings of the 30th annual international ACM SIGIR conference on research and development in information retrieval*, pp. 825–826. doi:10.1145/1277741.1277928

Steinberg, S. J., & Steinberg, S. L. (2006). *GIS geographic information systems for the social sciences: Investigating space and place.* Thousand Oaks, CA: Sage.

Stern, P., & Harris, C. (1985). Women's health and the self-care paradox: A model to guide self-care readiness—clash between the client and nurse. *Health Care for Women International, 6*, 151–163.

Strauss, A. (1987). *Qualitative analysis for social scientists.* Cambridge, England: University of Cambridge Press.

Strauss, A., & Corbin, J. (1998). *Basics of qualitative research: Techniques and procedures for developing grounded theory.* Thousand Oaks, CA: Sage.

STROBE Group. (2010). *STROBE statement.* Retrieved from http://www.strobe-statement.org/

Stroup, D. F., Berlin J. A., Morton, S. C., Olkin, I., Williamson, G. D., Rennie, D.,... Thacker, S. B. (2000). Meta-analysis of observational studies in epidemiology: A proposal for reporting. Meta-analysis Of Observational Studies in Epidemiology (MOOSE) Group. *Journal of the American Medical Association, 283*(15), 2008–2012. doi:10.1001/jama.283.15.2008

Tashakkori, A., & Teddlie, C. (1998). *Mixed methodology: Combining qualitative and quantitative approaches.* Applied Social Research Methods Series (Vol. 46). Thousand Oaks, CA: Sage.

Taylor, N. P. (2014, August 18). *Survey: Scientists talk on Twitter, network on ResearchGate.* Retrieved from http://www.fiercebiotechit.com/story/survey-scientists-talk-twitter-network-researchgate/2014–08–18

Teddlie, C., & Tashakkori, A. (2009). *Foundations of mixed methods research: Integrating quantitative and qualitative approaches in the social and behavioral sciences.* Thousand Oaks, CA: Sage.

Thouless, R. H., & Thouless, C. R. (1990). *Straight and crooked thinking* (4th ed.). Sevenoaks, England: Hodder & Stoughton.

Thouless, R. H., & Thouless, C. R. (2011). *Straight and crooked thinking* (5th ed.). Sevenoaks, England: Hodder & Stoughton.

Tong, A., Flemming, K., McInnes, E., Oliver, S., & Craig, J. (2012). Enhancing transparency in reporting the synthesis of qualitative research: ENTREQ. *BMC Medical Research Methodology, 12*(1), 181. doi:10.1186/1471–2288–12–181

Tong, A., Sainsbury, P., & Craig, J. (2007). Consolidated criteria for reporting qualitative research (COREQ): A 32-item checklist for interviews and focus groups. *International Journal of Qualitative Health Care, 19*, 349–357. doi:10.1093/intqhc/mzm042

Toulmin, S. E. (1958). *The uses of argument.* Cambridge, England: Cambridge University Press.

Tschannen-Moran, M., Woolfolk Hoy, A., & Hoy, W. K. (1998). Teacher efficacy: Its meaning and measure. *Review of Educational Research, 68*, 202–248. doi:10.2307/1170754

U.S. Census Bureau. (2012). *Annual estimates of the population for the United States, regions, states, and Puerto Rico: April 1, 2010 to July 1, 2012.* Retrieved from http://www.census.gov/popest/data/national/totals/2012/index.html

Vacha-Haase, T., & Thompson, B. (2000). Score reliability: A retrospective look back at 12 years of reliability generalization studies. *Measurement and Evaluation in Counseling and Development, 44*, 159–168. doi:10.1177/0748175611409845

Vicsek, L. (2010). Issues in the analysis of focus groups: Generalizability, quantifiability, treatment of context and quotations. *The Qualitative Report, 15*, 122–141. Retrieved from http://www.nova.edu/ssss/QR/QR15–1/vicsek.pdf

Voils, C., Hassselblad, V., Crandell, J., Chang, Y., Lee, E., & Sandelowski, M. (2009). A Bayesian method for the synthesis of evidence from qualitative and quantitative reports: The example of antiretroviral medication adherence. *Journal of Health Services Research and Policy, 14*, 226–233. doi:10.1258/jhsrp.2009.008186

von Elm, E., Altman, D. G., Gøtzsche, M., Vanderbroucke, S. J., and the STROBE Initiative. (2007). The Strengthening the Reporting of Observational Studies in Epidemiology (STROBE) Statement: Guidelines for reporting observational studies. *Annals of Internal Medicine, 147*, 573–577. doi:10.7326/0003–4819–147–8–200710160–00010

Vygotsky, L. S. (1978). *Mind in society: The development of higher psychological processes.* Cambridge, MA: Harvard University Press.

Wao, H. O. (2008). *A mixed methods approach to examining factors related to time to attainment of the doctorate in education.* Unpublished doctoral dissertation, University of South Florida, Tampa, FL.

Walsh, D., & Downe, S. (2005). Meta-synthesis method for qualitative research: A literature review. *Journal of Advanced Nursing, 50*, 204–211. doi:10.1111/j.1365–2648.2005.03380.x

Ware, M. (2006). *Scientific publishing in transition: An overview of current developments.* Bristol, England: Mark Ware Consulting. Retrieved from http://www.stm-assoc.org/2006_09_01_Scientific_Publishing_in_Transition_White_Paper.pdf

Watt, A., Cameron, A., Sturm, L., Lathlean, T., Babidge, W., Blamey, S.,… Maddern, G. (2008). Rapid reviews versus full systematic reviews: An inventory of current methods and practice in health technology assessment. *International Journal of Technology Assessment in Health Care, 24*, 133–139. doi:10.1017/S0266462308080483

Watters, A. (2011, January 10). *View your Prezi presentations anywhere via new iPad app.* Retrieved from http://readwrite.com/2011/01/10/view_your_prezi_presentations_anywhere_via_new_ipa#awesm=~oFGP4rrFr14jsS

Whittemore, R., & Knafl, K. (2005). The integrative review: Updated methodology. *Journal of Advanced Nursing 52*, 546–553. doi:10.1111/j.1365–2648.2005.03621.x

Wilcox-Pereira, R., Valle, R., Gonzales, V., Venzant, M., & Paitson, D. (2014, February). *The effect of faculty employment status on graduation rates among undergraduate students.* Paper presented at the annual meeting of the Southwest Educational Research Association, New Orleans, LA.

Williams, M. (2000). Intepretivism and generalization. *Sociology, 34*, 209–224.

Willinsky, J. (2005). Scholarly associations and the economic viability of Open Access Publishing. *Open Journal System Demonstration Journal, 1*(1), 1–25.

Witcher, L. A., Onwuegbuzie, A. J., Collins, K. M. T., Witcher, A. E., James, T. L., & Minor, L. C. (2006). Preservice teachers' efficacy and their beliefs about education. *Academic Exchange Extra.* Retrieved from http://www.unco.edu/AE-Extra/2006/10/index.html

World Health Organization Report. (2000). Retrieved from http://www.photius.com/rankings/who_world_health_ranks.html

Zimmer, L. (2006). Qualitative meta-synthesis: A question of dialoguing with texts. *Journal of Advanced Nursing, 53*, 311–318. doi:10.1111/j.1365–2648.2006.03721.x

NAME INDEX

Steinberg, S., 190
Stephenson, William, 261
Stern, P., 27
Strauss, A.L., 27, 231

Tashakkori, A., 170–1
Teddlie, C., 170–1
Tindall, C., 36
Toulmin, S.E., 162, 164
Turner, L.A., 209
Twitter, 42, 187, 208

Vache-Haase, T., 61
Voils, C., 260–1
Vygotsky, Lev, 36

Wao, H.O., 309
Ware, M., 23

Yo-Yo Ma, 275

Zachary, Dr Lois, 208
Zotero, 210–11, 232

SUBJECT INDEX

computer-assisted qualitative data analysis
    software (CAQDAS) *cont.*
  functions, 146–8
  major headings, 286
  overview, 128–9, 144
  programs available, 145–6
  scientometrics and bibliometrics, 264–5
  storage and organization, 148–9, 151
  see also QDA Miner
computer-mediated communication (CMC), 40, 41, 208–11
concept maps, 307, 308, 309–10
conceptual frameworks, 59–60, 289–93, 353
conceptual maps, 228
conclusions, 288–9
concurrent design, 380
concurrent mixed analysis, 256
concurrent validity, 167
conference papers, 198–201
conferences, 276–9
confirmation bias, 169
consensus information, 364, 365
consequential element, 171–3
consistency information, 364, 365
constant comparison analysis, 116–17, 226, 229, 231–2
constitutive definitions, 303–4
constitutive keywords, 103–4
construct validation, 171–2
constructivist philosophy, 53, 72, 73, 74
construct-related validity, 167–8
content maps, 307, 308, 309–10
content-related validity, 167
continuity of ideas, 320
continuum, research, 8
convergent design, 381
conversion design, 382
conversion mixed analysis, 256
copyright, 119, 187, 349
CORE process, xv–xvi, 20–1, 43–4
correlational research
  design, 371
  techniques, 50
correspondence analysis, 244, 248, 260
counterbalanced design, 377–8
counter-claim, 162
counter-factive, 162
covariation model, 364–5
credibility, 166, 168, 391, 392–4
crib sheets, 116
crisp set, 240
criterion-related validity, 167
critical dialectical pluralism, 54, 72, 74, 75, 211
critical eye, 174
critical stance, 76
critical theory, 74
critical thinking, xv, 43, 156–7
cross-case displays, 241–3

crossover mixed analysianas, 262
crossover mixed analysis, 256, 258–9
crossover trial, 379
cultural competence, xiii, 11, 32, 36–7, 73
cultural deficit model, 37
culturally progressive literature reviewer, 36–7, 39, 44, 45–6,
    78, 88
culture, 35–6, 45, 68–9, 233

dance, 275
data
  analysis *see* data analysis and synthesis
  collection, 49
  comparison, 258–9
  reduction, 114
  saturation, 179, 232, 280, 359
  synthesis *see* data analysis and synthesis
data analysis and synthesis
  analysis versus synthesis, 224
  approaches, methods and techniques, 225–7
  creating analysis questions, 225
  handling decisions and emergent issues, 227–9
  information sources, 224–5
  mixed analysis *see* mixed analysis
  mixed methods integration, 227–8
  qualitative *see* qualitative data analysis
  quantitative *see* quantitative data analysis
  saturation, 179, 232, 280, 359
  selecting the analysis, 265–7
databases, 57, 88–100, 137, 303
debriefing interviews, 207–8
deductive reasoning, 3, 6, 31
defensible, 16
deficit model, culture, 37
definitions, 303–4
degrees of difficulty, 360
Delicious, 42, 210, 232
Delphi method, 209–10
descriptive analysis, 248, 250–1
descriptive research design, 371
descriptive validity, 169
deselection, information *see* selection and deselection
designs, research, 371–95
development, 170, 288
dialectical pluralism, 53–4, 72, 75, 266
dialectical scaffold, 291, 292, 369
dictionaries, 194
digital sources, 13–14
disciplines, 89
discipline-specific beliefs, 68, 71
discourse analysis, 230, 233, 236–7, 359
Discourse Analysis-Based Research Synthesis (DARS), 236–7
discovery arguments, 283–4
discursive scaffold, 291, 292, 369–70
dissemination, 57
dissenting views, 305, 306